# NOVELS
## *for Students*

# *Advisors*

# NOVELS
## *for Students*

**Presenting Analysis, Context, and Criticism on Commonly Studied Novels**

### VOLUME 32

*Sara Constantakis, Project Editor*

*Foreword by Anne Devereaux Jordan*

**GALE**
CENGAGE Learning™

Detroit • New York • San Francisco • New Haven, Conn • Waterville, Maine • London

**Novels for Students, Volume 32**

Project Editor: Sara Constantakis

Rights Acquisition and Management: Beth Beaufore, Leitha Etheridge-Sims, Jackie Jones, Kelly Quin

Composition: Evi Abou-El-Seoud

Manufacturing: Drew Kalasky

Imaging: John Watkins

Product Design: Pamela A. E. Galbreath, Jennifer Wahi

Content Conversion: Katrina Coach

Product Manager: Meggin Condino

For product information and technology assistance, contact us at **Gale Customer Support, 1-800-877-4253.**
For permission to use material from this text or product, submit all requests online at **www.cengage.com/permissions.**
Further permissions questions can be emailed to **permissionrequest@cengage.com**

While every effort has been made to ensure the reliability of the information presented in this publication, Gale, a part of Cengage Learning, does not guarantee the accuracy of the data contained herein. Gale accepts no payment for listing; and inclusion in the publication of any organization, agency, institution, publication, service, or individual does not imply endorsement of the editors or publisher. Errors brought to the attention of the publisher and verified to the satisfaction of the publisher will be corrected in future editions.

*Gale*
27500 Drake Rd.
Farmington Hills, MI, 48331-3535

ISBN-13: 978-1-4144-4170-2
ISBN-10: 1-4144-4170-3

ISSN 1094-3552

This title is also available as an e-book.
ISBN-13: 978-1-4144-4948-7
ISBN-10: 1-4144-4948-8
Contact your Gale, a part of Cengage Learning sales representative for ordering information.

Printed in the United States of America
1 2 3 4 5 6 7 14 13 12 11 10

# *Table of Contents*

**ADVISORS** . . . . . . . . . . ii

**THE INFORMED DIALOGUE: INTERACTING
WITH LITERATURE** . . . . . . . . ix
*(by Anne Devereaux Jordan)*

**INTRODUCTION** . . . . . . . . . . xi

**LITERARY CHRONOLOGY** . . . . . . . xv

**ACKNOWLEDGMENTS** . . . . . . . xvii


**ATONEMENT** *(by Ian McEwan)* . . . . . . 1
   Author Biography . . . . . . . . 2
   Plot Summary . . . . . . . . . . 2
   Characters . . . . . . . . . . 6
   Themes . . . . . . . . . . . 8
   Style . . . . . . . . . . . 10
   Historical Context . . . . . . . 11
   Critical Overview . . . . . . . . 12
   Criticism . . . . . . . . . . . 14
   Sources . . . . . . . . . . . 26
   Further Reading . . . . . . . . 27

**THE BRIDGE OVER THE RIVER KWAI**
*(by Pierre Boulle)* . . . . . . . . . 28
   Author Biography . . . . . . . . 29
   Plot Summary . . . . . . . . . 29
   Characters . . . . . . . . . . 32
   Themes . . . . . . . . . . . 33

Style . . . . . . . . . . 35
Historical Context . . . . . . 36
Critical Overview. . . . . . . 38
Criticism. . . . . . . . . . 39
Sources . . . . . . . . . . 49
Further Reading . . . . . . . 50

**JOSEPH ANDREWS** *(by Henry Fielding)* . . . 51
Author Biography . . . . . . 52
Plot Summary. . . . . . . 53
Characters . . . . . . . . 56
Themes . . . . . . . . . 58
Style . . . . . . . . . . 60
Historical Context . . . . . . 61
Critical Overview. . . . . . . 63
Criticism. . . . . . . . . . 64
Sources . . . . . . . . . 69
Further Reading . . . . . . . 69

**THE LAST OF THE MOHICANS** . . . . . 70
Plot Summary. . . . . . . 71
Characters . . . . . . . . 75
Themes . . . . . . . . . 78
Style . . . . . . . . . . 80
Cultural Context . . . . . . . 81
Critical Overview. . . . . . . 82
Criticism. . . . . . . . . . 83
Sources . . . . . . . . . . 92

**THE LEARNING TREE**
*(by Gordon Parks)* . . . . . . . 93
Author Biography . . . . . . 94
Plot Summary. . . . . . . 94
Characters . . . . . . . . 98
Themes . . . . . . . . . 101
Style . . . . . . . . . . 103
Historical Context . . . . . 103
Critical Overview. . . . . . 105
Criticism. . . . . . . . . 106
Sources . . . . . . . . . 112
Further Reading . . . . . . 113

**THE PILGRIM'S PROGRESS**
*(by John Bunyan)* . . . . . . . 114
Author Biography . . . . . 115
Plot Summary. . . . . . . 116
Characters . . . . . . . . 120
Themes . . . . . . . . . 122
Style . . . . . . . . . . 124
Historical Context . . . . . 125
Critical Overview. . . . . . 127
Criticism. . . . . . . . . 128
Sources . . . . . . . . . 130
Further Reading . . . . . . 130

**A PLACE WHERE THE SEA REMEMBERS**
*(by Sandra Benitez)* . . . . . . . 131
Author Biography . . . . . . 132
Plot Summary. . . . . . . 132
Characters . . . . . . . . 135
Themes . . . . . . . . . 138
Style . . . . . . . . . 140
Historical Context . . . . . 140
Critical Overview. . . . . . 142
Criticism. . . . . . . . . 143
Sources . . . . . . . . . 145
Further Reading . . . . . . 146

**THE POWER OF ONE**
*(by Bryce Courtenay)* . . . . . . 147
Author Biography . . . . . . 148
Plot Summary. . . . . . . 149
Characters . . . . . . . . 153
Themes . . . . . . . . . 157
Style . . . . . . . . . . 159
Historical Context . . . . . 160
Critical Overview. . . . . . 162
Criticism. . . . . . . . . 163
Sources . . . . . . . . . 170
Further Reading . . . . . . 170

**STAYING FAT FOR SARAH BYRNES**
*(by Chris Crutcher)* . . . . . . . 172
Author Biography . . . . . . 173
Plot Summary. . . . . . . 173
Characters . . . . . . . . 178
Themes . . . . . . . . . 180
Style . . . . . . . . . . 182
Historical Context . . . . . 183
Critical Overview. . . . . . 185
Criticism. . . . . . . . . 185
Sources . . . . . . . . . 194
Further Reading . . . . . . 194

**A THOUSAND ACRES** *(by Jane Smiley)* . . 195
Author Biography . . . . . . 195
Plot Summary. . . . . . . 197
Characters . . . . . . . . 200
Themes . . . . . . . . . 203
Style . . . . . . . . . . 206
Historical Context . . . . . 207
Critical Overview. . . . . . 209
Criticism. . . . . . . . . 210
Sources . . . . . . . . . 222
Further Reading . . . . . . 223

**TO KILL A MOCKINGBIRD** . . . . . 224
Plot Summary. . . . . . . 225
Characters . . . . . . . . 229

Themes . . . . . . . . . 233
Style . . . . . . . . . . 236
Cultural Context . . . . . . . 237
Critical Overview . . . . . . . 238
Criticism . . . . . . . . . 238
Sources . . . . . . . . . 252

**TYPEE** *(by Herman Melville)* . . . . . 253
Author Biography . . . . . . 254
Plot Summary . . . . . . . 254
Characters . . . . . . . . 258
Themes . . . . . . . . . 260
Style . . . . . . . . . . 262
Historical Context . . . . . . 263
Critical Overview . . . . . . 264
Criticism . . . . . . . . . 265
Sources . . . . . . . . . 271
Further Reading . . . . . . 272

**THE WINGS OF THE DOVE**
*(by Henry James)* . . . . . . . . 273
Author Biography . . . . . . 274
Plot Summary . . . . . . . 275
Characters . . . . . . . . 277
Themes . . . . . . . . . 280
Style . . . . . . . . . . 283

Historical Context . . . . . . 283
Critical Overview . . . . . . . 285
Criticism . . . . . . . . . 286
Sources . . . . . . . . . 293
Further Reading . . . . . . 293

**A WRINKLE IN TIME**
*(by Madeleine L'Engle)* . . . . . . . 295
Author Biography . . . . . . 296
Plot Summary . . . . . . . 296
Characters . . . . . . . . 300
Themes . . . . . . . . . 302
Style . . . . . . . . . . 304
Historical Context . . . . . . 304
Critical Overview . . . . . . 306
Criticism . . . . . . . . . 307
Sources . . . . . . . . . 314
Further Reading . . . . . . 314

**GLOSSARY OF LITERARY TERMS** . . . 315

**CUMULATIVE AUTHOR/TITLE INDEX** . . 327

**CUMULATIVE NATIONALITY/
ETHNICITY INDEX** . . . . . . . 337

**SUBJECT/THEME INDEX** . . . . . . 345

# The Informed Dialogue: Interacting with Literature

When we pick up a book, we usually do so with the anticipation of pleasure. We hope that by entering the time and place of the novel and sharing the thoughts and actions of the characters, we will find enjoyment. Unfortunately, this is often not the case; we are disappointed. But we should ask, has the author failed us, or have we failed the author?

We establish a dialogue with the author, the book, and with ourselves when we read. Consciously and unconsciously, we ask questions: "Why did the author write this book?" "Why did the author choose that time, place, or character?" "How did the author achieve that effect?" "Why did the character act that way?" "Would I act in the same way?" The answers we receive depend upon how much information about literature in general and about that book specifically we ourselves bring to our reading.

Young children have limited life and literary experiences. Being young, children frequently do not know how to go about exploring a book, nor sometimes, even know the questions to ask of a book. The books they read help them answer questions, the author often coming right out and *telling* young readers the things they are learning or are expected to learn. The perennial classic, *The Little Engine That Could, tells* its readers that, among other things, it is good to help others and brings happiness:

> "Hurray, hurray," cried the funny little clown and all the dolls and toys. "The good little boys and girls in the city will be happy because you helped us, kind, Little Blue Engine."

In picture books, messages are often blatant and simple, the dialogue between the author and reader one-sided. Young children are concerned with the end result of a book—the enjoyment gained, the lesson learned—rather than with how that result was obtained. As we grow older and read further, however, we question more. We come to expect that the world within the book will closely mirror the concerns of our world, and that the author will *show* these through the events, descriptions, and conversations within the story, rather than *telling* of them. We are now expected to do the interpreting, carry on our share of the dialogue with the book and author, and glean not only the author's message, but comprehend how that message and the overall affect of the book were achieved. Sometimes, however, we need help to do these things. *Novels for Students* provides that help.

A novel is made up of many parts interacting to create a coherent whole. In reading a novel, the more obvious features can be easily spotted—theme, characters, plot—but we may overlook the more subtle elements that greatly influence how the novel is perceived by the reader: viewpoint, mood and tone, symbolism, or the use of humor. By focusing on both the obvious and more subtle literary elements within a novel, *Novels for Students* aids readers in both analyzing for message and in determining how and why that message is communicated. In the discussion on Harper Lee's *To Kill a Mockingbird* (Vol. 2), for example, the mockingbird as a symbol of innocence is dealt with, among other things, as is the importance of Lee's use of humor which "enlivens a serious plot, adds depth to the characterization, and creates a sense of familiarity and universality." The reader comes to understand the internal elements of each novel discussed—as well as the external influences that help shape it.

"The desire to write greatly," Harold Bloom of Yale University says, "is the desire to be elsewhere, in a time and place of one's own, in an originality that must compound with inheritance, with an anxiety of influence." A writer seeks to create a unique world within a story, but although it is unique, it is not disconnected from our own world. It speaks to us *because* of what the writer brings to the writing from our world: how he or she was raised and educated; his or her likes and dislikes; the events occurring in the real world at the time of the writing, and while the author was growing up. When we know what an author has brought to his or her work, we gain a greater insight into both the "originality" (the world of the book), and the things that "compound" it. This insight enables us to question that created world and find answers more readily. By informing ourselves, we are able to establish a more effective dialogue with both book and author.

*Novels for Students,* in addition to providing a plot summary and descriptive list of characters—to remind readers of what they have read—also explores the external influences that shaped each book. Each entry includes a discussion of the author's background, and the historical context in which the novel was written. It is vital to know, for instance, that when Ray Bradbury was writing *Fahrenheit 451* (Vol. 1), the threat of Nazi domination had recently ended in Europe, and the McCarthy hearings were taking place in Washington, D.C. This information goes far in answering the question, "Why did he write a story of oppressive government control and book burning?" Similarly, it is important to know that Harper Lee, author of *To Kill a Mockingbird,* was born and raised in Monroeville, Alabama, and that her father was a lawyer. Readers can now

see why she chose the south as a setting for her novel—it is the place with which she was most familiar—and start to comprehend her characters and their actions.

*Novels for Students* helps readers find the answers they seek when they establish a dialogue with a particular novel. It also aids in the posing of questions by providing the opinions and interpretations of various critics and reviewers, broadening that dialogue. Some reviewers of *To Kill A Mockingbird,* for example, "faulted the novel's climax as melodramatic." This statement leads readers to ask, "Is it, indeed, melodramatic?" "If not, why did some reviewers see it as such?" "If it is, why did Lee choose to make it melodramatic?" "Is melodrama ever justified?" By being spurred to ask these questions, readers not only learn more about the book and its writer, but about the nature of writing itself.

The literature included for discussion in *Novels for Students* has been chosen because it has something vital to say to us. *Of Mice and Men, Catch-22, The Joy Luck Club, My Antonia, A Separate Peace* and the other novels here speak of life and modern sensibility. In addition to their individual, specific messages of prejudice, power, love or hate, living and dying, however, they and all great literature also share a common intent. They force us to *think*—about life, literature, and about others, not just about ourselves. They pry us from the narrow confines of our minds and thrust us outward to confront the world of books and the larger, real world we all share. *Novels for Students* helps us in this confrontation by providing the means of enriching our conversation with literature and the world, by creating an *informed* dialogue, one that brings true pleasure to the personal act of reading.

## Sources

Harold Bloom, *The Western Canon, The Books and School of the Ages,* Riverhead Books, 1994.

Watty Piper, *The Little Engine That Could,* Platt & Munk, 1930.

*Anne Devereaux Jordan
Senior Editor,* TALL (Teaching and Learning Literature)

# Introduction

## Purpose of the Book

The purpose of *Novels for Students* (*NfS*) is to provide readers with a guide to understanding, enjoying, and studying novels by giving them easy access to information about the work. Part of Gale's "For Students" Literature line, *NfS* is specifically designed to meet the curricular needs of high school and undergraduate college students and their teachers, as well as the interests of general readers and researchers considering specific novels. While each volume contains entries on "classic" novels frequently studied in classrooms, there are also entries containing hard-to-find information on contemporary novels, including works by multicultural, international, and women novelists. Entries profiling film versions of novels not only diversify the study of novels but support alternate learning styles, media literacy, and film studies curricula as well.

The information covered in each entry includes an introduction to the novel and the novel's author; a plot summary, to help readers unravel and understand the events in a novel; descriptions of important characters, including explanation of a given character's role in the novel as well as discussion about that character's relationship to other characters in the novel; analysis of important themes in the novel; and an explanation of important literary techniques and movements as they are demonstrated in the novel.

In addition to this material, which helps the readers analyze the novel itself, students are also provided with important information on the literary and historical background informing each work. This includes a historical context essay, a box comparing the time or place the novel was written to modern Western culture, a critical essay, and excerpts from critical essays on the novel. A unique feature of *NfS* is a specially commissioned critical essay on each novel, targeted toward the student reader.

The "literature to film" entries on novels vary slightly in form, providing background on film technique and comparison to the original, literary version of the work. These entries open with an introduction to the film, which leads directly into the plot summary. The summary highlights plot changes from the novel, key cinematic moments, and/or examples of key film techniques. As in standard entries, there are character profiles (noting omissions or additions, and identifying the actors), analysis of themes and how they are illustrated in the film, and an explanation of the cinematic style and structure of the film. A cultural context section notes any time period or setting differences from that of the original work, as well as cultural differences between the time in which the original work was written and the time in which the film adaptation was made. A film entry concludes with a critical overview and critical essays on the film.

To further help today's student in studying and enjoying each novel or film, information on media adaptations is provided (if available), as well as suggestions for works of fiction, nonfiction, or film on similar themes and topics. Classroom aids include ideas for research papers and lists of critical and reference sources that provide additional material on the novel. Film entries also highlight signature film techniques demonstrated, and suggest media literacy activities and prompts to use during or after viewing a film.

## *Selection Criteria*

The titles for each volume of *NfS* are selected by surveying numerous sources on notable literary works and analyzing course curricula for various schools, school districts, and states. Some of the sources surveyed include: high school and undergraduate literature anthologies and textbooks; lists of award-winners, and recommended titles, including the Young Adult Library Services Association (YALSA) list of best books for young adults. Films are selected both for the literary importance of the original work and the merits of the adaptation (including official awards and widespread public recognition).

Input solicited from our expert advisory board—consisting of educators and librarians—guides us to maintain a mix of "classic" and contemporary literary works, a mix of challenging and engaging works (including genre titles that are commonly studied) appropriate for different age levels, and a mix of international, multicultural and women authors. These advisors also consult on each volume's entry list, advising on which titles are most studied, most appropriate, and meet the broadest interests across secondary (grades 7–12) curricula and undergraduate literature studies.

## *How Each Entry Is Organized*

Each entry, or chapter, in *NfS* focuses on one novel. Each entry heading lists the full name of the novel, the author's name, and the date of the novel's publication. The following elements are contained in each entry:

**Introduction:** a brief overview of the novel which provides information about its first appearance, its literary standing, any controversies surrounding the work, and major conflicts or themes within the work. Film entries identify the original novel and provide understanding of the film's reception and reputation, along with that of the director.

**Author Biography:** in novel entries, this section includes basic facts about the author's life, and focuses on events and times in the author's life that inspired the novel in question.

**Plot Summary:** a factual description of the major events in the novel. Lengthy summaries are broken down with subheads. Plot summaries of films are used to uncover plot differences from the original novel, and to note the use of certain film angles or other techniques.

**Characters:** an alphabetical listing of major characters in the novel. Each character name is followed by a brief to an extensive description of the character's role in the novel, as well as discussion of the character's actions, relationships, and possible motivation. In film entries, omissions or changes to the cast of characters of the film adaptation are mentioned here, and the actors' names—and any awards they may have received—are also included.

Characters are listed alphabetically by last name. If a character is unnamed—for instance, the narrator in *Invisible Man*—the character is listed as "The Narrator" and alphabetized as "Narrator." If a character's first name is the only one given, the name will appear alphabetically by that name.

Variant names are also included for each character. Thus, the full name "Jean Louise Finch" would head the listing for the narrator of *To Kill a Mockingbird*, but listed in a separate cross-reference would be the nickname "Scout Finch."

**Themes:** a thorough overview of how the major topics, themes, and issues are addressed within the novel. Each theme discussed appears in a separate subhead and is easily accessed through the boldface entries in the Subject/Theme Index. While the key themes often remain the same or similar when a novel is adapted into a film, film entries demonstrate how the themes are conveyed cinematically, along with any changes in the portrayal of the themes.

**Style:** this section addresses important style elements of the novel, such as setting, point of view, and narration; important literary devices used, such as imagery, foreshadowing, symbolism; and, if applicable, genres to which the work might have belonged, such as Gothicism or Romanticism. Literary terms are explained within the entry but can also be found in the Glossary. Film entries cover how the director conveyed the meaning, message, and mood of the work using film in comparison to the author's use of language, literary device, etc., in the original work.

**Historical Context:** in novel entries, this section outlines the social, political, and cultural climate in which the author lived and the novel was created. This section may include descriptions of related historical events, pertinent aspects of daily life in the culture, and the artistic and literary sensibilities of the time in which the work was written. If the novel is a historical work, information regarding the time in which the novel is set is also included. Each section is broken down with helpful subheads. Film entries contain a similar Cultural Context section because the film adaptation might explore an entirely different time period or culture than the original work, and may also be influenced by the traditions and views of a time period much different than that of the original author.

**Critical Overview:** this section provides background on the critical reputation of the novel or film, including bannings or any other public controversies surrounding the work. For older works, this section includes a history of how the novel or film was first received and how perceptions of it may have changed over the years; for more recent novels, direct quotes from early reviews may also be included.

**Criticism:** an essay commissioned by *NfS* which specifically deals with the novel or film and is written specifically for the student audience, as well as excerpts from previously published criticism on the work (if available).

**Sources:** an alphabetical list of critical material used in compiling the entry, with full bibliographical information.

**Further Reading:** an alphabetical list of other critical sources which may prove useful for the student. It includes full bibliographical information and a brief annotation.

In addition, each entry contains the following highlighted sections, set apart from the main text as sidebars:

**Media Adaptations:** if available, a list of audiobooks and important film and television adaptations of the novel, including source information. The list also includes stage adaptations, musical adaptations, etc.

**Topics for Further Study:** a list of potential study questions or research topics dealing with the novel. This section includes questions related to other disciplines the student may be studying, such as American history, world history, science, math, government, business, geography, economics, psychology, etc.

**Compare and Contrast:** an "at-a-glance" comparison of the cultural and historical differences between the author's time and culture and late twentieth century or early twenty-first century Western culture. This box includes pertinent parallels between the major scientific, political, and cultural movements of the time or place the novel was written, the time or place the novel was set (if a historical work), and modern Western culture. Works written after the mid-1970s may not have this box.

**What Do I Read Next?:** a list of works that might give a reader points of entry into a classic work (e.g., YA or multicultural titles) and/or complement the featured novel or serve as a contrast to it. This includes works by the same author and others, works from various genres, YA works, and works from various cultures and eras.

The film entries provide sidebars more targeted to the study of film, including:

**Film Technique:** a listing and explanation of four to six key techniques used in the film, including shot styles, use of transitions, lighting, sound or music, etc.

**Read, Watch, Write:** media literacy prompts and/or suggestions for viewing log prompts.

**What Do I See Next?:** a list of films based on the same or similar works or of films similar in directing style, technique, etc.

## *Other Features*

*NfS* includes "The Informed Dialogue: Interacting with Literature," a foreword by Anne Devereaux Jordan, Senior Editor for *Teaching and Learning Literature* (*TALL*), and a founder of the Children's Literature Association. This essay provides an enlightening look at how readers interact with literature and how *Novels for Students* can help teachers show students how to enrich their own reading experiences.

A Cumulative Author/Title Index lists the authors and titles covered in each volume of the *NfS* series.

A Cumulative Nationality/Ethnicity Index breaks down the authors and titles covered in each volume of the *NfS* series by nationality and ethnicity.

A Subject/Theme Index, specific to each volume, provides easy reference for users who may be studying a particular subject or theme rather than a single work. Significant subjects, from events to broad themes, are included.

Each entry may include illustrations, including photo of the author, stills from film adaptations, maps, and/or photos of key historical events, if available.

## *Citing Novels for Students*

When writing papers, students who quote directly from any volume of *Novels for Students* may use the following general forms. These examples are based on MLA style; teachers may request that students adhere to a different style, so the following examples may be adapted as needed.

When citing text from *NfS* that is not attributed to a particular author (i.e., the Themes, Style, Historical Context sections, etc.), the following format should be used in the bibliography section:

> "*Night.*" *Novels for Students*. Ed. Marie Rose Napierkowski. Vol. 4. Detroit: Gale, 1998. 234–35.

When quoting the specially commissioned essay from *NfS* (usually the first piece under the "Criticism" subhead), the following format should be used:

> Miller, Tyrus. Critical Essay on "*Winesburg, Ohio.*" *Novels for Students*. Ed. Marie Rose Napierkowski. Vol. 4. Detroit: Gale, 1998. 335–39.

When quoting a journal or newspaper essay that is reprinted in a volume of *NfS,* the following form may be used:

> Malak, Amin. "Margaret Atwood's *The Handmaid's Tale* and the Dystopian Tradition." *Canadian Literature* 112 (Spring 1987): 9–16. Excerpted and reprinted in *Novels for Students*. Vol. 4. Ed. Marie Rose Napierkowski. Detroit: Gale, 1998. 133–36.

When quoting material reprinted from a book that appears in a volume of *NfS,* the following form may be used:

> Adams, Timothy Dow. "Richard Wright: 'Wearing the Mask.'" In *Telling Lies in Modern American Autobiography*. University of North Carolina Press, 1990. 69–83. Excerpted and reprinted in *Novels for Students*. Vol. 1. Ed. Diane Telgen. Detroit: Gale, 1997. 59–61.

## *We Welcome Your Suggestions*

The editorial staff of *Novels for Students* welcomes your comments and ideas. Readers who wish to suggest novels to appear in future volumes, or who have other suggestions, are cordially invited to contact the editor. You may contact the editor via e-mail at: **ForStudents Editors@cengage.com.** Or write to the editor at:

Editor, *Novels for Students*
Gale
27500 Drake Road
Farmington Hills, MI 48331-3535

# Literary Chronology

**1628:** John Bunyan is born in November in Elstow, Bedfordshire, England.

**1678:** Part I of John Bunyan's *The Pilgrim's Progress* is published.

**1684:** Part II of John Bunyan's *The Pilgrim's Progress* is published.

**1688:** John Bunyan dies of a fever on August 31 in Holburn Ridge, England.

**1707:** Henry Fielding is born on April 22 in Somerset, England.

**1742:** Henry Fielding's *Joseph Andrews* is published.

**1754:** Henry Fielding dies on October 8 in Lisbon, Portugal.

**1789:** James Fenimore Cooper is born on September 15 in Burlington, New Jersey.

**1819:** Herman Melville is born on August 1 in New York, New York.

**1826:** James Fenimore Cooper's *Last of the Mohicans* is published.

**1843:** Henry James is born on April 15 in New York City.

**1846:** Herman Melville's *Typee* is published.

**1851:** James Fenimore Cooper dies on September 14 in Cooperstown, New York.

**1891:** Herman Melville dies of a heart attack on September 28 in New York, New York.

**1902:** Henry James's *The Wings of the Dove* is published.

**1912:** Gordon Roger Alexander Buchanan Parks is born on November 30 in Fort Scott, Kansas.

**1912:** Pierre-François-Marie-Louis Boulle is born on February 20 in Avignon, France.

**1916:** Henry James dies of pneumonia on February 28 in London, England.

**1918:** Madeleine L'Engle is born on November 29 in New York, New York.

**1926:** Harper Lee is born on April 28 in Monroeville, Alabama.

**1933:** Bryce Courtenay is born on August 14 in Johannesburg, South Africa.

**1941:** Sandra Benitez is born on March 26 in Washington, DC.

**1946:** Christopher C. Crutcher is born on July 17 in Dayton, Ohio.

**1948:** Ian McEwan is born on May on June 21 in Aldershot, Hampshire, England.

**1949:** Jane Graves Smiley is born on September 26 in Los Angeles, California.

**1952:** Pierre Boulle's *The Bridge over the River Kwai* is published.

**1960:** Harper Lee's *To Kill a Mockingbird* is published.

**1961:** Harper Lee's *To Kill a Mockingbird* is awarded the Pulitzer Prize for Fiction.

**1962:** Madeleine L'Engle's *A Wrinkle in Time* is published.

**1962:** The film *To Kill a Mockingbird* is released.

**1962:** The film *To Kill a Mockingbird* wins Academy Awards for Best Actor, Best Art Direction, and Best Screenplay.

**1963:** Gordon Parks's *The Learning Tree* is published.

**1989:** Bryce Courtenay's *The Power of One* is published.

**1991:** Jane Smiley's *A Thousand Acres* is published.

**1992:** Jane Smiley is awarded the Pulitzer Prize for Fiction for *A Thousand Acres*.

**1992:** The film *Last of the Mohicans* is released.

**1992:** The film *Last of the Mohicans* wins an Academy Award for Best Sound.

**1993:** Chris Crutcher's *Staying Fat for Sarah Byrnes* is published.

**1993:** Sandra Benitez's *A Place Where the Sea Remembers* is published.

**1994:** Pierre Boulle dies on January 20 in Paris, France.

**2001:** Ian McEwan's *Atonement* is published.

**2006:** Gordon Parks dies of cancer on March 7 in New York, New York.

**2007:** Madeleine L'Engle dies on September 6 in Litchfield, Connecticut.

# *Acknowledgments*

The editors wish to thank the copyright holders of the excerpted criticism included in this volume and the permissions managers of many book and magazine publishing companies for assisting us in securing reproduction rights. We are also grateful to the staffs of the Detroit Public Library, the Library of Congress, the University of Detroit Mercy Library, Wayne State University Purdy/Kresge Library Complex, and the University of Michigan Libraries for making their resources available to us. Following is a list of the copyright holders who have granted us permission to reproduce material in this volume of *NfS*. Every effort has been made to trace copyright, but if omissions have been made, please let us know.

**COPYRIGHTED EXCERPTS IN *NfS*, VOLUME 32, WERE REPRODUCED FROM THE FOLLOWING PERIODICALS:**

*African American Review*, v. 4, March 1, 1970. Reproduced by permission.—*America*, v. 187, July 15, 2002. Copyright 2002 www.america magazine.org. All rights reserved. Reproduced by permission of America Press. For subscription information, visit www.americamagazine.org.— *The Atlantic Monthly*, v. 289, March 1, 2002 for "The Beauty of the Conjuring: The Pernicious Power of Fine Storytelling Is a Central Theme in Ian McEwan's New Novel," by Claire Messud. Reproduced by permission of the author.— *Australian Screen Education*, winter, 2004. Copyright 2004 Australian Teachers of Media. Reproduced by permission.—*The Booklist*, v. 102, September 1, 2005; v. 103, May 15, 2007. Copyright © 2005, 2007 by the American Library Association. All reproduced by permission—*Brisbane News*, December 1, 2004. © 2009 Queensland Newspapers. Reproduced by permission of *Brisbane News* and the author.—*Critique*, v. 46, winter, 2005. Copyright © 2005 by Helen Dwight Reid Educational Foundation. Reproduced with permission of the Helen Dwight Reid Educational Foundation, published by Heldref Publications, 1319 18th Street, NW, Washington, DC 20036-1802.—*The English Journal*, v. 59, December 1, 1970; v. 94, November 1, 2004. Copyright © 1970, 2004 by the National Council of Teachers of English. All reproduced by permission of the publisher—*The Explicator*, v. 62, summer, 2004; v. 65, winter, 2007. Copyright © 2004, 2007 by Helen Dwight Reid Educational Foundation. All reproduced with permission of the Helen Dwight Reid Educational Foundation, published by Heldref Publications, 1319 18th Street, NW, Washington, DC 20036-1802—*Film & History*, v. 23, 1993. Copyright © 1993 Center for the Study of Film & History. Reproduced by permission.—*First Things: A Monthly Journal of Religion and Public Life*, v. 177, November 1, 2007. Copyright © 2007 Institute on Religion and Public Life. All rights reserved. Reproduced by permission.—*Horn Book Magazine*, v. 69, May-June, 1993. Copyright 1993 by The Horn Book, Inc., Boston, MA, www.hbook.com. All rights reserved. Reproduced by permission.—*The Journal of Blacks in Higher Education*, v. 40, summer, 2003. Reproduced by permission.—*Knight Ridder Tribune Business News*, January 15, 2006. Copyright © 2006, Detroit Free Press. Distributed by Knight Ridder/Tribune Business News. Reproduced by permission.—Gray, Ann M.G., 'The Power of One', page. 73, in *Library Media Connection*, v. 24, January 1, 2006. Copyright © 2006. Reproduced with permission of ABC-CLIO, LLC, Santa Barbara, CA.—*Literature/Film Quarterly*, v. 2, 1974; v. 34, 2006. Copyright © 1974, 2006 Salisbury State College. All reproduced by permission.—*The Midwest Quarterly*, v. 40, autumn, 1998. Copyright © 1998 by *The Midwest Quarterly*, Pittsburgh State University. Reproduced by permission.—*The Mississippi Quarterly*, v. 50, winter, 1996. Copyright © 1996 Mississippi State University. Reproduced by permission.—*The Modern Language Review*, v. 24, October 1, 1929 for a review of "The Pilgrim's Progress from This World to That Which Is to Come" by John Bunyan, by G. B. Harrison. Copyright © Modern Humanities Research Association 1929. Reproduced by permission of the author.—*Modern Language Studies*, v. 5, autumn, 1975 for "The Forbidden Fruit of 'Typee'," by Rita K. Gollin. Copyright © Northeast Modern Language Association 1975. Reproduced by permission of the publisher and the author.—*Papers on Language & Literature*, v. 16, summer, 1980. Copyright © 1980 by The Board of Trustees, Southern Illinois University at Edwardsville. Reproduced by permission.—*Publishers Weekly*, v. 240, July 1, 1993; v. 242, February 20, 1995. Copyright © 1993, 1995 by Reed Publishing USA. All reproduced from *Publishers Weekly*, published by the Bowker Magazine Group of Cahners Publishing Co., a division of Reed Publishing USA, by permission—*School Library Journal*, v. 51, November 1, 2005. Copyright © 2005. Reproduced from *School Library Journal*. A Cahners/R. R. Bowker Publication, by permission.—*The Writer*, v. 112, May 1, 1999 for "A Conversation with . . . Jane Smiley," by Lewis Burke Frumkes and Jane Smiley. Copyright © 1999 Kalmbach Publishing Company. Reproduced by permission of the author.

**COPYRIGHTED EXCERPTS IN *NfS*, VOLUME 32, WERE REPRODUCED FROM THE FOLLOWING BOOKS:**

Becker, Lucille Frackman. From "Pierre Boulle (1912-1994)," in *Multicultural Writers since 1945: An A-to-Z Guide*. Edited by Alba Amoia and Bettina L. Knapp. Greenwood Press, 2004. Copyright © 2004 by Alba Amoia and Bettina L. Knapp. All rights reserved. Reproduced by permission of ABC-CLIO, Santa Barbara, CA.—Creswell, Toby and Samantha Trenoweth. From *1001 Australians You Should Know*. Pluto Press Australia, 2006. Copyright © Toby Creswell and Samantha Trenoweth, 2006. Reproduced by permission.—Johnson-Woods, Toni. From "Popular Fiction 1960-2000," in *A Companion to Australian Literature Since 1900*. Edited by Nicholas Birns and Rebecca McNeer. Camden House, 2007. Copyright © 2007 by The Editors and Contributors. All rights reserved. Reproduced by permission.

# Contributors

**Bryan Aubrey:** Aubrey holds a Ph.D. in English. Entry on *To Kill a Mockingbird*. Original essay on *To Kill a Mockingbird*.

**Charlotte M. Freeman:** Freeman is a freelance writer and editor who holds a Ph.D. in English. Entry on *The Power of One*. Original essay on *The Power of One*.

**Cynthia Gower:** Gower is a freelance writer, novelist, and playwright. Entry on *The Wings of the Dove*. Original essay on *The Wings of the Dove*.

**Joyce Hart:** Hart is a published author and creative writing teacher. Entries on *Atonement* and *A Place Where the Sea Remembers*. Original essays on *Atonement* and *A Place Where the Sea Remembers*.

**Michael Holmes:** Holmes is an editor and writer. Entry on *The Last of the Mohicans*. Original essay on *The Last of the Mohicans*.

**David Kelly:** Kelly is a writer and an instructor in creative writing and literature. Entry on *The Learning Tree*. Original essay on *The Learning Tree*.

**Michael J. O'Neal:** O'Neal holds a Ph.D. in English literature. Entries on *Joseph Andrews*, *The Pilgrim's Progress*, *Typee*, and *A Wrinkle in Time*. Original essays on *Joseph Andrews*, *The Pilgrim's Progress*, *Typee*, and *A Wrinkle in Time*.

**Bradley A. Skeen:** Skeen is a classics professor. Entry on *The Bridge over the River Kwai*. Original essay on *The Bridge over the River Kwai*.

**Rebecca Valentine:** Valentine is a writer with an extensive background in literary theory and analysis. Entries on *Staying Fat for Sarah Byrnes* and *A Thousand Acres*. Original essays on *Staying Fat for Sarah Byrnes* and *A Thousand Acres*.

# *Atonement*

**IAN MCEWAN**

**2001**

Ian McEwan, whose novel *Atonement* was published in 2001, is known for his stories about dysfunctional relationships. Beginning in what appears to be an English idyllic country setting, where wealth and camaraderie seem to prevail, the author slowly introduces his readers to the darker side of a situation, one in which everything is turned upside down. Innocence is entangled with guilt, and falsehood obscures truth. At the center of this trauma is a thirteen-year-old girl named Briony, the youngest of the Tallis siblings. Briony wants to impress and is eager to call attention to herself. She also uses her broad imagination to twist circumstantial evidence into charges against her perceived enemies. Before the night is over, an innocent man will be marked for life. A guilty man will not be judged. And Briony will carry the weight of her actions and their consequences into adulthood. She will spend the rest of her life searching for atonement, a way to be forgiven for her wrongdoings.

Atonement* was shortlisted for the 2001 Booker Prize, the 2001 James Tait Black Memorial Prize, and the 2001 Whitbread Book Award. In 2002, the novel won the *Los Angeles Times* Book Prize and the National Book Critics Circle Award. *Time* magazine named *Atonement* the best novel of 2001, and the London *Observer* called McEwan's book one of the one hundred best novels ever written.

*Ian McEwan* *(David Levenson / Getty Images)*

## AUTHOR BIOGRAPHY

Ian McEwan is an award-wining British author, noted for his clear writing style and the dark psychological nature of his stories. He was born on June 21, 1948, in Aldershot, Hampshire, England, but grew up in the Far East, Germany, and North Africa, where his father, an officer in the British army, was posted. McEwan received a bachelor's degree in English from the University of Sussex and a master's degree in creative writing from the University of East Anglia (both in the United Kingdom).

In his late twenties McEwan published his first collection of short stories, *First Love, Last Rites* (1975), which won the 1976 Somerset Maugham Award. Three years later, he published his second collection, *In Between the Sheets* (1978). These stories received a lot of attention for their emphasis on deviant sexuality and dysfunctional family life. In that same year, McEwan produced his first novel, *The Cement Garden*, about four orphaned children and their struggles to survive. In 1981, *The Comfort of Strangers*, a story set in Venice, was published. This novel was shortlisted for the prestigious Booker Prize, which is awarded each year for the best novel written by a citizen of the British Commonwealth or Ireland.

In the following years, McEwan wrote *The Child in Time* (1987), *The Innocent* (1990), *Black Dogs* (1992), and *Enduring Love* (1997). These works were followed in 1998 by what most critics believe is McEwan's masterpiece, the Booker Prize–winning *Amsterdam*, a novel about three men—a composer, a newspaper editor, and a politician—who loved the same woman. The men meet one another at the woman's funeral and make a pact with one another, which sets off a great feud among them.

*Atonement*, published in 2001, was McEwan's next work. He has since published *Saturday* (2005) and *On Chesil Beach* (2007), which was also shortlisted for the Booker Prize. McEwan has also written plays, screenplays, and children's books. In 2008, he wrote the lyrics of an opera, *For You*. He has been married twice and has two sons. McEwan lives in London.

## PLOT SUMMARY

### Part One

Though Part One of McEwan's novel *Atonement* takes place on only one day in the middle of a hot summer, this first section makes up more than half of the novel. Part One is also divided into fourteen short chapters, whereas the rest of the novel has no chapter subdivisions. The setting is an English manor house in Surrey in the southeastern part of the England. It is 1935, and talk of England's becoming involved in a possible war in Europe has begun. The country estate belongs to the Tallis family. Jack Tallis, the father, a government official, is not at home, as is the normal case. Emily Tallis, the mother, is in bed with a migraine headache, a familiar condition. The children, therefore, are left on their own. Briony, the thirteen-year-old, has created a play, *The Trials of Arabella*, which she is rehearsing with her cousins, Lola, Jackson, and Pierrot Quincey. The Quincey children have come to stay with the Tallises while their parents go through a divorce. Leon, Briony's older brother, is coming from London for a visit, and Briony wrote the play to welcome him home.

Meanwhile, Cecilia Tallis, who is twenty-three, has returned home from Cambridge University for the summer. Though she does not fully understand her feelings, she is emotionally irritable. Her edginess has something to do with Robbie Turner, the son of the Tallises' housekeeper. Robbie, who is also twenty-three and returned from Cambridge, has grown up with the Tallis children and has always been a close friend. But

# MEDIA ADAPTATIONS

- In 2007, Focus Features Studios adapted McEwan's novel *Atonement* for the screen. Joe Wright directed the movie, which starred James McAvoy as Robbie and Keira Knightley as Cecilia; Saoirse Ronan played the thirteen- year-old Briony, Romola Garai portrayed her during the war years, and Vanessa Redgrave was the elderly Briony. Brenda Blethen portrayed Robbie's mother. The screenplay was written by Christopher Hampton. The movie was nominated for an Academy Award for best picture of that year.

- There are three audiotape versions of *Atonement*, a full- length recording performed by Jill Tanner and produced by Recorded Books (2002), another full version read by Carole Boyd and offered through Chivers Audio Books (2002), and an abridged version performed by Josephine Bailey and produced by Publishing Mills (2002).

in the past few years, Cecilia and Robbie have become uncomfortable in one another's company. A sexual tension has grown between them.

Briony witnesses a strange encounter between Cecilia and Robbie. Briony has taken a break from the frustrating play rehearsals. The young boys are not good actors, and Lola, who is sixteen and a bit more sophisticated than Briony, has assumed the lead role, one that Briony had coveted for herself. While standing at an upstairs window, Briony sees her sister talking to Robbie. She cannot hear their conversation, so she tries, in her inexperienced way, to interpret their body language. To her, it looks as if Robbie might be proposing marriage. If this is true, he is doing it in a very strange way. He looks as if he is commanding Cecilia to do something. In response, Cecilia takes off all her clothes but her underwear and jumps into a fountain and dives under the water. Briony, who writes overly dramatic romance,

thinks what she is watching is the total opposite of what should be happening. The hero should save the drowning maiden rather than demand that the maiden drown herself. After witnessing this strange scene, Briony swears she is done with writing romantic fantasy. She decides that watching real people and interpreting what they are doing is much more fascinating. She calls off the play.

In truth, what Briony witnesses is an argument between Cecilia and Robbie. In the course of trying to help Cecilia fill an antique vase with water, Robbie breaks off a piece. This ceramic piece drops into the fountain, and in a curious demonstration of self-reliance, Cecilia takes off her clothes and jumps into the fountain to retrieve it. Both Robbie and Cecilia later reflect on this confrontation and do not understand why they have both been acting so strangely. They admit they feel awkward around one another. Later, alone in his room, Robbie tries to comprehend what is behind this awkwardness and realizes that he is in love with Cecilia. He wants to explain his new feelings to Cecilia, but he fears he will be unable to speak the right words, so he attempts to write her a letter. He throws the first drafts away. Then he decides to just write what he is feeling. However, in one of his failed attempts, Robbie is a little too frank. He uses words expressing sexual desire. This note was fun to write for his own sake, but he would never use that kind of language with Cecilia.

After dressing to attend the celebratory dinner in Leon's honor, Robbie slips the note into an envelope and puts it in his pocket. On the way to the Tallises' house, he happens to meet Briony; he gives her the note and asks her to deliver it to Cecilia. After Briony runs into the house, Robbie realizes his mistake. He has given Briony the wrong note, the sexually explicit one. He runs to find Briony, but it is too late.

Briony cannot resist reading the note. She justifies her actions because she thinks a writer must know what goes on in the adult world. She is horrified by what she reads, believing that Robbie must be a monster who is about to attack her sister. As she wonders what she can do to protect Cecilia, she finds her cousin Lola crying. Lola has scratches on her arms, which she blames on her brothers. She says they jumped her. Since Lola has confided in her, Briony decides to tell her cousin about the note from Robbie.

Just before dinner, Briony hears noises in the library and opens the door to the darkened room. In the far corner she sees Cecilia and Robbie. Cecilia looks distressed and disheveled. After straightening her clothes and hair, Cecilia walks past Briony without saying anything. A few seconds later, Robbie does the same. Briony believes that Robbie has attacked Cecilia. What Briony does not know is that Robbie has explained his note to Cecilia. And Cecilia has confessed that she is in love with Robbie.

Emily, Briony's mother, joins everyone at the table for dinner. She is impressed by Paul Marshall, a friend of Leon's, who has made a lot of money from his candy-making company. Paul talks about his next professional move, which is to make a candy bar called Amo. It will be sold to the British military, and will make Paul even richer. Robbie notices fresh scratches on Paul's face and becomes suspicious when Lola's scratches are discussed at the table. But he does not say anything. Emily, however, believes that Paul is a perfect gentleman and regards him as a possible suitor for Cecilia. Emily does not like Robbie. This attitude is based more on Robbie's lack of money (he had been sent to Cambridge by Emily's husband) than on anything personal, though Emily is aware of a strange look on Robbie's face that she cannot interpret.

Throughout the dinner, Robbie and Cecilia think about their planned meeting somewhere private. Their passions are aroused, which is distracting them both from the meal and the table conversations. In a twist of events, just as dinner is completed, Pierrot and Jackson ask to be excused. Instead of going to the bathroom as they had suggested, they run away. The adults find the note the twins have left behind and go out to search for them.

Robbie is disappointed. He has hoped to be with Cecilia rather than hunting in the dark for the mischievous boys. Cecilia has taken off with her brother to search, while Robbie is left alone. Briony is also alone. As she searches the areas near the house, she happens upon Lola, who implies that she has been raped. Briony saw a dark figure slip away right before encountering Lola, but she has no real view of him. Despite this, she is convinced that it is Robbie. She bases her conclusion on Robbie's impassioned note to Cecilia. Briony appears to lead Lola into believing the attacker is Robbie. Lola was grabbed from behind, she tells Briony, and did not see the man's face.

Cecilia and Leon happen along and help Lola into the house. Briony runs upstairs to Cecilia's room and finds Robbie's note. Once Emily reads the note, she is sure that Robbie is the rapist. The police are called in. Shortly afterward, Robbie comes back with the two boys. He is caught totally off guard when he is arrested. Cecilia runs to him and says something that no one else hears. Robbie is put into the police car, and when the police try to leave, Robbie's mother, Grace, stands in the middle of the road. Finally, the police get Grace under control and drive away. Part One ends with Robbie's mother yelling at the Tallis family, telling them they are liars.

### Part Two

This section of the novel follows Robbie, who has been released from prison early on the condition that he volunteer for the British army. It is now 1939, and World War II has begun. Robbie has been in jail for four years. He did not see Cecilia while imprisoned, though they did write to one another. They plan a meeting before he is sent to France. But the timing is bad. Cecilia is working as a nurse and is having trouble getting time off. Meanwhile, emergency orders come in, and all military leave is cancelled. So Robbie and Cecilia can only meet briefly before he is sent to France.

The setting switches to France in 1940; the British troops have been defeated and are retreating. Robbie and two fellow soldiers, Corporal Nettle and Corporal Mace, have recently survived a bomb attack. Although the corporals outrank him, Robbie's education helps him to read maps and understand the country's geography. Although he is wounded, he does not tell anyone. The men have a long way to go with little or no food or water. Some farmers along the way provide what nourishment they can afford to share. As Robbie and the soldiers draw closer to Dunkirk, they join the masses of people—a mix of civilians and soldiers—who are following a main route to the northern French town. The British troops are making their way to the English Channel, where they hope to find boats ready to take them back home. From time to time, German airplanes fly over and drop bombs on the people or scatter a barrage of bullets through the crowds.

Throughout this section, Robbie reads letters he has received from Cecilia. She tells him that she no longer speaks to her family, that she wants nothing to do with them, especially with her sister, Briony. She does not believe she can ever forgive Briony. In her latest letter, Cecilia tells him that Briony has suggested that she is willing to recant her story against Robbie. Briony is hoping that the court will listen to her plea asking that all charges against Robbie be dismissed. She is willing to admit she made a mistake. This and Robbie's memory of Cecilia telling him, on the night of his arrest, that she will always love him and will wait for him, inspires Robbie to keep moving toward the beach so he can return to her. His wound is festering and he is becoming delirious owing to the infection as well as hunger, thirst, and exhaustion.

McEwan uses the British soldiers' long journey to the north of France to give an up-close view of World War II and its casualties. Body parts litter the landscape. Wounded citizens and soldiers sit along the roadside begging for assistance. Children and women die as they try to find shelter. Everyone knows that the German army is marching toward them. Belgium and the Netherlands have fallen under German control.

By the time Robbie and his fellow soldiers arrive at the beach at the English Channel, Robbie is in a semiconscious state. The two soldiers whom Robbie led safely through the war zone are now focused on saving him. Most of the men at the beach are equally desperate. There is no supply of food or water readily available. Robbie helps a local woman catch her pig, and she rewards him with food and drink. But the men have to be cautious about where they eat their food. Others might kill for the food Robbie and his friends have. This section closes with a rumor that a British boat is scheduled to arrive the next day. At the end of Part Two, Robbie is completely delirious.

### Part Three

Part Three also takes place in 1940, four years after that summer night when Robbie was arrested. The story turns its attention to Briony, who has become a student nurse, just as Cecilia had several years before. The hospital where Briony works is preparing for the wounded soldiers. One day, lines of army ambulances arrive, and terribly wounded soldiers are brought in. Briony must come to terms with the war. She attends to young boys with parts of their heads blown off. She smells the gangrene of infected wounds. She feeds soldiers who no longer have mouths. She thinks that one of these soldiers could have been Robbie. The thought of him being wounded, or dead, makes the guilt of what she has done even greater.

In the middle of this activity, Briony receives a response from a publisher to whom she has sent a short novel. Her story has been rejected, but the publisher writes a long explanation full of encouragement. He is impressed with her story's depth and style, but he notes several flaws and makes suggestions as to how Briony can change the story to make it publishable. Among other things, he suggests that she supply more details. One of his questions is "If this girl has so fully misunderstood or been so wholly baffled by the strange little scene that has unfolded before her, how might it affect the lives of the two adults?" Then he asks: "Might she come between them in some disastrous fashion?" This makes it clear that Briony's novel is based on what happened in Part One.

When Briony learns that her cousin Lola and Paul Marshall are to be married, she sneaks into the back of the church to watch the ceremony. She wants to make sure that both Paul and Lola see her. She wants them to know that she knows their secret and will never forget it. Briony believes it was Paul who had sex with Lola. Whether or not it was rape is never made clear. What readers do know is that neither Paul nor Lola come forth and confess that Robbie was not the rapist.

Taking care of the wounded soldiers and seeing Lola and Paul's wedding ceremony bring Briony's guilt to the forefront. She is now conscious of the pain she has caused her sister and Robbie and is determined to meet with Cecilia, who has not wanted anything to do with her.

Briony arrives at Cecilia's apartment and is surprised to find Robbie there. Robbie tells Briony that if she wants to help them, she is to write a letter to her family proclaiming his innocence. She is also to go to court to try to clear Robbie's name. Robbie is on his way to return to his army unit, so he and Cecilia leave Briony on her own.

### London, 1999

McEwan ends Part Three with a signature that reads: BT, London, 1999. Then he begins the last section of the novel with the heading, London, 1999. The "BT" in the signature, readers can assume, stands for Briony Tallis. Readers learn in this last section that what they have read prior to this is the novel that Briony had sent to her publisher. Only this last section is set outside the boundaries of Briony's novel.

Briony has been diagnosed with vascular dementia, a mental condition that will eventually strip her of all memory and kill her. She is seventy-seven and is on her way to the Tallis estate for a family birthday celebration in her honor. Before she leaves London, Briony puts all her affairs in order, including the notes on her novel. Her editors have said that, owing to the possibility of lawsuits, she cannot publish it until Lola and Paul Marshall have died. Fearing she might die before the Marshalls do, Briony has left instructions with her publisher on how to deal with her manuscript.

As Briony sits with her family and watches her great-grandchildren put on the play that she wrote when she was thirteen, she has an inner monologue with her readers. By the end of McEwan's novel, it is not clear if the story prior to this last section is a statement of fact, a fictionalized version of fact, or a complete fabrication. Since Briony is concerned about a lawsuit, readers might conclude that the story was based on fact. But Briony's inner monologue clouds this issue. She wonders if she ended her novel properly. She had different options. She could have had both Robbie and Cecilia die. Or she could have ended it happily. So readers do not know which parts of her novel were based on truth and which were not.

## CHARACTERS

### Betty
Betty is the Tallises' cook and housemaid. She appears in Part One as an easily irritated woman who scares Jackson and Pierrot with her stern voice.

### Doll
Doll is only briefly mentioned in Part One as one of the Tallises' servants.

### Sister Marjorie Drummond
Sister Drummond is a strong disciplinarian who teaches Briony and the other student nurses. She is very stern and rarely praises the nurses. However, when the wounded soldiers begin to arrive, Sister Drummond changes and treats the nurses more like equals.

### Fiona
Fiona is Briony's roommate and a friend at the hospital. She is a storyteller who breaks the tension of the nurses' training through her ability to make others laugh.

### Danny Hardman
Danny is the sixteen-year-old son of Mr. Hardman. He only appears briefly, but Robbie and Cecilia suspect Danny was the rapist.

### Mr. Hardman
Mr. Hardman is Danny's father. He works on the Tallis estate as a handyman and gardener.

### Corporal Mace
Corporal Mace is one of the two soldiers who travel with Robbie through France. He is described as a large-sized soldier and often protects Robbie, especially when they finally reach Dunkirk and Robbie is ill.

### Paul Marshall
Paul is Leon's rich friend and owns a candy company. Paul is the man who has sex with Lola Quincey. It is not made clear whether he raped Lola or whether Lola consented to his advances and was later ashamed of the act. Paul and Lola eventually marry. Paul becomes rich and politically influential in his later years. Because of this, Briony is advised not to publish her novel about him until Paul is dead.

### Corporal Nettle
Nettle is one of the two soldiers who walk across France with Robbie during the British retreat. He helps take care of Robbie as he grows weak from his wound. Nettle is mentioned at the end of the novel when Briony corresponds with him. Nettle provides information about the war for her book.

### Polly
Polly is a cook and housemaid for the Tallis family.

### Cecil Quincey
Cecil is Lola's father and makes his only appearance when Lola and Paul are married. In the beginning of the novel, Cecil is mentioned because he and his wife are getting a divorce.

### Hermione Quincey
Hermione is the sister of Emily Tallis. She is also the mother of Lola and the twins and the wife of Cecil. Hermione only appears in the story when Lola and Paul are married.

### Jackson Quincey

Jackson is one of Lola's nine-year-old twin brothers. Jackson is the twin who wet his bed and was made to wash out his sheets as punishment. He and his brother are disappointed when Briony cancels the play for which he has rehearsed. He runs away with his brother the night that his sister, Lola, is supposedly raped.

### Lola Quincey

Lola is the fifteen-year-old cousin of Briony. She comes with her twin brothers to stay with the Tallises while her mother and father are considering a divorce. Lola is two years older than Briony and a bit more sophisticated. She is emotionally upset, though, when Paul Marshall makes sexual advances. When Paul has sex with her in the garden, she either pretends not to know or truly does not know that it was Paul, and she allows Robbie to be charged with the crime. At the end of the novel, Lola reappears briefly. Briony notices that Lola is in much better health than she is. This makes Briony realize that her novel might not be published until after she herself dies because Lola might outlive her.

### Pierrot Quincey

Pierrot is one of Lola's nine-year-old twin brothers. Pierrot is the twin who thought acting in a play was just another way of showing off. Later, he was disappointed about Briony's canceling the show, so he runs away with his brother, Jackson.

### Briony Tallis

Briony could be considered the protagonist of this story. She is also the author of the story within the story, and the focus is on her for a large part of the novel. It is Briony who writes the play at the beginning of the story, who sees Robbie and Cecilia together, and who seeks the atonement that is the title of the story. She is guilty of accusing Robbie of raping Lola, though she later recants her accusation. Briony is thirteen when the story begins, and her imagination is very active. She views the adult world from a child's perspective, seeing adult acts through the lens of melodrama. When she was ten, she was in love with Robbie for a couple of days, and pretended to drown so Robbie would save her. There is one point in the story when Robbie wonders if this is the reason Briony lied about the rape of Lola.

In the third part of the novel, Briony worries about the weight of guilt she has carried since she realized the wrong she did to Cecilia and Robbie. She wants to make amends, but she does not know how she can give them the time that she took away from them. Also in the third part of the story, readers learn that Briony has written a novel that sounds very much like the novel McEwan has written. In the last section of the book, this is confirmed. Briony has written the first three parts of the novel. At the end of her life, she realizes that she may never see the book published because the book places the blame for Robbie's time in jail on Paul and Lola, and the book cannot be published until they have died.

### Cecilia Tallis

Cecilia is the older sister of Briony. As the story opens, Cecilia has just returned from Girton College at Cambridge University. She is confused about the agitation she experiences at the sight of Robbie. Later, she confesses her passion for Robbie. When Robbie is charged with the rape of Lola, Cecilia tells him she will always wait for him. Because the family did not support Robbie, Cecilia vows never to have anything to do with them. She enters nurse's training while Robbie is in jail. Cecilia's last scene in the novel takes place at her apartment, where Briony has come to ask for forgiveness. At the end of Part Three, Robbie and Cecilia are shown walking away from Briony to spend together the last few hours before Robbie has to report back to military duty. Briony, at the end of the novel, strongly implies that Cecilia might have died and might never have been reunited with Robbie.

### Emily Tallis

Emily is the mother of Briony, Cecilia, and Leon. She suffers from severe headaches and spends most of her time in bed. She has been all but abandoned by her husband, who she suspects is having affairs. She is quiet about her conclusions, sensing that when she and her husband grow old, he will return to her. Emily makes rash judgments about the people in her life, which are often off the mark. For example, she is impressed with Paul Marshall and considers him a great suitor for Cecilia. On the other hand, she does not trust Robbie, whom she views as some kind of deviant. Emily's perceptions are obviously tainted by wealth. Paul has it. Robbie does not. Emily is present only in Part One of the novel.

### Jack Tallis

Jack Tallis is Emily's husband and the father of Briony, Cecilia, and Leon. He is often not at home and does not appear in the novel, except through phone calls. Jack is, at first, very supportive of Robbie, at least financially. He pays for Robbie to attend Cambridge and in the beginning of the novel has agreed to send him to medical school. However, when Robbie is charged with rape, Jack does not come to his defense.

### Leon Tallis

Leon is Briony and Cecilia's older brother. When the story opens, Leon is coming home for a visit and the family is celebrating his return. Leon does not play a significant role in this story.

### Ernest Turner

Ernest is Robbie's father. He never makes an appearance in the novel. Ernest used to be the gardener on the Tallis estate. However, one day he left without a word and was never seen again.

### Grace Turner

Grace is Robbie's mother. She works as a housekeeper for the Tallises and lives in a cottage on the estate. When Ernest leaves Grace and Robbie behind, Jack Tallis signs the cottage over to Grace. However, after the Tallises do not come to Robbie's defense during his trial, Grace leaves the cottage behind. She does not reappear in the story.

### Robbie Turner

Robbie grew up on the Tallis estate. He was friends, from childhood, with Leon and especially with Cecilia. He is the son of Grace, the Tallises' housekeeper. Robbie comes to the story at a slight disadvantage as far as social class is concerned. Cecilia accepts him for who he is, but she suspects, when Robbie does not speak to her when they are both at Cambridge, that it might be his social standing that makes him feel awkward around her. Robbie exposes the real reason for his awkwardness and it has everything to do with the fact that he has fallen in love with Cecilia. Robbie is charged with the rape of Lola and spends four years in jail. He is released only because he volunteers to join the British army. He is wounded while in France. According to Briony's version of the story in her novel, he returns to England and meets again with Cecilia. However, it is suggested that Robbie might have died of his wounds at Dunkirk and therefore never saw Cecilia again.

## THEMES

### Guilt and Forgiveness

In McEwan's novel *Atonement* there are many characters who might or should feel guilt and seek atonement; however, there is only one character who does. That is Briony. Briony's accusation that Robbie has raped Lola sends Robbie to jail and alters not only the course of his relationship with Cecilia but his entire life. Instead of going to medical school, Robbie spends years in prison for a crime he did not commit.

McEwan does not go into why or how Briony admits her mistake in identifying Robbie as the criminal, but he does shows evidence of the guilt she suffers and her attempts to atone for her mistake. Briony foregoes her studies of literature and writing and enlists in nurse's training, for example. She wants to help others because she is responsible for causing her sister and Robbie pain. When she encounters wounded soldiers, her guilt runs even deeper. She realizes that one of these soldiers could have been Robbie. He might even have died in the war without ever seeing Cecilia again. All this might have happened because she sent him to jail.

Briony's other attempts at atonement are the writing of her novel about what happened that night on the Tallis estate. She also offers to explain Robbie's innocence to her parents and to the courts in hopes that Robbie's name will be cleared. None of this, however, will give Robbie and Cecilia the opportunities they have already lost.

There should be guilt on other characters' shoulders, too. Neither Paul Marshall nor Lola come forward to give evidence of Robbie's innocence. None of the Tallises, other than Cecilia, stand up for Robbie. But McEwan marginalizes these characters, keeping them in the background of the story. So readers have no idea what they are feeling.

### Truth

What is truth? McEwan seems to be asking this question throughout his novel. Does anyone know truth for sure? Is there anything that a person could claim was absolutely true? McEwan offers several versions of truth, such as the different versions of what happened at the fountain. Briony believes one truth about the situation, but this does not match what her sister believes. And even her sister, Cecilia, is not sure why she acted the way

# TOPICS FOR FURTHER STUDY

- Create a relief map of France, marking the various positions of the German, French, and British troops during the 1939–1940 time period of the British retreat. Show the journey that Robbie takes on foot, according to the details in the novel. However, also research the history of this time period and, as accurately as possible, list the casualties, the positions of the major conflicts, and the number of ships and number of soldiers who were evacuated from Dunkirk. Display your map, explaining the details to your class.

- Read Jane Austen's *Northanger Abbey*. Compare the protagonist of Austen's novel, Catherine Norland, with McEwan's character Briony Tallis. How are their personalities similar? How do they differ? How do the consequences of Catherine's misinterpretations affect the lives of the other characters in Austen's novel? Are the consequences as serious as those caused by Briony? Write an analysis and comparison of the two protagonists in these novels.

- Using the details provided, as well as the suggested state of Briony's mind at age thirteen, recreate Briony's play *The Trials of Arabella*. Creatively fill in any details that are not included in the novel. Then select players and perform the play for your literature class.

- Videotape a candid conversation between two adults. Ask their permission first, but encourage them to be as natural as possible. Record the tape from a distance. Then show the tape to a preteen and ask him or her to interpret what might have been going on in the conversation. Next, come to your own conclusions as to what might have been happening. Finally, ask the couple you videotape to explain what they were doing and talking about. Print all three interpretations, then present the tape and the three different interpretations to your class without identifying whose interpretations they are. Take a survey. Which of the interpretations do your classmates believe is the real one?

- Lead a discussion of McEwan's novel *Atonement* in your class. The purpose of this discussion is to provide possible answers for many of the unanswered questions in this novel. Some of the questions to be considered for discussion might include: Why did Briony accuse Robbie of raping Lola? Why did the Tallis family not help Robbie fight the charge? Did Paul rape Lola? If so, why did Lola protect him? Did Robbie die at Dunkirk? Did Cecilia die during the war? Create more questions if needed to keep the discussion lively.

she did in front of the fountain. Was she really angry at Robbie? Or was something else going on?

Briony is confused about a lot of things that happened on the night of the welcome home dinner. Was Robbie truly a crazed monster? Or was he in love? Was Lola really raped? Or was she complicit in the act but too embarrassed to admit it? McEwan continues to push the boundary between fiction and truth when he makes Briony the author of his own story. McEwan pushes so hard that he appears to be saying that nothing is true. Everyone can come to their own conclusion about what is truth.

## Family Dysfunction

McEwan's novels are known for having family dysfunction as a theme. In this novel, there are several families whose relationships suffer from poor communication and lack of compassion. In the Tallis family, the mother and father might as well be living separate lives. Their marriage is held together by a very fragile string. Mrs. Tallis suspects infidelity but will not mention it. She would rather have a partial marriage than no marriage at all. Her unhappiness makes her so sick she can barely attend to her children. The children hardly

*Saoirse Ronan as Briony in the 2007 film version of the novel* (Focus Features / The Kobal Collection / Bailey, Alex / The Picture Desk, Inc.)

know her and go about their lives without much adult intervention. When emotions become tangled and misunderstandings brew, the children have no one to help them untangle the knots. Briony and Cecilia's communication completely breaks down. Their older brother Leon, like his father, is almost always gone. The only way that Briony and Cecilia are able to define themselves is to completely cut themselves off from the other members of their family and put themselves together on their own.

Another example of dysfunction occurs in Robbie's family. Though his mother is supportive and nurturing, his father has abandoned his wife and son. The father simply disappears without offering a reason. This leaves his son wondering who his father was and why his father left him—questions that will remain unanswered.

Lola Quincey and her twin brothers do not fare much better. Both parents abandon them, leaving them to fend for themselves at the Tallis estate. With their parents gone, the twins turn to their sister, Lola, who is too young to explain their parents' absence. She is too young to ease

their pain. Lola is preoccupied with her own issues, which not only consume her but confuse her. The consequences are torturous. In her bewilderment, she sends a man to jail.

## STYLE

### *Metafiction*

Metafiction is a literary device used when the author of a work of fiction wants to call attention to the fact that what has been written has been fabricated. In McEwan's *Atonement*, metafiction is used when the author gives the impression that one of his fictional characters is the actual author of this piece of fiction. Through this device, McEwan questions the relationship between fiction and reality. McEwan waits until almost the end of the novel before he informs his readers that the most of the novel was (supposedly) written by one of his invented characters.

One of the purposes of metafiction is to make readers consciously aware that fiction is not the same as reality. Metafiction is used to demonstrate the difficulties in attempting to reconstruct reality through language. Up to the point of Briony's disclosure that she is the author of the first three parts of the novel, the story being told might feel real to readers. Because of this, readers become lost in the world that McEwan has created. Most novelists attempt to create fictional worlds that appear to be real. McEwan, however, wants the reader to be aware of how unreliable the fictional world is. When McEwan has Briony take over authorship of the novel and then also creates a scene in which she discusses various endings that she might have used, he emphasizes how uncertain language can be in representing the world. In other words, McEwan, through metafiction, demonstrates how easily words can change the world that is being described.

## Confusing Role of Protagonist

Although Briony is a dominant character in McEwan's novel, she shares the role with Robbie as protagonist in many ways. In the first part of the story, the narrator is omniscient, following both Briony and Robbie and listening to their thoughts. One might conclude that the two characters share the role of protagonist. In the second part of the story, Briony disappears as Robbie takes over the leading role. Readers follow Robbie through his challenges as he fights to stay alive. Then in the third part of the story, the focus returns to Briony and stays with her until the end of the story.

What makes the idea of Briony as protagonist ironic is that in the last section of the novel, Briony reveals that she is the author of the first three parts of the story. This turn of events makes it more difficult to define Briony as protagonist because readers become confused with the question of Briony's existence. Is she real? Or is she a fictional character? Is the story a fictionalized account of real events or is it a memoir? If the story is autobiographical fiction, how did Briony create the section about Robbie in the war? Was that part purely fiction?

Of course, McEwan is the real author, but he leaves a lot of questions unanswered, especially that of his protagonist. In the end, most readers probably will assume that it is Briony.

## HISTORICAL CONTEXT

### Great Britain and World War II

British leaders were busy trying to keep their economy from falling apart in the 1930s, as the Great Depression put more than two million of its citizens out of work. Thus, in 1938, the leaders of Great Britain were reluctant to go to war against Germany. The belief was that if they stayed out of the mounting conflict on the European mainland a second world war might be averted. In 1938, British Prime Minister Neville Chamberlain signed an agreement with Germany called the Munich Pact that essentially gave Hitler's forces permission to take complete control of Czechoslovakia. However, by 1939, Great Britain took a stand. They announced that if Germany invaded Poland, they would declare war. Though their military forces were underprepared, nine months later, on September 3, 1939, when German troops crossed the border into Poland and refused to withdraw, Great Britain (along with France) declared war on Germany. World War II had begun. After the declaration of war, all British men age twenty or older were drafted into the military.

In preparation for an all-out war, cities shut off their lights at night, food and supplies were rationed, and children living in large metropolitan areas of Great Britain were sent to live in the country. By the spring of 1940, Germany had swept through and gained control of France, Belgium, the Netherlands, Luxembourg, Denmark, Norway, and Romania. Britain was the next country on Hitler's radar.

Prime Minister Chamberlain had not been able to back up his claim that Hitler would not become a threat. In May 1940 Winston Churchill, who had been First Lord of the Admiralty and was considered more aggressive than Chamberlain, was elected prime minister. However, Churchill had been in office only a few weeks when Hitler went on a huge offensive and forced Britain to rescue its troops after a disastrous campaign at Dunkirk, France. Germany was encouraged by the large-scale evacuation of the troops, and from July until October 1940, German planes bombed Britain on a daily basis. The bombings continued into the spring of 1941. The United States offered support to Britain in 1941 in the form of guns and ammunition. On December 7, 1941, Japan bombed U.S. ships in Pearl Harbor, and the United States was drawn into the war. Churchill, who proved to be an inspiring leader, called on the citizens of England to work for the cause of defeating Germany. Women and old, retired men were asked to help in any way they could. Some worked as plane spotters. Others worked as night

# COMPARE
# &
# CONTRAST

- **1940s:** World War II engulfs Europe as Hitler's German forces moved toward France and Great Britain.

  **2000s:** War in Iraq and Afghanistan is fought by a coalition of military forces from the United States, Great Britain, and several other European countries.

- **1940s:** Women join the war effort by taking on jobs such as mechanics and nurses but are not actively involved in the fighting of World War II.

**2000s:** Women join the military services and are trained to fight on the battlefields in Iraq and Afghanistan.

- **1940s:** Circumstantial evidence can be used to send a man to jail for rape.

  **2000s:** Though circumstantial evidence can send a man to trial for rape, new techniques in DNA research can also help prove a man's innocence.

watchmen, looking for German spies who might have snuck into the country. Women, in particular, went to work on farms to help grow food for the surging numbers of men who were fighting abroad. Women also worked in great numbers in hospitals and in the armed forces as truck drivers and pilots. Even the future queen, Elizabeth II, volunteered as a mechanic in the British army.

In the end, the Allies won the war against Germany. However, in the process, Great Britain lost over 300,000 soldiers and more than 60,000 civilians.

### *Battle at Dunkirk*

British troops were sent to France to help the French army hold off the German forces. At one point, in May 1940, the British troops were cut off from their French compatriots and were surrounded by the German army, both on land and in the air. Realizing their impossible situation, the British troops were ordered to retreat to Dunkirk on the northern French coast. Winston Churchill, the British prime minister, sent orders for all ships and boats (military, commercial, and civilian) in the immediate area to go to Dunkirk and rescue as many soldiers as they could. Over 300,000 soldiers were evacuated. Masses of machinery and supplies that had previously been shipped into France to equip the

British soldiers were left behind for German troops to seize.

Today, Dunkirk, which is located just six miles south of Belgium, is France's third-largest sea harbor. The city of more than 250,000 people in its metropolitan area is connected by ferry with Dover, England.

### CRITICAL OVERVIEW

McEwan's award-winning novel *Atonement* was a best seller in both the United Kingdom and the United States. According to an article by Brian Finney, writing for the *Journal of Modern Literature*, *Atonement* was "greeted by most book critics as a masterpiece that unexpectedly stayed at the top of the best seller lists of the *New York Times* for many weeks." Finney continues, "Almost all American reviewers of the book have given it the highest praise possible." The same was not true for the British critics, however. Finney writes, "The few reviewers (largely British) who have voiced major reservations about the novel invariably focus on the concluding section in which it is revealed that Briony . . . has been the author of the entire novel and has taken a novelist's license to alter the facts to suit her artistic purposes." Finney explains that he read the novel

*Stokesay Court in Ludlow, Shropshire, UK, where the film adaptation of the novel was set* (© *John Snowdon /
Alamy*)

"as a work of fiction that is from beginning to end
concerned with the making of fiction."

Naturally, a lot that has been discussed
about *Atonement* focuses on the complexity
of the novel and the way McEwan twists the
narrative by having Briony take ownership of
its authorship. Peter Mathews, in his article for
*ESC: English Studies in Canada*, describes the
construction of the novel in this way: "Each
new chapter forces the reader to revise his or
her understanding of what was revealed earlier, sowing seeds of doubt that make the
text blossom into a set of irreconcilable uncer-
tainties." Mathews continues: "While the novel
demonstrates the potentially tragic results of
hasty judgment, its increasing ambiguity self-
reflexively turns this logic of shame back onto
the reader, so that the book's conclusion leaves
us, as witnesses, to ponder our own ability to
testify about the story that Briony has just
described." Later, Mathews writes: "McEwan's
novel thus possesses a complicated perspectivist
structure, a tactic that requires the reader continually to revise their view of particular events and
characters."

Also highlighting the complex structure of
McEwan's work, James Harold, writing for *Philosophy and Literature*, concludes that McEwan's
style and technique as demonstrated in this novel
"show us that an audience's participation in narrative is much more subtle and complex." Harold's
concluding remarks are that McEwan's novel is
remarkable because it takes "advantage of readers'
enormous flexibility in taking up different kinds of
viewpoints and deploying attention in creative and
sometimes conflicting ways."

An anonymous *Kirkus Reviews* critic finds
that McEwan owes a lot of his writing technique
to the famous British author Virginia Woolf, as
demonstrated by McEwan's combination of
"insight, penetrating historical understanding, and
sure-handed storytelling despite a conclusion that
borrows from early postmodern narrative trickery." Despite what this reviewer calls trickery, the
concluding remark is that *Atonement* is "master-
ful." Lawrence Rungren, writing for *Library Journal*, finds the novel to be "a compelling exploration
of guilt and the struggle for forgiveness." And
finally, Barbara Beckerman Davis, for *Antioch*

*Review*, states: "This is McEwan's most intricate book, but certainly his most ironic, deeply humane offering thus far."

# CRITICISM

## *Joyce Hart*

*Hart is a published author and creative writing teacher. In the following essay, she explores the unreliability of Briony, the supposed narrator of* Atonement.

In McEwan's novel *Atonement*, readers first assume that Briony Tallis is merely a character in the story. The narrator of the novel is unknown through most of the book and is assumed to be related to the author—a synthesized version of the author's writing voice. However, by the end of the novel, it is revealed that Briony is not only the author but that she has doubts about her portrayal of some of the characters. Upon reflection, this announcement throws details of the story into chaos. How can readers trust what Briony says or have confidence in her interpretations of what has happened? In other words, now that the narrator is identified, the complexities of the story increase in direct proportion to the decline in reliability of the supposed narrator, Briony. If readers are to assume that Briony is the narrator/author, they might begin to wonder what her motives were for writing the novel within the novel. Another issue to ponder is how this new information changes the story.

Briony is thirteen when the story opens. She is on the verge of adulthood—curious about the ways of adults but having no experience with which to compare them. In the first part of the story, it is obvious that Briony overreacts, misinterprets, and twists events to make them match her beliefs. In some ways, Briony, at the opening of the story, is somewhat humorous. Her overreactions are entertaining to read because for a while they have little consequence, except for Briony. For example, her judgment of Robbie as being a monster because of his lust for Cecilia is typical of a child who does not understand human sexual desires. At first, this judgment does no harm. Likewise, her belief that Cecilia has jumped into the water fountain because she wants to drown herself is born of Briony's juvenile concepts of love. She believes in the romance fantasy of a hero proving his love by saving the woman of his desires. Up to this point, Briony, as a character, may be tolerated and accepted as a typical young girl with a possibly

> RATHER THAN WORKING WITH THE WOUNDED SOLDIERS AS A WAY TO ATONE FOR HER SINS, COULD BRIONY JUST BE ADDING MORE REFERENCES TO DEMONSTRATE HOW GOOD SHE IS?"

overdeveloped imagination. Her conclusions affect no one but herself.

Toward the end of Part One, however, things become more dramatic. Briony's misguided observations and interpretations go awry. They become seriously consequential, deeply affecting the lives of the people around her. Briony alone claims to have recognized Robbie as the person who raped her cousin Lola. Even Lola does not know who that person was, or at least that is what Lola contends. To back up her accusation, Briony offers her mother the sexually explicit note that Robbie wrote to Cecilia. In today's courts, this probably would not be enough evidence to convict Robbie. However, in this novel, the note and Briony's accusation appear to be more than enough. Even when Robbie goes to jail, readers can almost forgive Briony, believing she is just a misguided young girl.

In Part Two, Briony disappears from the story line for the most part. There is mention of her in Cecilia's letters to Robbie and in Robbie's reflections. Briony, through a letter to Cecilia, hopes that her words will be enough to clear Robbie of the accusation of rape. Since the adults accepted Briony's evidence while she was merely thirteen, why would they not accept her withdrawing that evidence when she is an adult? Briony's words, she believes, are powerful. She has created stories most of her life. Why should she not be able to create new ones?

The other interesting insight into Briony and the way her mind works comes from Robbie, who remembers the incident in the pond when Briony was only ten. Briony had been swimming with Robbie and at one point dove into a part of the water that was dangerous enough that she might have drowned. Briony waited for Robbie to save her. She had fallen in love with Robbie and wanted him to prove his love for her. This piece of information makes the reader question Briony's

# WHAT DO I READ NEXT?

- McEwan's award-winning novel *Amsterdam* (1998), often called McEwan's best work, tells the story of Molly Lane, the subject of interest to the male characters who have gathered for her funeral. Molly has died a torturous death, and the men promise to euthanize one another if such a morbid fate comes their way.

- McEwan's *Enduring Love* (1998) is a thriller and a story of love. Joe Rose, the protagonist, attempts to stop a runaway hot-air balloon. In the group of men who are assisting him with the balloon is Jed Parry. After this shared traumatic rescue, Parry becomes obsessed with Joe, believing that Joe has fallen in love with him. The rest of the novel deals with the psychological torment that Joe suffers from the intrusion of Parry into his life. In the process, Joe's love for his girlfriend Clarissa as well as Joe's sanity are severely challenged.

- In an epigraph at the beginning of *Atonement*, McEwan quotes a passage from Jane Austen's *Northanger Abbey*, which was published posthumously in 1817. In Austen's novel, the protagonist, Catherine Morland, is portrayed similarly to McEwan's Briony. Both characters are first seen as naive as they become caught up in viewing the world through the influences of Gothic romance. Austen's story is a parody on the marriages of the English upper classes at the turn of the eighteenth century. It is also a coming-of-age story as the protagonist comes to terms with adult life.

- The 1952 novel *The Go-Between* by L. P. Hartley shares some similarity to a section of *Atonement*. *The Go-Between* tells the story of Leo Colston, an old man who is looking back at his youth and young adulthood. As a boy, Leo, a poor boy living among the upper class, plays the role of go-between, passing notes between two lovers. The notes go between Marian Maudsley, on whom Leo has a schoolboy crush, and Marian's boyfriend, the son of a farmer, Ted Burgess. When Leo discovers the content of the notes, he struggles to get out of his position as go-between, which ends in tragedy.

- Virginia Woolf's *Mrs. Dalloway* (1925) focuses on one day in the life of the protagonist, Mrs. Dalloway, as she prepares for a dinner party. The setting is post–World War I London, and the consequences of the war affect the people and their conversations. This novel is one of Woolf's most popular.

- *In the Time of Butterflies* (1995) by Julia Alvarez covers the lives of four sisters living under the brutal dictatorship of Rafael Leonidas Trujillo in the Dominican Republic during the early part of the twentieth century. The sisters, who work for underground rebels trying to overthrow Trujillo, face a different kind of war.

- *Book Thief*, a 2005 best-selling novel by Markus Zusak, deals with World War II through the eyes of a young German girl, Liesel. The young female protagonist attempts to escape from the horrors of the war by reading books. Before the war is over, Liesel and her adopted family hide a young Jewish boy from the Nazis.

- Anne Enright, a contemporary British author, writes about a different type of dysfunctional family in her novel *The Gathering* (2007). The protagonist comes from a family of twelve and returns home for the funeral of one of her brothers. As she works through her sorrow, she uncovers self-truths that almost destroy her marriage.

motives for accusing Robbie of the rape. Is she jealous because Robbie chose Cecilia over her? Does Cecilia's diving into the water fountain remind Briony of her own faked drowning? Is Briony's accusation of Robbie revenge rather than an innocent, though childish, misinterpretation?

While these questions swirl in the reader's mind, in Part Three, readers find Briony working hard as a student nurse and later as a compassionate woman who attends mortally wounded soldiers. She has forsaken her college education in order to serve her fellow citizens. She has followed in the footsteps of her sister. Briony may not have won Robbie's heart, but maybe she can win the heart of her sister. Briony might also be attempting to atone for her sin of betraying Robbie. Up until this point, all the above interpretations could be considered typical of many readers as they evaluate the character of Briony through the information that the narrator has so far provided. Then everything changes.

Once it is announced that Briony is the one who (supposedly) wrote the first three parts of this novel, readers might be drawn to reread those sections from this new perspective. All of the accounts of Briony's actions and thoughts then come under fire, as do the thoughts of the other characters. If Briony has authored the first three parts, this means that the story is not being told by an objective observer. Briony has written the story with a goal in mind. What is that goal? It could very easily be that Briony wants to tell the story in such a way that Robbie is shown as innocent and Lola and Paul Marshall are portrayed as guilty. Therefore, Briony writes about the scratches on Lola's arms and the scratches on Paul's face. Are these scratches based on fact or does Briony make them up to throw suspicion on these two characters. Was Paul the rapist? Or could it have been Danny Hardman, as Robbie and Cecilia suspected? If Briony really believed Paul and Lola were guilty of concealing the truth, why did she not confront them directly? What good does it do to tell a story about their alleged crime and then not publish it until after their deaths? So the next question that arises might be whether Briony wrote this story to punish Lola and Paul or to exonerate herself? Is she trying to say that, while she might be guilty for sending Robbie to jail unjustly, they are more guilty than she is?

Part Two is almost completely fictionalized since Briony merely pieces together notes from Corporal Nettle, who clarifies military terminology for her. Everything else comes from Briony's imagination. This means that Robbie's so-called reflection on the time Briony leaped into the pond so Robbie could save her could also be a fabrication. This drowning scene helps create a deeper understanding about why Briony might have made up her accusation against Robbie. The drowning scene makes Briony look as if she is hopelessly infatuated with Robbie as well as lost in her adolescent visions of romance. If the drowning scene is true, Briony might have felt spurned by Robbie when he chose Cecilia over her. This might have made readers feel more sympathetic toward Briony, as the faked drowning makes Briony look like a confused, love-struck little girl. If readers assume that Briony wrote the novel, why else would she have included the whole drowning scenario but to further prove her innocence?

What about Part Three? It is in this section that readers might, at first, come to admire Briony and to feel sorry for her. She suffers with the men who die in her arms. But is this just more of Briony's creative manipulation? Rather than working with the wounded soldiers as a way to atone for her sins, could Briony just be adding more references to demonstrate how good she is?

Of course all of these questions are worthless speculation, since Briony herself is fictional. These questions merely reflect what the real author, McEwan, wants readers to experience in this novel. McEwan turns the story on its head by insinuating that Briony is the author and narrator. The point McEwan appears to be making is that readers should not rely on any fictive narrator. Narrators of novels are unreliable just because they are creative constructs—made up by the author. Even though readers' minds naturally want to put all the pieces together by the end of the story, to sum them all up as if everything were true, McEwan's message, through this novel, seems to be telling readers not to do that so easily. McEwan seems to be warning that fiction authors sometimes play games with the reader's mind. After all, fiction is merely a collection of synthesized, unreliable details, as Briony points out by questioning her options on how to end the novel.

**Source:** Joyce Hart, Critical Essay on *Atonement*, in *Novels for Students*, Gale, Cengage Learning, 2010.

## Pilar Hidalgo

*In the following essay, Hidalgo compares McEwan's storytelling style to that of famous British novelists.*

> **THE BRILLIANT NARRATIVE TECHNIQUE OF
> *ATONEMENT* DOES NOT FULLY EXPLAIN THE
> CRITICAL ACCLAIM THAT GREETED THE NOVEL, OR
> THE NATURE OF THE EXPERIENCE IT PROVIDES."**

In his review of *Atonement* for *The Times Literary Supplement*, Robert Macfarlane observes that "the question of how the past is represented in language has become the central obsession of British fiction over the past three decades" (23). I would argue that the tendency has been far more marked in the 1990s and the early 2000s, when British novelists have engaged with the past in ways that have little to do with the traditional forms of historical fiction or with the self-conscious parody of the historiographic metafictions of the previous decades. The complex reassessment of the Victorian past undertaken by A. S. Byatt in *Possession* (1990) and continued, with a slant toward the impact of Darwinism, in her *Angels and Insects* (1992), by Graham Swift in *Ever After* (1992), plus Hilary Mantel's vivid imagining of living during the French Revolution in *A Place of Greater Safety* (1992) or Beryl Bainbridge's reconstruction of Samuel Johnson's relationship with the Thrale family in *According to Queeney* (2001) are just a few examples that bear out Byatt's comment about "the extraordinary variety of distant pasts British writers are inventing, and the extraordinary varieties of forms in which these pasts have been constructed" (*On Histories and Stories* 36).

The attraction of the past has proved so strong that it has reached writers long known for their immersion in the present and the creation of self-enclosed fictional worlds. Ian McEwan's novels of the 1990s marked a departure from the suffocating atmosphere of his early fiction, which is best symbolized perhaps by the body of the mother encased in cement in *The Cement Garden* (1978) or the surreal quality of the unnamed city of Venice in *The Comfort of Strangers* (1981). Perhaps it was inevitable that, as he grew older, McEwan would leave behind the cool analysis of incest, sadism, and abjection that had gained him notoriety and would explore the power of evil in twentieth-century European history.

In the introduction to the edition of his television plays, McEwan spoke of his intention to write about Word War II:

> Three years later I read *The People's War*, a social history of World War II, and resolved to write something one day about the war. I come from an Army background and although I was born three years after the war ended, it was a living presence throughout my childhood. Sometimes I found it hard to believe I had not been alive in the summer of 1940. (*The Imitation Game* 15–16)

An event in the summer of 1940, the retreat of the British Expeditionary Army to Dunkirk, features in *Atonement*, but the story the novel tells is far more complex and nuanced than a mere fictional account of one of the great military disasters in British history. The epigraph, the well-known moment in the conversation between Henry Tilney and Catherine Morland in *Northanger Abbey* in which the young man tells Catherine how unfounded her surmises about General Tilney have been, relates to *Atonement* in two ways. In an interview with Jeff Giles in *Newsweek*, McEwan says that in his notebooks he called *Atonement* "my Jane Austen novel" (Giles 94); and in a long conversation focusing on *The Child in Time, Enduring Love*, and *Atonement*, he makes explicit the connection embedded in the epigraph:

> What are the distances between what is real and what is imagined? Catherine Morland, the heroine of Jane Austen's *Northanger Abbey*, was a girl so full of the delights of Gothic fiction that she causes havoc around her when she imagines a perfectly innocent man to be capable of the most terrible things. For many, many years, I've been thinking how I might devise a hero or heroine who could echo that process in Catherine Morland, but then go a step further and look at, not the crime, but the process of atonement, and do it through writing—do it through storytelling, I would say. (Reynolds and Noakes 20)

The Jane Austen connection is thus twofold. On the one hand, Briony Tallis, like Catherine Morland, is a heroine whose perception is distorted by literature and an imperfect knowledge of the world. On the other, in the first part of *Atonement*, set in 1935, the country house as a literary motif makes ironic intertextual allusions to *Mansfield Park* (the rehearsal of a play that finally is not performed, Robbie Turner's fleeting interest in landscape gardening, the sexual predator from London) and to twentieth-century works of fiction such as E. M. Forster's *Howards End* and Evelyn Waugh's *Brideshead Revisited*. Thus, in his exploration of the gap between what is real and what is imagined, McEwan deploys a variety of stylistic devices and narrative techniques that give the novel its multilayered texture. Hermione Lee put it this way in her review of *Atonement* for *The Observer:*

> *Atonement* asks what the English novel of the twenty-first century has inherited, and what it can do now. One of the things it can do, very subtly in McEwan's case, is to be androgynous. This is a novel written by a man acting the part of a woman writing a "male" subject, and there's nothing to distinguish between them. (Qtd. in Reynolds and Noakes 185)

*Atonement* is structured in three parts and a final, much shorter section titled "London, 1999." The point of view, crucial in a story that so dramatically foregrounds perception, is shared by four characters in part 1, set in the Tallis family's country house in Surrey during the summer of 1935. Part 2 records the retreat to Dunkirk from the perspective of Robbie Turner, now a private in the British Army; in part 3, the action is simultaneous to that of part 2, as we follow the preparations to receive the casualties from Dunkirk in a London hospital where Briony is a probationary nurse. The three parts are narrated in the third person, and at the end of part 3 the identity of the narrator turns out not to be what the reader (at least this particular reader) had expected. The final section is told in the first person by Briony Tallis, and the time is now fifty-nine years after the events narrated in parts 2 and 3.

The central consciousness belongs to a writer and, in part 1, to a thirteen-year-old girl. If we accept (and I do) Hermione Lee's point about the presence of the history of the English novel in *Atonement,* part 1 appears as a rich depository of motifs and narrative techniques. As a young girl who cannot understand the world of adults, Briony descends both from Jane Austen's Catherine and Henry James's Maisie, although the country house motif points to Austen as the central influence at work. The use McEwan makes of the country house is ironic: the Tallis family background is anything but distinguished (the grandfather had kept an ironmonger's shop and made the family fortune with patents on padlocks and bolts), and the house itself is not only ugly but something of a fake, from the derelict island temple that echoes the original Adam-style building to the portrait in the dining room that depicts an aristocratic family with no connections to the present owners of the house.

When Hermione Lee observes that in *Atonement* "historical layers of English fiction are invoked—and rewritten" (184), she has in mind Austen and E. M. Forster's novels of social misunderstanding; she also detects echoes of Elizabeth Bowen in part 1 of the novel (qtd in Reynolds and Noakes 185). (Incidentally, Bowen is mentioned in part 3 as one of the critics who offers advice on Briony's novella.) The use of an Italianate fountain as the site for an apparently trivial moment in the lovers' story may contain an allusion to the Italian fountain in Evelyn Waugh's *Brideshead Revisited.* If this is so, it would be another ironic reversal because the country house that gives title to Waugh's novel is the ideological, aesthetic, and emotional center of the novel. When the lovers in *Brideshead Revisited* meet by the fountain near the end, we witness a crucial moment: the first stirrings of guilt in Julia, which will eventually lead to her return to the Catholic faith and her parting from Charles.

The dinner scene in part 1 may recall the long dinner party in the first section of *To the Lighthouse,* although the contrast between the hostess (and the food) in each novel is more marked than the similarity. The cluster of intertextual connections in part 1 (to which we can add the love relation across class lines in L. P. Hartley's *The Go-Between*) is part of the rich verbal texture of the novel and engages the reader's literary memory. The presentation of Briony's nascent literary imagination allows the reader to follow her development (at times unsuspectedly) from folk tales, written when she was eleven, through melodrama to modernist and finally realist fiction:

> Six decades later she would describe how at the age of thirteen she had written her way through a whole history of literature, beginning with stories derived from the European tradition of folk tales, through drama with simple moral intent, to arrive at an impartial psychological realism which she had discovered for herself, one special morning during a heat wave in 1935. (*Atonement* 41)

Briony's writing, of which we see samples at different points in *Atonement,* foregrounds issues of genre and narrative technique. In fact, the wealth of covert literary allusion in part 1 and its leisurely pace signal a departure from McEwan's previous fiction that is not fully accounted for by his avowed indebtedness to Jane Austen. I think we must look for a connection at a deeper level than that of the epigraph from *Northanger Abbey* or the introduction of the country house motif. If the style and subject matter of *Atonement* surprised readers and critics, the narrative technique is no less novel, precisely because it is rooted in the tradition of the English novel. As David Lodge observes:

> In *Atonement* (2001), Ian McEwan, who has tended to favour first-person narration in his previous novels and stories, seems to be telling his story in a rather old-fashioned way, entering into the consciousness of several different characters and rendering their experience in third-person discourse that makes extensive use of free indirect style. (86–87)

I part company from Lodge when he claims that the introduction of the first-person epilogue turns the novel into a postmodernist metafiction (87). It is true that the reader discovers on the last page of part 3 that he or she has been deceived about the nature of the narratorial voice of the novel, but to my mind the metafictional element lies not so much in this jolt to the reader's trust as in the subtle deployment in part 1 of narrative forms developed by the English novel in the nineteenth and twentieth centuries, a development that is mirrored by Briony's own evolution as a storyteller.

The use of free, indirect speech in rendering the consciousness of the characters is, of course, a narrative device pioneered by Jane Austen; McEwan introduces a further refinement when he gives two consecutive versions of the same event. The first version comes in third-person narration and thus has authorial sanction; the second is filtered through Briony; and because it is a misreading of what the reader has just seen, it anticipates the crucial moment when Briony will commit her crime and send an innocent man to prison.

Cecilia has been arranging wild flowers in a valuable vase that she is to take to the guest's bedroom. She decides to get water from the fountain and on her way there meets Robbie Turner. The two young people have known each other since childhood (Robbie is the son of the Tallis family's cleaning lady) and both have just come down from Cambridge, where they moved in different circles. There is a new awkwardness between them that Cecilia attributes to class resentment. Once they reach the fountain, Robbie tries to help Cecilia by taking the vase from her; she holds on, with the result that a section of the lip of the vase is broken off and falls to the bottom of the basin. The vase has great sentimental value for the family, particularly for Cecilia's father, because it had been given to his only brother, killed in the First World War, by the mayor of a small French town in gratitude for having saved the lives of a number of its citizens. Robbie begins to unbutton his shirt, but before he can go further, Cecilia strips to her underclothes, climbs into the water, retrieves the pieces, and walks away from him.

In the next chapter, the point of view shifts to Briony, who is worried about the way the rehearsals of her play are going. She looks from one of the nursery's windows and sees her sister Cecilia and Robbie standing by the fountain. Briony first reads the scene according to her experience of folk tales: as a young man of humble origins aspiring to the hand of a princess. She immediately begins to make mistakes when she interprets Robbie's gesture as a command that Cecilia dared not disobey. The transition in Briony's imagination from romance to realism is marked at this moment by a terrible irony whose full impact the reader will discover much later:

> Briony had her first, weak intimation that for her now it could no longer be fairy-tale castles and princesses, but the strangeness of the here and now, of what passed between people, the ordinary people that she knew, and what power one could have over the other, and *how easy it was to get everything wrong, completely wrong.* (39, emphasis added)

Briony's perception of Robbie as in some undefined way threatening her sister is reinforced when she reads the sexually explicit message that he sends to Cecilia by mistake and later when she finds the young man in the library engaged in what she takes to be an assault on her sister. The narrative order is reversed here: we see first the abrupt end of the scene by Briony's coming into the library, and in the next chapter, while all the characters are having dinner, Robbie remembers what had happened a half hour before in the library and thus contradicts Briony's interpretation.

The reader is made aware of the perils of perception and, at the same time, of the narrative devices through which literature encodes experience. We see indirectly a wonderful example of this when in part 3, Briony, now a probationary nurse in a London hospital in 1940, receives a letter of rejection from Cyril Connolly, editor of the prestigious literary journal *Horizon*. From Connolly's comments, the reader realizes that Briony's novella is a fictionalized account of the fountain scene in part 1, written in the high-modernist style.

Connolly praises Briony's work and singles out an image that in fact had appeared on page 38 of *Atonement* (something that the reader can only notice in retrospect). The reader also will need a careful second reading of the novel to perceive that Connolly's corrections concerning the provenance of the vase and the square in Rome, where stands the fountain after which the one in the Tallis country house is modelled, have been silently incorporated into the body of *Atonement,* but he complains about the feeble characterization and lack of development in her novella. The critic's comments contrast with Briony's own views on modern fiction, conveyed in free indirect style a few pages before: "A modern novelist could no more write characters and plots than a modern composer would a Mozart symphony" (281). Connolly compares Briony's method of presentation with Virginia Woolf's and adds that Elizabeth Bowen has taken an interest in the novella and saw in it traces of *Dusty Answer,* Rosamond Lehmann's first novel. Briony's writing is thus placed in the tradition of the British female novel of the 1920s and 1930s.

The literary memory embedded in Connolly's critique of Briony's novella involves a revision of modernist fiction from the standpoint of the late 1930s (Connolly's) and late 1990s (McEwan's through his surrogate narrator). Although this episode appears in part 3, it is in part 1 that works of English literature are woven into the narrative texture and characters comment openly on literary matters, from Robbie's disagreement with Leavis's valuation of English literature as "the most vital pursuit of an enquiring mind" (91) to Mrs. Tallis's disparagement of literature as an academic subject. We may conclude that literary memory is central in part 1 because the story focuses on the present, whereas the characters' past is not yet determining, as it will be in the other sections of the novel. Part 1 contains scattered references to Hitler and the need for rearmament, but the story it tells is firmly centered on the emotions, the terrible consequences of mistaken perceptions, and the shaping of a writer's imagination.

The leisurely pace and rich verbal texture of part 1 gives way in part 2 to a more straightforward narration. The time is 1940—five years after the events of part 1—and the point of view is Robbie Turner's, now a private in the British Expeditionary Forces in France. Here, McEwan draws on the historical memory of a military disaster that came to symbolize in the national imaginary the determination to fight on and on his own family history (his father had taken part in the retreat to Dunkirk). Little narrative space is left for ironical allusion and reimagining the literary past; and the emphasis is on objects, bodies, and the physical sensations of hunger, thirst, and fear. While Robbie and his two mates struggle to survive on the road to Dunkirk, his memories of the past five years acquaint the reader with what happened after the dramatic ending of part 1.

The action of part 3 is roughly simultaneous to that of part 2, but the central consciousness is Briony's and the setting is London. These two sections of *Atonement* have much to do with the reappraisal in the novels of Graham Swift, Julian Barnes, Martin Amis, and McEwan himself of what Byatt calls "their fathers' war" (*On Histories* 12). Reappraisal is not perhaps the correct word because none of those writers offers a novel interpretation of the Second World War. What McEwan does in *Atonement* is to present, through research into the circumstances of a particular episode early in the war, the influence on two individuals (Briony and Robbie as the victim of her crime and the lover of her sister) who were closely related in part 1 and now are very differently positioned: Robbie fighting for his life in France and Briony training as a nurse in a London hospital.

The detailed account of Briony's life at the hospital shows the extent of McEwan's research into the medical and nursing practices of the period. But no amount of research could have achieved what I regard as one of the highlights of the novel: Briony's experience of nursing the casualties of the retreat. The description of what shrapnel and fire can do to the human body is not new in literature, but in part 3 of *Atonement* McEwan offers a rare combination of precision and a compassionate lack of sentimentality that has few precedents. When Briony glimpses the interior of bodies through the terrible wounds the soldiers have sustained, "she learned a simple, obvious thing she had always known, and everyone knew: that a person is, among all else, a material thing, easily torn, not easily mended" (304). The story of the dying French boy-soldier to whom Briony speaks in her school French is impressive and needs no justification for its inclusion in *Atonement*.

Another episode connects at a deeper level with the plot of the novel. Briony extracts with forceps the pieces of shrapnel embedded in an airman's leg and explains to him the danger of their sinking into his flesh and carrying the infection into his bloodstream and, thus, into his heart or his brain. Again, we do not grasp the full significance of this until much later.

The emotional impact of this section should not obscure those elements in part 3 that link the different strands of storytelling. We discover the identity of Lola's rapist, not so much of a surprise, perhaps, as the striking revelation on the last page of part 3. I have no doubt that the pages dealing with the nursing of the wounded in *Atonement* will become a classic of the literary representation of the aftermath of war; nevertheless, if we look at the novel as a whole, part 3 is also the section in which the reader has access to crucial information concerning not only the past (what really happened on that fateful night back in 1935) but also the future, although in this latter case vital information is withheld until the end of the novel.

The last section, "London, 1999," is told in the first person by Briony, who speaks on a momentous day: it is her seventy-seventh birthday, and her doctor has just told her that she is suffering from vascular dementia; sooner or later she will lose her memory and then control of all intellectual and physical activity. Before leaving London to attend a birthday party organized by her family, Briony goes to the Imperial War Museum to return material she has been using in writing her last novel. On her way to this repository of national memory, Briony passes houses that she and several members of her family have formerly inhabited: "Beyond a certain age, a journey across the city becomes uncomfortably reflective. The addresses of the dead pile up" (355).

The birthday party is held in the old Tallis country house, now the luxurious Tilney hotel (a last reference to *Northanger Abbey*). Briony experiences a haunting retrieval of the past. A third-generation family member recites the prologue for *The Trials of Arabella,* which she had written fifty-four years earlier, and the grandchildren of her brother and her cousins perform the play whose rehearsal she had given up at thirteen. Early the next morning, Briony reflects that just as the war had frustrated her plan to redress some of the consequences of her crime, she cannot

achieve atonement as a novelist because there is no higher form to which she can appeal or that can forgive her: "It was always an impossible task, and that was precisely the point. The attempt was all" (371).

When McEwan calls *Atonement* "my Jane Austen novel," he knows that she is the last writer readers and critics would have associated with him. I have already traced the debt to Austen in the novel. But Austen's historical and ideological context is long gone; and her fiction, like that of the other writers *Atonement* engages with at different points, is part of the multilayered texture of a work infused with late twentieth-century issues and values. Although it is right to see *Atonement* as McEwan's masterpiece to date and a breakthrough in his career, we should not overlook the continuities with his previous fiction. The claustrophobic atmosphere that McEwan explored in his early stories and in *The Cement Garden,* what Kiernan Ryan has called "the blighted Eden of adolescence" (19), started to give way to a new awareness of the recent past in *The Innocent* (1990) and *Black Dogs* (1992), just as the emotional bleakness of the early works was transmuted into the warm celebration of family love in *The Child in Time* (1987). In his analysis of this work, Slay perceives both the mapping of new fictional and emotional territory and the connection with early themes: "for underlying much of the brutality, violence, and chaos of McEwan's canon is a subtle yet prevailing optimism" (217).

We see this qualified optimism in the moment of revelation that June Tremaine experiences in *Black Dogs* after her terrifying encounter with the beasts:

> A malign principle, a force in human affairs that periodically advances to dominate and destroy the lives of individuals or nations, then retreats to await the next occasion; it was a short step from this to a luminous countervailing spirit, benign and all-powerful, residing within and accessible to us all; perhaps not so much a step as a simultaneous recognition. Both principles were incompatible, she felt, with the materialism of her politics, and she left the Party. (19)

June's moment of recognition in *Black Dogs* takes place in France in the aftermath of the Second World War and is connected with the activities of the Gestapo during the Occupation, but "the malign principle" manifests itself in the novel in the more ordinary cruelty of a father's mistreatment of his son during a meal in a restaurant. It seems to me that here, as in *The Child in Time* and *The Innocent*, McEwan is drawing parallels between historical and private experience. D. J. Taylor, for one, thinks that he is more successful in the private realm, at least as far as *The Child in Time* is concerned:

> As an examination of the way in which families function, the novel [*The Child in Time*] is masterly. As an examination of the way in which people formally react to political contingency it strikes me as fundamentally flawed. (59)

I believe that in *Atonement* McEwan achieves the welding of historical experience and individual lives that had perhaps eluded him in his novels tackling the effects of Thatcherism on British society (*The Child in Time*), Anglo-American relations during the early cold war years in Berlin (*The Innocent*), and the fall of the Berlin Wall (*Black Dogs*), which had been prefigured at the end of *The Innocent*. Although, in part 1, the manifold allusions to the history of English literature (mostly, but not exclusively, fiction) foreground the complex cultural processes that account for the ways in which characters react to and interpret a shocking assault on a young girl, in part 2 we witness history in the making, before it becomes part of the national mythology, and history as it involves an individual for whom the reader feels strongly.

History and fiction mingle again in part 3 when Briony nurses the casualties of a war that will thwart her plans of atonement. The first-person postscript brings together the historical, private, and fictional strands: Briony finishes the last version of her novel, returns to the Imperial War Museum the documents that have helped her in her research, and attends the birthday party at which a play is performed that she had written sixty-four years earlier. The sense of an ending is more poignant because Briony has just been told that she is going to lose her memory.

The brilliant narrative technique of *Atonement* does not fully explain the critical acclaim that greeted the novel, or the nature of the experience it provides. The intelligent deployment of literary devices is not self-conscious but part of a story of love, death, evil, and a child's incomprehension of the word of adult emotions. It is a strong story, and in telling it the author creates three strong characters, Briony and the lovers. With truly Austenian irony, McEwan triumphantly does what Briony at eighteen thinks a modern novelist cannot do: write characters and plots.

> THIS IS, OF COURSE, VINTAGE MCEWAN: THE STRUGGLE BETWEEN THE INTERNAL LIFE, SO MUCH MORE VIVID THAN THE LIVES OUTSIDE IT, AND THE UNBENDING FORCE OF REALITY IS A THEME HE HAS LONG EXPLORED."

**Source:** Pilar Hidalgo, "Memory and Storytelling in Ian McEwan's *Atonement*," in *Critique*, Vol. 46, No. 2, Winter 2005, pp. 82–91.

## Claire Messud

*In the following review, Messud focuses on the novel's main character, comparing her to other famous heroines.*

Encountering Ian McEwan's prose is rather like meeting an extremely good-looking person. We experience a strange confusion of expectations. Rationally, it seems that this extraordinary surface must suffice, and yet we project and imagine far more than could ever be realized: this person, so attractive, cannot be, and yet must be, also brilliant and charming and witty; this prose, so fluid and elegant, so vivid and meticulous, cannot possibly carry, and yet must certainly carry, a narrative of great moment, insights of otherwise ineffable grandeur.

Experience teaches us, however, that good looks betoken nothing certain about their possessor; and it might be unwise to presume that McEwan's novels owe us anything greater than the textures and odors his diction so powerfully elicits, or than the satisfying musical rhythms of his sentences. Add to these not inconsiderable gifts his power to compel—because McEwan forces his readers to turn the pages with greater dread and anticipation than does perhaps any other "literary" writer working in English today—and we have before us so fine and controlled a stylist that we may imagine we cannot ask for more; surely these are pleasures enough.

But as McEwan himself, vivisectionist of the human psyche, knows so well, we are a voracious, even an insatiable, species. Beautifully evoked scenes prompt a search for meaning, an analytical will. We want not merely to be carried away—we want to know why. We want form and content seamlessly to unite, so that the story before us has about it a solid inevitability. McEwan, aware of this desire, wants to comply; it is a desire that he, too, clearly feels. In the past his fiction has acceded to that urge for narrative tidiness, often at the expense of the truest realism. But his memorable new novel, *Atonement,* makes clear that he is painfully alive to the dangers of that desire: the pernicious power of fine storytelling is one of the book's central themes.

Briony Tallis, thirteen at the novel's opening, is its writerly protagonist. As we meet her, she is preparing her first play, *The Trials of Arabella,* for a performance to mark her elder brother's visit home. *Atonement*'s lengthy and magnificent opening section—a tour de force that in scope and in prolonged intensity outstrips the opening of McEwan's earlier novel *Enduring Love* (1997)—is set in Surrey at the height of summer in 1935. Briony hovers at the end of childhood but lives her fantasies with an adult fierceness, wondering to herself, "[Was] everyone else really as alive as she was? For example, did her sister really matter to herself, was she as valuable to herself as Briony was? Was being Cecilia just as vivid an affair as being Briony?" Although she knows rationally that this must be so, she is also enamored of herself *as a writer,* and believes that writing imbues her with greater powers.

> A story was a form of telepathy. By means of inking symbols onto a page, she was able to transfer thoughts and feelings from her mind to her reader's. It was a magical process, so commonplace that no one stopped to wonder at it. Reading a sentence and understanding it were the same thing . . . There was no gap during which the symbols were unravelled.

Hers is a childish and arrogant faith, dangerously let loose upon the household that surrounds her. That communication is composed of vast gaps and desperate, distant signals is something Briony will learn through suffering—her own, eventually, but more immediately other people's.

*Atonement* like all McEwan's novels, is suspenseful, and it would not do to reveal all the events that unfold in this single summer evening before the war. What can be said is that Briony—awaiting the arrival of her brother, Leon, and his friend Paul Marshall while suffering the presence of her cousins Lola, Jackson, and Pierrot Quincey—witnesses a curious scene in the garden between her elder sister, Cecilia, just down from Cambridge, and a young man named Robbie Turner, a servant's son and a protégé of Tallis *père* who has grown up alongside the Tallis children. Cecilia is carrying flowers in a vase, over which the pair tussles, and then Cecilia strips to her underwear and plunges into the garden's fountain while Robbie looks on. Briony is old enough to recognize the complexity of what she witnesses but perhaps not old enough to see that it is a matter of reality, not of story.

> She could write the scene three times over, from three points of view; her excitement was in the prospect of freedom, of being delivered from the cumbrous struggle between good and bad, heroes and villains. None of these three was bad, nor were they particularly good. She need not judge. There did not have to be a moral. She need only show separate minds, as alive as her own, struggling with the idea that the other minds were equally alive.

And yet by her very construction of events Briony passes judgment, determines "good" and "bad": as the evening unfolds, her interpretation of each action and interaction around her is shaped by her understanding of what she has seen, and although she believes absolutely in the inevitability of the story she constructs, we can see that it is partial, in both senses of the word. Needless to say, the story Briony tells has terrible consequences.

This is, of course, vintage McEwan: the struggle between the internal life, so much more vivid than the lives outside it, and the unbending force of reality is a theme he has long explored. He has frequently led us into the fantasy worlds of the unsavory, from the haunting pedophile narrator of the early story "Butterflies"; to the menacingly nerdy Leonard Marnham, of *The Innocent* (1990), whose fantasies of violence against his girlfriend, Maria, are so powerful that he comes to believe she must share them; to the stalker Jed Parry, of *Enduring Love,* and his effects on the psyche of Joe Rose. For McEwan, the internal life may be a form of ideology as well as fantasy, a framework through which his characters construe and misconstrue the world. In *Black Dogs* (1992), June Tremaine's spiritual interpretation of her attack by a pair of slavering beasts on an isolated path in France in 1946 leads her to separate from her husband, Bernard, whose rationalist view guides him to politics.

But Briony is a storyteller, and in this she differs from her predecessors: she undertakes to shape and describe the world around her with, significantly, a pretense of objectivity. In so doing, however, she confuses imagination and reality as forcefully as do Leonard Marnham and the pedophile of "Butterflies." When her nine-year-old twin cousins, Jackson and Pierrot, go missing, Briony embarks on a search, and imagines them drowned in the swimming pool.

> It made sense, surely, to see if the twins were there, fooling about with the hoses, or floating face-down, indistinguishable at last in death. She thought how she might describe it, the way they bobbed on the illuminated water's gentle swell, and how their hair spread like tendrils and their clothed bodies softly collided and drifted apart. The dry night air slipped between the fabric of her dress and her skin, and she felt smooth and agile in the dark. There was nothing she could not describe.

Suddenly Briony's powers of description are McEwan's, the seductions of her luscious vocabulary his. The twins have not drowned; and yet Briony has drowned them. Of what else might she be capable? The glorious prose (isn't this enough? we have wondered) is revealed to be the ultimate peril.

If Briony and McEwan are in some measure indistinguishable in this novel (and only in the novel's conclusion do we discover how profoundly this is so), there remains, owing to McEwan's subtleties, a distance between them, a distance that articulates itself in a new raggedness of form and in a self-conscious insistence on the novel's story-ness. In these two elements *Atonement* most closely resembles *Black Dogs*. That book is a tale told in retrospect, and convolutely, through the intermediary of the narrator, Jeremy, son-in-law of the Tremaines. The scene in which June is attacked, the crux of that novel, is not revealed until the end; but it defines all that has come before, symbolically and intellectually as well as narratively, just as *Atonement*'s opening section fatefully determines what will ensue. *Atonement* differs from *Black Dogs*, however, in that its asymmetrical, telescopic structure almost resists the McEwan penchant for resolution: part one is followed by three segments, two of which take place at the beginning of World War II—one in France, recording the fate of Robbie Turner, and the other in London, where Briony is becoming a nurse at St. Thomas's hospital. Each of these three segments is essential yet strangely discrete; and an attendant and intriguing diminuendo as the novel progresses is reversed only in the book's fourth and final

section. Set in near-contemporary London, this brief first-person narrative ties the novel together. It does so neatly—perhaps too neatly for this reader's taste (and with a twist, of course)—but that very neatness is suspect in light of all that has come before, and we know that McEwan, too, knows it to be suspect.

This formal self-consciousness is inseparable from the other ways in which the story insists on its story-ness. True, McEwan has toyed with it before—in the opening sentence of *Black Dogs*, for example: "Ever since I lost mine in a road accident when I was eight, I have had my eye on other people's parents." We are compelled to continue, even as we absorb the sign that this is a story we are being told. In real life it is mercifully rare that children lose both parents in a car accident; in fiction, however, it happens with alarming frequency. To be thus orphaned, and to be seeking to replace missing parents, is to call upon a host of fictional forebears: Jeremy is letting us know that he is a *character,* however deftly and roundly drawn, rather than a person. So, too, the opening of *Amsterdam* (1998), which gathers Molly Lane's lovers at her funeral, echoes not experience as we know it but rather fiction and film (*The Man Who Loved Women,* for example). But these suggestions of artificiality are mere traces, and hence seem unwitting evidence of the well-made story rather than an intended exposition of its inner workings.

The opening of *Atonement,* on the other hand, overtly summons a number of literary references, and thereby insists rather volubly on its fictionality. It recalls *Northanger Abbey* in its epigraph, and *Mansfield Park* in its theatrics, as Briony prepares *The Trials of Arabella* for the stage. In the depiction of Briony herself—"she kept a diary locked by a clasp and a notebook written in a code of her own invention"—we see many heroines of girls' fiction from Enid Blyton novels to *Harriet the Spy*. In the solid, prosperous (but modern, and hence fake) Tallis house, set in its parkland, and in the gathering of guests in that house, we find echoes of the interwar house-party genre (Evelyn Waugh, say, or Anthony Powell; or that masterpiece of cinema, Jean Renoir's *The Rules of the Game*). Then, too, there are the characters' names: Leon, Briony, and Cecilia are overdone enough; but what of the Quincey cousins, Lola, Jackson, and Pierrot? *We are characters,* these names announce. And this is a story.

Paradoxically, it is apparently this very acknowledgment, this frank playfulness, that liberates McEwan to follow his characters more honestly than ever before, with less bending to the demands of narrative satisfaction. Gone are the grotesqueries of Leonard and Maria's dismembering Otto in *The Innocent,* the sexual menace of the mythical Nazi hounds in *Black Dogs,* the histrionic kidnapping and gunplay of *Enduring Love.* There are memorable descriptions of hideous events in the second and third sections of *Atonement,* but they are depictions of the surreality of war. These sections are not stylishly impressive or slick in the way of the book's first 150 pages; nor are their comedies as evident. They lead us not into the psyches of the unhinged but into the psyches of ordinary people in an unhinged time. Seeing as they see, thinking as they think, we draw something new, smaller and quieter, from McEwan's gifts. Robbie, while retreating across France, reflects, "No one would ever know what it was like to be here. Without the details there could be no larger picture." And yet, thanks to McEwan, we are granted those details.

> [Robbie] had been going for about ten minutes when he saw Mace's head on the grass by a pile of dirt. It was about twenty-five yards away, in the deep green shadow of a stand of poplars. He went towards it, even though he suspected that it would be better for his state of mind to walk on. He found Mace and Nettle shoulder-deep in a hole. They were in the final stages of digging a grave. Lying face-down beyond the pile of earth was a boy of fifteen or so. A crimson stain on the back of his white shirt spread from neck to waist.

We are given access, too, to the trials that Briony—a mere nursing probationer at St. Thomas's hospital—must bear. She is sent, for instance, to dress the face of a patient, Private Latimer.

> [She] could see through his missing cheek to his upper and lower molars, and the tongue glistening, and hideously long. Further up, where she hardly dared look, were the exposed muscles around his eye socket. So intimate, and never intended to be seen.

There is nothing storylike about these visions, nothing tidy, no narrative advantage to their telling. Reading McEwan's work, we often find it impossible to slow down, so powerful is the pull of "What next?" In *Atonement* that pull lures us through the first section at breakneck speed, and reasserts its sway in the last. But in the second and third segments of the book a strange and fine thing happens: we are free to linger in the moment, to savor the exquisite, agonizing aptness of McEwan's images and the delicacy of his touch as he records, in fiction, the true horrors of war, and makes new the ordinary realizations those horrors force upon us—Robbie's longing for children, say, and Briony's recognition "that a person is, among all else, a material thing, easily torn, not easily mended." We see at last that the beauty of the conjuring is indeed enough; and that its meaning—in all its ambiguities—lies before us.

**Source:** Claire Messud, "The Beauty of the Conjuring," in *Atlantic Monthly,* Vol. 289, No. 3, March 2002, pp. 106–10.

### John B. Breslin
*In the following review, Breslin outlines the plot of* Atonement *and explains how it follows the great tradition of English novels.*

I first began reading Ian McEwan when *Black Dogs* came out a decade ago; subsequently I started collecting and reading all his novels. Combining a shrewd narrative sense with acute psychology, he often manages to pick subjects that push him and his reader into the borderlands of ordinary life where the bizarre and the everyday regularly collide or intersect.

*Atonement* fits that pattern but in a decidedly more naturalistic way; indeed, it may be the least eccentric of all, consciously echoing, as it does, the novels of Jane Austen (who provides the epigraph) and Henry James with their omniscient narrators, expansive plots and acute awareness of class. In fact, the first half of the novel might be labeled a drawing room comedy that takes a tragic turn, while the second gives us a war story with all its horror and grittiness.

The year is 1935, England's hottest summer in memory. The Tallises live in an inherited country house outside London. Mr. Tallis works long hours in London for the government, secretly estimating the damages to be expected from air attacks and, incidentally, avoiding his wife's migraines and listless supervision of their two grown and one teenage child. And then there is Robbie Turner, son of the housekeeper, who has grown up with the Tallis children and has become Mr. Tallis's social betterment project. Cecilia Tallis and Robbie have just come down from Cambridge, where he took top honors and she just got by, and where they moved in decidedly different social and intellectual circles.

Renegotiating their relationship on home turf is proving awkward, a fact not lost on Briony, Cecilia's 13-year-old sister and a burgeoning writer. Gifted with a perception beyond her years, Briony lacks judgment and only half-aware sets in motion the novel's tragic event. After a disastrous dinner party, a harried search ensues for the 9-year-old visiting twin nephews of Mrs. Tallis, who have decided to run away. Briony sets off on her own and stumbles in the dark upon a sexual encounter between the twins' older sister and a mysterious figure she believes to be Robbie, for reasons that have more to do with her suspicions than her eyesight. Under questioning, likelihood soon becomes certitude, and Robbie is hauled off to trial and jail, but not before his outraged mother attacks the police car with an umbrella and Cecilia manages a last embrace, bringing the first act to a close.

Act 2 plunges us into World War II. Robbie joins up as a private to get out of prison and soon finds himself by force of character leading a motley pair of corporals on the hasty retreat to Dunkirk after Britain's first, disastrous invasion of France. But before that he has a brief reunion in London with Cecilia, who has cut off all contact with her family. Their faith in and love for each other are their sole sustenance, along with Briony's promise to recant her testimony.

Robbie carries Cecilia's last letter as a talisman against the aimless slaughter that surrounds him. His determination to return carries him past mad officers intent on one last stand against the Stukas and the sadism of his own frustrated comrades at Dunkirk. Reflecting on Briony's possible motivation shocks him back to an early memory of her capriciousness, risking her life in the local river to prove that he would risk his to save her.

The third act follows Briony's wartime penance as a nurse and her emerging career as a writer. She meets Robbie and Cecilia briefly to confess her sin but is ready neither to forgive nor forget, and both are astounded by the identity of the real culprits, whose wedding she has just attended.

This is a capacious novel, written with a keen awareness of the "great tradition" of English fiction; it is also considerably longer than any of McEwan's earlier ones. Had it not been for the Booker Prize he received for *Amsterdam,*

a superb thriller, in 1998, *Atonement* might well have won Britain's most prestigious literary award last year. Happily, it may also be the one by which most readers in America will remember him, since it held a longtime spot midway on The New York Times best-seller list, a literary standout amid the usual collection of espionage, murder and romance novels.

Ian McEwan's rich sense of irony will no doubt appreciate all of these publishing anomalies, since the concluding pages of *Atonement* offer their own twist on the book you have just read. Suffice it to say that the book's tragic and comic elements achieve a fitting resolution that does justice both to the harsh realities of the "real world" and the more satisfying requirements of the imagination.

**Source:** John B. Breslin, "Lies and War," in *America*, Vol. 187, No. 2, July 15, 2002, pp. 22–23.

## SOURCES

Davis, Barbara Beckerman, Review of *Atonement*, in *Antioch Review*, Vol. 61, No. 1, Winter 2003, pp. 179–80.

Finney, Brian, "Briony's Stand Against Oblivion: The Making of Fiction in Ian McEwan's *Atonement*," in *Journal of Modern Literature*, Vol. 27, No. 3, 2004, pp. 68–82.

Harold, James, "Narrative Engagement with *Atonement* and *The Blind Assassin*," in *Philosophy and Literature*, Vol. 29, No. 1, 2005, pp. 130–45.

"Ian McEwan," in *British Council: Contemporary Writers*, http://www.contemporarywriters.com/authors/?p = auth70 (accessed June 1, 2009).

*Ian McEwan.com*, http://www.ianmcewan.com/bib/books/atonement.html (accessed May 18, 2009).

Lord, Walter, *The Miracle of Dunkirk*, Combined Publishing, 1998.

Mathews, Peter, "The Impression of a Deeper Darkness: Ian McEwan's *Atonement*," in *ESC: English Studies in Canada*, Vol. 32, No. 1, 2006, pp.147–60.

McEwan, Ian, *Atonement*, Anchor Books, 2003.

Review of *Atonement*, in *Kirkus Reviews*, Vol. 69, No. 23, December 1, 2001, p. 1637.

Rungren, Lawrence, Review of *Atonement*, in *Library Journal*, Vol. 126, No. 19, November 15, 2001, p. 97.

Waugh, Patricia, *Metafiction: The Theory and Practice of Self-Conscious Fiction*, Routledge, 2005.

"World Wars, World War Two," in *British Broadcasting Corporation (BBC)*, http://www.bbc.co.uk/history/world wars/wwtwo/ (accessed June 2, 2009).

# FURTHER READING

Ambrose, Stephen, *The Good Fight: How World War II Was Won*, Atheneum, 2001.

Well stocked with photographs, this book provides a visual, as well as written, explanation of U.S. involvement in World War II. The reader is not overwhelmed with details, as the author focuses on specific events, such as D-Day, the bombing of Hiroshima, and the Nazi concentration camps. The extensive use of photographs helps to bring the story alive.

Banting, Erinn, *England—The People (Lands, Peoples, Cultures)*, Crabtree Publishing, 2004.

This book provides an overview of British history. Included are the people, their kings and queens, and their culture. Topics such as the mystery of Stonehenge, the notorious King Henry VIII and his many wives, and unusual foods such as blood pudding are explored in this easy-to-read account.

McGlashan, Kenneth Butterworth, *Down to Earth: A Fighter Pilot's Experiences of Surviving Dunkirk, the Battle of Britain, Dieppe, and D-Day*, Grub Street Publishing, 2007.

The author of this wartime account was only nineteen years old when he fought against the Germans at Dunkirk for Britain's Royal Air Force. Dunkirk was not the only part of World War II that McGlashan was a part of, and his honest account of his experiences are captured in this book.

Campbell, Kumari, *United Kingdom in Pictures*, Atheneum, 2001.

Take a tour of the United Kingdom through photographs and easy-to-read accounts of the historical places and beauty of this land. Included in this visual tour are places in Ireland and England, including the British Parliament. Topics include the geography, the history, and the culture of the people.

Childs, Peter, *The Fiction of Ian McEwan*, "Readers' Guides to Essential Criticism" series, Palgrave Macmillan, 2005.

Childs offers not only an introduction to McEwan's works but also an appreciation of the range of critical approaches to his fiction. Reviews from scholarly articles as well as from popular newspapers are provided together with explanations of what the reviews mean. Interviews with the author are also included.

McGowen, Tom, *World War II*, Children's Press, 1993.

Written for junior high school students, this book provides an historical background into the military battles and political changes that occurred during World War II.

# The Bridge over the River Kwai

**PIERRE BOULLE**

**1952**

French novelist Pierre Boulle's 1952 *The Bridge over the River Kwai* competes with his 1963 novel *Planet of the Apes* for the honor of being his most widely read work. Both are known to a broad audience through their film adaptations. *The Bridge over the River Kwai* takes place within a Japanese prison camp during World War II and superficially resembles a whole genre of works, often semi-autobiographical, with the same setting, from James Clavell's *King Rat* to the 1983 film *Merry Christmas Mr. Lawrence*, based on the memoirs of Laurens van der Post. However, Boulle later wrote his own memoir, *My Own River Kwai*, about the wartime experiences that lay behind his novel, which suggests a deceptively complex relationship between history and literature. Reading the two works together makes it clear that *Bridge over the River Kwai* bears an allegorical relationship to Boulle's own wartime experiences, something that is not intuitively clear from the novel alone. The true theme of Boulle's novel seems closer to other literature inspired by the war such as George Orwell's *Nineteen Eighty-Four*, which is concerned not with the recording of experiences, but with analyzing how the ideological conflicts of the war attacked not merely the bodies of soldiers and civilians who suffered in concentration camps, but the very foundation of human identity.

*Pierre Boulle* *(Time & Life Pictures / Getty Images)*

## AUTHOR BIOGRAPHY

Pierre-François-Marie-Louis Boulle was born on February 20, 1912, in the city of Avignon in Provençe in southern France. His father was a successful lawyer and the greatest influence on the young Boulle. He spent much of his time duck hunting and capturing birds with his young son, introducing him to what Boulle considered a bucolic paradise. Boulle later said that those were the happiest years of his life and the source of all his later inspiration as a writer. But Boulle's idyllic youth was cut short in his fifteenth year when his father died. After receiving an engineering degree from the École Supérieure d'Électricité, Boulle worked as an engineer in France and then in 1936, like many Europeans of that era, sought his fortune in the colonies. He became an engineer on a rubber plantation in the British colony of Malaya, just north of Singapore. After the outbreak of World War II, Boulle was drafted into the French army as part of the universal conscription that was then the norm in European states. He was assigned to various military units in the French Colony of Indochina (modern Vietnam) but saw no action. After the fall of France in June 1940, Indochina passed to the control of the

Vichy government, the puppet state set up by the Nazis to control France and her colonial empire. Boulle recoiled from this and returned to British territory where he joined Free French forces, which continued to resist the Axis powers. After the Japanese entry into the war in 1941, Boulle was sent back to Japanese-occupied Indochina as a secret agent or commando with orders to blow up bridges that were important to the Japanese war effort. He was caught in 1942 and remained in prison until his escape in November 1944. These wartime exploits, for which he was awarded the Légion d'sHonneur, the Croix de Guerre, and the Médaille de la Résistance, formed the basis of his novel *The Bridge over the River Kwai.*

After the war, Boulle attempted to return to his plantation work, but by 1949 he had returned to France where he lived with his sister and cared for his niece as though she were his own daughter and began a quickly successful literary career. He became internationally prominent in 1952 with *The Bridge over the River Kwai,* which won for him the prestigious Prix Sainte-Beuve French literary award. He continued prolifically producing novels, short stories, plays, and essays until 1990. Only about half of his works have been translated into English. After *The Bridge over the River Kwai,* his best-known work is his 1963 novel *The Planet of the Apes.* Boulle died in Paris, France, on January 30, 1994.

## PLOT SUMMARY

### Part 1: Sections 1–8

Boulle establishes that *The Bridge over the River Kwai* concerns the "insuperable gap between East and West." While the belief in this gap has as much to do with prejudice as real cultural differences, it is nevertheless real in the sense that it motivated the actions on both sides of the war. The novel tells the story of the conflict between two colonels, the Japanese Colonel Saito and the British Colonel Nicholson. The latter is the commander of a British battalion that is taken captive in Malaya after the British headquarters in Singapore announces a general surrender. Nicholson distinguishes himself by an exact adherence to the letter of the law. He forbids his men to flee to Dutch-controlled territory to continue the fight against the Japanese, but at the same time he wins much better treatment for his men than many units receive because his insistence to the Japanese

## MEDIA ADAPTATIONS

- *The Bridge over the River Kwai* was filmed in 1957 by director David Lean as *The Bridge on the River Kwai*. It starred William Holden, Alec Guinness, and Sessue Hayakawa and won seven Academy Awards, including Best Picture.

about proper conduct, including their adherence to the Hague Convention on prisoners of war (POWs), makes a deep impression on their captors.

Colonel Nicholson and his battalion are moved up-country from Singapore into Siam (modern Thailand) to begin work on the new railway between Bangkok and Rangoon in Burma. Once the POWs are in their new camp on the river Kwai, its commandant, Colonel Saito, explains that within six months they will have to build two short stretches of railroad on either side of the river and a bridge connecting them. In a vicious speech in which nearly every other sentence is 'I hate the British!' and in which he threatens to execute the entire battalion if they are uncooperative, he gives the order that British officers will work alongside the enlisted men performing manual labor. Nicholson informs Saito that the Hague Convention forbids compelling POW officers to do manual labor, and that his officers will do no such thing. For his trouble Nicholson is repeatedly beaten by Saito himself and by his guards, and his officer corps is threatened by having machine guns trained on them. But Major Clipton, the medical officer, prevents the intended massacre by telling Saito that he and the men in the hospital have seen everything and that if he kills anyone, he will have to kill them all; that would go beyond even the bounds for the treatment of POWs set by the Japanese army.

Nicholson is put into solitary confinement, where he is beaten, starved, dehydrated, and forced to live in his own excrement, but he resists this pressure and refuses to cave in to Saito's

demands. The British POWs are deeply moved by their colonel's resistance to the unlawful demands of their Japanese captors. Believing they are following his example, they ruin all of the work assigned to them during his punishment through sabotage and malingering. After Saito realizes he has no further pressure to put on Nicholson, he releases the British colonel and accedes to his demand to spare the officers manual labor. Nicholson inspects the men and their work on the railroad, or rather their sabotage of it. He comes to the conclusion, at first surprising to the other officers, that they must now show the Japanese that, as Englishmen and as Europeans, they know how to command men and will oversee the work of their soldiers to build the railroad faster and better than the Japanese could ever have done.

### Part 2: Sections 9–15

The scene shifts to the office of a third colonel, Colonel Green in Calcutta in India, who is in command of Force 316, a group of commandos. They are known as 'The Plastic and Destruction Co. Ltd.' because their mission is to use plastic explosives to blow up bridges behind enemy lines. On the basis of intelligence reports, Green decides to send Major Shears and two other agents, Captain Warden and the young Joyce, into Siam to build up a cadre of partisans from among the disaffected natives and blow up bridges on the Bangkok-Rangoon railway, preferably beginning with a suitable bridge just at the moment the first train passes over it in order to inflict maximum psychological as well as physical damage on the enemy.

Back on the river Kwai, Nicholson's chief subordinates, Reeves and Hughes, come to the conclusion that the Japanese are actually interfering with the work of the men in building the bridge and that the Japanese design is technically disastrous. They persuade their superior to intervene to make the construction a purely British matter, overseen and designed by themselves and the other officers. This leads to a conference with Colonel Saito. The Japanese commandant must decide between the loss of face (humiliation) before his own men by being bullied into acquiescence by Nicholson as the cost of building the bridge more quickly, or the loss of face (which might end in suicide) before his superiors if the work falls behind schedule. In the end he submits to Nicholson, even putting his own camp guards to work on the British plan for the bridge. Work proceeds under the British plan and the British command. Clipton, the medical officer, at first believes or hopes that all of the detailed preparations and planning are just a ruse to cause further delay, but in fact Nicholson is in earnest about building the bridge and building it as perfectly as possible, certainly better than the Japanese could have done. He tells the engineer, Captain Reeves, "We've got to show we're superior to these savages."

The bridge-destroying commandos of Force 316, having airdropped into Siam, reconnoiter the various bridges being built by POW slave labor and begin to focus their attention on the one crossing the Kwai. The construction of the bridge has proceeded rapidly, the men setting aside their natural tendency to sabotage anything wanted by the Japanese in deference to their respect for the ordeal Colonel Nicholson has undergone.

## Part 3: Sections 16–20

Shears and his commandos and the Thai partisans they have organized finally decide that they will begin their campaign of destruction by blowing up the bridge over the Kwai. They are at first interested in it because the height and width of the span will make it the most difficult for the Japanese to repair. When Joyce, an engineering draftsman, actually sees the bridge, he realizes it is built to a greater scale of size and strength than the other bridges. "It's a big job. It's properly built. It's nothing like any other Japanese bridge." They choose to destroy it first precisely because they think it will inflict a psychological blow on the Japanese sense of pride.

As the bridge nears completion, Colonel Nicholson visits Clipton, the medical officer. Clipton has the power to certify prisoners to be excused from duty because of sickness. Given the constant exhausting labor required of the POWs, their starvation diet, and the rigors of a tropical climate that must be borne without the possibility of protection from disease-carrying mosquitoes and other parasites, more and more men are becoming too ill to work. In Nicholson's view this drain on the labor supply is putting the work on the bridge behind schedule, and he prevails upon Clipton to release at least some men from hospital. Since Clipton is reluctant, Nicholson falsely tells him that "Saito has threatened to take drastic steps," hinting that malingerers would be executed or tortured. The colonel justifies this to himself as a "white

lie." In this way Nicholson compels even British soldiers who are lame or have lost the use of an arm to work on the bridge.

## Part 4: Sections 21–24

In the final section of the book, the narrative is told only from the viewpoint of the commandos. The action carried out by Shears and his team of commandos and partisans in preparing to blow up the bridge is based on the commando training that Boulle received during the war. Its presentation is meticulous, clinical, and emotionless, concentrating on boring, degrading tasks such as laying electrical wire and tying explosives to pilings while floating in water under the bridge in the dark of night so that one's skin starts to peel from becoming waterlogged. It is the opposite of a thrilling spy story such as might be found in popular genre literature. The action is likened to a dream in which one performs the same meaningless task over and over again.

The commandos know that the first train is to pass the bridge on a certain date at 10:00 AM. The day before, the majority of the British POWs (excepting the sick) are evacuated from the camp to move on to other projects since their work on the bridge is done. The commandos prepare the bridge with explosives that night. However, dawn reveals that the level of the river is dropping and has exposed the explosives that are affixed to the bridge pilings. Also exposed is the wire running to where Joyce is hiding in vegetation on the bank, waiting to detonate the bridge as the first train, loaded with vital supplies as well as Japanese dignitaries including generals, crosses over it. Colonel Nicholson, the only remaining POW officer, inspects the bridge with Saito minutes before the train is to arrive. Nicholson notices the packs of explosives tied to the bridge piers but dismisses them as flotsam caught on the timber. Then he sees the wire running from the bridge to the detonator and starts to follow it, with Saito close behind, toward Joyce. Joyce kills Saito and attempts to explain to Nicholson that he is a fellow British officer and tell him what his mission is. The colonel, enraged at hearing the words "Blow up the Bridge!" shouts out "Help!" to alert the Japanese guards on the bank above and actually strangles and tries to kill Joyce. Shears swims across the river but is wounded and captured by the Japanese guards. There is no longer any possibility of blowing up the bridge. But as it crosses, the train nevertheless sets off a booby trap prepared by Captain Warden and derails, sending the engine over the side. Warden, observing from a mortar post too far away to help at the scene, sees that Joyce is not dead from Nicholson's attack and is reviving. Knowing that his two captured comrades will be tortured in a particularly hideous way for attempting to assassinate Japanese generals, he uses his mortar to kill them, and Colonel Nicholson as well, and then to sow panic among the Japanese troops until he is out of ammunition. He finally escapes and eventually returns to India to report on the matter to Colonel Green.

## CHARACTERS

### Major Clipton

Although the novel is told by an impersonal narrator, much of it takes advantage of Clipton's viewpoint because he alone among the POW officers is not caught up in the plan to build the bridge. He is the medical officer of Colonel Nicholson's battalion. Conveniently for his role in the narration, "Clipton, however, was by nature objective, and had the rare gift of being able to examine a problem from every angle." Despite his best efforts, Clipton fails either to persuade Nicholson of the folly of his actions or to significantly hinder him.

### Colonel Green

Green is the commander of Force 316, commandos dedicated to destroying infrastructure behind enemy lines. He is very distrustful of military bureaucracy. He complains that he suspects vital information is often held back by the intelligence services and won't be seen by anyone until the intelligence officers publish their memoirs after the war.

### Major Hughes

Hughes is one of Nicholson's chief subordinates in the POW camp. Before the war he had been the owner of a mining company and is an expert in controlling men. He oversees the actual construction work on the bridge.

### Joyce

Joyce is the third commando who goes on the mission to destroy the bridge over the Kwai. Before the war he worked as an engineering draftsman, essentially drawing the same girder in variations on the plans for a prefabricated bridge over and over again for two years. He viewed the war as an escape from the tedium of that job. All of the plans to blow up the bridge are based on Joyce's reconnoitering of the bridge and on his sketches; because of his understanding of the bridge's structure, he is able to include in the sketches details of where to place the explosives. Young and eager for combat, at the moment of truth when he must kill Colonel Saito in order to protect the arrangements to blow up the bridge, Joyce is nevertheless only able to bring himself to do so by drawing on his hatred of his repetitive office job and transferring it to the acts of blowing up the bridge and killing in hand-to-hand combat. Inexperienced as he was, Joyce had no hope of realizing in time that it was even more important to his mission to kill Colonel Nicholson.

### Colonel Nicholson

Colonel Nicholson is the main character of *The Bridge over the River Kwai*. He was in charge of a British battalion fighting the Japanese and, after the capitulation of Allied resistance in Malaya, he surrendered his unit and continued in charge of his men as an intermediary with the Japanese POW system. His personality is composed of a "sense of duty, observance of ritual, obsession with discipline, and love of the job well done." In Nicholson's case these traits add up to an arrogance that is highly effective in dealing with bureaucracy, both that of his own army during his twenty-eight-year career and with that of the Japanese army once he becomes a POW. He has a deep belief in the superiority of the West and particularly of the British over the Japanese. He focuses on building the bridge over the Kwai as a means of demonstrating that superiority, paradoxically ignoring the fact that it is aiding the Japanese in making war on Britain. He is eventually consumed and destroyed by this desire, not only alerting the Japanese to the commando attack against the bridge, but even trying to kill a fellow British officer to protect the bridge.

### Captain Reeves

Reeves is one of Colonel Nicholson's chief subordinates. Before the war he had been a civil engineer in India and had built many bridges similar to that over the Kwai. He becomes responsible for the design of the bridge and is able to set aside any mental reservation about building a superior bridge for the enemy as the work becomes the holy grail of his career:

[Reeves] had always dreamed of tackling a really big job without being badgered every other minute by administrative departments or maddened by interfering officials who ask ridiculous questions and try to put a spoke in the wheels on the pretext of economy, thereby frustrating every creative effort.... He could already feel the breeze of creative inspiration fanning those hungry flames which overcome every obstacle in their path.

## Colonel Saito

Saito is the Japanese colonel in command of the POW camp and tasked with building the bridge over the Kwai. He was given the assignment largely because he is considered incompetent for more important duties. He is an alcoholic and given to uncontrollable fits of rage when drunk. He is described as a Dr. Jekyll and Mr. Hyde depending on his sobriety or intoxication. "The hatred he felt for the prisoners was intensified by all the humiliation he had suffered from not having seen any action" during the fighting so far. In general he was motivated by "racial pride, a mystic belief in authority, the dread of not being taken seriously, a strange sort of inferiority complex which gave him a jaundiced, suspicious outlook on life, as though he was in perpetual fear of being laughed at." Boulle expands at length on the theme of Saito's actions being driven by his personal insecurities and insufficiencies: "his actions were all due to fear of one kind or another: fear of his superiors, ... and fear of his subordinates, in whose eyes he was 'losing face' [being humiliated] through his obvious inability to exact obedience" from the British. When Nicholson and Saito inspect the bridge on the day that the first train is to cross, it is obvious to the commando Major Shears from their body language that Nicholson is the one in command.

## Major Shears

Shears is an ex-cavalry officer who was trained as a highly efficient commando and is a member of Force 316. He and his team are airdropped into Siam by the British army to destroy the bridge on the Kwai. He is to some degree an autobiographical character based on Boulle himself. During the war Boulle served in a French cavalry regiment and after fleeing to British India to join the Free French forces, he was trained by Unit 136 in commando tactics. After a period of service in China, he was sent, following the Japanese attack on the Allies, into French Indochina on a mission to destroy bridges. However, Boulle lacked Shears's ruthless efficiency. In his memoir, *My Own River Kwai*, Boulle presents himself as more nearly a fool archetype who was captured almost immediately after he entered the country.

## Captain Warden

Warden is a commando sent into Siam with Shears on the mission to destroy the bridge over the Kwai. Before the war he was a university professor and linguist, and thus is the only member of the team to understand the local Thai languages spoken by the native partisans they work with. He is a particularly logical thinker and uses that ability to devise a plan to plant explosives on and near the bridge that will not only destroy it but will tie it up for months with derailments after it is repaired. His training in languages and his superior intellect recall Dr. Georges Béchamp, a Free French Consul in China who was eventually imprisoned in Indochina with Boulle according to his memoir, *My Own River Kwai*.

# THEMES

## Atrocity

Although the Japanese never signed the Geneva Conventions, they did sign the Hague Convention (as Colonel Nicholson repeatedly points out), which regulated the particular treatment of POWs. The Japanese military also had its own criminal code, closely based on Great Britain's, which forbade the inhumane treatment of prisoners, attacks against civilians, and many other categories of action that are usually thought of as war crimes or atrocities. Nevertheless, the Japanese military completely disregarded the rules of war in their conduct during World War II, to a degree that would seem incredible except for arguably worse violations by Germany and the Soviet Union. The very basis of *The Bridge over the River Kwai* is the Japanese decision to use Allied POWs as slave labor, which itself was a serious war crime (not only the requirement that officers participate in manual labor, as Colonel Nicholson seems to believe). Moreover, the enslaved POWs, as well as tens of thousands of local civilian slaves, were treated in an especially barbaric way, denied adequate nutrition, and forced to work at a pace and in a manner calculated to eventually kill them. In fact, Boulle hardly touches the surface of the atrocities committed by the Japanese on the

# TOPICS FOR FURTHER STUDY

- James Clavell's 1962 novel *King Rat* takes place in the Changi POW camp in Singapore, which Colonel Nicholson and his battalion briefly pass through. Clavell's and Boulle's novels are among the best-known fictional treatment of the lives of Allied POWs of the Japanese during World War II. Prepare a paper comparing and contrasting the themes or styles of the two works. As an alternative, use the film adaptations of the two works instead of or in addition to the novels.

- In many ways David Lean's film *Bridge on the River Kwai* is a faithful adaptation of Boulle's *The Bridge over the River Kwai*, but in other respects it is a fundamental transformation. Prepare an oral presentation discussing the similarities and differences between the two, illustrated with excerpts from the novel and short clips from the film.

- An Internet search of blogs reveals that in the last few years thousands of entries have been posted by tourists after visiting the bridge on the river Kwai in Thailand. Look at a representative sample of blog entries and report to your class on what knowledge the bloggers have of what they saw. Is their information based on the film or on the novel or does it come from tourist guides? How many were inspired to seek out historically accurate information? How many to read the novel? Do any of the blogs reveal a sophisticated understanding of the problems of myth, history, and fiction involved in their touristic experience?

- British novelist J. G. Ballard was born and grew up in the international community in Shanghai. In 1943 he was interred in a concentration camp by the Japanese authorities and spent the years between the ages of thirteen and fifteen separated from his parents and trying to survive in that environment. That history is the basis of his 1984 novel *Empire of the Sun*. It was made into a film in 1987 by Stephen Spielberg. How does that film adaptation of the novel compare with David Lean's adaptation of Boulle's novel? How do the directors transform their source material in the new medium? Make a Power-Point presentation using clips from both films.

---

Burma railway. Actions described merely as "beatings-up, the butt-end blows, and even worse forms of brutality" added up by war's end to tens of thousands of deaths. The commandos plotting to blow up the Kwai bridge also observe the POWs at work on it and learn more about them from local natives. They were "working almost naked in the scorching sun, working without a break under strict surveillance." They assume that the POWs are under the oppressive orders of the Japanese: "Knowing the Japs as they did, they could well imagine how far their brutality would go in order to get a job like this one finished." In short, the POWs are "living in a continual nightmare." In other theaters of war the Japanese committed still worse atrocities, including medical experiments that included vivisection, the use of germ warfare, and systematic acts of cannibalism meant to terrorize other groups of POWs, occupied civilian populations, and Allied soldiers. In contrast to Germany, in Japan only a small number of top military and political leaders were prosecuted in war crimes trials conducted by the victorious Allies, but thousands more Japanese soldiers were tried and imprisoned or executed by local authorities where the atrocities had taken place. Nevertheless, by 1958 all Japanese soldiers convicted of war crimes had been pardoned or had their sentences commuted, frequently by Douglas MacArthur, the military governor of occupied Japan. One explanation frequently offered for Japanese war crimes is the then current Japanese view that other Asians as well as the European and American Allies were racially inferior to the Japanese and so did not have to be treated as human beings. Ironically, an important factor in motivating Colonel Nicholson's behavior in *The Bridge over the River Kwai* is his own sense of racial superiority over the Japanese.

### Race

The novel is told primarily from the point of view of the British officers who are its main characters. They are naturally hostile to the Japanese they are fighting, doubly so because they have been captured by their enemies and are mistreated to the extent that individual Japanese officers and soldiers will later be tried for war crimes because of the atrocities they committed against the POW workers on the Burma railway. This hostility takes many forms, including the regular use of the derogatory slur "Japs," and the frequent comparisons of the Japanese to monkeys or apes, making them less than human, which were common ways of speaking during the war. However, in Boulle's novel the British are permeated by a more fundamental racism. The ultimate expression of this sort of racism is found in some of the works of the British author Rudyard Kipling. Warden finally says of Colonel Nicholson: "I'm sure he had read the whole of Kipling as a boy, and I bet he recited chunks of it as the construction gradually took shape above the water. 'Yours is the earth and everything that's in it, and—which is more—you'll be a man, my son'—I can just hear him!" The quotation is from Kipling's poem "If." The attitude of the British officers more generally recalls that of Kipling's "The White Man's Burden," which argues that European colonialism was justified by the need for Europeans to civilize the barbarous populations of the colonial empires.

However, Boulle undercuts the conventional beliefs of his characters with irony. When the commando Joyce has surveyed the camp and seen what is going on there, he responds with a typically racist dismissal of the Japanese and praise for the relative superiority of Nicholson. "Monkeys dressed up as men! The way they drag their feet and slouch around, you'd never take them for anything human. Colonel Nicholson's a model of dignified behavior. A born leader, that's how he struck me, sir." Joyce's racist attack is motivated by the hatred he feels toward the Japanese because he believes they have tortured and brutalized the British POWs to make them

*Alec Guinness as Colonel Nicholson in the 1957 film version of the novel* (AP Images)

build the bridge. The reader, however, knows that in fact it is Nicholson who is overseeing the construction of the bridge and who has usurped the authority of the Japanese in every detail; it is Nicholson, with his preconceived racial stereotypes, who is acting in an inhuman manner.

## STYLE

### Irony

Irony is a rhetorical device in which words seem to mean one thing but upon further reflection actually mean something quite different, usually the exact opposite of the surface meaning. Considerable humor is often found in examining the contrast between the two meanings, but it is more likely a bitter rather than a gleeful humor. Sarcasm is the simplest form of irony, as when a student is told that many hours of homework have been assigned over the weekend and replies, 'Wonderful!' Boulle's sense of irony in *The Bridge over the River Kwai* is highly refined. It begins with simple one-line gags such as Colonel Nicholson telling Reeves, the construction engineer,

"That's quite clear. As you say, even a child could understand. That's the sort of demonstration I like." On the one hand, Nicholson is praising the captain for giving a clear explanation. But on the other hand, it also means Nicholson is admitting, without admitting it to himself, that his own mentality is best suited to understand a simplified explanation. Or again, Reeves complains to the colonel that the incompetent orders of the Japanese engineer are undermining the success of the bridge: "It'll never stand up, sir. I'm absolutely ashamed to be taking part in such sabotage." He is exaggerating the incompetence of the Japanese engineer, suggesting that it is as dangerous to the success of the bridge as sabotage. But on the other hand, Reeves, as a British officer, is sworn to fight the Japanese and it is, in fact, his duty to sabotage rather than aid the Japanese war effort. Reeves is the one who no longer knows how to do his duty. This leads to the larger irony that is the main theme of *The Bridge over the River Kwai* as a whole. Colonel Nicholson seizes on one part of his duty, to demonstrate the superiority of the British over the Japanese (and that is a duty owed more to the prejudices and traditions of his culture than to the British army), and exaggerates it so that it becomes his single obsession. Despite the fact that the Japanese used meticulous and detailed planning to capture Malaya and Singapore, defeating the British in a victory that was, to a large degree, brought about by British incompetence, Nicholson, intends to show the Japanese that the British, not the Japanese themselves, are the ones who know how to build a bridge, how to discipline men, and how to wage war. But in doing so, he completely ignores his principal duty, which is to defeat the Japanese, who, in 1942 when the novel is set, had a real chance of conquering India and driving the British entirely out of East Asia. Boulle drives home the irony in a description of the bridge itself as "a masterpiece which was to prove the superiority of the West—this bridge, which was to be used by the Japanese trains on their triumphant advance to the Bay of Bengal [i.e., India]."

### Adventure Story

The story of men fighting in war and going on perilous journeys to face unknown dangers is as old as literature itself, going back to ancient Greece and the Homeric epics *The Iliad* and *The Odyssey*. It continues today as one of the most popular genres of entertainment, in film as well as in novels. A subgenre of the adventure story is the spy story, in which an agent must assume a covert identity and make his way through deadly enemies and perhaps hostile armies to carry out some vital secret mission in the fashion of Rudyard Kipling's *Kim* or Ian Fleming's James Bond. Such a story is implicit in *The Bridge over the River Kwai* in the mission of Force 316 to airdrop into Japanese-occupied territory and blow up the bridge on the Kwai. And while it is his own story, as Boulle, who served as a commando during the war, reveals in his memoir *My Own River Kwai*, he does not exploit its dramatic potential. Rather it exists in the text of the novel as an anti-story, working against the purposes of the 'hero,' Colonel Nicholson, providing the ultimate irony of the novel when Nicholson actually attempts to kill his fellow British officer rather than letting him carry out his (and Nicholson's own) duty to blow up the bridge. In the film version by David Lean this adventure story consumes the plot of the novel so that the story of the commando played by William Holden becomes as important as that of Nicholson, who comes to his senses at the last moment and in fact carries out the mission of destroying the bridge.

## HISTORICAL CONTEXT

### World War II

General hostilities began in Asia with the Japanese annexation of Manchuria in 1931 and the invasion of China in 1936, because of which all Western powers, including the United States, put Japan under a trade embargo. After an attempt to probe into Siberia in the summer of 1941, in the course of which the Japanese army was badly defeated by the Soviet Union, Japan decided to attack and annex Southeast Asia, then controlled by various colonial powers including Great Britain, the Netherlands, France, and the United States in order to secure the raw materials needed by its economy.

After France was conquered by Nazi Germany in 1940, the Germans set up a puppet state, called Vichy after the French town where it was declared. French colonial officials throughout the world decided to collaborate with the Axis powers of Germany and Japan, rather than join the Free French forces who continued to resist Axis aggression in concert with Great Britain. Japan gained effective control of French Indochina (modern Vietnam, Cambodia, and Laos)

# COMPARE
# &
# CONTRAST

- **1940s:** Waterboarding was routinely used as a method of torture by the Japanese and after the war it figured in many prosecutions for war crimes, despite the fact that the same technique was often used in American police investigations until about that time.

  **Today:** Widely condemned as torture, waterboarding was nevertheless authorized for use by the American military during the Iraq War during the George W. Bush administration.

- **1940s:** The world is engulfed in a global conflict, World War II, that engages all of the great powers and combatants from every continent.

  **Today:** The balance of world power has shifted so dramatically that the United States is the only nation able to project power on a global scale, with the result that wars are limited either to policing actions or regional or local conflicts.

- **1940s:** The third world was organized into colonial empires overseen by one of several great European powers.

  **Today:** The rather arbitrary divisions of the old colonial empires into separate provinces continues in the form of independent nations that emerged from colonialism in the aftermath of World War II.

- **1940s:** Japan was an aggressive, expansionist power that ruthlessly pursued an empire across all of East Asia and the Pacific.

  **Today:** The Japanese constitution forbids military aggression and Japan has become a peaceful world economic and democratic power.

---

when its Vichy-controlled regime admitted Japanese forces.

On December 7, 1941, hoping to neutralize the ability of the United States to intervene in Asia, Japan attacked the U.S. fleet at Pearl Harbor and sank seven battleships. At almost the same time (but on December 8 because of the international dateline), Japanese forces in Indochina attacked the British colony of Malaya (and also occupied Siam) and its heavily fortified naval base on the island of Singapore. The British naval force defending Singapore was quickly sunk by Japanese aerial attacks, largely because the British commanders had failed to take necessary precautions, believing that the Japanese air force and naval aviation were too incompetent to pose a serious threat. The fortress at Singapore proved useless because its guns had been supplied only with armor-piercing shells meant to attack an invading naval force but ineffective against the Japanese troops invading in numerous small craft across the narrow Singapore straits. Because of failures of British planning and a contemptuous underestimation of Japanese military power and efficiency, Singapore, along with all Allied forces still in isolated pockets of resistance on the Malaya peninsula, was compelled to surrender on February 15, 1942. It is at this point that *The Bridge over the River Kwai* begins, with Colonel Nicholson surrendering his battalion in Malaya to the Japanese.

Japan organized the Asian colonies it had "liberated" (i.e., conquered) into the Greater East Asian Co-prosperity Sphere. This organization was ostensibly intended to foster the independence of Asian peoples from colonial rule, but in reality it was merely an attempt to disguise Japan's ruthless economic and political exploitation of its occupied territories.

Japan quickly pressed on with its offensive into the British colony of Burma and succeeded in attacking India, but its forces could not advance further. This was not because of British resistance since most of the troops in India had been shifted to fight in Africa or the Near East against the Germans and Italians (and a large number of

*Tourists walk over the bridge on the River Kwai* (AP Images)

native Indian troops had been captured at the fall of Singapore), but because it was impossible to sustain an offensive without reinforcements and supplies that could scarcely be moved through the mountainous jungles of Burma.

This is the reason the Japanese need the Siam-Burma railroad built over the Kwai, as Colonel Saito explained: "to provide a way through to Bengal for the army which has liberated [Burma and Malaya]...from European oppression. Japan needs this railway to continue her victorious advance, to enable her to overrun India, and so bring this war to a rapid conclusion." Slave labor drawn both from Allied POWs and local civilian populations was used to build the railroad (as was also true of countless other projects throughout Japanese-occupied territories). At the same time, the slave laborers were systematically starved and brutalized in order to control them. Between 50,000 and 100,000 men died working on the railroad.

By the time it was completed, the strategic balance of power had shifted against Japan and no renewed offensive into India ever became possible. Although there was a real bridge over the river Kwai, it was several hundred miles downstream from the location given in the novel and no commando raid ever took place against it. The bridge was eventually destroyed by Allied bombers in 1945. After completing the railway, the prisoner community in Southeast Asia fared relatively well compared to captives of the Japanese in other areas, but, nevertheless, tens of thousands continued to die of starvation and disease until the end of the war in 1945.

## CRITICAL OVERVIEW

Boulle's *The Bridge over the River Kwai* met with early and widespread critical acclaim as one the best of the novels that dealt with the experiences of Allied POWs. It won the French Prix Sainte-Beuve literary award in 1952. Boulle's principal English critic, Lucille Frackman Becker, in *Pierre Boulle*, considers it his masterpiece. However, the novel eventually (especially after the release of the film version) became involved in controversy. Boulle knew the bare facts—that the Japanese had built a railway through Burma to support an invasion of India using Allied POWs as slave labor, killing 80,000 of them in the process (actually most of these victims were conscripted laborers, not POWs, demonstrating the slightness of Boulle's acquaintance with the historical facts). But he did not investigate historical actualities much further than that. He simply looked at an atlas of Siam and saw that any railway in the area would have to cross the river Kwai at some point. He made it close to the border with Burma. In fact, British POWs did construct a bridge across the Kwai, but 200 miles downstream near Bangkok.

As Ian Watt, a survivor of the POW laborers on the bridge who later became an academic, points out in articles in the *Partisan Review* and the *Observer*, the impact of the film on the popular imagination not only conflated the identity of the two bridges, but tended to replace the actual historical memory of the building of that bridge with the events of the film, which had grown into a sort of myth. Indeed, Becker points out that "Tours are organized from Bangkok to visit 'The Bridge over the River Kwai' . . . and each year thousands of tourists visit this 'historic' spot."

The main point of contention, however, was apprehension on the part of many surviving POWs that their commander, Colonel Philip Toosey, was slandered by the portrayal of Colonel Nicholson in the novel and the film. In fact, Watt asserts that any officer who collaborated to the degree Nicholson does in the novel would have been assassinated by his subordinates. At least two monographs, *The Man behind the Bridge* by Peter Davies and *The Colonel of Tamarkan* by Toosey's granddaughter Julie Summers, refute any such identification, pointing out that Toosey ensured that construction of the bridge was shoddy and personally introduced termites into the structure. But as Summers concedes, the model for Nicholson was not Toosey, but the Vichy officials Boulle dealt with in his own war experiences. He used the British army as the setting because his own captors had reminded him of British officers in the writings of Rudyard Kipling, not because he had any knowledge of Toosey.

## CRITICISM

### Bradley A. Skeen

*Skeen is a classics professor. In this essay, he explores the philosophical and ideological content of* The Bridge over the River Kwai *in light of*

> THE PHENOMENON OF WILLING, EVEN ENTHUSIASTIC COLLABORATION WITH A RECENTLY HATED ENEMY IS REMARKABLE, WHETHER IN THE FICTIONAL EXAMPLE OF NICHOLSON OR THE HISTORICAL REALITY OF VICHY."

*Boulle's own memoirs and the larger intellectual framework provided by Orwell's* Nineteen Eighty-Four.

*The Bridge over the River Kwai* is set among British POWs in Siam, but it is not a historical novel meant to tell the story of that group or arising from their experience. It has a quite different and, for Boulle, more personal origin. Boulle wrote his memoir of his wartime experiences, *My Own River Kwai*, shortly after returning to France. That he published the memoir only after the success of *The Bridge over the River Kwai* led to many questions about its inspiration. He revealed that the novel truly concerns his own wartime experiences. "The background is . . . contained in this series of adventures. It is there implicitly; it is not perceptible at first sight. I did not know this myself and became aware of it only after several years of anguished introspection." *The Bridge over the River Kwai* is an allegory of Boulle's war, a symbolic telling of French war experiences.

The Nazi conquest of France created two successors to the French Republic: the Free French or French military units that escaped to British territory and continued to fight to liberate France, and the puppet Vichy regime that collaborated with the Axis. Surprisingly perhaps, the administrators of the French colonial empire accepted the Vichy government, although the Nazis were in no position to enforce their rule outside metropolitan France. This created a situation where thousands of French government officials and ordinary citizens throughout the world collaborated with the Axis. It is this situation that Boulle is commenting on with Colonel Nicholson's collaboration with the Japanese. Boulle is trying to explore the psychological factors that might bring about such a reaction.

# WHAT DO I READ NEXT?

- J. G. Ballard's 2008 memoir *Miracles of Life* concentrates on his youth growing up in the international community in Shanghai from his birth in 1930 until the end of World War II. Ballard spent the end of that period, 1943–1945, in a Japanese concentration camp. This book provides clarification about many points in his previous fictional account of his time in the camp, *Empire of the Sun.*

- The PBS television series *Secrets of the Dead*, devoted to forensic archaeology, maintains a Web site featuring an episode on the Burma railway (http://www.pbs.org/wnet/secrets/previous_seasons/case_kwai/index.html) with video interviews of POWs who worked on the railway and several pages devoted to the way in which archeology has thrown light on the historical understanding of the period.

- Kenji Tokitsu's 2004 *Miyamoto Musashi: His Life and Writings* presents translations of the writings of one of the greatest Samurai of the feudal period together with near-contemporary biographies. This material throws light on the Japanese mindset of Bushido that still influenced the private and collective actions of the Japanese during World War II.

- Richard J. Golsan's 2000 study *Vichy's Afterlife: History and Counterhistory in Postwar France* deals with the difficult subject of how the Vichy period has been understood in postwar France. The issues of collaboration and human rights violations were so widespread, and potentially affected so many French politicians, judges, businessmen, and other leading figures that Vichy has been as much purposefully forgotten as recalled. Even Boulle found Vichy disturbing enough to approach through allegory in *The Bridge over the River Kwai.*

- The 2007 collection of conference papers edited by Kei Nemoto *Reconsidering the Japanese Military Occupation in Burma (1942–45)* shows how perceptions of Japan's war and its attendant atrocities are being revised in contemporary Japan.

- The Far East POW Community (http://www.fepow-community.org.uk/) is a Web site maintained by survivors of Japanese POW and concentration camps and their families. It has numerous pages of blogs, articles, poetry, and other resources that illuminate the experiences of the POWs both in the camps and recovering in civilian life.

- For a view of the Japanese occupation by a family in the Philippines, read *When the Elephants Dance* (2002) by Tess Uriza Holthe.

Boulle's war was bound up in this division, since, as a Free French commando, he was sent into Vichy-governed French Indochina with the mission of blowing up bridges to hinder the Japanese war effort. Once in the country, Boulle sought out a certain Major F., who he had been told would be friendly to his mission. Instead, the major declared his loyalty to Vichy and immediately arrested him. Boulle was interrogated by other French officials, of whom he says, "He wasn't a bad fellow, the police commissioner. He was only doing his duty as a commissioner, as Major P. was doing his duty as a public prosecutor, and the hefty gendarme his duty as a hefty gendarme." Boulle felt he could not blame them for just following their orders. With his customary irony he merely notes that they did not even waterboard him during the fifteen days of interrogation, but only deprived him of sleep and food. During his trial, after refusing to admit that the Free French were a foreign army with respect to France, he was asked in regard to his fighting to liberate France and the French empire from

Axis occupation, "Do you regret it?" In effect he was being asked how it was possible to not be a supporter of Vichy. At the time he did not understand the question. He was condemned to serve fourteen years in prison for treason. As the war began to go against the Axis, the Vichy authorities treated Boulle and his fellow prisoners with more and more leniency, until after the Normandy invasion it was the prison guards themselves who arranged their escape. Boulle never says so explicitly, but they clearly expected their former prisoners might put in a good word for them at any future trials for treason or war crimes.

Boulle helped himself, as he says, mostly unconsciously, to come to an understanding of the Vichy mentality in *The Bridge over the River Kwai*. When Colonel Nicholson and his men are first put to work on the bridge, the colonel simply wants to have the laws of war enforced. But after he is tortured (somewhat more roughly than Boulle himself was), Nicholson comes to a new understanding. He examines the work on the bridge and observes that his men have obstructed the progress of the railway at every turn so that absolutely nothing has been accomplished. Captain Reeves makes a joke of how successful their efforts at obstruction have been: "I don't think we need worry about the invasion of India if this is the line they say the're going to use." Nicholson's response is quite surprising:

> I can see we'll have to take a very firm line if we want to regain control of the men.... As of today, we've got to put a stop to this disgraceful inefficiency. We can't have the men going absent at the slightest provocation.... I don't think I need to remind you of the need for firm action at the first sign of sabotage or malingering. A railway line is meant to run horizontally, and not twist about like a switchback, as you so rightly observed, Reeves.

Nicholson is speaking as if he were an officer building a bridge for his own army rather than for the enemy. The reader slowly learns Nicholson is intent not on hindering construction, which every other POW realizes is his duty, but on building the bridge as quickly and as well as possible. He does not think of this as collaboration, but the opposite. He is determined to humiliate the Japanese by showing that the British can make a better bridge than they ever dreamed of and to demonstrate the racial superiority of the British over the Japanese. At one point, Nicholson says of the Japanese: "They're what I've always said they

were: primitive people.... They can't do a thing by themselves. Without us, they'd still be living in the age of sailing ships and wouldn't own a single airplane.... As far as I can make out, they're only just capable of making a footbridge out of jungle creepers." This is part of Nicholson's core belief system, which has been badly damaged by the recent stunning victories of the Japanese over the British. Showing up the Japanese by outdoing them in the matter of the bridge will restore that belief, regardless of how incompatible it is with his larger duty. Perhaps Boulle is suggesting that the French bureaucrats and soldiers who embraced Vichy had their core identity shattered by the Nazi conquest of France and had to rebuild themselves in whatever way they could, even if that meant reestablishing their internal order and the internal order of France in willing collaboration with the triumphant enemy.

In any case, Nicholson's single-minded pursuit of what he sees as part of his duty—humiliating the Japanese—while ignoring the whole, makes him a collaborator. Without realizing it, he begins to work for the success of the East Asian Co-prosperity Sphere exactly as his Japanese captors intended. He infects his fellow POWs with the same goals. Nicholson is not the only man who needs to rebuild his lost sense of superiority. Captain Reeves believes that the Japanese are incapable of the design and planning necessary for building a bridge. He tells Nicholson of the Japanese plans, "never in the whole of my career have I seen such carelessness and lack of system." He is further convinced that it is because the Japanese are inherently inferior to Westerners: they are "savages." But Reeves is also seduced by the possibility of personal achievements that had been impossible under the old order, but that can now be fulfilled. In the end Nicholson himself goes much further, for he attacks his own comrades—the commandos—who were sent to carry out the duty in which he failed and destroy the bridge.

The phenomenon of willing, even enthusiastic collaboration with a recently hated enemy is remarkable, whether in the fictional example of Nicholson or the historical reality of Vichy. Boulle is not the only postwar novelist to consider it. Boulle's narrative technique is not to explore directly what is going on in the minds of his characters, but to show it through their actions. George Orwell in his 1948 novel *Nineteen Eighty-four* deals with the same problem, but in a more systematic way. Like Boulle's, Orwell's novel is allegorical. It supposedly explores a different reality that might have emerged from the crucible of World War II, but its subject is actually the real world that did emerge, treated, as it were, under a different name. The society that Orwell describes in scientific detail has remarkable similarities to the society of Boulle's POW camp. The society of Orwell's totalitarian state of Oceania has a rigid and naked hierarchy of power, dominated by the Party whose ideology is Ingsoc (English socialism). The core principle of Ingsoc is *doublethink*. "*Doublethink* means the power of holding two contradictory beliefs in one's mind simultaneously, and accepting both of them." The process of *doublethink* must be conscious or it could not achieved, but it must also not enter the conscious mind at all or else it would be insincere. It requires the ability "to tell deliberate lies while genuinely believing in them," as well as to deny any fact, but also to recall the fact when necessary. It is only through *doublethink* that the followers of Ingsoc can embrace a system that operates in a manner diametrically opposed to its claimed self identity, resolving its contradictory slogans, "War is Peace," "Freedom is Slavery," and "Ignorance is Strength."

Orwell produced a perfect description of the process that must be going on in Colonel Nicholson's mind. Nicholson's personal psychological needs require him to build the bridge. His military duty requires him to destroy the bridge. At one point Nicholson explains to Clipton that the bridge will remain unpainted, since it could only be painted with white lime, "and a fine target that would make for the planes, wouldn't it! You seem to forget there's a war on!" In the same sentence Nicholson demonstrates his dedication to safeguarding the bridge, but just as clearly shows that in fact he remembers there is a war on and so must be aware of what he, as a soldier, ought to be doing. The conflicts are both resolved and unresolved, conscious and unconscious. The ability to engage in *doublethink* is protected by "*crime-stop* . . . the power of not grasping analogies, of failing to perceive logical errors, of misunderstanding the simplest arguments if they are inimical to Ingsoc." Nicholson does this too, remaining impervious to ironic criticism from Clipton such as: "To think that, without us, [the Japanese] would have built their bridge in a swamp and it would have capsized under the weight of their trains loaded with troops and supplies!" Another process operative in *doublethink* is "*blackwhite* [which] has two mutually contradictory meanings.

Applied to an opponent, it means the habit of impudently claiming that black is white, in contradiction of the plain facts. Applied to a Party member, it means a loyal willingness to say that black is white when Party discipline demands this." Nicholson embraces this concept when he rationalizes that his driving his men to literally work like slaves, even requiring the sick and wounded to work, is serving the virtuous purpose of teaching the Japanese a lesson, which for him is all that is left of the war and his duty. But it does not appear that way to Joyce the commando when he observes the POW workers. "They're nothing but skin and bone. Most of them are covered with ulcers and jungle sores. Some of them can hardly walk. No civilized person would even think of making men work in such a crippled state. You ought to see them, sir. It's enough to make you weep . . . absolute skeletons, sir. I've never seen such a ghastly sight. It's utterly criminal." Joyce thinks that he has witnessed a war crime perpetrated by the Japanese, but he has actually seen the results of Nicholson's *doublethink*.

Captain Warden's final report to Colonel Green begins with a headline that shows he at least very much realized the *doublethink* in which Nicholson engaged. "'Two men lost. Some damage done but bridge intact thanks to British colonel's heroism.'" While the first inclination might be to read it as the colonel's heroism resulting in the derailment, it is rather his heroism on behalf of the enemy that saved the bridge. Warden finally suggests of Nicholson, "Perhaps he really had a genuine ideal? An ideal as sacred as our own? Perhaps the same ideal as ours?" In that case the ideals that they were fighting for would be no different than the ideals that lead to collaboration; they would both be mere covers for the organization of power. This question is an embryonic form of Orwell's conclusions about the nature of life in the modern world.

**Source:** Bradley Skeen, Critical Essay on *The Bridge over the River Kwai*, in *Novels for Students*, Gale, Cengage, 2010.

### Lucille Frackman Becker

*In the following essay, Becker gives a biographical account of the life and works of Boulle as well as an overview of the author's views on colonialism.*

The French novelist and short story writer Pierre (François Marie-Louis) Boulle was born in Avignon on February 20, 1912, to Eugène and

Thérèse (Seguin) Boulle. In an autobiographical work titled *L'ilon: Souvenirs,* published when he was 78 years old, Boulle evoked images of his early years in Provence, eschewing strict chronology to follow the order of memory. These images, he wrote, "with their mixture of joy, of anguish, of hope, and of disappointment, constitute a store of riches which I never tire of counting, as an old miser counts his coins" (7). His native Provence would provide the background for *Le bon Léviathan* (1978), *Miroitements* (1982), and *A nous deux, Satan!* (1992).

The most important person during his formative years was his father, a brilliant lawyer whose legal world of Avignon is portrayed by Boulle in the novel *La face* (1953). Despite his great love and respect for his father, he did not feel that he himself was suited for the law, and, after completing his secondary studies at the lycée, he went to Paris to study science and engineering at the Sorbonne. The style and content of his fiction bear the mark of his scientific education; he attributes to it his "somewhat cruel taste for the bizarre together with great formal simplicity and rigorous logic" (*My Own River Kwai,* 26). It is also apparent in his essay on cosmology, *L'univers ondoyant* (1987), and in his works of science fiction, most notably *La planète des singes* (1963).

Boulle received his *licence ès sciences* in 1931 and an engineering diploma from the École supérieure d'electricité in 1933. He then worked as an engineer for two years in Clermont-Ferrand. Boredom, restlessness, and a desire to travel led him to accept a position abroad as an electrical engineer. So, at the age of 24, he left France for a rubber plantation in British Malaya. A fictionalized account of his years in Southeast Asia until the outbreak of World War II can be found in *Le sacrilège malais* (1951), Boulle's only novel of an autobiographical nature. In the pages of this work, we find atmosphere, local color, characters, and incidents that reappear in the novels and short stories set in Asia: *Le pont de la rivière Kwaï* (1952), *Le bourreau* (1954), *L'épreuve des hommes blancs* (1955), *Les voies de salut* (1958), *Les oreilles de jungle* (1972), *Les vertus de l'enfer* (1974), *Histoires perfides* (1977), and *Le malheur des uns . . .* (1990).

The account of Boulle's war years in Southeast Asia as a Resistance fighter and as a secret agent in Indochina can be found in *Aux sources de la rivière Kwaï,* published much later in 1966. At the outbreak of World War II in 1939, he enlisted in the French army in Indochina. After the collapse of France, he went to Singapore and joined the Free French, who trained him as an intelligence agent and saboteur. On December 7, 1941, when Japan attacked Pearl Harbor, the Pacific Islands, Malaya, and the British possessions in China, the Free French decided to transfer their mission to Kunming, China. From Kunming, Boulle departed by mule train for a desolate Chinese mountain post en route to Moung-La, a Thai village on the banks of the Nam-Na River, six miles from the Indochinese border. After several months of fruitless efforts to infiltrate Indochina, then held by Vichy forces, he entered the French colony in 1942 after a hair-raising descent of the Nam-Na River on a raft he had constructed of bamboo held together by rushes. He was promptly arrested by the French authorities, and in October 1942 he was court-martialed, found guilty of treason, reduced to the ranks, deprived of French nationality, and sentenced to hard labor for life. During his time in prison, having nothing to do—for, ironically, no job was assigned to this man sentenced to forced labor for life—Boulle began to write to pass the time. On little bits of paper filched here and there, he scribbled some recollections of his adventures during the raft trip on the Nam-Na. In September 1944, when Allied victory appeared certain, the prison authorities decided to organize Boulle's "escape," and he spent the rest of the war with the Free French in Calcutta.

Sick with malaria and dysentery, Boulle returned to Paris on January 3, 1945, where he was awarded the French Légion d'Honneur, the Croix de Guerre, and the Médaille de la Résistance. He returned to the rubber plantation in Malaya in 1945 in an attempt to resume his life where the war had interrupted it, but he was unable to follow this sensible course, for the war had made him incapable of doing an ordinary job. In 1948, he decided abruptly that writing was to be his life; he left his job, went back to Paris, sold all his possessions, moved into a little hotel on the Left Bank, and started writing a novel, taking a vow to undertake nothing else ever again. "I have kept my word," Boulle wrote at the end of *Aux sources de la rivière Kwaï.* "I have done practically nothing else ever since, and this foolhardy decision, taken some twenty years ago among the fireflies piercing the equatorial darkness of a Malayan plantation, still strikes me today as the worthy conclusion to a series of incongruous adventures" (*My Own River Kwai,* 214).

## MAJOR MULTICULTURAL THEMES

Five of Boulle's novels provide a guide to colonial mentality within the framework of a broad historical overview of Southeast Asia during the first three-quarters of the twentieth century: from the re-creation in *Le sacrilège malais* of the early years of colonialism inherited from the nineteenth century, through World War II, which was to undermine that colonialism (in *Le pont de la rivière Kwaï* and *L'épreuve des hommes blancs*), to the nationalistic liberation movements unleashed by the war that would put an end to colonialism (*L'épreuve des hommes blancs* and *Les voies de salut*), and, finally, to the casting off of what Kipling called the "White Man's burden" (in *Les oreilles de jungle*). Dr. Moivre, a character in *L'épreuve des hommes blancs* who serves as Boulle's alter ego, expresses the author's ideas on colonialism: "From a strictly moral point of view, the expropriation of one nation by another could not be justified by any means or by any argument which had even the remotest claim to rationalism" (*The Test,* 83). In the same novel, Boulle refutes another colonialist misconception that maintains that the ordinary people of Southeast Asia immediately loved the white strangers who came to their lands and would willingly sacrifice themselves on their behalf. On the contrary, the Malay fishermen in the novel refuse to help the white men in their desperate flight from the Japanese. Their only concern is for survival, and they are indifferent to the outcome of the war being waged around them. The new Japanese order is as alien to the Malays as the European organization had been.

## SURVEY OF CRITICISM

Louis Allen, in his 1986 article, finds Boulle's novel *Le pont de la rivière Kwaï* successful in depicting the courage of resistance but a failure in its account of the nature of the Japanese enemy. Lucille Frackman Becker, in her literary biography of Pierre Boulle (1996), details the author's experiences in Southeast Asia and devotes a chapter to an in-depth analysis of the novels situated there. Edgar C. Knowlton (1982) observes that the use Boulle makes of his firsthand experience in Southeast Asia is persuasive in its sympathy for the cultures, languages, and peoples of the area. Judith D. Suther (1983) discusses several French novels on U.S. involvement in Vietnam, including Boulle's *Les oreilles de jungle,* which she characterizes as arch satire on the continued U.S. saturation bombing of Vietnam following the Tet Offensive

of 1968. Ian Watt (1959) analyzes *Le pont de la rivière Kwaï* in the light of his own experiences as a Japanese prisoner of the war who was forced to work on the Burma-Siam railway. Although Boulle's picture bears a little direct resemblance to what Watt saw on the Kwai, Watt feels that the author's ultimate purpose was to dramatize the ridiculous disparity between the West's rational technology and its self-destroying applications. The translation of the novel into film is the object of studies by Michael Anderegg (1984), Ian Watt (1968), and most critics of Boulle's oeuvre.

**Source:** Lucille Frackman Becker, "Pierre Boulle," in *Multicultural Writers since 1945: An A-to-Z Guide,* edited by Alba Amoia and Bettina L Knapp, Greenwood Press, 2004, pp. 90–93.

### Georges Joyaux

*In the following essay, Joyaux chronicles the accuracies, inaccuracies, trials, and tribulations involved in the adaptation of the novel to the screen.*

*The Bridge Over the River Kwai,* Pierre Boulle's third novel, was first published in 1952. An English translation followed in 1954, but it was not until 1957, after Columbia Pictures produced its own version of the novel in film form, that Boulle's masterpiece really achieved world-wide notice. By now, the movie has been seen by millions (it has been shown three times on prime television time, though not yet on the late-night TV); the novel has gone through several re-editions in French, including the well-known and widely-read *livre de poche* series; the original English translation published by Vanguard Press has been followed by several others, also in paperback; and by 1962, the novel had been translated into some twenty other languages.

At the same time, several of Boulle's other works have been widely circulated: *The Face,* originally published in 1953, was later made into a successful TV film in the United States, and more recently, his *"conte philosophique," The Planet of the Apes,* first published in 1963, was made into a science-fiction film whose success soon led to a sequel. *The Return to the Planet of the Apes,* which, in turn, called for a *Beneath the Planet of the Apes.* The vein has not yet run dry, and Twentieth-Century Fox has just produced *The Conquest of the Planet of the Apes.*

> THERE IS FAR MORE CONSISTENCY IN THE NOVEL'S HERO THAN THERE IS IN HIS COUNTERPART IN THE MOVIE, AND HIS *SUCCESSFUL* HEROISM AT THE END OF THE NOVEL IS THE LOGICAL OUTCOME OF WHAT THE READER HAS LEARNED ABOUT HIM FROM THE START."

Boulle is first and foremost a brilliant storyteller whose concern with the absurdities and perplexities of life provides his readers with both entertainment and intellectual stimulation. His works, whether they be detective stories, war and spy adventures, science fiction or historical novels, constitute a rich mine of basic narratives; and it is not surprising that they should have caught the eye of the movie and TV producers, whose needs for good "yarns" are necessarily endless.

It is equally true that the passage from one medium (novel) to another (film) causes some transformations, and in the following pages I intend to compare Boulle's novel with its movie version and discuss the changes which the original novel underwent as it was adapted to the needs and possibilities of a new medium.

Discussing the movie version of his novel, Boulle summed up his reservations as follows:

1. A denouement similar to the novel, the image of the bridge intact, and a few outbursts of rage on the part of Warden, following the failure of his mission.

2. Twenty to twenty-five minutes shorter; the American's role reduced, his discussions with Warden abridged, a few "silences" on the part of Nicholson instead of his reflections aloud; and, naturally, the understanding nurse assigned to other activities.

3. Five to ten minutes longer: on the *building* of the bridge, the sweat blood and tears which this work, designed to prepare the Japanese invasion of India, cost the British soldiers. With these corrections, the film would have fulfilled my wildest dreams—such as it is, however, it is not bad at all.

The first, and by far more significant, difference between the novel and the movie, a difference which in fact amounts to a complete transformation of Boulle's original intent, is in the way each ends. Boulle asserts, in the interview mentioned above, that he began his novel with the last scene, when Nicholson "jumps on Joyce, subdues him, and calls the Japanese soldiers for help in an effort to preserve his work, the bridge, at all costs." "Help!" Boulle continues, was the first word written, and the novel was then built to lead to this word and this situation.

Whereas the movie ends with a bang, so to speak, as the bridge majestically (but not unexpectedly) collapses into the Kwai river, following the explosion prepared, but not set off, by the British commandos, the novel ends with a *whimper*. This whimper is summed up in the telegram sent by Warden to his superiors in Calcutta: "Two men lost. Some damage done, but bridge intact thanks to British Colonel's heroism." These contrasting climaxes, a lavish spectacular and a perplexing riddle, embody to a large extent, the respective characteristics of the two works, for Boulle's intellectual stimulation is conspicuously absent from the movie.

It is clear that we are dealing with two different media. On the one hand, the novel afforded Boulle, master of the understatement and possessor of a rapier-like wit, innumerable occasions to apply his talents. The world of the printed word is eminently favorable to the handler of the litotes, and Boulle made good use of this rhetorical device in his suspenseful account of Nicholson's indomitable efforts to build the perfect bridge—for the enemy. On the other hand, the movie makers likewise knew how to make the best of the possibilities inherent to their own medium, but also they knew what was expected of them; understandably, they could not resist the long-established and always-successful race between the commandos and the onrushing train, neither could they resist the temptation of a grandiose "spectacle"—the collapse of the bridge and the oncoming Japanese train. Here, the case was clearly that of a picture worth a thousand words, though none of these words appeared in the novel itself. One might add, furthermore, that since the bridge had to be built, it was to some extent logical to get as much mileage from it as possible; in a way, its eventual destruction was to be expected from the start.

Still, the matter of the bridge itself could be accepted—though not approved—were it not for another and far more important issue: Nicholson's conduct in the last sequences of the movie and in the last pages of the novel. In the film, after the British Colonel subdues Joyce, the plunger operator, he calls out for help to the Japanese soldiers. Shears, another commando, swims frantically across the river in a desperate attempt to do what Joyce has been unable to do, namely to kill the "right" colonel and set off the explosion. Nicholson, who recognizes Shears (they had argued earlier as to the responsibilities and duties of POWS), seems suddenly *awakened* as he wonders. "What have I done?" Though Shears fails in his task, it seems that Nicholson will take over and carry out the Commandos' mission: dazed, but apparently aware *now* of what he has done and is doing, he turns around and walks deliberately towards the plunger. As he reaches it, weak, wobbling and stunned by the ongoing shooting, he falls backwards upon the plunger, thus setting off the explosion just as the approaching inaugural train reaches it. Though it seems clear, from the moment he recognizes Shears, that he has now "seen the light" and that he is set upon correcting his wrong doing, his final gesture is no gesture at all, and the film sequence indeed *stresses* the accidental quality of the event. It seems strange that once the producers decide to set Nicholson straight and awaken him to the full realization of what he had done, they should not carry out their interpretation to its full consequence and have him destroy his own creation in the same deliberate way in which he had carried out its construction. Is it that the producers tried, though too late, to return to the original intent of the novel, aware as they were (and as their hero, Nicholson, was) of their betrayal of Boulle's meaning?

Or maybe it was only the result of the "give and take" which must have taken place between author and producers as the latter proceeded to adapt the novel for the new medium. As Pierre Boulle pointed out in the same interview:

> I do not agree with the movie's end: namely the destruction of the bridge and the remorse which seems to overcome Nicholson when he exclaims: "What have I done?" This is the issue which led to the longest discussions between the producers and myself. Eventually I yielded, cowardly, and accepted their point of view; today I am sorry I was not more insistent.

Not only does such a distortion mutilate the personality of Boulle's Nicholson, but it robs the movie of Boulle's most characteristic slant, the "extravagance" of this world, an extravagance

made explicit from the very beginning through the epigraph he borrowed from Joseph Conrad:

> No, it was not funny; it was rather pathetic, he was so representative of all the past victims of the Great Joke. But it is by folly alone that the world moves, so it is a respectable thing upon the whole. And, besides, he was what one would call a good man.

This view was further reinforced by Boulle when he wrote in the Preface to the textbook edition of his novel: "Maybe the value of an act is of no importance, what matters is the passion one brings into it." Such attitudes, however, are not in line with the majority's beliefs and neither are they what the average reader looks for when he turns to entertainment as an escape from the daily routine and drudgery.

Furthermore, one should not forget the problem posed by the Motion Picture Production Code; its directives have, until recently, guided and at times seriously limited the activities of the movie makers: "No picture shall be produced which will lower the moral standards of those who see it. Hence, the sympathy of the audience should never be thrown on the side of crime, wrong doing, evil or sin." The Code, which embodied the long-entrenched and long-cherished concept of "Poetic Justice" and which found its best expression in the old "Crime Does Not Pay" series, became a necessity as soon as it became evident that the new medium, film, "was a most potent factor in shaping national minds and morals." Thus, it became incumbent upon the few to formulate guidelines for the protection of the many.

Nicholson's change of heart in the movie allows for the righting of his wrong doing, and the final image of the bridge's collapse illustrates in an impressive visual way the failure of evil and wrong-doers to win the day. The paradoxes and absurdities of life are eliminated, and, in the long run, good and reason prevail as befits the fictional world created by Hollywood.

The personage of Shears (played by William Holden) and his role represent another major change between the novel and the movie. In the novel a British Colonel leads the Commandos assigned to destroy the bridge; in the film the producers introduce an American soldier who is a prisoner and who impersonates an officer. He is present when Nicholson and the ragged, sickly regiment reach the camp and line up in the stereotyped "stiff upper-lip" British style. It is significant that the camera then moves to Holden-Shears, even before it focuses on Colonel Saito, the camp commander and, one would expect, Nicholson's natural and logical enemy. We watch Holden-Shears bury some of his dead fellow-prisoners and then use a dead man's lighter to bribe the guards to be placed on the sick list. After a quick glance at Saito, the camera again returns to Holden, who comments, "We're going to be a busy pair of grave diggers," as he continues watching the newcomers file in, as erect and undaunted as their Colonel.

Even the big scene when Saito and Nicholson clash head on as to whether officers should be required to work manually is overshadowed by the first face-to-face encounter between Nicholson and Shears. To Nicholson, who has just made the point that "his men will remain *soldiers,* and not become *slaves*"—a point with which one can hardly argue, at least until the bridge is completed and turned over to the Japanese—Shears replies: "I hope they can remain *soldiers,* as for me, I am a *slave.*" Though he is far from really becoming a slave, Shears is willing to play this role as far as others are concerned, that is, to accept his transformation into an object-slave, if that is what it takes to remain alive. He is the stereotyped, resourceful and rugged individualist who plays by his rules and bides his time while waiting for the right occasion to escape and return to civilization. Can it be also that the producers remembered the great success William Holden met with in an earlier movie, *Stalag XVII,* in which he played a similar role?

Thus, from the start, the lines are clearly drawn between the British Colonel, "Empire builder" à la Kipling ("sense of duty, observance of ritual, obsession with discipline, and love for the job well done, were all jumbled together in this worthy human repository") and the civilian-turned-soldier American who knows all the tricks and who prefers to live by the only law known to the animal world in which he is trapped, the survival of the fittest. We know by now that Shears will eventually succeed in escaping and that his clash with Nicholson, which will obviously resume, will turn to his advantage in the long run since he symbolizes the "will to live."

Following his escape, Shears is rescued and brought back to civilization, where he enjoys all the comforts and pleasures granted to those who have gone to hell and returned. The fact that he is acquainted with the conditions at the Kwai River Camp makes his decision to return there with the Commandos on the suicidal mission all the more meaningful and endears him further to his audience. Though he is not anxious to "volunteer," and no one really expects him to do so (after all he is not really an officer and therefore not expected to be as concerned as they are with duties and responsibilities), we know that he will go along "when the chips are down." Even then, however, it is made to appear as if he were "forced" to volunteer. Needless to say, he does not let us down any more than he will in his final but futile and self-sacrificing attempt to fulfill his mission.

The return trip through the Burmese jungle provided the producers, cameramen and special effects crew numerous opportunities to display their talents in conjunction with varied resources afforded by the film media. As expected, Shears is at his best with the female native guides and bearers; and the equally expected encounter with the Japanese patrol, during which the leader, Warden, is disabled, makes it possible for the Yank to "rise to the occasion" and assume the leadership.

Thus, though he is not in charge of the raiding party (a position he never assumed in the novel), he "steals the show" throughout the trek through the jungle and henceforth for the rest of the movie. Indeed, his importance seriously challenges Nicholson's and the bridge's, thus destroying the unity established in the novel. As Boulle insisted on several occasions, the whole book was written to lead to the final scene when Nicholson calls upon his Japanese jailors to help him thwart his own countrymen's efforts at destroying the bridge. Both Nicholson and the bridge share the spotlight in the novel, and the other characters exist only in so far as they can help the reader to understand him. There is far more consistency in the novel's hero than there is in his counterpart in the movie, and his *successful* heroism at the end of the novel is the logical outcome of what the reader has learned about him from the start. An inexorable logic has allowed Boulle to create, starting from the colonel of the prologue—who attracts all the sympathy of the reader—the colonel of the last scene whose conduct, though astounding and clearly reprehensible, remains nevertheless consequential and understandable.

Boulle, as was pointed out earlier, was well aware of the excessive importance attributed to

Shears by the movie producers, not only along the lines mentioned above (he is at the very center of the "action") but also, and perhaps more significantly, as a counter-weight to Nicholson's unexpressed but clearly implicit views. Shears plays this role in two ways: first, in his early encounter with Nicholson—which, as was noted, established their respective positions—and next, in his many discussions with Warden, also a stickler-for-rules and another representative of the "stiff-upper-lip" approach. Altogether, one feels that Shears has been introduced in the movie to "moralize" about war and its consequences (suffering and death) and to side with the concrete, life, as opposed to the abstract. As he says to Warden (in the movie): "You make me sick with your heroics . . . This is a game, this war, for you and Nicholson . . . How to die like a gentleman? How to die by the rules? What matters . . . is to live like a human being."

Boulle, on the contrary, did not intend to "moralize."

> As far as I am concerned, my novel is neither militaristic nor anti-militaristic, nor for that matter is it "istic" in any other way . . . I intended it to be the illustration of a general "absurdity" which could as well have been located in other times, other places and with other personages.

He defines "absurdity" as: "The lack of congruity between the motives explaining a certain conduct and the results achieved when one follows to the letter the 'good' principles motivating this particular behavior." Later on, reminiscing about the origin of the novel, he explained further:

> I have undoubtedly been influenced by the conduct of *Vichyites* during the German occupation of France, officers and civil servants who let themselves be caught into a *de facto* betrayal of their motherland as a result of too strict an attachment to the rules of military discipline.

In 1966, in an autobiographical account of his own adventures in Indochina, Boulle further enlightened his readers as he recalled some of his unpleasant encounters with the French "legal" authorities—in this case a Commandant to whom he had turned for help in a vain attempt to continue the struggle against the Axis forces:

> I wish for the Allies' victory, but I do consider the Gaullists as misguided persons who are acting against the best interests of France. I am and I shall remain faithful to the *Maréchal* [Marshall Pétain] who wants to maintain discipline at all cost. Discipline is essential today. And it is therefore impossible for me to help you.

Though Boulle himself singled out Shears's moralizing and philosophizing as one of his reservations about the movie, one must acknowledge that Shears is not the only one to express his thoughts aloud. Colonel Nicholson, whose views in the novel are made clear mainly in terms of the "silences" with which he answers his soldiers' and officers' comments (it might suffice here to recall his first inspection tour following his successful confrontation with Saito), talks much more in the movie. Thus, while walking proudly across the bridge after its completion, he explains himself to Saito—and to the spectators:

> "Tomorrow is the twenty-fifth anniversary of my enlistment . . . I have not been at home for more than ten months in those twenty-five years. Still, it was a good life! At times, one realizes he is nearer the end than the beginning, and he wonders: 'What's the sum total of my life?' 'Is there a difference in my having been here at all?' To night . . ."

Though he does not finish his explanation at this time, since he is interrupted by his men who have prepared an appropriate celebration, the message is clear: and, were there any doubt, it is dismissed shortly thereafter when he addresses his men:

> "When we return home—the war cannot last forever—you'll feel proud of what you have accomplished here. This bridge will remain as an example to all . . . You have survived with honor and you have turned defeat into victory."

It is interesting to notice that the movie's protagonists are generally much more talkative than their counterparts in the novel. As was suggested earlier, Boulle, an expert in the art of saying the most with the least amount of words—and by the eloquent "silences" of his main character—left a large amount of freedom to his readers with respect to their interpretation of the novel. The producers, on the other hand, though they used the "image" eloquently at times (one cannot forget the close-ups of Nicholson, Shears and Saito in the early parts of the movie), made their characters express their views more often and at greater length. As Boulle pointed out, "It is surprising that the novelist would have [and indeed did in the novel] had his characters speak less than the producers did in their movie."

One must assume that the film makers, aiming primarily at a mass audience, felt that they should instruct and altogether lead their public to palliative conclusions while providing them with entertainment, rather than with an aesthetic experience.

As for Boulle's last reservation, the film does lack the novel's stress on "the sweat, blood and tears" of the British soldiers driven mercilessly by their jailors as well as by their own Colonel. As a matter of fact, the last "suspenseful" sequence—the final efforts of the commandos, the onrushing Japanese train, the blowing up of the bridge, and the accompanying "regalia"—is longer than the few feet of film dealing with the actual construction of the bridge and the pain and suffering that went into it.

Again, this was to be expected from the moment the emphasis was shifted from Nicholson and his bridge to the opposition between Shears and the Nicholson-Warden alliance. In the novel, it is undeniable that Nicholson occupies the center stage; and his bridge, symbol of his life-long ambition and indomitable spirit, is the link which holds the various parts of the novel together. In the movie, on the contrary, Nicholson's role, counterbalanced as it is by Shears, no longer stands out—as is evidenced by the choice of co-stars to play the respective parts.

Furthermore, it is not only the actual material construction of the bridge which is slighted in the movie, but also the whole matter of the initial preparations: "When it comes to bridge building. Western mechanical procedures entail a lot of gruelling preliminaries which swell and multiply the number of operations leading to the actual construction." What is at stake here is the so-called superiority of the Occidental over the Oriental, a theme largely ignored in the movie version though it provided Boulle with many opportunities for tongue-in-cheek comments at the expense of his protagonists.

Finally, the construction of the bridge offered many (particularly Nicholson's lieutenants) an unexpected opportunity to release their psychological "hang-ups," unhampered by petty, tradition-bound administrations, routine procedures, budget limitations, and incomprehensible fear of innovation. Thus, Reeves, the brain behind the construction, and Hughes, the specialist of the "assembly-line" approach, make Nicholson's project *theirs* as much as *his* when they become as blind as their leader:

> Reeves . . . sacrificing his sleep at the end of each tiring day in order to see his craftsmanship take shape in a masterpiece which was to prove the superiority of the West—the bridge which

was to be used by the Japanese trains on their triumphant advance to the Bay of Bengal.

It is interesting to notice that many of the characters in the novel—Nicholson, Reeves, Hughes—let their passions take over their intellect. Their emotions are in command; they are all equally unable to "see" their situation objectively and comprehend what they are doing. Nicholson will build his bridge for the enemy with the complete and unlimited cooperation of his lieutenants and soldiers; meanwhile, Joyce's failure to grasp the situation and kill the "right" colonel will cause the mission to abort.

Still, despite the many modifications the novel underwent in the hands of the film makers, the movie met with tremendous success. It contained all the elements needed to be received favorably by the public at large, abroad as well as in the United States: a good "story"; a lot of action; enough suspense—though of the kind that is artificially yet acceptably maintained; engaging, sympathetic, well-portrayed characters whose faults are redeemed *in extremis* by a "return on the right track"; impressive photography and highly successful special effects.

Pierre Boulle might have spoken for many other viewers when, after stating the reservations mentioned above on the basis of a comparison between novel and movie, he concluded:

> . . . altogether, I have enjoyed the movie very much and I must say that I have admired without reservations, its technique, its photography, the interpretations of the different characters, and the constant care with which the minutest details have been handled.

**Source:** Georges Joyaux, "*The Bridge Over the River Kwai*: From the Novel to the Movie," in *Literature/Film Quarterly*, Vol. 2, 1974, pp. 174–82.

## SOURCES

Becker, Lucille Frackman, *Pierre Boulle*, Twayne's World Authors Series, No. 859, Twayne Publishers, 1996.

Boulle, Pierre, *The Bridge over the River Kwai*, translated by Xan Fielding, Vanguard, 1954.

———, *My Own River Kwai*, translated by Xan Fielding, Vanguard, 1967.

Davies, Peter N., *The Man behind the Bridge*, Continuum International, 1991.

Dower, John, *War without Mercy: Race and Power in the Pacific War*, Pantheon, 1986.

Esposito, Vincent J., ed., *The West Point Atlas of American Wars, Vol. II, 1900–1953*, Praeger, 1959.

Kipling, Rudyard, *Rudyard Kipling's Verse: Inclusive Edition 1885–1918*, Doubleday, Page & Co., 1919, pp. 371–72, 645–46.

Summers, Julie, *The Colonel of Tamarkan: Philip Toosey and the Bridge on the River Kwai*, Simon & Schuster, 2005.

Watt, Ian, "Bridges over the Kwai," in *Partisan Review*, Winter 1959, pp. 83–94.

——, "The Myth of the River Kwai" in *Observer*, September, 1968, pp. 18–21.

## FURTHER READING

Bourke, Roger, *Prisoners of the Japanese: Literary Imagination and the Prisoner-of-War Experience*, University of Queensland Press, 2006.

> Bourke surveys the depiction of British and Commonwealth POWS of the Japanese in literature and film and devotes a chapter to Ian Watt's criticism of The Bridge over the River Kwai.

Houston, Jeanne Wakatsuki, and James D. Houston, *Farewell to Manzanar: A True Story of Japanese American Experience during and after World War II Internment*, Houghton Mifflin, 1973.

> Jeanne Houston's first-person account of life in a Japanese American internment camp during World War II is told through the eyes of a child. This novel has become a staple in school curriculums across the country.

Parkin, Ray, *Wartime Trilogy: Out of the Smoke; Into the Smother; The Sword and the Blossom*, Melbourne University Publishing, 1999.

> This is a reissue of one volume of the three-part memoir of an Australian POW who worked on the Siam-Burma railway. It is generally considered among the finest literary achievements produced by World War II POWs. Parkin tries to come to terms with his experience through Asian philosophy.

Velmans, Loet, *Long Way Back to the River Kwai: Memories of World War II and After*, Arcade, 2003.

> The memoir of a Dutch POW who worked on the Bangkok-Rangoon railway is a vivid, detailed account of the experiences of a Japanese-held POW.

Waterford, Van, *Prisoners of the Japanese in World War II: Statistical History, Personal Narratives, and Memorials Concerning POWs in Camps and on Hellships, Civilian Internees, Asian Slave Laborers, and Others Captured in the Pacific Theater*, McFarland, 1994.

> This is a compilation of useful and interesting information relating to POWs in Japanese hands.

# Joseph Andrews

## HENRY FIELDING

## 1742

Henry Fielding's first novel is generally referred to by the abbreviated title *Joseph Andrews*, but the complete title is *The History of the Adventures of Joseph Andrews and His Friend Mr. Abraham Adams*. It recounts the comic adventures of a young footman (servant) and his absent-minded friend, Parson Adams, as they travel from London back home to the countryside. Fielding characterized his novel as a comic epic-poem in prose, linking it not only with the fictional prose of such contemporaries as Daniel Defoe and Samuel Richardson but also with the classical epic poems that were being imitated by eighteenth-century British poets.

Fielding's impetus for writing the book, which is among the first true novels written in English, was the enormous success of Richardson's *Pamela* (1741). The book was an epistolary novel, a novel written in the form of "epistles," or letters. It tells the story of a virtuous serving girl who resists the efforts of her master to seduce her. Fielding was outraged at what he regarded as the moral hypocrisy in Richardson's book, for it depicted virtue as a commodity, a valuable asset for a woman. He also believed that the epistolary form was creaky and necessarily led to too much irrelevant detail. Accordingly, in 1741 he wrote and published anonymously *Shamela*, a brief travesty—that is, an extravagant parody—of Richardson's novel. With *Joseph Andrews*, his intention was to continue his satiric attack on Richardson by tracing the career of Pamela's brother, Joseph, but soon the

*Henry Fielding* (The Library of Congress)

satire evolved into something much larger—a genuine novel that delighted readers with its comic characters and situations, its erudition, and its philosophical asides. Originally published in London in 1742, the novel has been a challenge for modern textual editors, for in the decade after its first publication it went through five editions, each one incorporating the author's revisions, but also incorporating new printer's errors.

## AUTHOR BIOGRAPHY

Henry Fielding was born on April 22, 1707, at Sharpham Park in Somerset, England. He was educated at Eton beginning in 1719, and after several years in London as a man-about-town and writer in the 1720s, he studied law at the University of Leiden in Holland. Lacking money to continue his education on the continent, he returned to London and embarked on a career as a playwright. Perhaps his most famous play was *Tragedy of Tragedies; or, the Life and Death of Tom Thumb* (1731), a farcical play that mocked English tragedies.

Fielding's career as a playwright was short-lived, in part because his satirical plays criticized the government, leading the British Parliament to pass the Theatrical Licensing Act of 1737. This law, which required plays to be submitted to a government censor, made it virtually impossible for a theatrical company to stage a play that was critical of the government, which was precisely the kind of play Fielding wrote. Accordingly, he turned to the law to support himself, his wife, and their two children.

Fielding by no means abandoned the literary scene. He continued to write plays, and he contributed to literary and political journals, writing for Tory journals under the name Captain Hercules Vinegar. He carried on a literary feud with Colley Cibber, England's much maligned poet laureate. After he was made a justice of the peace, Fielding issued a facetious arrest warrant for Cibber, charging him with murdering the English language.

Fielding became a novelist almost by accident. He turned to prose fiction in response to what he regarded as the moral outrages of Richardson's novel *Pamela*. After the success of his answer to Richardson, *Joseph Andrews*, he wrote *The Life and Death of Jonathan Wild, the Great* (1743), a novel about a notorious underworld figure. He then wrote his masterpiece, *Tom Jones* (1749), a robust, comic tale about a foundling whose parentage, and therefore class and social status, is uncertain. A later novel, *Amelia*, was published in 1751.

Meanwhile, Fielding was active in other affairs. He founded and wrote for a literary journal, using the publication to attack hack journalists and starting what came to be called the "Paper War" of 1752–1753, an ongoing battle of words among writers and journalists in London's newspapers and journals. He also wrote satirical articles for newspapers and other journals. In 1748 he was appointed to the position of London's chief magistrate, and a year later, with his half-brother John, he founded the Bow Street Runners, London's first police force. A noted humanitarian, he offered proposals for alleviating the plight of the poor and argued for judicial reform, prison reform, and the abolition of public hangings.

By 1750, Fielding's health was beginning to deteriorate and he had to walk with crutches. In 1754 he traveled to the milder climate of Portugal in a futile search for some relief, but he died from the accumulated effects of gout, asthma, jaundice, and dropsy on October 8, 1754. He was buried in the English cemetery in Lisbon.

## PLOT SUMMARY

### Book I

#### CHAPTERS I–IV

The opening chapters of *Joseph Andrews* introduce the title character. Joseph is presented as the brother of Pamela, the central character in Samuel Richardson's novel by that name. As a youngster, "Joey" was employed by Sir Thomas Booby as a stable boy. He proved to be diligent and incorruptible, so when he turned seventeen, he moved up to the position of footman to Sir Thomas's wife, Lady Booby. The reader is then introduced to the scholarly Abraham Adams, the absent-minded parish parson, who has little direct contact with the Booby family because of an ongoing dispute over his income, which is paid out of the proceeds of the Booby estate. Adams is drawn to Joseph in large part because of the boy's innocence and sweet singing voice in church. The Boobys regard Adams as little more than a domestic servant. The only person in the Booby household who retains any respect for Adams is Mrs. Slipslop, a gentlewoman who waits on Lady Booby. On a trip to London, it become apparent that Lady Booby is attracted to Joseph, making her the subject of gossip.

#### CHAPTERS V–X

Sir Thomas dies, and the widow redoubles her efforts to seduce Joseph by calling him to her bedroom. Joseph, though, affirms his commitment to remaining chaste and resists his mistress's advances. Joseph writes letters to his sister Pamela, expressing his confusion about Lady Booby's advances and his fears that he will be dismissed. Lady Booby again tries to seduce Joseph, and when her efforts fail, she dismisses him from her service. She also dismisses a chambermaid, Betty, who, according to Mrs. Slipslop—who herself nurses a secret passion for Joseph—is pregnant with Joseph's child. Lady Booby tries to dismiss Mrs. Slipslop as well, but relents, knowing that her reputation is in the hands of her attendant. Joseph collects his wages, dons new clothing, and sets out for his home at the Booby county seat.

#### CHAPTERS XI–XIII

Joseph is eager to return to the countryside because of his love for Fanny Goodwill, who lives on a nearby farm. He and Fanny have loved each other since they were children but have been out of touch. On his journey, he takes shelter at an inn. After he resumes his journey, he is beaten,

robbed, and left in a ditch by highwaymen. Travelers in a coach reluctantly take him to an inn owned by Mr. and Mrs. Tow-wouse. He is met with indifference from the coach passengers, Mrs Tow-wouse, and the doctor called to attend him, as well as from Barnabas, a clergyman who offers him empty advice. Only Betty, a maid, treats Joseph with kindness. (This is not the same Betty who worked for the Boobys.)

#### CHAPTERS XIV–XVI

Parson Adams arrives at the inn and discovers that the injured man is Joseph. Adams is on his way to London to seek publication of his sermons. One of the thieves who assaulted Joseph is caught, and a bundle of Joseph's stolen clothing is found. Joseph is delighted that he has recovered a small piece of gold that is a memento of Fanny. After Betty convinces Mrs. Tow-wouse that Joseph is not just a vagabond, given the piece of gold and his acquaintance with Adams, the landlady treats Joseph with more respect. The captured thief escapes because of the carelessness and corruption of the constable, Thomas Suckbribe. Adams recognizes that Joseph is not well enough to travel, so he tries to persuade Mr. Tow-wouse to allow him to remain at the inn. He tries to borrow money from the innkeeper, offering his volumes of sermons as security for the loan.

## CHAPTERS XVII–XVIII

A coach has arrived at the inn. Barnabas knows one of the occupants, and Adams is delighted to learn that the man is a bookseller. Adams's discussion with the bookseller about publishing the clergyman's sermons leads to discussions of religious doctrine, which Barnabas joins. The discussion is interrupted by the uproar created when Mrs. Tow-wouse discovers her husband in an amorous embrace with Betty. Betty resisted his advances in the past, but she has become attracted to Joseph and tried to throw herself at him. When she fails, her passions remain aroused and she submits to Mr. Tow-wouse's advances.

## Book II

### CHAPTERS I–IV

After an introductory chapter about the practice of authors of dividing novels into books and chapters, the action recommences. Joseph and Adams decide to go on their separate ways until Adams discovers that his wife did not pack his sermons, so he decides to travel back home with Joseph. Joseph discovers that he does not have money to pay for his horse's boarding, so the stable owner will not release it. Meanwhile, Adams has set out on foot and arrived at an inn. Mrs. Slipslop arrives in a coach. Adams learns that she has paid for the horse's boarding, releasing the horse and Joseph. When Joseph catches up, the three board a coach. When the coach passes a house, one of the ladies riding in the coach begins a story about Leonora, who lives as a recluse in the house. Leonora jilted her lover Horatio in favor of Bellarmine, a dashing man who only wanted her money. Before the lady can finish the story, the coach arrives at an inn.

### CHAPTERS V–VI

Joseph has fallen from a horse and is laid up with an injury at the inn. The mistress of the inn does not want her husband to waste time caring for a mere footman. Adams is outraged, and a fistfight breaks out. After the fight is resolved, the parties board the coach, though one of the travelers, Miss Grave-airs, does not want to ride with a footman inside the coach. The issue is resolved when her father appears and takes her away. In the carriage, Mrs. Slipslop makes advances to Joseph. The lady then resumes the story of

Leonora, who learned of Bellarmine's bad faith and retired to the home the party had passed.

### CHAPTERS VII–IX

Adams, who has become lost, encounters a hunter. The two have discussions about the military, bravery, and politics. Adams wants to catch up with the coach, now ahead of him on the road, but it is getting late. The hunter invites Adams to spend the night at his nearby home. The two men hear a woman screaming. Adams runs to her rescue and gets into a fight with a man who is trying to force himself on the woman. Adams fells the attacker and thinks he may have killed the man.

### CHAPTERS X–XV

Adams learns that the woman is none other than Fanny, who had learned of Joseph's condition and set out to find him. Fanny's attacker accuses Adams and Fanny of trying to rob him. He and a group of accomplices take the pair into custody for trial. The judge turns out to be ignorant and incompetent, and he believes the rogues' story. Adams and Fanny are saved by a squire who recognizes Adams as a parson, thus changing the judge's mind. Fanny's attacker escapes while his accomplices bicker about how much reward money each of them would have received if Adams and Fanny had been convicted.

Adams and Fanny take shelter from a storm at an inn. They hear the sound of someone from another room singing a ballad. Fanny, realizing that the singer is Joseph, faints, and Joseph revives her with kisses. Adams is delighted to see the lovers reunited, but Mrs. Slipslop is jealous and refuses to recognize Fanny. Joseph and Fanny renew their love and ask Adams to marry them, but the parson refuses to marry them on an impulse. The following morning the party is about to leave the inn, but again Adams and Joseph have no money. Adams departs to secure a loan from a nearby fellow clergyman. The clergyman, Mr. Trulliber, is more a pig farmer than a cleric. He believes Adams is there to buy pigs, but when he discovers Adams's true purpose, he refuses to make the loan. Adams returns to the inn, where he learns that the innkeeper's wife has agreed to extend credit. She changes her mind after she goes to the Trulliber farm to fetch the coat Adams had forgotten and Trulliber defames Adams. The party is rescued by a kind peddler at the inn, who offers to pay the party's bill.

## CHAPTERS XVI–XVII

Adams, Joseph, and Fanny encounter a good-natured gentleman on the road. They join the man at an inn, where he offers them hospitality, at his home, and horses, and even promises Adams a parish after the present minister dies. It turns out that all of the man's promises are empty and that he has disappeared. The innkeeper explains that he is not surprised, for the man has made similar empty promises in the past. He and Adams have a spirited discussion about benevolence, traveling, and necessities versus luxuries that is interrupted as Joseph and Fanny appear and the three travelers resume their journey.

## Book III

### CHAPTERS I–V

Book III begins with a chapter in which the narrator discusses the writing of biography. In Chapter II, the action recommences with the travelers pausing at the side of the road to rest. They see some strange, ghostly lights, so they flee and are taken in by a Mr. Wilson, a kindly man, and his wife. Wilson assures the travelers that they have not seen ghosts, only sheep stealers. He then narrates the story of his life, a story that bears some resemblance to Fielding's own life. Wilson had tried to become a fine gentleman in London, but his life was a shambles, marked by debt and a failed career as a playwright. He purchased a lottery ticket that won three thousand pounds, but he had to sell the ticket for food. After serving a term in prison, he received money from Harriet Hearty, the daughter of the man who had purchased the ticket. The two eventually married and retired to the countryside, where they enjoy a peaceful life. Wilson, though, notes that his eldest son had been taken by gypsies years ago. He says that he would be able to identify the son because of a birthmark on his chest. The travelers take their leave, Wilson having promised to visit Adams within the week.

### CHAPTERS VI–XIII

The most brutal episode of the novel begins as Adams dozes by the roadside. A pack of hounds chases a hare, then turns on Adams. Adams and Joseph drive the hounds off. The hunter, a local squire, invites the party to have dinner at his house. He and his companions treat the travelers maliciously. They also have designs on Fanny. The three travelers flee to an inn, but three of the squire's companions pursue Fanny. After a fight, Adams and Joseph are left tied to the bedposts

and the terrified Fanny is carried away. On the road, two horsemen approach, and one recognizes Fanny. He turns out to be Peter Pounce, Lady Booby's steward, traveling home ahead of her to Booby Hall. The party returns to the inn and releases Adams and Joseph. After Joseph drubs one of their assailants, he, Adams, Fanny, and Pounce set out for Booby Hall.

## Book IV

### CHAPTERS I–III

All the major characters are back at Booby Hall, where Lady Booby's passion for Joseph is again inflamed. At church, Adams announces the upcoming marriage of Joseph and Fanny, raising Lady Booby's ire. She threatens to dismiss Adams, who refuses to bend to her will, and she consults with Scout, a lawyer who agrees to help her stop the marriage.

### CHAPTERS IV–VI

With the conniving of Scout, Joseph and Fanny are arrested and tried on a trumped-up charge: Joseph is accused of cutting a hazel twig on Scout's property. Lady Booby's nephew, Mr. Booby, and his wife, Pamela (Joseph's sister), arrive at Booby Hall. Mr. Booby attends the trial and is outraged. He persuades the judge to release Joseph and Fanny into his custody. He dresses Joseph in fine clothes, and the three return to Booby Hall, to Lady Booby's delight.

### CHAPTERS VII–VIII

Lady Booby persuades her nephew to try to talk Joseph out of the marriage. Even Pamela tries to dissuade Joseph from marrying Fanny. Fanny is assaulted by a young gentleman (who later is identified as Beau Didapper), then by his servant, but Joseph rescues her, and the two depart for the home of Adams. There they discover Mrs. Adams berating her husband for opposing Lady Booby. Adams is grief-stricken by the news that his son has drowned, but later the boy, Dick, appears. He had been rescued by the same peddler who had earlier helped Adams.

### CHAPTERS IX–XI

Lady Booby and her entourage arrive at the Adams home. She tries to arrange a match between Fanny and Beau Didapper. A fight breaks out when Joseph sees Didapper trying to fondle Fanny. Adams leaps to Joseph's defense, armed with the lid of a pot. After the two men are separated, Joseph and Fanny leave, but they return with the peddler and invite the Adams family to dinner.

**CHAPTERS XII–XIV**

The peddler has discovered Fanny's parentage. Years before, he had a mistress, who revealed to him that she and a group of gypsies had stolen a child and sold it to Sir Thomas Booby. The child's parents were a Mr. and Mrs. Andrews, so it appears that Joseph has fallen in love with his own sister. The peddler repeats his story at Booby Hall.

Adams is involved in a burlesque incident. Didapper, still lusting after Fanny, jumps into what he believes is Fanny's bed but is in fact Mrs. Slipslop's. When Mrs. Slipslop screams for help, Adams, naked, runs to her aid. Yet, in the dark, Didapper escapes. Adams, though, believes that he has seized Didapper when in fact he has seized Mrs. Slipslop. Lady Booby appears to find Adams in bed with Mrs. Slipslop, but she finds evidence that in fact Didapper had been the culprit. Adams is exhausted, and when he goes to bed, he mistakenly enters Fanny's room and curls up in Fanny's bed. Joseph discovers him the next morning, but soon the confusion is resolved.

**CHAPTERS XV–XVI**

The mysteries surrounding the parentage of Joseph and Fanny are sorted out. Gaffar and Gammar Andrews, Joseph's parents, arrive. Mr. Andrews denies that Fanny is his daughter, but Mrs. Andrews confirms the peddler's story. She had given birth while her husband was away at war, but the child was stolen by gypsies, who had left Joseph in her place. Mrs. Andrews decided to raise the boy as her own son. The peddler then asks Joseph whether he has a birthmark on his chest. Joseph indeed does, suggesting that he is the son of Mr. and Mrs. Wilson. The Wilsons arrive on their promised visit to Adams. Mr. Wilson inspects Joseph's birthmark and confirms that Joseph is his long-lost son. Joseph and Fanny are not brother and sister. Adams performs the marriage of Joseph and Fanny at Mr. Booby's house. Mr. Booby gives Fanny money, which the couple uses to purchase a small estate. Mr. Booby also gives Adams a decent living as a parish minister and arranges to reward the peddler with a job as an exciseman (one who appraises imported goods for tax purposes). Lady Booby returns to London, where she links up with a young captain and soon forgets about Joseph.

# CHARACTERS

### Abraham Adams

Adams is the parson on the Booby estate. On the one hand, as Joseph's sidekick, he is a comic character. He is absent-minded and totally innocent. He knows little of the ways of the world, and he knows even less about money. On the other hand, he is the moral center of the novel. He, like Joseph, is incorruptible. He is charitable and kind, and he serves as a worthy moral compass for Joseph, for the world's evils do not affect him in any way.

### Mrs. Adams

Mrs. Adams is Parson Adams's wife. Unlike her husband, she is much more concerned with worldly interests, and she treats her husband badly.

### Joseph Andrews

Joseph is described as handsome and incorruptible. He resists Lady Booby's efforts to seduce him. He is driven by his love for Fanny, which enables him to overcome temptations and to deal with the many thieves, corrupt judges and lawyers, and other rogues that cross his path. He is believed to be a person of common ancestry, and as such he works as a stable boy and then as a footman for Sir Thomas and Lady Booby. In the end it is revealed that he is really the son of a gentleman, Mr. Wilson, suggesting that the gentlemanly qualities he exhibits throughout are indications that he is a true gentleman—in contrast to other characters who have the external trappings of fashion but are in fact corrupt, weak, dishonest, or hypocritical.

### Barnabas

Barnabas is a hypocritical clergyman who is more interested in his stomach than in his or anyone else's soul.

### Betty

Two characters named Betty appear in the novel. One is a chambermaid to the Boobys. Mrs. Slipslop falsely claims that Betty is pregnant with Joseph's child. The other is a maid at the Towwouses's inn. She becomes enamored of Joseph, who resists her, but her passions having been aroused, she allows Mr. Tow-wouse to take liberties with her.

## Lady Booby

In some respects, Lady Booby is the most vital character in the novel. She lusts after Joseph, but she often finds her reason warring with her passion. She is vain, selfish, shallow, and drawn to life in the city, placing her in stark contrast to Joseph. While she does everything in her power to impede the marriage of Joseph and Fanny, her conflicting emotions create in the reader some small measure of sympathy, for she succumbs to the same passions that might afflict any other person.

## Mr. Booby

Mr. Booby is Lady Booby's nephew and the husband of Pamela, Joseph's sister.

## Sir Thomas Booby

Sir Thomas Booby is Lady Booby's husband and Joseph's master. He dies early in the novel.

## Bookseller

Parson Adams has conversations about religious doctrine and about the possibility of publishing his sermons with an unnamed bookseller, who arrives at the inn where Joseph is laid up with his injuries.

## Beau Didapper

Didapper is a dissolute young gentleman who tries to rape Fanny. Lady Booby later tries to arrange a match between him and Fanny.

## Fanny Goodwill

Fanny is believed to be the common, illiterate daughter of a farmer on the Booby estate. She, like Joseph, is incorruptible. In the novel's climax, it is revealed that she is in fact the daughter of Gaffar and Gammar Andrews, but that she and Joseph are not, as feared, brother and sister. Fanny is presented as a perfect person—loyal to Joseph, modest, and capable of depth of feeling—in contrast to such women as Lady Booby and Mrs. Slipslop.

## Miss Grave-airs

Miss Grave-airs is a prudish coach traveler who refuses to allow Joseph, supposedly a mere footman, to ride inside the coach with her.

## Leonora

Leonora is the lead character in a tale told by one of the travelers who accompany Joseph and Adams. She jilts her lover, Horatio, in favor of a dashing man, Bellarmine, who is interested in her only for her money.

## Pamela

Pamela, presumably the same young woman from Samuel Richardson's novel *Pamela*, is Joseph's sister and the wife of Mr. Booby, Lady Booby's nephew.

## Peddler

The peddler first appears when he helps Adams by paying his bill at an inn. He later appears as the rescuer of Adams's son, who was in danger of drowning. The peddler plays a key role in sorting out the ancestries of Joseph and Fanny.

## Peter Pounce

Peter Pounce is the Boobys' dishonest steward.

## Scout

Scout is a sly, hypocritical lawyer who bends to Lady Booby's will in trying to block the marriage of Joseph and Fanny.

## Mrs. Slipslop

Mrs. Slipslop is a gentlewoman who waits on Lady Booby, despite an unspecified "small Slip in her Youth." She is described as corpulent and short, with pimples on her face, a nose that is too large, and eyes that are too small. She adds comedy to the novel by speaking in malapropisms, which are distorted or misused words. (The word *malaprop* later came from Mrs. Malaprop, a character in Richard Brinsley Sheridan's 1775 play *The Rivals*.) Thus, for example, she says "contract" when she means "contrast," or "ironing" when she means "irony." She is enamored with Joseph. She is something of a foil to Lady Booby, since both are attracted to Joseph but they are of different social classes.

## Tom Suckbribe

Suckbribe is the corrupt and lazy constable who allows the thief who robbed Joseph to escape.

## Surgeon

The unnamed surgeon, who reluctantly attends Joseph after he is beaten and robbed, fails to exhibit the kind of benevolence and fellow feeling that Parson Adams shows.

## Lady Tittle and Lady Tattle

These two minor characters gossip about Lady Booby's familiarities with Joseph in London.

## Mr. Tow-wouse

Tow-wouse is the landlord of the inn to which Joseph is taken after he is robbed and beaten. He is essentially of a kindly disposition, but he is under the thumb of his wife.

### Mrs. Tow-wouse

Mrs. Tow-wouse is the wife of the innkeeper to whose inn Joseph is taken after he is robbed and beaten. She is reluctant to provide care for a mere foot passenger and vagabond, though she relents when she learns of Joseph's connection with Adams, a parson. After she catches her husband taking liberties with a maid, she makes it clear that she will hold his adultery over his head for the rest of his life.

### Parson Trulibber

Parson Trulibber is more of a farmer than a cleric. He raises and sells pigs, and he refuses to make a loan to Parson Adams when the latter needs money to pay an inn bill.

### Mr. Wilson

Wilson is a kindly man who takes in the travelers and tells them the story of his life. His eldest son had been taken by gypsies years ago, but he knows he could recognize his son by a birthmark. In the novel's climactic scene, it is revealed that Joseph is his long-lost son.

## THEMES

### Charity and Benevolence

The overriding theme of *Joseph Andrews* concerns the true nature of charity, benevolence, and, more generally, sound morals. Throughout, Joseph proves to be incorruptible, firmly resisting the flattery of Lady Booby and others. Parson Adams, too, is an innocent, and although his innocence often gets him embroiled in comic misadventures, his moral compass is always true. In contrast to these men, along with the equally steadfast Fanny Goodwill, Mr. Booby (Lady Booby's nephew), Mrs. Wilson, and the peddler who helps sort out the novel's complications, the rest of the novel's cast is a rogue's gallery of hypocrites, thieves, and sexual predators. Characters such as Beau Didapper, the lawyer Scout, Barnabas, and Parson Trulliber fail to exhibit any measure of charity or benevolence, instead showing vanity, corruptness, shallowness, scorn for those of a lower social class, greed, jealousy, and the like.

This concern with the nature of true morality and goodness is expressed in some way in virtually every chapter of the novel. One example is Joseph's monologue on morality, when he says:

> Now would not one great Act of Charity, one Instance of redeeming a poor Family from all the Miseries of Poverty...or any such like Example of Goodness, create a Man more Honour and Respect than he could acquire by the finest House, Furniture, Pictures or Clothes that were ever beheld?

### Social Class

Throughout *Joseph Andrews*, Fielding depicts characters from a wide range of social classes, from the knight Sir Thomas Booby and his wife, Lady Booby, to innkeepers, highwaymen, servants, attorneys, parsons, and others. Fielding takes a satiric view of birth and its role in determining social class; indeed, the entire novel turns on the question of the title character's birth and ancestry. Fielding takes up this theme in a discussion of Joseph's antecedents:

> But suppose for Argument's sake we should admit that he had no Ancestors at all, but had sprung up, according to the modern Phrase, out of a Dunghill,...Would it not be hard, that a Man who hath no Ancestors should therefore be render'd incapable of acquiring Honour, when we see so many who have no Virtues, enjoying the Honour of their Forefathers?

The outcome of the novel undermines the century's common assumptions about social class. Joseph, it turns out, is in reality not just an orphaned servant but the son of a respected gentleman. This ending seems fitting, for throughout Joseph has exhibited the qualities of a gentleman, in contrast to other characters who are "gentlemen" and "ladies" in name only.

### Appearance versus Reality

*Joseph Andrews* persistently explores the issue of appearance versus reality. It raises the question of who is just, kind, moral, or genuinely religious—and who is not—in spite of appearances. Lady Booby is a member of the upper class, and yet she lusts after Joseph. Parson Adams is a bumbling character, yet he is good at heart. Mr. Wilson led the life of a London man-about-town, but it was all a charade; he wrote love letters to himself, for example. Barnabas possesses the guise of a parson, but he has little interest in religion and instead likes to discuss legal issues. Fanny appears to be a poor, illiterate girl, but in reality she turns out to be related to the Booby family. And of course Joseph himself

# TOPICS FOR FURTHER STUDY

- Conduct Internet research on how people lived in early eighteenth-century England, focusing on one aspect of their lives. Possibilities include clothing, food, inns, transportation, medicine, the legal system, and housing. Present your findings, possibly in a PowerPoint presentation or sketchbook, using as many visuals as possible.

- In eighteenth-century England, crime was rampant, particularly robbery and burglary. So-called highwaymen often robbed travelers, and many of these highwaymen gained reputations as colorful, almost romantic figures. Investigate the history of highwaymen during the eighteenth century. Write and perform a skit that captures how highwaymen might have operated.

- Many novels and movies are structured around the adventures of a hero and his or her sidekick as they are on the road. The sidekick often contributes to the hero's education. Read another novel with a sidekick and write a report on the character's similarities to and differences from *Joseph Andrews*'s Adams. Possibilities include Samwise Gamgee, Frodo Baggins's sidekick in J. R. R. Tolkien's *Lord of the Rings*, Friday in Daniel Defoe's *Robinson Crusoe*, or Ron Weasley, the hero's sidekick in J. K. Rowling's Harry Potter novels.

- In eighteenth-century England, religion was a topic of widespread discussion in government, in newspapers and journals, and in literature. Discussion of religion made reference to groups such as the Methodists, Deists, Free-Thinkers, latitudinarians, Dissenters, Nonconformists, and others, along with reference to such doctrines as justification by faith. Conduct research on one religious group or concept from this time period. What influence did it have on religious discussion and practice? Describe your findings in a report.

- Sherman Alexie's *Reservation Blues* (1996) is a novel about a Native American rock band that embarks on a tour of the United States. As such, it uses the same journey motif around which *Joseph Andrews* is structured. Read *Reservation Blues* and make a chart showing the similarities and differences between the two novels and their treatment of the effects of the surrounding culture on the journey and the lead characters.

- In L. Sprague de Camp's Novarian series, a sequence of fantasy stories (1968–1989), one of the central characters embarks on a journey to return home to his true love, much as Joseph Andrews does. During his journey, he encounters a wide range of adventures, and much of the commentary in the stories is satirical. Read some of the stories in the series, perhaps focusing on *The Goblin Tower* (1968), *The Clocks of Iraz* (1971), and *The Unbeheaded King* (1983), collected under the title *The Reluctant King* (1985), and write an essay that compares *Joseph Andrews* and de Camp's novels.

appears to be nothing more than a servant, but in reality he is the son of a country gentleman.

## *City versus Country*

A common theme in eighteenth-century literature is the contrast between the city and the countryside. The city, in this case London, is a place that is corrupt and artificial. It is a place of intrigue, gossip, and loose morals. This theme is particularly apparent in Mr. Wilson's narration of his life. In London, he led a false existence. He fell into debt, turned to hack journalism to earn money, and came to rely on a lottery ticket. People in London are imprisoned for debt. They adopt poses—such as Wilson's feigned interest in the theater, which he attended just to

*Illustration from* The Adventures of Joseph Andrews *(© Lebrecht Music and Arts Photo Library / Alamy)*

be seen, not because he was interested in the play—and they are corrupted by wealth. The narrative arc of *Joseph Andrews* follows the title character's escape from the city and Lady Booby's lust (and, to a lesser extent, the lust of Mrs. Slipslop). In contrast, it is in the countryside where the plot complications are sorted out and people find benevolence, happiness, and a secure future.

## STYLE

### Omniscient Narrator

*Joseph Andrews* is narrated by a third-person omniscient narrator. In narration of this type, characters are referred to as "he," "she," and "they" by a narrator who is omniscient, or all knowing, meaning that the narrator can enter into the characters' minds. Different authors handle the technique of omniscient narration in different ways. Many authors create narrative voices that provide detailed narration about characters' inner lives—their thoughts, emotions, and perceptions. In *Joseph Andrews*, Fielding's narrative voice tends to restrict itself

to external action and dialogue, although the narration sketches in descriptions of the characters and their backgrounds.

What is especially noteworthy about Fielding's use of omniscient narration is that his "narrator" is not at all hidden or disguised. The narrator frequently refers to himself as "I" and intrudes into the narration in many places, for example: "But I pass by these and many others, to mention two Books lately published, which represent an admirable Pattern of the Amiable in either Sex." The narrator goes on to satirize Fielding's contemporaries, the poet laureate Colley Cibber and Samuel Richardson, the author of *Pamela*. Similarly, the narrator intrudes to offer a discussion of why the novel is divided into chapters and books, and engages in an extended discussion of writing biography. At one point he makes a digression for the sole purpose, he says, of lengthening a short chapter. These authorial intrusions are nearly always witty, sarcastic, or philosophical observations on characters, situations, or literary matters. Collectively, they create an image of a wise, literate, sometimes genial, sometimes acerbic host who is guiding the reader through the world he has created.

### Mock-Heroic

The mock-heroic style imitates the lofty language of heroic Classical epics but applies it to trivial subjects. Its purposes can vary. One is to satirize the heroic style of those epics. Frequently, though, it serves the purpose of emphasizing the un-heroic nature of the modern age, in contrast to the presumed heroism of the Classical period. Instances of mock-heroic can be found throughout *Joseph Andrews*. When Joseph is about to have an interview with Lady Booby, Fielding uses the mock-heroic style, with Classical references:

> Now the Rake *Hesperus* had called for his Breeches, and having well rubbed his drowsy Eyes, prepared to dress himself for all Night.... Now *Thetis* the good Housewife began to put on the Pot in order to regale the good Man *Pheobus*, after his daily Labours were over. In vulgar Language, it was in the Evening when *Joseph* attended his Lady's Orders.

### Irony

Fielding relies on irony throughout *Joseph Andrews*. Sometimes he creates irony of situation, where events turn out in a way different from what the reader has been led to expect. In this sense, the revelation of Joseph's parentage is highly ironic. Much of his irony, though, is irony of language, often delivered in chatty asides to the reader. For instance, the narrator digresses into a discussion of "high" people and "low" people:

> Be it known, then, that the human Species are divided into two sorts of People, to-wit, *High* People and *Low* People. . . . High People signify no other than People of Fashion, and low People those of no Fashion. . . . Now the World being thus divided . . . a fierce Contention arose between them.

The narrator goes on in this vein for more than two pages, appearing to offer a sober social analysis but in reality undercutting people of fashion.

### Dialogue

Fielding often uses dialogue as a way of presenting character. One clear example is Mrs. Slipslop, whose affectations of being a gentlewoman are undercut by her use of malapropisms, or distorted or misused words, such as "convicted" rather than "convinced," or "respect" rather than "suspect." The hypocrisy of such characters as Lady Booby and snobbishness of such characters as Miss Grave-airs are revealed through their spoken words, reflecting Fielding's earlier work as a playwright.

Fielding does not follow the modern practice of beginning each character's speech on a separate line. The dialogue between characters is usually run together within a paragraph. Book printing and paper in the eighteenth century were expensive, so books typically included little of the white space modern readers are accustomed to. In this way, a book required fewer pages.

### Character Names

Like many writers from this period and into the nineteenth century, Fielding used names to satirize characters or to give the reader some indication of the character's true nature. Mrs. Slipslop, Miss Grave-airs, Thomas Suckbribe, and the Boobys are clear examples. Fanny Goodwill's name indicates her essentially moral nature. Some characters' names are simply comic, including Peter Pounce and Mr. Tow-wouse. The names of the author's most sympathetic characters, though, including Joseph Andrews, Mr. Wilson, and Abraham Adams, are more commonplace, suggesting that they represent a norm against which other characters are measured.

### Interpolated Tales

The narration of *Joseph Andrews* is interrupted by interpolated tales. These are stories told by one of the characters that become almost like short stories within the novel. For example, an unnamed lady in a coach with Joseph and Adams tells the story of Leonora, the "Unfortunate Jilt." Later, Mr. Wilson gives an extended narration of his life. This was a common narrative device in eighteenth-century fiction, derived from Cervantes's *Don Quixote* and from earlier tale-telling works such as *Thousand and One Nights* and Giovanni Boccaccio's *Decameron* (1350–1353). The technique has continued to be used in modern literature, including the award-winning graphic novel *Watchmen*, by Alan Moore and Dave Gibbons. The interpolated tale usually has a thematic connection to the surrounding novel, shedding further light on themes and characters. Mr. Wilson's narration is in many particulars a narration of Fielding's own life.

## HISTORICAL CONTEXT

At least two historical trends are relevant as backdrops to *Joseph Andrews*. Perhaps the more important concerns disputes over religion. By the eighteenth century, residents of England were predominantly members of the Anglican Church, or Church of England. At least two religious groups posed a challenge to Anglicanism. One was Catholicism. Although Catholics were in the minority and were generally reviled, they remained a strong and vocal presence. In the political arena, many in England feared rebellion being stirred by the Stuart line. The Stuarts (sometimes spelled Stewarts) were the Scottish royal line that laid claim to the British throne after Queen Elizabeth I died childless in 1603. Elizabeth, like her father, Henry VIII, was a Protestant, but the Stuarts were sympathetic to Catholics. Over the next century, six Stuart monarchs ruled England, and the last of the Stuarts, James II, was himself Catholic. In 1701, the Act of Settlement established the German Hanoverian line on the British throne, bringing an end to Stuart rule. However, the Stuarts in exile maintained their claim to the throne, and in 1715 and again in 1745, Jacobite revolts attempted to restore the descendants of the last Stuart monarch, James II, to the throne of England. (*Jacobite* derives from the Latin version of "James").

# COMPARE
# &
# CONTRAST

- **1740s:** Travel is slow, uncertain, and exhausting, with people getting from place to place on foot, on horseback, or in carriages and wagons on unpaved roads that can often be muddy and impassable.

  **Today:** Travel in motorized vehicles over paved roads and highways is the norm, reducing travel time and making travel much safer and more comfortable.

- **1740s:** Travelers are often robbed by highwaymen, who operate freely in part because there is no police force; travelers typically have to defend themselves if they can, and injuries often have to be treated at the nearest inn or home.

  **Today:** Modern police forces, combined with organized transport systems and better communications, make traveling safer and reduce the risk of a traveler being robbed, though modern carjacking still occurs.

- **1740s:** Social classes are sharply defined, with country squires and members of the nobility owning large tracts of land and deriving income from the land's resources, while poorer people often work as laborers on the land or as servants.

  **Today:** While classes of rich and poor continue to exist, a large middle class of people enjoys relative comfort without being landowners or employing servants.

The other threat to the Church of England came from a variety of dissenting religious sects. In *Joseph Andrews*, the characters take part in an extended discussion of religious doctrine. Reference is made to two major religious evangelists, George Whitefield and John Wesley, along with a number of other religious writers and thinkers, including John Toland, Thomas Woolston, and Bishop Benjamin Hoadly. Reference is also made to Methodists and "Free-Thinkers." These figures and movements were central to an ongoing debate about salvation and the means by which a Christian achieves it. Some were proponents of the orthodox doctrine of justification by faith, meaning that faith alone determined whether a person would achieve salvation after death. Others, however, disputed this notion, arguing that true religion, and hence salvation, were founded on sincerity and good works, not on external forms of worship. In *Joseph Andrews*, Adams discourses on religion and politics, referring to conflicts between so-called High Churchmen—that is, orthodox Anglicans—and various groups of dissenters and nonconformists. The Tory High Churchmen attacked the Whig Party for its presumed willingness to tolerate dissenters.

Fielding was a great admirer of Bishop Hoadly, who was regarded as a heretic by more orthodox clerics because of his belief that how a person lived his or her life, not simply faith, was the earmark of true religion. Fielding believed that the doctrine of justification by faith led to hypocritical behavior, corruption, and worldliness, for it said in effect that a person could behave badly yet reach heaven. In *Joseph Andrews*, Parson Adams puts it succinctly:

> can any Doctrine have a more pernicious Influence on Society than a Persuasion, that it will be a good Plea for the Villain at the last day; *Lord, it is true I never obeyed one of thy Commandments, yet punish me not, for I believe them all?*

Religious hypocrites—indeed, all forms of hypocrisy and corruption—are regularly lampooned in Fielding's novels.

Also relevant to an understanding of *Joseph Andrews* is the political situation during Fielding's lifetime. Fielding was a young man when Sir Robert Walpole, the First Lord of the Treasury, assumed the functions of prime minister. (At the time, England did not officially recognize a prime minister, but Walpole was a dominant member of the cabinet and as such was the country's de facto

*Fielding's home* *(Hulton Archive / Getty Images)*

prime minister.) Walpole served in this capacity for twenty-two years, a period that spanned most of Fielding's adult life, and Fielding was a staunch political opponent of Walpole and his Whig Party. On the surface, his novel *Jonathan Wild*, for example, is about a notorious gangster by that name, but the book was in actuality a thinly disguised satire on the Walpole government. It suggests that Walpole's Whig administration functioned like a gang of thieves, and the full title's reference to "Jonathan Wild the Great" was a direct slap at Walpole, who was widely referred to by the epithet "the Great Man."

Fielding shared the widely held belief that Walpole retained his position through corruption and control of patronage. His disdain for the Walpole government was heightened by the passage of the 1737 Theatrical Licensing Act, which required that new plays be submitted to a government censor before they could be performed. In *Joseph Andrews*, Fielding makes reference to a British defeat at Carthagena in the West Indies, which many people, including Fielding, blamed on the Walpole administration's policy of keeping trained troops at home to intimidate political

opponents while sending raw troops against Spanish forces in the battle. Some evidence, though, suggests that in the final years of Walpole's administration, Fielding backed off on his criticism because he became a recipient of Walpole's favors.

## CRITICAL OVERVIEW

The more modern practice of reviewing individual works of literature in periodicals had not taken hold when Fielding wrote. Many comments on *Joseph Andrews* were made in personal correspondence, as well as in more general discussions of Fielding's work as a whole or of contemporary literature and writing. Early commentary on *Joseph Andrews* focuses on the simple question of whether the reader enjoyed the book, given that it represented a new species of writing: a comic "biography" that was not a biography of an actual person. While many readers approved of Fielding's art, some did not. In a 1742 letter to Samuel Richardson, Dr. George Cheyne refers to the author's "wretched Performance." Richardson himself, the object of Fielding's satire, missed no opportunity to revile Fielding; in a 1749 letter to Lady Dorothy Bradshaigh, he refers to Fielding's "lewd and ungenerous" satire of his work.

In general, though, contemporary readers commented favorably on *Joseph Andrews*. In a review of the novel, which he had recently translated into French, Pierre François Guyot Desfontaines calls it "a judicious and moral novel full of salt and pleasures." In 1751, Francis Coventry, in *An Essay on the New Species of Writing*, calls Fielding's novel "a lively Representative of real Life." In a similar vein, novelist Tobias Smollett, in *Continuation of the Complete History of England* (1761), calls attention to the author's conscious attempt to imitate Cervantes (the author of *Don Quixote*), saying that Fielding's work was "transfused" with Cervantes's genius and that Fielding was able to ridicule "the follies of life with equal strength, humour and propriety." In "An Essay on the Life and Genius of Henry Fielding, Esq." (1762), Arthur Murphy, like a number of contemporary readers, is particularly appreciative of Parson Adams, whom some readers regarded as the novel's major character. Murphy's remarks are typical: "Nothing could be more happily conceived than the character of Parson Adams for the principal personage of the work; the humanity, and benevolence of affection, the goodness of heart, and the zeal for virtue." After continuing to comment favorably on Adams at great length, Murphy praises the novel as a whole, saying that it "abounds with situations of the truly comic kind; the incidents and characters are unfolded with fine turns of surprise." He concludes by calling *Joseph Andrews* the "sun-rise of our author's genius."

*Joseph Andrews* is no longer new, so modern critics focus on the question of whether the novel is more than just entertainment. These critics take a variety of approaches to the novel. Paul Baines, for example, in his essay "Joseph Andrews," focuses on the novel's thematic underpinnings, where the action serves to progressively strip the major characters of their goods and money, forcing them to fall back on "honesty, fellow-feeling, courage." Baines concludes: "Having demonstrated high-value moral essence, the characters are then prepared for a reasoned shift in social status: Adams is promoted out of his poverty, and Joseph and Fanny take up their rightful roles within the minor gentry."

As his book's title suggests, Simon Varey, in *Joseph Andrews: A Satire of Modern Times*, focuses more on the novel's satiric elements. "The main satiric target of *Joseph Andrews* is hypocrisy, as the preface promises. Parson Barnabas, Parson Trulliber, Lady Booby, and many other characters behave in ways that belie their motives." Robert Alter's focus is more on characterization. In *Fielding and the Nature of the Novel*, he writes that "Fielding's ability to envisage both positive and negative aspects in his ostensibly one-sided characters is especially important in his presentation of the figures he wants us to admire." In this regard, he examines the character of Mrs. Slipslop, who, despite her pretensions, hypocrisy, and conniving nature, still possesses a warmth and vitality that engage the reader. Richard J. Dircks's *Henry Fielding* examines the genre of the novel, noting that it has roots in "Aristotle's distinction between comedy and tragedy in the drama," and that "the comic epic in prose is related to the serious epic in a manner similar to the relationship between comedy and tragedy in the drama."

## CRITICISM

### Michael J. O'Neal

*O'Neal holds a Ph.D. in English literature. In this essay on* Joseph Andrews, *he discusses the literary genre of comedy as it applies to the novel.*

# WHAT DO I READ NEXT?

- Henry Fielding's masterpiece *Tom Jones* (1749) is a comic adventure that traces the career of a character who bears many similarities to Joseph Andrews.

- *Shamela* (1741), which is often printed alongside *Joseph Andrews* in the same binding, is a brief parody of Samuel Richardson's *Pamela*, the novel that prompted Fielding to write both his parody and *Joseph Andrews*.

- Richard Scrimger's contemporary young-adult novel *Into the Ravine* (2007) is a comic picaresque novel in the tradition of *Joseph Andrews*.

- *Benjy Lopez: A Picaresque Tale of Emigration and Return* (1980) by Barry B. Levine is a nonfiction biography that employs the picaresque tradition to recreate the experiences of a Puerto Rican immigrant to New York City, who then returns to Puerto Rico.

- Daniel Venegas is the author of *Las aventuras de don Chipote o, cuando los pericos mamen*, or *The Adventures of Don Chipote; or, When Parakeets May Suckle Their Young*, a 1928 picaresque novel about a Mexican immigrant who travels through the American Southwest and encounters misadventures and rogues and suffers at the hands of bosses and the authorities.

- In his young-adult novel *Finn* (2001), Matthew Olshan adapts the picaresque tradition by creating a female hero, Chloe, and her sidekick, an illegal Mexican immigrant who is pregnant. The novel turns on its head some of the conventions of the picaresque novel as used by Mark Twain in *Huckleberry Finn*.

- For a brief overview of British history during the time Fielding wrote, the *Kingfisher Children's Encyclopedia of British History* (2005) is a place to start. Despite the title, the encyclopedia's audience is young adults.

That *Joseph Andrews* is a comedy seems readily apparent. Fielding engages in pure comedy when Didapper, lusting after Fanny, assaults her in her bedroom, and Parson Adams runs in, naked, to save her, seizes hold of her while her attacker escapes, then discovers that "Fanny" is really Mrs. Slipslop. To top it all off, Adams stumbles off to bed, only to wind up in Fanny's bed. Readers respond with laughter, much as they would while watching a modern movie that is billed as a madcap comedy.

Fielding himself took great pains to try to explain to his readers precisely what *Joseph Andrews* is. In his preface to the novel, he calls it a "comic epic-poem in prose," distinguishing the novel from "romance" on the one hand and pure "burlesque" on the other. He wanted, he said, to conform to "nature" because "Life every where furnishes an accurate Observer with the Ridiculous." The comic writer, he says, is to "be the least excused for deviating from Nature." Accordingly, his effort was to depict flesh-and-blood men and women, not idealized characters (as in romance) or characters who are reduced to absurd monsters (as in burlesque).

In everyday usage, comedy is defined by laughter. If a work induces laughter, it must be comic; if it does not, then the work is something else. Literary historians, though, would argue that laughter does not define comedy. Rather, laughter is a symptom of comedy, but only one symptom, and not a necessary one at that, for there exist dark comedies that prompt reflection and other emotions, but not mirth. If Fielding's novel is a comedy, what really does that mean? Put differently, what were the conventions within which Fielding was writing that make *Joseph Andrews* an exemplar of the comic tradition?

Comedy can be thought of as one of four major literary types. Its opposite, of course, is tragedy. The other two are romance and satire. By reaching deeply into the history of literature, these literary types can be seen as archetypes that represent a fundamental response to the natural order. Tragedy is winter, a time of darkness, fear, even of death. The natural cycle turns to bring springtime, the season of romance, of festivity, when admirable characters innocently look forward to a world with infinite possibility. Comedy represents the archetype of summertime, when all is green and alive. Wishes are gratified, but heroes and heroines have achieved a measure of self-awareness and growth by overcoming obstacles.

But summer inevitably gives way to autumn, the season of decline toward death, reminiscent of satire. Each of these types can shade off into the adjacent one; just as the line between summer and autumn sometimes blurs, so too the satirical comedy contains elements of both satire and comedy.

Comedy is the genre of the social group. The basic plot of a comedy consists, broadly, of three steps. In the first, there is an existent society. This is the society that Lady Booby inhabits, a social order marked by vanity, selfishness, hypocrisy, and an emphasis on material wealth. In the second step, the hero confronts the society, challenging its norms, values, and arbitrary laws. The journey motif in *Joseph Andrews* allows Joseph to confront an ongoing series of rogues, thieves, and others who serve to impede him in his quest to be reunited with the woman he loves. In the third stage, the society is reclaimed or reformed through the efforts of the hero. The hero's social order, in effect, replaces the earlier social order, which is accomplished as rewards are distributed: Joseph and Fanny marry, Parson Adams obtains a new living, and even the peddler is rewarded. Yet Fielding's comedy shades off into satire, for the existent society is not entirely replaced: Lady Booby goes off to London, entirely unrepentant.

*Joseph Andrews* adheres to the conventions of comedy in nearly all particulars. The existent society is dominated by obstructing characters. These are characters like Lady Booby, Scout, and Mrs. Slipslop who form a block that impedes Joseph in his attainment of his goal. Such a society is dominated by older characters, particularly parents or parent-like figures, who stand in way of the younger characters and are often imposters of some sort, like Mrs. Slipslop or the hunter who makes promises to the travelers but fails to keep them. The existent society is defined by an emphasis on money and wealth, and it is ruled by ritual (including religious rituals), habits, tradition, and arbitrary law; Joseph is not admitted to a coach because Miss Grave-airs refuses to occupy a coach with a mere servant, and Joseph is imperiled by accusations that he cut a twig. Most importantly, the existing society is defined by a fixed illusion. Joseph was born into a social class that tells him he can be only a servant; Fanny is apparently the daughter of a mere farmer.

The conventions of comedy replace, at least in part, the existing society. The heroes and heroines are young, vital, and energetic, just as Joseph and

Fanny are. They place little emphasis on money and material possessions, instead seeking a life of accomplishment, virtue, and goodness; although Joseph and Fanny receive money in the end, the money is not an end in itself but the means to an end. The characters are freed from the conventions and arbitrary laws that restricted their lives. The world of illusion is replaced by a real world when Joseph's and Fanny's parentage is sorted out. Joseph and Fanny, along with Parson Adams, find their places in a new social order, represented by the countryside and the potential fecundity of marriage.

Comedy is almost necessarily the depiction of types, or as Fielding puts, "I describe not Men, but Manners; not an Individual, but a Species." Comedy, unlike tragedy, is not interested in dissecting the frailties of the individual—of a Hamlet or a King Lear. Comedy is a social celebration, where the promise of springtime ripens into the fullness and maturity of summer. Joseph, through his tribulations and with the moral guidance of Parson Adams, attains the fullness and maturity of summer and thus can serve as an exemplar of an improved social order.

**Source:** Michael J. O'Neal, Critical Essay on *Joseph Andrews*, in *Novels for Students*, Gale, Cengage Learning, 2010.

## I. B. Cauthen, Jr.

*In the following essay, Cauthen explains how Fielding uses the three stories to play variations upon a theme of moral justice.*

In his *Henry Fielding* F. Homes Dudden has criticized the novel *Joseph Andrews* for four "evident" weaknesses. For him, the novel is "too rambling and haphazard," and its denouement is unsatisfactory; moreover, he censures Fielding for too frequently indulging "in farcical absurdities" in the episodes of the book. Finally, he condemns the "digressions":

> the main narrative is interrupted by the interpolation of two independent stories—'The History of Leonora, or the Unfortunate Jilt,' and 'The History of Two Friends'—and by the extensive life-history of Mr. Wilson. The introduction of such digressions, though in accord with the common usage of the Spanish and French fiction-writers—to say nothing of earlier examples in classical epics, medieval romances, and Eastern tales—can hardly be justified on artistic grounds. Moreover, in the first of his intercalated stories (which is also the more

> IN THIS GENRE-MAKING NOVEL FIELDING USES THREE STRUCTURALLY DISCRETE STORIES AS A MEANS OF PLAYING A VARIATION UPON A BASIC THEME, HOSTILITY TO PRETENSION."

interesting and humorous) Fielding absurdly causes the narrator to repeat no fewer than five whole letters from memory. Wilson's history, indeed, comprises some matter relevant to the plot..., but it would have been definitely an advantage had the greater part of it been omitted. (I, 351–357)

Mr. Dudden's fellow-commentators agree with such a criticism of the digressions, although they advance various excuses for them. Ethel Thornbury, like Mr. Dudden, sees them as only a manifestation of the contemporary practice which had the sanction of epic usage; but she concedes that Fielding works them into his central story by making them "have an ethical bearing upon the problem of the hero's life." Cross, however, sees the stories introduced only to fill up an uneventful hour, although "at times perhaps Fielding lets his narrative stand perfectly still as a burlesque of the suspense characteristic of Richardson." Saintsbury's excuse for them (in his Everyman introduction) is likewise traditional: "divagations of this kind existed in all Fielding's Spanish and French models,...[and] the public of the day expected them." But if these digressions can be defended on other grounds, we may be able to give them a virtue other than Saintsbury's "grand and prominent [one] of being at once and easily skippable."

The three stories are placed at almost regular intervals throughout the novel: Leonora's story appears in Book II, chapters 4 and 6, Mr. Wilson's life-history occurs in III, 3, and the story of Paul and Leonard in IV, 10. The third and last story is not finished, perhaps for a reason other than that Beau Didapper "offered a rudeness to [Fanny] with his hands," for which he received from Joseph "a sound box on the ear." The two completed stories and the interrupted third one, I believe, are closely related to Fielding's aesthetic theory of his novel—the exposure of ridiculous human frailty and folly. By holding "the glass to thousands in their closets,...they may contemplate their deformity, and endeavor to reduce it, and thus by suffering private mortification may avoid public shame." The novel, therefore, is designed both to entertain and, more importantly, to instruct by laying bare the "only true source of the ridiculous"—affectation. This affectation, according to Fielding, proceeds either from vanity or from hypocrisy: vanity makes men affect "false characters, in order to purchase applause," while hypocrisy is the concealing of "our vices under an appearance of their opposite virtues" in an endeavor to avoid censure. Vanity is thus a disproportional exaggeration of a trait which, in itself, may be virtuous enough; hypocrisy is the living lie.

> From the discovery of this affectation [Fielding declares] arises the Ridiculous, which always strikes the reader with surprise and pleasure; and that in a higher and stronger degree when the affectation arises from hypocrisy, than when from vanity; for to discover any one to be the exact reverse of what he affects, is more surprising, and consequently more ridiculous, than to find him a little deficient in the quality he desires the reputation of.

If the "digressions" can be related to this theory which underlies the novel, they furnish their own justification.

The first story, told to while away a journey, concerns the lovely Leonora, "an extreme lover of gaiety" who never missed a public assembly "where she had frequent opportunities of satisfying a greedy appetite of vanity." She is attracted by Horatio, a young barrister, to whom she always listens attentively "and often smiled even when [his compliments were] too delicate for her comprehension." When Horatio proposes to her, Leonora is "covered with blushes" and refuses him with "as angry a look as she could possibly put on"— although, of course, she "had very much suspected what was coming." But eventually she accepts Horatio. At this inopportune moment, a stranger who owns a coach and six arrives in town and Leonora is attracted to him because of his pretty equipage. He is the French fop Bellarmine who immediately becomes interested in Leonora: she "saw herself admired by the fine stranger, and envied by every woman. . . . Her little heart began to flutter within her, and her head was agitated with a convulsive motion. . . . She could not disengage her thoughts one moment from the contemplation of [her present triumph]. She had never tasted anything like this happiness." Thus Bellarmine's gaiety and gallantry possessed the heart of the vain Leonora in a day, demolishing poor

Horatio's work of a year. Upon the advice of her aunt, Leonora jilts Horatio, who in turn wounds Bellarmine in a duel, which, of course, makes Leonora love her foppish heart-flutterer more than ever.

However, when Bellarmine goes to Leonora's father to draw up the marriage papers, he learns that he is to get Leonora without a shilling of dowry; he breaks off his engagement, and Leonora, brokenhearted over losing both him and Horatio, "left the place where she was the subject of conversation and ridicule" and retired to a small place in the country.

In this digression, Leonora is held up as an object of ridicule for her vanity in her beauty, her pleasure in being admired by other women for Bellarmine's attentions, her pride in his coach and six, his French clothes, his superficial culture, and for her refusal of the honest and unaffected Horatio. Bellarmine is the hypocrite—his love is not for Leonora, but for Leonora's father's money. He gives the appearance of a sincere lover, but he is in reality only a fortune hunter. The unmasking of the hypocrite and the exposure of Leonora's vanity carry out Fielding's general purpose for the novel in this digression.

In the same way, Mr. Wilson's story contributes to the general purpose. Like Leonora, Mr. Wilson is a vain young person who is excessively ambitious of obtaining a fine character. By frequenting public places in London, he learned to master "fashionable phrases, . . . to cry up the fashionable diversions, and [to know] the names and faces of the most fashionable men and women." His reputation for intrigue he made secure by writing letters to himself; his life was one of sauntering about the streets, going to coffee-houses, attending Drury Lane and Lincoln's Inn Fields, and indulging in small talk in drawing rooms. In such a life, he confesses, he admired himself. Nor was he unique: at the Temple, where he lived, he found the beaus "the affection of affection." Here he met "with smart fellows who drank with lords they did not know, and intrigued with women they never saw." Where they talked and did nothing, Wilson seems to have done everything and talked little: he kept a series of mistresses, intrigued with the "wife to a man of fashion and gallantry," received "some advances . . . by the wife of a citizen," and fell in with "a set of jolly companions, who slept all day and drank all night." Later, he "became a great frequenter of playhouses" and continued to accomplish his own ruin until he could be saved only by the *deus ex machina* of a lottery ticket. He then reformed, married the woman who generously gave him the lottery ticket, and managed her father's estate until he saw he was no business man. He then retired to the country where he now leads an idyllic life with his family.

Midway in this story of a typical fop, Fielding gives us the moral of it and its purpose. By his observations of London life, Wilson concludes that

> the general observation, that wits are most inclined to vanity, is not true. Men are equally vain of riches, strength, beauty, honours, etc. But these appear of themselves in the eyes of the beholders, whereas the poor wit is obliged to produce his performance to show you his perfection.... Vanity is the worst of passions, and more apt to contaminate the mind than any other: for, as selfishness is much more general than we please to allow it, so it is natural to hate and envy those who stand between us and the good we desire. Now, in lust and ambition these are few; and even in avarice we find many who are no obstacles to our pursuits; but the vain man seeks preeminence; and everything which is excellent or praiseworthy in another renders him the mark of his antipathy.

Wilson's story thus is the biography of a vain wit, a ridiculous, affected, and at times hypocritical fop. He suffers for his vanity, and the reader is both amused and instructed by the edifying account of his own unmasking and his reform. He no more deserves Harriet Hearty than Dorimant in Etherege's *Man of Mode* deserves his Harriet. But he has sense enough to reform himself, even as Fielding's readers were encouraged to amend their ways by "private mortification."

The third story, the interrupted tale of Leonard and Paul, has reached its climax when Joseph Andrews throws the listeners into consternation by his defense of Fanny. Read to visitors by Parson Adams' small son, the story concerns a couple who bicker incessantly over every detail of their lives; a friend advises them on this marital problem, first telling the husband to surrender to his wife when he is most convinced that he is in the right. Unfortunately, he gives the same advice a little later to the wife, and consequently he finds himself "the private referee of every difference." When the couple, however, compare his decisions, they find he has decided in favor of each upon every occasion, and he becomes, of course, the only thing the couple has in common—a mutual enemy.

Here again, as in the stories of Leonora and of Mr. Wilson, is an exposure of vanity, this time about the vanity of being preëminently correct. Both Leonard and his wife are so insistent upon their correctness that they become equally vain: as Mr. Wilson had said, men are vain of "riches, strength, beauty, honours, &c." He could have easily added "and of truth as they want to see it." Certainly the vanity of Leonard and his wife contaminates their minds as they each seek preëminence over the other in each argument. Nor is the hypocritical attitude that their friend Paul proposes a solution to their vanity. Indeed, no solution is given, nor is there one to give except the self-reform or the consequent suffering that concludes the other two digressions that precede this one. No wonder Fielding, manipulating his characters, lets Didapper offer that rudeness to Fanny only to be rewarded with a box on the ear. The conclusion of the story is for the reader to write: the way the reader lets the story end is an exercise in how well he has learned from what he has already read in the novel.

These three digressions, therefore, need not be so utterly condemned nor halfheartedly defended as they have been. Although they may not be as artistically successful today as they were in the eighteenth century, they are closely related to Fielding's aesthetic of the novel, the exposure of affectation that arises from vanity or hypocrisy. By the very nature of this relationship, they assume an artistic purpose that should be considered historically as well as in the light of Fielding's own avowed intention in writing the novel. And while the "digressions" probably cannot acceptable to modern aestheticians of the unified novel, they are far from the traditional digression—they are, instead, much more akin to the exemplum, a story told with moral intent. Although such a device had often been used in literature before the time of Fielding, there is no model as far as I know in the novel for such stories. In this genre-making novel Fielding uses three structurally discrete stories as a means of playing a variation upon a basic theme, hostility to pretension. He had no model in the young art of novel-making for this kind of thematic repetition, the exemplum whose characters, setting, and events are completely unconnected with the main story.

Admittedly these digressions—or exempla—stand outside the episodic structure of the book, but they are discussions that go even beyond the announced theme of affectation. They are concerned with three important phases of life which the novel proper cannot include. For here we have a discussion of courtship, of married life, and of the vain young man beginning his career. In these three discussions Fielding continues his exposure of affectation that underlies the whole novel; in the novel itself this exposure takes place in character and incident: Mr. Wilson may inveigh against vanity and Parson Adams, agreeing with him, may be vain enough to want to read a sermon on vanity; Peter Pounce may be the uncharitable hypocrite who would turn the poor out to pasture, an unmasking that drives Parson Adams from the carriage; Mrs. Slipslop may affect learning as Lady Booby affects chastity—they all are victims of Fielding's stripping of a character to its essentials. In the same way, these stories unmask the vices of hypocrisy and vanity in courtship, in marriage, and in the life of the rake. By their inclusion Fielding has doubled his emphasis on his theme—the laying bare of the only true source of the ridiculous. As Parson Adams commented upon Steele's *Conscious Lovers,* this novel—with its exempla—has things in it "solemn enough for a sermon."

**Source:** I. B. Cauthen, Jr., "Fielding's Digressions in *Joseph Andrews*," in *College English*, Vol. 17, No. 7, April 1956, pp. 379–82.

## SOURCES

Alter, Robert, *Fielding and the Nature of the Novel*, Harvard University Press, 1968, p. 80.

Baines Paul, "*Joseph Andrews*," in *The Cambridge Companion to Henry Fielding*, edited by Claude Rawson, Cambridge University Press, 2007, p. 59.

Cheyne, George, "Letter to Samuel Richardson, March 9, 1742," in *Henry Fielding: The Critical Heritage*, edited by Ronald Paulson and Thomas Lockwood, Routledge & Kegan Paul, 1969, p. 118.

Coventry, Francis, "An Essay on the New Species of Writing founded by Mr. Fielding: with a Word or Two upon the Modern State of Criticism," 1751, in *Henry Fielding: The Critical Heritage*, edited by Ronald Paulson and Thomas Lockwood, Routledge & Kegan Paul, 1969, p. 263.

Desfontaines, Pierre François Guyot, Review of *Joseph Andrews* in "Observations sur les écrits modernes," 1743, in *Henry Fielding: The Critical Heritage*, edited by Ronald Paulson and Thomas Lockwood, Routledge & Kegan Paul, 1969, p. 126.

Dircks, Richard J., *Henry Fielding*, Twayne Publishers, 1983, p. 45.

Fielding, Henry, *Joseph Andrews*, edited by Martin C. Battestin, Wesleyan University Press, 1967, pp. 18, 21, 32, 37–38, 45, 82, 156, 189, 233–34.

Murphy, Arthur, "An Essay on the Life and Genius of Henry Fielding, Esq.," 1762, in *Henry Fielding: The Critical Heritage*, edited by Ronald Paulson and Thomas Lockwood, Routledge & Kegan Paul, 1969, pp. 421, 423.

Richardson, Samuel, "Letter to Lady Dorothy Bradshaigh, 1749," in *Henry Fielding: The Critical Heritage*, edited by Ronald Paulson and Thomas Lockwood, Routledge & Kegan Paul, 1969, p. 186.

Smollett, Tobias, "Continuation of the Complete History of England," 1761, in *Henry Fielding: The Critical Heritage*, edited by Ronald Paulson and Thomas Lockwood, Routledge & Kegan Paul, 1969, p. 403.

Varey, Simon, *Joseph Andrews: A Satire of Modern Times*, Twayne Publishers, 1990, p. 26.

## FURTHER READING

Battestin, Martin C., with Ruth R. Battestin, *Henry Fielding: A Life*, Routledge, 1989.
   From a leading Fielding scholar, this is the fullest biography of Fielding, though some scholars believe that some of the information it contains is too speculative. It supersedes earlier biographies by incorporating new information about Fielding's early life and his career as a magistrate.

George, M. Dorothy, *London Life in the Eighteenth Century*, 1925, reprinted by Capricorn Books, 1965.
   As the title suggests, this volume gives the reader an introduction to the social, cultural, and material life of Londoners during Fielding's lifetime. Readers can learn about coffeehouses, parks, insane asylums, and other features of life during Fielding's time.

Pringle, Patrick, *Hue and Cry: The Story of Henry and John Fielding and Their Bow Street Runners*, Morrow, 1955.
   As London's chief magistrate, Fielding and his half-brother John created the Bow Street Runners, the city's first police force, whose story is told in this volume.

Rawson, Claude, *Henry Fielding*, Routledge & Kegan Paul, 1968.
   Part of the publisher's Profiles in Literature Series, Rawson's volumes identifies and explains themes and techniques in Fielding's novels, relying heavily on extensive quoted passages.

Rogers, Pat, *Henry Fielding*, Paul Elek, 1979.
   This volume is regarded as among the best short biographies of Fielding.

# *The Last of the Mohicans*

**1992**  Director Michael Mann released his film adaptation of the classic frontier tale *The Last of the Mohicans* in 1992, fifty-six years after the appearance of the 1936 black-and-white adaptation, which largely shaped his vision. Various other versions of the story were produced during the twentieth century, but Mann has said that the 1936 film, which he first saw at age three or four, is "the first sense memory" he has of a motion picture (as quoted by Gary Edgerton). As befits the hallowed place that movie must have retained in the director's mind, Mann's own adaptation could attribute its modest success—earning around $75 million at the domestic box office—above all to its ability to immerse the viewer's imagination in the wilderness and war of the frontier of northern New York in 1757. Critics, however, did not prove especially positive about the film—which is rated R for violence—faulting its appeal for being more visceral than intellectual, emphasizing the thrilling battle scenes and the costars' steamy glances.

The original version of *The Last of the Mohicans*, James Fenimore Cooper's 1826 novel, was likewise criticized for its catering to popular taste, trading in familiar "Indian novel" motifs such as ambushes in the wilderness and captivity with life-or-death consequences. Despite its popular nature, however, few would call the novel accessible to the modern reader, particularly due to the density of Cooper's language. Mark Twain left Cooper's literary reputation languishing for

© *Photos 12 / Alamy*

decades when he fiercely critiqued the romantic-fiction author in a humorous 1895 essay titled "Fenimore Cooper's Literary Offenses." However, other critics have since seen fit to redeem Cooper, and *The Last of the Mohicans*, the second in his series of five Leatherstocking novels, remains a foundational work in the American canon. The mythology that Cooper established has appealed to numerous screenwriters and comic-book artists over the years, and Mann's film has sustained the informal tradition of adaptation that has given each generation a fresh vision of this renowned American story.

## PLOT SUMMARY

### 1. Main Titles

After background text giving the year of 1757 and the circumstances of the French and Indian War, forest panoramas (wide, unobstructed views) provide the background for the opening credits. (The particulars of the scenes as referred to here are from the director's expanded edition of the film, the only version available on DVD in the United States and Canada.)

### 2. The Deerslayers

Hawkeye, Chingachgook, and Uncas are dashing through the forest chasing a deer. Hawkeye kills it with his long-barreled rifle (in the novel referred to as "kill-deer"). Chingachgook offers a prayer for the animal's spirit.

In the novel, in chapter 3 Hawkeye has a deer in his sights, but Uncas objects because he has found the tracks of a nearby party of hostile Maquas; the rifle would be too loud. Thus, Cooper gives the glory of the kill not to the white man with his gun but to the young Indian with his arrow and knife.

### 3. The Cameron House

The three hunters arrive at the rural cabin of John Cameron, to be welcomed by the family and share news of their fur trapping around Horican (now called Lake George). Jack Winthrop reports that a militia is being raised to fight against the French.

The plot line concerning Cameron's cabin and the settlers who enlist was invented for the film. Not a single scene in the novel takes place in such a permanent settlement, with Fort Edward and Fort William Henry being the only Anglo American settings. Thus, this plot line serves to

# FILM TECHNIQUE

- Mann's production team devoted much attention to accurately reproducing the sounds of the wilderness and of the battles fought there by the British, French, and Indian forces. Footsteps on leaves and the birds and insects of the forest give way to the firing of cannons and guns and the desperate shouts and screams of men at war. The film won its only Academy Award in 1993 for Best Sound.

- The novelist Cooper effectively situates his reader in the wilderness by giving detailed descriptions of characters' experiences in seeing things from a distance, through the trees of the forest, or at night, when the dimness renders the world indistinct. In one of the book's most comical scenes, Heyward, for a while, believes himself to be viewing an Indian village from afar, with the residents crawling oddly about on all fours—until he is made aware that he is watching not people but beavers. Mann reproduces such effects for the film by often showing indistinct shots of the characters as screened by tree trunks—such as when Magua leads the ambush of the defeated British—or as positioned at a great distance, as in the final scene along the cliffs.

- Another priority for the production team was the historically accurate replication of items and settings. From the clothing of the British and Indians to their guns and tomahawks to the inner and outer wooden works of the impressive reconstruction of Fort William Henry, the viewer is immersed in the textures of the era. Such attention to material detail allows the camera to linger on images of the people and objects, greatly enhancing the visceral experience of the film—the viewer's "reliving" of history—though occasionally at the expense of moving the story along.

---

ground the film in the daily lives of the American colonists and to portray their relations with the British.

## 4. A Call to Arms

At an assembly held at Cameron's cabin, a Mohawk chief announces that his tribe will join the British to fight the French and their Indian allies. Cameron asks whether enlisted settlers would be allowed leave to defend their homes; the British officer declares that they should foremost fight the French in defense of Britain. Jack, inclined to enlist, says those interested shall go to Albany, New York, to negotiate terms with General Webb. White settlers and Indians play lacrosse together.

## 5. The New Major

Major Heyward rides into Albany, where the settlers are meeting with Webb, who says he will agree to their demand for leave from military service if they are needed at their homes. Heyward objects to Webb's bending of royal policy; Webb disparages the French and says that in any case, militia will not be needed at Fort William Henry, where Heyward is being dispatched.

In the novel, Heyward and the Munro sisters depart for Fort William Henry not from Albany but from Fort Edward.

## 6. The Scotsman's Daughter

Duncan finds Cora, and they have dinner together. She rejects his dry romantic overtures, but he says they would be a logical match. Alice arrives, excited for their coming adventurous trip to Fort William Henry.

The novel's scene prior to the daughters' departure for Fort William Henry, in chapter 1, is reported as if seen from a distance. The film's invention of this dinner thus highlights the romantic tension between Cora and Duncan; in the novel, Duncan is interested in the younger, prettier Alice rather than with Cora.

## 7. The War Party

The regiment of British soldiers drums its way into the forest. Elsewhere, Chingachgook, Uncas, and Hawkeye find the trail of the Huron war party. On the march, Magua backtracks alongside the troops and suddenly attacks two of them, and other Indians fire from the forest. A battle ensues, with the Indians massacring the Redcoats until the Mohicans and Hawkeye arrive, killing off the Hurons, though Magua escapes.

In the novel, Munro's daughters travel along a different route from that which the soldiers take to Fort William Henry, and no battle such as this one occurs. Rather, the small party led astray by Magua happens upon Hawkeye and the Mohicans, who move to seize Magua before he slips away. This film battle, then, effectively replaces the novel's ensuing firefight at the cascades (chapters 7–8) and hand-to-hand combat in the forest (chapter 12).

## 8. To Fort William Henry
Hawkeye, Chingachgook, and Uncas are guiding Duncan, Cora, and Alice to Fort William Henry, climbing a path alongside a river. Uncas takes a long look at Alice. Heyward disparages Hawkeye, who intends to travel to "Ken-tuck-ee" rather than join the war effort. The novel includes several such scenes of walking and conversation.

## 9. The Faces of War
At John Cameron's cabin, the party comes upon a scene of ruin and death. The Mohicans recognize the work of an Ottawa war party. Cora wishes the bodies buried, but Hawkeye declines (in the interest of leaving no evidence of their passage there).

## 10. A Stirring in the Blood
The men of the party are holding defensive positions in a glade. Hurons approach, but they retreat upon realizing the glade is a burial ground. Cora asks Hawkeye about his family; he was orphaned and adopted by Chingachgook, and then he and Uncas were sent to school. The circumstances make Cora romantically interested in Hawkeye.

This scene reflects chapter 13 of the novel, where the glade features a dilapidated block shelter from an earlier war (accounting for the burial ground). In the novel, Hawkeye and Cora do not develop an intimate relationship.

## 11. The Siege
Trekking through the woods, the party sees the fireworks of the ongoing battle at Fort William Henry, which is being bombarded by French cannons. The party reaches the fort surreptitiously by canoe. Munro reports having sent word for the girls to stay away, but the couriers were evidently intercepted, and Magua was treacherous; Munro's requested and much-needed reinforcements are not coming. Hawkeye asserts that the colonists should be released to defend their homes, but Munro refuses.

The party's arrival at the fort aligns with the close of chapter 14 of the book, although in the

novel they approach over land, through fog, rather than by water. At the fort, the scenes about the colonial militia were invented for the film.

## 12. Magua's Hate
At the French camp, Montcalm interviews Magua, who confirms the success of their deceptions. Magua expresses his need for vengeance against "the gray hair"—that is, Munro—and his children.

This scene does not occur in the novel. Instead, the reader learns of Magua's desire for vengeance through a conversation between Magua and Cora in the forest.

## 13. The Look of Love
Cora bandages Uncas. Hawkeye gazes at Cora; they smile. In the novel, Cora does not participate in activity in the fort's infirmary.

## 14. A Run to Fort Edward
The British forces engage the French while a courier departs for Fort Edward, with Hawkeye and Uncas firing from the fort to provide cover. The novel instead relates in chapter 15 an unsuccessful attempt by Hawkeye to break the French lines to deliver a letter.

## 15. Final Decisions
Hawkeye and Jack argue for dismissal for the colonists so that they can protect their homes. However, Munro suggests that the Ottawa raiding party may have been mere thieves, and Heyward provides an erroneous report confirming the notion. Munro says that militia may not leave and threatens capital punishment. Heyward again entreats Cora to marry him, but she definitively refuses. In the novel, Heyward instead successfully entreats Munro for permission to marry Alice in chapter 16.

## 16. The Escape Plan
The mood in the fort is solemn. The militia make plans for escape, expressing prerevolutionary sentiments, with Hawkeye involved but remaining behind because of his interest in Cora.

## 17. Lovers
Cora leaves the infirmary to find Hawkeye. They share intimate affections.

## 18. Sedition
British soldiers storm the Indian quarters and arrest Hawkeye for sedition. Cora defends him

before her father, enraging Duncan, who recognizes her infatuation with the frontiersman. Munro asserts that Hawkeye will hang for sedition. These threads of the narrative are all inventions of the film.

### 19. The Whole World's on Fire

Cora tells the jailed Hawkeye of his sentence. He confirms his love for her and warns her to keep close to her father if the fort falls. The French breach the fort's walls with cannon fire. Cooper does not describe the particulars of the battle in terms at all equivalent to the staged firefight and violence of the modern action-film battle scene.

### 20. Terms for Surrender

At a parley (a negotiation between the opposing sides) outside the fort, Montcalm reveals that he has captured a letter from Webb revealing that the general is withholding reinforcements and advises surrender. Heyward speaks of fighting until death, but Munro accepts terms for an honorable surrender. Such a meeting occurs in chapter 16 of the novel.

### 21. Magua's Pain

Before dawn, Magua complains to Montcalm that the Indians yet desire fulfillment in battle. Magua's children were killed by the British, and he was enslaved, during which time his wife remarried. Montcalm pointedly expresses his wish not to "fight the same men twice," though he cannot break the terms of surrender allowing the British to leave unharmed and bearing their arms.

In chapter 17 of the novel, Montcalm meets Magua as such but insistently urges the Huron chief to respect the truce forged between the combatants.

### 22. The Defeated

The British file out of the fort past the French and their Indian allies. Hawkeye remains a prisoner. This scene occurs in chapter 17 of the novel.

### 23. Magua Strikes

Later that day, in a clearing, an enemy Indian strikes the line. The other Indians stalk through the surrounding forest until Magua leads them in a battle cry, and they open fire on soldiers and citizens alike, slaughtering many. Magua kills Munro. Hawkeye rushes to Cora's defense, saving her life, and Chingachgook and Uncas help the sisters flee.

Cooper situates this massacre earlier, just inside the forest by the plains around the fort. Cooper portrays this scene not as premeditated but as a spontaneous outburst of Indian anger inspired in part by covetousness of the goods of the departing citizenry. Magua does incite the massacre with a battle cry in the novel. Cooper gives no accounting of the actions of Hawkeye and the Mohicans through the surrender of the fort and the massacre.

### 24. Escape

Hawkeye, Uncas, Chingachgook, Cora, and Alice escape over the lake by canoe, as does Heyward—who still has Hawkeye's death sentence in mind—with other soldiers. They go down a river, abandoning their canoes when they hit an impassible waterfall.

Starting at this point, the plot of the film diverges significantly from that of the novel. Cooper has Magua carry the unconscious Alice from the battle scene, followed by Cora, who is somehow protected by the song of the psalmist David Gamut (who is absent from the film). Hawkeye, the Mohicans, Heyward, and Munro then begin tracking Magua's party three days later.

### 25. The Falls

The fleeing party takes refuge inside caverns sheltered by the waterfalls, hoping they will not be found. Hawkeye tells Cora of Munro's death. Uncas embraces Alice.

This scene loosely accords with chapter 6 of the novel, in which the same characters take refuge in caverns among the cataracts prior to reaching Fort William Henry.

### 26. Stay Alive . . .

Torch-bearing Hurons are seen approaching the caverns. Hawkeye and the Mohicans debate the merits of escaping via the falls. Cora implores them to go, and he asserts that he will find them. The Hurons arrive and imprison Cora, Alice, and Duncan. Hawkeye and the Mohicans wash up downriver and track the Hurons.

In chapters 7 and 8 of the novel, Hawkeye and the Mohicans defend against a prolonged attack at the cascades; when the situation becomes desperate, they escape via the falls, as they do in the film, and then track Magua's party.

### 27. Trophies of Honor

At a Huron encampment, Magua appeals to the great sachem, or wise leader, for recognition as a war hero and expresses his desire to burn the women at the stake as trophies. Hawkeye and the Mohicans arrive to witness the gathering, and Hawkeye walks unarmed into the village, suffering a few blows. Magua reports that he wants to enrich the Hurons, who could become traders. Hawkeye denounces Magua's conduct before the sachem, pleading for the release of the prisoners.

The novel features two loosely similar Indian judgment scenes, one in such a Huron encampment in chapter 24 (with Uncas's life at stake), and one in a Delaware encampment in chapters 28–30 (with the fates of Hawkeye, Heyward, the Munro sisters, and Uncas at stake), as presided over by the elder Tamenund. The film eliminates the plot line involving the neighboring Delaware tribe.

### 28. Heyward's Choice

The sachem declares that Magua should take Alice as his wife, Heyward should be released as a gesture to the British, Cora should burn at the stake, and Hawkeye should go free. Magua is disgusted, and he and his men leave to instead appeal to the Hurons of the lakes. Hawkeye wants to sacrifice himself for Cora, but Duncan, who is translating into French for the Hurons, offers himself instead. He burns until Hawkeye mercifully shoots him from the forest.

In the book, Tamenund ultimately allows the release of everyone but Cora, who, having been entrusted to the Delawares as a prisoner, must be returned to Magua to honor their agreement. No one burns at the stake.

### 29. To Save Alice

Uncas leads as they pursue Magua's party up the ridge of the mountain. Reaching the head of the party by shortcut, Uncas kills the several Hurons in the lead before Magua kills him. Rather than let herself be captured by Magua, Alice intentionally falls off the ridge to her death.

In the book, after a final battle in which the Delawares rout the Hurons (not included in the film), Magua and two others escort Cora up the mountain. One Huron kills Cora before being slain by Uncas, who is then killed by Magua.

### 30. A Father's Revenge

Chingachgook and Hawkeye catch up to the party and kill the trailing Hurons. As Hawkeye and the other Hurons watch, Chingachgook slays Magua. Cooper gives this act of vengeance to Hawkeye instead, who shoots Magua from afar.

### 31. Last of the Mohicans

Chingachgook, now the last of the Mohicans, prays for Uncas on the mountaintop. Cora and Hawkeye embrace. Chingachgook foretells the end of the frontier and of people like his "white son," Hawkeye. Cooper sets Chingachgook's last words about Uncas and his people within an elaborate funeral ceremony held among the Delawares for both Uncas and Cora.

## CHARACTERS

### Nathaniel Bumppo
*See* Hawkeye

### John Cameron
Cameron, formerly an indentured servant in Virginia, is emblematic of the perseverance that brings fulfillment on the frontier. He wishes above all to protect his family and home, joining the militia with reservations. The Cameron family does not appear in Cooper's novel, nor do any other colonial militiamen.

### Rebecca Cameron
John Cameron's wife evokes the image of Uncas settling down with a wife to raise a family, thus sustaining his bloodline. She is killed when the cabin is raided.

### Chingachgook
Father of Uncas and adoptive father of Hawkeye, Chingachgook, despite ultimately proving to be the title character, plays a supporting role in the film. He is fierce in battle, but the younger Hawkeye and Uncas lead in most of the action. Instead, the elder Mohican offers connections to the spiritual and philosophical aspects of life. He prays for the killed deer and meditates on the fate of his people after he avenges Uncas's death.

Perhaps the most significant change to Chingachgook's character from the novel is the civilization of his appearance. Cooper introduces the Mohican in striking terms: "His body, which was nearly naked, presented a terrific emblem of death, drawn in intermingled colours of white and black," and his head is shaved clean save for the "chivalrous scalping tuft." In the film, the Hurons are portrayed in minimal native attire and with shaven heads and painted faces, but Chingachgook and Uncas both have long hair, unpainted faces, and enough clothing to cover their entire bodies. Practically speaking, this allows the viewer to easily distinguish the "good" Indians from the "bad" ones, but the unavoidable implication that Westernized Indians are preferable to "savage" ones calls to mind historical oppression and discrimination. Russell Means, the actor who portrayed Chingachgook, is a well-known American Indian activist.

### Hawkeye

As played by the dashing Daniel Day-Lewis, Hawkeye fulfills all the expectations of the male lead in a historical romance: he is fiercely individualistic and yet bound by his sense of honor; he is calm under pressure and often stoic, yet passionate for ideals and, above all, for a certain woman. Better than any other character, he successfully negotiates both the Indian and white moral universes. He chafes under British authority, showing the distinctly American sentiments that would soon inspire the Revolution.

Day-Lewis, who is actually British himself, won the Academy Award for best actor two years before this film's release (for the 1989 film *My Left Foot*), and Mann certainly meant to showcase him as a romantic lead. Accordingly, Mann's transformation of Hawkeye's character from that of the novel (in which his name is written "Hawk-eye") is profound. To begin with, Hawkeye's assertion to Heyward after the Huron ambush that he is no military scout is in stark opposition to the novel, in which he is precisely a military scout, often referred to as "the scout" by the narrator. Cooper endows Hawkeye with a demeanor that is Indianized and yet distinctly Anglo American in terms of his orientation toward military-style goals. Mann's Hawkeye, to the contrary, makes clear that he "is not subject to much of anything at all," as he tells the recruiting British officer, and he feels free to disregard British military authority, helping the militiamen escape the fort. He declines to escape himself only because of his professed interest in Cora—marking another significant departure from the novel, in which Hawkeye demonstrates no love interest at all. In fact, Cooper's Hawkeye confesses to making no claims to even understanding romantic love:

"I have heard that there is a feeling in youth, which binds man to woman, closer than the father is tied to the son. It may be so. I have seldom been where women of my colour dwell; but such may be the gifts of nature in the settlements." Undeniably, for the purposes of producing a successful film, Mann was shrewd to depart from the novel give his charismatic lead actor a sense of romantic love.

### Major Duncan Heyward

In the film as well as in the novel, Heyward (played by Steven Waddington) exemplifies the morals and codes of a British soldier, offering a distinct foil (contrast) to the Indianized Hawkeye. He chastises General Webb for seeming to compromise royal policy. He aspires to gallantry in seeking the hand of Cora in marriage, but his entreaties are driven more by logic than by emotion, and Cora is justifiably indifferent to him. Viewers are likely to scorn him as inferior to Hawkeye in character, but Heyward redeems himself by offering his life in exchange for Cora's freedom, thus allowing Cora and Hawkeye to be reunited.

The Heyward of the novel is similarly ignorant of the ways of the wilderness, but his affections lie instead with Alice. As Cooper has it, Heyward and Alice survive, and they eventually marry, suggesting the propagation of white society in place of any thriving or revival of Indian society.

### Magua

As the villain whose motive for revenge against Munro drives the narrative, Magua is accorded more screen time and characterization than either of the Mohicans. His two conversations with Montcalm reveal how his children were killed by Mohawks fighting for "Grey Hair," while he was enslaved and lost his wife. This back story differs slightly from Cooper's: in the novel, Magua dishonored himself among the Hurons by becoming a drunken rascal, and he earned the punishment of whipping for disorderly conduct. In contrast, the Magua of the film was originally an innocent victim of British wartime pursuits. Thus, Mann has in a way portrayed Magua as more honorable—and yet his vindictiveness is enhanced, as evidenced by his savage murder of Munro. Critics generally agree that Magua is admirably portrayed by Wes Studi, now a highly regarded veteran film actor.

Beyond his thirst for revenge, Magua's appeals to the sachem reveal his interest in enriching the Hurons and aligning his people's values with Western capitalism—interests that do not surface in the novel. Rather, Cooper's Magua, always artfully eloquent, appeals to his elders' sense of justice, convincing the Hurons that Uncas should die and convincing the Delawares that his escaped white prisoners, as members of an oppressive and unjust race, should be returned to him. The pace of the film leaves little room for the original Magua's deliberate and subtle eloquence to be conveyed.

### General Montcalm

Montcalm, head of the French forces, claims to be an honorable gentleman for a soldier, but his actions belie this. The terms of the British surrender at Fort William Henry say that the British soldiers should be allowed to leave in peace, but Montcalm communicates quite clearly to Magua that he would be pleased if his Indian allies would attack them. Cooper implicates Montcalm less directly; Montcalm suggests no such course of vengeance in the corresponding conversation in the novel, and yet the Indian massacre occurs much closer to the fort. Montcalm could easily deploy his soldiers to quell the Indians, but he does not.

### Alice Munro

Alice, the fair-haired daughter of Colonel Munro, is above all an image of white innocence, even naïveté. In the film, she is traumatized by the killing and war, and perhaps especially in her weakness, she appeals to Uncas, who embraces her when her strength falters in the caverns under the falls. Thereafter, she is ushered around by the Hurons until, following Uncas's death, she tumbles to her own demise. In the novel, she is actually unconscious for much of the second half of the book.

### Colonel Munro

Colonel Munro is a tragic figure at the head of tragic circumstances, including the abandonment of his forces by his commanding general and his forced surrender. His lack of sympathy for the colonial militia, which is justified by his military integrity, is symbolic of the broader failures of the British to accommodate the human needs of American colonists. When the departing British are massacred, Magua gains a measure of revenge by gruesomely murdering Munro.

Cooper's Munro essentially becomes narrative deadweight after surviving this massacre, and so Mann's decision to give Munro a sensational death scene instead is unsurprising.

### Cora Munro

Madeleine Stowe's portrayal of Cora Munro is very faithful to Cooper's vision of the character. Though of privileged birth, she proves open-minded enough to rise to the challenges of the wilderness, maintaining her composure even in the face of grave danger and emotionally supporting her sister. Mann even has her kill a Huron with a pistol in the course of the massacre after Fort William Henry.

Much significance is attached to Cooper's rendering of Cora as bearing African blood, Munro having met her mother in the West Indies. Although Duncan is conscious of a prejudice against blacks "as deeply rooted as if it had been engrafted in his nature," the Delawares hold Cora (who had stayed with them for some time as a prisoner) in the highest esteem: "That she was of a blood purer and richer than the rest of her nation, any eye might have seen." Whatever racial commentary Cooper intended to convey through the character of Cora and her unfulfilled romantic pairing with Uncas, it is lost to the film, in which Cora is as white as Alice and pairs instead with Hawkeye.

### The Sachem

The sachem, or wise elder, of the Hurons decides the fates of Magua's prisoners. The sachem's role is analogous to that of the Delaware elder Tamenund in the novel.

### Uncas

Although still a main character in the film, Uncas (played by Eric Schweig, of Inuit descent) has less of a role than he does in the novel. Cooper portrays Uncas as nearly godlike in his physical presence. Alice gazes at "his free air and proud carriage, as she would have looked upon some precious relic of the Grecian chisel," while Heyward considers Uncas "an unblemished specimen of the noblest proportions of man." Accordingly, Uncas's senses and skills as a tracker are more finely tuned than Hawkeye's. The second half of the novel revolves around Uncas's capture by the Hurons, his escape with Hawkeye's help, his trial before the Delawares, and his leading the final battle against the Hurons—none of which occurs in the film. In the book, Uncas dies when, after "leaping frantically, from a fearful height" in an attempt to save Cora, Magua seizes the opportunity to stab him in the back; in a fair fight, Cooper's Uncas would undoubtedly have vanquished Magua. In the film, Uncas is simply outdueled by Magua.

### Jack Winthrop

Winthrop spearheads the colonists' participation as militia in the ongoing French and Indian War. He argues with Munro over being granted leave and then coordinates the colonists' escape from military duty at Fort William Henry. The inclusion of the colonial militia plot line, especially as signified by Winthrop, gives the film a more future-oriented historical context than the novel, with the sentiments of the militia foreshadowing the American Revolution of twenty years later.

### Other Characters

The one significant character from the novel not included in the film is David Gamut, the peculiar psalmist who bumbles along but plays incidentally crucial parts during the episodes of captivity among the Hurons. The broad revision of those episodes for the film allowed for the easy elimination of David's character. In the novel, Cooper's inclusion of the psalmist provides not only comic relief but an opportunity to reflect on the many differences between the man who is devoted to his faith—evidently at the expense of essential physical abilities—and the men who are devoted to existential fulfillment as warriors. Cooper also uses Gamut to contrast Western spirituality with Indian spirituality.

### THEMES

### The Character of Native Americans

Richard Slotkin, in his introduction to the novel, writes that "in the prefaces to *The Last of the Mohicans* Cooper makes it plain that the view of Indian character is a foremost issue. In its largest dimension, the question goes beyond the specifics of Indian ethnography to pose a question about the moral character of man in an uncivil or pre-civilized condition." Cooper approaches this theme in a variety of ways, especially through ruminations by the talkative Hawkeye, who is likely to hold forth on whatever is on his mind at any given time, even in the midst of a suspenseful firefight. Hawkeye, of course, has a unique

perspective on both white and Indian ways, and he comments on and analyzes them at will. Furthermore, the plot of the second half of the novel revolves around issues such as the manner in which the Huron and Delaware tribes uphold justice; the spiritual beliefs of the tribes; and the comportment of individual Indians in debate, in neighborly relations, and in battle.

The film greatly reduces the presence of this theme, both in dialogue and in the workings of the plot. In that Mann chose to give priority to the action sequences and the romantic pairing of Hawkeye and Cora, the many conversations between Hawkeye and his companions, particularly the ignorant but curious Heyward, are reduced to so few exchanges as to leave room for little more than plot exposition and character development. What little philosophical or ethnographic discussion remains, in turn, is focused not on the character of American Indians but on the relationships among the British, the colonists, and the Indians, especially in view of the looming Revolutionary War, which Cooper hints at not at all. With respect to the plot, all of the intricate aspects of the second half of Cooper's novel, as framed among the Delaware and Huron tribes, were eliminated for the film, which sacrifices depth by including only the one scene in the Huron encampment.

The viewer is left, then, to infer notions about Indian nature from the images of the lead Indian characters, Chingachgook, Uncas, and Magua. Magua is in some respects a caricatured Indian villain, bloodthirsty and bent on revenge against white people who have incidentally wronged him. Interestingly, the Mohicans are distinguished from most of their fellow Indians, who are clad in minimal warrior attire, by their full-length garments. The film accounts for this difference by making Chingachgook an Indian who approves of Anglo American society enough to have submitted both Hawkeye and Uncas to Western education at Eleazar Wheelock's school (which would become Dartmouth College, in New Hampshire). In fact, the original aim of this school was to provide Native Americans with both secular and religious education so that they might return to their tribes as missionaries. Thus, in associating the Mohicans with this school, the film Westernizes them and coincidentally extracts much of the "Indianness" that characterizes the novel and that Cooper intended to highlight. For example, whereas Cooper refers often to Uncas's extraordinary

# READ.
# WATCH.
# WRITE.

- Cooper provides some interesting descriptions of water in *The Last of the Mohicans*, especially in a soliloquy of Hawkeye's on the nature of the waterfalls early in chapter 6. Examine the dramatic and symbolic roles played by water in the novel, and then analyze the extent to which Mann has conveyed these roles in his film by incorporating images of water and events in and around water. Create a PowerPoint presentation using different images of water to illustrate these roles.

- Reviewers and critics have reacted in a variety of ways to the portrayal of Native Americans in Mann's film, often depending on whether they have read Cooper's novel or not. Write a personal reflection paper inspecting your emotional and intellectual responses to Mann's portrayals of Native Americans. First, relate your own degree of previous exposure to any American Indian culture, religion, or history. Then describe your responses, both at first and after thinking about the movie, to the Indian characters, roles, and actions in the film. Conclude by considering why the movie might have created these particular portrayals.

- David Gamut is perhaps the most curious character in Cooper's novel, with his role and actions communicating much about kinesthetic intelligence (that is, having to do with movement), musical enchantment, and spirituality. Write an essay considering the themes developed in the novel through David's character, and then reflect on his absence from the film, discussing whether his themes are filtered into other characters and how the film benefits or suffers from his absence.

- Whereas Hawkeye and Heyward are quite companionable in the novel, they are much at odds in the film, especially due to their clashing affections for Cora. Examine this relationship, using film clips as part of a presentation to illustrate how it bears on the acting styles and approaches of Daniel Day-Lewis and Steven Waddington. How do the two actors contrast each other through their physicality, speech, and expressions? To what extent do their interactions provide narrative tension? What might have been the results if Mann had been loyal to Cooper's novel and not established animosity between Hawkeye and Heyward?

---

grace and natural beauty, Mann instead highlights the physical form of Day-Lewis as Hawkeye. Hawkeye removes his shirt in the course of the opening deer hunt, while Uncas does not, and he also appears shirtless when he is arrested for sedition. In an examination of adaptations of the story, Martin Barker concludes that Mann unfortunately exhibits "an overall tendency to make Hawkeye the most Indian character of all." Cooper's Hawkeye, on the contrary, typically defers to his Mohican companions on matters of expertise and wisdom, particularly in the course of tracking the Hurons. Accordingly, in the novel, Hawkeye's many offhand remarks and speeches on Indian and white nature

communicate the notion that no white man could ever equal the gifts and abilities of a pure-hearted Indian and warrior like Uncas.

## *Life on the Frontier*

In a departure from Cooper's novel, the film devotes a degree of thematic attention to the circumstances faced by American colonists who forged their livelihood on the frontier, which was ever shifting as the trappings of civilization moved steadily westward. The colonists who assemble at John Cameron's cabin, in northern New York, are portrayed as honest, hardworking, and principled, ever concerned with the fundamental effort of survival. When the British

© *Archives du Feme Art | Photos 12 | Alamy*

officer convinces the colonists of the danger to their families posed by the French, they hesitantly but dutifully bear arms. The peril of life on the frontier is made evident when Hawkeye and company return to the Cameron residence to find a scene of death, with the cabin ravaged by a raiding Indian war party allied with the French. When Cora inquires about the victims, Hawkeye reveals his high opinion of the Camerons, who left indentured servitude in Virginia to risk lives of independence. This personal degree of independence is equated with national independence, which Americans would soon be fighting the British to achieve.

## STYLE

### Romanticism

Cooper's 1826 novel is situated by critics firmly within the romantic literary movement, which originated late in the eighteenth century. As Jacquelyn Kilpatrick observes, "Romanticism emphasized Nature as an elemental force and

focused largely on the testing of one's spirit, two 'naturals' for Cooper's setting. It also stressed the rise and fall of nations and the importance of heroes and heroic deeds." Cooper's development of the wilderness itself as a character in *The Last of the Mohicans* has been identified as one of the novel's greatest strengths, and Mann's vision is loyal to this essential aspect. From the opening scenes onward, panoramas of the wilderness, distant shots that show the towering forest canopy, and glances through the trees and into the underbrush—such as when Cora glimpses a wildcat—effectively place the viewer in the natural world. In turn, in many scenes the musical score drops away to leave only the sounds of the wilderness and of the passage of humans through it.

That Mann seems to have given priority to immersing the viewer in the frontier setting at the expense of, say, ideological reflection and development of the Indian characters is no accident. In his essay on the film, Gary Edgerton quotes Mann in an interview, "I wanted history to become as vivid and real and immediate as if it were being lived right now." Indeed, much of the appeal of the medium of film, especially as supported by modern budgets and cinematic technology, is its ability to transport viewers not just to foreign places but to bygone eras as well. While critics may dismiss a romantically immersive but thematically lightweight film as second rate—Edgerton disparages Mann for exhibiting "a good deal of unreflective faith in the ability of surface realism alone to capture a sense of historicity and human drama"—there is distinct value in the historical film that successfully captures the casual viewer's imagination. Many people watch movies not to contemplate but to escape; in making his film an engrossing venue of escape, Mann at least leads viewers to a basic awareness of what North America looked and felt like before the native tribes were violently swept across the continent and onto reservations. Though it does not reflect any scene from the novel, Mann's portrayal of the game of lacrosse played by white settlers and Indians together may be to many viewers a stirring vision of how successful cohabitation with Indians, rather than national oppression of them, might have led to a very different modern America. And for every viewer who is afterward drawn to Cooper's novel, to there find the complex thematic treatment that no film adaptation of reasonable length could truly reproduce anyway, Mann can feel that much more justified in having designed his film to be above all a captivating romantic vision.

### Action/Adventure

As is Mann's film version of *The Last of the Mohicans*, Cooper's original work is replete with action and adventure. In fact, some critics, as Slotkin notes, "thought Cooper compromised his art by pandering to a popular thirst for sensational action scenes." The novel has been adapted to the screen over a dozen times largely because the action and suspense alone make the tale so absorbing to viewers. Mann's film, released in 1992 to decent returns, prefigured the success of *Braveheart* (1995), which established the precedent of a three-hour running time for an Oscar-worthy, battle-laced historical epic. *The Last of the Mohicans* reaches the credits after an hour and fifty-two minutes, which thus almost seems short given the possible breadth of the subject matter. If Mann had directed the film a decade later, he might have seen fit to expand the movie beyond its action/adventure/romance essence so as to more fully address the profound themes of Cooper's novel.

## CULTURAL CONTEXT

### Establishment of an American Mythology

Situating his tale in American history, Cooper stresses how events of the recent past have led to the point in history when his fictionalized Mohican tribe reaches the end of its line. (The real-life Mahican and Mohegan tribes, both models for Cooper, survive in the modern era.) In his introduction, Slotkin notes how Cooper's tale "is a deliberate and rather elaborate fabrication of 'myth' for fictional purposes. Its effect is to unite the fragmentary history of the Indians into a single story of origin, rise to grandeur, intermarriage, decline, and fall." Kilpatrick further notes that Cooper belonged to a circle of literary and artistic minds who expressly intended to create an American mythology, in part to "establish a strong national personality for America, with a mythology that tied the American people, a large percentage of whom were recent immigrants, into a cohesive whole with a unifying 'history.'" Cooper's Mohicans, originating on the part of the northeastern seaboard first colonized by Europeans, are among the first tribes to be displaced and, consequently, to die off, and part of Cooper's aim is to address the circumstances that account for this symbolic tribe's tragic historical turn.

The text is ambiguous with regard to whether the white settlers who first displaced the Mohicans should be held accountable for the tribe's fate. That portion of the tribe's history is not fully explicated in the course of the novel, being addressed primarily when Uncas reveals his identity to the Delawares; and many of the references in that chapter come in the extensively metaphorical language used by the Indians, yet leaving the reader without any specific accounting of how the Mohicans were whittled down to so few. Meanwhile, the notion of a tribe becoming extinct is made more palpable by the Delawares' slaying of all the warriors of the neighboring Huron tribe in the final battle. While the sum of the acts of the colonial and American governments against North American Indians may be referred to as constituting genocide, Cooper's evocation of the decimation of one tribe by another suggests that even such mass injustice against a people can be construed—dangerously—as part of the "inevitable" course of history. Indeed, as Kilpatrick chillingly notes, "In Cooper's day the assumption was that all such indigenous people would eventually be swept away." Commentators frequently draw on Cooper's other writings and expressed ideologies in analyzing *The Last of the Mohicans* and drawing conclusions about the meanings of his symbolism. Yet Cooper does not present his mythological tale in a way that allows the reader to state definitively that the author is either condoning or condemning the roles that his race and his nation have played in the devastation of the continent's Native American communities.

### The Revolutionary War

The primary cultural context that Mann evokes in his film is that of the coming Revolutionary War, which would begin less than twenty years after the events of 1757 that are portrayed. While Mann certainly also evokes the tragedy of the extinction of the Mohicans, he mostly does so indirectly. In one of the earliest scenes, mention is made at John Cameron's cabin of the possibility of Uncas settling down with a family; but Cooper's plot line in which Uncas rises to his inherited chiefdom among the Delawares and leads them to victory in battle against the Hurons was eliminated. As such, the issue of Chingachgook and Uncas's

heritage surfaces again in the film only after Uncas is killed by Magua, making the Mohicans' demise more of a framework than an actual theme or plot focus. Instead, Mann gives thematic priority to the colonial militia's ultimate rejection of British rule, which was failing to address the colonists' humanitarian needs, circumstances that foreshadow the upcoming Revolutionary War. Given the patriotic stirrings that Americans are supposed to feel in reflecting on the birth of their country—which are likely evoked as well by the Fourth-of-July-worthy fireworks over Fort William Henry—Mann as director perhaps realized the commercial merits of allowing patriotic fervor to compete with, if not overshadow, the tragic demise of the Mohicans in his film.

### CRITICAL OVERVIEW

Upon viewing the film, critics seemed to gather that Mann's intentions lay more along the lines of impressing and entertaining the average viewer—rather than doing as much justice to Cooper's novel as possible. *New York Times* critic Janet Maslin, wondering why the story would

© *Pictorial Press Ltd | Alamy*

be adapted yet again, wryly suggests that the viewer think of "thrilling scenery and Daniel Day-Lewis running bare-chested through the forest if you want to grasp the real impetus behind this latest Cooper revival." She adds, "The film makers may have done a better job making their own tomahawks and rebuilding Fort William Henry than of breathing sense into their material, but the results are still riveting." While disparaging the director's "uncertain staging" of scenes and the resulting choppiness, she commends the "superb tableaux" and "moments of high drama" achieved in the wilderness, and she especially appreciates what she considers the "enlightened and uncommonly interesting treatment of the story's Indian characters."

Critics approaching the film from the literary perspective have been somewhat less kind in their assessments, with most judging that Mann made insufficient effort to address the thematic complexities of Cooper's tale. In the journal *Sight and Sound*, Martin Barker states that "Mann has made a clever, beautiful, but in the end, hollow film, celebrating cultural pluralism but depoliticizing racial politics." He considers the wistful mountaintop scene at the film's close to be "an oversimplified and ultimately meaningless promise of simple renewal, in which all issues of power, oppression and injustice are snuffed out by a rhetoric of vague hope and kindness." Similarly, Gary Edgerton notes in the *Journal of American Culture* that Mann "generally opts for romance and nostalgia" over thematic complexity. In an essay in *Hollywood's Indian: The Portrayal of the Native American in Film*, Jeffrey Walker likewise comments that "Mann's decision to turn *The Last of the Mohicans* primarily into a love story and to ignore the essence of the Native American theme is the strangest and most damaging plot twist of all." Edgerton concludes that the film "remains another vivid reminder of how difficult it is for our culture to adequately imagine any credible solutions to the multiracial challenges that still confront us."

# CRITICISM

## *Michael Allen Holmes*

*Holmes is an editor and writer. In this essay, he considers the implications of Mann's changes to the familial relationship between Hawkeye and the Mohicans.*

> MANN PROFESSED TO HAVE HONORABLE INTENTIONS IN DIRECTING HIS ADAPTATION OF COOPER'S NOVEL, ESPECIALLY WITH REGARD TO THE TREATMENT OF THE NATIVE AMERICAN CHARACTERS."

One of the most critically lamented aspects of Michael Mann's 1992 adaptation of James Fenimore Cooper's 1826 novel *The Last of the Mohicans* is the extent to which the director neglected the complex Native American themes developed by the original author. As Gary Edgerton notes in his essay on racial matters in the film, although Mann professed an intent "to revise the negative stereotyping of Native Americans in *The Last of the Mohicans* from Cooper through Hollywood's many versions," the film "never provides an expanded and in-depth portrayal of Amerindian life and culture." Almost all aspects of Cooper's plot revolving around the heritage and birthright of Uncas, who as the last in the line of the Mohicans assumes a brief but glorious chiefdom among the Delawares before his tragic death, were eliminated for the film. Arguably, Mann's faults go further than simple neglect: in light of the familial relations that he establishes between Hawkeye and the Mohicans, the presentation of certain images associated with the title theme may leave the viewer with an inappropriate impression about the resolution of the tale.

In the novel, Hawkeye is understood to be a peer of Chingachgook's, though either's exact age is unclear. Hawkeye does communicate, when they hear the cries of the frightened horses from the caverns at the falls, that of himself, Chingachgook, and Uncas, "two of us have ranged the woods for more than thirty years." He later more precisely remarks of his own experience, "I have listened to all the sounds of the woods for thirty years, as a man will listen, whose life and death depend on the quickness of his ears." One might assume that Hawkeye, raised as an Indian, began ranging the woods and developing such acute sensory awareness when he was an adolescent, perhaps between ten and fifteen years of age. Thus, he and

# WHAT DO I SEE NEXT?

- The 1971 British Broadcasting Corporation miniseries *The Last of the Mohicans*, directed by David Maloney, with a total running time of 320 minutes, provides fewer thrills than Mann's film but follows the plot of Cooper's novel more closely.

- The film *Geronimo: An American Legend* (1993) recounts the story of the Apache warrior Geronimo, played by Wes Studi (who played Magua in Mann's film), in the style of a traditional western, with Gene Hackman, Jason Patric, and Robert Duvall costarring and Walter Hill directing.

- *Dances with Wolves* (1990), directed by and starring Kevin Costner, is a film about a Civil War soldier who befriends the local Sioux tribe at his outpost on the western frontier. The film won seven Academy Awards in 1991, including Best Picture and Best Director.

- *The Patriot* (2000), starring Mel Gibson and Heath Ledger and directed by Roland Emmerich, is set not long after *The Last of the Mohicans*. It recounts the participation of a farmer-soldier in the American Revolution.

- Dustin Hoffman stars in *Little Big Man* (1970), directed by Arthur Penn, which tells the story of the only white survivor of the Battle of Little Bighorn while examining American expansionism in the West.

- Director and star Mel Gibson's *Braveheart* (1995) expanded on the formula of *Last of the Mohicans*, providing romance, international intrigue, and intense battle scenes, all in a historical context. *Braveheart* takes place in thirteenth-century Scotland; it received the Academy Award for Best Picture of 1996.

- *Smoke Signals* (1998) is an independent film produced primarily by American Indians, with Chris Eyre directing, a screenplay by novelist Sherman Alexie, and young Indian actors as the stars. The story revolves around a road trip taken by two friends who live on the Coeur d'Alene reservation in Idaho.

---

Chingachgook could be estimated to be around forty or forty-five years or older, with Uncas being perhaps twenty or twenty-five. As such, Hawkeye would be something of an uncle figure to Uncas. When he is explaining to Duncan and Alice why he must attempt to save Uncas from execution by the Hurons despite the low likelihood of success, he compares the romantic love linking Duncan and Alice to the closeness with which "the father is tied to the son," and he speaks warmly of how he "taught the lad [Uncas] the real character of a rifle." The narrator refers to "the decided preference that the sturdy woodsman gave to one who might, in some degree, be called the child of his adoption." Thus, the generational difference between Hawkeye and Uncas is made quite clear.

Mann's film establishes distinctly different familial relationships between Hawkeye and the Mohicans. The brief prologue text that opens the movie refers to "three men, the last of a vanishing people," thus positioning Hawkeye not simply as a close friend of the Mohicans but as one of them. The following scene establishes a level of equality between Hawkeye and Uncas, who keep pace with each other in chasing the deer; Uncas stands by Hawkeye's side as he fires the gun, while Chingachgook catches up afterward to offer a prayer. Later, in the scene in the forest when Hawkeye and Cora are chatting while entrenched on the burial ground, Hawkeye makes clear his relationship to the Mohicans in noting that he was adopted by Chingachgook as a very young boy. Although the particular circumstances of this adoption—of a white boy by an Indian who is among the last of his tribe—are unique, to the modern viewer, any adoption is understood to make one legally a true part of the adoptive family. And indeed, Hawkeye uses the phrasing, "my father told me,"—"father" rather than "adoptive father." All in all, the viewer surely gathers that Hawkeye is to be understood as a brother to Uncas and a legitimate part of the Mohicans' family.

Along with matters of family relations, then, come questions of inheritance. Critics frequently refer to the way in which, as the last Mohicans pass beyond the earthly world, someone or some group can be understood to inherit the history and the land that they have left behind. Jacquelyn Kilpatrick, for example, summarily notes that "in Cooper's story the Indians are a noble but vanishing impediment to settlement," with Hawkeye being framed as the "isolated man of the wilderness who would 'inherit' the land." Yet in Cooper's text, Hawkeye, as a peer of Chingachgook, makes no claims to being in a position to "inherit" the land that has been taken from the Native Americans after Uncas is gone. Rather, as Slotkin notes in his introduction to the novel, Hawkeye "mourns the passing of Uncas and shares the Indians' fate of disappearing without a trace of progeny in the American future." As Hawkeye confirms in speaking to Chingachgook in the final scene, "I have no kin, and I may also say, like you, no people." The two lead characters who do survive to reproduce are Duncan and Alice, who retreat into the safety and comfort of the settlements. Thus, as Slotkin observes, "Only the pure-whites . . . will marry and produce heirs. The future belongs to Heyward and Alice." The white people, then, are the "inheritors"—or, more accurately, the usurpers—of the land.

Mann's film uses the theme represented by the title more as a framework than as a thread of the plot; the tragedy of the Mohicans reaching the end of their line is not revisited until the final scene, after Uncas's untimely death. In this scene, Chingachgook solemnly refers to himself as the "last of the Mohicans"—yet after he utters these words and looks at Hawkeye with profound sadness, his image is eclipsed by that of Cora as she steps into the frame, and the shot then transitions to a long close-up of Cora and Hawkeye embracing. Moments later, Chingachgook speaks directly of how the frontier will be pushed farther and farther westward, until there is nowhere left for the people of his race to go. The Mohican then evokes the inevitable prospect of Hawkeye and Cora raising a family together: "The frontier place is for people like my white son and his woman, and their children." The implication, then, is that in this version of the

story, contrary to Cooper's tale, Hawkeye, as the adopted son of the last of the Mohicans, is indeed the legitimate inheritor of the land—not a usurper, as Heyward and Alice are in the novel—and he will reproduce with Cora to people the land he has inherited.

Mann professed to have honorable intentions in directing his adaptation of Cooper's novel, especially with regard to the treatment of the Native American characters. As a reviewer for *Rolling Stone* notes, "Mann has slagged Cooper for romanticizing and disempowering the Indians. But . . . Mann falls into the same trap" in transferring the focus of the story away from the Mohicans and onto Hawkeye. The most conspicuous example of this transfer of focus is perhaps to be found on the film's theatrical poster and prevailing image: Clad in his woodsman's garb, Daniel Day-Lewis, as Hawkeye, is portrayed running toward the camera with his knife drawn, presumably in the heat of battle. In the background are blurred images of other combatants, some Indian; certainly none are meant to be identified as either Chingachgook or Uncas. Gracing Day-Lewis's image, of course, is the title of the movie, *The Last of the Mohicans*. Thus, despite Chingachgook's identification of himself as the last of the Mohicans in the film's closing scene, by virtue of the images in that scene and especially this frozen action image of Day-Lewis that visually defines the film, the viewer is likely to be left with the impression, whether distinct or subconscious, that Hawkeye *is* the "last of the Mohicans." Mann could not have been unaware that theatergoers casually viewing the poster without necessarily being familiar with the film would be left with this impression. His decision to allow for this gross misidentification, perhaps motivated in part by an awareness of the subtle commercial appeal of ambiguity, might be dismissed as mildly irresponsible, or it might leave one feeling as though Mann is just another white man slyly taking advantage of Native American history and culture.

**Source:** Michael Allen Holmes, Critical Essay on *Last of the Mohicans*, in *Novels for Students*, Gale, Cengage Learning, 2010.

## *Jeffrey Walker*

*In the following review, Walker criticizes many film versions of Cooper's novel, claiming few of them remain true to the text and Cooper's storytelling.*

> IN THEIR VERSIONS OF *THE LAST OF THE MOHICANS*, FILMMAKERS HAVE REWRITTEN COOPER'S PLOT, MISCAST AND MISLABELED HIS CHARACTERS, MODERNIZED HIS DIALOGUE, MISUNDERSTOOD HIS THEMES, AND MISREPRESENTED HISTORY."

Since its initial two-volume publication on 6 February 1826 by the Philadelphia publishing house of Carey and Lea, James Fenimore Cooper's *The Last of the Mohicans; A Narrative of 1757* has probably generated more attention from Hollywood filmmakers than virtually any other American novel. From its first adaptations in 1909, as a D. W. Griffith one-reeler and in 1911 as two different one-reelers by the Powers and Thanhouser Film Companies, to its latest incarnation in 1992 as a Michael Mann potboiler, more than a dozen interpretations of the novel have appeared in various forms: from silent picture, to Mascot serial, to animated version, BBC television series, and Hollywood epic. Considering the popular reception of the novel in Cooper's day, and the mythic story it spins about American frontier heroes, this attention seems deserved. Most Americans, if they have not read the novel (and most have not), have nonetheless read about it or read abridged versions of it, and our own popular culture has embraced it in a number of curious ways. Mark Twain made Cooper and his "offenses" against literary art in the Leather-Stocking tales part of his traveling lecture shows. More recently, the anti-hero of television's *M\*A\*S\*H*, Captain Benjamin Franklin Pierce, we are told, received his sobriquet "Hawk-eye" because the Cooper tale was supposedly the only novel his father had ever read.

That most Americans have never read *The Last of the Mohicans* is not surprising. Until the Fenimore Cooper family agreed to cooperate in the production of a responsibly-edited series of Cooper's fiction and non-fiction in the mid-1960s, *The Last of the Mohicans* (appearing in 1983 as part of that NEH-sponsored, CSE-sealed, SUNY Press-published series) was available for readers only in a plethora of corrupt texts. And

while the absence of reliable Cooper texts has been partially responsible for Cooper's less than highly touted reputation as a man of letters, Twain certainly had something to do with this offense against the American literary canon. The fact remains that the novel has been praised more often for what it did not do, rather than for what it did. Film versions of the novel illustrate this strange reaction to Cooper's masterpiece and explain the distortion of the text, yet ironically Hollywood filmmakers are probably as responsible for generating interest in Cooper's novel over the years as literary critics or college and university professors. In translating Cooper's work for the screen, they highlight and make popular those elements of *The Last of the Mohicans* that have little to do with Cooper's original story, but have everything to do with twentieth-century American popular culture and taste. While most of the directors do a sterling job of presenting Cooper's mise en scene, none of their film versions of the novel accurately reproduce Cooper's plot, and few come close to understanding Cooper's theme. Despite these problems, film versions continue to be made because Hollywood sees the novel containing the ingredients of an American film classic, if for all the wrong reasons.

When *The Last of the Mohicans* appeared in 1826, it was hailed by some as an American masterpiece. In the 18 February 1826 issue of the Philadelphia *National Gazette*, Robert Walsh remarked that

> Never since the days of our childhood has Fairy hand sported so with our feelings... Never has necromancer, or poet, held us so long enchanted. The work, from the beginning to the close, is one tissue of harrowing incidents, beautiful and chaste imagery, and deep pathos, and what adds to the charm, is, though we yield a willing credence to every turn of the narrative, we *know* that every thing is true. (163)

William Leete Stone's review in the New York *Commercial Advertiser* of 6 February 1826 concurred with Walsh's praise of Cooper's novel:

> "It is American books," says a late English Review, "that are wanted of America; not English books, nor books made in America by Englishmen. We want, in a word, from the people of North America, books, which, whatever may be their faults, are decidedly, if not altogether, *American*." Well, here they have one—a description of the aboriginal character—in all its native, wild, and lofty grandeur—powerful, warm, rich, glowing, and animated, from the

hand of a master, though they may be unwilling to acknowledge him as such. (238)

Such contemporary reviews of the novel addressed issues that have affected the literary interpretation of *The Last of the Mohicans* in the almost two centuries since its publication, but have had seemingly little impact on the twentieth-century filmmaker's response to the text. Historically praised either for the inclusion of harrowing incidents in his fictions or for the creation of truly American books, Cooper has been generally misinterpreted and misrepresented by filmmakers. Almost all of the film adaptations have concentrated on his plots, always to the novel's detriment, and the result has been chaos with Cooper's text.

With the exception of the 1920 silent version of *The Last of the Mohicans* (directed by Maurice Tourneur and Clarence Brown, and starring Wallace Beery as Magua, Barbara Bedford as Cora, Albert Rosco as Uncas, Harry Lorraine as Hawk-eye, and Theodore Lerch as Chingachgook), none of the other versions come close to reliably retelling the story. In this 1920 interpretation, the directors concentrated on the relationship between Cora and Uncas, with Hawk-eye reduced to almost a secondary position. It is generally faithful to the novel, although it includes an extremely long section on the Fort William Henry massacre and introduces a villainous British officer who lusts for Cora and betrays the fort to the French. These are minor distortions in the text in comparison to those in later versions.

In 1924, for example, Pathe produced a composite film of *The Leatherstocking Tales* directed by George B. Seitz. With Harry Miller as Leatherstocking and David Dunbar as Chingachgook, the film also features Edna Murphy as Judith Hutter and Lillian Hall as Hetty Hutter (both characters from *The Deerslayer*, not the *Mohicans*), and depicts such historical figures as Montcalm, Braddock, and George Washington. Columbia Pictures produced a similar distortion in 1947 called *The Last of the Redmen*. In addition to making Hawk-eye an Irish scout and Cora Munro a redhead, the film also introduces a new character into the text, Davy Munro, the Munro girls' kid brother, as well as a standard bromide of the classic western, the circling of the wagon train. Equally western in its *mise en scene* is Harold Reinl's direction of a 1965 German adaptation called *The Last Tomahawk*. Set in the American West of the 1880s, the action takes place at Ranch Munro and contains such imaginative variations as a chest of government gold, an exploding mountain, and a cavalry charge.

In the 1930s, two film versions of the novel were produced. The first, a Mascot serial directed by Reaves Eason in 1932, is a classic twelve-chapter nail biter that includes almost as many textual distortions of the novel as it has cliffhanger endings. Known chiefly for its casting of Harry Carey as Hawk-eye, the twelfth installment ends with an equally bizarre violation of textual integrity: Chingachgook is killed, Uncas lives, and Hawk-eye tells the young Mohican that he is the last of his race. The second cinematic version filmed in the 1930s is probably the most famous of all the film adaptations, primarily because its script was used as the source for the 1992 Michael Mann blockbuster. Based on a screenplay by Philip Dunne and directed by George B. Seitz, who remade his 1924 silent film in 1936 for United Artists, *The Last of the Mohicans* stars Randolph Scott as Hawk-eye and Binnie Barnes as Alice Munro. Seitz introduced most of the plot changes used in the 1992 film, but the chief plot difference portrays Seitz's Hawk-eye and Alice Munro as the two white star-crossed lovers rather than Mann's Hawk-eye and Cora. In spite of his misrepresentation of Cooper's novel, which has Uncas, the Native American, and Cora, the part-white woman herself the product of miscegenation, as the principals in an interracial romance, Seitz's plot twist was not surprising in 1936, given Hollywood and the Hay's Office's horror of miscegenation. It would have been distasteful to Cooper, too, not only because of the violation of plot, but also because he attempted in his Leather-Stocking tales to deemphasize the love interest of the European Gothic novel.

When Michael Mann produced his 1992 film, the Hawk-eye and Cora love affair took center stage. In choosing to pair Hawk-eye with the dark-haired Cora and Uncas with the fair-haired Alice, Mann revised Cooper's original story which showed Hawk-eye as a "man without a cross" (and without a girlfriend) and Uncas drawn to Cora, a dark-haired mulatto, rather than to the blonde Alice, a coupling representing Cooper's own attitudes toward miscegenation. Of all the many revisions of Cooper's novel that appear in the 1992 version, Mann's decision to turn *The Last of the Mohicans* primarily into a love story and to ignore the essence of the Native American theme is the strangest and most damaging plot twist of all. It is one thing to borrow scenes from other Leather-Stocking novels (the canoe chase from *The Pathfinder*, for example); to invent scenes (Hawk-eye's shooting of Duncan Hayward to prevent his suffering at the burning stake, Magua's killing of Colonel Munro); or to mismatch lovers (Duncan and Cora rather than Duncan and Alice, Uncas and Alice rather than Uncas and Cora) to sell theater tickets. But to manipulate the story's plot in an attempt to make history more vivid and realistic for the contemporary filmgoer is questionable directing and screenwriting. To focus on the love affair between American literature's most strongly individualistic, anti-authoritarian, and anti-British mythic hero and Cora Munro is to miss the essential theme and flavor of Cooper's classic tale. As James Franklin Beard informs us in his historical introduction to the SUNY edition of the novel, *The Last of the Mohicans* is not finally about such peripheral action as two lovers (particularly white ones), but about the "unremitting, frequently violent, always exasperating contest between the Native Americans and the intruders, white immigrants and settlers of every description" (xxx) and its consequences: the destruction of the last vestiges of a race of Native Americans.

In the current climate of political correctness, where the rights and heritage of all Americans demand celebration and recognition, it is unusual that none of the filmmakers who have translated *The Last of the Mohicans* for the stage have taken this theme into consideration. Cooper's early nineteenth-century reviewers certainly recognized his strengths and his weaknesses as a writer and social critic. An anonymous pundit wrote in the pages of the July 1826 issue of the *North American Review* that

> we do not find that he [Cooper] describes with great effect the secret workings of the passions of the human heart; or that he moves our affections, by any other than mere external agents, and such commonly as are calculated to excite no softer or more sympathetic emotion than terror or surprise (153).

Charles Sealsfield agreed in his 12 February 1831 *New York Mirror* essay on the newly published Bentley Standard Novels series of Cooper's novels that "Our author does not excel in painting civilized men and manners; and, least of all, civilized women" (252). Cooper, of course, was not, nor did he intend to be, a novelist of manners. As another anonymous critic pointed out in his biographical sketch of Cooper in the June 1838 issue of the *Southern Literary Messenger,*

> In painting Indian scenes of still life, or in delineating the warrior and hunger, the battle or the chase, our novelist, as he is the first who seized upon subjects so full of interest for the romance, so is he alone and unrivalled in this branch of his art (375).

An earlier anonymous writer's diagnosis in *The New-York Mirror* concurs:

> In this novel the American aborigines are introduced with better effect than in any work of fiction that has ever been written. The gentle Uncas and his valiant sire, the field-like Magua, and the venerable patriarch of the Delawares, are perfect masterpieces of their kind... They are immensely superior to all that Chateaubriand, or any others, have made to delineate the character of the American savage (39).

Cooper's strengths certainly did not lie in his portrait of domestic toilets, and the contemporary reviews showed it; instead reviewers like the critic in the April 1826 issue of the *Literary Gazette* admired his Native Americans and praised them as "original and interesting" portraits never "so well, so truly, and so vividly drawn as in his pages" (198).

How then has twentieth-century America and Hollywood strayed so far from Cooper's original theme in *The Last of the Mohicans?* What is it about Cooper's story that readers and filmmakers have refused to understand or acknowledge? Does the problem lie in ignoring the source and history of Cooper's tale, or perhaps in falling prey to the bad reputation Cooper as novelist has received in American literature ever since Mark Twain penned his hilarious satire of "Fenimore Cooper's Literary Offences" and condemned Cooper forever as a second-rate hack? The problem, I would argue, lies somewhere in between. On the one hand, American readers have not stopped laughing long enough over Twain's essay to recognize that it was not serious literary criticism, but primarily a tour de force in the history of American humor. To some degree this has prevented American readers and filmmakers from listening closely enough to what scholars have been claiming, either as Cooper's contributions to American literature, or to what we have learned about the historical background and composition of the novel.

When Twain wrote his grossly exaggerated lampoon in the July 1895 issue of the *North American Review*, he accused Cooper of literary incompetence by attacking his use of imprecise language, his development of improbable characters, and his creation of impossible plots in the Leather-Stocking novels (in particular, *The Deerslayer*, *The Pathfinder*, and *The Last of the Mohicans*). In recent years, as the *Writings of James Fenimore Cooper* series has worked to produce seventeen textually-reliable editions of his novels, we have learned that Cooper was not the careless slipshod writer Twain portrayed him to be in his essay. While it is true that the editions of his novels were remarkably corrupt because compositors had difficulty reading his script, because he did not read proof against printer's copy, and because numerous resettings had left a heavy toll of corruptions, Cooper did revise, as the textual evidence discovered by the editors of the Cooper series has demonstrated conclusively. In *The Last of the Mohicans*, for example, Cooper, in a letter from Paris dated 29 August 1831 to his publishers Colburn and Bentley, noted that "There are errors in the Preface of the Mohicans, and in one instance bad grammar—'As the verdure of their native forests *fall*.' Verdure is the nominative case of fall, and it should have been *falls*" (*L&J* II: 137). Such authorial revisions were commonplace with Cooper. Furthermore, Twain's charges have also been challenged and disproven by Lance Schachterle and Kent Ljungquist in their rejoinder to Twain appropriately called "Fenimore Cooper's Literary Defenses: Twain and the Text of *The Deerslayer*." In their essay, they attempt to prove that Twain's charges against Cooper's art are both fallacious and inaccurate. Based upon their own work as Cooper editors, they determine that "By carefully manipulating Cooper's texts, willfully misreading, and sometimes fabricating evidence, Twain leaves the reader with the impression that he has polished Cooper off." However, "By looking at Twain's treatment of plot, characterization, and especially diction in *The Deerslayer*, [they] lay bare Twain's rhetorical strategy and satirical distortions" (402). Despite the overwhelming evidence they present in their essay that Cooper was a careful craftsman, most uninformed American readers continue to laugh at Cooper. Hollywood has unfortunately contributed to this offense against literary history by repeatedly telling the wrong tale of *The Last of the Mohicans*.

Cooper first conceived the idea for his novel in early August 1824. As James Franklin Beard tells the story, *The Last of the Mohicans* was born out of an excursion Cooper took with four young English noblemen (Edward Stanley, Henry Labouchere, Evelyn Denison, and John Wortley) to Glens Falls and Lake George. While there,

Cooper was struck by the scenery at the falls and declared, recorded in a footnote in Stanley's journal appended to his description of the Falls, that he had to "'place one of his old Indians here'—*The last of the Mohicans* was the result." Beard notes that "The word Indian or Indians in both accounts is probably significant; for The Leatherstocking Tales had not yet been conceived as a series, and the introduction of Hawk-eye may have been an afterthought" (*Mohicans*). If Stanley's note and Beard's interpretation of Cooper's words are correct, then *The Last of the Mohicans* as a novel focusing *exclusively* on the character of Hawk-eye as its central hero is as much an American literary myth as are the Hollywood films that not only place him at the center of their adventure tale, but also represent him as the principal male lead in a love story.

Of course, Hawk-eye's role in the novel is certainly important and central to the significance of the action, but it is not necessarily as the quintessential American white hero that this centrality functions. Following the massacre at Fort William Henry, Hawk-eye recognizes that the decisions made by his fellow white men (Munro, Heyward, Montcalm) have led to an unmitigated disaster. As he discusses with Chingachgook and Uncas the path they should take to recover the Munro sisters,

> he arose to his feet, and shaking off his apathy, he suddenly assumed the manner of an Indian, and adopted all the arts of native eloquence. Elevating an arm, he pointed out the track of the sun, repeating the gesture for every day that was necessary to accomplish their object (199).

This scene is crucial, not only because Hawk-eye shakes off his apathetic mood, but also because he undergoes a metamorphosis and realizes that the "manner of an Indian" is one he must assume to successfully rescue the women. It is in the second half of the novel that Cooper reinforces his decision to select the Native American (and his ways) as the hero and the subject of his story.

Cooper's interest in Native Americans and their story appears throughout *The Last of the Mohicans*. He was certainly aware of the significance of statements by Chief Justice John Marshall in 1823 and President James Monroe in 1824 that would be the basis of the official Federal Indian Removal Policy instituted years after the publication of his novel, as well as the popularity of Indian captivity narratives throughout the colonial period of

American history and historical treatments of the massacre of Fort William Henry, all of which he used as inspiration for his narrative of 1757. Cooper's task, as Beard suggests, "whether or not he formulated it consciously, was to invent an infrastructure to make the outrage dramatically intelligible and humanly meaningful" (*Mohicans*). *The Last of the Mohicans* was that infrastructure.

Seventeen years after the publication of *The Last of the Mohicans*, Cooper wrote to Rufus Wilmot Griswold telling him that his book was "an experiment, being quite original as to manner and subject" (*L&J* IV: 343). A year later, in another letter to Griswold, he remarked that his narrative was "an original book...I do not know where to find its model. It succeeded perfectly, forming a totally new class of romance" (*L&J* IV: 461). Noting the book's originality, Cooper implies that *The Last of the Mohicans* was not a novel intended to continue the story of Leather-Stocking saga first addressed in *The Pioneers*, or simply a tale that would address his fascination from youth with Indian culture; instead, as he said in the introduction to the 1831 Bentley Standard Novels edition, "the business of a writer of fiction is to approach, as near as his powers will allow, to poetry" (*Mohicans*). Cooper of course intended this to imply that he would de-emphasize realism and, as Beard notes, present "himself as a writer of romance, stressing the tragic element Aristotle identified as endemic in epic structure" (*Mohicans*). *The Last of the Mohicans* fits this definition, but it becomes not so much a romance demonstrating Hawk-eye and his woodsmanship, as it develops into a tragic tale of the extinction of a Native American race and the recognition of man's mortality.

Cooper did not write *The Last of the Mohicans* because he wanted to vilify Native Americans or to celebrate the manifest destiny of the white man. He examined human nature and did not care much whether he exposed the evils of one race or another. Magua is probably the blackest villain in Cooper's fiction, but Montcalm's inability (or unwillingness) to anticipate and prevent the Fort William Henry massacre does not speak well for Europeans. Similarly, those characters who promote their own education and sophistication as the chief virtues of the civilized world (Montcalm again, Colonel Munro, Duncan Heyward, the Munro sisters) have little or no compassion or understanding of human nature. Even Hawk-eye and the two Mohicans commit their own acts of transgression in the course of the narrative and do not escape blame for the tragedies that befall either race. Cooper was far more interested in exploring larger moral issues in *The Last of the Mohicans*, something that Hollywood has not recognized in its adaptations of the novel.

To explore these ideas, Cooper did not write a Gothic romance; instead he constructed a plot that borrowed from several popular genres of the period, ones that were certain to address moral issues in 1826 America and to evoke emotional responses from his readers. Certainly the most prominent genre appearing in *The Last of the Mohicans* is the Puritan captivity narrative. Cooper adopts many of its conventions and invents some new variations so as to transform the captivity genre into his own secular adventure story. By doubling the number of captivities, Cooper also doubles the number of the traditional attack-capture-escape scenes in the novel and makes the center-piece of the tale—the massacre at Fort William Henry—more atrocious and dehumanizing. Cooper also invents two heroines instead of one, doubling the love interest that he does borrow from the British Gothic romance. He introduces the psalmist David Gamut into the novel for comic relief and to satirize the Calvinist theme of the triumph of the godly over the savage wilderness and the pagans who inhabit it. And by describing Magua and his actions in both Miltonic and Shakespearean terms to broaden his historiographic strategy (his use of literary allusion in the novel is extensive), Cooper borrows and modifies for his own use traditional literary tropes. But *The Last of the Mohicans* is anything but a traditional novel.

Almost every convention and motif Cooper adopts in his narrative of 1757 helps him address in one way or another the conflict between Native Americans and European settlers. His use of two captivity narratives not only provides structure for the novel (the first occurs in Chapters 1–17 and describes the journey to Fort William Henry and the events leading up to the massacre; the second in Chapters 18–33 charts the course of Hawk-eye and the Mohicans as they track Magua and the captive Munro sisters), but also provides an important context for the tragic conclusion. Following the massacre scene in Chapter 17, Cooper describes almost immediately in the very next chapter the change in the season: "The whole landscape, which, seen by a favouring light, and in a genial temperature, had been found so lovely, appeared now like some pictured allegory of life, in which objects were arrayed in their harshest but truest colours, and without the relief of any shadowing." The grass is arid, the mountains are barren, the wind blows unequally; as Cooper paints it in allegorical terms, "it was a scene of wildness and desolation; and it appeared as if all who had profanely entered it, had been stricken, at a blow, by the relentless arm of death." The world of the novel has abruptly changed, but so too has the character of the participants also changed. Munro and Heyward, the heroes of the European world of the first half of the novel, seem impotent, while Uncas, "*who moved in front*" (italics mine), takes the lead in the chapter following the massacre and discovers the tell-tale signs of Magua and the fleeing party. Magua is transformed from the victim of the European settlement of the colonies to its destroyer, the "Prince of Darkness, brooding on his own fancied wrongs, and plotting evil." It is Uncas and Magua who become the central figures in the second half of the novel; as the *last* of the Mohicans, Uncas asserts his mythic stature in a battle on a mountain top with Magua, not only to determine the winner in a struggle between good and evil, but also to decide the destiny of a race. Uncas's ultimate death not only signifies the end of the Mohicans, but in a larger context, the end of a time in history. In the final paragraph of the novel, Tamenund, the Delaware sage, elegizes that "The pale faces are masters of the earth, and the time of the red-men has not yet come again."

Cooper's decision to concentrate on the end of a race and on the dramatic battle between white and red, rather than on the romantic adventures of a frontiersman in *The Last of the Mohicans*, surfaces everywhere in the novel. Hawk-eye, for all his centrality in the tale, never serves as the romantic lead or as the hero of the story, the role that Hollywood has assigned him in all of their adaptations of Cooper's work. In the first half of the novel, Cooper casts Hawk-eye as a guide to lead Heyward and the Munro sisters to Fort William Henry. In the second half, Cooper uses him again as guide, this time to prepare Uncas to seek his destiny in the land of the Delawares. While he voices many of Cooper's concerns regarding the settlement of America by Europeans throughout the novel, fulfills his role as sharpshooter when the events demand, and serves as the stage manager of much of the plot

in the tale, he guides, but never *directs* the action. Similarly, none of the other white male characters in the novel take the lead in anything other than their own culpability. Duncan Heyward never understands that the methods of white warfare will not work in the wilderness; Colonel Munro's and Montcalm's blindness to the realities of "honor" (whether white or red) brings destruction; David Gamut's belief in the goodness of men is both facetious and ironic. Hollywood has consistently portrayed these impotent Europeans in their true light in all of the film versions of *The Last of the Mohicans*, but scriptwriters and directors continue to misrepresent Hawk-eye and the Native Americans in the tale.

Even the two heroines in the tale surface on film as the opposite of what Cooper intended them to represent. It is Cora Munro, the dark-haired sister to the fair-haired Alice, that Cooper intends to fall in love with Uncas. By using Cora, the product of two races, not Alice, as the love interest of Uncas (and in an even more aberrant moment, of Magua), Cooper intensifies the tragic consequences of their fatal attraction and heightens the importance of Uncas's responsibilities towards his hereditary responsibilities and customs. While the Hollywood of the 1930s could not have portrayed on celluloid such an interracial relationship, the Hollywood of the 1990s certainly could write into the script such a match. To pair Hawk-eye with either woman or to match Uncas with the fair-haired Alice, as Hollywood filmmakers continue to do, is to misunderstand the very essence of Cooper's theme in *The Last of the Mohicans*. Cooper did not condone interracial relationships; his attitude toward interracial marriage was pragmatic. In his *Notions of the Americans* (1828), he explained that "As there is little reluctance to mingle the white and red blood . . . I think an amalgamation of the two races would in time occur. Those families of America who are thought to have any of the Indian blood, are rather proud of their descent; and it is a matter of boast among many of the most considerable persons of Virginia, that they are descended from the renowned Pocahontas" (490). For Cooper, neither interracial marriage (the proposed match of Uncas and Cora) nor miscegenation (Colonel Munro and his mixed blood mistress) was a racial judgment, but instead a plot device.

As a plot device, the suggestion of interracial marriage or miscegenation raises important issues in the novel on a number of levels. As a product of an "unnatural union" (her mother was "the daughter of a gentleman of those isles, by a lady, whose misfortune it was, if you will . . . to be descended, remotely, from that unfortunate class, who are so basely enslaved to administer to the wants of a luxurious people!"), Cora herself is tainted. Yet it is Cora who anticipates a marriage with a red man, and it is Cora who is the object of both the lust and protection of Magua. As a tainted woman, however, Cora also is the only character in the novel who represents Christian forgiveness. As Robert Milder reminds us, she "pardons Magua for his obscene proposal to her and his malignant ferocity with a Christ-like 'he knows not what he does,' . . . and in the trial scene . . . she is cast in the role of the eloquent advocate for mercy, Shakespeare's Portia" (426–27). Milder concludes that "Cora's history establishes her as a symbol for the injustice done the Negro," and "she is made to embody both the problem itself and the potential solution to the problem . . . As the product and victim of racial injustice Cora represents the sufferings of the Negro in the New World; as the most eloquent and admirable Christian in the book she offers a principle of reconciliation founded upon the equality of souls before God" (427–28). Everyone loves her: Magua, Uncas, Alice, Colonel Munro, and Duncan Hayward, ironically a southerner himself. It is unusual in another sense that Hollywood has not grasped the significance of Cooper's treatment of Cora and developed her role in their versions of *The Last of the Mohicans* as something more than the love interest of Hawkeye, who in the novel admires her also, but certainly is not in love with her.

Hollywood has seldom missed an opportunity to tell a story on film about interracial relationships, independent men and women, Native Americans, and the historical truth behind the real violence that generated American culture. They missed it this time, however. Filmmakers should follow D. H. Lawrence's advice for readers in regard to Cooper, and trust the (text of the) tale, not the (misunderstood reputation of its) teller (2). Although *The Last of the Mohicans* seems a natural choice for the wide screen, at least by those who believe that Fenimore Cooper was a writer of children's frontier adventure stories, it is a tale, however, with a far more profound significance than Hollywood has given it in any of its superficial film interpretations. None of them are accurate representations of Cooper's novel. Hollywood has regrettably conducted its own campaign against historical and textual veracity and committed its own set of literary offenses. In their versions of *The Last of the Mohicans*, filmmakers have rewritten Cooper's plot, miscast and mislabeled his characters, modernized his dialogue, misunderstood his themes, and misrepresented history. As Mark Twain himself would have to confess, "Counting these out, what is left is Art. I think we must all admit that" (12).

**Source:** Jeffrey Walker, "Deconstructing an American Myth: Hollywood and *The Last of the Mohicans*," in *Film & History*, Vol. 23, No. 1–4, 1993, pp. 103–16.

## SOURCES

Barker, Martin, "First and Last Mohicans," in *Sight and Sound*, Vol. 3, No. 8, August 1993, pp. 26–29.

Bird, S. Elizabeth, "Savage Desires: The Gendered Construction of the American Indian in Popular Myth," in *Selling the Indian: Commercializing and Appropriating American Indian Cultures*, edited by Carter Jones Meyer and Diana Royer, University of Arizona Press, 2001, pp. 62–98.

Buscombe, Edward, *"Injuns!" Native Americans in the Movies*, Reaktion Books, 2006.

Cooper, James Fenimore, *The Last of the Mohicans*, Penguin Books, 1986.

Edgerton, Gary, "'A Breed Apart': Hollywood, Racial Stereotyping, and the Promise of Revisionism in *The Last of the Mohicans*," in *Journal of American Culture*, Vol. 17, No. 2, Summer 1994, pp. 1–20.

Kilpatrick, Jacquelyn, "Keeping the Carcass in Motion: Adaptation and Transmutations of the National in *The Last of the Mohicans*," in *Literature and Film: A Guide to the Theory and Practice of Film Adaptation*, edited by Robert Stam and Alessandra Raengo, Blackwell, 2005, pp. 71–85.

Maslin, Janet, Review of *The Last of the Mohicans* (1992), in *New York Times*, September 25, 1992.

Review of *The Last of the Mohicans*, in *Rolling Stone*, http://www.rollingstone.com/reviews/movie/5947353/review/5947354/the_last_of_the_mohicans (accessed August 20, 2009).

Slotkin, Richard, Introduction to *The Last of the Mohicans*, by James Fenimore Cooper, Penguin Books, 1986.

Twain, Mark, "Fenimore Cooper's Literary Offenses," in *North American Review*, Vol. 161, 1895, pp. 1–12.

Walker, Jeffrey, "Deconstructing an American Myth: *The Last of the Mohicans*," in *Hollywood's Indian: The Portrayal of the Native American in Film*, edited by Peter C. Rollins and John E. O'Connor, University Press of Kentucky, 1998, pp. 170–87.

# The Learning Tree

**GORDON PARKS**

**1963**

*The Learning Tree* is a 1963 novel about an African American family, the Wingers, living in rural Kansas in the 1920s. The book is centered on the experiences of Newt Winger, the youngest son, a young man who wants to go to college and achieve great things, even though he is told to expect his life to amount to little. Over the course of three years, Newt has his first experiences with death, sex, love, and terror. He sees cruelty and compassion, and he witnesses more violent events than readers would think possible. The racial divide that was so much a part of American life at the time is not prominent in all of the sorrows and joys that these characters experience, but it is always an element in the Wingers' lives.

Newt Winger's story is based on the life of the novel's author, Gordon Parks, who grew up under very similar circumstances. By the time the book was published, Parks had become the artistic success that Newt dreams about, having become an award-winning photographer and professional musician. When *The Learning Tree*, his first published novel, was made into a movie in 1968, Parks wrote the screenplay himself, composed the soundtrack, and directed it, becoming the first African American to direct a major Hollywood movie.

*Gordon Parks* (AP Images)

## AUTHOR BIOGRAPHY

Gordon Roger Alexander Buchanan Parks was born on November 30, 1912, in Fort Scott, Kansas. He was the youngest of fifteen children. His father was a tenant farmer. When his mother died in 1928, Parks went to live with his sister in St. Paul, Minnesota, but his brother-in-law soon forced him to leave, and he was on his own at age sixteen. He slept in railroad cars and attended school briefly before dropping out, then worked several menial jobs, such as waiter and busboy. Those jobs introduced him to musicians, and Parks taught himself to play the piano. He worked as a musician in a brothel and then toured with a dance band, which broke up in New York City in 1933. There, Parks worked for the government in the Civilian Conservation Corps.

In 1933, he married Sally Alvis and moved to Minnesota, where they raised three children. Parks worked as a railroad porter, and on a stop in Chicago he visited the Art Institute and developed an interest in photography. He bought a camera and moved his family to Chicago, eventually making a name for himself as a photographer. In 1941, he won a Julius Rosenwald fellowship for his photography.

Parks worked as a photographer for a few government agencies until, in 1948, he was hired as a staff photographer by *Life* magazine, starting a relationship with the magazine that would continue over the next twenty-four years.

In the 1950s, Parks became involved in film and television production. He divorced Sally in 1961 and married Elizabeth Campbell the next year; the couple stayed together for eleven years and had one child, Leslie. Parks published a few books about photographic technique, then in 1963 he published his first novel, *The Learning Tree*. His next book, *A Choice of Weapons* (1966), was the first of three autobiographies.

In 1968, Parks wrote and produced the movie version of *The Learning Tree*. Three years later, however, he became internationally famous as the director of *Shaft* (1971), a detective movie that ushered in an era of black filmmaking. He followed it up the next year with *Shaft's Big Score* (1972), a sequel that he admitted he did in order to work with a big studio budget. Around the same time, his son, Gordon Parks, Jr., directed *Super Fly*, which is another of the most famous entries in the Black Exploitation, or "Blaxploitation," film genre of the 1970s.

Parks directed a few more films, including *The Super Cops* in 1974 and *Leadbelly*, a biography of blues guitar legend Huddie Ledbetter, in 1976. His third marriage was to Genevieve Young, from 1973 to 1979. Parks was awarded the National Medal of Arts by President George Bush in 1988. In 1989, *The Learning Tree* was included with twenty-four other films to be preserved in the National Film Registry by the U.S. Library of Congress.

Parks died of cancer in New York City on March 7, 2006.

## PLOT SUMMARY

### Chapter 1
*The Learning Tree* takes place in the small Kansas town of Cherokee Flats in 1925. The first chapter opens with the novel's protagonist, twelve-year-old Newt Winger, examining ants in a cornfield. He is so engrossed in his work that he does not notice a cyclone approaching.

# MEDIA ADAPTATIONS

- The film version of *The Learning Tree* was directed by Parks, the novel's author, who also produced the movie, wrote the screenplay, and wrote its musical score. The film had the distinction of being the first major studio motion picture to be directed by an African American, and it was placed on the National Film Registry of the U.S. Library of Congress in 1989. Starring Kyle Johnson and Alex Clarke, the movie was released in 1969. Warner Home Video released *The Learning Tree* on VHS in 1994.

- In 2000, HBO produced a comprehensive biographical look at the life of Parks. The documentary *Half Past Autumn: The Life and Works of Gordon Parks* is narrated by Alfre Woodard. It is available on DVD from HBO Home Video.

Big Mabel, a local girl, alerts him just as the storm strikes, and they find refuge in a neighbor's shed, where, huddled with Mabel for warmth, Newt has his first sexual experience. Returning home after the storm, Newt finds that a neighbor's house has collapsed and killed the neighbor. That night, Reverend Broadnap visits the Winger home as he is traveling around the town, and Newt resents the food that is taken from his dinner to feed the reverend.

## Chapter 2

Newt's father, Jack Winger, helps stabilize a church steeple that was damaged by the cyclone. While he is up there, he looks out over the town, seeing his son-in-law Clint going into Chappie's bar with Doc Cheney. He sends Newt over to the bar to help the drunken Clint home. At the home of Judge Cavanaugh, where she works as a housekeeper for this white family, Newt's mother, Sarah, finds the judge's oldest son, Chauncey, in bed with a girl and insists that he get her out before his father finds her there. Later, the family is told

that Jack has gone to the hospital. Thinking that he has been injured in the steeple reconstruction, they race to his side, only to find that he has volunteered to participate in a skin graft for a girl whose mother accidently burned her. Later, an inebriated Clint chases his wife, Rende, back to the Wingers' home, threatening to shoot her, but Sarah slaps his face and forces him to give up his gun.

## Chapter 3

The chapter opens depicting a church service presided over by Reverend Broadnap. After church, Newt and his friends go swimming in the river, then they go to Jake Kiner's orchard to steal peaches. Kiner comes out and chases them with a whip, but the biggest of the group, Marcus Savage, beats Kiner up. Newt tells Marcus that he is not going to lie to the police about what he saw, making an enemy of him. He does tell the police that Marcus was the one who beat the old man. Newt's parents make him go to Kiner and apologize, and the old man accepts the apology but says that he will have to work off his debt to him. Marcus, unrepentant, is sentenced to a year in reform school.

A week later, Newt sees the local policeman, Kirky, sneaking up on an illegal dice game that Clint and Doc Cheney are playing. He warns them, but Kirky shoots Doc Cheney for running away. Cheney's body falls in the river and is lost. The police hire Newt and his friends to dive in the river to find the body. The sight of Cheney's floating corpse haunts Newt at night. As he contemplates the meaning of death, he cannot sleep until he throws the money he was paid out the door.

## Chapter 4

Newt and his friends go to the ballpark, where they pay a man named Cap'n Tuck to alert them when they can see up the dress of a woman seated in the bleachers. That night, Tuck takes the money he has earned at the ball game to the bar, where he and Big Mabel get drunk. They steal a car, and, trying to outrun the police, they crash and are both killed. When Newt is passing by Mottsy's Funeral Parlor, two boys who live there lock him in with the corpses of Tuck and Mabel, and he passes out.

## Chapter 5

Newt works with his blind uncle, Rob, selling brooms door-to-door. At one home a boy calls to his mother that a "nigger" is at the door selling brooms, and Newt becomes so enraged that he pushes his way in and punches the boy. The boy's mother comes out and shouts the same insult at him. Later, walking Uncle Rob home, Newt tells him about the incident, and Uncle Rob decides that they had all acted badly.

On September 13 of that year, a calf is born. Since it is Newt's thirteenth birthday, his father presents the calf to him as a present.

Newt's mother takes him with her to Judge Cavanaugh's house. Newt is friends with the judge's youngest son, Rodney, who has scientific instruments and displays and talks to him about scientific principles, piquing Newt's interests. In the next room, they hear Rodney's older brother Chauncey arguing with his father.

At Spit's School for Wayward Boys, Marcus Savage is sentenced to shoveling snow. He hits the guard with the shovel and runs away, but after getting lost in the snow, he turns himself in and is sentenced to solitary confinement.

## Chapter 6

At the start of Christmas break, Newt starts dating Arcella Jefferson. On the way home from her house one night he runs into his sister Rende with her two children; they are running from Clint, who is drunk. Once again, his mother slaps Clint and takes his gun from him.

## Chapter 7

On Christmas morning, the Wingers exchange their presents. Arcella comes over with a gift for Newt, a book of short stories, and Newt gives her a locket. At the reform school, Marcus receives a card from the boys back home. Reverend Broadnap and a few of the church people from home come to see him, but he is embarrassed because the white guard, Charlie Crapper, is watching them, so he becomes violent and throws them out, tossing his card from the boys back home onto the floor.

## Chapter 8

The newspaper reports that the public high school will not be accepting any black freshmen in the coming year because of budget constraints. Newt has been looking forward to being able to use the resources at the high school, since the facilities at the school provided for black students are practically nonexistent. His mother contacts other parents to form the Negro Parent-Teacher Association to block the move, even though some of the black educators fear that supporting the association might cost them their jobs. At a public meeting in April, Sarah Winger stands up and presents the position of the parents of the black students, and her husband Jack stands up to support her.

Marcus Savage is brought home from the reformatory to live in the dilapidated shack that he shares with his violent, drunkard father, Booker.

## Chapter 9

Newt is chosen to present the graduation speech at his grammar school. One day he and the other boys run into Marcus, who is still angry at them. Just before a fight starts, Newt's older brother Pete approaches. When the other boys leave, Pete suggests that Marcus should look for a job, and he says that he will put in a word with Chappie Logan, who owns a bar. Marcus goes to Chappie as soon as Pete leaves the bar, and he is hired.

Pete gives Newt boxing lessons to learn to support himself.

At the graduation ceremony it is announced that the Negro Parent-Teacher Association has been successful, and the graduates will move on to the white high school. Newt gives a successful graduation speech. Afterword, his brother Pete gives him money to take Arcella out for ice cream. The ice cream parlor is crowded, and Newt is uncomfortable. The man behind the counter assumes without asking that he wants his order to go, and Newt agrees, but on the way out his friend Waldo Newhall invites Newt and Arcella to join their table. They do so hesitantly, but then the manager comes and tells them they must leave because they are black.

## Chapter 10

Newt's light-skinned cousin Polly comes to visit around the Fourth of July.

At the carnival that comes to town for the holiday, Newt and his friends decide to participate in a free-for-all fight, during which ten participants begin and the last two standing in the ring win prize money. They decide to arrange things so that they will win without any danger, but at the last minute Marcus Savage joins the competition. As the crowd shouts racist curses at them, the fight comes down to Newt and Marcus. Newt wins, making Marcus, who has always been the strongest of the group, hate him more.

Newt is so humiliated at the way the mob treated the black men like fighting animals that he gives up the money he has won.

One day when he is walking with his cousin Polly, Newt is attacked by some white boys who object to seeing an interracial couple. Before he is beaten up, Waldo Newhall comes to his rescue. That night Newt's mother tells Polly that it might be a bad idea for her to spend the summer with the family, that racial tensions are too high. After discussing the situation with her niece, Sarah collapses into a chair, claiming to have a dizzy spell, although later in the novel a serious heart condition develops.

## Chapter 11

While walking with Newt, Arcella comments on how handsome Chauncey Cavanaugh is, making Newt jealous. Soon after that, Newt finds himself falling into trouble at his new high school. He has an argument with his English teacher and guidance counselor, Miss McClintock, who tells him to forget training for college because a black man like him would not be able to go to college anyway. When he argues with her, he is given after-school detention and is not able to walk Arcella home for a few days. After that, Arcella becomes ill and stops going to school.

Newt tells his mother what Miss McClintock had told him, and his mother goes to talk to the school's principal, Mr. Hall. Mr. Hall talks to Newt and tells him that there is some truth to what Miss McClintock said, but that she was born in a different generation and times are changing.

Newt stops at Arcella's house, and she will not say what is wrong with her. He knows that they are drifting apart, though he does not know why.

## Chapter 12

Newt continues to drop off Arcella's homework, but she will not speak to him. One day Newt's father meets him at the door and tells him that Arcella's parents were over to see him, and that Arcella is pregnant. Newt denies being the father. Arcella admits that the father is Chauncey Cavanaugh. Later, Newt takes a Christmas present over to the Jefferson house and finds that Arcella and her parents and all of their furniture are gone. Judge Cavanaugh comes to visit Sarah, who is sick, and tells her that he will make Chauncey work to pay for the baby, but a few days later Chauncey runs away from town.

## Chapter 13

In spring, Newt begins working for Jake Kiner on his farm. Kiner has also hired Silas Newhall, a disreputable drunkard and the father of Newt's friend Waldo. One day Silas shows up drunk, and Kiner has to fire him. Later, Newt runs into Silas coming out of Chappie's bar, and Silas insists that he will get his pay for that day.

## Chapter 14

When Kiner goes out of town one morning, Newt slips up to the loft in the barn to take a nap. He is awakened by the sound of Booker Savage breaking into the storeroom. Kiner and Silas enter, arguing over the back wages, and they fight. When Silas is knocked out, Savage and Kiner fight, and Kiner is killed. Savage leaves the murder weapon in Silas's hand.

When he hears his father questioned by the police, Marcus Savage comes to suspect that his father is responsible for the attack on Jake Kiner. Booker admits that he is, but he swears Marcus to secrecy. Though Marcus hates his father, he hates the legal system more, so he stays quiet.

## Chapter 15

As Silas Newhall's trial approaches, Newt feels torn about not telling anybody what he had seen that day, but he fears that if the locals found out that Savage, a black man, killed the white Kiner, there would be trouble for all of the black people in the town. Eventually Newt tells his parents, who make him tell the judge. The judge has him talk to the prosecuting attorney, and they are all amazed when the prosecutor closes his case without mentioning this eyewitness. The Wingers talk to the defense attorney, who brings this new evidence up in the trial. On his way to the stand, Booker Savage grabs a policeman's gun and runs into a locked room, where, finding himself trapped, he kills himself.

## Chapter 16

Fearing what Marcus might do for revenge, Newt stays near home, but when his friend Earl Thompson stops by in his father's car, he agrees to go to a nearby town to pick up a saddle with him. On the way back, Earl does not want to stop at the railroad crossing because the car is running out of gas. It stalls on the tracks and the two boys jump out, but in the ensuing wreck Earl loses his foot.

Sarah Winger's heart condition has worsened, and her grown children—Roy, Clara, and

Lucille—have come to town to be with her. Clint talks with Roy, who lives in Chicago, about how much he would like to travel the world, and how his wife Rende and their children are holding him back.

### Chapter 17

Clint becomes drunk and chases Rende to the Winger house with a shotgun. With his wife bedridden, Jack Winger tries to face Clint, who nearly shoots him. When the police arrive, they are determined to kill Clint, who is hiding in the cornfield in the dark, but Sarah insists on being brought out in the rain to face him. Clint surrenders to his mother-in-law, as always. The excitement is too much for Sarah, however, and the next day she is dead.

### Chapter 18

To overcome his fear of death, Newt spends the night in the parlor with his mother's casket, and he wakes in the morning feeling peaceful. After the funeral, he packs to go and live with his sister Clara. He arranges to meet his friends at the river for one last swim.

Marcus steals money and a gun from Chappie and goes to take his revenge on Newt. His first shot hits one of the other boys in the leg, and then the gun jams. He attacks Newt with a knife, but Newt is not afraid anymore. When the police show up, Marcus runs for the river. Instead of diving, as he has before, he slips and falls onto the rocks and is killed.

## CHARACTERS

### Polly Bates

Polly is Newt's light-skinned cousin, whose father was the son of a Georgia plantation owner and his black servant. After the death of Newt's aunt, Polly's father, who is lightskinned, remarried to a white woman, and he wants to raise Polly in white society, although the girl does not feel comfortable among whites. When she comes to stay with the Winger family for the summer, the people in the town cast disapproving looks, thinking that she is a white girl socializing with black people. After Newt is attacked by white kids when he is walking with her, Sarah Winger tells her niece that it would be best if she left.

### Big Mabel

Big Mabel is five years older than Newt. She rescues him when a cyclone catches him unprepared out in a field, and he has his first sexual experience with her. She is drinking with Cap'n Tuck when he decides to steal a car, and Mabel dies with him in the ensuing crash.

### Reverend Lucius Broadnap

When he is first introduced into the story, Reverend Broadnap is presented as a greedy character, lustily helping himself to a meal at the Winger house. In subsequent chapters, however, he proves to be a leader of his congregation. He brings the community together after the ravages of the cyclone, and he is instrumental in leading the Negro Parent-Teacher Association in its drive to keep black freshmen at the high school. He also leads some parishioners to visit Marcus Savage at a school far from Cherokee Flats on Christmas Day.

### Chauncey Cavanaugh

The eldest son of the town's judge, Chauncey is a playboy. He is caught by Sarah with a girl who has stayed overnight in his room, though she helps him hide the girl from his father. After he is found to be the father of Arcella's child, Chauncey runs away from town instead of facing his responsibilities.

### Judge Jefferson Cavanaugh

Newt's mother works as a housekeeper for Judge Cavanaugh. Despite the divisions between the races in Kansas in the 1920s, he visits Sarah when she is ill. In court cases, Judge Cavanaugh proves to be temperate. He sentences Marcus Savage to juvenile detention with great regret, and he tries to keep firm control on the sensationalistic trial of Silas Newhall. Once Booker Savage is accused and commits suicide, Judge Cavanaugh admonishes the whites in the courtroom who called for the black murderer's death, saying that they are as guilty as the murderer.

### Rodney Cavanaugh

Rodney is a friend of Newt. They have a mutual interest in science. He is Judge Cavanaugh's younger son. Being from a wealthy family, Rodney has tools, such as a microscope and preserved butterflies, that he uses to explain scientific principles.

### Doc Cheney

The black doctor in Cherokee Flats is a hopeless alcoholic. The town policeman shoots him when he is fleeing an illegal poker game, and Newt and his friends are hired to find his body in the river.

### Clara

Clara, Newt's older sister, lives in Minnesota. She is the more aggressive and opinionated sister, frequently giving Newt orders about how he should live his life. At the end of the novel, Newt is set to go and live with Clara.

### Clint

Clint is married to Newt's sister Rende. He loves his wife and children when he is sober, but Clint tends to drink too much. When he is drunk, he becomes resentful because he has never been able to travel the world as he wants to, and he becomes violent against Rende. When he threatens to shoot her, the only person who can stop him is his mother-in-law, Sarah.

### Charlie Crapper

Crapper is the guard at Spit's School for Wayward Boys. He goads Marcus into fights and then beats him with a club.

### Doctor Timothy Cravens

Doc Cravens is a white man who was raised by Jack and Sarah Winger after his father died and his mother ran away. He went away to school, but he came back to Cherokee Flats after becoming a doctor. Doc Cravens is thirty-five when the novel begins and is dedicated to his profession, and so has no family life.

### Harley Davis

Davis is a young lawyer who defends Silas Newhall. He is inexperienced, but he believes in Silas's innocence.

### Jappy Duncan

Jappy is one of Newt's friends.

### Beansy Fuller

Beansy is Newt's best friend. He the opposite of Newt—his intelligence is limited, and he is unathletic. Still, they spend their summer days together, and Beansy is one person that Newt can talk to about his troubles.

### Arcella Jefferson

Newt notices Arcella when she moves to town, and he shyly asks her out. They become boyfriend and girlfriend. She rejects his sexual advances because she is afraid of the consequences, but later she becomes pregnant by Chauncey Cavanaugh, a white playboy.

### Jake Kiner

Jake owns a nearby farm. When he catches Newt and his friends stealing peaches from his orchard, he comes at them with a whip, but Marcus Savage takes the whip away and brutally beats Jake. Jake forgives the other boys, though he continues to act stern. Years later, he lets Newt come to work on his farm. He also hires Silas Newhall, when everyone else says that Silas is a worthless drunk, but he is also strict enough to fire Silas when he shows up for work inebriated. Jake is murdered by Booker Savage while he is in the middle of an argument with Silas.

### Jason Kirky

Kirky is the town's police officer. He can be cruel toward the black citizens, as when he chases Doc Cheney from a card game and then shoots him to death because he will not stop. Though he often acts callous and racist, he has enough respect for the Wingers to hold off killing Clint when Sarah tells him that she can handle the drunken man.

### Chappie Logan

Chappie is a huge man who owns the bar in town where the worst elements of society gather. When Marcus goes to work for him, he learns that Chappie has an exotic past: he was once in the circus, and he has signed pictures from performers who remember him fondly.

### Lucille

Lucille is one of Newt's older sisters who lives away from Cherokee Flats. Lucille, also called Lou, lives near her sister Clara in Minneapolis. She is the more easygoing sister, but Newt would not want to live with her because she is too religious.

### Miss McClintock

Miss McClintock is the school guidance counselor who tells Newt that it he should not study for college because the odds of a black person getting admitted to college or being able to pay for it are so slim.

### Stewart McCormack

McCormack is the prosecutor in the Silas Newhall trial. Newt tells him of seeing Booker Savage commit the murder, but McCormack suppresses the information and goes on with the prosecution of an innocent man, probably to avoid the racial conflict that might erupt over a black person killing a white person.

### Skunk McDowell

Skunk is one of Newt's friends.

### Silas Newhall

Silas is a hopeless alcoholic with two decent children. No one in town will hire him until he asks for a job from Jake Kiner, but then Jake has to fire him when he shows up drunk for work. When he is accused of killing Jake, he is in such an alcoholic stupor that he cannot say for certain that he did not.

### Waldo Newhall

Waldo, who is white, is one of Newt's friends. When Newt is being attacked for walking with Polly, who looks white, Waldo steps in and fights on Newt's side. After graduation, when the ice cream shop is full of white people, Waldo invites Newt and Arcella to sit with him. Waldo's father goes on trial for a murder that Newt knows he did not commit, making Newt suffer terrible guilt.

### Rende

Rende is Newt's older sister. She does not live in the Winger house; she lives with her husband, Clint, and their two small children. When Clint reaches a certain point of drunkenness, he threatens Rende's life, and the only security she can find is to run off to her parents' home. Throughout the course of the novel, Rende becomes pregnant and gives birth to a third child.

### Booker Savage

Booker is the father of Marcus Savage. He makes very little money running a junkyard, and what he does make he spends on liquor. He kills Jake Kiner while stealing from him, and he almost escapes punishment. When he is accused, Booker steals the sheriff's gun and escapes, but the room he has run into is locked, so he kills himself.

### Marcus Savage

Marcus is presented in the book as Newt Winger's opposite. While Newt was raised in a loving and supporting family, Marcus was raised by a bitter, alcoholic father. Marcus's one claim is that he has grown faster than the other boys and is clearly stronger than them. They are just children when he beats Jake Kiner and puts him in the hospital, and when he is tried for his crime he is contemptuous and unremorseful. His self-esteem suffers greatly when Newt beats him in the carnival boxing match. In the end, the rage that builds up inside Marcus makes him go after Newt with a gun and then with a knife, and he dies trying to escape the law.

### Earl Thompson

Earl is one of Newt's friends. When they are a little older, he drives the family car on an errand. The car is hit by a train, and Earl loses his foot. In the hospital, he is able to joke about his loss.

### Cap'n Tuck

Cap'n Tuck hangs around under the bleachers at the baseball stadium. When he finds that he can see up a girl's skirt, he brings boys to look, for a fee. While drinking with Big Mabel, he steals Chauncey Cavanaugh's car, and, trying to outrace the police, crashes the car and dies.

### Jack Winger

Newt's father, Jack Winger, is a quiet man who is not inclined toward talking about his feelings. The book establishes his steadfast morality early when he volunteers his own skin to help out a young burn victim in need of a transplant. He tries to be harsh, to raise Newt to be tough in a tough world, but Jack knows more about what his son is going through than he is ever willing to say. In a scene at the end of the book, after his wife's death, Jack looks at his sleeping son and understands why the boy sleeps beside the casket of his mother. He knows that he cannot raise Newt and sends him away to live with his sister, but Jack clearly loves his son.

### Newt Winger

Newt Winger is the protagonist of this story. He is twelve at the beginning of the book and nearly fifteen when it ends. In that time, the events that transpire bring him into adulthood. He has his first sexual experience with Big Mabel, and he encounters death face-to-face when he is hired to find the body of Doc Cheney in the river. He falls in love with Arcella Jefferson and then loses her when she becomes pregnant with another man's child. He experiences racial prejudice, both implied and overt.

Even though there are many social factors that are pressuring Newt to fail, he continues to believe in himself. Much of the credit for this is due to the stable family environment that he has been raised in. His father feels that his intellectual ambitions are too high and will never be attainable for a black man, but he does nothing to stop Newt and, in fact, stands up for his education when the high school tries to keep black freshmen from enrolling. Newt's mother encourages Newt wholeheartedly in his studies. His older brother Pete teaches him to defend himself by fighting, and his older sister Prissy jokes with him, keeping his ego in check.

After the death of his mother, Newt learns to face his fears. He faces his adversary, Marcus Savage, who has always intimidated him. When Marcus dies, Newt is ready to leave Cherokee Flats, the only town he has ever known, and go out to explore the wide world.

### Pete Winger

Newt's older brother Pete is a war veteran, and he has felt the unfair force of discrimination in Cherokee Flats. He works only when work is available. His preferred work seems to be as a cowboy: He is hired to ride cattle to market, and he makes extra money competing in the rodeo.

### Prissy Winger

Newt's older sister Priscilla is his good-natured antagonist. She lives to catch him doing what he should not be doing and to tell their parents so that he can get in trouble.

### Rob Winger

Newt's uncle on his father's side is blind, having been near an exploding bomb twenty-five years earlier. He lost some fingers in the same unexplained event. He sells brooms door-to-door for a living, sometimes with Newt's help.

### Roy Winger

Roy is Newt's older brother who lives in Chicago. He returns at the end of the novel when their mother is dying, spinning tall tales about life in the big city.

### Sarah Winger

Newt learns empathy from his mother. She is a force of righteousness. This is shown when several times in the book Clint is wildly drunk and threatening to kill his wife, Newt's sister, but Sarah is able to speak directly and cut through

his drunken insanity. When Newt has a problem, such as the school guidance counselor belittling his ability because he is black or the murder he witnessed, he eventually brings it to his mother, because he knows that she will be morally correct. Sarah is respected by the white people in the town, such as Judge Cavanaugh and Doctor Cravens, because they remember favors that she has done for them over the years.

## THEMES

### Coming of Age

*The Learning Tree* is often referred to as a coming-of-age novel because it depicts major events in the life of the protagonist, Newt Winger. These events change the way the twelve-year-old boy views the world. This theme is established in the very first chapter, in which Newt has his first sexual encounter, an experience that in itself has been the basis for numerous coming-of-age stories. As the novel progresses, Newt falls in love, encounters his first dead human, takes his first job, stands up to a bully, testifies at a trial because he believes it is the right thing to do, lives through the death of his mother, and moves away from the only home he has ever known. These are all standard events in the coming-of-age tradition. They are events that authors use to push an immature character into a mature point of view. As a result of his experiences, Newt is no longer the boy that he was at the beginning of the story, idly gazing at ants and wondering about the world around him. He grows into the decisive man of action that he is at the story's end.

### Death

Newt's emerging understanding of death is a running theme throughout *The Learning Tree*. Parks introduces the theme of death in the first chapter, when Newt's sense of triumph at having survived the cyclone and having had his first sexual experience comes to an abrupt halt with the discovery that a neighbor has been crushed to death under the debris of his house. This theme continues through chapter 3, wherein Newt lightheartedly accepts the job of diving for Doc Cheney's body but finds that the sight of it haunts his dreams. The theme of death is pushed even further in chapter 4, when the Mottsy boys lock Newt in a room with the bodies of Big Mabel and Cap'n

# TOPICS FOR FURTHER STUDY

- Research modern methods of handling juvenile offenders like Marcus Savage. Write up a treatment program for him that would be more conducive to his rehabilitation than the novel's depiction of having him thrown into Spit's School for Boys.

- Conduct a trial for Silas Newhall. Instead of resolving the issue with testimony from an eyewitness, emphasize the fact, which is mentioned in the book but not used, that Silas is left-handed but the murderer appears to be right-handed. Both prosecution and defense should use illustrations and/or models to support their cases.

- Throughout the book, Marcus has a vendetta against Newt. Imagine that they live in the twenty-first century, and that they have computers. Write the correspondences between the two boys on e-mail or Twitter.

- Newt's blind uncle describes the exotic colors that he likes to imagine for people. Create pictures of members of the Winger family as they might appear in Uncle Rob's mind, and write a brief explanation about why he would have given them the characteristics that you gave them.

- Read *Elijah of Buxton* (2007), by Christopher Paul Curtis, concerning a boy raised on an Ontario, Canada, settlement for escaped slaves in the 1840s. Prepare a PowerPoint presentation for your class that compares and contrasts what it was like to be a black person living outside of the United States during slavery and what it was like to be a black person living in the United States during the Jim Crow era of the 1920s.

---

Tuck. When the boys turn out the lights, Newt is so overcome with emotion that he passes out.

Parks resolves Newt's fear of death at the end of the book, when Newt makes the decision to spend a night in the room with his mother's casket. By willingly facing his fear of death, he is freed, so that after the funeral he is calm and assures his father that everything will be all right in the future.

## Race

Race plays an important role in the lives of the characters in this book. Entire episodes that are central to the plot show dramatically the ways in which black people are treated as second-class citizens in this rural Kansas community. When Doc Cheney is shot by a white policeman, for instance, there is no inquiry about whether the shooting was warranted: a white law officer is allowed to do whatever he wants to do to a black suspect, and no one from either side of the race spectrum would question his judgment. Later, Newt knows that Booker Savage, a black man, is the true murderer of Jake Kiner, a white man, but he holds back telling what he knows for fear that the news of a black-on-white crime will unleash a wave of white vigilante violence against the innocent black people of the town.

The book is filled with examples of racial inequality. For one thing, it is the black students who are made to suffer when budget constraints affect the high school: they are forced to continue their schooling in the all-black school, which has much worse facilities and fewer learning materials. Newt and his cousin Polly are attacked in broad daylight for walking down the street together because their attackers cannot accept the idea of a black person walking side by side with a person who appears to be white. Newt's guidance counselor, Miss McClintock, tells Newt not to waste his time with college because he will only be eligible for menial jobs anyway. Principal Hall explains that her ideas are from an earlier generation, but that they are also based in reality; he tells a story about seeing the valedictorian of his college class working as a railroad porter. After graduation, Newt and Arcella are allowed to buy ice cream, but they are not allowed to sit in the ice cream parlor with their white friends. At the free-for-all at the carnival, Newt and his friends find out that the promoter has hired the black and Hispanic men to fight against each other for the entertainment of whites, who savagely shout for their blood. There are compassionate white people in this novel, such as Newt's friends Waldo and Rodney and Rodney's father, Judge Cavanaugh, but the social order is fixed to ensure that racial inequality will be continued.

*Scene from the 1968 film adaptation of the novel*
*(Winger / The Kobal Collection / The Picture Desk, Inc.)*

## STYLE

### Autobiographical Novel

Many of the details about Newt Winger's life correspond to details from the life of the novel's author. Parks was a young teenager in 1925, as is Newt; Parks was the youngest child of a large family, as is Newt; Parks grew up in a rural Kansas town, as Newt does; Parks left Kansas to live with his sister in Minnesota at the age of sixteen after his mother's death, as does Newt. Many of the details of Parks's early years are given in the first of his three autobiographies, *A Choice of Weapons*, which was published three years later, in 1966.

Although there are many ways in which the events of the novel resemble events from his life, Parks has used a free hand in crafting a story with dramatic elements to make it more interesting than the ordinary life. The novel starts with the excitement of a cyclone ripping through town and with Newt's first sexual experience, and in the following pages it keeps hitting readers with more and more exciting experiences. There are more adventures centering on the Winger family than would normally occur in one small town. The events of the novel might have each occurred

to different people, but Parks weaves them all together as the experiences of one family. Because this is a work of fiction, readers should not assume that these events actually happened, regardless of the ways in which Newt's life resembles the life of Parks.

### Courtroom Drama

Although most of this novel is about Newt Winger's life and his adventures, the book reaches a height of excitement while following a story that Newt is involved in only tangentially. The murder of Jake Kiner, in chapter 14, certainly affects the Winger family, because Newt is a silent witness to it and also because it has potentially devastating implications for all of the black citizens of Cherokee Flats. For most of chapter 15, however, Parks relegates Newt to the edges of the narration, instead focusing on the details of the trial of Silas Newhall.

The courtroom drama is a standard of popular entertainment. It is a situation that has inherent tension: for the writer, it allows the opportunity to systematically reveal hidden information about life-and-death matters. Although chapter 15 reveals much about Newt's thoughts, it also follows the procedure in the courtroom: the swearing in of witnesses, the questioning, the introduction of evidence, and the arguments that the lawyers make for their respective cases. All of this culminates with the guilty party being revealed and, in this particular case, killing himself. The novel's readers have information presented to them, just as the jury in a trial does, with the key difference that the readers know from the previous chapter which character is really guilty of the crime.

Although chapter 15 of *The Learning Tree* follows the tradition of the courtroom drama, Parks ends it with a twist that brings the focus off of the murder case and back to Newt's social situation. Racial tensions begin to flair before Judge Cavanaugh makes a speech that shames those who tried to turn things into a fight of whites against blacks. In this way, the brief diversion into courtroom drama gives way, and Newt's story is continued.

## HISTORICAL CONTEXT

Parks published *The Learning Tree* in 1963, in the midst of the social change that is referred to as the Civil Rights era. The following year would

# COMPARE & CONTRAST

- **1920s:** Many African Americans still live on farms. Like the Wingers, they are sharecroppers residing on land owned by white farmers.

  **1960s:** After the great migration of the early part of the century, millions of African Americans have moved from the farms of the South and are living in large cities of the North, creating crowded urban conditions and poverty.

  **Today:** As with most other demographic groups, large numbers of African Americans have moved from cities to live in the suburban and exurban areas that surround them.

- **1920s:** Laws and social traditions create limited potential jobs for minorities, so that a school guidance counselor, like the one in the novel, could be sincere in advising a black student to not bother going to college.

  **1960s:** Racial boundaries are broken down. James Meredith's enrollment at the University of Mississippi in 1962 marks a turning point in the fight against segregation.

  **Today:** College enrollment figures have declined for white students in recent decades, while enrollment figures for African Americans and other minorities have doubled.

- **1920s:** A police officer could shoot a black man in the back, as Kirky does to Doc Cheney in the book, and no one would ask any questions.

  **1960s:** During the racial turbulence of the 1960s, police violence against an unarmed black man could set off race riots that would spread from city to city.

  **Today:** Social groups are vigilant in watching for signs of racial injustice, addressing such events nonviolently with media attention and lawsuits.

- **1920s:** The sight of a light-skinned person living with her dark-skinned relatives is so shocking that she would have to move away to protect the safety of all, as is portrayed through the character of Newt's cousin, Polly.

  **1960s:** Interracial dating is still unusual. Although racial equality is often talked about, blacks and whites seldom interact socially.

  **Today:** The United States has become so comfortable with mixed marriages that a man of mixed black and white parentage is elected president in 2008.

---

see one of the greatest breakthroughs in the struggle for racial equality that the United States had ever encountered, the passage of the Civil Rights Act of 1964. The country had lived with laws that accepted and encouraged inequity throughout its entire history. After the Civil War ended in 1865, national politicians accepted laws that favored whites over blacks in an attempt to placate the slaveholding states that had seceded from the Union and to smooth over the differences that had led to the war. Though slavery was outlawed by the Thirteen Amendment, conditions for black citizens scarcely improved in the postwar period. Southern states passed a series of laws that amounted to legalized discrimination, referred to as Jim Crow laws, named after a buffoonish black character from a minstrel play. These laws were enacted to maintain the status quo and to avoid the social upheaval that was expected to occur if black citizens were allowed equal voting rights and rights of ownership that would allow them to compete fairly with whites. In effect, they froze the prevailing social order where it was when slavery ended. In 1896, in the case of *Plessy v. Ferguson*, the U.S. Supreme Court ruled that it was fair to offer black citizens different social services, with the assumption that all citizens would be offered relatively similar opportunities.

As Parks shows in the differences between the black high school and the white high school in the novel, this doctrine of "separate but equal" was very rarely fair when put into practice. For years, even in the northern states that had no tradition of slaveholding, black citizens were limited as to where they could buy houses or where they could live, and black students were kept out of the better-funded public schools. There were different areas for white hotels and white theaters that were separate from those areas designated for black hotels and theaters. In almost every case, when particular facilities were limited for use by black citizens, those facilities were either substandard to begin with or were left untended and allowed to fall into disrepair.

After World War II, concerted efforts were made to correct the blatant unfairness of race relations in the United States. In the 1950s, the Civil Rights movement began congealing, slowly winning legal and public relations battles that changed opinions about what was acceptable. In the legal case of *Brown v. the Board of Education of Topeka* in 1954, the Supreme Court overturned the principle of *Plessy v. Ferguson* and determined that the idea of "separate but equal" could never really be fair. The 1955 Montgomery bus boycott, led by Dr. Martin Luther King, Jr., became a celebrated cause throughout the land. In 1957, federal troops were sent to Little Rock, Arkansas, to defy the state's governor and ensure that the city's schools would be desegregated. By the start of the 1960s, young whites, mostly high school and college students, traveled to the South to join with African Americans in the fight against inequity.

By 1963, the year *The Learning Tree* was published, President John F. Kennedy had introduced a Civil Rights bill that would assure all citizens of the United States equal protection, fair voting standards, and legal recourse against job or housing discrimination. There was considerable opposition to the bill in southern states, but Kennedy's assassination in November 1963 made it politically difficult to fight against a cause that he had championed. Kennedy's successor, Lyndon Johnson, followed in the fight for equal rights, and the Civil Rights Act became law in 1964. Although one bill could not assure racial equality, this law did give black Americans the support of the national government whenever they were faced with systematic unfairness.

*Tornado wreckage* (*Image copyright Amy K. Planz, 2009. Used under license from Shutterstock.com*)

## CRITICAL OVERVIEW

When *The Learning Tree* was published in 1963, the United States was going through a period of heightened awareness about the country's racial divisions. Because of this, reviewers tended to put the book into a context of what it had to say about race. The book has often been acclaimed for what it adds to the discussion of race, even though reviewers have, from the beginning, looked at its storytelling as being less than admirable. For instance, David Dempsey, in his review for the *New York Times Book Review* upon the novel's initial publication, stated that "Color furnishes the plot devices of the story without predetermining the moral judgments," which he found to be a welcome difference from other, more preachy, race-oriented books, and he decided in the end that "The real value of the novel is in its insight into group mores. . . ." His overall decision about the writing, however, was that "[t]his is the sort of plot that you can take or leave alone, and my own inclination is to leave it alone." Writing in the *New Yorker*, Whitney Balliett found the reverse. The human story was what worked for Balliett, not the social commentary:

> When the book deals with the Wingers' home life, it is quiet reminiscence, and one wishes that Parks had fanned his story out from this dignified center instead of arranging it in a series of violent happenings that eventually make the Wingers seem overblown gods and goddesses.

While its initial critics faulted this novel for the sensationalistic elements in its plot structure, it has, nonetheless, remained in print. Part of its continuing appeal is due to the groundbreaking movie adaptation that was released six years after the book's publication. While the movie made no significant changes to the story, it has the historical distinction of being the first movie to be written, produced, directed, and scored by an African American. Critics have pointed to other books that have conveyed the experiences of blacks in rural America in the 1920s in more realistic ways, but the story that Parks tells is exciting and cinematic, and it has captured the imaginations of generations of readers.

## CRITICISM

### David Kelly

*Kelly is a writer and an instructor in creative writing and literature. In the following essay, he questions whether Newt's fear of death in* The Learning Tree *is truly an important part of his character.*

In writing his 1963 debut novel *The Learning Tree*, Gordon Parks has been accused of throwing in gratuitous, crowd-pleasing elements. It is, after all, a story that starts with a tornado on the first page and sex on the fourth, and goes on to chronicle shootings and beatings, bare-knuckle boxing, solitary confinement in juvenile detention, teen pregnancy, race-baiting, spousal abuse, a school board human rights standoff, a murder trial, the loss of a minor character's foot, and more. It is full of oafish authority figures and snarling white men and drunks and kindly folks of both races. On each page there is some aspect that is not very nuanced, but they all add up together to give the novel its charm and vitality.

Critics who fault the book for being packed with clichéd elements or sensationalistic events seem to be missing the point. It is one thing to give a gratuitous nod to a targeted mass reading

> READERS HAVE FOLLOWED NEWT THROUGH HIS MANY ADVENTURES, AND THEY CAN SEE THAT THERE HAS BEEN NO ACTIVE 'STIGMA.' REVIVING AN EARLIER THEME IS NOT THE SAME THING AS CLAIMING THAT IT HAS BEEN AN OBSESSION ALL ALONG."

audience, but quite another to be careless about serious character development. Tossing in the sorts of things that art-minded critics would like to see in a work should not work, because these are the people who are supposed to see through such pandering, but Parks does this as well, and when he does, it stands out even more than his rough-hewn plot devices. He gives his main character, Newt, a fear of death that borders on existential panic: In theory, it looks like something that would give a novel intellectual weight, and Parks makes it look even more substantial than it should by weaving it skillfully into the story. In the end, though, the book's musings on mortality come off as its most forced aspect.

When the fear of death is present in the story, in the first few chapters, it controls the reader's understanding of young Newt. It arrives unexpectedly, with the onset of a cyclone on a bucolic summer day: One moment he is looking at ants, and the next a killer storm is all around him, and he is bleeding from a gaping wound. This taste of death is quickly undone, though, by his first sexual experience, but in a few pages death is back, as he finds a house that has collapsed on a man. Newt wonders if the man might have survived, but the woman who seduced him, Big Mabel, dashes that hope, telling him to look carefully at all the blood, that survival is unlikely.

This is all pretty traumatic material. Even more traumatic is the next chapter, in which Newt and his mother have to go to the hospital because they know that his father is there, though they have not been told why. On the day after the cyclone, with death and catastrophe on his mind, it is natural that Newt would be considering his father mortally ill. The prospect of the death of a father, especially one who has been as powerful a presence as Jack Winger has been to Newt, leaves the boy shaken, even after he knows that his father

# WHAT DO I READ NEXT?

- Critics have noted similarities between *The Learning Tree* and Harper Lee's *To Kill a Mockingbird*, published in 1960. Both books are about growing up in rural areas and concern race relations, and both have a dramatic trial at their climaxes.

- Soon after *The Learning Tree* was published, in 1966, Parks published the first volume of his autobiography, *A Choice of Weapons*. In this book, he outlined the early part of his life, which was often quite similar to the experiences that he gave to Newt in the novel. Not currently in print, the 1986 edition from Minnesota Historical Society Press is available in libraries and in used-book collections.

- Tony Johnston's novel *Bone by Bone by Bone* tells the story of two boys, one black and one white, whose friendship in 1950s Tennessee is endangered by a father who is a hateful member of the Ku Klux Klan. Listed as a 2008 Best Books for Young Adults by the American Library Association, it was published in 2007 by Roaring Brook Press.

- Elena Castedo's 1990 novel *Paradise* concerns a young person coming of age while surrounded by a loving family. Castedo's book takes place in an unnamed Latin American country, and her family, instead of being African Americans in a country run by whites, has emigrated from Spain during the time of the dictator Francisco Franco's regime.

- Critics often compare *The Learning Tree* to Richard Wright's *Black Boy*, a 1945 autobiography that is frequently read in schools. *Black Boy* concerns Wright's brutal childhood in segregated Mississippi at roughly the same time that Parks's book takes place.

- Parks is best known for his many artistic successes as a novelist, a photographer, a film director, and a composer. His poetry was seldom published, but some prime examples can be found in the collection *Eyes with Winged Thoughts: Poetry and Images*, published in 2005.

---

will be all right. On the walk home, he starts a conversation with his mother about death, asking if it will indeed happen to everyone and whether it will hurt. She tells him that her religious conviction makes the idea of dying easier, and she gives him the "learning tree" simile, about how life can be viewed as a tree of learning, to help him put all of the horrible and random things about life into some sort of perspective. What she says does not make a lot of sense when weighed against the imponderable mysteries of existence, but that does not matter: what matters is who says it, not what is being said. Sarah Winger has such moral authority that her presence beside him and her certainty in the overall goodness of life, at least as a learning experience, are enough to sweep his fear away.

The novel continues to press on with Newt's fear of death through the next few chapters. In

chapter 3, he and his friends negotiate a sum to dive into the river to find the body of a black man, the drunken Doc Cheney, who has been shot in the back by the white sheriff while he had been running from a dice game. The sight of the corpse floating in front of his face in the water haunts Newt at night until he makes a symbolic gesture, an almost religious ritual: throwing his diving fee out the front door, into the darkness. In chapter 4, some mean kids shove Newt into the mortuary and lock him in with two dead bodies, plunging the room into darkness for good measure. Newt screams in terror and then, his emotions overloaded, passes out.

In the first two cases where his fear of mortality bubbles up, after seeing his father in the hospital and after seeing the corpse underwater, Newt talks to his mother, who calms him. After he is revived at the mortuary, though, he jumps to his feet and runs off into the night. The book's narrative then takes one of its few digressions from what Newt is feeling and doing. It cuts from the image of the boy running away to a newspaper story, published two days later, that summarizes the drama of Newt's brother Pete finding the boys who tormented him, beating them, being arrested, and being released by the judge. All this is conveyed in just two sentences.

The offhanded way in which Newt's night of terror ends might seem a bit casual, given the circumstances. If fear of death is what drives Newt, starting with the crushed, bloody body found after the storm and on through this event that is so distressful that his brain forces himself to shut down in a faint, then it would seem that the author should follow through with his character and show readers the consequences that ensue. Instead, readers see Newt's back as he runs off into the night.

But the way that Parks turns away from the action to a newspaper summary written days later is actually very appropriate. It is not just Newt who runs away from the macabre situation at the mortuary, but the narrative abandons the situation as well. After building up the fear of death in each of the first four chapters, the novel turns a corner and becomes a different type of story. Nobody dies in chapter 5: Newt works the fields, concentrates on his interest in science, and meets Arcella Jefferson, who is to be the love of his life. There are deaths in the rest of the novel, most notably the murder that Newt witnesses and keeps quiet about, and the death of his mother. These are important events in his life, certainly, but they are not the sorts of mind-numbing psychological traumas that blast him awake at night or that make his brain switch itself off.

One explanation for this change in the novel's focus could be that the events of chapters 5 through 18 are meant to show how Newt functions in the world, carrying his fear of death with him through ordinary life experiences. If this is meant to be the case, though, it is not very skillfully done. Much happens in this book, and Parks records Newt's reactions to what happens pretty carefully, but his reactions are seldom linked to the concept of death. For example, a case could be made that a young man who is being suppressed in his career path, as Newt feels he is when his guidance counselor at high school tells him to forget college, is afraid of being locked into a narrow life that is a one-way trip to the grave: that case could

be made, but Parks never mentions death during that important event in Newt's life. When his girlfriend becomes pregnant and leaves town, Newt shows no reaction that could be considered the equivalent of his passing out in the mortuary. He does not even have a heartfelt discussion with his mother about it. Even when he sees a man beaten to death before his eyes, Parks does not give Newt anything near the trauma of seeing the dead corpse he was looking for underwater. If the point is that Newt has matured, that his life experiences have enabled him to grow beyond the fears that gripped him in the early chapters, there should still be some mention of those fears, if only for comparison.

In chapter 19, after his mother's death, Newt thinks about her tranquility at the end, and how he respects that: "Now, this morning, it was creating within him a near-fanatical desire to rid himself of this stigma that had dogged his soul since the day of Doc Cheney's death," the narrator explains. He goes on to think about "worm-bored coffin sides, everlasting decay, dust piling forever upon eternal dust—entombed in the still, suffocating blackness." This is powerful writing, and these would be powerful emotions, if they rang true. But it is too late. Readers have followed Newt through his many adventures, and they can see that there has been no active "stigma." Reviving an earlier theme is not the same thing as claiming that it has been an obsession all along.

*The Learning Tree* begins with Newt Winger being introduced to the concept of death, and it ends with him overcoming his fear of death by spending the night beside his mother's coffin, so there is every reason to believe that this is a novel about a boy who learns what death is and how to control it. The problem with that interpretation is that death is absent from much of the book. This is an interesting novel, and it has much to say about social relations in rural Kansas in the 1920s. Parks tells fascinating stories, but when he tries to inject philosophical weight into his book, the result stands out as a halfhearted effort.

**Source:** David Kelly, Critical Essay on *The Learning Tree*, in *Novels for Students*, Gale, Cengage Learning, 2010.

### Milton Moskowitz

*In the following essay, Moskowitz describes the life of the writer before and after achieving commercial success with* The Learning Tree.

" BUT PARKS HAS NEVER BECOME BITTER

ABOUT THE RACISM HE ENCOUNTERED—AND HE

CREDITS HIS MOTHER, SARAH PARKS, FOR IMBUING IN

HIM A SPIRIT THAT ENABLED HIM TO SUCCEED

AGAINST ALL ODDS."

Make a man of yourself up there. Put something into it, and you'll get something out of it.

The quote above was the advice Gordon Parks received in 1927 from his mother when he was 15 years old and living on the farm his father worked at Fort Scott in the Kansas prairie. Gordon was the youngest of her 15 children. She knew she was dying and had just arranged for Gordon to move to St. Paul, Minnesota, to live with his older sister, Maggie Lee.

Gordon Parks, now 90 and living in a glass-sheathed skyscraper near the United Nations in New York City, may have thought of that advice last May 17 when he traveled to Storrs, Connecticut, to accept a doctorate of fine arts from the University of Connecticut. And it may have occurred to him again a week later when he traveled to Amherst College in western Massachusetts to accept another honorary degree.

These days, when institutions of higher learning look ahead to their spring commencements, they cast about to find people of color to honor. It's akin to an act of atonement for actions of previous years when applicants of color were routinely turned away. Recipients of these honorary degrees have ranged from Mike Tyson to Toni Morrison. However, this quest for honorees has probably landed on Gordon Parks' doorstep as often as at any other address in the United States. The two degrees he received last May were the thirty-ninth and fortieth he has collected.

It's a remarkable achievement considering the fact that Gordon Parks never graduated from high school. That, too, has been rectified—twice. In 1993, without having to take a test, he was awarded a high school degree by Lawrence High School in Lawrence, Kansas, home of the University of Kansas. Then, last July a delegation from his hometown, including a former mayor, made its way to Parks' apartment in New York to present him with a diploma from the Fort Scott

high school. They may not have been aware that 77 years ago Miss McClintock, a white high school teacher in Fort Scott, who served as an adviser to black students, had told them: "Don't waste your parents' money on college. You'll wind up as porters and maids." Gordon Parks remembered this advice and when he received his thirtieth honorary degree, he dedicated it to her "for pushing me to find her wrong."

Parks' apartment, overlooking the East River, is a veritable cornucopia of certificates, plaques, medallions, paperweights, and what-have-you celebrating the accomplishments of a Renaissance man who was essentially self-taught. And in many disciplines. He is no doubt best known for his photography but he admits being a "restless soul," and so he has tried his hand, successfully, at poetry, painting, films, journalism, fiction writing, and musical composition. He was driven by a catechism of his mother's: "If a white boy can do it, so can you. So don't ever give me color as a cause for failing."

This ability to float from one field to another was honed during his late teenage years in the Twin Cities after he was literally thrown out of his brother-in-law's home in St. Paul and left to fend for himself. He lived for two weeks on a trolley car. At age seven he had begun to bang on the Kimball upright in his family's home, and he had learned to play by ear—and that skill enabled him to get a job playing piano in a Minneapolis brothel. During the late 1920s and into the 1930s jobs did not so much come his way so much as he sought them out himself. He washed dishes in a restaurant, bused tables in a hotel, worked as a waiter in the fancy Minneapolis Club, served in the Depression-born CCC (Civilian Conservation Corps) and played guard on the touring House of David basketball team. And then he took a series of jobs as a waiter on railroad dining cars. Riding the Pullman cars gave him a chance to see other parts of the country, and for him these were learning experiences. As he once put it, "The important thing is not so much what you suffered—or didn't suffer—but how you put that learning to use."

Putting that learning to use is the essential core of Gordon Parks' life.

Reading magazines that had been discarded on the trains he worked, Parks came across photographs of migrant workers shot by the remarkable group of photographers assembled by the Farm Security Administration during the Depression:

Arthur Rothstein, Russell Lee, Carl Mydans, Walker Evans, Ben Shahn, John Vachon, Jack Delano, Dorothea Lange. They made a powerful impression on him, as did the paintings in the Art Institute, which he visited on a stop in Chicago.

He began to read: John Steinbeck, Erskine Caldwell, and Margaret Bourke-White. He remembers going to a Chicago movie theater in 1937 and seeing a newsreel showing Japanese war planes bombing the *U.S.S. Panay* gunboat in the Yangtze River in China. After the newsreel ended, a voice on the theater intercom announced: "And here is Norman Alley, the photographer who shot this remarkable film." Alley rose from the audience, took a bow and told about his experience. "I was enthralled," Parks wrote in his 1965 memoir, *A Choice of Weapons.* "He had no way of knowing it, but he had just changed my life. I sat through another show, and even before I left the theater I had made up my mind I was going to become a photographer."

When the Northern Pacific train he was working on reached Seattle, he went to Abe Cohen's pawnshop and for $12.50 bought a German camera, the Voigtlander Brilliant—and he began taking pictures. He never stopped taking pictures after that. And he never stopped looking for new opportunities. Having studied copies of *Vogue* discarded by train passengers, he fantasized about doing fashion photography—and he went to every large department store in the Twin Cities, offering his services. His diligence finally paid off when Frank Murphy's, a high-end boutique in St. Paul, gave him a chance to shoot pictures of models wearing the store's clothes. Parks' photos were soon on display throughout the store. One day Marva Louis, wife of heavyweight boxing champion Joe Louis, visited the store and, impressed by the Parks' photos, told him: "I think you are wasting your time here. Why don't you come to work in Chicago? I could get you a lot of work there."

He did, in 1940, working out of the Southside Art Center, where he divided his time between taking pictures of life in the black ghetto on the Southside of Chicago and portraits of society matrons. His work in Chicago led to a Julius Rosenwald fellowship, and in 1942 he joined the fabled Farm Security Agency's stable of photographers in Washington, D.C.

Roy Stryker headed this photographic team, and he became an important mentor of Parks, dispatching him to shoot pictures depicting black life in the nation's capital, which was then largely segregated. It was about this time that *12 Million Black Voices: A Folk History of the Negro in the United States* was published. It featured photographs selected by Edwin Rosskam and a searing essay by Richard Wright, a self-taught writer whose novel, *Native Son,* had been published in 1940. This book became Parks' bible, especially the passage:

> The seasons of the plantation no longer dictate the lives of many of us; hundreds of thousands of us are moving into the sphere of conscious history. We are with the new tide. We stand at the crossroads. We watch each new procession. The hot wires carry urgent appeals. Print compels us. Voices are speaking. Men are moving! And we shall be with them.

A few years later Parks met Wright, who gave him a copy of his novel inscribed: "To one who moves with the tide."

Parks' career blossomed after World War II. He moved to New York City to join a photographic department that Stryker had formed at Standard Oil Company of New Jersey (now Exxon/Mobil). He began shooting fashion pictures for *Vogue.* And in 1949, two years after Jackie Robinson began to play for the Brooklyn Dodgers, Parks broke the color bar at *Life* magazine. He was hired there as a staff photographer and a few years later he was posted to *Life*'s Paris bureau. Parks completed more than 300 assignments for *Life,* and his work is part of photographic history.

In 1997, when the Corcoran Gallery of Art in Washington, D.C., mounted a Gordon Parks retrospective that traveled to 30 cities, the exhibit included 277 of his photographs, and certainly one of the amazing aspects of this show was the diversity of subjects. They show that Gordon Parks was comfortable pointing his camera at gang fights in Harlem, chain gains in Alabama, Ingrid Bergman and Roberto Rossellini at Stromboli, the plains of his native Kansas, Paris fashion shows, Muhammad Ali, the favela in Rio de Janeiro, Duke Ellington, and black Muslim rallies in New York and Chicago. This is very characteristic of Gordon Parks. He enjoyed hanging out with Malcolm X and Eldridge Cleaver, but he is also an avid tennis player and an accomplished skier. There is very little in the world that does not interest Gordon Parks.

Parks once explained: "When the doors of promise open, the trick is to quickly walk through them." He himself has walked through many doors. In the early 1960s, a colleague at *Life,*

Carl Mydans, a famous photographer in his own right, read something Parks had written about a storm he once witnessed in Kansas and he suggested that they have lunch with Evan Thomas, a Harper & Row executive. As Parks relates the story, Thomas opened the conversation by saying: "Look, I want your novel. It's your first novel and we can only offer you $5,000." Parks started to respond, "But Mr. Thomas, I...", which prompted Thomas to add: "Perhaps we can go to ten, but no more." Parks' answer: "What I was trying to say, Mr. Thomas, was that I probably can't write a novel, but since you offered me all this money, I'm damn sure going to try."

His "damn trying" led 18 months later to *The Learning Tree,* a novel published in 1963 to wide acclaim and to great commercial success: it was a best-seller. Set in the Kansas locale where he grew up, the town is called Cherokee Flats (Parks' mother was part Cherokee). The novel's opening page has a father saying: "Son, the only thing worse than lazy Negroes is lazy white trash 'cause they're born white, with a God-given chance from the start."

The success of *The Learning Tree* opened another door for Parks. It became a motion picture that Parks produced and directed, returning to Fort Scott to film it. It moved into theaters in 1969, the first Hollywood movie directed by an African American. Parks also wrote the screenplay and the musical score. In the 1970s Parks directed the two Shaft movies starring Richard Rountree—*Shaft* and *Shaft's Big Score*—plus *The Super Cops* and *Leadbelly*.

One reason we know so much about Gordon Parks is that he has written endlessly about himself. He has written three full-length memoirs: *A Choice of Weapons* (1965), *To Smile in Autumn* (1979), and *Voices in the Mirror* (1990). *The Learning Tree,* while fictional, deals with the Kansas town where he grew up. And *Half Past Autumn,* the book published by Little, Brown in 1997 in conjunction with the Corcoran retrospective contains a long autobiographical essay by Parks, along with comments on his work.

And today, as he approaches his ninety-first birthday this November, Gordon Parks is still at work. Last year he published a new book, *The Sun Stalkers,* a novel based on the life of the English landscape painter, Joseph M. W. Turner. It was his eighteenth book. *Life* magazine still calls upon him to write essays. He did so after the September 11 attacks on the World Trade Center, and he recently completed a commentary for a special *Life* issue on "Pictures That Changed the World." And yes, he has completed some 500 pages of—surprise—another memoir.

Parks has already made it clear, in his memoirs, that he considered his parents "my just heroes." He has cited their "compassion and generosity" as they raised a large family in a two-bedroom house. "Not once, during those years, did I hear my mother or father raise a voice against one another, nor, for that matter, against their children." Racism was rampant in Kansas during Parks' childhood, and he once wrote that he considered himself "lucky to be alive especially when I remember that four of my close friends died of senseless brutality before they were twenty-one."

But Parks has never become bitter about the racism he encountered—and he credits his mother, Sarah Parks, for imbuing in him a spirit that enabled him to succeed against all odds. In his last memoir, *Voice in the Mirror,* he depicts his mother as someone "who would have defied God himself if what he willed her to do would harm another human being. Without considering the consequences, she once took a homeless white child into our house to feed and clothe until a distant relative came to his rescue. When a judge sentenced three older black boys to three months' imprisonment for roughing me up and throwing me off a truck, she asked the court to rescind its decision and allow her to mete out the punishment. The judge bowed to her wishes and the three were sentenced to three months' worth of Wednesday night prayer meetings."

Parks himself has great compassion, and you can see that in his photographs. Philip Brookman, curator of photography and media arts at the Corcoran Gallery, concluded that Parks' "greatest achievement remains that, while still young, he overcame both personal and social adversity to fulfill his potential to dream, to express the lessons of his early life, and to impart them to future generations."

**Source:** Milton Moskowitz, "Gordon Parks: A Man for All Seasons," in *Journal of Blacks in Higher Education,* Vol. 40, Summer 2003, pp. 102–104.

## J. R. S.

*In the following review, J.R.S. explains the depth and delicacy with which Parks handles racial discrimination in his storytelling.*

The episodes from the novel chosen for recording focus on events in the lives of two black boys, Newt Winger and Marcus Savage, and on the contrast and the conflict between them. Newt's thinking is shaped by his wise and loving mother, Marcus' by his surly, shiftless father. When Marcus is caught and lashed by a farmer whose peach orchard he had been raiding, he turns on the farmer and beats him brutally; as a result, he is sentenced to a term in the reformatory. Later, the same farmer is murdered by Marcus' father, who was caught stealing peach brandy after a fight between the farmer and a drunken white man, in which the latter is knocked unconscious, found still dazed when the farmer's body is discovered, and charged with the crime. Newt has seen the whole affair, and eventually testifies at the trial; Marcus' father then seizes a revolver from the sheriff and kills himself. Newt's mother shortly thereafter dies of a heart attack. In the final scene Marcus tries for revenge against Newt, but is shot and killed by the sheriff.

The action of the story is plainly violent and potentially sensational, yet sensationalism is not its purpose. Rather, we are led to see clearly into the minds and feelings of a number of people, both black and white. Racial discrimination is one inevitable theme, which appears in the reformatory, in the speeches and actions of the sheriff, in the eviction of Newt and his date from an all-white drugstore, and in the advice given Newt by a high school counselor, who tells him that he must never dream of going to college—this last all the more damnable because the discrimination is entirely unconscious. To counterbalance these examples, we see the humane high school principal, deeply shocked by what goes on in his school, and the trial judge of the murder case, who lectures the courtroom crowd after the suicide of Marcus' father. Only the last episode in the album contains some language which will trouble the squeamish, but hardly seems excessive in the circumstances. Students who enjoy the story only because it is exciting are likely to find that it has also given them much to think about.

**Source:** J. R. S., Review of *The Learning Tree*, in *English Journal*, Vol. 59, No. 9, December 1970, pp. 1315–16.

### Harry L. Faggett

*In the following review, Faggett describes the careful attention to and significance of Parks's use of race relations to tell his story.*

Sensationalism is the order of the day, and Gordon Parks' *The Learning Tree* conforms. The author makes use of every conceivable instance to present the violent and the spectacular in his amazingly credible (intended so, anyway) melodrama of a Negro family, solid citizens of the Midwest:

Destruction, death and sex during a cyclone; callous killing by a (white) two-gun-toting sheriff; race hatred, persecution and exploitation: a wild ride in a stolen auto ending with broken bodies on an undertaker's table; more bodies dragged from a river bottom; a black woman chased home by a drunken husband . . . then finally the tearful demise and funeral of the mother—all these related in convincing detail, allowing the truth of first-hand observation to shine through. Briefly, this is the story of the Wingers of Cherokee Flats, Kansas: Jack and Sarah Winger with their children, Pete, Rende, Prissy and young Newt the hero (probably a portrait of Gordon Parks, himself).

They have the usual black-and-white race problems, but there are no overtones of malice or of intense hatred in the author's treatment. With some effort someone might even discover some vestiges of the power and passion of Pasternak's *Dr. Zhivago*—Pasternak's use of atmosphere and scene too, perhaps; but Parks' purpose and propaganda are too obvious for pure artistry.

One major flaw in the work lies in a few "loose ends" of the tale left untied—flying in the breeze. Noteworthy in this respect is the author's failure to devise any punishment for the repulsive sheriff, Kirky. This vicious killer is still running loose at the end of the story without suffering—without any payment whatsoever for his crimes in the name of the law.

Life is your "Learning Tree" says Sarah Winger to her thirteen-year-old son, Newt. We are all God's children—the fruit of that same tree, she tells him. Some good, some bad, black and white alike. And this theme is significantly dramatized in a court of law when Newt's testimony clears the name of an accused white man and convicts a burly black killer.

**Source:** Harry L. Faggett, Review of *The Learning Tree*, in *African American Review*, Vol. 4, No. 1, March 1970, p. 34.

## SOURCES

Ball, Jane, "Gordon Parks," in *Dictionary of Literary Biography*, Vol. 33: *Afro-American Fiction Writers after 1955*, edited by Thadious M. Davis, Gale Research, 1984, pp. 203–208.

Balliett, Whitney, Review of *The Learning Tree*, in the *New Yorker*, November 2, 1963, p. 209.

Dempsey, David, "Witness to a Killing," in *New York Times Book Review*, September 15, 1963, p. 4.

"Gordon Parks Biography," in *Biography Channel Online*, http://www.biography.com/articles/Gordon-Parks-37379 (accessed June 5, 2009).

Parks, Gordon, *The Learning Tree*, Fawcett Crest, 1976.

Rivo, Lisa E., "Parks, Gordon, Sr.," in *African American National Biography*, edited by Henry Louis Gates, Jr. and Evelyn Brooks Higginbotham, Oxford University Press, 2008.

U.S. Department of Education, "Fast Facts: College Enrollment," in *National Center for Education Statistics*, http://nces.ed.gov/fastfacts/display.asp?id = 98 (accessed June 8, 2009).

## FURTHER READING

Donloe, Darlene, *Gordon Parks*, Holloway House, 1992.
   Donloe provides an overview of Parks's life and artistic contribution.

Levy, Peter B., *The Civil Rights Movement*, Greenwood Press, 1998.
   This book gives a clear and concise explanation of the changes that affected American race relations, roughly from the 1920s, when *The Learning Tree* takes place, to the late 1990s, and beyond.

Myers, Lois E., and Rebecca Sharpless, "'Of the Least and the Most': The African American Rural Church," in *African American Life in the Rural South, 1900–1950*, edited by R. Douglas Hurt, University of Missouri Press, 2003, pp. 54–80.
   This scholarly article analyzes the importance of church life in building a community feeling among rural black Americans, identifying social elements that would be as true in the Kansas of the novel as they would in the South at the time.

Walker, Vanessa Siddle, *Their Highest Potential: An African American School Community in the Segregated South*, University of North Carolina Press, 1996.
   The school that Walker focuses on, Caswell County Training School, operated in Virginia from 1934 to 1969. This book focuses on the school's success in making its students into scholars, but readers can use it to understand the difficulties facing Newt in the novel.

# The Pilgrim's Progress

### JOHN BUNYAN

### 1678–1684

John Bunyan, a seventeenth-century English writer and cleric, was deeply embroiled in the religious controversies of his time. He served in the military during the English Civil War, endured a lengthy spiritual crisis, and spent twelve years in prison because of his Puritan religious beliefs. Much of his voluminous writing was nonfiction and outlined his theological positions. He became most famous, though, for one fictional work, *The Pilgrim's Progress from This World to That Which Is to Come: Delivered Under Similitude of Dream*, the tale of Christian's journey to the Celestial City. Usually known by the simpler title *The Pilgrim's Progress*, the book is an allegory, meaning that its characters, rather than representing real people, signify abstract ideas that teach a lesson or moral. *The Pilgrim's Progress* was immensely popular among people of all social classes, and for generations it was standard reading. In many homes just two books could be found: the Bible and *The Pilgrim's Progress*, and the book is reputedly the most widely read book ever written in English.

*The Pilgrim's Progress* was published in two parts. Part I, published in 1678, focuses on the allegorical journey of the main character, Christian, who passes through the Slough of Despond, the Valley of Humiliation, Vanity Fair, and other places in his quest to reach the Celestial City. Part II, published in 1684, focuses on Christian's wife, Christiana, as she makes the

*John Bunyan* (The Library of Congress)

same journey accompanied by her neighbor Mercy and escorted by Great-heart. The travelers defeat monsters such as Giant Despair to reach their destination. The two parts were first published in a single volume in 1728.

## AUTHOR BIOGRAPHY

John Bunyan was born in 1628 near Elstow, Bedfordshire, England. His early life was marked by hardship. His father was a tinker—that is, a metalworker who mended pots and pans—and Bunyan lost his mother and two of his sisters when he was a teenager. The family was poor, and Bunyan received little formal education. He became estranged from his father after the latter remarried, prompting him to join the parliamentary army during the English Civil War (1641–1651). After completing his service in the war, he returned home and married a woman who brought with her a dowry consisting entirely of two books of theology. Bunyan credited these books with sparking his interest in religion. He later claimed that in the late 1640s and early 1650s he led a dissolute life (his claims were greatly exaggerated, though he did have a reputation for cursing) and that he one day heard a voice that condemned him for his sinfulness. It was from this point on that he pursued a religious life.

In 1653, Bunyan was baptized into the Baptist Church. During the 1650s, though, he struggled with his faith and went through periods of despair, caused in large part by the death of his wife and of his spiritual mentor. In 1655, though, he was made a deacon at the Baptist church in Bedford, England. He became embroiled in a religious dispute with the Quakers (more formally, the Religious Society of Friends), for he believed that the Quakers' religious views placed too much emphasis on inner feeling and not enough on the literal word of the Bible. This controversy led to the publication of his first theological works, including *Some Gospel-Truths Opened* (1656). A war of words with Quaker theologians ensued and lasted for several years.

Bunyan ran into trouble with the law beginning in 1658. He had become a popular preacher, but when the monarchy was restored in 1660, he became the object of persecution because he did not follow the beliefs set out by the official Church of England (also called the Anglican Church), which had just been reinstituted by King Charles II (the son of the beheaded King Charles I). Meetinghouses were closed down, and nonconforming preachers (those who refused to follow the guidelines of the Anglican Church) were subject to arrest. In 1660 Bunyan was arrested and imprisoned for not preaching in conformity with the Church of England. He was released briefly in 1666 (the year of the publication of his spiritual autobiography, *Grace Abounding to the Chief of Sinners*), but he continued to preach, so after a period of just a few weeks he was imprisoned again. He was not released until 1672, when King Charles II issued a declaration of indulgence, an edict that extended toleration to religious nonconformists. In 1675 he was imprisoned again after the king withdrew the declaration. Ironically, it was the Quakers who helped to secure a pardon and his release after about six months.

For the remainder of his life, Bunyan continued to preach. Although he was officially a Baptist, his religious outlook was essentially Puritan. He continued to write theological works—some sixty books and tracts in total—and he published what is arguably his second-most famous book, *The Holy War* (1682). Bunyan's name, however, will likely forever remain linked with *The Pilgrim's Progress* (1678, 1684), which he began writing when he was in prison. In 1688, he was riding from London to Reading in a heavy rain when he caught a cold and developed a high fever. He died in Snow Hill, London, on August 31. He was buried in the Bunhill Fields cemetery in London.

## PLOT SUMMARY

### Part I

#### AUTHOR'S APOLOGY; SECTION 1

*Pilgrim's Progress* is a continuous narrative that is not divided into chapters, so Section 1 and the subsequent sections are arbitrary divisions, each encompassing a stage of Christian's journey in Part I, and of Christiana's journey in Part II.

An unnamed narrator falls asleep in a den where he dreams of Christian, who is told by Evangelist that he must leave the City of Destruction carrying a burden on his back. Christian leaves after trying to persuade Obstinate and Pliable to go with him. Obstinate refuses, but Pliable agrees, though he becomes discouraged and returns home after the two enter a muddy pit called the Slough of Despond. Christian forges on and meets Worldly Wiseman, who tries to persuade Christian to put down his burden. Christian continues on his journey until he comes to a Wicket Gate, where he tells the story of his journey so far to Goodwill. Goodwill sends him to the nearby house of the Interpreter, where he sees a picture of a man in a crown (presumably Christ) and watches as a man sweeps, representing the Old Testament, and a woman washes, representing the New Testament. He also watches as a man pours water on a fire while another pours oil on it. The fire is the fire of faith, which the devil is trying to extinguish with water while Christ feeds it with oil. A man comes into the room, armed, and fights a crowd, representing the notion that a fervent pilgrim must show bravery. The Interpreter takes Christian into a darkened room, where a man sits in an iron cage of despair, for he had once been confident that he would reach heaven, but he is experiencing a crisis of faith. The Interpreter tells Christian that the

# MEDIA ADAPTATIONS

- A 2008 version of Bunyan's book, titled *Pilgrim's Progress: Journey to Heaven*, directed by Danny R. Carrales and starring Dan Kruse, was released on DVD by Christiano Film Group. For Spanish speakers, the DVD is available under the title *El Progreso Del Peregrino: La Jornada Hacia El Cielo*. Running time is 105 minutes.

- An earlier movie version (originally released in 1977), directed by Ken Anderson and starring Liam Neeson, was released on DVD by VCI Video in 2006. Running time is seventy-two minutes.

- An animated version of *The Pilgrim's Progress* was directed by Scott Cawthon and released on DVD by Cawthon Entertainment in 2005. Running time is sixty-five minutes.

- An operatic version of the book was written by Ralph Vaughan Williams and performed by the Royal Opera Chorus. It was released as an audio CD by Chandos in 1998 and is available as an MP3 download.

- An audiobook version of *The Pilgrim's Progress*, read by Max McLean, was released by The Listener's Bible in 2007. Running time is five hours and twenty-two minutes.

- An audiocassette reading of Part II of *The Pilgrim's Progress*, focusing on the journey of Christiana, was released by Orion's Gate in 1995; an "amplified" version was released in 1999. It was adapted and produced by Jim Pappas; the running time is about six hours.

fear he is feeling is good, for it will motivate him during his journey.

#### SECTION 2

Christian continues his journey. He arrives at the Wall of Salvation, which fences in an area where there is a cross and a tomb. Christian's burden falls from his back. Three Shining Ones appear and give him a certificate that he will need to enter the Celestial City. Christian follows the straight and narrow path along the Wall of Salvation. He encounters Sloth, Simple, and Presumption, then sees Formalist and Hypocrisy, who come from the town of Vain-Glory, trying to scramble over the wall. The two are taking a shortcut in an effort to reach the Celestial City. Christian climbs a hill called Difficulty until he comes to an arbor, where he falls asleep, leaving his certificate exposed. After two men awaken him to warn him of lions, Christian realizes that he has lost his certificate and retraces his steps to find it. He takes refuge at a pilgrims' hostel called Palace Beautiful (in some editions called House Beautiful).

One of the daughters of the house, Discretion, admits him to the hostel after he identifies himself. He then tells Discretion and her sisters, Piety, Prudence, and Charity, about his family and his journey so far. After they all eat, the women give Christian a tour of the hostel, which contains various Christian mementos, such as the slingshot David used to slay Goliath. The women give Christian weapons and food and send him on his way. He enters the Valley of Humiliation, where he encounters a grotesque monster named Apollyon, who claims Christian as his subject. Christian and Apollyon fight. Christian almost succumbs, but he manages to save himself. He then enters the Valley of the Shadow of Death, a desert filled with pits. He hears demons and is frightened, but he soothes himself by remembering that Christ will protect him. He sees the bones and ashes of other pilgrims. The valley is ruled by Pagan and Pope, but Christian is unafraid of these decrepit rulers.

**SECTION 3**

Christian encounters a townsman, Faithful, who has fled the City of Destruction. He tells Christian that the people in the city talk about their impending doom, but no one takes it seriously. He also tells Christian that Pliable returned to the city, covered with mud from the Slough of Despond; Help has rendered aid by pulling Christian from the Slough of Despond. Faithful goes on to narrate his adventures in the Slough of Despond, where he was tempted by Adam, who offered him one of his three beautiful daughters. Faithful resisted Adam's offer, but he was struck down by Moses because he was secretly tempted. Christian and Faithful are joined by an old acquaintance, Talkative, who seems pious and devout because he talks about

religious topics, but Christian knows it is all talk. Talkative leaves them after he is unable to distinguish between speaking against sin and abhorring sin.

Christian and Faithful again encounter Evangelist, who praises them for the progress they have made. He tells them that their next obstacle will be a city called Vanity, which sells cheap merchandise at a market called Vanity Fair. The people in Vanity worship Beelzebub. When Christian and Faithful arrive at Vanity, they are mocked and locked in a cage. Both refuse to repent and are sentenced to death. Faithful is burned at the stake, but Christian escapes. He gains a new companion, Hopeful, along with By-ends, who sees religion as nothing more than a means of getting ahead in the world. Christian chastises him and drives him away. He and Hopeful come to the plain of Ease, where a man named Demas tempts them with silver and visions of wealth. Christian and Hopeful, though, refuse to be tempted by worldly riches. They encounter a man who says that he knows a shortcut to salvation, but they fall into a pit and almost drown during a terrible storm. They take shelter at the Doubting Castle, presided over by Giant Despair. Despair and his wife, Diffidence, punish them for trespassing by locking them up and beating them. In despair, Christian and Hopeful contemplate suicide, but Christian remembers that he has a key called Promise that allows them to escape the castle.

**SECTION 4**

At the Delectable Mountains on the outskirts of the Celestial City, Christian and Hopeful eat and rest in an orchard owned by Lord Emmanuel. Shepherds offer to protect them and warn them that nearby hills, Error and Caution, have led other pilgrims astray: Error caused some pilgrims to hold false beliefs about resurrection, and wandering about on Caution were blind pilgrims who had tried to take a shortcut, wound up in the Doubting Castle, and had their eyes put out. The pilgrims see a view of the Celestial City through a telescope. They continue on their journey after the shepherds warn them not to fall asleep on the Enchanted Ground and to avoid Flatterer.

The travelers encounter Ignorance, who tells them that their journey is too hard and that he knows an easier route to the Celestial City. Ignorance also asserts that living a good life is sufficient to reach the Celestial City. Christian and

Hopeful outpace him and arrive at an alley filled with devils. Again they encounter an old acquaintance, Little-Faith, who endlessly complains because he had been set upon by thieves and robbed of his money and a jewel that was his birthright. Continuing on, Christian and Hopeful encounter Flatterer, who entangles them in a net, but a Shining One arrives to cut them free. They then encounter Atheist, who claims that the Celestial City does not exist. Christian and Hopeful discuss sin and backsliding among the faithful, which helps them ward off sleepiness as they cross the Enchanted Ground. Again they encounter Ignorance, who rejects the pilgrims' view that revelation is the path to salvation.

**SECTION 5**

Christian and Hopeful again discuss backsliding, with Christian citing the example of Temporary, whose faith was not strong enough to enable him to reach the Celestial City. They then encounter a river that blocks their access to the city. Christian goes into the river but despairs of crossing it. Hopeful reminds him of Jesus Christ, who will help him. The men emerge from the river, and the Shining Ones guide them up the hill to the city's gates. The king of the city orders that the gates be opened. Christian and Hopeful see that they have shed their earthly garments in the river. They are now clothed in garments of gold. Ignorance is shut out of the city and sent to hell.

The narrator awakens from his dream. In the conclusion to Part I, he invites readers to interpret the dream. He cautions his readers, though, not to focus on the details of the dream or to read it as entertainment but to search for the essence of the message.

## Part II

**INTRODUCTION; SECTION 1**

Writing in his own voice, Bunyan calls Part II of his book Christiana, addressing the book as though it were a living creature. He then imagines that Christiana, Christian's wife, raises objections to Part II of the book: that people will not believe that Bunyan really wrote it, that it will make people angry, that some readers will object to the use of allegory, and that some readers will dismiss both books as mere romance. Bunyan answers each of these objections, then turns the narration back over to the narrator, who falls asleep and dreams of Sagacity. The narrator asks Sagacity about Christiana and her

four sons. Sagacity knows them and tells the narrator that they had packed up to journey to the Celestial City. The narrator then turns the story over to Sagacity, who narrates the first portion of Christiana's journey.

Christiana persuades Mercy to accompany her on her journey. After Christiana, her four sons, and Mercy cross the Slough of Despond, Sagacity returns the task of narration to the narrator. The travelers come to a gate guarded by a ferocious dog. The gatekeeper knows of Christian and admits Christiana and her sons. Mercy remains outside the gate and is terrified until she remembers a passage from the Gospel of Matthew. She knocks at the gate and is admitted. The women ask the gatekeeper about the dog. The dog belongs to a neighbor but performs a useful function by driving away beggars; true pilgrims are not frightened by the dog. The gatekeeper feeds the travelers and washes their feet.

**SECTION 2**

As the travelers proceed, the boys climb over a wall and take fruit, but Christiana chastises them because the fruit belongs to the devil. They encounter two Ill-Favored Ones and cover their faces. The Reliever comes from a nearby house and drives the Ill-Favored Ones away. They arrive at the house of the Interpreter, who shows them scenes in his Significant Rooms. They see a man raking muck; he is more concerned with earthly matters than with looking up to heaven. They also see a room with a spider, representing sin. In another scene they see a butcher killing a sheep, suggesting that true believers should accept death. In a garden, the beautiful flowers do not quarrel out of jealousy. A robin is eating a spider, just as professors of religion fail to live their religion sincerely and secretly eat sin. After asking the women what prompted their journey, the Interpreter gives them new clothing and sends them on their way. He also sends his servant, Great-heart, to accompany them. They come to the place where Christian had lost his burden, then encounter Simple, Sloth, and Presumption, who are hanging in chains. They arrive at the hill called Difficulty, where Great-heart urges them on to the Prince's arbor, where they rest and eat.

**SECTION 3**

At the same spot where Christian lost his certificate, the party stops to rest and eat. Christiana, though, forgets her bottle, prompting Great-heart to explain that pilgrims must guard against sleepy forgetfulness. The travelers then arrive at the place where Christian saw the lions. The lions' owner, Grim, tells them that they may not pass. Great-heart draws his sword and kills Grim, and the lions are chained up so that the travelers can proceed. They then arrive at the Palace Beautiful, where the mistresses Piety, Prudence, and Charity are delighted to see them and take them in. Mercy tells Christiana about a dream she had in which she was being mocked until a winged creature came to her and clothed her in beautiful clothes, earrings, and a crown. Prudence talks with the sons, whose names are Samuel, James, Joseph, and Matthew, and is satisfied that they are knowledgeable about Christian beliefs.

Mr. Brisk comes and seems interested in marrying Mercy until he discovers her making clothing for the poor. Put off by her religious enthusiasm, he never comes again. Matthew becomes ill from the devil's fruit that he had eaten, but a doctor, Skill, arrives with medicine, which cures the boy.

After a month, the travelers resume their journey. They come across a monument commemorating Christian's victory over Apollyon. They arrive at the Valley of the Shadow of Death, where darkness engulfs them and snares entangle their feet. A giant named Maul accosts Great-heart, telling him that the party cannot pass. He accuses Great-heart of having kidnapped the two women. Great-heart and Maul do battle for a hour before Great-heart cuts off the giant's head.

### SECTION 4

At the spot where Christian met Faithful, the travelers come upon Old Honest, who initially thinks they are thieves until he learns that Christiana is Christian's wife. Great-heart inquires about a pilgrim named Fearing, whom he had escorted to the Celestial City. Fearing was frightened that he would be sent to hell because he was not sure that he was fully committed to reaching Celestial City. The party discusses how fear can motivate pilgrims and how all pilgrims are beset by failures.

When the pilgrims encounter the robbers that robbed Little-Faith in Part I, they seek shelter at the house of Gaius. They remain there for a month. Gaius talks at length about religious subjects. He defends women; Eve may have been

responsible for the fall of man in the Garden of Eden, but Mary was the mother of Christ and of human salvation. Gaius proposes that they hunt down Slay-good, a giant that has been tormenting pilgrims. They find Slay-good about to eat a pilgrim named Feeble-mind and kill him.

Matthew, the eldest son, marries Mercy, and James, the youngest son, becomes engaged to Phoebe, Gaius's daughter. Feeble-mind and a handicapped pilgrim, Ready-to-halt, join them. Along the way they lodge at the home of a character named Mnason, who introduces the pilgrims to his friends, including Contrite. Samuel and Joseph each marry one of Mnason's daughters. Great-heart and Mnason's friends slay a dragon with seven heads that has been terrorizing the neighborhood. The pilgrims climb a hill called Lucre, where Christian had been tempted with silver. Christiana instructs her daughters-in-law to turn their babies over to a man who cares for pilgrims' children. Great-heart, Old Honest, and the four boys kill Giant Despair, tear down his castle, and rescue Despondent and Much-afraid. The travelers arrive at the Delectable Mountains, where they encounter shepherds who show them Mount Innocent and Mount Charity. In thanks for the party having killed Giant Despair, the shepherds give Mercy a mirror that reflects back the face of Christ.

### SECTION 5

The pilgrims encounter Valiant-for-truth, who was inspired by Christian's story, which has spread widely, to ask the Lord for help in fighting off a groups of thieves. Accompanied now by Valiant-for-truth, the weary travelers come to the Enchanted Ground, where they struggle against the temptation to sleep. They try to rouse Too-Bold and Heedless, but the sleepers only mutter incoherently. After the travelers pass through the Enchanted Ground, they encounter Standfast, who has successfully resisted the temptations of Madam Bubble.

The travelers arrive at the land of Beulah, the location of the Celestial City. Christiana receives from the Master a letter summoning her to see him. The other pilgrims bid farewell. Ready-to-halt leaves his crutches as a legacy to his son. The narrator concludes by saying that he has no knowledge of what happened to Christiana's sons, although he has heard that they are alive.

# CHARACTERS

### Apollyon

Apollyon appears only briefly in the allegory, but he is important in conveying Bunyan's message. His name is taken from the pagan Greek god Apollo, who represented a number of aspects of the human condition, notably beauty. Yet Apollyon is an ugly creature, half man and half beast. The beastly parts encompass all of material creation: He is part fish, part dragon, and part bear, suggesting that he partakes of water, earth, fire, and air. He is also representative of medieval feudalism, for he claims Christian as his vassal and subject. Christian defeats Apollyon, suggesting his ability to defeat the forces of materialism and assert his freedom from worldly institutions.

### Mr. Brisk

Mr. Brisk is Mercy's suitor until he discovers her interest in religion and in sewing clothes for the poor.

### By-ends

By-ends values Christianity for its social and worldly advantages.

### Christian

Christian, like most characters in an allegory, is not a fully rounded character. He is the hero and central character of Part I, and he clearly represents all Christians who embark on the quest for salvation in a world that tries to block that quest. He is driven entirely by his goal of reaching the Celestial City, or heaven, and all other matters fade into the background for him. He experiences some temptation and occasionally fear, but he readily overcomes these emotions as he pursues his single-minded quest. Interestingly, during his journey, he never brings up his family, which he has left behind in the City of Destruction, although he does show emotion about his family when he is asked about it at the Palace Beautiful.

### Christiana

Christiana is Christian's wife and the heroine of Part II. Her decision to leave the City of Destruction can be seen as more heroic than Christian's, for she has responsibilities that hold her there. In many respects she is a more complex character than Christian. Her husband's quest is entirely single-minded, but Christiana is more attuned to the world around her. She bears the responsibility of caring for her four children, and she takes Mercy along with her as a companion. She is able to achieve victories that eluded Christian, such as the defeat of Giant Despair. She gives more thought to other people, such as when she gives a tip to the porter at the Palace Beautiful; while Christian sees money as evil, Christiana recognizes that money has its uses and can be used for a good purpose.

### Demas

Demas is a worldly figure who tempts Christian with silver and dreams of wealth.

### Discretion, Piety, Prudence, and Charity

These four are the mistresses of the Palace Beautiful. Charity is able to get Christian to show emotion, making him cry when she asks him about his family.

### Evangelist

Evangelist, as the bearer of Christ's message, spurs Christian to undertake his quest for the Celestial City.

### Faithful

Faithful accompanies Christian until he is burned at the stake for refusing to worship Satan at the city of Vanity.

### Fearing

Fearing is a pilgrim who is uncertain about his commitment to reaching the Celestial City.

### Feeble-mind

Feeble-mind is a pilgrim of limited intelligence who joins Christiana's group after almost being slain by Giant Slay-good.

### Flatterer

Christian is cautioned to avoid Flatterer on his journey to the Celestial City.

### Formalist and Hypocrisy

Rather than following the straight and narrow path along the Wall of Salvation, these two try to climb the wall and take a shortcut to the Celestial City. A formalist is someone who is more concerned with the outward forms of religion than its essence.

### Gaius

Gaius takes Christiana's party into his home and shelters them. Two of his daughters marry two of Christiana's sons.

### Giant Despair

Giant Despair imprisons Christian and Hopeful in his castle, the Doubting Castle. In Part II, Great-heart and Christiana's sons slay the giant.

### Giant Slay-good

Giant Slay-good, a giant that terrorizes the neighborhood, is killed by Great-heart as he is about to devour Feeble-mind.

### Goodwill

Christian tells the story of his journey to Goodwill, who guards the Wicket Gate.

### Great-heart

Great-heart is Christiana's protector and companion in Part II. He seems almost to fill the role of a surrogate husband to Christiana during her perilous journey. He also in some ways represents an expansion of Christian. While the latter is focused entirely on his own quest for salvation, Great-heart displays a more instinctual recognition of the needs of others. He also displays great benevolence, such as when he aids Feeble-mind and Ready-to-halt in their efforts to reach the Celestial City.

### Grim

Grim's lions attack Christiana and Mercy; he is killed by Great-heart.

### Heedless and Too-Bold

Heedless and Too-Bold are a pair of pilgrims who succumb to sleep near the end of their journey and can only babble nonsense when they are awakened.

### Help

Help is a pilgrim. He pulls Christian from the Slough of Despond.

### Hopeful

Hopeful becomes Christian's companion after Faithful is executed. He saves Christian from the river outside the gates of the Celestial City.

### Ignorance

Ignorance tries to distract Christian from his path by claiming that he knows an easier way to get to the Celestial City.

### Ill-Favored Ones

These are two figures who try to bring harm to Christiana and Mercy.

### Interpreter

The Interpreter is one of Christian's spiritual guides. He takes Christian in and shows him the Significant Rooms, where Christian learns that everyday objects can have religious significance.

### Little-Faith

Little-Faith complains because he had been set upon by thieves and robbed of his money and a jewel that was his birthright.

### Madam Bubble

Madam Bubble cares only for worldly amusements and offers herself and her money to the pilgrim Standfast.

### Matthew, Joseph, Samuel, James

These are Christiana's sons. Matthew, the oldest, eats fruit from the devil's garden and becomes ill. He later marries Mercy.

### Maul

Maul is a giant who accuses Great-heart of kidnapping Christiana and Mercy before Great-heart kills him.

### Mercy

Mercy is Christiana's companion in Part II, and she later marries Matthew, Christiana's oldest son.

### Mnason

Christiana's party takes shelter at Mnason's home. His name appears to come from the biblical book of Acts, chapter 21, where an old disciple accompanies Paul on a journey and provides hospitality for him.

### Obstinate

Obstinate is one of Christian's fellow townsman in the City of Destruction; he refuses to undertake the quest for the Celestial City.

### Old Honest

Old Honest is an aged pilgrim who tells Christiana and Mercy of the fate of Fearing.

### Pliable

Pliable begins the quest with Christian, only to become discouraged and turn back after encountering the Slough of Despond.

### Ready-to-halt

Ready-to-halt, who walks with crutches, joins Christiana's party at the urging of Great-heart.

### Reliever

Reliever rescues Christiana and Mercy from the Ill-Favored Ones.

### Sagacity

Sagacity briefly functions as the narrator near the beginning of Part II. His name is a synonym for wisdom.

### Shining Ones

The Shining Ones are presumably angels. They give Christian his certificate and clothe him when he arrives at the Celestial City.

### Sloth, Simple, and Presumption

Christian encounters these three figures together at the Wall of Salvation.

### Standfast

Standfast is a pilgrim who resists the temptations of Madam Bubble.

### Talkative

Talkative is a pilgrim who places more value on the words of religious discourse than on true religion.

### Temporary

Temporary is a backslider, a figure who begins the pilgrimage but then gives up.

### Valiant-for-truth

Valiant-for-truth, a knightly pilgrim, joins Christiana's party after having driven off attackers.

### Watchful

Watchful is the porter at the Palace Beautiful.

### Worldly Wiseman

Worldly Wiseman is unsuccessful in his efforts to persuade Christian to give up his foolish quest and be satisfied with his worldly life.

## THEMES

### Journey

One of the most important themes in *The Pilgrim's Progress* is the importance of the spiritual journey that each person has to make. Doom awaits the citizens of the City of Destruction, but those who are willing to undertake a spiritual journey can escape destruction and arrive at the Celestial City, or heaven. Along the way, though, the pilgrim/traveler encounters many obstacles: despair, despondency, the temptations of wealth and sensual pleasure, and in particular a lack of understanding of the divine word. The journey, then, is a physical journey, but what is of more importance is the spiritual journey.

### The Wilderness versus the City

The journey of *The Pilgrim's Progress* is framed by two cities. One is the City of Destruction, where people face doom if they do not undertake a spiritual journey. At the other end is the Celestial City, the goal of the pilgrimage and of every true Christian. In between is the wilderness, with such features as the Slough of Despond, the hill of Difficulty, and the Valley of the Shadow of Death. Along the way, though, Christian and Faithful encounter the city of Vanity, where baubles and gewgaws are sold and where Faithful is burned at the stake for refusing to worship Satan. Vanity is a worldly city, in contrast to the city the pilgrims are trying to reach, which is a celestial, unworldly city. The worldly city, as it often is in literature, is depicted as a place of corruption, greed, sensual pleasure, and other distractions on the path to salvation. The wilderness that the pilgrims must pass through is representative of biblical wildernesses, such as that in which the Old Testament Jews wandered for forty years, or that in which Christ wandered for forty days.

### Knowledge

A key theme in *The Pilgrim's Progress* is the importance of knowledge, particularly the knowledge contained in the Bible as God's revealed word. During their journey, the pilgrims arrive at places of refuge where they are essentially instructed in Christian doctrine. Christian dismisses the pilgrim Ignorance because he is unable to read and understand the message of the Bible. Christiana receives her summons to the Master in the form of a letter, which she must be able to read in order to understand its message. Remember

# TOPICS FOR FURTHER STUDY

- Investigate the history of the English Civil War, which began in 1641 and continued intermittently until 1651. What names were given to the two sides in the war? What positions were they fighting for? What was the outcome of the war? Which side did Bunyan fight on? Make a chart outlining your findings.

- In seventeenth-century England, religion was a topic of widespread discussion, and sometimes dispute. In addition to the Church of England (the Anglican Church) and the Catholic Church, there were a variety of religious sects: Quakers, Baptists, Puritans, the "Diggers," the "Levellers," and others. Additionally, debate raged over such matters as predestination versus free will. Conduct research on one religious group or concept from during this time. What influence did it have on religious discussion and practice? Discuss your findings in a written report.

- In seventeenth-century England, disputes arose about proper conduct. Many Puritans (a group that included Bunyan, although he called himself a Baptist) opposed practices such as sports, Maypoles, festivals, plays, masques (short dramas, usually allegorical, performed by masked actors), mumming (pantomimes), and other "pagan" activities that they regarded as sinful. Many of these were rural activities. Using the Internet, investigate the history of one or more of these activities. Locate visuals that you can use in a PowerPoint presentation about the activity and why Puritans regarded it as sinful.

- Just as Christianity split as a result of the Protestant Reformation, Islam split in its early days as a result of a dispute about who should succeed Muhammad as the leader of Islam. The result was the First Fitna, or First Islamic Civil War (656–661). Later in that century, the Second Fitna (680s) created additional turmoil. Research the history of the First Fitna and/or Second Fitna and make a chart drawing comparisons to the religious wars of seventeenth-century Europe.

- The religious disputes of the seventeenth century, in which Bunyan played a part, continue to influence religious debate in the twenty-first century. Make a PowerPoint presentation explaining some of the religious issues that continue to be debated, and be ready to explain how each issue's roots extend back to Bunyan's time. As an example, consider laws that prohibit the sale of liquor on Sunday, the role of religion in politics, or abortion rights.

- Read *The Shack* by William P. Young. This novel, suitable for young adults, is a work of theological fiction, as is *The Pilgrim's Progress*. Write a brief report explaining how the two works differ in the nature of the central characters' encounters with God.

---

that illiteracy was still widespread at the time Bunyan was writing. *The Pilgrim's Progress* is, among other things, thus a plea for people to learn to read so that they can read their Bible and absorb the wisdom it contains.

## Community

The two parts of *The Pilgrim's Progress* form an interesting contrast. In Part I, Christian's journey is essentially solitary. He abandons his family to undertake his spiritual quest, and although he acquires companions along the way, he does not really need them. Part II, though, strikes a very different tone. Christiana's journey is much more of a communal one. Her four sons and Mercy accompany her, and along the way the party of pilgrims grows as others join her. She is willing to take under her protection those who are

*Scene from* The Pilgrim's Progress *(© Timewatch Images / Alamy)*

weak or otherwise handicapped, including Ready-to-halt and Feeble-mind. Marriages and childbirth take place during her journey. Perhaps Bunyan is making a gender distinction, suggesting that men tend to journey alone while women are more socially attuned. Perhaps he is simply suggesting that sometimes a spiritual quest is a solitary endeavor, sometimes a communal one. Or perhaps he saw Part II as a corrective to Part I, suggesting that the quest for salvation necessarily involves the broader community and that Christian's more solitary quest misrepresents the true nature of Christianity.

## STYLE

### Allegory

*The Pilgrim's Progress* is an allegory, and as such it is often not regarded as an actual novel as the word is commonly used. In a novel, the author creates a fictional world in which more or less "real" characters function in recognizably human ways. The novel is fundamentally about those characters—their actions, their motivations, their backgrounds, and their interactions. An allegory, on the other hand, is more like a fable or a parable. It conveys a secondary meaning that is not always explicitly stated in the narrative. Thus, on the surface *The Pilgrim's Progress* is a tale about a journey from one city to another, but clearly the journey is an allegorical representation of the path of a Christian to heaven. Further, allegorical characters are types rather than individuals. In *The Pilgrim's Progress*, all of the characters represent a type of person in the context of a Christian's efforts to achieve salvation. Most represent moral qualities. Christian and Christiana meet those who would tempt them from their path, such as Madam Bubble. They meet other types of obstacles, such as Giant Despair. Some are not fully committed to the task, such as Fearing. Some try to take shortcuts, such as Hypocrisy. In the same vein, place names indicate the obstacles the pilgrims face. Clear examples as the Slough (pronounced "sloo") of Despond, the Valley of the Shadow of Death, and the Celestial City.

There is a wide range of types of allegories. At one end of this spectrum are subtle allegories; an example might be Herman Melville's novel *Moby Dick*, in which Captain Ahab's quest to find and destroy the white whale seems to stand for *something*, though what that something is has long been debated by scholars. In contrast, *The Pilgrim's Progress* is sometimes referred to as a "naïve" allegory. This word is not intended as a disparagement. It simply indicates that the allegorical significance of the book is easy to determine.

### Biblical Language

At the time Bunyan wrote *The Pilgrim's Progress*, two broad literary styles were vying for supremacy, and in fact still are. One was the style of Shakespeare, who ransacked Greek, Latin, and French to add a cornucopia of new words to the English language. Even today, the word *Shakespearean* is used to refer to a style that reflects Shakespeare's overflowing inventiveness. The other was the style of the King James Bible, commissioned by England's King James I, who plucked from obscurity a classics scholar and parson named John Bois. Bois completed his translation of the Bible in 1611 in a style that relied on short, natural sentences and a spare vocabulary. While Shakespeare employed about 30,000 different words in his poems and plays, Bois used only about 8,000 words, creating a tight, muscular prose style.

This prose style was favored by writers such as Bunyan, as well as later writers such as Robert Frost and Ernest Hemingway. The opening words of *The Pilgrim's Progress* are indicative of this style: "As I walked through the wilderness of this world, I lighted on a certain place where was a den, and I laid me down in that place to sleep, and as I slept I dreamed a dream. I dreamed, and behold I saw a man clothed with rags." Out of forty-eight words in this passage, only one has as many as three syllables (wilderness) and only three have two syllables (lighted, certain, behold)—and one of those is simply a past tense form. The remaining forty-four words are a single syllable, and with the exception of the word *certain*, every word in the passage is of Anglo-Saxon origin (as opposed to Latin). It is perhaps this simplicity of style that has made Bunyan's work popular among people of all ages and social classes for over three hundred years.

### Symbolism

Most of the symbolism of *The Pilgrim's Progress* lies on the surface and can be readily interpreted. Thus, characters' names stand for moral qualities. Place names often stand for obstacles. Some of the symbolism, though, is a bit more subtle. For example, the pilgrims' journeys are often interrupted by their stay in homes and castles. Some of these, such as the castle of Giant Despair, are prisons that prevent the pilgrims from reaching their goal. Others, though, are places of refuge and rest. Here the characters eat, sleep, and in particular engage in conversation. The house of the Interpreter and the Palace Beautiful are two clear examples of homes that have symbolic meaning.

Gates are used symbolically as obstacles that stand in the way of the pilgrims. Goodwill allows Christian to pass through the Wicket Gate because he is on his way to the Celestial City and has his certificate to prove it, but Formalist and Hypocrisy have to climb the Wall of Salvation because they are not allowed to pass

through the gate. Similarly, in Part II, Christiana and her party come to a gate guarded by a ferocious dog. The gatekeeper tells them that he knows who is worthy to pass on by how they react to the dog. At the Celestial City, the pilgrims must pass through gates, which can be thought of as the gates of heaven.

Some of the symbolism is more subtle still. For example, Little-Faith is robbed of his money and of a jewel that was his birthright. It is not immediately clear what the jewel represents. One possibility is his faith. Another is that it alludes to the story in the book of Genesis about Esau selling his birthright to his brother Jacob for a bowl of potage, or porridge, depriving himself of the blessings of inheritance. Another more subtle symbol is Christian's certificate, given to him by the Shining Ones. Christian never reads it, but he needs it to gain admittance to the Celestial City. Its symbolic significance is not immediately apparent, but it could refer to the notion of God's plan for humankind, "written" but not always revealed to humans.

## HISTORICAL CONTEXT

England was a tumultuous country during Bunyan's lifetime. When Bunyan was about thirteen, in 1641, long-simmering tensions in English politics erupted into civil war. The struggle was between King Charles I and his supporters, called Royalists or Cavaliers, and Parliament, whose supporters were called Parliamentarians or Roundheads. The name Roundhead came from the fact that many Parliamentarians were Puritans who wore their hair closely cropped, in contrast to the more fashionable Royalists, whose hair was long and often fell in curls. A breed of spaniel that Charles I favored is still called the Cavalier King Charles spaniel.

The Roundheads were led by the Puritan Oliver Cromwell, whose New Model Army defeated the king's forces in 1645. Charles I was taken prisoner, but he escaped, and war broke out again in 1647. (Many historians use the terms First English Civil War and Second English Civil War to distinguish the conflicts.) Again the king's forces were defeated, and Charles I was executed for treason in 1649. At

# COMPARE & CONTRAST

- **1680s:** The Scientific Revolution, the name often given to the scientific and mathematic events of the seventeenth century that laid the foundations of modern experimental science, was drawing to a close with the publication of Sir Isaac Newton's *Principia Mathematica* in 1687.

  **Today:** Scientists take for granted and daily use the principles of experimental science laid down in the seventeenth century.

- **1680s:** Religion is a subject of intense dispute between different Protestant denominations and between Protestantism and Catholicism.

  **Today:** Despite differences in doctrine and forms of worship, Christian denominations, including Catholicism, generally maintain respectful and cooperative relationships.

- **1680s:** Few children receive a formal education; upper-class boys might attend a grammar school, where conditions are often harsh and brutal; girls are taught domestic skills at home.

  **Today:** Virtually all children receive a formal academic education until they reach the age of eighteen, with many receiving formal education beyond that age.

- **1680s:** Men typically wear breeches and a waistcoat with a frock coat over it. The fashion is for men to wear wigs but no beards. Women typically wear a shift under a long dress, often consisting of two parts, a bodice and a skirt.

  **Today:** Standards of dress are much less formal and uniform, with both men and women wearing a wide variety of clothing styles that people in the seventeenth century would have regarded as shockingly immodest.

---

this point, England was declared a republic (as opposed to a monarchy), and its government under Oliver Cromwell—and briefly under his son Richard after Oliver's death—was variously called the Commonwealth, the Interregnum, or the Protectorate. The Protectorate governed England from 1653 to 1660, when Charles I's son Charles returned to London. He assumed the throne as Charles II the following year.

This event, generally called the Restoration, unleashed English society's pent-up desires for art, literature, theater, fashion, and pleasure after the strictures of Puritan rule—and Charles II's own hedonistic lifestyle was almost a source of relief to the English people. Although Charles II personally favored a policy of religious tolerance, he acceded to Parliament's desire to restore the supremacy of the Anglican Church by agreeing to the Clarendon Code, a series of laws that enforced religious conformity and made "meeting houses" and nonconformist worship illegal. Nevertheless,

in 1672 he issued the Royal Declaration of Indulgence, an edict that extended tolerance to nonconformists and Catholics, though he later withdrew the edict under pressure from Parliament. In 1679, the so-called Popish Plot raised a stir when it was revealed that Charles II's brother and heir, James II, was a Catholic. This revelation led to a division between the Whig Party, which favored the exclusion of Catholics from public office, and the Tory Party, which opposed such exclusion. When a plot to assassinate Charles II and James II was uncovered, many Whig leaders were forced into exile or even killed. Catholics were blamed for the Great Fire of London in 1666, though it was later determined that the fire started in a bakery. Charles II dissolved Parliament in 1679 and ruled without Parliament until his death in 1685, three years before Bunyan's death. In 1688 the so-called Glorious Revolution deposed King James II and replaced him with King William and his queen, Mary.

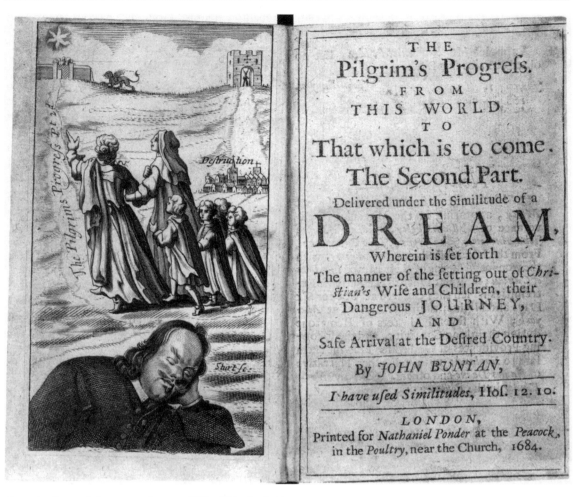

*Frontispiece of the second part of* The Pilgrim's Progress *(MPI / Getty Images)*

## CRITICAL OVERVIEW

*The Pilgrim's Progress* was an immediate popular success. The book went through some eleven editions during Bunyan's lifetime, and over the following centuries it was translated into more than a hundred languages and became a fixture in many people's homes. During the eighteenth century, though, the book and its author were not held in high regard by the literary community precisely because of that popularity, particularly among common folk. In a 1784 poem, "Tirocinium," the English poet William Cowper praises Bunyan for his story, but also mentions later in the same poem that Bunyan's name is not well liked (quoted in Southey).

Nevertheless, *The Pilgrim's Progress* earned praise from a number of important literary figures. In 1830, England's poet laureate, Robert Southey, published an edition of the book that included "A Life of John Bunyan." Commenting on an improvement in the book's reputation, he writes that "the opinion of the multitude has been ratified by the judicious." He goes on to say that it is "a book which makes its way through the fancy to the understanding and the heart: the child peruses it with wonder and delight; in youth we discover the genius which it displays; its worth is apprehended as we advance in years, and we perceive its merit feelingly in declining age." That same year, the English poet Samuel Taylor Coleridge wrote a review of Southey's edition in his *Table Talk*. He calls the book a "wonderful work" and concludes, "I could not have believed beforehand that Calvinism could be painted in such exquisitely delightful colours" (quoted in Mackail). Also in 1830, the English historian and man of letters Thomas Babington Macaulay, again alluding to the book's reputation, writes: "That wonderful book, while it obtains admiration from the most fastidious critics, is loved by those who are too simple to admire it" (quoted in Hale). He goes on to note that in the eighteenth century, Samuel Johnson, "the most pedantic of critics and the most bigoted of Tories," stated that it was "one of the two or three works which he wished were longer."

Numerous other nineteenth-century critics expressed admiration for *The Pilgrim's Progress*. In *The Hero as Divinity, Heroes and Hero-Worship*, Thomas Carlyle calls the book "an Allegory, and a beautiful, just and serious one" (quoted in Moulton). The American poet John Greenleaf Whittier, in *John Bunyan: Old Portraits and Modern Sketches* (1849), is more effusive: "In reading the concluding pages of the first part of 'Pilgrim's Progress,' we feel as if the mysterious glory of the Beatific Vision was unveiled before us. We are dazzled with the excess of light. We are entranced with the mighty melody; overwhelmed by the great anthem of rejoicing spirits" (quoted in Moulton).

## CRITICISM

### Michael J. O'Neal

*O'Neal holds a Ph.D. in English literature. In this essay, he discusses Bunyan's viewpoints on women as reflected in the allegory in* The Pilgrim's Progress.

John Bunyan lived in an era when men enjoyed privileges and freedoms that were denied to women, so it is not difficult to apply modern standards of gender relations to his life and work and find instances of sexism. He grew up inheriting an older Christian tradition that looked upon women as a source of temptation. The principal basis for this view was the biblical story of Eve in the Garden of Eden. It was Eve who succumbed to the blandishments of Satan. Out of vanity she ate of the Tree of Knowledge of Good and Evil, then tempted Adam to do the same. This act represented the fall of mankind into sin, requiring a redeemer in the form of Jesus Christ. During the seventeenth century, the story of Adam and Eve was given renewed vigor with the publication of John Milton's epic poem *Paradise Lost* (1657). This poem, which slowly unfolds the fall of man and Satan's

rebellion against God and heaven, impressed upon readers the notion that feminine wiles were Satan's wiles and that it was the duty of Christian men to resist them.

Nevertheless, Bunyan should perhaps be given some credit for being ahead of his time in reflecting attitudes that accorded more respect to women and to a feminine outlook. Women played important roles in his life. In 1644 he was devastated by the death of his mother and two of his sisters. His relationship with his father was strained. He married in 1649, but after giving birth to four children, his wife, Mary, died, casting Bunyan into a Slough of Despond similar to that described in *The Pilgrim's Progress*. As a minister, he had daily contact with large numbers of women. It has been estimated that fully two-thirds of the worshippers who attended Baptist and nonconformist meeting houses during this time were women, and many of these women refused to adopt passive roles in the church.

*The Pilgrim's Progress*, in its two parts, can be thought of as the yin and yang of masculine and feminine. In Part I, the focus is clearly on the solitary male hero, Christian. Christian leaves his wife and family to embark on his quest for salvation. He takes no one from the City of Destruction with him. Along the way he picks up companions, notably Faithful and Hopeful, and although these companions help him in his quest, Christian does not need them and could have succeeded in his quest alone. The world of Part I is almost entirely a masculine world. Its priorities are the ego of the hero in a world of struggle, dominance, and ultimately transcendence of the world. It is a world where any kind of sensual pleasure, even food and sleep, is to be regarded with suspicion, as a distraction from the path of salvation. It is a world of darkness and shadows, of cages and pits, where the masculine ego asserts its dominance over the flesh.

Part II, in contrast, is a highly feminine world. Now the hero is a heroine, Christian's wife, Christiana. She embarks on the same quest as her husband, but the tone of the quest is entirely different. Part II elevates the supposedly feminine values of community, nurturance, benevolence, and compassion. Christiana does not set off alone but is part of a community that includes her four sons and her neighbor and friend, Mercy. Marriages and childbirth take place along the way. While Christiana faces obstacles similar to those that her husband faced, she and her party also stay in

# WHAT DO I READ NEXT?

- Bunyan's *A Book for Boys and Girls: Country Rhymes for Children* (1686) is a collection of poems that teaches religious lessons, each using images and themes of the countryside.

- *The Chronicles of Narnia* (1950–1956), a series of seven fantasy novels by C. S. Lewis, contains Christian allegorical elements.

- Philip Pullman's trilogy of fantasy novels, *His Dark Materials* (1995–2000), is a young-adult series that has been described as rejecting the Christian themes of C. S. Lewis's *The Chronicles of Narnia*.

- Jonathan Swift's *A Tale of a Tub* was written in the 1690s, shortly after Bunyan's death, and published in 1704. The book is a satirical allegory about three brothers, each representing a branch of Christianity, as they make their way in the world.

- Egyptian writer Naguib Mahfouz is the author of *Children of Gebelawi* (1959), sometimes translated from the Arabic as *Children of the Alley*. The book is an allegory about the history of monotheistic religions.

- Ingmar Bergman's *Wood Painting*, written in 1954, is a one-act play that became the basis for the Swedish film producer's most famous film, *The Seventh Seal* (1956), an allegory about a knight pursued by Death in a land rendered a wasteland by a plague.

- *The Purple Flower*, a one-act play by the African American writer Manta Bonner, published in 1928, is an allegory of race relations and oppression as members of the Us strive to climb a hill, where can be found The Purple Flower-of-Life-at-Its-Fullest.

- Madeleine L'Engle's *A Wrinkle in Time* (1962) is a science-fiction allegory that contains Christian themes and features a struggle between good and evil in the universe.

- *Miracles of Our Lady* is the English title of *Milagros de Nuestra Señora*, a series of twenty-five devotional poems about the Virgin Mary written by the Spanish poet Gonzalo de Berceo in the thirteenth century. The introductory poem is subtly allegorical.

- Nathaniel Hawthorne's *The Scarlet Letter* (1850) is a classic novel of Puritanism in America with strong allegorical elements.

---

pleasant homes, where hospitality is extended and some sensual pleasure, including food, is not just tolerated but looked on with approval. Old Honest is not regarded as having failed by falling asleep under an oak; Christiana longs to find a place where she can find rest. Christiana herself, it is suggested, has some physical charms, and Mercy is described as alluring. The shepherds give Mercy a mirror, but rather than being regarded as a "feminine" bauble, the mirror reflects the face of Christ, suggesting that women as well as men are made in the image of God. Mercy herself gives expression to a more fruitful, sensual view of human experience: "They that go rightly through this Valley of Baca make it a well, the rain that God sends down from heaven upon them that are here also filleth the pools. This valley is that from whence also the King will give to them vineyards, and they that go through it shall sing."

In Part II, Bunyan explicitly counters the mythology that women are seductresses like Madam Bubble. He does this through the character Gaius:

> I will now speak on the behalf of women, to take away their reproach. For as death and the curse came into the world by a woman, so also did life and health. God sent for his Son, made of a woman. Yea, to show how much those that came after did abhor the act of their mother, this sex, in the Old Testament, coveted children, if happily this or that woman might be the mother of the Saviour of the world.

Gaius goes on to list the roles that women played in the life of Christ: They washed his feet, they anointed him at his burial, they wept as he went to his death, they watched by his tomb, they announced his resurrection. Gaius concludes: "Women therefore are highly favoured and show by these things that they are sharers with us in the grace of life."

Perhaps by modern standards, Bunyan's revisionist view of women might not seem like much of an advance in gender relations. Tradition, his church, and the social mores of the time, though, enforced a viewpoint that said that women were the author of sin and the fall of mankind. That Bunyan was able to entertain an alternative view—to see women as "sharers with us in the grace of life"—is a credit to his far-reaching imagination and perhaps helps explain why his explicitly religious, Puritan text has remained popular for more than three centuries.

**Source:** Michael J. O'Neal, Critical Essay on *The Pilgrim's Progress*, in *Novels for Students*, Gale, Cengage Learning, 2010.

# SOURCES

Bunyan, John, *The Pilgrim's Progress*, Dodd, Mead, 1979, pp. 11, 233, 254.

Carlyle, Thomas, "The Hero as Divinity, Heroes and Hero-Worship," 1840, in *Library of Literary Criticism of England and American Authors*, Vol. 2: 1639–1729, edited by Charles Wells Moulton, Moulton Publishing, 1901, pp. 394–95.

Coleridge, Samuel Taylor, "Table Talk," May 31, 1830, in *Coleridge's Literary Criticism*, edited by J. W. Mackail and Henry Froude, 1908, pp. 148–49.

Cowper, William, "Tirocinium," 1784, in *The Pilgrim's Progress, with a Life of John Bunyan*, edited by Robert Southey and John Murray, 1830, p. iv.

Macaulay, Thomas Babington, Review of *Southey's Edition of the "Pilgrim's Progress,"* 1830, in *Literature: A Fifth Reader*, edited by Edward Everett Hale, Jr., and Adaline Wheelock Sterling, Globe School Books, 1901, p. 110.

Milton, John, *Paradise Lost*, edited by Alastair Fowler, rev. ed., Longman, 2007.

Southey, Robert, ed., *The Pilgrim's Progress, with a Life of John Bunyan*, John Murray, 1830, p. v.

Whittier, John Greenleaf, "John Bunyan, Old Portraits and Modern Sketches," 1849, in *Library of Literary Criticism of England and American Authors*, Vol. 2: 1639–1729, edited by Charles Wells Moulton, Moulton Publishing, 1901, p. 395.

# FURTHER READING

Brown, John, *John Bunyan: His Life, Times and Work*, Read Books, 2008.

> Although first published in 1885, Brown's volume is still considered the standard biography of John Bunyan.

Coffey, John, and Paul C. H. Lim, eds., *The Cambridge Companion to Puritanism*, Cambridge University Press, 2008.

> This volume is a collection of essays on all aspects of Puritanism, both in England and in early America.

*The Kingfisher Children's Encyclopedia of British History*, Kingfisher Books, 2005.

> This volume provides a good general introduction to British history at the time Bunyan wrote. Despite the title, the encyclopedia's audience is young adults.

Leeming, David Adams, and Kathleen Morgan Drowne, *Encyclopedia of Allegorical Literature*, ABC-CLIO, 1996.

> This volume encompasses all aspects of allegory in the Western tradition, from parts of the Bible to modern fiction. It also includes works from Africa, the Middle East, South America, and other cultures.

# A Place Where the Sea Remembers

## SANDRA BENITEZ

## 1993

Sandra Benitez's 1993 novel *A Place Where the Sea Remembers* takes place in the 1980s in the fictitious seaside town of Santiago, Mexico, where residents, like people in other small towns, whisper secrets about one another. Through a series of short vignettes, most of them focusing on one or two characters at a time, Benitez demonstrates how the lives of this small village are closely intertwined. Each chapter provides a story of the people who struggle to make a living while trying to make sense of their world. Woven through the stories is the presence of Remedios, a healer, who listens to her neighbors' complaints and shares their joys and sorrows until she can no longer take in any more of their emotions. Then she heads to the sea, which she describes as a great vessel of stories. It is at the edge of the sea that she renews her spirit. But there is one particular day, when Remedios goes to the ocean not to refresh herself but to claim the body of someone who has drowned. It is with Remedios patiently waiting at the edge of the waves that the story both begins and ends. Whose fate, readers wonder at the end of the opening chapter, has cast the victim into the raging water? Who are the people standing along the cliffs, and why are they also waiting for the body to appear? Benitez answers these questions in her stories throughout this novel.

*A Place Where the Sea Remembers* won the 1993 Minnesota Book Award, and for her accomplishment, Benitez was named the first

*Sandra Benitez* *(© 2003 Ed Bock. Reproduced by permission)*

winner of the Barnes and Noble Discover Great
New Writers Award (1993). *A Place Where the
Sea Remembers* was the author's first published
novel.

## AUTHOR BIOGRAPHY

Benitez was born on March 26, 1941, in Washington, D.C. Benitez's mother was born in Puerto
Rico and Benitez claims that her mother's culture
has influenced her work. It was through her
father's job at the U.S. State Department that
the family lived in Mexico and later in El Salvador for most of Benitez's childhood and early
adulthood. These experiences would also have a
strong effect on the topics of Benitez's writing.
Her youth also included time spent in Missouri,
on a farm owned by her paternal grandparents.
This is where, Benitez reports from her personal
Web site, that she learned the benefits of hard
work.

Benitez was almost forty years old when she
began to write fiction. She would work at her
craft for another thirteen years before seeing her
first novel, *A Place Where the Sea Remembers*,
published. Later, Benitez published her second
novel, *Bitter Grounds* (1997), which follows the
lives of three El Salvadoran women. Since then,
Benitez has written two more novels, *The Weight
of All Things* (2000), about a young boy caught
in the middle of a civil war in El Salvador, and
*Night of the Radishes* (2003), which draws on the
author's experiences living in Minnesota and
Mexico. In 2005, Benitez turned to nonfiction,
completing a memoir called *Bag Lady*, a story of
the author's struggle with a serious illness and
her triumph over it.

Besides writing, Benitez teaches writing at
the University of Minnesota and the University
of San Diego. She has also presented at writers'
conferences, including the prestigious Bread
Loaf Writers' Conference in Vermont. In 2004,
she was named the National Hispanic Heritage
Award Honoree for literature. Benitez lives in
Minnesota with her husband, Jim Kondrick.

## PLOT SUMMARY

### Chapters One and Two

Benitez's novel *A Place Where the Sea Remembers* is written in a nontraditional style. Rather
than each chapter following the same main characters, the author has chosen to focus on different characters in different chapters, sometimes
one at a time. In the opening chapter, readers are
introduced to Remedios, an old female healer.
Remedios is pictured standing at the edge of the
waves at a local beach. She is waiting for a
drowned body to appear. There are other people
standing along the cliffs. They are also waiting.
However, Remedios senses that the body will
appear exactly where she is standing. She has a
special way of communicating with the ocean,
she believes. She dips her fingers into the water
and tastes the salt. This is how she hears the
stories that the ocean wants to tell her.

In chapter two, readers meet Candelario
Marroquin, who is painting the front door of
his house in his favorite color—blue. He is celebrating his recent promotion at don Gustavo del
Norte's restaurant. While before, Candelario
was a waiter earning meager wages, he is now
the salad maker. He will wear a bow tie and a
cummerbund (a special cloth around his waist)

to mark his newly earned prestige. He will also earn more money. As he paints the door, Candelario sees his wife, Chayo, and sister-in-law, Marta, walking along the dry riverbed that runs in front of his house. They are coming back from the beach, where Chayo sells the paper flowers she makes to tourists who visit the small fishing town of Santiago, Mexico. Candelario is pleased that Marta's pregnancy is not yet showing. This means that the neighbors have not yet begun their gossip about the young sixteen-year-old who is not married. Candelario knows the people talk about him and his wife because they have been married for two years and Chayo has not yet become pregnant.

When Chayo and Marta reach the house, Candelario hears that Marta is planning to have an abortion. Chayo warns Marta that many women have suffered from complications after having an abortion. Marta, however, is willing to take that chance. Chayo then tells Marta that having an abortion will permanently harm Marta's soul. This does not deter Marta from her plan. She says she hates the baby. Marta was raped by a man named Roberto. Candelario speaks up, though his words surprise him. He tells Marta that he and Chayo will raise the child. Chayo supports her husband's decision. Marta is overjoyed with relief. "I will hate the child less if you raise it," Marta tells Candelario.

A few months later, Candelario tells his wife that his boss, don Gustavo, is expecting special guests at his restaurant. The doctor, Federico, and his wife, Maria Elena, are from Guadalajara. The doctor provides medical services for the local children and also performs illegal abortions. For these guests, don Gustavo wants Candelario to serve Caesar salad, a special salad that don Gustavo has personally taught Candelario to make. Candelario has tasted the salad in the past and vowed never to taste it again. He cannot understand how anyone could eat it. However, he trusts his boss and does what he is told. Candelario prepares the salad carefully, but when he serves it, there are complaints. The doctor and his wife tell don Gustavo and Candelario that the salad has been made improperly and they cannot eat it. Don Gustavo blames Candelario for this error. He denies that Candelario has followed his instructions and fires him.

### Chapters Three and Four

Chapter three returns to Remedios, the healer. The hut in which she lives is described. It sits on top of a hill overlooking the ocean. The hut is

small and is filled with dried herbs and grasses that she uses as medicines. She lights a bundle of aromatic sticks and watches the smoke flow over her body. Then she chants, ending with the words: "I am she who knows."

Fulgencio Llanos, a photographer, is introduced in the next chapter. He thinks about the unusual event that happened the day before. He was able to take a picture of El Santo, the masked wrestler. El Santo was very popular but no one had ever seen his face. Fulgencio is sure that he will be able to sell the photograph for a lot of money. But right then, he was tired and missed his girlfriend, Lupe Bustos. He was anxious to get to her restaurant so he could order his customary dish of shrimp. Fulgencio is almost fifty and has spent most of his adult life traveling around Mexico with his camera.

Fulgencio needs a ride back to Santiago and while taking a moment to drink a beer in a local cantina, a "gringo" walks in. After talking for a few minutes, the man, whose name is Jaime, offers Fulgencio a lift. He has an old red Cadillac parked outside. Fulgencio decides Jaime is a strange kind of hippie. No hippie he has ever seen has driven a red Cadillac. When he gets to the car, he notices it is filled with a wide assortment of merchandise: straw hats, machetes, T-shirts, radios, and calculators.

Halfway to Santiago, Jaime slows down and makes a turn to Playa de Oro, a place with a beautiful beach that Jaime wants to see. He promises it will be only a short delay. While driving there, Fulgencio panics. He believes that Jaime is setting him up. He is concerned that Jaime wants to rob him of his camera. When they get there, Jaime gets out, but Fulgencio insists on staying in the car. It is very dark now. So once Jaime gets out, Fulgencio can no longer see him. He plans his escape, for he knows it is too dangerous to wait for Jaime to come back. Before he leaves, he reaches into the back of the car for one of the machetes. Just then Jaime returns and misunderstands what Fulgencio is doing. He forces Fulgencio out of the car and takes off fast back down the road, leaving Fulgencio alone in the night. After the car leaves, Fulgencio realizes that his camera and all his equipment, including the photograph of El Santo, are in the car. This was the plan all along, Fulgencio believes. The gringo was out to steal his things. But after walking a few minutes, Fulgencio comes across a strange shadow on the side of the road. It is his valise with all his photographic equipment inside. Fulgencio crouches on the ground, realizing what a mistake he has made in judging Jaime wrongfully. He laughs at himself and calls himself a fool. His mistake, however, also makes him rejoice. He decides he will celebrate his good fortune with Lupe.

## Chapters Five and Six

Chapter five focuses on Marta, who is working at her job in the hotel. Her clothes are fitting tighter because of her pregnancy. She finds a magazine and flips through the pages, dreaming of her ideal job, which is working for some rich woman who adores her. Luz, Marta's friend, walks into the room. Luz looks for money left behind in the room. She has two children she is raising by herself and needs the extra money to help pay bills. Tito, her husband, has run off with another woman, Tula Fuentes, to El Paso. Luz has asked Remedios to intercede with her magic and make Tito come back.

Later, on her way home, Marta stops to see her sister. Chayo tells her that they cannot take her baby because she is now also pregnant. She cannot raise two children at once. Marta runs home. Luz lives in the same rooming house, and Marta tells her what has happened. Luz tries to soothe Marta, telling her that after the baby comes, she will learn to love it. After Marta leaves, Tito, Luz's husband, appears in the courtyard outside the rooming house. Marta considers the situation and decides to trust in Remedios's powers. Marta goes to the healer and wants her to make Candelario change his mind and still take her child. Remedios believes that it is wrong for Marta to leave her baby and go north. She will not do anything for Marta.

Marta decides to plead with Candelario to change his mind. When she goes to her sister's house, Candelario confesses that he is not the one who does not want Marta's baby. It is Chayo. Marta is angry. She leaves her sister and goes to Pico Lara, a *brujo*, or a witch doctor. He agrees to put a spell on Chayo's baby.

Chapter six describes a very brief image of Remedios outside her hut, offering some corn to a magpie.

## Chapters Seven and Eight

One of the village teachers, Rafael Beltran, is spotlighted in chapter seven. Rafael has never been married. He lives with his mother, who is overweight and prone to illnesses and physical complaints. Rafael constantly bends his ways to please his mother. On his way home from the school, he passes the clinic of Esperanza Clemente, a woman he admires but never has gotten close to, mostly because he is consumed with taking care of his mother.

One day, Rafael travels to the edge of town to visit one of his students, Beto Burgos, who has recently missed a lot of school. Beto's mother, Concha, opens the door to greet Rafael. She tells him that Beto has stayed home to help his father catch fish. While he stands at the door, Rafael sees Ines, the girl who works in his house. Concha tells him that the girl lives with an old man, who is not good to her. A few days later, when Ines is preparing dinner for Rafael, she becomes ill. She collapses in a pool of blood. Rafael calls Esperanza, who tells him that Ines is having a miscarriage. Rafael then learns that the old man Ines lives with is her husband. When Rafael's mother learns that Ines is pregnant, she suspects that Rafael is the father. Meanwhile, Esperanza, who knows that Ines's husband beats her and probably caused the miscarriage, has made arrangements with a family she knows in Guadalajara. They agree to take in Ines.

Cesar Burgos, in chapter eight, tries to rouse his son Beto, who is curled up in bed. Concha Burgos, while traveling to her parents' home for a visit, was killed in a bus accident, along with her two other sons. Beto is despondent. He barely eats. In an attempt to renew his son's enthusiasm, Cesar has begun to build a shrine to his departed wife and sons. The shrine is made of wood and is shaped like a chapel. Cesar thinks the shrine is too dull but does not know how to brighten it. He has asked for Beto's help, but the boy refuses.

Cesar insists that Beto go out with him on the boat. It is difficult to do an adequate job fishing with just one person. The weather is stormy and the fishing is not good. Cesar thinks about how good life was when his wife was alive, and the memories cause him to cry. He admits his fears to his son. He is concerned that as a father he is a failure. When they arrive back home, Beto pulls out three jars from under his bed. Inside are shells he has been collecting. Beto then begins to glue the seashells onto the shrine that his father has built. Cesar joins him.

Before Cesar and Beto travel to the place where the bus that Concha was in went over the cliff, they stop at Chayo's house to buy some of her paper flowers. Chayo offers food and Beto eats heartily. Then they go to the place of the accident and erect the shrine in memory of Concha and the boys. While there, Beto tells his father he should be dead. If he had gone with his mother and brothers he would have saved them. If he could not, then he, too, should be dead. His father comforts him, telling him how much he needs him.

### Chapters Nine and Ten

Chapter nine offers another short glimpse into the life of Remedios. She goes to the sea to release all the stories that people have told her. She knows that people feel relieved when they tell her their stories, so she does the same with the sea.

Justo Flores is the topic of the chapter ten. He is often referred to as the Birdman because he has trained three canaries to perform for tourists at the beach. He also has a dog, named Yoyo. On this particular day, Justo receives a telegram. He cannot read, but he fears the telegram contains bad news. Although he now lives alone, he has a wife and nine children living in other parts of the country. He knows the whereabouts of only two of his children, his oldest daughter, Justina, and his fifth-born daughter, Ernestina. At the beach, Justo finds a young couple and asks that they tell him what is in the telegram. The telegram is from Ernestina, telling him that Justina is dead. The reason Justina had refused to talk to her father was that after her mother died, Justo's second wife refused to allow Justina to live with them. Readers are not told the reason for this. Justo had not fought for Justina's case and had abandoned her.

### Chapters Eleven and Twelve

Esperanza Clemente, the nurse and midwife, has invited Marta to live with and work for her. Marta has given birth to a son she has named Richard, and who is now two years old.

Rafael, the teacher, asks Esperanza to come to his house to treat his mother, dona Lina. He is concerned that if his mother is not feeling well, she will not take the trip he has planned for her. Dona Lina accuses Rafael of wanting to get rid of her. He is sending her to visit his brother, Tomas, who owns a big house in Veracruz. Rafael tells Esperanza that he thinks this trip for his mother will be good for him and Esperanza. Esperanza does her best in the next days to make dona Lina strong enough to travel. After

dona Lina leaves, Rafael asks Esperanza to go out with him. Rafael tells Esperanza that for the first time in his life, since his mother has left, he feels happy. The two of them go out again. Esperanza, after she senses that Rafael is truly interested in her, confesses that she is not a virgin. She, like Marta, was raped when she was a teenager. Rafael takes several days to consider what Esperanza has told him. When he finally comes back, he apologizes for allowing what she has told him to affect him in a negative way.

Esperanza is called to Candelario's house on an emergency. His son, Tonito, is having an allergic reaction to ant bites. Tonito is taken to the hospital and is saved. Readers discover that Chayo and Marta have not spoken to one another in years since Chayo discovered that Marta put a curse on her son.

In Chapter twelve, Remedios is dreaming that she is traveling among the stars. In the dream, she briefly recalls her youth. She also meets with various spirits.

### Chapters Thirteen and Fourteen

Two years have passed. Tonito, Chayo's son, is now four. Chayo prepares food for Esperanza and Rafael's wedding. At the wedding, Tonito asks his parents if Richard, Marta's son, can spend the night with them. On their way home, a rainstorm hits. In the middle of the night, someone yells from outside. The storm has filled the riverbed and a pig is stuck in a tree that has fallen into the rushing water. The people try to capture the pig, but the rain water is too strong. Chayo looks up in time to see a child slip down the muddy banks and fall into the rushing water. At first she thinks it is Tonito. But when she finds Tonito, she knows it was Richard. Candelario tries to save the boy but is unsuccessful.

The story ends much as it had begun. Remedios is squatting on the beach near the waves, waiting for Richard's drowned body to appear. Marta and Chayo are standing on a nearby cliff, also waiting.

## CHARACTERS

### Rafael Beltran

Rafael Beltran, a teacher in the village, lives with his mother, dona Lina. Every day, after school, rather than socializing with his fellow teachers, Rafael hurries home to be with his mother. His mother dominates his life. Only when he sends his mother to his older brother Tomas does Rafael feel a sense of happiness. This prompts Rafael to develop a relationship with Esperanza Clemente.

### Beto Burgos

Beto is the son of Cesar and Concha Burgos. He is also a student of Rafael's. Beto becomes depressed after his mother and his two younger brothers die in a bus accident. Beto believes he is responsible for their deaths. When Beto confesses his thoughts to his father, Cesar tells him that he is wrong. This helps Beto pull himself out of his depression.

### Cesar Burgos

Cesar is the husband of Concha and the father of Beto. Cesar is a fisherman. Cesar breaks down emotionally after he loses his wife and two sons in a bus accident. When he exposes his feelings of sorrow to his son Beto, this helps Beto to better understand his own emotions. Cesar and Beto make a shrine to commemorate their missing family. This helps them to heal their sorrows.

### Concha Burgos

Concha is Beto Burgos's mother and Cesar's wife. Concha was a nurturing woman who devoted her life to taking care of her family. She dies in a bus accident.

### Lupe Bustos

Lupe is the girlfriend of Fulgencio Llanos. She owns a small restaurant in Santiago. She does not appear in this novel except through Fulgencio's thoughts.

### Ines Calzada

Ines is fourteen years old and an Xochimilca Indian. She is hired by dona Lina to cook for her and her son. Later, Rafael learns that Ines is married to a very old man who beats her. His beating leads to Ines miscarrying the child. After this, Esperanza arranges for a family in Guadalajara to take Ines into their home.

### Esperanza Clemente

Esperanza is a nurse and midwife. She lives down the street from Rafael Beltran. When she was a teenager, she was raped. She did not become pregnant, but she feels she has been soiled by the incident. When Rafael opens up his emotions to her, Esperanza feels compelled to tell him of her past. Because of her past, Esperanza is very sympathetic to Marta and offers her a home and a job at her clinic.

### Ernestina

Ernestina is Justo Flores's fifth-born daughter. He sometimes visits Ernestina, who lives in Guadalajara. Ernestina sends her father a telegram, telling him that Justina, his first-born daughter, has died.

### Tia Fina

Tia Fina is Marta's aunt. Marta shares a room in a small rooming house with her aunt. Tia attempts to counsel Marta about motherhood. Her role in this story is very limited. Later in the novel, readers learn that Tia Fina has died.

### Justo Flores

Justo is an old man who lives in the same rooming house as Marta. He has trained birds to perform tricks for tourists at the beach. Justo receives a telegram, which he cannot read, but he fears it contains bad news. When he finds someone to read it, he learns that his oldest daughter has died.

### Tula Fuentes

Tula is the woman whom Luz's husband has run away with. Luz believes that Tula cast a magic spell on Tito to lure him away from her.

### Luz Gamboa

Luz is a twenty-two-year-old mother of two. She is Marta's friend. They work in the same hotel. Luz tells Marta that Remedios is working a spell on her husband, Tito, who has left her for another woman. Luz wants Tito to come back.

### Jaime

Jaime, who is called a "gringo" (a non-Hispanic), arrives in a small town outside of Santiago just as Fulgencio, the photographer, is about to hitch-hike home. Jaime offers Fulgencio a ride in his old Cadillac that is filled with articles he intends to sell. Though Fulgencio later mistrusts Jaime, the white stranger proves he is trustworthy by not stealing Fulgencio's camera and equipment.

### Justina

Justina is Justo Flores's oldest daughter. She was born with a twisted foot. Justo has not spoken to Justina in a long time. Justina was still angry at her father for his having abandoned her. Justo receives a telegram later, telling him that Justina has died.

### dona Lina

Dona Lina is Rafael Beltran's mother. She is overweight and overbearing in her constant need of her son. She also exhibits her prejudice when she talks about Ines, the Indian girl whom dona Lina has hired as a maid. She does not understand why her son bothers to educate an Indian girl.

### Fulgencio Llanos

Fulgencio Llanos is a traveling photographer. He is the first person to photograph a very popular masked wrestler without his mask. Fulgencio learns a lesson when he accepts the offer of a ride with a stranger then becomes frightened that the stranger wants to rob him. The incident makes Fulgencio more deeply appreciate his good life.

### Candelario Marroquin

Candelario is Chayo's husband and Tonito's father. At the beginning of the story, he loses his restaurant job. When his unwed sister-in-law plans an abortion, Candelario offers to raise her baby. He hopes that this child will inspire him and Chayo to have a child of their own. Even though Chayo later refuses to raise Marta's child because she has become pregnant with her own child, Candelario sticks to his promise. He tells Marta that it is only Chayo who has changed her mind. Also, when Richard, Marta's son, falls into the river, it is Candelario who jumps in the rushing waters and tries to save the child.

### Chayo Marroquin

Chayo is the wife of Candelario, the sister of Marta, and the mother of Tonito. Chayo makes paper flowers and sells them to tourists. When Chayo becomes pregnant, she feels it would be too difficult to raise two babies at once and takes back her promise to raise her sister's soon-to-be-born child. When Chayo learns that Marta has put a curse on Chayo's unborn baby, she refuses to forgive her sister. Not until Marta's own son, Richard, drowns do the sisters come back together.

### Tonito Marroquin

Tonito is Chayo and Candelario's son. When Tonito is four years old, his mother fears that he has fallen into the swollen river outside their home. However, it is his cousin, Richard, who is presumed drowned.

### don Gustavo del Norte

Gustavo is the restaurant owner who teaches Candelario how to make a Caesar salad. When dinner guests complain that the salad has not been made correctly and is therefore unappetizing, Gustavo puts all the blame on Candelario and fires him.

### Roberto Ramos

Roberto is the man who raped Marta. He never makes an appearance in the story. He is the father of Marta's son, Richard.

### Remedios

Remedios is an elderly woman who has been trained as a healer. She gathers plants and animals in order to cure people. Remedios appears in very brief chapters devoted completely to her, though her presence in this novel is not strong enough to call her the protagonist. She is often pictured as chanting, dreaming, or otherwise in touch with a more spiritual part of the world.

### Marta Rodriguez

Marta is Chayo's sister. She is sixteen at the beginning of the novel. She has been raped and is pregnant. She asks her sister and brother-in-law to raise the baby. Otherwise, Marta is willing to have an abortion. When her sister later refuses to raise Marta's child, Marta has a curse put on her sister's baby. At the end of the story, Marta's son drowns.

### Richard Rodriguez

Richard is Marta's son. He drowns, at age four, in the arroyo after a big storm.

### El Santo

El Santo is called the masked wrestler and is a very popular figure in Mexico. He wears a mask when he is performing, and no one knows his true identity. It is El Santo's photograph that Fulgencio, the photographer, sells to a newspaper in Mexico City.

### Tito

Tito is married to Luz, but he runs off to El Paso with another woman, leaving Luz to care for their two children. Luz has a spell cast to make Tito come back to her, which he does, but only for a short while.

# TOPICS FOR FURTHER STUDY

- Create a Web site that would match Marta's fantasy job. In other words, pretend you are a wealthy U.S. citizen looking for a young Mexican woman to become your house-keeper. Create a Web site hoping to attract the best applicant. On your Web site, create the type of environment that Marta dreams about. Be extravagant. Collect pictures of luxurious mansions. Create a work schedule and describe the working conditions that Marta fantasizes about. Share your creation with your class.

- Research the economies of small towns in Mexico that might be representative of the town Santiago in Benitez's novel. Find out what a typical restaurant owner might earn and compare this with the amount of money a salad maker receives. What does a typical tourist vendor make? What about local doctors and midwives? What is the amount a fisherman might earn? After collecting your data, do the same research for a small town in the United States. How do the figures compare? Include cost of living in your analysis. Create graphs and other statistical formats and present your report to your class.

- Read Rudolfo A. Anaya's *Bless Me, Ultima* (1972) and compare it with Benitez's novel. How do the overall tones of the books compare? Are there issues of poverty in both? Describe the theme of old traditional ways versus modern ways in both books? Do they differ? Which novel provides a deeper understanding of the female healer and how is this done? Then read several examples of book reviews from national newspapers, such as the *New York Times*. Write a 500-word review for each book, stressing the novels' strengths as well as weaknesses.

- Build a memorial shrine, such as described in chapter eight of Benitez's novel. Mimic the structure, size, paint color, and shell decorations as closely as you can. Read about the practice of creating shrines like this in Mexico and explain the significance and the tradition to your class as you exhibit the shrine you have created.

---

### Tomas

Tomas is Rafael's older brother. Rafael sends his mother to Tomas when he needs a break from her.

## THEMES

### Tragedy

The theme of death weaves through Benitez's novel from beginning to end. The story opens as people are standing at the beach waiting for a drowned body to float to shore, setting a somber mood that will overshadow many of the book's characters. All the deaths in this story are dramatically tragic. In other words, the deaths cause more than sad responses. For example, there is the death of Concha and her two sons in a bus accident. This is a very sad event, but the tragedy is portrayed through Beto, the son who does not die. Beto feels guilty about his mother's death. He believes that he has become a burden for his father because he cannot shake off his depression. His father worries because Beto does not eat or speak. Beto finally admits to his father that the reason he feels guilty is that he might have prevented his mother's and brothers' deaths if he had taken the trip with them. The tragedy is that the young boy feels so responsible that he wishes he, too, had died.

Benitez creates another tragedy in the death of Justina, the daughter of Justo Flores. Justo, the man who trains birds, has not spoken to Justina in many years. Their estranged relationship began

*Traditional fishermen* (© *A.T. Willett* / *Alamy*)

when Justo married another woman after Justina's mother died. Justo's new wife did not want to raise Justina. Justo and his daughter have not spoken since. The tragedy comes into play when Justo receives news about Justina's death. It is then that he realizes he will never have another chance to bridge the gap between them.

A more central tragedy is the death of Marta's son, Richard. Marta did not want to give birth to this baby, since it was conceived as a result of rape. She considers having an abortion. Later, Marta decides to keep the boy and appears to be doing a good job of mothering him. Though Marta had placed a curse on her sister's baby after her sister refused to raise Marta's baby, it seems that the curse falls on her own child. The tragedy occurs after Marta has surrendered herself to the raising of her child and then her son, Richard, drowns.

### Trust

The theme of trust is brought up in several different chapters. It is hinted at in the opening scene, in which Remedios trusts her intuitions and makes a stand on the beach where she feels the body of

young Richard will appear. In the next chapter, Candelario trusts his boss, don Gustavo, as he learns to make a Caesar salad. When guests complain about the salad, Candelario trusts that don Gustavo will own up to his mistake. Readers, and Candelario, learn that don Gustavo is mean hearted and cannot be trusted.

Marta trusts her sister when Chayo agrees with her husband that they will raise Marta's baby. This trust is sabotaged when Chayo gets pregnant and changes her mind about taking Marta's baby. Throughout the rest of the story, that break in trust between the two sisters sets off a long string of events. The wounds that the lack of trust cause are not remedied until tragedy strikes and Marta's son drowns.

Chapter four is also focused on the theme of trust. First, Fulgencio trusts the so-called gringo, Jaime. Jaime is a stranger, but Fulgencio accepts Jaime's offer of a ride to the next town. When Jaime takes a detour away from their planned destination, Fulgencio begins to lose that trust. He has no reason for this except that Jaime is a stranger, so the trust is not based upon past experiences the two of them shared. Fulgencio knows very few details about what Jaime is doing in Mexico or what he does for a living. Jaime offers almost no conversation to fill in the gaps, so Fulgencio becomes very suspicious. Fulgencio's fears escalate when Jaime stops the car to investigate a deserted beach. When Jaime comes back to the car and sees Fulgencio reaching for a machete, Jaime then jumps to conclusions and also becomes distrustful of Fulgencio. The mutual lack of trust in this situation is based on lack of personal knowledge as well as on both men's fears. Jaime turns the issue around at the end when he leaves Fulgencio's camera and equipment on the side of the road for Fulgencio to find. Fulgencio realizes too late what a fool he was not to trust the white stranger.

## STYLE

### *Linked Short Stories*

Benitez's novel is composed in an unusual style. In a traditional form, a novel develops its story line and characters through a series of chapters. Although this novel is divided into chapters, the links between chapters are only loosely connected. Each chapter reads more like a short story, with the focus on brief glimpses into the lives of particular characters. One chapter focuses on Candelario and Chayo, for instance, and the next one focuses on Raphael, the school teacher. Although some of the characters bump into one another in later chapters, the bonds among them are often peripheral. For example, there is a chapter devoted to Cesar and his son Beto, making them main characters for the duration of that section. Those two characters also show up in a chapter devoted to Rafael, but they are only in the background in Rafael's chapter.

By creating this style for her storytelling, Benitez covers a lot of territory, as if the narrator was visiting with several members of a neighborhood. The reader learns details about the individual characters but seldom witnesses all the characters interacting with one another. The effect is that readers feel like they have had brief glimpses of the characters but have not spent enough time with them to really get to know them.

### *Lack of a Protagonist*

There is no protagonist, or main character, in this story. Traditional novels usually employ one character through which the story is told. In Benitez's novel, there are some characters who return from one chapter to the next, and the reader becomes better acquainted with them than with others, but there is no one character the reader can point to and say, this is a story about him or her. The closest this novel comes to having a protagonist might be Remedios. She has the most chapters devoted to her; however, those chapters are extremely brief. She is only faintly involved in the lives of the other characters.

Another element in traditional novels is the development of the protagonist, referred to as the character arc. The protagonist grows from what he or she was at the beginning to what he or she becomes by the end of the story. In Benitez's novel, some characters do change, such as Marta, who begins by hating her unborn son to becoming a good mother and then suffering the loss of her child. Rafael also changes, from being a browbeaten son to finding his independence from his mother. Beto, the young boy who loses his mother, also transforms himself as he recovers from his depression. But none of these characters hold the limelight long enough to be called a protagonist.

## HISTORICAL CONTEXT

### *Mexico—History and Culture*

Initially, before the Spanish invasion of the early 1500s, the people of Mexico were of an advanced Amerindian descent. The Maya people are considered to be the most highly developed of the ancient Mexican cultures, having developed a written language and an understanding of many aspects of science, such as astronomy and mathematics. The dates of these people have been traced back as far as 1500 BCE with signs of their existence ceasing sometime around 900 CE.

Replacing the Maya appear to be a group known as the Toltec. The Toltec were known as warriors, and they claimed land as far north as what later became the southwestern part of the United States. Like the Maya, the Toltec also disappeared. The range of their era is listed as somewhere between tenth century CE and the eleventh century. Other minor groups that flourished for short periods between the eleventh and sixteenth centuries include the Chichimeca and the Tarasco, both Amerindian cultures. However, the major group that developed and next influenced

# COMPARE & CONTRAST

- **1980s:** The oil-based economy that flourished in the 1970s in Mexico suffers its worst recession in fifty years as oil prices plummet.

  **2000s:** The Mexican economy, which depends largely on exports to the United States, suffers from the economic downturn in the U.S. economy.

- **1980s:** According to the World Bank, 21 percent of the Mexican population lives in poverty.

  **2000s:** The World Bank calculates a decrease in national poverty in Mexico, but between 4 and 9 percent of the population still lives on less than one dollar per day.

- **1980s:** A report from the United Nations estimates that 800,000 abortions per year are performed in Mexico despite the restrictions the Mexican government puts on this procedure. This figure suggests that about 24 percent of females of childbearing age have had an abortion.

  **2000s:** Though some local Mexican governments have legalized abortion, many doctors refuse to perform the procedure because it is against their beliefs.

---

Mexican culture was the Aztec, who were the prevalent culture in Mexico from the early fourteenth to the beginning of the sixteenth century. The Aztec were based in Tenochtitlàn, the capital city of a large empire. The city was considered an architectural marvel for that time, with a series of canals, marketplaces, and temples. The Aztec had a highly organized society, with ruling monarchs, a well-defined priesthood, armies, and a distinct merchant class. The arrival of the Spanish would put an end to the rule of Mexico by Amerindians.

The Spanish conqueror Hernando Cortés landed in Mexico in 1519 and set up a Spanish town. The Aztec, upon hearing that a white-skinned man had been seen, believed Cortés fulfilled an old prophecy of the arrival of an Aztec god. Though the Aztec attempted to stop him, Cortés proved victorious, as he pushed through Mexico, conquering millions of Aztec with an army of less than 1,000 soldiers and the help of an epidemic spread of disease. Cortés's victories were celebrated in Spain, and thus the Spanish influence in Mexico began.

With the Spanish came Catholicism. Spanish people were devout in their Catholic beliefs and began to spread their faith throughout the villages and towns of Amerindians. Between the sixteenth century and the nineteenth century, it has been estimated that more than 12,000 Catholic churches were built in Mexico. The Catholic missionaries who arrived set up schools to teach the indigenous people not only how to read and write but how to practice Christian principles.

As Spanish influence grew, so too did the development of relationships between Amerindian people and the Spanish, eventually giving rise to a mixed-blood population, referred to as mestizos, who now make up the vast majority of Mexico's population. Culturally, the Spanish were considered at the top of the social ladder in Mexico, followed by mestizos. At the bottom of the ladder were the pure-blood indigenous people, the Amerindians, who provided much of the manual labor in the building of new cities. As the population of Amerindians declined, African slaves were imported to do the hard labor, thus adding a new segment to the culture and society of Mexico.

According to the Central Intelligence Agency's *World Factbook*, the 2009 estimated population of Mexico is slightly over 111 million. Of that, 60 percent are mestizo, a mix of Amerindian and Spanish; 30 percent are purely or predominantly Amerindian; 9 percent are white; and 1 percent are listed as other. Roman Catholics make up 76 percent of the population.

*Mexican seaside city (Image copyright Martin Garnham, 2009. Used under license from Shutterstock.com)*

With the richness of Mexico's history come other cultural mixtures, such as those found in the healing practices. Traditional western medicine is used, as well as ancient healing forms from Amerindian, Spanish, and African traditional medicine. The older practices include more than just the lifting or applying of curses, as popularly portrayed. Often natural herbs, along with an understanding of the patient's underlying psychology, are considered in the treatment process.

## CRITICAL OVERVIEW

*A Place Where the Sea Remembers*, Benitez's first published novel, has received favorable reviews. One element that is consistently referred to by many critics as the novel's strength is the language Benitez uses in the telling of this story. Such were the comments from Chris Bohjalian, writing for the *New York Times*. Bohjalian stated that throughout her story, "Ms. Benitez's descriptions of people and places are crisp, and the staccato rhythms of her prose are just right for this dark fable of a story." Continuing with the emphasis on Benitez's mastery of language,

the *Library Journal*'s Harold Augenbraum and Shirley E. Havens praised Benitez as "a true artist with words."

Other critics focused their attention on the characters that Benitez develops in *A Place Where the Sea Remembers*. Martha Frase-Blunt, writing for the publication *Hispanic*, described the novel by stating: "Sandra Benitez mines the lives of ordinary Mexican people and delivers a collection of simple stories, simply told, that shine with gem like intensity." In conclusion, Frase-Blunt wrote: "Benitez's prose is spare, yet she succeeds in drawing very real characters. The unique individuals who populate *A Place Where the Sea Remembers* are, indeed, unforgettable."

In a review for *Publishers Weekly*, an anonymous critic found that "Benitez's unsparing vision into the stark realities of village residents' lives offers a poignant counterpoint to superficial vacation snapshots of Mexico." Robert Kendall, writing for the *Hispanic Times Magazine* told the story of how Benitez almost gave up her writing career before it had barely begun. However, while she reassessed her situation, she "continued to write her little stories eventually weaving them together in a powerful novel."

Kendall also commented on the lifelike characters that Benitez created for this novel. Her "moving depiction of characters," Kendall wrote, "become so real you think they are the next door neighbors." And finally, Mary Margaret Benson, writing for the *Library Journal* found this novel to be "another welcome addition to the growing body of Latina literature."

## CRITICISM

### Joyce Hart

*Hart is a published author of over thirty books and a creative writing teacher. In this essay, she interprets the lessons the author implies in* A Place Where the Sea Remembers*: that her characters learn from practicing, or not practicing, the act of forgiveness.*

In *A Place Where the Sea Remembers*, Benitez wraps her novel in a study of forgiveness. She develops several different models, demonstrating the benefits of forgiveness as well as the torment that can occur when forgiveness is seemingly impossible to attain. In her novel, Benitez's characters, from young children to the elderly, learn lessons in forgiving themselves as well as forgiving others. In the process, Benitez lays bare, through her characters, the benefits as well as the sorrows that forgiveness, or the lack of it, can cause.

Beto is the youngest character who must deal with issues of forgiveness. He must learn the difficult lesson of forgiving himself. Beto mistakenly believes that he could have saved his mother from her tragic death. In his grief, Beto thinks that had he been with his mother, he might have kept the bus from falling over the cliff. Even if he could not have stopped the accident from happening, he imagines that somehow he could have cushioned the fall for his mother and brothers or could have rescued them from the crush of metal when the bus came to its final stop. Not being at the scene of the bus accident makes him feel responsible for his mother's and brothers' deaths. Beto's psychology suffers from his fantasies of saving his family. As he wraps himself in his mother's cloak and refuses to eat, he probably replays the crash scene over and over in his mind, trying to force the real events into other, happier conclusions. His inability to forgive himself pushes him closer to his own death. He stops responding. He stops eating.

> BENITEZ RESTATES HER CASE THAT ALTHOUGH FORGIVENESS IS DIFFICULT, THE CONSEQUENCES OF NOT FORGIVING MIGHT BE EVEN MORE DEVASTATING."

He grows weaker every day. It is only when he witnesses his father's sorrow that Beto begins to venture outside of his self-created shell. He is not the only one who is suffering, he realizes. But Beto has other problems, too. Even after confessing to his father that he feels responsible for the deaths, Beto also has to learn to forgive himself for the burden he has become for his father. His father worries about his son. Beto's inability to forgive himself for what he considers his selfish actions has driven him to the point of both physical and mental illness. Beto's father finally clears up the boy's confusion about being responsible for the deaths. Beto also hears his father say that Beto is the one whom his father now needs. It is not until Beto is able to rid himself of his guilt that he is able to forgive himself.

In Beto's situation, Benitez demonstrates how being unable to forgive can be detrimental to one's health. This theme continues, in a different way, when Benitez explores the character of Rafael, the school teacher. The youngest of three brothers, Rafael has resigned himself to taking care of his always ailing and also demanding mother. He sacrifices most of the pleasures of his life to make sure that he is at home every minute that he is not teaching. He has no social life, because his mother takes up so much of his time and energy. Rafael also absorbs his mother's verbal abuses without complaint. For example, she accuses him of not loving her. Later, she even insinuates that Rafael is the father of Ines's miscarried baby. Through all of the sacrifices that Rafael makes for his mother's sake, he never talks back to her. He never complains to anyone about the demands that she places on his life. Although he is obviously a patient man and a loving son, it takes more than that to put up with his mother's torments. The undercurrent that Benitez suggests is that Rafael is a man

# WHAT DO I READ NEXT?

- Benitez's second novel, *Bitter Grounds* (1998), won the American Book Award and covers the lives of three generations of El Salvadoran women. The setting is a coffee plantation in the midst of a civil war in the country. Both rich and poor women are depicted in this story as the author explores the hardships and the friendships of her characters.

- Benitez's *The Weight of All Things* (2002) has received positive reviews for her story about a nine-year-old boy and the effect of the El Salvadoran civil war on his life. The young protagonist's mother is killed, and he must fend for himself. His travels, at times, put him in the hands of people on both sides of the war, the government army and the rebels.

- In 2006, Benitez published her memoir, *Bag Lady*, a story about a chronic disease that challenged the author's life. Critics have stated that the story, though true, reads as seamlessly as Benitez's fiction. Benitez uses humor as well as straightforward honesty to tell her astonishing story.

- Rudolfo A. Anaya wrote what has become a classic tale that encapsulates some of Hispanic American myths and beliefs in his novel *Bless Me, Ultima* (1972). In this story a young boy learns about the old ways through a healer, Ultima, who comes to live with his family. Several times Ultima saves the lives of some of Antonio's family. Ultima sees something special in Antonio and begins to teach him the secrets she has learned.

- In 1919, Sherwood Anderson wrote the unconventional book *Winesburg, Ohio*. It contains twenty-two related short stories, similar in format and style to Benitez's novel. The various characters in these stories live in a small, Midwestern town, and the stories share common themes of loneliness and frustration. This book is often placed on publishers' best one hundred books lists.

- Judith Ortiz Cofer, who grew up in Puerto Rico and learned the art of storytelling from her grandmother, published a novel in 2003 called *The Meaning of Consuelo*. The narrator of this novel is a young girl who relates stories from her experiences of growing up in Puerto Rico during the 1950s. The beauty of the island as well as the cruelty of a harsh dictatorship shape this story.

who knows how to forgive. Rafael constantly forgives his mother's pettiness, her selfishness, and her small-mindedness. However, when one of Rafael's brothers finally offers to take care of their mother, Rafael celebrates. He comments that only then has he felt happiness. With this character, Benitez seems to suggest that Rafael's ability to forgive his mother for all her demands and abuses should be well rewarded. She demonstrates her belief by having Rafael find love and eventually getting married.

Benitez also provides a character in this story who is unable to forgive in Justina. Though she never makes an appearance in the story, readers learn about her through her father, Justo. Though Justina's story is never fully developed, readers are told that Justina was born with a twisted foot and when her father remarried, his new wife did not want to take on the responsibility of raising Justina. Justo did not fight for her, so Justina felt abandoned. Forgiving her father was apparently unfathomable for Justina. She shut him out of her life. Justina's inability to forgive affects her father. Though his feelings are not directly exposed, Benitez has Justo asking a younger daughter about Justina, wondering if Justina might be willing to see him. So readers know that Justo is interested in his daughter, but he is not able to make a bolder step. He tracks Justina through someone else. It could be that Justo's guilt is so great that it keeps him from pursuing Justina more directly. Whatever the reason, when Justo receives the telegram that Justina has died, he senses what has happened without reading it. Justo's love for his daughter causes him to fall apart emotionally when he learns of Justina's death. She has gone to her grave without forgiving him. In this case, Benitez seems to issue a warning that one should not wait for forgiveness to come but rather seek out forgiveness. Justo fell short of this.

Chayo also has problems with forgiveness. She cannot forgive her sister, Marta, for placing a curse on Chayo's unborn baby. Despite the closeness that the sisters once shared, Chayo cannot fathom how Marta could have been so selfish or so cruel. Even after Marta pays to have the curse released and repents for her sins, Chayo can still find no room for forgiveness. She believes Marta's reasons for placing the curse were superficial and selfish. Marta wanted to move to the United States and be free from the responsibilities of motherhood. She wanted Chayo to bear the responsibility of raising her child. With this information in hand, Chayo does not have enough of an open heart to find forgiveness in this situation.

Benitez presents a good case for Chayo's refusal to forgive Marta. However, she also shows Chayo's coldhearted side. Forgiveness is not an easy process. In some cases, it takes the mind and the heart of a saint, someone who has transcended human nature to forgive. Chayo does not seem capable of rising to that level. She prefers holding onto her grudge against her sister. The author implies that the result of this grudge, of Chayo's inability to forgive, is a different type of curse. Chayo's grudge turns on her sister and plants its own curse on Marta's child, ripping him away and tossing him into the raging river. It is not until after this tragedy that Chayo finds the grace to forgive. But forgiveness, in this case, comes with a high price. And as a result, Chayo's forgiveness is tainted with guilt. Even though Chayo did not pay to have a curse put on her sister's child, she feels responsible for Richard's death. He was in her care the night he drowned. At first, when Chayo saw Marta's son slip into the water, Chayo thought it was her own son who was being carried away. Naturally Chayo was relieved when she discovers that her child was safe. But the price for her son's safety was the death of Marta's son. Again, the author might be issuing a warning through the character

of Chayo. Benitez restates her case that although forgiveness is difficult, the consequences of not forgiving might be even more devastating.

**Source:** Joyce Hart, Critical Essay on *A Place Where the Sea Remembers*, in *Novels for Students*, Gale, Cengage Learning, 2010.

### *Publishers Weekly*

*In the following review, a* Publishers Weekly *critic points out that Benitez is noted for her sympathetically portrayed characters and stark illustrations of the realities of Hispanic life.*

Latina writer Benitez begins her excellent debut novel with a painful event—the wait for a drowned body to float to shore—and works backwards, retracing the myriad, seemingly insignificant steps that led to the character's death. As in *Like Water for Chocolate*, this novel sympathetically explores the lives of Mexican women caught in a mystical, fatalistic world. Chayo, a flower seller, and her sister Marta, a chambermaid, live in a poverty-stricken village by the sea. When 15-year-old Marta is raped and becomes pregnant, seemingly barren Chayo and her husband, Candelario, agree to take the child. Soon after, however, Chayo discovers that she too is expectant and reneges on the promise. Livid, Marta arranges with el brujo, the witch doctor, to put a curse on her sister's child. Both women bear sons, and a remorseful Marta tells her sister about the curse, which she claims to have had removed by la curandera, the healer. But when Chayo's son almost dies after being bitten by fire ants, the sisters' relationship once more deteriorates and, inexorably, the tragedy presaged in the book's opening chapter comes to pass. Benitez's unsparing vision into the stark realities of village residents' lives offers a poignant counterpoint to superficial vacation snapshots of Mexico.

**Source:** Review of *A Place Where the Sea Remembers*, in *Publisher's Weekly*, Vol. 240, No. 29, July 1993, p. 236.

## SOURCES

Augenbraum, Harold, and Shirley E. Havens, "Word of Mouth," in *Library Journal*, Vol. 119, No. 10, June 1, 1994, p. 200.

Avila, Elena, and Joy Parker, *Woman Who Glows in the Dark: A Curandera Reveals Traditional Aztec Secrets of Physical and Spiritual Health*, Tarcher, 1999.

Benitez, Sandra, *A Place Where the Sea Remembers*, Scribner Paperback Fiction/Simon and Schuster, 1993.

Benson, Mary Margaret, Review of *Bitter Grounds*, in *Library Journal*, Vol. 122, No. 14, September 1, 1997, p. 214.

Bohjalian, Chris, "The Fatal Caesar Salad," in *New York Times*, October 31, 1993, p. A25.

Central Intelligence Agency, "Mexico," in *The World Factbook*, https://www.cia.gov/library/publications/the-world-factbook/geos/MX.html (accessed June 10, 2009).

Frase-Blunt, Martha, Review of *A Place Where the Sea Remembers*, in *Hispanic*, Vol. 7, No. 3, April, 1994 p. 72.

Kendall, Robert, Review of *A Place Where the Sea Remembers*, in *Hispanic Times Magazine*, Vol. 18, No. 3, May-June 1997, p. 39.

Malkin, Elisabeth, and Nacha Cattan, "Mexico City Struggles with Law on Abortion," in *New York Times*, August 25, 2008, p. A5.

"Poverty in Mexico—Fact Sheet," in *The World Bank*, http://web.worldbank.org/WBSITE/EXTERNAL/COUNTRIES/LACEXT/MEXICOEXTN/0,contentMDK:20233967~pagePK:141137~piPK:141127~theSitePK:338397,00.html (accessed May 14, 2009).

Review of *A Place Where the Sea Remembers*, in *Publisher's Weekly*, Vol. 240, No. 29, July 1993, p. 236.

Ruiz, Ramon Eduardo, *Triumphs and Tragedy: A History of the Mexican People*, W. W. Norton, 1992.

*Sandra Benitez Web site*, http://sandrabenitez.com (accessed May 13, 2009).

United Nations, "Abortion Policies: Mexico," in *United Nations Population Division Department of Economic and Social Affairs*, http://www.un.org/esa/population/publications/abortion/doc/mexico.doc (accessed May 18, 2009).

U.S. Department of State, "Background Note: Mexico," in *Bureau of Western Hemisphere Affairs*, http://www.state.gov/r/pa/ei/bgn/35749.htm (accessed June 10, 2009).

# FURTHER READING

Behnke, Alison, *Mexicans in America*, Lerner Publications, 2004.

> Written for junior high school students, this book provides an historical background into immigration as well as social issues that Mexicans face when they move to the United States.

Dahl-Bredine, Phil, and Stephen Hicken, *The Other Game: Lessons from How Life Is Played in Mexican Villages*, Orbis Books, 2008.

> The lives of Mixtec villagers are explored in this book through personal interviews of people who have lived in small towns that have existed for thousands of years in the southern part of Mexico. These people discuss their lives, their families, and how they work and make a sustainable living. The author wrote the book believing that these small villages might offer contemporary options for life in bigger towns.

Garcia-Oropeza, Guillermo, and Cristobal Garcia-Sanchez, *One Hundred and One Beautiful Small Towns in Mexico*, Rizzoli, 2008.

> Enjoy the scenery of some of Mexico's most beautiful small towns through photographs and stories that recall the towns' histories. This book also offers an overview of the culture of Mexico and the influence of the ancient Maya traditions. Small coastal towns, as well as hilltop villages, are included in the publication.

Hellman, Judith Adler, *Mexican Lives*, New Press, 1994.

> Hellman offers stories of both the rich and poor who live in Mexico. A small subsistence farmer talks about his dreams of selling gourmet fruit, and a housewife tries to make a decision about her life's savings, whether to help her son migrate to the United States or buy a sewing machine with which she can earn more money. Hellman brings these stories together to provide a well-rounded view of Mexican life and culture.

Koch, Peter O., *The Aztecs, the Conquistadors, and the Making of Mexican Culture*, McFarland, 2005.

> Koch provides a detailed history of the ancient tribes of Mexico, their defeat, and the circumstances, influences, and events that evolved into what has become Mexican culture.

Madigan, Dan, *Mondo Lucha a Go-Go: The Bizarre and Honorable World of Wild Mexican Wrestling*, Rayo, 2007.

> Masked wrestling is fast becoming an international craze, and it all began in Latin America. Madigan traces its history and displays vivid photographs of some of the most interesting characters in the extreme ringside action.

Merrell, Floyd, *The Mexicans: A Sense of Culture*, Westview Press, 2003.

> Merrell provides an overview of Mexican history in order to explain what has gone into making contemporary Mexican culture. He provides information on the wide variety of ethnic cultures that are found in Mexico, such as Amerindian, African American, and European. Also included are stories about daily life, artistic pursuits, and politics.

Monsivais, Carlos, *Mexican Postcards*, Verso, 1997.

> Mexican culture, in context and in contrast to American culture, is explored in this book. One popular topic is music, as in Latino hip-hop. The author also explores the differences and sometimes the conflicts between contemporary and traditional lifestyles.

Rosay, Rosalina, *Journey of Hope, Memoirs of a Mexican Girl*, AR Publishing, 2007.

> The author recounts her life from childhood in the small town of Guanajuato, Mexico, to her attempt to escape poverty by immigrating illegally to the United States.

# The Power of One

## BRYCE COURTENAY

## 1989

*The Power of One* is the first novel by Bryce Courtenay, a writer who was born in South Africa but has lived in Australia since 1958. It was first published in 1989 in Great Britain and Australia, as well as the United States. Loosely based on Courtenay's own biography, *The Power of One* follows a small, weak, English-speaking white child as he navigates a world where the strong dominate the weak, where the white population keeps the black population in a state of semi-slavery, and where the two major white ethnic groups, the English and the Afrikaans-speaking Boer, are locked in a struggle for power. Peekay finds himself caught between the two worlds. To the Boers, he is a *rooinek* (meaning "red-neck," after the English soldiers' sunburned necks), whereas to the English, his ability to speak Afrikaans and his love of boxing mark him as someone who is not a true gentleman. Peekay also speaks several African languages, and throughout the novel, he consistently sees the black people around him as full human beings. This is another sign of Peekay's difference, for the South Africa in which he is being raised is a world built on the ideas that whites are superior to blacks and that blacks owe whites deference and subservience. In a nation divided by ethnic and racial hatreds, Peekay's ability to move between worlds is exceptional, and it causes him problems as often as it opens doors to him.

Peekay escapes the brutality of his world through education. He befriends Doc, an elderly

*Bryce Courtenay* (*AP Images*)

professor, who teaches him to play the piano, to identify rare cacti, to play chess, and not to hate anyone. When Doc is incarcerated as an enemy alien during World War II, he is given much more freedom than an ordinary prisoner because he is an artist and scientist. Peekay learns that becoming an educated person can set him apart from the brutality of the prison. Along with Doc, the characters of Mrs. Boxall and Miss Bornstein both contribute to Peekay's education and take on the challenge of teaching the black prisoners how to read, write, and do basic math. Throughout the novel, Peekay's success in school is what sets him apart and allows him to escape the cycle of brutality in which he is mired.

Despite his education, Peekay is no stranger to violence. Beaten as a child, he encounters a boxer on a train who teaches him that by being smart and quick, small people can escape victimhood. Peekay takes this lesson to heart and determines to become the welterweight champion of the world when he grows up. He trains as a boxer, and although he learns to distinguish

boxing from fighting, he is not above using a dirty trick in a street fight. The lure of violence is always a challenge for Peekay, as he is a poor boy in a violent nation where the strong take what they want from the weak. It is finally through a combination of education and violence that Peekay escapes South Africa. His education wins him a scholarship to Oxford University in England, but he earns the money he needs to get there by doing brute physical work in the copper mines of Rhodesia. This is the central tension of *The Power of One*, whether to succeed through wit and speed or through brute strength. In the end, Peekay must combine the two qualities in order to escape his country and move into the world.

## AUTHOR BIOGRAPHY

Courtenay was born on August 14, 1933, in Johannesburg, South Africa. His mother, Maude, was single when he was born and in precarious mental health throughout his childhood, so she placed him in an orphanage as an infant. The orphanage was populated with mostly Afrikaans-speaking Boer children who marked him as the enemy, as they do Peekay in the novel. The boys at the orphanage bullied and beat him regularly. In order to defend himself from the bigger boys, Courtenay learned to box. He also learned to tell stories as a means of self-defense. When the bigger boys threatened to hit him, Courtenay offered them a story. To ensure his safety, he would break off before the end, telling the bullies that if they hit him, he would never tell them what happened.

During a Sunday expedition to gather firewood for the orphanage, Courtenay nearly cut off a finger. The orphanage matron sent the boy to walk seven miles to the nearest doctor. The doctor kept him overnight, and when Courtenay awoke the next morning, he discovered a box of English books near the bed. English books were forbidden in the Afrikaans-speaking town where the orphanage was located, so Courtenay stole a leather-bound volume by hiding it under his sweater. "It was the most beautiful thing I had ever seen," Courtenay said in an interview. "I knew I needed to know what was in this book." When a female teacher arrived at the orphanage from Johannesburg several years later, she taught him to read English, tutored him, and signed him up for the entrance examination to a fashionable boys' school in Johannesburg. He scored well enough to win a full scholarship. Courtenay did well academically, but during vacation, when the other children went home, he spent holidays in Johannesburg's parks with the homeless. "They were wonderful to me," he told Lou Fortescue in an interview with an Australian newspaper, *The Telegraph*.

After finishing school, Courtenay was accepted to the London School of Journalism. To raise the money he needed, Courtenay signed on to work in the copper mines of what was then northern Rhodesia (now Zimbabwe). It was dangerous work, blasting rock through a big metal cage known as a grizzly. Courtenay began his work as a "grizzly man" with eleven other boys his own age. When he left the mines fourteen months later, six of them were permanently injured, and three had died.

In London, Courtenay studied journalism and met his future wife, Benita, who convinced him to return to her native Australia. Courtenay emigrated with her in 1958. They were married and had three sons. Courtenay got work at an advertising agency in the newly created television division. He rose through the ranks of several advertising firms before starting his own agency, which he eventually sold, earning him enough money to follow his dream of becoming a writer. Since that time he has published more than fifteen novels, including *The Power of One*, and he consistently appears on the best-seller lists in Australia.

# MEDIA ADAPTATIONS

- *The Power of One* was adapted for film by Robert Mark Kamen and directed by John Avildsen (*Rocky, The Karate Kid*). The film, released in 1992, stars Morgan Freeman as Geel Piet and Daniel Craig, in his first major movie role, as the Judge. This film is considerably different from the novel, changing Peekay's family story, eliminating the episode with Hoppie Groenewald on the train, and adding a love story to Peekay's sojourn in Johannesburg. The movie version spends more time on the problem of apartheid, and it recasts the Judge as a Johannesburg policeman. The film features gorgeous photography of Africa and is inspiringly scored by the South African musician Johnny Clegg.

- *The Power of One* is available as a twenty-one-hour audiobook, narrated by Humphrey Bower in 2004. Bower also recorded the audiobook of the abridged young-adult version of the novel. This version is only nine hours long, and like the printed version of the abridged novel, focuses on the story of Peekay's childhood, ending with the concert.

## PLOT SUMMARY

### Book One, Chapters 1–15

#### CHAPTER 1

*The Power of One* is narrated in the first person, although the narrator remains nameless for several chapters. At the age of five, our narrator is separated from his beloved Zulu nanny and sent to boarding school. On his first day there, he is subjected to a brutal and terrifying trial in which the other boys drag him to the shower room and urinate on him. The narrator is so young that he routinely wets his bed in the night; the matron beats him for it, and the other children nickname him "Pisskop." When the boy returns home for the summer, he confides in his nanny about the bedwetting. She sends for Inkosi-Inkosikazi, a Zulu medicine man, who leads the boy on an imaginary journey to give him strength. The medicine man also teaches the boy how to hypnotize a chicken.

#### CHAPTER 2

Pisskop takes his chicken, named Granpa Chook, back to school with him. The Judge returns and shows off a swastika tattoo, and then tells Pisskop that Adolf Hitler is coming to drive the English into the sea. The next morning, Granpa Chook is nearly turned into soup by the matron, until he demonstrates a talent for catching bugs. England declares war on Germany, and the headmaster of the school leads the children in chants of "Heil Hitler." Pisskop enrages a teacher by reciting the multiplication tables and then suffers a beating at the hands of the headmaster.

When the kind, English-speaking doctor arrives to tend to him, the matron tells Pisskop to lie and tell the doctor he fell out of a tree.

**CHAPTER 3**

The Judge declares Pisskop a prisoner of war and sentences him to march around the playground every afternoon. In order to prevent the Judge from beating him, Pisskop offers to do his math homework. Nevertheless, Pisskop's status as a prisoner of war remains unchanged. Once the Judge finds out he will graduate, he institutes a last torture session, in which the boys rub feces on Pisskop's face. Granpa Chook, the chicken, comes to his rescue by defecating from a tree branch into the Judge's open mouth. The boys turn on the chicken and kill him. Devastated by the death of his friend, Pisskop buries Granpa Chook in a pile of stones and returns to the school.

**CHAPTER 4**

The matron informs Pisskop that his grandfather has moved to a town called Barberton. She buys him a pair of canvas sneakers called tackies. Harry Crown asks the boy's name. When he replies "Pisskop," the shopkeeper is appalled and renames him P. K. (Peekay). Peekay is delivered into the care of Hoppie Groenewald, the conductor of the train. He takes Peekay under his wing, settles him into a compartment, tells him he can take off his shoes, and explains how boxing works. Hoppie treats Peekay to dinner when the train stops for a break.

**CHAPTER 5**

In the morning, Hoppie takes Peekay to the dining car for an enormous breakfast, during which he explains betting and Peekay wagers his only shilling. In Gravelotte, the town where the fight is to take place, Hoppie takes Peekay into a store run by an Indian family to buy shoes that fit. The shopkeeper recognizes Hoppie as "Kid Louis" and refuses their money. Peekay is shocked to find out that Hoppie has been drafted and takes this as a sign that Hitler has arrived in South Africa. Hoppie tells him that South Africa is fighting on the British side, and he then teaches the boy to tie his new shoes.

**CHAPTER 6**

Big Hettie, the cook in the railway kitchen, sits Peekay beside her at the top of the stands. Hoppie wins the first five rounds easily, but in the seventh round, Smit nearly knocks Hoppie out. He comes back, and he finishes the round by landing a solid uppercut on Smit. Smit resorts to dirty tricks, head butting Hoppie in the eleventh round. The referee calls the fight on a foul, but Hoppie insists on continuing the fight. In round fourteen, Smit lands what seems to be a knockout punch, but Hoppie rises from the canvas and knocks the big fighter out with a blow to his jaw. It takes four big railwaymen to get Big Hettie down from the top of the stands. Hoppie finds Peekay and utters the phrase that will become Peekay's motto: "First with the head, and then with the heart."

**CHAPTER 7**

Peekay wakes up in a railcar berth. He discovers Big Hettie passed out on the bunk below him. While Peekay is in the corridor, Big Hettie slides off the bunk and appears to be suffocating on her skirt. Peekay manages to slide her legs off the bunk, alleviating her respiratory distress, but she lodges between the bunks. The conductor, Pik Botha, and Peekay try to raise the fallen woman, but to no avail. They manage to prop Big Hettie up with pillows, and to pass the time, Big Hettie tells Peekay stories about her lost love, the bantamweight fighter. Big Hettie seems to be having more and more trouble breathing. They arrive at the next station; Big Hettie is in serious distress. "You will be a great fighter, I know it," she whispers, just before dying, lodged between the berths.

**CHAPTER 8**

Peekay arrives in Barberton, where his mother picks him up with her minister from the Apostolic Faith Church. When Peekay asks about his nanny, his mother tells him he is too old for a nanny. Peekay keeps asking but no one will tell him what has happened to his nanny. Eventually, Peekay forces his mother to tell him that she sent the nanny back to Zululand, because she would not convert to the Apostolic Faith Church and so is "possessed by the devil." Peekay runs out of the house and climbs a high hill until he finds on a rock where he can sit and think.

**CHAPTER 9**

Doc finds Peekay sitting mournfully on the rock and takes his picture. Doc is a German professor of music who collects cacti and who makes Peekay laugh hilariously with his trademark word, "absoloodle." Peekay and Doc become fast friends. Upon returning home, Peekay's mother says that he has mocked the Lord and sends him to go to bed without supper. Several days later, the Professor calls on Peekay's mother and asks her to let him teach the boy music in exchange for Peekay's talent at finding cacti. Peekay's mother hesitates and then agrees. Doc not only teaches the boy about nature but takes him to the library and teaches him to play the piano.

**CHAPTER 10**

Doc is arrested under the Aliens Act of 1939. The arresting officer handcuffs Doc and knocks him to the ground. When Peekay throws himself at the officer, the officer kicks him in the head and breaks his jaw. Peekay awakens in the hospital with his jaw wired shut and discovers that the local newspaper has accused Doc of being a German spy. Peekay gets Marie, his nurse, to smuggle a note to Mrs. Boxall with a full account of what happened. Mrs. Boxall takes the letter to the military judge, who clears Doc of all espionage charges. Doc must still remain in jail as an enemy alien, but Peekay is given permission to visit him. When Peekay finds out that there is a boxing team at the prison, he begs to join. The kommandant demands that Doc play a surprise concert for the town. Doc confides to Peekay that he has terrible stage fright. As Doc takes the stage, a riot nearly ensues between the Boer and the English, but Doc quells it by playing Beethoven.

**CHAPTER 11**

Doc and Peekay settle into prison life. Peekay trains with the boxing team. Doc is spared the work duties to which most prisoners are subjected. Marie, the kind nurse, comes to work for Peekay's mother and brings supplies back from her parents' farm on weekends. She brings tobacco from the farm, and Peekay smuggles it to Geel Piet, who runs the prison black market. Eventually, Peekay begins smuggling letters too, and Mrs. Boxall starts "The Earl of Sandwich Fund for the Poor" to raise money for stamps and to help the black prisoners' families. Peekay wins his first real fight. The black prisoners nickname Peekay the "Tadpole Angel."

**CHAPTER 12**

Peekay goes to the district championships, and Geel Piet presents him with black leather boxing boots that the prisoners have made for him. The new warden, Sergeant Borman,

threatens Piet. Doc trades the kommandant a concert performance for the opportunity to attend Peekay's fight. His opponent is much bigger, but Peekay wins his qualifying round and proceeds to the finals, where he is matched with a boy nicknamed "Killer Kroon." Peekay nearly loses the fight twice, once when he is accidentally knocked over (a knockdown ends the fight) and again when Kroon manages to pull down Peekay's pants. The referee calls no knockdown on both occasions, and Peekay wins the fight on footwork and points.

**CHAPTER 13**

Lieutenant Smit praises Piet's coaching abilities. The prison photographer takes a photo of the team. When Smit invites Piet into the shot, everyone but Doc, Peekay, and Gert moves out. A new teacher named Miss Bornstein arrives at Peekay's school, and he falls in love with her. She moves him into her class and begins to tutor him. When Smit is promoted, Borman is promoted behind him. Lieutenant Borman increases his violent behavior toward the black prisoners and menaces Geel Piet. Doc looks forward to his promised freedom at the end of the war, and Peekay discovers that Borman has been sent from Pretoria to start a new chapter of the Oxwagon Guard, a violent pro-Afrikaans group. Borman's menace increases as Peekay and Doc prepare for Doc's release.

**CHAPTER 14**

Doc agrees to return to the prison to play for the inspector in exchange for the opportunity to play for the prisoners. Lieutenant Borman tries to stop it, claiming that the prisoners will riot. Doc plays, and each tribe sings its part beautifully. After the concert, Peekay discovers the body of Geel Piet in the boxing ring, where he had been beaten to death. Captain Smit promises Peekay that he will avenge Piet. Doc returns for the inspector's concert and plays "Requiem for Geel Piet." The inspector praises Doc's music and says that Geel Piet must have been a great man to inspire it. The prison boxing team gives an exhibition, after which the boys are told to go back into the darkened gymnasium and to remain very quiet. As they watch, Captain Smit and Klipkop enter the room, with Borman between them. They confront Borman with the rolled-up canvas upon which Geel Piet bled to death. Captain Smit then beats Borman until he confesses to murdering Piet, rolls him in the bloodstained canvas, and tells him he is cursed.

### CHAPTER 15

Peekay distributes tracts for the Apostolic Faith Church as part of the letter-writing program. When Peekay begins tucking tobacco into the tracts, his "ministry" becomes very popular. Lieutenant Borman begins to suffer from intestinal cancer. Miss Bornstein, Mrs. Boxall, and Doc all prepare Peekay to take the entrance exams for a private school, the Prince of Wales school, in Johannesburg. Peekay passes the exam and wins a full scholarship, but he is nearly prevented from attending by the expense of buying the proper school uniforms. His friends all rally to purchase the proper fabric and accessories, and Miss Bornstein's father, who was a tailor before fleeing Hitler's Germany, makes him the proper clothes.

## Book Two, Chapters 16–22

### CHAPTER 16

At the Prince of Wales school, Peekay meets Morrie Levy, who becomes his best friend. Peekay is assigned to "fag," or act as a servant, for the head boy in his dormitory. The legend of the Tadpole Angel has traveled to Johannesburg, and the black servants at the school quietly take up many of his duties as fag. Peekay joins the boxing team, and Morrie volunteers to manage it. Peekay uses Geel Piet's eight-punch combination to win his first fight. Before the fight starts, a number of blacks arrive, and after Peekay finishes fighting they chant "Onoshobishobi Ingelosi" (Tadpole Angel).

### CHAPTER 17

Peekay and Morrie spend the next two years taking bets, or "running book," on school fights to provide Peekay with spending money. When Peekay suggests that they lend money to boys at the school, Morrie is appalled. He has been sent to the Prince of Wales school to scrub himself of the stigma of being Jewish, but Peekay convinces him to open up the "Boarder's Bank." Peekay continues to box, and people continue to attend his matches, leading chants before matches. Miss Bornstein sends Peekay letters with questions and discussion points about his schoolwork. He shares these letters with Morrie, and they print and sell them as "The Miss Bornstein School of Correspondence Notes." Each year the headmaster, St. John Burnham, chooses six boys for

the group known as Sinjun's People. Morrie and Peekay make a lot of money setting up a bet on who will be picked and are thrilled to discover that they have both been picked for the group.

### CHAPTER 18

Peekay returns home between terms to discover that not much has changed in Barberton. The prison letter-writing effort has expanded to include a school for prisoners. Gert has been promoted to corporal, has learned English, and has become devoted to Doc and to Mrs. Boxall. Peekay resumes boxing with the prison squad, smuggling tobacco to prisoners, and he discovers that Doc learned to play ragtime jazz in New Orleans many years ago. During the day, Miss Bornstein tutors Peekay for the Oxford University entrance exams.

### CHAPTER 19

Doc convinces Peekay to take an overnight hike to a waterfall. They find what appears to be an ordinary cave, at the back of which is an opening that leads to a second, enormous chamber filled with white stalagmites and stalactites that shine like crystal. At the end of the cavern is a ledge of rock that looks like an altar. Doc speculates on how marvelous it would be to die in such a place and makes Peekay promise never to tell anyone about the cave. Peekay is made uncomfortable by the excitement the old man shows. It is a long hike home, and at the end of the hike Doc is exhausted.

### CHAPTER 20

Peekay returns to school and takes up the tutorials with Singe 'n' Burn. Morrie has arranged for Peekay to train with Solly Goldman, the best professional boxing trainer in South Africa. To pay for it, they come up with one last betting scam. Morrie sets up a bet against the Afrikaans school, giving three-to-one odds that Prince of Wales will beat them in rugby. Prince of Wales has never beaten this school, and as a condition of making the bets, one of the fighters demands a rematch with Peekay. Peekay wins in the third round, knocking out the bigger fighter. Peekay's boxing win inspires the rugby team to win. They make enough money to pay for two years of training with Solly Goldman. Peekay goes home for the Christmas holidays and discovers that Doc has had pneumonia. When Peekay sees his old friend, he bursts into tears and begs him not to die. Doc assures him it is not yet his time.

## CHAPTER 21

The Nationalist Party wins the general election and institutes apartheid. Solly and Mr. Nguni set up an illegal fight for Peekay in a black township. Peekay agrees to fight the black boxer, Gideon Mandoma, in front of ten thousand spectators. Just before the fight, he discovers that his opponent is the son of his nanny. In the fifth round, Peekay knocks Mandoma to the canvas, but he recovers. They fight hard, and Peekay finally gets a chance to use the Solly Goldman thirteen-punch combination, winning the fight. Afterward, Peekay and Mandoma declare themselves brothers. Peekay breaks down in the showers. He hears Doc's voice in his head, calling from the crystal cave, and is sure that Doc has died.

## CHAPTER 22

Peekay returns to Barberton and joins in the search for Doc, but he does not lead them to the crystal cave because he had promised Doc that he would never tell anyone about it. After the search ends, he hikes alone to the cave opening, where he finds Doc's pocket knife, buried in the cliff. There is a note tied to the knife with a piece of music written on the back. Reassured by Doc's note, he returns to Barberton and then goes back to school, where he discovers that Goldman is training Gideon Mandoma. Mandoma challenges Peekay to teach him English, and Peekay and Morrie start a Saturday school. Peekay and Morrie translate "Miss Bornstein's Famous Correspondence School" into three African languages for textbooks. The school is successful, but they are raided by the police. The police threaten Singe 'n' Burn, Morrie, and Peekay, and they all narrowly escape arrest. In the end, they decide to work through Mr. Nguni to distribute their textbooks as a correspondence course.

## *Book Three, Chapters 23–24*

### CHAPTER 23

Peekay finishes school and wins the South African schools' featherweight title. Although he passes the Oxford entrance exams, he does not get a scholarship. Peekay returns to Barberton and hikes to the cliff outside Doc's cave. There he goes into a dream state and talks to Doc about his problems. Peekay emerges from the dream, and a poisonous snake emerges from the cave. The huge snake rises in front of his face, while Peekay remains absolutely still. As

the snake leaves without hurting him, Peekay decides to go to northern Rhodesia to work in the copper mines. In Rhodesia he trains to be a "grizzly man," learning how to use explosives to move raw ore through an enormous steel sieve. Peekay spends the first four months in a course run by the School of Mines. Peekay is rescued from a bar fight by an enormous Russian called Rasputin, and despite their lack of a common language, they become friends over a shared love of chess and classical music.

## CHAPTER 24

Despite the dangers, Peekay pushes himself to keep working on the grizzlies without a break. A near-miss accident leaves him feeling that he is invincible, but that night, the rock breaks loose and Peekay is buried under several tons of rubble. Rasputin digs for seven hours until he finds Peekay protected by a narrow ledge. Peekay is saved, but the Russian dies of exhaustion and blood loss. Peekay is shocked that Rasputin left him a life insurance settlement, which means he has enough money for three years at Oxford. Before he leaves, Peekay encounters a miner on a rampage in the bar. When the huge Afrikaner lunges at Peekay, he recognizes the Judge by his tattoo. Peekay takes on the crazed miner and beats him to a bloody pulp, using the combinations that Geel Piet and Solly Goldman have taught him. As the Judge goes down, face smashed, hand and arm broken, covered in blood and vomit, Peekay cuts a Union Jack symbol over the swastika tattoo. Then he carves his initials into the Judge's arm, and walks out of the bar into the African night, illuminated by the full moon.

# CHARACTERS

## *Sergeant Borman*

Sergeant Borman (later promoted to lieutenant) is a brutal prison warden sent to Barberton from Pretoria to establish a chapter of the Oxwagon Guard, a neo-Nazi group dedicated to the restoration of the Boers to political power. He terrorizes the black prisoners with both physical violence and appeals to their superstition. Borman kills Geel Piet on the evening of the performance of *Concerto of the Great Southland.* He is beaten in turn by Lieutenant Smit and Klipkop, and he dies a painful death from rectal cancer. He is converted on his deathbed by Marie to the Apostolic Faith Church.

### Jaapie Botha
*See* the Judge

### Pik Botha
Pik Botha is the second train conductor Peekay meets on his trip home from his first boarding school. Botha is a persnickety, by-the-books sort of man who makes much of his status as a born-again Christian and member of the Apostolic Faith Church. He is kind to Peekay and to Big Hettie when she is stuck between the bunks.

### Mrs. Boxall
Mrs. Boxall is the head librarian at the Barberton Library and the cultural columnist for the local newspaper. It is Mrs. Boxall who convinces the judge to hear Peekay's testimony in order to clear Doc of espionage charges after he is arrested. She volunteers to serve as the post office for the letters Doc and Peekay smuggle out of the prison, and she starts the Earl of Sandwich fund to pay for the postage. Eventually, the fund expands to help the families of black prisoners with clothing and monetary help.

### St. John Burnham
*See* Singe 'n' Burn, Sinjun

### Harry Crown
Harry Crown runs the general store in the town where Peekay's first boarding school is located. He is the first Jewish person Peekay meets, and his kindness and prosperity make a big impression on the boy. He fits Peekay with his first pair of shoes and packs him several lollipops for his train journey.

### Dee and Dum
Dee and Dum are twin sisters who work as kitchen maids for Peekay's mother. They nominally convert to the Apostolic Faith Church and so make the transition from the farm to Barberton. When Doc is sent to prison, Dee and Dum take over the cleaning and upkeep of his cottage. When he is in Johannesburg, Peekay buys them a sewing machine, with which they earn some extra money sewing clothes. When Doc becomes too old to teach music anymore, Dee and Dum help support him with their sewing earnings, and after Doc's death, Peekay installs them in the cottage permanently.

### Doc
Doc, whose full name is Karl Von Vollensteen, is Peekay's dearest friend and father figure. He befriends Peekay when he is a small boy and directs his education in music, science, logic, chess, and mountaineering. Doc is a German national, a concert pianist who fled to Africa after freezing up on stage in Berlin. Because he is a German national, he is imprisoned in the Barberton Prison for the duration of the war. Peekay is given full visiting privileges while Doc is in prison, and the two devise a scheme to smuggle tobacco, sugar, and salt into the prison, and to take dictation and smuggle letters in and out as well. Doc's prison career is capped off with a performance of his *Concerto for the Great Southland*, which is built around the traditional songs of the major black African tribes. Doc, along with Mrs. Boxall and Miss Bornstein, coaches Peekay for the entrance exams to the Prince of Wales school in Johannesburg. On one of his vacations from boarding school, Doc and Peekay discover a magical cave full of crystalline formations high in the hills above town, and it is to this cave that Doc eventually returns and where he takes his own life.

### Gert
Gert is one of the Afrikaans wardens in the Barberton prison. He is a heavyweight boxer, and he becomes a stalwart friend to Doc and Mrs. Boxall, fixing her car and doing odd jobs around Doc's cottage. In return, they teach him English. Although Gert is Afrikaans, he lacks the brutality of some of his fellow wardens.

### Solly Goldman
Solly Goldman is the best amateur boxing coach in South Africa. Morrie Levy arranges for Peekay to train with him, after arranging one last betting scheme in order to pay Goldman's fees. Solly Goldman also arranges the fight in Sophiatown with Mandoma, and then he takes on the training of Mr. Nguni's black boxers.

### Granpa
Granpa is Peekay's grandfather. When the book begins, they all live on Granpa's farm, but after an outbreak of Newcastle disease forces Granpa to kill his chickens, they move to Barberton. Granpa is devoted to the rose garden he built for his late wife, and although he is consistently kind to Peekay, he is an ineffectual figure.

### Granpa Chook

Granpa Chook is a semi-feral "kaffir" chicken that Peekay becomes attached to when he is a small child. After the witch doctor, Inkosi-Inkosikazi, teaches Peekay how to hypnotize the chicken, Peekay decides that he will take Granpa Chook back to boarding school with him to be his only friend. Granpa Chook nearly becomes soup when Mevrou discovers him, but his talent for finding and killing kitchen bugs saves him. The Judge and the other boys kill Granpa Chook on Peekay's last day at the school.

### Hoppie Groenewald

Hoppie Groenewald is a train conductor and the railway boxing champion of the Transvaal region. He takes Peekay under his wing when he leaves his first boarding school and treats the boy with some of the first true kindness he has known. Hoppie teaches Peekay what boxing is, shows him the speedball, and takes him to his big fight against Jackhammer Smit. It is from Hoppie that Peekay learns the motto that will sustain him through many challenges: "First with the head, then with the heart, that's how a man stays ahead from the start."

### Big Hettie

Big Hettie is the cook in the railway kitchen. She is an enormous woman who keeps an eye on Peekay during Hoppie Groenewald's fight. She is kind to him, sharing the contents of her food hamper with Peekay both at the fight and on the train afterward. On the train after the fight, she becomes stuck between the lower bunks. Despite the best efforts of Pik Botha and Peekay, she cannot be set free, and as they pull into Kaapmuiden, she dies.

### Inkosi-Inkosikazi

Inkosi-Inkosikazi is a Zulu medicine man and the descendant of the last great Zulu warrior. Nanny calls him for help when Peekay confides that he is being beaten for wetting the bed. Inkosi-Inkosikazi leads Peekay on an imaginary journey on which he conquers his fears by navigating three waterfalls, before emerging as the "little warrior of the king." The medicine man tells the boy, "When you need me you may come to the night country, and I will be waiting." Inkosi-Inkosikazi also teaches Peekay the trick of hypnotizing a chicken so its head remains inside a circle drawn in the dirt; this shared knowledge, Inkosi-Inkosikazi tells Peekay, makes them brothers.

### The Judge

The Judge, whose name is Jaapie Botha, is Peekay's nemesis at his first boarding school. A much bigger boy, the Judge is a brutal Afrikaner with Nazi leanings. He declares Peekay a prisoner of war and leads a group of boys who subject Peekay to continual physical abuse. Although Peekay earns a reprieve for doing the Judge's homework, once school ends, the Judge leads the boys in one last orgy of violence against Peekay, which ends in the death of Granpa Chook. Many years later, Peekay discovers that his diamond driller at the mine is the Judge, and when the Judge goes crazy from gelignite fumes, Peekay finally defeats his old enemy in a brutal fistfight.

### Klipkop

Klipkop is a warden at the Barberton prison and one of Peekay's boxing coaches. Klipkop is Afrikaans for "stonehead," and although his real name is Johannes Ouendaal, Klipkop tells Peekay that he does not mind the nickname, which he got because he can take so many punches to the head. Klipkop is occasionally brutal to the black prisoners, but is generally kind to Peekay, and he helps Lieutenant Smit beat Sergeant Borman after Borman murders Geel Piet.

### Morrie Levy

Morrie Levy is Peekay's closest friend at the Prince of Wales School. Morrie is Jewish and comes from a wealthy family. He becomes Peekay's boxing manager and teaches him how to make and handle money, a skill that does not come naturally to Peekay. Morrie has been sent to the Prince of Wales school to lose the ethnic markers of his Jewishness so he will fit more comfortably into the higher echelons of white South African society. He is Peekay's first real friend, and he is instrumental in getting Peekay into Sinjun's People, the elite study group led by the school headmaster.

### Marie

Marie is originally Peekay's nurse when he is hospitalized after the officer who comes to arrest Doc kicks Peekay in the head, breaking his jaw. She translates for him when he testifies on Doc's behalf. Later, she comes to work for Peekay's mother. Marie becomes an enthusiastic convert to the Apostolic Faith Church, and when Doc dies, no one has the heart to prevent her from claiming that she had converted the old man at the end. Marie is also the source of the tobacco that Peekay smuggles into the prison, as her parents grow it on their farm.

### Mevrou

Mevrou, which means "mistress" in Afrikaans, is the matron of Peekay's first boarding school. She is a terrifying figure, devoid of warmth, who beats him for wetting his bed and who fails to protect him from the bigger boys who terrorize him.

### Mother

Peekay's mother suffers a nervous breakdown at the beginning of the novel, thus necessitating his removal to the brutal boarding school. When she recovers, she becomes a convert to the Apostolic Faith Church, and Peekay's lack of faith is a constant source of aggravation and sorrow to her. She works as a dressmaker to support Peekay and his grandfather, and she and Peekay have a cordial but emotionally distant relationship.

### Gideon Mandoma

Gideon Mandoma is a young black fighter whom Peekay boxes in a big fight in Sophiatown. Mandoma is the son of Peekay's beloved nanny, and because she was Peekay's wet nurse, who breast-fed him when his mother could not, Mandoma was separated from his mother as a baby. After the fight, Mandoma and Peekay declare themselves brothers, and Peekay starts a school in part to educate Mandoma and his friends.

### Nanny Mandoma

Peekay's nanny raised him as a young child and provided him with his most solid sense of being loved. It is she who calls Inkosi-Inkosikazi when Peekay is being abused for bed wetting. Peekay's mother sends the nanny back to Zululand when they move to Barberton, in part because she will not convert to Christianity and in part because she is jealous of Peekay's love for her.

### Mr. Nguni

Mr. Nguni is a Zulu boxing promoter from the black townships. From the time of Peekay's first fight in Johannesburg, Mr. Nguni leads groups of black spectators to watch him. Later, he arranges the fight in Sophiatown with Gideon Mandoma.

### Johannes Ouendaal

*See* Klipkop

### Geel Piet

Geel Piet is a lifelong criminal who becomes Peekay's most important boxing coach while he is on the Barberton Prison team. Geel Piet means "yellow Peter" in Afrikaans; Piet is named this because he is half black and half white. Because he does not belong to either race, he is seen as a traitor to both, and prison becomes the only place where he finds even the smallest success. Piet and Peekay run the successful smuggling operation, and it is Piet's refusal to tell Sergeant Borman who is smuggling the letters that leads to his brutal death. Piet teaches Peekay his two most cherished boxing moves, the eight-punch combination and the head-butt known as the Liverpool Kiss.

### Rasputin

Rasputin is an enormous Russian miner who lives in the cottage next to Peekay when he is working in the Rhodesian copper mines. Rasputin rescues Peekay from a bar fight, and they become fast friends over a shared love of chess and classical music. When Peekay is nearly killed in a mine accident, it is Rasputin who saves him, losing his own life in the process.

### Singe 'n' Burn

Singe 'n' Burn and Sinjun are both nicknames the boys have for the headmaster of the Prince of Wales School, St. John Burnham (in British English, the first name *St. John* is often pronounced *Sinjun*). A liberal who studied at Oxford, he chooses six boys each year as Sinjun's People and tutors them in the art of becoming Renaissance men, that is, well-rounded scholar-athletes in the liberal arts model. Peekay thrives under the rigorous intellectual challenges of Sinjun's teaching methodology; however, he is disappointed when Sinjun balks at the proposed Saturday school for black boxers. It is only after Peekay and Morrie bring Mandoma to make his case personally that Sinjun relents and allows them the short-lived school.

### Sinjun

*See* Singe 'n' Burn

### Jackhammer Smit

Jackhammer Smit is Hoppie Groenewald's opponent in the fight in Gravelotte. He is Lieutenant Smit's brother.

### Lieutenant Smit

Lieutenant Smit is Peekay's head boxing coach on the Barberton Prison team. Although he is capable of casual brutality toward Geel Piet and the other black prisoners, it is Lieutenant Smit who avenges Piet's death by beating up Sergeant Borman and wrapping him in the bloodied boxing canvas. He is Jackhammer Smit's brother.

### Kommandant van Zyl

Kommandant van Zyl is the commander of the Barberton prison. Although he treats the black prisoners with the same casual brutality as the other wardens, he arranges for Doc to have the maximum freedom he can while he is detained, sends a crew to bring Doc's piano to the prison, and allows Peekay free access to Doc. He is also responsible for curing Doc's stage fright by forcing him to play first for the townspeople and then for the inspector of prisons.

### Professor Karl Von Vollensteen

*See* Doc

## THEMES

### Identity

The central theme of *The Power of One* is Peekay's quest to forge his own identity, regardless of what others might think of him. He calls this "the power of one" and claims that it is based on assuming "the role of the loner, the thinker, and the searching spirit who calls the privileged and the powerful to task." Although Peekay is nearly always a solitary figure throughout the book, he does not begin as someone capable of calling the powerful to task—that is, making them take responsibility for their harmful actions—indeed, he spends the first section of the book being brutally abused by a pack of bigger, more powerful boys. This instills in him a determination to overcome adversity and to escape persecution and vulnerability in the future. Watching Hoppie Groenewald triumph over Jackhammer Smit, Peekay comes to realize that with the right skills, "small can beat big," and it is then that he determines to grow up to become the welterweight champion of the world. Peekay seizes upon boxing as a means to gain power in the world, since boxing gives him the physical skills to survive in a world of casual violence where the strong prey upon the weak.

## TOPICS FOR FURTHER STUDY

- Recall a time when you or someone you know was bullied in school. What were the circumstances? What did you do? Recount your experience in a brief narrative essay. Use descriptive language to recount the incident.

- Watch the movie version of *The Power of One* and write a paper describing how the movie is different from the novel. Include whether you would have made the same choices as the filmmakers. If not, what would you have done differently? What choices would you have made if filming this story?

- Doc argues that the true soul of South African music is in the voices of its people. Research South African singers and listen to several recordings of South African traditional and pop music. Then, prepare an oral and audio presentation in which you play musical excerpts and discuss your reactions to the music.

- Do you think that Peekay should have beaten up the Judge so brutally in the final scene of the novel? When Peekay fights the Judge, is he boxing or is he fighting? What is the difference as it has been taught to Peekay throughout the novel? What does it mean that the novel ends on this violent note? Write an essay on this topic, using quotations from the book.

- Peekay chooses Granpa Chook as his first friend. Have you ever felt that an animal was your true friend? Prepare a collage using photographs and written reminiscences of your animal friend. Explain in words and pictures what was so special about your relationship.

Peekay's dedication to boxing also sets him apart, not just from his family but from the English community at large. His adversaries are almost exclusively Afrikaans, and when he reaches the posh English boarding school in Johannesburg, he discovers that boxing is not a

*Apartheid in South Africa* (AP Images)

sport his classmates are particularly interested in nor one at which they excel. Peekay's other act of self-assertion is to name himself. We never learn the character's given name, and the first name by which he is called is the insulting name the boys at the boarding school give him, Pisskop. Although it is Harry Crown, the kindly Jewish shopkeeper, who renames him Peekay (P. K., for Pisskop), it is Peekay's assertion that this is his one and only name that sets him apart throughout the novel. Peekay is fatherless and forgoes a surname, traditionally the name of one's father, as if he has sprung from the soil of Africa of his own making. His self-naming and his insistence on a single name are emblematic of his belief in the power of one. They match his assertion that "the courage to remain separate" is what will allow him to succeeded despite his small size, his lack of money, and his entrapment in a nation riven by racial and ethnic prejudices.

## *Violence*

Violence and brutality are at the heart of *The Power of One*, for the book is set in a nation where violent means are used to keep the black majority population subjugated to a white minority who have declared themselves superior. Peekay's earliest experiences of the world are of being a small, weak child at the mercy of larger children and adults who despise weakness and seek to eliminate it through violence. Even after he escapes the violent boarding school, Peekay spends the bulk of his childhood in a prison, and although he is free to come and go, the threat of violence against him or the people he cares about is a constant pressure. Although Peekay is exposed to the civilizing influences of Doc's musical and botanical instruction and the rigorous liberal arts education that Miss Bornstein and St. John Burnham give him, it is boxing that remains Peekay's most compelling interest. Despite the presence of rules and referees to enforce them, boxing is an inherently violent pursuit, and the novel revels in the details of Peekay's victories and the physical harm he inflicts on his opponents. In the end, Peekay can escape only by passing through the final spasm of violence that is his experience in the Rhodesian mines. The mines are a violent world populated by violent men who are menaced by the constant physical dangers of their work. Although there is some culture there, as represented by Rasputin's love of classical music and chess, in the end Peekay must survive both the violence of the mine collapse and his brutal fight with his old enemy the Judge in order to escape the violence and brutality of colonial Africa for the civilizing influence of Oxford University.

## Nature

When the violence of human relationships becomes too much to bear, Peekay escapes to the natural world, which is consistently portrayed as a place of beauty and plenty, a source of solace. Although Peekay cannot physically escape the brutality of the boarding school, when he must have a break from it, he retreats to the "night country" world of waterfalls and natural beauty that Inkosi-Inkosikazi gave him for strength. It is in the natural world that he and Doc find their greatest happiness, meeting on the ledge above Peekay's house when he is heartbroken to discover that his beloved nanny has been banished to Zululand. He first takes to the natural world for solace; there he meets Doc, who, like Inkosi-Inkosikazi, instructs him in the ways of this place. With Doc, Peekay learns not only to love the natural world but to study and observe it in detail, and it is this knowledge that serves him as solace late in the book when Doc disappears. In their last big adventure together, Peekay and Doc discover a magnificent cave filled with crystal rock formations, and it is to this cave that Doc goes when he decides it is time to die. Again, Peekay takes to the natural world for solace, using the skills Doc taught him to discover the hidden pocketknife and Doc's last words to him. At the novel's end, after Peekay has defeated the Judge, his emotions are described as natural phenomena; his inner landscape is described as a desert river filled with stones over which flows clear, cool water. While the human world in *The Power of One* is always fraught with imminent violence, the natural world serves throughout the book as a refuge and a place of healing.

## STYLE

### Bildungsroman

Bildungsroman is a German word meaning "formation novel." In English, it refers to the story of

a young person's education and development. A bildungsroman may have autobiographical elements of the writer's life, as *The Power of One* does, because this sort of novel often follows the development of an artist as he or she passes through the trials of childhood and adolescence. *The Power of One* is a typical bildungsroman in that it follows Peekay from his earliest education to young adulthood and focuses on the trials that form his character. Peekay's determination to become an extraordinary person is typical of this kind of novel, as is the manner in which he triumphs over adversity through hard work and perseverance. Other examples of a bildungsroman are Charles Dickens's *David Copperfield* and James Joyce's *Portrait of the Artist as a Young Man*.

### First-Person Narrative

A first-person narrative is one in which the book is narrated by a character who speaks in his or her own voice, as though addressing the reader directly. The hallmark of a first-person narrative is that the narrator refers to himself or herself in the first person—that is, as "I." In *The Power of One*, Peekay tells his story to the reader directly, and because Peekay's version of events seems to be corroborated by the other characters in the novel, we can consider him a reliable narrator. Many bildungsromans are told using a first-person narrator, since they usually begin with the voice of a young child, and using the first-person voice allows the author to show how that child's perception changes as he or she grows. Peekay is exceptional in this regard, an exceptionality that the character notes on those occasions when he retrospectively wonders how he could have perceived something sophisticated at such a young age (such as his attraction to Miss Bornstein or his precocity with language, for example).

### Melodrama

Melodramatic works are characterized by stark contrasts between good and evil, heroes and villains. *The Power of One* tends toward melodrama in the way that it presents central characters like Peekay and Doc as almost entirely good and nearly without flaws. Peekay suffers many external challenges in his quest to grow up, but his character rarely struggles when deciding whether to do the right thing. In contrast, a character like Sergeant Borman is so wholly evil that he becomes a stock character, someone who is only and always a villain. However, there are other characters in *The Power of One* who are characterized as neither wholly good nor wholly bad—for instance, Lieutenant Smit casually beats a black prisoner in his first scene but later avenges the death of Geel Piet. Another way that *The Power of One* works against the conventions of the melodrama is evident in the character of Morrie Levy. The money-lending Jew is a stock character with a long history in both drama and literature. The classic example is the character of Shylock in Shakespeare's play *The Merchant of Venice*. Traditionally, this character is a villain who preys on gentiles by charging outrageous interest rates and demanding timely payment no matter what mitigating circumstances might ensue. Courtenay seeks to overturn this stereotype by portraying Morrie Levy as a modern banker who provides a useful service by lending money under reasonable terms, rather than as a greedy moneylender engaging in usurious conduct. Although the term *melodramatic* is often used as a pejorative, this type of story has a long history as a dramatic form, originating in musical theater. Most melodrama in contemporary times appears in film.

## HISTORICAL CONTEXT

### Boer War

The Boer War was fought from 1899 to 1902, when the British, who were actively engaged in expanding their empire around the globe, decided to take control of the extensive gold fields in the Transvaal, a province of South Africa under Boer control. The British expected a quick victory, as they vastly outnumbered the Boer forces, but they found to their surprise that the Boer had several things in their favor: they were fighting in rugged terrain that they knew well, they were skilled riflemen, and the British lines of communication were so long that they were easy to break. The Boers fought a guerilla war: a war in which a smaller force uses tactics of ambush and surprise to defeat a larger, more traditional military force. By 1901, the tide turned as the British began to use scorched earth tactics. They burned Boer farms and then rounded up the women and children and confined them to concentration camps. These camps had poor hygiene, and food was scarce. The death of more than twenty thousand Boer women and children became an international scandal. These are the camps for which the Judge and the other boys hold Peekay responsible; when he is a child, they terrorize him in retribution for these camps. The brutal tactics of the British eventually prevailed, and the Boer War was settled in 1902 with the Peace of Veerniging. In 1910, the Union of South Africa was formed as an independent dominion of the British Commonwealth.

### World War II and South Africa

When Great Britain declared war on Hitler's Germany in 1939, the Union of South Africa was led by the anti-British Nationalist Party. The Nationalist Party was not merely anti-British; it was actively pro-Nazi, adapting anti-Semitism as an official plank in its party platform and lobbying against the acceptance of Jewish refugees from Hitler's Germany. The debate over whether to enter the war was one of the most heated of South African history, with Jan Smuts (later to be prime minister) defeating Barry Hertzog, who was the head of the Nationalist Party. Smuts argued that since the Union of South Africa was constitutionally obligated as a member of the British Commonwealth to support Great Britain, to break with them would only increase the international chaos brought on by the war in Europe. The rift between Afrikaners who supported the war effort and those who supported the Nazi party was to remain a virulent force in Nationalist politics, and pro-Nazi sympathies in the Nationalist Party long outlived the course of World War II. In *The Power of One*, when the war breaks out, Peekay is in boarding school deep in the Boer part of the country. He is led to believe that South Africa is supporting Hitler, and it takes him until his encounter with Hoppie Groenewald on the train to discover the truth, that South Africa is actually fighting on the side of the British.

### Apartheid

Although racial segregation had been practiced in South Africa since the first white colonists arrived, it was not until after the 1948 elections that brought the Nationalists into power that racial segregation was codified into law. Known as apartheid (an Afrikaans word meaning "separateness"), this collection of laws classified people into official races: white, black, Indian, and coloured (mixed-race). Under apartheid, blacks were stripped of citizenship and forcibly removed to separate *bantustaans*, or

# COMPARE
# &
# CONTRAST

- **1930s:** Economic chaos and the rise of communism lead to the rise of fascism as a political movement in many parts of Europe. Germany, Italy, and Spain all have fascist governments, and the Nationalist Party in South Africa shares many characteristics with those European parties. There are also viable fascist political movements in England, France, and the United States.

  **1980s:** As memories of World War II fade, neo-fascist groups rise in many European and South American countries as well as in the United States. While these groups make some political gains, especially in France, Austria, Italy, and Great Britain, they do not succeed in garnering substantial legislative power.

  **Today:** Fascism is no longer a viable political philosophy; however, it lingers in those countries where the Nazis took refuge, including South Africa and many South American countries. In the United States, pockets of fascist thought remain in movements such as the neo-Nazi and antigovernment militias.

- **1930s:** Anti-Semitism (hatred toward or discrimination against Jews) is an important force in South Africa, especially among those Afrikaners who admire Hitler. Anti-Semitism is as old as the Jewish religion itself, but the 1940s bring the event that we have come to know as the Holocaust or the Shoah. As Germany takes power over European territory, Jewish citizens are systematically rounded up and shipped to concentration camps, where they are either murdered or worked to death. Although this is the most virulent form of anti-Semitism, the prejudices that Morrie Levy describes in *The Power of One* and against which he rebels are also examples of anti-Semitism.

  **1980s:** In the United States during the 1980s, several neo-Nazi groups including the Aryan Nation propagandize that the problems of white working-class men are not the result of massive economic changes, but are the fault of shadowy Jewish financiers. They rely on the discredited Protocols of the Elders of Zion, a well-known hoax document, for their evidence and declare their intentions to colonize large swaths of the Pacific Northwest. Over time, however, they are largely discredited, and their movement loses momentum.

  **Today:** Although prejudice can probably never be eliminated altogether, today's most modern nations such as those in Europe and the United States prohibit legal discrimination on the basis of religion or race. In most countries outside of Israel and the Middle East, Jewish identity is an ethnic and religious designation like any other.

- **1930s:** The United Party in South Africa is formed, combining part of the National Party with the South African Party. The two groups share a common goal: favoring the white minority, who could vote, over the black majority, who could not. By the end of the 1940s, apartheid will become official law in South Africa.

  **1980s:** The world community begins to demonstrate against apartheid (segregation between races), which has been official law in South Africa since 1948. In 1985, the governments of both the United States and the United Kingdom impose stiff economic sanctions on South Africa, and international opposition to apartheid grows at a steady pace. University students around the world hold sit-ins and demand that their schools divest themselves of their South African investments. There is worldwide demand for the release of Nelson Mandela, an anti-apartheid activist, from prison and the dismantling of the apartheid laws.

  **Today:** Apartheid has been officially dismantled and is no longer the policy of South Africa. However, the nation still struggles with the economic and social problems that are the legacy of apartheid.

*Afrikaans school* (AP Images)

homelands. The township of Sophiatown, where Peekay boxes Gideon Mandoma, was bulldozed in 1959. The people who lived there were forced to move farther from the city center to Soweto, which was supposed to be a planned city but wound up becoming a notorious slum. Blacks were required to carry passes at all times documenting that they had permission to be in white areas, they were forbidden to own land or businesses, their education was severely curtailed, social contact between members of different races was forbidden, and it was illegal for whites to marry members of any of the other races. Although the African National Congress (ANC) was founded in 1912 to work against white oppression of blacks, it was not until the 1940s that it started to gain influence as a revolutionary force. It was the ANC Youth League that nurtured a generation that would eventually free South Africa from apartheid, leaders such as Nelson Mandela, Oliver Tambo, and Walter Sisulu. The international community punished South Africa for its repressive racial politics,

forcing the country to withdraw from the British Commonwealth in 1961, and in 1985 both the United States and United Kingdom imposed economic sanctions on the country. After decades of negotiations and international protest, apartheid laws were gradually revoked between 1990 and 1993, a process that culminated in the election of Nelson Mandela as president in 1994. Despite the repeal of legal apartheid, the social and economic effects of the decades of apartheid policies continue to haunt South Africa, and the nation still struggles to overcome them.

## CRITICAL OVERVIEW

*The Power of One* was an international best seller, and it has remained in the list of the top one hundred most popular books in Australian libraries since it was published. However, the critics have not been as kind to the book as its fans. Christopher Lehmann-Haupt, writing for the *New York Times*, criticizes the formulaic aspects of the book, noting that it "has everything: suspense, the exotic, violence; snakes, bats and Nazis; mysticism, psychology and magic; schoolboy adventures, drama in the boxing ring and disasters in a copper mine." However, Lehmann-Haupt acknowledges that despite the wealth of incident, sometimes cloying language, naive storytelling, and some unbelievable incidents, the book is a compelling read that engages the reader. A *Publishers Weekly* reviewer calls the book an "epic melodrama," and a contributor to *Kirkus Reviews* describes it as "a fast-paced book with an old-fashioned, clean-cut hero, easily identifiable villains, no sex, and saintlike sidekicks. All done in sturdy, workmanlike prose." In an interview with Karin van Heerwaarden for an Australian Web site, *The Blurb*, Courtenay refers to himself primarily as a storyteller, claiming, "I have unquestionably the education and the understanding and the craftsmanship to affect a literary style.... It's the last thing that I would do." Because he considers himself a storyteller, he is also very enthusiastic about audiobooks, claiming they allow him to reach a much wider audience and, in particular, reach out to people who might not be particularly literate or have good reading skills. Like most novels written for a popular audience, *The Power of One* has been largely overlooked by serious literary critics; however, its large following and popularity are a testament to the power of Courtenay's storytelling.

## CRITICISM

### Charlotte M. Freeman

*Freeman is a freelance writer and editor who holds a Ph.D. in English. In this essay, she examines the political implications of Peekay's determination to act as an individual and to treat others as individuals in* The Power of One. *In a political environment where racial and ethnic identity is determined by the state and enforced with violence and oppression, to assert the primacy of one's individuality is a political act.*

While at first *The Power of One* appears to be an ordinary coming-of-age story, because it is set during the rise of the Afrikaans nationalist movement, Peekay's quest for individual identity takes on a political dimension. Nationalist movements like the one in which Peekay grows up

> TO DEVOTE ONESELF TO DEVELOPMENT OF THE INDIVIDUAL IN AN ENVIRONMENT THAT INSISTS THAT THE INDIVIDUAL IS ALWAYS SUBORDINATE TO THE GROUP IS TO REBEL AGAINST THAT SOCIETY."

value the group above the individual, and they seek to enforce social conformity with ruthless hostility to outsiders and random violence against the weak. Although Peekay is portrayed as an exceptional person, possessing a precocious intellect, a gift for boxing, and a talent for friendship, it is his devotion to developing "the power of one" that marks Peekay as transgressive—that is, breaking boundaries. To devote oneself to development of the individual in an environment that insists that the individual is always subordinate to the group is to rebel against that society. If family is the first group to which we belong as individuals, Peekay's act of self-naming can be seen as a rejection of one of the core concepts of Afrikaans nationalism, that the sins of the fathers are borne by their children. Another major marker of group identity is language, and in a nation like South Africa where many languages are spoken, the language people use marks and reinforces their position of power or weakness in the political hierarchy. Peekay refuses to be bound by a single language, choosing whenever possible to address others in their own language, thus rejecting the exercise of power inherent in the imposition of one language upon another. Finally, nationalist movements use random violence against the weak as a means to instill terror in their victims and consolidate power among their allies. After being victimized as a child, Peekay takes up boxing as a means of seizing power in a world where power relations are enforced through brutality and violence. While Courtenay has written what appears to be a classic coming-of-age story, a novel in which a weak child triumphs over his circumstances through pluck and courage and native intelligence, he has also created, in Peekay, a character who embodies the kind of individualism that the Nationalist Party had to quell in order to seize power and enforce apartheid in South Africa for forty years.

# WHAT DO I READ NEXT?

- In 1992, Courtenay published *Tandia*, a sequel to *The Power of One*. Set during the darkest days of apartheid, the novel continues the story of Peekay and his fight against the dominant power structure of South Africa.

- *Kaffir Boy*, published in 1986, is Mark Mathabene's story of how he escaped the townships outside of Johannesburg. His family is poor and illiterate, and his father tries to prevent his education, but Mathabene perseveres, teaching himself to read English and to play tennis. In this way, he manages to earn a tennis scholarship to an American college and escape apartheid-era South Africa.

- *Martha Quest* (published in England in 1952 and the United States in 1964) is the first book in a five-book series, *The Children of Violence*, by Nobel winner Doris Lessing. Martha, the central character in these books, is a semi-autobiographical portrait of Lessing and her escape from what was then called Rhodesia (now Zimbabwe). The novel portrays how difficult it can be for well-meaning people to break free of repressive systems of thought and belief.

- A classic of African literature, Alan Paton's *Cry the Beloved Country* was published in 1948, the year apartheid was established in South Africa. It tells the story of a black pastor who travels to Johannesburg only to find that his sister has slipped into a life of prostitution and that his son has killed a white man. Paton's novel explores the human and emotional consequences of the brutal politics of South Africa on both Pastor Kumalo and Mr. Jarvis, the white father of the murder victim, as both men struggle to come to grips with the entwined fate of their sons and the valley in which they both reside.

- In *The Long Walk to Freedom: The Autobiography of Nelson Mandela*, published in 1995, Mandela recounts his journey from a tribal childhood to his life as a law clerk in Johannesburg and his growing political involvement. Much of the book was written during Mandela's twenty-seven years of imprisonment on Robben Island, and it recounts the complex negotiations that led to his release. This is a remarkable life story of a winner of the Nobel Peace Prize and the first black president of South Africa.

- In 2000, South African journalist and poet Antjie Krog published *Country of My Skull: Guilt, Sorrow, and the Limits of Forgiveness in the New South Africa*, an account of the Truth and Reconciliation Commission, which she covered as a journalist. The commission, which was presided over by Archbishop Desmond Tutu, heard testimony by whites who committed crimes against blacks under apartheid in the hopes that an honest and open account could be the first step toward national healing. Krog's book documents the cost of that effort on all who took part.

- An abridged version of *The Power of One* for young-adult readers was released in September 2005 by Delacorte Press. Courtenay wrote this after receiving many letters from teachers requesting a version suitable for use in primary schools. This young reader's novel omits the more upsetting episodes in the adult version, and it ends with the uplifting prison concert.

---

Peekay has no father, and the book never gives any explanation for this situation. Peekay has a grandfather on his mother's side, and he has a father figure in Doc, but his actual paternity is a mystery. As readers, we never learn Peekay's given name; the first name we hear anyone address him by is the nickname given to him at boarding school, "Pisskop." In

Afrikaans, this means "piss head," but it is also slang for a drunk or a vagrant. A hostile nickname like this marks someone as a weakling and makes that person a target for scapegoating and violence. The concept of the scapegoat comes from an ancient Jewish tradition: on Yom Kippur, the annual Day of Atonement, the community rid itself of its members' shortcomings by symbolically placing the sins on a goat and then driving it into the wilderness. In common usage, the term has come to refer to any individual upon whom a group lays blame and toward whom it expresses hostility and violence. Peekay is the scapegoat in his first boarding school, which is populated by the sons of the defeated Boers. They believe that "the sins of the fathers had been visited upon the sons, unto the third generation." Peekay is English, which means he is a descendant of the forces who defeated the paternal ancestors of the boarding school boys and who incarcerated their maternal ancestors in deadly concentration camps. "I was infected," Peekay notes. In his first experience away from home, he learns that fatherhood is a source of infection, blame, and punishment. Thus his first act of self-identification is to excise his surname, the name of his father. It is the kind Jewish shopkeeper, Harry Crown, who rejects the hated nickname Pisskop and renames the boy P. K. (or, as the boy hears it, Peekay), but it is Peekay himself who rejects the infection of fatherhood by refusing to use a surname at all. For the rest of the book, he answers only to his own name, the name he chose to keep, which carries no paternity whatsoever. In a nation rapidly moving toward a political system built on the rigid classification of people into ethnic and racial groups, this act of self-naming is a radical stance. By dropping his surname, Peekay asserts that he belongs to no group larger than himself, not even a family. He is singular and individual.

Nationalist regimes gain much of their power by declaring that the purity of a single group renders that group superior to all others. The pressure to maintain this pure state results in a pervasive social anxiety about potential infection and pollution, which leads in turn to the enforcement of rigid boundaries between groups of people. In South Africa, the Afrikaans population positioned itself as the one true South Africa and declared the English, the coloured, and above all the blacks to be inferior groups that must be contained and controlled in order to prevent further erosion of the purity of the

Afrikaans culture. Although Peekay is victimized for his ethnicity in the early sections of the book, he refuses to emulate his tormentors by concluding in turn that all Afrikaans are bad people. Instead he develops his theory of the power of one, a power defined by "the courage to remain separate, to think through to the truth, and not to be beguiled by convention or the plausible arguments of those who expect to remain in power." He seeks not only to develop the power of one within himself but to recognize it in others, and his primary means of doing so is to speak to people, whenever possible, in their own language. Peekay's facility with languages is one of his talents, and we see his facility in English, Afrikaans, and tribal languages such as Zulu and Shangaan. Peekay also he uses the etiquette of different groups instead of imposing his upon them. Illustrations of how rare this is in Peekay's world range from the prison, where blacks must take orders and beg mercy in Afrikaans, to Peekay's own mother, who banishes Nanny Mandoma because she will not forsake her religion for the Apostolic Faith Church. Peekay's facility for languages is portrayed not as a dangerous breakdown of social order, which might expose him to the infection of outside influence, but rather as an important form of social currency. For example, when he firsts meets Klipkop and Lieutenant Smit, he addresses them using the polite form of Afrikaans address, allowing him to curry favor with those who are bigger and more powerful. Later, however, when he greets Mr. Nguni using the polite Zulu phrase, "I see you, Nguni," and in turn allows Mr. Nguni to address him by name, it is the act of a social superior using the language and codes of a social inferior to signal that he has no hidden agenda and is approaching the fight negotiations in good faith. In the South Africa in which Peekay grows up, crossing linguistic boundaries must be undertaken with caution, as it is a threat to the regime. When he extends his personal linguistic boundary crossing to the black boxers by teaching them to read and write in English, the regime takes notice of his transgression and shuts down the Saturday school. It is one thing to "see" others as a Zulu might, but trying to extend the power of one to those the regime has marked as outsiders is too big a threat to the Nationalist social and political order, and so they shut him down.

The primary means by which Peekay seeks to develop his power of one is boxing. In the boxing ring, Peekay can hope to harness the physical violence of his world. In a social and political environment characterized by scapegoating and random violence, the rule-bound world of the boxing ring offers a place where "Small can beat big if you have a plan." The character of the Judge is in many ways a microcosm of the characteristics of the Afrikaner Nationalist Party that takes power at the end of the novel. The Judge is big, mean, and ruthless, and he scapegoats Peekay in order to consolidate his own power among the other boys. The Nationalist Party is portrayed in the novel as similarly powerful. When Peekay's Saturday school is raided, not even the headmaster of Peekay's posh Johannesburg boarding school can fight back against it. Superior intellect is, in this case, no match for brute force. Peekay learns about boxing from Hoppie Groenewald, the train conductor who treats him with some of the first true kindness he has known from an adult. Hoppie shows him that boxing is a place where violence is contained by enforceable rules and where a small man can beat a larger one if he is smart and quick. Instead of rejecting violence altogether after his experience in the first boarding school, Peekay determines to learn to fight back, and he spends most of the novel determined to become the welterweight champion of the world. Peekay is enormously successful in the boxing ring. He remains undefeated for many years, and even when he beats the black son of his nanny, Gideon Mandoma, the fight is seen as so fairly fought that the huge crowds of black spectators accept his victory as just. Outside the boxing ring, however, life is not so simple. There are no clear rules, and although Geel Piet warns him against street fighting, against ruining his skills by succumbing to the lure of brute violence, Peekay develops enough skill as a street fighter to remain undefeated in that realm as well. However, by Book Three, when Peekay finds his precocity and intelligence stymied when he does not get the Rhodes Scholarship and cannot find a way to get to Oxford on his own, he decides it is time to confront the brutal reality of African life directly. He claims he is going to the mines to test himself, to develop the physical strength he needs to compete as a welterweight, and to make the money he needs to go to university. However, Peekay discovers that in the mines he must confront brute force for the first time since he was a child in that boarding school, and although he survives the mining

accident that nearly kills him, the story closes on an episode of true violence. Until the final fight, Peekay has adhered to the rules and codes of boxing that rule in the ring. In the final scene of the novel, Peekay encounters a miner, driven insane by fumes from mining explosives, and recognizes him by his tattoo. If the Judge's childhood brutality represents the clumsy tactics used by the Afrikaans to obtain and consolidate power, then the crazed and violent man Peekay encounters in the final scene of the novel represents the fruits of that effort: a world defined by a violence that is insane and insensible to reason and that seeks to impose its will no matter what the cost. In defeating the Judge, Peekay performs his one and only act of dominance in the novel: He carves a Union Jack and his initials over the Judge's swastika tattoo and then ensures that it will overwrite the older tattoo by smearing it with blood so it will become infected. Peekay finds a way to harness violence in the boxing ring, but his experience there also gives him the skills he needs when confronted with a true fight against an enemy for whom there are no rules.

Although Peekay defeats the Judge at the end of the novel, it is still clear that Peekay alone is not the savior that the black boxing spectators believe him to be. Peekay can beat the Judge, a single man in a single fight, and he can even survive the horrific accident in the mine, but those are individual achievements. Although Peekay's insistence on developing the power of one allows him to succeed as an individual in a harsh world, and although his devotion to individualism is a rebellion against a political system bent on collectivization, in the end Peekay's effect upon his surroundings is unknown. He must go to England to complete his education, and the book gives no indication of whether he will return to his country or not. Although *The Power of One* relies on the political situation as one of the antagonistic forces that Peekay must overcome, the book ends on this singular victory, Peekay's revenge upon the Judge, demonstrating that just as Peekay is primarily concerned with his development as an individual, so the novel also chooses the individual over the political collective. The book might be set in the midst of a charged political situation, but it is, in the final analysis, not a political novel, but a personal novel.

**Source:** Charlotte M. Freeman, Critical Essay on *The Power of One*, in *Novels for Students*, Gale, Cengage Learning, 2010.

### Toni Johnson-Woods

*In the following essay, Johnson-Woods puts into perspective Bryce Courtenay's fame as an Australian writer, comparing him to no other.*

Increasing globalization of the publishing industry has caused tremendous changes in Australian publishing. Many Australian publishing houses have been subsumed under multinational publishing concerns, so it is no surprise that more Australian authors such as Colleen McCullough and Bryce Courtenay have become international success stories. McCullough's first novel *Tim* was published in both Australia and the United States in 1974; but it was *The Thorn Birds* (1977), and the successful television mini-series based on it, that secured her worldwide fame. McCullough's switch from Australian-centered romantic stories to ancient Rome in the Masters of Rome series (1990–2002) marked her arrival as an author of weightier subject matter. McCullough continues to resist pigeonholing by publishing across genres, producing detective, romance, and historical fiction.

Like McCullough, Bryce Courtenay has cast his literary net wide. His first novel *The Power of One* (1991) became an instant hit in Australia, was translated into several languages and has been produced as a film. Though *The Power of One* was set in South Africa, Courtenay has since written historical novels set in colonial Australia (*The Potato Factory, Tommo & Hawk, Solomon's Song*), Europe (*Sylvia*), and Russia (*The Family Frying Pan*). Courtenay's novels are popular in Australia but only *The Power of One* is available in the United States.

**Source:** Toni Johnson-Woods, "Popular Fiction 1960–2000," in *Companion to Australian Literature Since 1900*, Camden House, 2007, p. 399.

### Cassandra Spratling

*In the following review, Spratling comments on the young-adult edition of* The Power of One.

To help kick off New Year reading, how appropriate that there's a version of the coming-of-age novel *The Power of One*, by Bryce Courtenay condensed for young readers. The timing is perfect for a couple reasons. The

powerful message can be a resolution of self-motivation for the year. And it comes at a time when the nation will celebrate the birthday of Martin Luther King Jr., a man whose life story testifies to the power of one.

In this story, the power of one is demonstrated through the life of Peekay, an enormously sensitive and intelligent boy. Peekay grows up in South Africa when Hitler's hatred is wreaking havoc on the world and the cruelty of racism and discrimination is evident all around him.

Peekay becomes the victim of bullies who harass and taunt him for no other reason than he speaks English. And his young mind finds it impossible to comprehend why he's supposed to hate and belittle blacks, when the woman who most loved him was his black nanny.

Peekay's early years are miserable and lonely after he's sent to live in a boarding school. But Peekay soon learns the power one person has when using his brain and his heart.

A man who befriends him and fills him with the desire to become a boxer first teaches the lesson. Other men become crucial father figures, too, including a professor who teaches him to play piano and a mixed-race man who teaches him to box.

This story is so beautifully and vividly written that it can't help but have a positive impact in making readers think about the pain of prejudice as they feel the triumph of the power of one.

**Source:** Cassandra Spratling, "Free Press Book Club for Kids: Teens Can See How One Person Might Make a Big Difference," in *Knight Ridder/Tribune Business News*, January 15, 2006, p. 1.

### Toby Creswell and Samantha Trenoweth

*In the following essay, Creswell and Trenoweth discuss Courtenay's background, the sales of* The Power of One, *and how that changed the author's life.*

Bryce Courtenay, the prolific novelist, came from the most humble beginnings. He was born in Johannesburg, South Africa, in 1933, the illegitimate son of a seamstress who suffered from mental illness. His father was a travelling salesman. Almost at birth Courtenay was placed in an orphanage in the Northern Transvaal where he grew up. However, a scholarship to a private school led to a further scholarship to study journalism in London. He met his wife Benita, an Australian, and in 1957 they married and migrated to Sydney.

Courtenay took a job in advertising as a copywriter and became creative director at McCann Erickson and J. Walter Thompson and later at George Patterson Advertising. Courtenay's campaigns such as 'Louie the Fly' and 'Mr Sheen' created household icons.

Courtenay had three sons: Brett, Adam and Darnon. The latter was born with haemophilia and died at age 24 from AIDS, contracted through a blood transfusion. The family tragedy was a watershed. Not only did it put an unmendable strain on the marriage but it gave Courtenay the impetus to retire from advertising and devote himself, at the age of 55, to writing novels.

Sales of *The Power of One,* set in South Africa, topped seven million. The book was also adapted for the screen. Courtenay is not a literary novelist but plays to his strengths, such as narrative and character. Since the *Power of One,* Courtenay has written nearly 20 books and almost all of them are bestsellers. He is Australia's most popular novelist and is currently living in the Hunter Valley, NSW.

**Source:** Toby Creswell and Samantha Trenoweth, "Bryce Courtenay," in *1001 Australians You Should Know*, Pluto Press, 2006, p. 66.

### Ann M. G. Gray

*In the following review, Gray praises the novel for its careful portrayal of apartheid in the 1940s.*

Courtenay has created a condensed, young-adult version of his well-known novel. The story deals with the journey of a young white boy toward adulthood in the South Africa of the 1940s. When Peekay is five years old he is sent to boarding school, where the older students abuse him. After Peekay's grandfather loses all the chickens on his farm, Peekay has to leave the school for financial reasons. He befriends an older man, Doc von Vollensteen, who teaches him to play the piano. When the war breaks out, Doc, a German, is imprisoned for his own safety, and Peekay becomes a daily visitor to the prison. He, Doc, and a black prisoner, Geel Piet, devise a way to smuggle sugar, salt, and tobacco to the prisoners, and they set up an elaborate letter writing system that allows prisoners to send letters home to their families. Now known as the Tadpole Angel and much beloved by the prison population, Peekay eventually wins a scholarship to school. Courtenay does a wonderful job of describing life in South Africa, and readers get a feeling for the bitterness of apartheid. This would be a good book to use in conjunction with the study of apartheid.

**Source:** Ann M. G. Gray, Review of *The Power of One*, in *Library Media Connection*, Vol. 24, No. 4, January 2006, p. 73.

### Sue Gifford

*In the following review, Gifford praises Courtenay for the powerful characters and accurate dialogue in his writing.*

The opening chapters of this haunting autobiographical novel, set in small-town South Africa during World War II, are as bleak and violent as anything written for young people. Five-year-old Peekay is the only English-speaking boy in a harsh Afrikaans-language boarding school. He is urinated on by a pack of older boys, and then beaten for it by the matron. Although he endures many losses, he grows through his experiences. His goal is to become a boxer, and the story shows how hard work can lead to success. Peekay forges loving relationships with adults, most notably Doc, a German professor. When Doc is detained as an enemy alien, Peekay's life becomes intertwined with the local prison. It is there that he learns to box and becomes a secret ally of the black prisoners. Courtenay's deft and chillingly accurate characterization of the Afrikaner prison warders. The author is unsparing in his portrayal of the brutality meted out to prisoners and in his depiction of racist speech. Courtenay's ear for dialogue is impressive, and he consistently captures the cadences of South African speech. Peekay's story is written in a direct, almost childlike style, which sometimes seems bland, but readers will be swept along by the events in the protagonist's life. The book packs a powerful emotional punch, evoking horror, laughter, and empathy. It is a condensed version of the first part of Courtenay's adult book of the same title, and the ending feels artificial and unresolved. In all, this is an extraordinary and unusual survival story, and one that should inspire young people feeling battered by the circumstances of their own lives.

**Source:** Sue Gifford, Review of *The Power of One*, in *School Library Journal*, Vol. 51, No. 11, November 2005, pp. 130–31.

## Hazel Rochman

*In the following review, Courtenay's handling of racism is discussed.*

"I went in under the arm with a quick upper-cut and caught him in the ribs." The sports action is exciting in this story about Peekay, a white English-speaking boy in rural South Africa during World War II, who becomes a talented boxer and dreams of being welterweight champion of the world. With the help of several mentors, including an Afrikaner, a German botanist and pianist, a Coloured (mixed-race) worker in the local jail, a brave librarian, and a Jewish teacher, Peekay not only wins the local boxing championship but helps desperate African chain-gang prisoners send letters home. The original book was published for adults and made into a movie with Morgan Freeman; this effective condensation for YAs gives a sense of personal uplift, despite the virulent racism, but American teens won't get the complex political history. What is timeless is the picture of the sport and the kid who takes on the giants and wins.

**Source:** Hazel Rochman, Review of *The Power of One*, in *Booklist*, Vol. 102, No. 1, September 1, 2005, p. 115.

## Phil Brown

*In the following interview, Brown expounds on an experience talking with Bryce Courtenay, and on Courtenay's early life.*

A tough start in life helped shape best-seller Bryce Courtenay's literary output

Christmas is near so it must be time for another "lousy" book from Bryce Courtenay. Now, before anyone takes offence, this is simply what the author reckons the critical response to his new offering, the 842-page epic, *Brother Fish*, will be.

"I've done 16 books and there are around 320,000 copies of this one in bookshops now. But the critics will almost certainly say, 'This is another lousy book by Bryce Courtenay,'" he says, with a wry smile. His readers beg to differ and have done so ever since *The Power of One*, published in 1989, made him an international, best-selling author.

Since then, the pocket dynamo and former ad man, who didn't start writing until his 50s (he's now a spry 72), has been prodigiously playing literary catch-up by producing some of

Australia's favourite books (often based on his passion: Australian history) including *The Potato Factory, April Fool's Day, Tommo & Hawk* and *Jessica*.

In a recent article in *The Australian*, the statistics of his success were given by tonnage, something that no doubt amused the literary critics who either ignore or lambaste him. He has, the article pointed out, sold more than 2 million books, "the equivalent of 7000 tonnes of books in Australia alone," and his fiction is read in 75 countries in 11 languages. His new releases routinely sell 300,000 copies in hardback alone and are eagerly awaited by devoted fans.

Which is why, on a drizzly Brisbane morning, I'm meeting with this publishing superstar, weighed down by his brick of a new book—an historical saga about the lives of two veterans of the Korean War and a Russian woman emigre.

"Going to interview someone interesting?" the cabbie asked me en route.

"Yes, Bryce Courtenay," I replied, straining to hold the book up. "Never heard of him," the cabbie responded. So fame is relative, I suggest, after telling Bryce about that exchange over coffee.

"It's nice when people do know who you are," he admits. "But anyone can be a celebrity nowadays—they are being manufactured regularly. I'm just the same old s—bag that I've always been."

He laughs, but the laughter fails to entirely mask a vulnerability, which is endearing and underpins his inspirational life.

This is a bloke who probably shouldn't be famous; who has suffered and made it against the odds. Though it's something he's not overly keen to play up.

But how could he have written a book as empowering as The Power of One without having struggled hard himself?

His own travails started when his mother "dumped" him in an orphanage in backwoods South Africa.

"I was in the orphanage from about six months of age," he recalls, and the look on his face shows the emotional memory lingers. "In defence of my mother, who had a series of nervous breakdowns, she did take me out now and then, but in many ways that was worse."

In the orphanage, he was bullied by the mostly Boer boys for having a British, rather than an Afrikaner, name.

"I knew, even then, that I was destined to be a writer," he says. "To survive, I told stories and when I was beaten up every day, I said, 'Look, I'll tell you a story if you stop.' Then I threatened not to tell them the next episode if I got beaten again. It was tough, but it could have been tougher if I hadn't been born with blue eyes and white skin."

He learnt to defend himself by boxing (like Peekay, the protagonist in *The Power of One*) and eventually won a scholarship to a private school. He studied journalism in England and never returned to South Africa. His fate would have been sealed if he had, he explains, after he was branded a communist for starting a weekend school for Africans while still a teenager.

"I guess I took the cowardly way out by not going back," he says. "So I tried to find a new country and thank God I found this one."

In Australia, he charted a successful career in advertising and, with wife Benita, raised three sons—Adam, Brett and Damon, a haemophiliac who contracted AIDS and died on April 1, 1991.

This heart-rending story is told in Bryce's most personal and powerful book, *April Fool's Day* (Damon's dying words to his father were: "Thanks for a wonderful life dad, but please write this book.").

His marriage didn't survive the tragedy, but Bryce has found happiness again with his partner, Dorothy Gliksman, and the couple live in the Yarramalong Valley, near Sydney.

Bryce smiles at the mention and you feel that he deserves to be happy as well as successful, and though he may not be the critic's choice, it doesn't seem to matter. "Nothing of what I write is for posterity anyway," he says, wistfully. "But it has an immediacy and people are kind enough to read it and enjoy what I write.

"As for the rest of it, well, the tide comes in and out, and the footprints we leave on the beach will soon be washed away."

**Source:** Phil Brown, "The Power of Bryce," in *Brisbane News*, December 1, 2004, p. 10.

## SOURCES

Baldick, Chris, *The Oxford Dictionary of Literary Terms*, Oxford University Press, 2008, pp. 35, 201.

Barnard, Rita, *Apartheid and Beyond: South African Writers and the Politics of Place*, Oxford University Press, 2007.

Bunting, Brian, "The Rise of the South African Reich," in *African National Congress*, 1969, http://www.anc.org.za/books/reich.html (accessed June 4, 2009).

"Bryce Courtenay Tops Author Survey," in *The Age*, http://www.theage.com.au/ (accessed June 6, 2009).

Courtenay, Bryce, *The Power of One*, Random House, 1989.

Cuddon, J. A., *The Penguin Dictionary of Literary Terms and Literary Theory*, Penguin, 1999.

Fortescue, Lou, "Bryce Courtenay's Emotions Catch Up at Wisdom Exhibit," in *Daily Telegraph*, October 16, 2008, http://www.news.com.au/couriermail/story/0,23739,24507137-953,00.html (accessed June 6, 2009).

Lehmann-Haupt, Christopher, "Everything but Sex (Lack of Time)," in *New York Times*, http://www.nytimes.com/ (accessed May 30, 2009).

Review of *The Power of One*, in *Kirkus Reviews*, April 1, 1989, Vol. 57, pp. 484.

Sharp, Anette, "Sad Serenade for Courtenay," in *Sydney Morning Herald*, March 12, 2007, http://www.smh.com.au/news/people/sad-serenade-for-courtenay/2007/03/11/1173548008005.ht ml (accessed May 30, 2009).

"South Africa," in *Encyclopaedia Britannica*, http://www.britannica.com/EBchecked/topic/555568/South-Africa/259494/The-apartheid-years (accessed November 9, 2009).

Steinberg, Sybil, Review of *The Power of One*, in *Publishers Weekly*, April 7, 1989, Vol. 235, No. 14, p. 129.

Thompson, Peter, "Talking Heads: Interview with Bryce Courtenay," in *Australian Broadcasting Corporation*, August 5, 2006, http://www.abc.net.au/talkingheads/txt/s1630548.htm (accessed May 31, 2009).

van Heerwaarden, Karin, "Courtenay's Crusade," in *The Blurb*, http://www.theblurb.com.au/Issue72/Courtenay.htm/ (accessed May 31, 2009).

## FURTHER READING

Barthorp, Michael, *Slogging over Africa: The Boer Wars, 1815-1902*, Cassell, 2002.
   This book is a history of the conflict that broke out when the English, flush with victories against native armies across Africa, decided to take on the Boer farmers of the Transvaal in order to secure the gold and diamonds that lay beneath their territory.

Bebey, Francis, *African Music: A People's Art*, Lawrence Hill Books, 1999.
   This book describes the forms, musicians, and instruments of African music, as well as its place in the life of the people. A discography classified by country, theme, group, and instrument is also included.

Citino, Robert Michael, *Germany and the Union of South Africa in the Nazi Period*, Greenwood Press, 1999.

This book examines the foreign policy of Nazi Germany toward the Union of South Africa from 1933 to 1939. A major focus is about efforts by the German Foreign Office to exploit both racial prejudices and tensions between the English and Boer populations to sway the South African population to the Nazi cause. Their goals were to gain strategic control of South Africa's mineral wealth and win control of the Cape of Good Hope.

Conan Doyle, Sir Arthur, *The Great Boer War*, McClure, Phillips, 1902.

The author of the Sherlock Holmes stories and novels was knighted for his work as a doctor during the Boer War and for this written defense of the war. Conan Doyle argued in this pamphlet (later published as a book) that the concentration camps were necessary housing for the displaced women and children of the Boer fighters and that the high mortality rate was not the fault of the British but an inevitable consequence of crowded conditions and poor hygiene.

Silverman, Jeff, ed., *The Greatest Boxing Stories Ever Told*, Lyons Press, 2004.

This anthology collects stories about boxing from sources as diverse as Homer, James Baldwin, and Joyce Carol Oates. Boxing is a subject that has long attracted great writers, and this collection addresses many aspects of the sport, from victories against all odds to dealing with shady promoters to death in the ring.

# Staying Fat for Sarah Byrnes

## CHRIS CRUTCHER

## 1993

*Staying Fat for Sarah Byrnes*, published in 1993, is Chris Crutcher's sixth young-adult novel and remains one of his most controversial because of the issues it explores and because of its use of profanity. Crutcher is a child protection advocate and therapist, and his novels are inspired by the stories he hears in his work.

High school seniors Sarah Byrnes and Eric Calhoune have been best friends for years. Both have grown up as outcasts, Eric because of his weight—his nickname is Moby, after Moby Dick, the famous fictional whale—and Sara because of disfiguring facial scars. When Eric begins swimming on the school team, he starts to lose weight. Sarah Byrnes expresses concern that he will leave her behind as he sheds weight, so Eric continues to overeat. Her friendship is more important to him than gaining popularity. When Sarah Byrnes is satisfied her friend will not forsake her, Eric slims down.

When Sarah Byrnes is admitted to a psychiatric hospital because she refuses to speak, Eric visits her. The conversation is one-sided, and Eric is more worried for his friend's safety more than ever before. He knows it is up to him to uncover the secret of her pain. When he does, he realizes he must choose between keeping her secret and keeping her safe. In making that choice, he puts his own safety at risk.

*Staying Fat for Sarah Byrnes* explores the topics of friendship, child abuse, religious

*Chris Crutcher* *(Reproduced by permission)*

tolerance, and abortion. Crutcher's examination spares no beliefs.

## AUTHOR BIOGRAPHY

Crutcher was born on July 17, 1946, in Dayton, Ohio. He grew up in the small logging town of Cascade, Idaho, and graduated from Eastern Washington State College (now Eastern Washington University) with a bachelor's degree in psychology and sociology.

Crutcher eventually became a primary and secondary school teacher, a career that included a stint as teacher of at-risk students from kindergarten through high school. That job eventually led him to a job as a therapist and child protection advocate. He was thirty-five years old when he began writing novels. His first, *Running Loose*, was published in 1983.

By the time he published *Staying Fat for Sarah Byrnes* in 1993, Crutcher had already published four more novels and a collection of short stories. By 2010, he had published twelve young-

adult books, a collection of stories, and an autobiography titled *King of the Mild Frontier*.

Crutcher's work is known for its gritty realism, and nearly every novel he has written has been banned in some middle school and high school libraries across the country. In 2008, he was sixth on the American Library Association's Top Ten Banned Authors list. Despite being the target of censorship, Crutcher's novels have been honored with dozens of awards, including the California Young Reader Medal for *Staying Fat for Sarah Byrnes* (1997), the American Library Association's Margaret A. Edwards Lifetime Achievement Award (2000), and the *Writer* magazine's Writers Who Make a Difference Award (2004).

Crutcher has also been a contributing columnist to several journals and Web sites and has traveled the country giving lectures and making bookstore appearances. He continued his work as a therapist in Spokane, Washington, where he also enjoyed sports and music. Motion picture versions of several of Crutcher's novels have been planned.

## PLOT SUMMARY

### Chapters 1–2

The novel *Staying Fat for Sarah Byrnes* opens with Eric Calhoune explaining that he is the only child of a thirty-six-year-old mother. His father left before Eric was born and has never been an active part of his life. Eric, nicknamed Moby, swims on his school team. Mrs. Lemry, his swim coach, is also one of his favorite teachers.

Eric visits Sarah Byrnes at the psychiatric ward of Sacred Heart Hospital for the first time. Sarah Byrnes is his best friend; he is her only friend. She had been horribly burned when, at age three, she pulled a pot of boiling spaghetti on top of herself. Her face and hands are badly disfigured as a result. This disfigurement has made Sarah Byrnes an outcast. Eric had also been an outcast once, because he was fat, but he has since lost weight.

Eric describes Sarah Byrnes as he sees her sitting there in the hospital: "Without her spirit behind her eyes, Sarah Byrnes is truly one of the ugliest human beings outside the circus." When the nurse explains to Eric that Sarah is not responding to anyone, he tells her that Sarah Byrnes will only respond to her full name; she

# MEDIA ADAPTATIONS

- *Staying Fat for Sarah Byrnes* was recorded on audiocassette in 1993 by Recorded Books.

thinks it is ironic that with injuries caused by burns, her last name is "Byrnes," and she wants everyone to think about that.

Eric believes she can hear him. During his visit, he remembers *Crispy Pork Rinds*, the underground newspaper that Eric and Sarah Byrnes had published and passed around their junior high school. It featured stories they wrote about people who had bullied them. Mr. Mautz, the principal, ordered them to stop publishing the paper.

The inspiration for *Crispy Pork Rinds* had been Dale Thornton, a bully who beat up Sarah Byrnes when she refused to give him her lunch money. Dale had been held back in school so often that he could drive by the time he was in eighth grade. The first edition of the newspaper was printed shortly after Dale beat up Sarah Byrnes, and he was the feature story.

## Chapters 3–4

Steve Ellerby picks up Eric from his house to go to a Saturday swim practice. Ellerby drives an old sedan nicknamed the Christian Cruiser. Their classmate Mark Brittain had unsuccessfully tried to get Ellerby banned from the school parking lot. Mr. Mautz, now the vice-principal at the high school, was on his side, but principal Patterson refused the request.

Ellerby and Eric conspire to wear Mark out during swim practice, a sort of psychological game they like to play with him. After the workout, Eric returns to the hospital. The counselor who is treating Sarah Byrnes asks Eric whether she has any other friends who could visit to remind her of familiar things. Eric mentions Dale Thornton, though he admits that Dale dropped out of school

after eighth grade and no one has really seen him since.

Eric remembers the day Dale found out he had been the butt of Sarah Byrnes and Eric's journalistic prank. Mr. Mautz hated Dale as much as he hated Eric and used the newspaper as a weapon against both. Mr. Mautz pulled Dale into his office and told him that Eric published that newspaper, knowing Dale would hunt down Eric and beat him up. Eric and Sarah Byrnes decided to befriend Dale and use him as protection against other bullies. In return, they would print one story of Dale's choosing each edition.

Later, Eric meets his mother's latest boyfriend, Carver Middleton. Eric is not impressed.

## Chapters 5–6

In middle school, Sarah Byrnes and Eric had befriended Dale by appealing to his sense of being used by Mr. Mautz. "He got Eric good and didn't have to lift a finger because he had a goon do it for him."

Mark, his girlfriend Jody Mueller, Ellerby, and Eric are in Contemporary American Thought (CAT) class. Eric has had a crush on Jody for three years. Mrs. Lemry wants to know what psychological, spiritual, or social issue each student will research and present to the class. Ellerby volunteers. He chose religion as his issue and has the class listen to a song. Ellerby interprets the song as saying that God created the world and then stood back to watch what humans would do with it, from a distance.

Ellerby says the song makes him think of fairness. For Sarah Byrnes, he says, the world is a cruel place. Ellerby considers his own life good and fair for the most part. "If God is fair, how do you explain me and Sarah Byrnes on the same planet?"

Eric returns to the hospital to visit Sarah Byrnes and finds her father, Virgil Byrnes, there with her. As Mr. Byrnes is leaving, he asks Eric if Sarah Byrnes talks to him, and Eric says no. Mr. Byrnes demands that Eric report to him if she ever does.

Eric remembers when Dale and Sarah Byrnes got into an argument over what to publish in *Crispy Pork Rinds*. Dale wanted to publish a story about another outcast kid; Sarah Byrnes tried to explain that the paper's purpose was to punish the bullies, not the victims.

In his anger at Sarah Byrnes's teasing him for his stupidity, Dale had lashed out and told her that she was not so smart herself. He told her he knew her scars did not come from an overturned pot of spaghetti. Eric told Dale not to slander people, and Dale insisted he was being truthful. "Ain't no slander. Just fact." He and Sarah Byrnes recognized each other, he said, because both of them come from abusive families. Realizing someone knew the truth, Sarah Byrnes said she no longer wanted to print the paper. Privately, she told Eric she did not want Dale Thornton hanging around so much.

Eric began swimming that summer, and he and Sarah Byrnes drifted apart. Sarah Byrnes thought it was because Eric was losing weight from all the exercise, and he no longer needed a reason to hang out with her. In an effort to prove his friendship, Eric ate as much as humanly possible. After a year of staying fat for Sarah Byrnes, she told him he was off the hook and should just be healthy.

Ellerby drives Eric into a scary part of town to locate Dale, whom they find living in a run-down shack with a dilapidated garage. Eric asks Dale whether he remembers Sarah Byrnes. Dale asks how she is—calling her "Scarface"—and Eric reports her status. He asks Dale whether he knows what really happened to Sarah Byrnes, and Dale explains that he knows her father caused her injuries because he has lived that kind of life, too.

## Chapters 7–8

Eric is surprised when Jody leaves a note on his desk asking him for his phone number. That evening, he recounts the day's events—minus the part about Jody's note—to a silent Sarah Byrnes. Still suspecting that his friend is able to talk and just refuses, he surprises her by sharing the fact that he recently talked to Dale, who repeated the claim that Sarah Byrnes's father caused her scarring.

Upon hearing this, her head jerks, and Eric tells her he knew she could talk all along. He decides not to let the nurse know Sarah Byrnes can talk, figuring she must have a good reason for taking shelter in a psychiatric ward.

Dale approaches Ellerby and Eric on the sidewalk outside Eric's house. He has given more thought to Sarah Byrnes and wants to set the record straight. He explains that he and Sarah Byrnes got to be better friends once Eric

started swimming, and she helped Dale through some tough times. She told him the story behind her scars, and though she swore him to secrecy, he wants to help her get out of the hospital. He tells Eric and Ellerby that Sarah Byrnes's father held her face against a burning wood stove when she was three years old.

CAT class is spent debating abortion, which Mark completely opposes. Eric calls Mark heartless, and the two participate in a fifteen-minute debate. Eric likens Mark's tone to that of Mr. Mautz. As class ends, Jody and Eric set a time for a date at the Burger Barn.

## Chapters 9–10

Eric visits Sarah Byrnes, and she begins talking, but only to him. She explains that her burns happened during a fight her father and mother were having. Mr. Byrnes was holding his wife's head under a sink full of water, drowning her slowly. Three-year-old Sarah Byrnes ran at him and knocked him off his balance. He picked her up and held her face out in front of him, arms straight. He walked his daughter right into a burning wood stove and refused her reconstructive surgery so that it would be a reminder to obey him. He threatened to burn the rest of her if she ever told, and while Sarah Byrnes was in the hospital, her mother abandoned her.

Eric learns that Sarah Byrnes recently saw signs that her father was losing his mind again, so she stopped talking in order to be admitted into the hospital for safety. She swears Eric to secrecy, and he understands that this is the only way she can have control over something so big and so powerful.

Eric and Jody go on their date, and she confides in him that she had gotten pregnant by Mark and was forced by him to have an abortion. She explains that he does not want anyone to know; he believes that having a baby would have prevented him from effectively spreading the word of God. Although she did not want the abortion, Jody went through with it, thinking that Mark knew better than she. Eric assures Jody that he does not think badly of her for what happened.

Mrs. Lemry notices that Mark seems to be falling apart, and she urges Eric and Ellerby not to push him so hard. Mark accuses Eric of stealing his girlfriend, and Eric defends himself, telling Mark that she asked him out. Realizing the situation is out of his control, Mark calls

Jody names and says he stayed with her out of pity. He warns Eric that she will fill his head with lies because there is something seriously wrong with her.

When Eric talks to his mother about Jody, she questions his motives, suggesting that he is seeking revenge on Mark. Carver surprises Eric by stepping in to take his side in the discussion.

## Chapters 11–12
Eric sneaks a notebook and pen under Sarah Byrnes's mattress so that she can write down what she wants him to do or what she plans on doing. He tells her about Jody, and Sarah Byrnes cries when she learns of Jody's abortion because often during her life, she has wished that she had been aborted.

Using the notebook, Sarah Byrnes tells Eric that the real reason she came to the hospital was that she was having suicidal thoughts. These thoughts scared her, and she wanted a safe place to relax so that she could think through the idea and decide whether she really wanted to die. Once at the hospital, she felt cared for, for the first time in her life. She knows that if she talked, they would send her home, so she chose to remain mute.

After reading the notebook, Eric decides to confide in Mrs. Lemry. After reading the notebook herself, she tells Eric she agrees with a point Sarah Byrnes makes in it: If she can find her mother and convince her to testify against her father, everything will be straightened out.

Eric visits Dale late one night to find out whether Sarah Byrnes ever told him anything about her mother. He is trying to help locate her, and he thinks Dale might have some valuable information. Sarah Byrnes had told Dale that her mom always wanted to be a singer or dancer and that her dream was to go to Reno, Nevada.

Mr. Mautz calls Eric to his office to find out more about CAT class. When Eric refuses to provide evidence to support Mr. Mautz's idea that the class is out of control, Mr. Mautz gets angry. It becomes clear that Mark, a fellow attendee at Mr. Mautz's church, had complained to him about the course, saying that Mrs. Lemry was allowing Christian values to be trashed and that Ellerby and Eric were taunting him.

Eric warns Mrs. Lemry that Mr. Mautz was questioning him about CAT class. Mrs. Lemry talks to Eric about Sarah Byrnes and tells him

she is willing to invest time and money in helping her if that is what Sarah Byrnes really wants. Eric realizes he needs to somehow make it okay that he confided Sarah Byrnes's secret to Mrs. Lemry. Sarah Byrnes is furious when Eric tells her what he did.

## Chapters 13–14
Sarah Byrnes finds refuge in the apartment above Mrs. Lemry's garage. She attends CAT class for the first time. Mr. Mautz sits in to observe, and the discussion about abortion continues. Mark restates his earlier argument that abortion is always wrong and says God demands that all individuals take responsibility for their own actions. When Mrs. Lemry reminds him that not everything is about Christianity, Mark disagrees.

Sarah Byrnes sits directly across from Mark, and she challenges him, asking whether he truly believes all life is equal. When he replies that of course it is, she walks across the room to his desk and makes him look at her. When his gaze quickly drops, she demands he keep looking at her.

Sarah Byrnes asks Mark whether a woman who is certain her husband will disfigure or kill her baby should still have that baby. Mark replies that all life is sacred and deserves a chance. He admits he would not choose the chance that Sarah Byrnes had, and she says she would not choose it either. After more preaching from Mark, Jody blurts out that she aborted his baby. The class is stunned, and Mark gathers his books to leave. Before he goes, he calls Jody a filthy liar.

Mark tries to kill himself that night but fails. The next day, Mr. Mautz informs Mrs. Lemry's class of the event. He blames the class, its students, and Mrs. Lemry. She throws him out of her classroom and opens up a discussion about the event. Jody falls apart, feeling responsible for Mark's choice. Mrs. Lemry reminds the class that every person is responsible for his or her own choices, and no one believes that more than Mark. Class ends when Mrs. Lemry is called to the office.

Eric invites Jody to his house for dinner and shares the story of CAT class with his mother and Carver. After listening intently, Carver announces that his own father killed himself. It took decades for him to understand that he was not responsible for that choice his father made. He agrees with Mrs. Lemry, and his willingness to share such an intimate story comforts Jody.

Eric visits Sarah Byrnes and Mrs. Lemry, during which he learns they are going to take a road trip to Reno. Principal Patterson is gone for three days, which makes Mr. Mautz acting principal. Mrs. Lemry figures it is a good time to take a three-day leave of absence.

## Chapters 15–16

Mrs. Lemry and Sarah Byrnes head off to Reno. Mr. Mautz calls Eric and Ellerby out of study hall and into his office, where Cal Brittain, Mark's father, is waiting. Together, the men tell the boys that they do not hold them responsible for Mark's breakdown. The boys see through the ruse and realize the men are actually placing the blame squarely on their shoulders. Ellerby calls his father and asks him to come to the school.

When Mr. Ellerby arrives, his son tells him what is going on. Mr. Brittain tells the pastor that Mark is repentant for what he has done but blames his suicide attempt on Eric and Ellerby's humiliation of him. Mr. Brittain demands that Mr. Ellerby get control of his son.

Mr. Ellerby requests to speak to Mr. Mautz without Mr. Brittain, so Mr. Brittain leaves. Mr. Ellerby suggests that there were other factors leading to Mark's breakdown. He points out the immense pressure to be perfect put on him by his father and the church. Mark is not allowed to make mistakes or to fail. This pressure, Mr. Ellerby explains, is why there is a separation of church and state. The two have different functions and can fulfill their potential only when there is no overlap. Mr. Mautz loses his temper and says there should exist no separation of the two, but that he does not expect Mr. Ellerby to understand because he is a pastor who supports female ministers, gay rights, and sex education. Mr. Ellerby warns Mr. Mautz that he will be watching him and that there had better be no harassment of his son on school grounds.

The Ellerbys leave, and Eric is left alone with Mr. Mautz. The door opens, and Mr. Byrnes walks through. A nervous and fearful Eric admits that he does know where Sarah Byrnes is but refuses to tell. He warns Mr. Mautz that he has no idea what Mr. Byrnes is capable of. Eric turns to Mr. Byrnes and tells him,

> I don't know how you fooled Mr. Mautz, but I'll bet it wasn't hard. I'm not fooled, though. And what you better do is leave me alone and leave Sarah Byrnes alone and hope we keep our mouths shut. She's not coming back to your place. Ever.

Mr. Mautz sends Eric back to class while Mr. Byrnes tries to control himself.

Eric is in his car on the way home from Ellerby's house when Mr. Byrnes pops up in the back seat. He cuts Eric's cheek with a knife and Eric slams on the gas pedal. He stops the car and escapes, only to have Mr. Byrnes catch up with him. With a knife to his throat, Eric confesses that Sarah Byrnes is in Reno. Mr. Byrnes cuts him, tears his hair from his scalp, and throws a knife into his shoulder as Eric runs away.

## Chapters 17–18

Mark visits Eric in the hospital and admits to lying about Jody. He tells Eric that he is in therapy and has a lot to work through. He asks Eric to apologize to Jody for him.

Mrs. Lemry and Sarah Byrnes find Julie, Sarah Byrnes's mother, who abandoned her daughter fourteen years ago. Julie apologizes to Sarah Byrnes, telling her she knew she should not have run out on her little girl. She also knows, however, that she is weak. Julie refuses to testify against Mr. Byrnes, and Sarah Byrnes is abandoned by her mother for the second and last time.

Sarah Byrnes sneaks in after visiting hours to tell Eric that she is leaving. She knows she is not safe as long as Mr. Byrnes is around, so she will head to a group home in Kansas that takes care of disfigured children. She understands that what kept her alive was the hope that her mother would return to save her. Without that hope, the dream of at least partial happiness dies. Eric sneaks out of the hospital, and he and Mrs. Lemry track down Sarah Byrnes before she gets on the bus.

## Chapter 19–Epilogue

Mark returns to school and makes a public apology to his classmates and Jody in particular. He admits to having lied.

Carver announces to Eric and his mother that he is taking a short trip. The next time Eric sees him, he is on the television screen, handcuffed and being pushed into a police car. Using skills learned in a Special Forces unit during the Vietnam War, Carver had gained access to Mr. Byrnes's house and beaten him until he was unrecognizable. Although he had not intended to beat Mr. Byrnes, once he tried to subdue him, it became clear that Mr. Byrnes would fight to the death. Carver is sentenced to six months of work release for his crime.

Mrs. Lemry and her husband adopt Sarah Byrnes. She will attend one year of community college until she decides what university she wants to attend. Ellerby and Eric are both accepted into college, and as the novel ends, Eric is looking forward to a summer spent with Jody.

## CHARACTERS

### Cal Brittain

Cal Brittain, Mark's father, is a rigid, by-the-book Christian who has pressured his son with unrealistic expectations all his life. When Mark tries to kill himself, Mr. Brittain blames Ellerby and Eric. His unrelenting dedication to absolutes prevents him from seeing the role he played in his son's desperation, and at the end of the book, he has not changed.

### Mark Brittain

Mark Brittain is a classmate of Eric and Sarah Byrnes. He is a devout Christian who takes every opportunity to preach the doctrine of his faith. Despite his commitment to his religion, Mark is known to be intentionally mean to people. Mark uses the Contemporary American Thought class to share his beliefs with others, but the way in which he presents those beliefs—as the only possible right beliefs—offends some people.

Mark is the voice of absolutism in the novel. From his perspective, there is only right and wrong, black and white, with no gray areas. He is unforgiving until forced to scrutinize his own behavior and hypocrisy, and only then does he begin to understand that theory does not always translate into reality.

### Sarah Byrnes

Sarah Byrnes is a high school senior who has been horribly disfigured by burn scars on her hands and face. Although she tells people the burns came from overturning a boiling pot of spaghetti onto herself, the truth is that her father intentionally burned her at the age of three and then refused to get her reconstructive surgery so that she would learn a lesson.

Whereas Eric hides his pain behind a mask of comedy, Sarah Byrnes hides hers behind a biting sarcasm and tough defense. She refuses to let insults and nicknames like Scarface intimidate her, yet she is lonely. Sarah Byrnes longs to lead a normal life, but with an incomprehensibly brutal father and an absent mother, she believes her friendship with Eric is all she has.

Sarah Byrnes's tough exterior is her defense mechanism, her way of dealing with the world. She knows she is physically ugly; she knows her presence makes people uncomfortable. However, she has made it her life's mission to force those who would ignore her to deal with her. One of the ways she does so is to insist on the use of her full name, allowing her last name to remind people of the scarring of her burns. She insists that people around her push past the boundaries of their comfort level, and in that way, she demands their personal growth.

### Virgil Byrnes

Virgil Byrnes is Sarah Byrnes's inhumanly cruel father. Eric describes him as "one of those shadowy people you can't imagine ever having been a kid; the kind of man a dog circles warily, his hackles at attention." Mr. Byrnes's inhumanity fills a room; just the mention of his name causes Sarah Byrnes to physically shrink into herself.

### Eric Calhoune

Eric Calhoune, only child of a single mother, is the novel's narrator and the best friend of Sarah Byrnes. Like Sarah Byrnes, Eric has spent his entire school career as an outcast. For most of his life, he was so overweight that his classmates nicknamed him Moby, after the fictional whale Moby Dick.

Eric loses the weight when he joins the school swim team, but inside, he still sees himself as a fat kid. When he flirts with his crush, Jody Mueller, he does it with the lack of confidence of a teen who has spent his whole life being ridiculed. He says, self-deprecatingly, "If you ever want a boyfriend who encourages freedom of expression, dial 1-800-FAT-BOY."

Being marginalized has given Eric a well-developed sense of compassion for others, but he recognizes the damage his experience has caused as well:

> In truth, the only reason I don't allow people up close and personal with my emotional self is that I hate to be embarrassed. I can't afford it. I spent *years* being embarrassed because I was fat and clumsy and afraid. I wanted to be tough like Sarah Byrnes, to stand straight and tall, oblivious to my gut eclipsing belt buckle, and say, "Up yours!" But I was paralyzed, so I developed this pretty credible comedy act—I'm the I-Don't-Care-Kid—which is what I assume most other kids do.

Eric has a very clear understanding of how the world works. He grasps the concept that people are who they are because of how they respond to their life experiences. He is arguably the most well-developed character in the novel.

## Mr. Ellerby

Although he wears the clerical robe and collar, Mr. Ellerby is not a traditional Episcopalian minister. He is big in stature, with movie-star good looks and a presence that commands whatever room he is in. He supports equal rights for homosexual people, the idea of women in the pulpit, and sex education for students. These beliefs make him suspect in the eyes of Mr. Mautz and Mark's father. In the novel, Mr. Ellerby is the voice of tolerance.

## Steve Ellerby

Steve Ellerby—called simply Ellerby—is Eric's close friend and an all-around obnoxious kid. Altar boy and son of a preacher, Ellerby drives an old, powder-blue sedan nicknamed the Christian Cruiser, from which he blares old gospel tunes. After Eric and Sarah Byrnes, Ellerby is third on Mr. Mautz's Most Wanted list.

Although Ellerby seems to go out of his way to annoy people, he is actually a thoughtful—though sometimes disrespectful—person who is as quick to take the blame as he is to lay it at someone else's feet. Ellerby is a Christian who believes more in the messages of the Bible than in rigid rules of right and wrong.

## Ellen Lemry

Mrs. Lemry is the swimming coach and teacher of the Contemporary American Thought (CAT) class. She appreciates Eric as a person who genuinely cares about people and issues. Mrs. Lemry calls him Eric the Well Read because he is intelligent and well informed, but she also calls him Double-E, for Eric Enigma. She considers him a mystery: "a jock who doesn't compete in his best sport, a student who doesn't excel where his aptitude is highest," and a person with a group of friends "straight out of 'The Far Side.'"

Mrs. Lemry is a teacher who does not let her personal beliefs interfere with her teaching. She clearly respects all students and demands that they respect each other. She will not, however, tolerate Mr. Mautz, whose attitude towards teens fosters animosity.

Although she does not know Sarah Byrnes at the beginning of the book, Mrs. Lemry befriends the youngster and drives her to Reno to try to locate her mother. Ultimately, Mrs. Lemry and her husband adopt Sarah Byrnes, giving hope to the reader that Sarah Byrnes will find fulfillment. Mrs. Lemry is the voice of reason in the novel.

## Mr. Mautz

Mr. Mautz had once been the principal of the middle school and is now the high school's assistant principal. He is a power-hungry man who wields his authority without reason, simply because he can. Mr. Mautz is described as one of those adults who looks but does not *see*. If an adult and a child were to tell him two different versions of an event, Mr. Mautz would automatically believe the adult.

Mr. Mautz dislikes Eric because he believes him to be a smart aleck who thinks he can outwit everyone else. Mr. Mautz is a manipulative, misguided man who abuses his power when it serves his purpose. Eric thoroughly dislikes him. He considers himself a righteous Christian; he believes he has God on his side when he attempts to blame Eric for Mark's suicide attempt. Mr. Mautz embraces the integration of church and state.

## Carver Middleton

Carver Middleton, an accountant, is Eric's mother's latest boyfriend and apparently a bit of a geek. He is also a Vietnam veteran. Carver is a thoughtful man, given to quiet observation. He is a rather minor character for most of the novel, but the successful conclusion of the story depends wholly on his actions.

Carver's experience as a victim of child abuse allows him to empathize with Sarah Byrnes's situation. He recognizes the gift of true and unwavering friendship that Eric offers Sarah Byrnes, and he makes a huge personal sacrifice in an effort to keep both of these young people safe.

## Moby
*See* Eric Calhoune

## Mom

Eric's mother gave birth to her son when she was just eighteen years old; she was and remains single. She is beautiful and understanding, but Eric is aware that she does not guide and mentor him the way mothers usually do. He feels that she treats him "like an extracurricular activity." One day, he knows, he will have to deal with this issue head-on. She relates to her son more as a friend than a parent, but the two share a close bond.

### Jody Mueller

Jody Mueller is Eric's love interest and Mark Brittain's former girlfriend. Jody's character is also devoutly Christian, but she tends to be balanced in her views, not quite so sure that there is only one truth.

Jody is attracted to Eric, and the two eventually date. Everyone assumes it was Eric who made the first move, but in reality it was Jody. She finds Eric's sense of humor and compassion appealing, and she confides in him.

### Dale Thornton

Dale Thornton is a bully who was held back in school so many times that he had a legitimate driver's license in eighth grade. He picked on Eric mercilessly and gave Sarah Byrnes the nickname Scarface. When she refused to hand over her lunch money to him one day in middle school, Dale beat her until she could no longer stand. She refused to surrender, though, and eventually the two became friends of sorts. Sarah Byrnes was quite possibly the first, if not the only, person Dale could ever respect.

With a physically abusive father and a mother who ran out on the family with an uncle, Dale is a victim, as are Sarah Byrnes and Eric. His bullying is a way of taking some control over his life. By the novel's end, Dale has found a way to live outside himself by helping those very people he once terrified.

## THEMES

### Appearances versus Reality

The difference between appearances and reality is a major theme in the novel. In high school, life for many young people is all about appearances and keeping up with each other. This novel reveals how different reality can be.

Sarah Byrnes appears to be a monster. She is horrifying to look at, and she talks tough. Despite her attempts to exude self-confidence, Sarah Byrnes is a frightened, lonely girl who just wants to fit in. She wants to be normal, something she will never experience.

## TOPICS FOR FURTHER STUDY

- How would changing the ending of the novel change the meaning of the work as a whole? Rewrite the last scene and read it to your classmates and explain why you chose that ending.

- Compare and contrast the religious beliefs of Steve Ellerby and Mark Brittain. On poster board, diagram their similarities and differences.

- Although Sarah Byrnes and Eric are best friends, she confides in Dale Thornton about how she got her scars. Why do you think she chose Dale instead of Eric? Write your response in an essay using facts or quotes from the text to support your opinion.

- In small groups, hold a debate on a controversial topic. Choose the side you do *not* agree with and present its arguments. Research the topic, set a time limit for each member of the team, and select a panel of judges to score the debate.

- Research Chris Crutcher's other young-adult titles. Choose one that sounds interesting to you and read it. Create a PowerPoint presentation comparing its themes to those found in *Staying Fat for Sarah Byrnes*.

- What do you consider to be the most revealing scene in the novel? Draw a picture of that scene and explain to your classmates what it reveals.

Mark Brittain is another character who seems so self-assured. When his religious convictions are challenged, however, he quickly loses control of his temper. In Contemporary American Thought class, Mark "explodes" during the discussion about abortion. He is absolutely sure of himself and that what he is saying is the only truth, but when the truth about his actions—his demand for Jody to have an abortion—comes to light, he cannot bear the pressure or the humiliation of his hypocrisy. Mark tries to kill himself. He is not the self-assured boy he presents himself to be.

Jody Mueller is the vehicle through which Eric realizes that appearances can be deceiving. Eric considers Jody to be the classiest girl in MacArthur High. She surprises him by admitting to having an abortion. On their date, Jody tells Eric the whole story.

> You can't imagine the emptiness. There's a piece that isn't getting talked about in class. Mark took me to the clinic, but he dropped me off two blocks away because he though somebody might recognize him. When I came out, I was just *lost*. . . . I just wanted to cry and have somebody hold me.

Eric realizes that Jody is not as confident as she seems to be, nor is Mark the epitome of Christian values he wants his peers to think he is. "God, nothing is as it appears," Eric says.

At the very end of the book, Eric takes away a major lesson: "One thing I do know: Families can get pretty messed up while they're looking pretty good."

### Nature of Friendship

At the core of *Staying Fat for Sarah Byrnes* lies the friendship of Sarah Byrnes and Eric Calhoune. Both are marginalized—not accepted by their peers—because they are different from most of their classmates. However, when Eric has the chance to break free of that limitation, he chooses not to because he values his friendship with Sarah Byrnes more than he values his individual place in society. For an entire year, he stays fat so that his friend can feel secure that she will not be left behind. And Sarah Byrnes, though she may never have felt completely assured, values her friend's individual happiness enough to eventually let him lose the weight and gain a larger circle of friends.

Eric puts his own life in danger to keep Sarah Byrnes safe. It takes a physical attack, with a knife at his throat and blood running down his neck, to force Eric to tell Mr. Byrnes where his daughter is. Although his feeling of terror is intense, his feelings for Sarah Byrnes are more so.

Although Dale Thornton's friendship for Sarah Byrnes is on a different level, he comes through for her when he is most needed. His connection to her is their shared victimization; both have parents who brutally beat them throughout their childhoods. Dale is the only person who does not believe Sarah Byrnes about how she got her scars.

Although Dale had dropped out of sight three years before Sarah Byrnes enters the psychiatric ward, Eric remembers him as being the only friend she had. When Dale willingly helps her out as she struggles to stay away from her father and locate her mother, he does so out of a sense of communion with her. He knows she survived beatings just as he did, and he relates to her in a way no one else can.

Several other friendships of various natures develop throughout the novel: Mrs. Lemry and Sarah Byrnes, Mrs. Lemry and Eric, and Carver Middleton and Eric.

### Moral Relativism versus Moral Absolutism

Mark's beliefs represent moral absolutism: There are rules that apply to every person in every situation and they must be obeyed. Cal Brittain and Mr. Mautz are moral absolutists as well.

This absolutism is most evident during the CAT class discussion of abortion. Mark yells, "There's a law higher than that! Don't you understand? There is a *higher law*! And it's not flexible!" For Mark, this law is Christian doctrine. In his eyes, there is only one correct way to interpret that doctrine, and anyone whose interpretation differs from his is wrong.

Steve Ellerby and his father, an Episcopalian minister, are also Christians, but they interpret those "laws" differently. They take into consideration the circumstances of each individual situation before deciding to what extent those laws apply. They operate from a theory of moral relativism: The morality of a choice or action depends upon the circumstances surrounding it.

Jody Mueller also embraces moral relativism. In CAT class, Mrs. Lemry asks Jody whether she agrees with Mark's absolutism. Jody replies, "I'd like to agree with Mark, but every time I think something is absolute, it turns out not to be. So I guess I don't know."

Mark's rigid thinking leads to his breakdown and subsequent suicide attempt. Having been raised in a family where standards are incredibly high and failure is not an option, Mark has no coping skills when it comes to dealing with a mistake. His unforgiving moral absolutes tell him abortion is wrong, but the reality of becoming a father before he graduates from high school is unimaginable to him. Therefore, Mark forces Jody into a permanent and life-altering decision—the abortion—that he believes is wrong, but he continues to preach against abortion. Mark is mentally unhealthy and recognizes that as the book comes to a close.

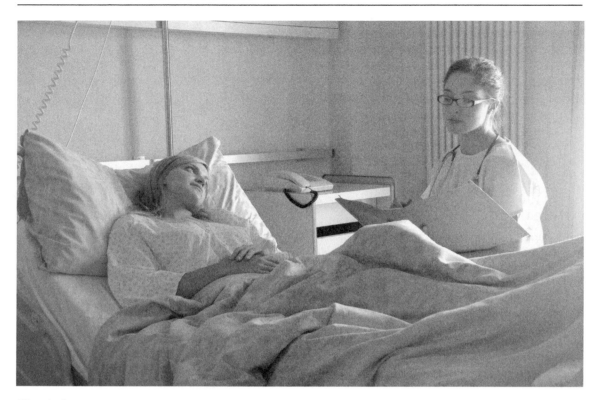

*Hospital room* *(Image copyright Olly, 2009. Used under license from Shutterstock.com)*

## STYLE

### First-Person Narrative

The novel is told from the point of view of Eric Calhoune. He speaks in terms of "I" and offers opinions on the events and characters that make up the story. First-person narrative gives a story an immediate and authentic feel. Readers tend to feel directly involved, as if they are sharing the narrator's experience.

### Coming-of-Age Novel

*Staying Fat for Sarah Byrnes* can be described as a coming-of-age novel, also known as a bildungs-roman. In this type of story, the main character is young, usually in his or her teens, and under-goes turmoil that leads to personal growth and development. This maturity is attained only after a loss of innocence. In Crutcher's novel, the coming-of-age story applies to Sarah Byrnes, Eric, and Mark.

### Realism

Realism is a literary technique in which a story seems believable and authentic. *Staying Fat for*

*Sarah Byrnes* uses realistic language, social sit-uations, and settings. Because readers can recog-nize their own experiences in these realistic details, they can relate to the story and empa-thize with the characters.

Some stories—*The Wonderful Wizard of Oz*, for example—are better told in a nonrealistic way. The subject matter or message (as determined by the author) usually dictates the use or lack of realism.

### Heroes and Heroines

This novel is full of heroes and heroines, people who display exceptional courage and strength. While the word *heroes* may conjure up images of masked crusaders in capes, the heroes in this story fit the definition in a more realistic sense.

Sarah Byrnes is the obvious heroine in the book. Having survived an abusive childhood by relying solely on her own strength, she epitomizes the concept of heroism. Eric is also a hero, though, because he forsakes his own desires and needs to protect a friend. Mrs. Lemry is another heroine, for she goes out of her way—and far beyond her obligations as a teacher—to establish a

# COMPARE & CONTRAST

- **1990s:** Overall national support for abortion rights is on the decline, as is the number of abortions performed in the United States. There are more protests—and more violent incidents—at U.S. abortion clinics. According to the National Abortion Federation (NAF), the number of incidents of picketing outside clinics increases from 292 in 1991 to 2,898 in 1992.

  **Today:** Issues surrounding abortion remain timely and controversial. The NAF reports that incidents of picketing hit an all-time high of 11,244 in 2003. The same year, federal laws are passed restricting abortion rights.

- **1990s:** According to Prevent Child Abuse America, reports of child abuse rise 33 percent over the course of the decade. By 1999, there have been more than one million confirmed child abuse cases since the beginning of the decade. One factor is the severe economic strain: Unemployment has skyrocketed, and substance abuse along with it.

  **Today:** A National Child Abuse and Neglect Data Systems report indicates that physical

child abuse has declined by 48 percent since 1992. The Crimes against Children Research Center identifies several reasons for the downward trend: sustained economic improvement, an overall increase in the number of law enforcement and child protection personnel, and more aggressive prosecution and prison sentences. Experts agree, however, that most child abuse goes unreported.

- **1990s:** Young-adult fiction is formulaic, using similar plots with similar uninteresting characters who do the same thing over and over. *Staying Fat for Sarah Byrnes* is therefore a target of censorship for its use of profanity and mature themes.

  **Today:** Sales of teen fiction skyrocket, and the market caters to older readers. The teenage population is considered more sophisticated, and more authors explore mature subjects. Crutcher's work is no longer the exception to the rule in terms of content or treatment of themes.

---

relationship with Sarah Byrnes and help her find a sense of normalcy in her life. On a lesser level, even Dale Thornton is a hero in this novel. Dale spent his life as an outcast, both at school and at home. Like Sarah Byrnes, he is an abuse survivor, and he steps out of his comfort zone to track down Eric and explain to him what he thought he needed to in order for Eric to help Sarah Byrnes. Dale puts the needs of someone else, someone he no longer is in contact with, before his own.

## Dialogue

As is often the case with young-adult fiction, the author relies on dialogue, the quoted conversations between characters, to give the reader insight into characters' feelings, thoughts, and beliefs. The dialogue supplements the narration, that is, the reporting of what happens.

## Flashback

Flashback is a technique used to fill in the reader on events that happened before the main story took place. In *Staying Fat for Sarah Byrnes*, the reader learns through flashbacks the history and evolution of the friendship between Sarah Byrnes and Eric, the rise and fall of *Crispy Pork Rinds*, and Dale Thornton's role in the events.

## HISTORICAL CONTEXT

### The Novel as a Reflection of Reality

At the time Crutcher wrote *Staying Fat for Sarah Byrnes*, he was working full time as a therapist in the field of child abuse and neglect. The issues he

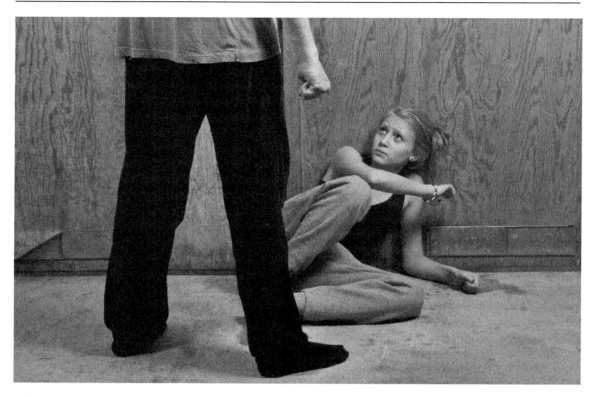

*Abuse* (*Image copyright Dodorema, 2009. Used under license from Shutterstock.com*)

deals with in that novel are ones that he repeatedly heard about in his job.

In his essay "A Dangerous Thing," Crutcher explains the effect those children and their stories have on him.

> I am struck by the fact that the kids I hear them from populate our classrooms. They do not tell their stories because many of them feel shame because they are treated that way, and they hold the secret, the only real power they have over their situations. They would rather be angry or depressed than vulnerable, and so they sit, many of them believing they are alone.

Crutcher was motivated to write about Sarah Byrnes and a host of other characters in other novels because he wanted to give those children a voice, a familiar landscape. He wanted to let them know they were not alone. However, the 1990s was a stale period in the field of young-adult literature. Most teen fiction published touched lightly, if at all, on issues its readers were facing. Crutcher broke through that invisible barrier by publishing stories that reflected the reality that teens across the nation faced on a daily basis.

*Staying Fat for Sarah Byrnes* covers a lot of ground: child abuse, religion, bullying, intolerance, and individualism. By using language heard in middle and high school hallways throughout the country, Crutcher gave his readers a story they want to hear because they can relate to it. Some parents and other adults feel differently, and nearly all his work has been censored in some places.

Time and hindsight have proven Crutcher to have been a writer before his time, a visionary. What was labeled unacceptable in the 1990s is finding a more mainstream place in young-adult publishing. Censors still target his work, but more and more authors are writing books with a commitment to realism rather than entertainment, and more and more young adults are reading them.

### Making It Safe by Making It Fiction

Crutcher uses his fiction to reach students who are marginalized or lonely. He understands that some adults believe children's reading selections should be censored, but he cautions against censorship as a tool to protect children. He explains in his essay:

When a teacher looks out over his or her classroom, he/she is looking at one in three girls who have been sexually mistreated, one in five boys. That doesn't take into consideration the number of kids who have been beaten, locked up, or simply never allowed to be good enough. Stories are buffered in fiction and therefore allow discussion of issues that would not otherwise be brought up. They save many students.

In the 1990s, this idea of using fiction as a sort of therapeutic tool was not common. At times, the censorship of Crutcher's work overshadowed the message of his novels. With the passage of time, the value of his work has been recognized more widely.

## CRITICAL OVERVIEW

*Staying Fat for Sarah Byrnes* was an immediate hit among most readers and critics. A *Publishers Weekly* reviewer writes, "Such superlatives as 'riveting' and 'powerful' can only hint at the craftsmanship on display in this transcendent story of love, loyalty and courage." The book received the American Library Association's award for Best of the Best Books for Young Adults and numerous other honors.

Young-adult readers praised the novel for realistically presenting high school life and the issues they face on a daily basis. In an interview published in *TeenReads.com* in 2000, Crutcher describes a letter he received from a girl who had just read the novel. Crutcher explains the gist of the girl's letter: "I'm not one of those people on the outside; but I have treated people like that. After reading your book, I'm going to make a conscious choice to treat people better." Many adults appreciated the novel as well. In the same interview, Crutcher shares a letter he received from a woman who called the book "one of the three best books I've ever read."

Like all of Crutcher's novels, *Staying Fat for Sarah Byrnes* has been censored in schools across the United States. Those critical of the novel cite his use of profanity, as well as his treatment of the themes of religion and teen pregnancy. Crutcher responded to attacks on the novel in an October 2005 essay in which he states,

> Good stories are one of few resources we have left to make connections with kids. They provide a level playing field for adults to talk about real life with kids, while allowing both to keep their personal safety. It's a lot easier to talk

about the struggles of a character in a book than it is to divulge personal information, and therefore make connections they would otherwise be unable to make.

Crutcher defends his controversial choice of theme and use of profanity in his essay by pointing out that stories must be told realistically in order to be received realistically.

Educators and librarians generally agree with the author's stance on censorship and realism in his novels. In spite of widespread censorship attempts, *Staying Fat for Sarah Byrnes* continues to be required reading in many American high schools.

## CRITICISM

### *Rebecca Valentine*

*Valentine is a freelance writer and editor who holds a bachelor's degree in English with an emphasis on literary analysis. In this essay, she explores how, in* Staying Fat for Sarah Byrnes, *Crutcher shows that knowledge carries with it a sense of responsibility.*

Crutcher's *Staying Fat for Sarah Byrnes* is a novel rich with well-developed characters whose flaws and virtues are equally evident. Although one primary story line commands most of the reader's attention, each character has his or her own individual story that feeds into Sarah Byrnes's quest for a normal life. Through these characters, Crutcher sends his readers the message that once an individual has knowledge of a detrimental situation, he or she also has a responsibility to try to bring about a positive change.

At one point in the novel, Steve Ellerby admits to his friend Eric Calhoune that although he has known Sarah Byrnes most of his life, he has made it a point to stay away from her because he does not like thinking of her pain. He recognizes that his behavior is cowardly, "because once a thing is known, it can't be *un*known."

The fact that what is known cannot be ignored is a pervading theme of *Staying Fat for Sarah Byrnes*, and Crutcher uses it to teach readers that they cannot run away from a situation just because it is unpleasant. That very belief was the catalyst for Crutcher's own decision to become a writer even though it meant leaving behind a full-time position as a child therapist.

In an interview with Heather Vogel Frederick of *Publishers Weekly*, Crutcher explains that

# WHAT DO I READ NEXT?

- In Crutcher's 2007 novel *Deadline*, eighteen-year-old Ben Wolf chooses not to undergo treatment for his leukemia in hopes he can lead a normal life his senior year of high school. Ben keeps his fatal disease a secret from his classmates and parents, and only as the book progresses does he realize the price of keeping secrets.

- *Speak*, written by Laurie Halse Anderson in 2006, is the story of high school freshman Melinda Sordino. A series of events traumatizes Melinda, and she slowly loses her ability to speak, despite the fact that she is screaming inside.

- *The Astonishing Life of Octavian Nothing, Traitor to the Nation, Vol. 1: The Pox Party* (2006) is the story of an African American teen raised in a household of radical philosophers. Author M. T. Anderson sets his novel in Boston during the American Revolution. As Octavian grows up, he realizes he is the subject of an experiment to determine the intellectual capacity of Africans.

- Sherman Alexie's novel *The Absolutely True Diary of a Part-Time Indian* (2007) explores the cultural identity and self-identity of fourteen-year-old Native American Arnold Spirit. Arnold was born with a medical condition known as water on the brain (hydrocephalus). As a result, his head is too big for his body and his defect makes him the target of bullies. His saving grace is his natural basketball ability coupled with an easy sense of humor. Arnold's drawings accompany the text throughout the book.

- *The Good Thief* (2008), written by Hannah Tinti, is the story of twelve-year-old Ren, an orphan who is missing his left hand and does not know why. When Benjamin Nab shows up, Ren finds that this stranger may be the key to both his future and his past.

- Leslie Connor's 2008 novel *Waiting for Normal* revolves around twelve-year-old Addie, who lives with her neglectful mother in a street-side trailer in New York. This is the story of one girl's search for community and what it means to be a family.

his work opened his eyes to the plight of abused and neglected children and thus gave him the responsibility to do something about it.

> What's known can't be unknown. As a writer and a human being, I can't turn my back on it. I have to keep myself in a position where I can scream and yell and be obnoxious about getting something done.

In *Staying Fat for Sarah Byrnes*, Crutcher forces several of his characters to come to the same conclusion. In the aforementioned scene, Ellerby realizes he had been taking the easy way out by not ever reaching out to Sarah Byrnes, despite knowing that she suffered. He is shamed by his behavior, and he spends the rest of the novel helping Eric help Sarah Byrnes.

Eric himself has always known that Sarah Byrnes suffered, and he ignores his own personal comfort and safety to do what he feels is right. For an entire year, he remained fat when he could more easily have lost weight and enjoyed a level of health he had never known. When Sarah Byrnes is hospitalized, Eric is the only one who visits her in the hope of learning what happened and how he can help. When Sarah Byrnes goes into hiding and her father threatens Eric with physical violence to learn her whereabouts, Eric endangers his very life by safeguarding her secret.

Dale Thornton, himself physically abused and neglected by a parent, is the one person who knows exactly how Sarah Byrnes got her scars. Her situation is the most "known" to him.

However, he does nothing overt to help her until Eric approaches him in search of knowledge. Dale had done something, though: He kept quiet. From his perspective, keeping the abuse a secret was the best he could do for his friend because he understood—in a way no one else in the story could—what could happen to Sarah Byrnes if he ever betrayed her confidence.

Once Eric tells Dale that Sarah Byrnes is in the psychiatric ward, Dale cannot stop thinking about her. He goes out of his comfort zone to search out Eric and tell him what he knows about Sarah Byrnes's past. When Eric asks Dale whether he is making up the story, Dale gets angry. Eric reminds himself that "to Dale the very worst thing in the world is to be called a liar." Ellerby, who hears Dale's story, asks why he never went to the authorities, an implication that Dale could have helped Sarah Byrnes and chose not to. Dale's reply indicates he operates from a sense of shared experience with Sarah Byrnes, one neither Eric nor Ellerby can fully grasp:

> Those guys don't listen to jokers like me. I give my word to Scarface I'd keep my mouth shut, an' that's just what I done. 'Cept for now. Don't wanna see her rottin' in some crazy house, like I said. Maybe we ain't such good friends anymore, but we was once.

Crutcher uses the character of Dale to illustrate that sometimes inaction can be thoughtful action, even if appearances say otherwise. Eventually Dale understands that remaining quiet no longer serves Sarah Byrnes, and he tells the truth to someone he knows will believe him, someone who will take the facts and use them to help Sarah Byrnes. In both instances, Dale acts responsibly, as best he knows how from his own life experiences.

Mark Brittain also illustrates the idea that once something is known, it cannot be unknown.

Mark lives his life in service to his beliefs, which are built on rigid rules. His world is black and white; actions are right or wrong, virtuous or sinful. Mark is not a likeable character because of his rigidity. Sarah Byrnes heatedly points out his hypocrisy when she publicly denounces him for preaching his Christian beliefs all over school yet not acting on them, especially when it comes to treating her as his equal.

Mark believes abortion is sinful, an unforgivable wrong. However, when Jody becomes pregnant with his baby, he pressures her to commit the very sin that he speaks out against. He then commits another sin by lying about Jody, claiming that she is making up the whole story just to make him look bad.

Mark attempts to kill himself because he cannot face the person he has become, the mistakes he has made. When he lives and realizes he will eventually have to face his peers again, he understands that knowing what he—and everyone else—now knows about himself means no one can ever *not* know it. Therefore, he publicly apologizes to his peers and to Jody. He begins seeing a therapist to help him figure out how to deal with his issues. In short, he takes responsibility.

Mr. Ellerby visits Mark and offers to help him explore different perspectives on Christianity. When Mark declines the offer, Mr. Ellerby replies, "Mark, you're only seventeen years old, and you've already tried to take your own life. I'd say that means something's not working." Mark agrees to meet with Mr. Ellerby. Though he may not particularly like Mark, Mr. Ellerby knows about his situation and his religious background and therefore takes on the responsibility of helping him heal.

Mrs. Lemry takes great responsibility for Sarah Byrnes's situation. She takes time off work to go to Reno in search of Julie, Sarah Byrnes's mother. She allows Sarah Byrnes to live in her home until she can figure out what to do next. Ultimately, she adopts Sarah Byrnes. By law, all Mrs. Lemry is required to do as a teacher is report the abuse to her principal. Mrs. Lemry goes above and beyond what was expected of her.

Carver Middleton is arguably the most surprising character in the novel. Until the very end, Carver is a minor figure. The reader never learns much about Carver, and that omission does not affect the story in any way. As the story progresses, Carver reveals that his father killed himself and that Carver believes that he could have prevented the suicide. Because he knows how it feels to feel guilty for someone else's bad decision, he does something he rarely does: He speaks up and interjects his opinion in a situation that does not involve him. Carver listens as Jody and Eric report Mark's suicide attempt. Jody expresses her feelings of guilt, and Eric explains that Mrs. Lemry told the class they were in no way responsible for Mark's choice. Carver surprises everyone and shares his experience with his father. He then counsels the teens that they absolutely were not responsible for what happened. He could have said nothing, but knowing the feeling of unwarranted guilt gave him the responsibility to speak up.

By the end of the novel, Carver has become one of the most important characters. Life falls into place because Carver takes responsibility for helping Sarah Byrnes get control of her life. And he takes responsibility because he knows, having been a soldier in the Special Forces unit during the Vietnam War, what it's like to be hunted. Carver takes matters into his own hands and captures Virgil Byrnes. He knows that without Mr. Byrnes on the loose, Sarah Byrnes can begin to lead as normal a life as possible. Carver explains his thoughts in a television interview:

> But I sat by for several months, watching the fallout from this man's actions. His daughter, who is severely scarred for life, was in the psychiatric unit at Sacred Heart, completely shut down. My girlfriend's son was in a constant state of hopeless turmoil, trying to repair what was beyond repair.... People were falling in his wake like flies.... Sometimes sacrifices have to be made. This seemed like a good place to make mine.

Carver knows he will be punished for breaking the law and taking matters into his own hands. He is fairly certain he would spend time in jail, away from his girlfriend and Eric, yet he feels an obligation to help because he knows the situation. Getting Mr. Byrnes out of the picture allows Sarah Byrnes to be adopted and begin building a sense of self-esteem. Because Eric knows his friend is going to be okay, he can move on and build a fulfilling life. Crutcher indicates to the reader that life settles into place for many of the other characters as well: Ellerby, Jody, and Mark.

In an interview with Teri S. Lesesne for the journal *Emergency Librarian*, Crutcher describes a hero: "Heroes stand up when it is easier to sit down. They are visible when it is easier to be invisible." By this definition, many of the characters in *Staying Fat for Sarah Byrnes* are heroes. Their heroism lies in the fact that they have knowledge and accept the responsibility to do something powerful with that knowledge.

**Source:** Rebecca Valentine, Critical Essay on *Staying Fat for Sarah Byrnes*, in *Novels for Students*, Gale, Cengage Learning, 2010.

### Theoni Soublis

*In the following essay, Soublis recounts a student's response to* Staying Fat for Sarah Byrnes.

Young adult novels are still changing my life. I teach Reading in the Secondary Content Areas, where I encourage preservice teachers from all disciplines to incorporate reading into their classes. In doing so, of course, I discuss Rosenblatt's reader-response theory. One of the required novels is Chris Crutcher's *Staying Fat for Sarah Byrnes*. I expect emotional responses to the novel's issues of child abuse, body image, religion, friendships, and abortion. But I was never prepared to hear a response like Erik Winkler's. His response was so powerful that I asked Erik to collaborate with me on this article so that we could capture the moment from my perspective as a teacher and his perspective as a student.

Erik's reading response

The similarities are there right away: He is named Eric and so am I. He swims competitively and so do I. While I could stop my enjoyment and reflection on the novel there, it would not be serving myself or the book justice.

Sarah says, "Every day I live with it is one more day I've lived with it; I'm a little fuller up. Nothing changes. I have to be tough or funny every minute. If I let up for a second, it gets me. It gets me when I'm half awake in the morning and forget who I am" (102). What gets Sarah is the pain of a lifetime. What gets me is the pain of a lifetime. For the longest time, and even to this day, the first thing I say to myself when I walk into a room is, "Just don't act like a faggot." Sarah has to be tough or funny. I have to mask the tone of my voice, the way I sit, conduct my body language, or how I look at people.

Like Sarah, I know what it is like to wake up and not be happy with what is in the mirror. Too bad mirrors are only skin deep. The ugliness I see in myself is not so much physical as it

*Young male swimmer* (*Image copyright Epic Stock, 2009. Used under license from Shutterstock.com*)

is metaphysical. The seed of self-hatred that was planted in me long ago still germinates within. I wish I could remember who or how it was planted, but the roots are too deep and far too tangled inside of my head; it would be too thorny to figure that out now.

Like Eric, I put all of my pain into the water. Swimming has literally saved my life. The numerous mornings when I do not want to get out of bed, it is swimming that comes to my rescue. The many years of waking up at five in the morning have given me the tenacity and discipline to be able to kick myself, drag my head off of my pillow, and start the day. From dealing with my everyday troubles, to the huge obstacles I have had to conquer, swimming has provided me with the mental intensity needed to challenge them. I face issues as I would a hard practice. . . . I tell myself, "OK, Erik, figure out a way to make it through this. NO GIVING UP." When, in my gut, all I want to do is run away, swimming has given me the confidence to confront things head on and stand my ground to take on the charging bull.

While many people in my situation run to mind-altering substances to cope with personal struggles, I sprint to the pool. The swimming is an emotional oasis for me. There is no better

feeling in the world than burying my face into a soft towel after a difficult practice. No matter my sexuality, the water has always seen me indifferently. In a world that feels so wrong for me sometimes, the water always feels so right. Underwater, I am in a world where I feel safe and clear in mind.

As Erik was reading his response to the class, I had so many reactions burning through me. I was proud of Erik's courage, impressed with his writing quality, thankful to have him as a student and, most of all, grateful that he soon would become a powerful and passionate teacher. But coupled with those positive thoughts were the negative thoughts I had about one of Erik's classmates, Scott.

Scott is an exercise science major, a baseball coach, and an aspiring future teacher. He is motivated, enthusiastic, and disciplined. Aware as I was of Scott's outstanding qualities, I was shocked at the horrific thoughts that were consuming me about Scott as Erik came out of the closet in his reading response. I was thinking, "If you make a snide remark. . . ." or "If you even smirk. . . ." I felt like I was being pulled in two

> I EXPECT EMOTIONAL RESPONSES TO THE NOVEL'S ISSUES OF CHILD ABUSE, BODY IMAGE, RELIGION, FRIENDSHIPS, AND ABORTION. BUT I WAS NEVER PREPARED TO HEAR A RESPONSE LIKE ERIK WINKLER'S."

directions: (1) monitoring all the students' reactions and (2) waiting to respond to Scott's nonverbal communication. For some reason, stereotypes of athletes I have held for years started to consume me. As I recognized a new stereotype entering my consciousness I tried to suppress it, to let it go, to talk myself out of fearing the reactions that Scott could be having. After all, I preach about encouraging diversity in the classroom, fighting stereotypes, and leaving biases in the hallway. How could I possibly have these thoughts about Scott? I felt guilty.

To my surprise, it was Scott who was to have the liberating reaction. As Erik finished reading his compelling passage, I scanned the room for reactions. There were tears, mine included. There were looks of hope, pride, and comfort on the faces of Erik's friends. But it was Scott's reaction that prevailed. Just as Erik completed his reading, Scott (who was seated next to Erik in a small circle of seven) extended his hand, firmly shook Erik's hand, and said, "That's the bravest thing I have ever seen anyone do."

I was shocked. More tears flowed from my eyes. Scott reminded me why I respect my career as I do. For the past decade I have been examining my stereotypical beliefs and biases that came from parents, media, friends, and experiences. Rosenblatt's theory may have been developed to assist students to become more active readers and participants in their learning, but the theory does not end with the students. For teachers, reader response continues to run deep. The tool surpasses classroom pedagogy and theoretical practices. It reminds us that, as teachers, we are agents of change and, to be successful facilitators, we too must create change in our lives. As we continue to grow as learners, we bring our newly constructed beliefs into our teaching

situations, which allow for opportunities such as this to flourish.

I continued to reflect on the interaction between Erik and Scott for another semester. Recently, I asked Erik how he felt about that pivotal day in class. He told me:

> As I read my response aloud in class that day, I could feel the emotion welling inside, not knowing whether tears or laughter would come. After finishing I waited, holding my breath, so as not to break the silence. I was so relieved when Scott reached over to me, looked me in the eyes, shook my hand, and complimented me in front of the small group we made. I'll never forget, because at that exact moment, I began to swallow the much-needed sunlight I had been waiting for my whole life. A group of unbiased people, who had no previous connections or attachments to me, embraced my words and allowed me to articulate my hardships in life. During that instant in time, because my comrades understood the novel, they understood me. I felt respected and warm inside.

> Who would have thought that a little book could give me the courage and strength to do something that two years ago I never would have been able to do?

What had I done throughout the semester to create a safe environment for Erik to share such personal details with the class? One of my objectives as a teacher educator is to generate a classroom atmosphere that can transcend bias and create opportunities for such intimate situations. Part of that objective includes building honesty, trust, loyalty, and respect between the students and me and among the students themselves. Literature discussions open a door for students to discuss their personal lives and experiences in such a way that any threat of ridicule is erased.

The reader responses were shared on the last day of the semester. Erik was the fourth of six students to read. I don't recall the three before him or the two after. Erik's writing has gripped me and has been a part of me ever since. When class was over that day I knew I couldn't keep this story to myself. I had to share it with other educators who have the influence to generate such responses from their students. Don't let the opportunity slip away.

**Source:** Theoni Soublis and Erik Winkler, "Transcending Bias through Reader-Response Theory," in *English Journal*, Vol. 94, No. 2, November 2004, pp. 12–14.

## Heather Vogel Frederick

*In the following interview with Frederick, Crutcher explains the source for his stories and characters.*

Chris Crutcher is probably about the last name the folks in his hometown ever expected to see on the cover of a book. Growing up in the tiny, isolated community of Cascade, Idaho, Crutcher says he was a "famous non-student" who recycled his older brother's homework and only read one book cover-to-cover the whole four years he was in high school.

Today, Crutcher has six critically acclaimed young-adult novels under his belt (each of which has been named an ALA Best Book), and a seventh, *Ironman* (Greenwillow), due out in April. His adult suspense novel *The Deep End* (Morrow, 1992) was one of four whodunits President Clinton reportedly purchased while Christmas shopping, and three of his YA stories have been optioned by Hollywood.

Crutcher's work is marked by his willingness to go toe-to-toe with the many pitfalls of adolescence: relationships, divorce fall-out and parent/child power struggles, He has also tackled grittier issues like child abuse and abortion (*Staying Fat for Sarah Byrnes*, 1993); racism and accidental death (*Running Loose*, 1983); and suicide, teen pregnancy and sexual molestation (*Chinese Handcuffs*, 1989). His honest look at life, as well as the humor with which his fast-paced stories are laced, have earned him the respect and popularity of his readers and the praise of critics. Far from being mere "problem" books, however, his stories are both thoughtful and tough, rooted solidly in Crutcher's decade-plus of experience as a child and family therapist at the Spokane Community Mental Health Center.

On a recent winter morning, PW visited with Crutcher in his modest Spokane, Wash., home. The soft-spoken writer sits with his Reeboks propped casually on his living room coffee table. It's a comfortable, masculine room (Crutcher has never married and lives alone, although he currently shares his home with his girlfriend's teenage son), dominated by the enormous L-shaped desk at which he works, generous bookshelves and an oversized television set ("a tax write-off," he admits sheepishly, now that he's a working screenwriter).

His recent transition from full-time therapist to full-time writer wasn't an easy decision,

> CRUTCHER OFTEN WRITES IN THE FIRST PERSON, PARTLY DUE TO THE INFLUENCE OF THAT ONE NOVEL HE READ IN HIGH SCHOOL, HARPER LEE'S *TO KILL A MOCKINGBIRD*. HE RECALLS SCANNING THE FLAP TO SEE IF HE COULD WEASEL OUT OF ACTUALLY READING THE BOOK FOR AN EXAM."

Crutcher admits. Burnout had nothing to do with it; it was simply a question of too much to do, and too little time. "When it came down to it," he says, "I could not give up writing."

And as he begins to talk about his craft, it's quickly clear why. Storytelling is Crutcher's passion. "I'm only interested in telling stories that I care about," he says. "So they have to connect someplace. If I don't feel passionate I can't write—I have to have that kind of heat to tell a story."

More often than not, the "someplace" to which his stories connect is his own life, and his books are populated with people and places from the rich landscape of his 48 years. The passion emerges in the memorable voices of his characters, such outspoken, irreverent voices as Louie Banks in his first novel, *Running Loose* (who quits football in protest after his coach orders a "hit" on the black quarterback of an opposing team) and the unforgettable Angus Bethune in the short-story collection *Athletic Shorts* (1991). Rotund, wisecracking Angus calls his two sets of parents (a lesbian couple and a homosexual couple) "a shade to the left of middle on your normal bell-shaped sexual curve."

### FEROCIOUS CHILD ADVOCATE

Despite the middle-age disguise (salt-and-pepper hair and beard), an adolescent fervor is evident not only in the more obvious clues—the jeans and worn leather jacket Crutcher sports, the motorcycle parked in the garage—but also in the intensity of emotion that emerges as he discusses issues about which he cares deeply. He's a ferocious child advocate, and the relaxed raconteur can disappear in a flash, his wiry runner's build suddenly taut as a bowstring as he talks of the hell he's seen in his work with abused children, troubled adolescents, violent men and battered women.

"What's known can't be unknown," he says. "As a writer and a human being, I can't turn my back on it. I have to keep myself in a position where I can scream and yell and be just obnoxious about getting something done."

Crutcher hasn't severed all ties with the mental health community, and he continues to "scream and yell" through his work on the Child Protection Team in Spokane, an organization of professionals who review the roughest cases.

Writing provides him with another forum, as well as with a modicum of catharsis. "When you write, you can to some degree at least control the outcome," he says. "When you're in mental health you don't get to do that."

Not surprisingly, Crutcher's books have incurred the wrath of conservative school districts and would-be censors. He can joke about it: *Running Loose* was banned in the Cascade schools, which was especially ironic as he had "almost 100% sales in Cascade. If you didn't have a copy, you had to deal with my mother. There isn't a house in town that didn't have the book, you just couldn't get it at school." Still, despite his humor, censorship clearly nettles him.

"It's a way of protecting kids that I don't think protects them," he says, adding soberly that censorship "is insidious, and I think it's tightening up. When I see the abortion pickets and people getting killed and this idea that politics and morals and spiritual beliefs all go hand-in-hand, it scares me, because I know what these people are doing to books.

A flash of the rebel surfaces again as he notes that he's not willing to let the climate goad him to self-censorship. In fact, he adds with a grin, "I'm likely to punch it up out of orneriness."

His fourth book, *Chinese Handcuffs,* which has caused the biggest stir so far, is a case in point. Among other things, it deals with an ugly case of sexual molestation. *Booklist* refused to review it, and it almost wasn't named an ALA Best Book, but Crutcher thinks that the sheer amount of fan mail it generated might have worked in its favor.

In defense of his subject matter, Crutcher tells of an incident at a writing workshop he held for students in Houston. "Usually you get a few people who stay around afterwards who are real wounded," he says. "This one girl waited until all the other kids were gone, and then she said, 'I don't have a question or anything, but I just want you to know that when I read *Chinese Handcuffs* I thought you knew me.'" The implication of her words stunned him, especially when she explained that, because she had realized that "somebody else must know about this," she was able to talk to someone about her plight. "And that," Crutcher adds pointedly, "was when everybody was saying that I put too much in this book, and I was taking a lot of heat for loading it down."

## A LATE START

Crutcher's path to writing was a circuitous one. The middle of three children, he is a distance runner and swimmer and occasional triathlete. Not surprisingly, sports figure heavily in all of his YA novels. In Cascade, Crutcher recalls, "it didn't matter if you were a good athlete or not. You tried out for the football team with a stethoscope—if you could breathe you could play. And if you didn't show up, they'd come get you."

After graduating from Eastern Washington State, Crutcher held a hodgepodge of jobs, ending up teaching at what he calls a "ragtag alternative school"—which reappeared years later in *The Crazy Horse Electric Game* (1987). Coincidentally, college friend and writer Terry Davis was on a Stegner Fellowship at nearby Stanford University.

"We'd meet once a week and he would bring *Visionquest* [the novel he was writing at the time] and we would take it apart chapter by chapter," says Crutcher. "This was an opportunity to get my hands dirty and see that a first draft is rough, and to watch how he polished it."

Crutcher eventually left his teaching job to concentrate on his first book. "I just sat down and wrote, in longhand, in a notebook, and it all came together. I loved the process."

He was also pleased with the product, *Running Loose,* and sent it off to his friend Terry Davis to critique. Davis phoned Crutcher the minute he finished reading it—at 2 a.m.—and said he was going to call his agent in the morning. By the end of the week, Crutcher was under contract with Liz Darhansoff.

*Running Loose* was published by Greenwillow in 1983, where he's been ever since. He praises his longtime editor, Susan Hirschman, not only for her editorial skills but also for her courage. "Susan has stuck by me," he says. "She has a real sense of noncensorship. Everybody respects her, and nobody's going to muscle her around."

Crutcher often writes in the first person, partly due to the influence of that one novel he read in high school, Harper Lee's *To Kill a Mockingbird*. He recalls scanning the flap to see if he could weasel out of actually reading the book for an exam. After a peek at the first page, however, he got "swept away," finishing it, he notes drily, "about three weeks after the test." Years later when he sat down to write, he couldn't get the book out of his head. And indeed, just as the voice of Scout Finch is synonymous with *To Kill a Mockingbird,* so is Louie Banks with *Running Loose.*

Any number of things can serve as what Crutcher calls "fuel pellets" for a story. *Running Loose* started with a conversation he overheard in a locker room about a racist coach who encouraged his players to eliminate a black player. "I thought somebody ought to kick his butt," he recalls, "but I was too afraid to walk around the lockers and have the basketball team beat me up, so I waited 15 years and wrote a book."

Sometimes the motivation is less specific. "When I started *The Crazy Horse Electric Game,"* he admits, "all I wanted to do was tell a bunch of bad puns." The puns remained, as did the title, which Crutcher pulled out of thin air before coming up with a plot to go with it. The story, about a star athlete who is left brain-damaged after a waterskiing accident and subsequently runs away from his problems—and his home—and winds up at an alternative school in San Francisco, deftly blends sports, action and humor into a moving coming-of-age tale.

At speaking engagements, Crutcher says he reads just as often from his adult novel as he does from his YA novels, and he is often frustrated by the limits that categorization places on a good story. He gets a lot of mail from adults about his YA books and wishes there would be more effort in general to market YA books to a crossover audience. "I am somehow going to single-handedly tear off the border between young adult and adult," he states firmly.

He is now hard at work on the screenplay of *Sarah Byrnes* as well as the novel he began last year while his mother was dying, a work he describes as "probably the most autobiographical" book he's written. He maintains a low profile locally and likes it that way. "Frankly, I don't know if the neighbors have any idea what

I do," he says, tongue only partially in cheek. "They probably think I'm a deadbeat."

One is left with the definite impression that he doesn't mind if they do. The fact is, the life of a writer suits him just fine. He smiles. "I'm having a helluva good time."

**Source:** Heather Vogel Frederick, "Chris Crutcher: What's Known Can't Be Unknown," in *Publishers Weekly*, Vol. 242, No. 8, February 20, 1995, pp. 183–84.

### Nancy Vasilakis
*In the following review, Vasilakis praises Crutcher's vivid characterizations.*

At eighteen Eric Calhoune is an overweight swimmer whose nickname is Moby, though he's not as fat as he used to be and would be even thinner were it not for his friendship with Sarah Byrnes. Eric's success on the swimming team and the weight loss that is the by-product of his strict physical regimen are so threatening to that long-standing relationship, however, that he forces himself into gluttony in order not to jeopardize it. The author has created one of his strongest female characters to date in the physically maimed Sarah Byrnes, who at the age of three was severely burned on the face and hands when her father pushed her into a wood stove. These two teenagers form a close bond based on much that they have in common. In addition to the "terminal uglies," they both have parents—Sarah's mother and Eric's father—who left their families, and they both have been granted a larger than normal allotment of intelligence and courage. They share a great deal of anger, too, repressed in Eric but smoldering and quick to surface in Sarah Byrnes. In their last year in high school, she has an apparent catatonic episode and is institutionalized. Eric's attempts to help his friend find her way back into the world make up the bulk of the narrative. Although the central issue of the novel is the insidious and far-reaching effects of child abuse, minor characters introduce several other topics of current interest, such as abortion and religious fundamentalism—perhaps too superficially and a bit sensationally given the serious nature of these issues. As is usually the case in this author's novels, the book's strength lies in the characterizations. Crutcher possesses a novelist's greatest asset: an ability to create people who are real and believable and about whom the reader can care deeply.

**Source:** Nancy Vasilakis, Review of *Staying Fat for Sarah Byrnes*, in *Horn Book*, Vol. 69, No. 3, May-June 1993, p. 336.

## SOURCES

"Crutcher Bio," *Chris Crutcher Web site*, http://www.chris crutcher.com (accessed June 24, 2009).

Crutcher, Chris, "Past Interview," in *Teenreads.com*, February 18, 2000, http://www.teenreads.com/authors/au-crutcher-chris.asp (accessed June 24, 2009).

———, "A Dangerous Thing," in *Powells.com*, http://www.powells.com/essays/crutcher.html (accessed June 24, 2009).

———, *Staying Fat for Sarah Byrnes*, Harper Tempest, 1993.

Frederick, Heather Vogel, "Chris Crutcher: What's Known Can't Be Unknown," in *Publishers Weekly*, Vol. 242, No. 8, February 20, 1995, pp. 183–84.

Goodnow, Cecilia, "Teens Buying Books at Fastest Rate in Decades," in *Seattle Post-Intelligencer Online*, March 7, 2007, http://www.seattlepi.com/books/306531_teenlit08.html (accessed June 24, 2009).

Ledford, Heidi, "Child Abuse Leaves Lasting 'Scars' on DNA," in *Nature*, http://www.nature.com/news/2009/090220/full/news.2009.113.html (accessed June 24, 2009).

Lesesne, Teri S., "Banned in Berlin: An Interview with Chris Crutcher," in *Emergency Librarian*, Vol. 23.5, May-June 1996, pp. 61–63.

"New Study Tallies Child Abuse during the 1990s," in *Salt of the Earth*, April 2001, http://salt.claretianpubs.org/stats/2001/04/sh0104.html (accessed July 15, 2009).

Review of *Staying Fat for Sarah Byrnes*, in *Publishers Weekly*, Vol. 242, No. 8, February 20, 1995, p. 207.

Robinson, B. A., "Violence & Harassment at U.S. Abortion Clinics," in *ReligiousTolerance.org*, http://www.religioustolerance.org/abo_viol.htm (accessed June 24, 2009).

## FURTHER READING

Beck, Debra, *My Feet Aren't Ugly! A Girl's Guide to Loving Herself from the Inside Out*, Beaufort Books, 2007.
> Beck provides the tools necessary for girls to develop self-confidence, self-respect, and fulfilling relationships in this nonfiction handbook for teens.

Horsley, Heidi, and Gloria Horsley, *Teen Grief Relief*, Rainbow Books, 2007.
> This short book shares the stories of teens who have lost family members or close friends. The writers advise teens on how to cope with the loss, understand parents, and find balance after experiencing a life-altering event.

Gerali, Steven P., *How to Stay Christian in High School*, NavPress, 2004.
> *Staying Fat for Sarah Byrnes* has several characters who are faced with contradictions or crises in their Christian faith. This book by Steven P. Gerali provides advice to teens on how to maintain a Christian outlook and commitment in the face of daily temptation and pressures.

Werlin, Nancy, *The Rules of Survival*, Puffin, 2008.
> This novel explores the topic of child abuse through the eyes of its seventeen-year-old narrator. Matt and his two younger sisters must deal with their mother's violent and frightening behavior.

# A Thousand Acres

**JANE SMILEY**

**1991**

Jane Smiley's *A Thousand Acres* was published in New York in 1991 and won the Pulitzer Prize for Fiction the following year. Primarily set in rural Iowa in 1979, the story revolves around a dysfunctional farm family headed by patriarch Larry Cook. With the realization that he is aging, Cook decides to incorporate his thousand-acre farm and divide it among his three daughters. When the youngest daughter expresses doubt about the wisdom of her father's plan, she is excluded from the contract. This sets in motion a series of life-altering events that leads to the physical and psychological breakdown of the Cook family.

*A Thousand Acres* is a contemporary retelling of William Shakespeare's seventeenth-century drama *King Lear*. Both stories focus on the relationships between a father and his daughters and explore themes of gender roles, the dynamics of family relationships, and sibling rivalry. But whereas the daughters in *King Lear* behave badly out of their own sense of greed and selfishness, those in Smiley's novel are responding to their current situation after surviving a lifetime of emotional and sexual abuse at the hands of their father. The results in both cases are the same.

## AUTHOR BIOGRAPHY

Jane Graves Smiley was born in Los Angeles, California, on September 26, 1949. While still

*Jane Smiley* *(© Ellen Isaacs / Alamy)*

a child, Smiley and her parents moved to Missouri, where her father was employed by the U.S. Army and her mother furthered her career as a journalist. For Smiley, storytelling was a family activity shared around the dinner table. Earning a degree in English literature from Vassar College in 1971, then, seemed a natural turn of events.

While at college, Smiley met and married Yale University student John Whiston. The couple divorced in 1975. Smiley's subsequent marriage to William Silage also ended in divorce, but not before producing two children: Phoebe and Lucy. In 1987, the author married Steve Mortensen. Together they had a child, Axel James, before divorcing in 1997.

Smiley graduated with a Ph.D. from the University of Iowa. She began teaching at Iowa State University in 1981, one year after publishing *Barn Blind*, her first novel. She continued teaching creative writing workshops in Iowa through 1996, despite the fact that she had, in the meantime, relocated to California. Smiley wrote and published four more works of fiction before publishing *A Thousand Acres*, the novel

that elevated her to best-seller status. In addition to earning her the 1992 Pulitzer Prize for Fiction, the book won its author the 1992 National Book Critics Circle Award for Fiction.

Smiley's fiction continued to earn her accolades. *The All True Travels and Adventures of Lidie Newton* won the 1999 Spur Award for Best Novel of the West. Her 2001 novel *Horse Heaven* was short-listed for the Orange Prize the following year. Smiley surprised her readers in 2009 with the publication of *Laura Rider's Masterpiece*, her first attempt at satire. In addition to books, Smiley has written hundreds of essays for magazines, including the *New Yorker*, *Harper's*, and the *New York Times Magazine*. She is a regular contributor to the popular online news site the *Huffington Post*.

Smiley has published several works of nonfiction as well. *A Year at the Races: Reflections on Horses, Humans, Love, Money, and Luck* (2004) chronicles her obsession with horses. In 2005, she wrote *Thirteen Ways of Looking at the Novel*, a study of the form and function of the novel.

Smiley has been the recipient of the distinguished O. Henry Award three times, and her 1981 novel *At Paradise Gate* won the Friends of American Writers Prize. The writer was elected into the membership of the American Academy of Arts and Letters in 2001 and belongs to the American Academy of Arts and Sciences.

## PLOT SUMMARY

### Book 1, Chapters 1–7

*A Thousand Acres* begins with a homecoming party for Jess, wayward son of farmer Harold Clark. All of Zebulon County, Iowa, is invited to welcome back this favorite son, who was traveling for thirteen years. It is during the party that Larry Cook, owner of the county's largest and most profitable farm, surprises his three daughters and their partners with a spontaneous announcement. Larry plans to retire and divide his thousand-acre farm among his daughters Ginny, Rose, and Caroline, who would form a corporation.

Ginny and Rose are already farm wives; they know the potential advantages to inheriting such a large acreage. Youngest sister Caroline had defied her father's wishes and chose a different lifestyle as an attorney in the city. She is the one person who does not outwardly react to Larry's news with even reluctant enthusiasm. When she expresses her doubt, Larry cuts her out of the agreement, and she returns home hurt and angry.

Ginny, the narrator of the novel, has her own doubts about the plan. Having spent her life being the peacemaker of the family, however, she chooses not to express them to Larry. To Jess she admits, "I was thinking that my father is acting crazy. I mean, I wasn't actually thinking it, I was panicking about it."

The three sisters could not be more different. Ginny is a woman for whom privacy is important. She rejoices and suffers privately. Her life's greatest burden is the fact that she is unable to have children. Her husband, Ty, knows about only three of her five miscarriages. Her desire to have her own children makes her a loving aunt to Rose's two girls, Pammy and Linda.

Rose is more outspoken than her older sister. A breast cancer survivor at thirty-four, Rose has a more realistic outlook on life. Unlike Ginny, Rose does not make excuses for or accept the bad

## MEDIA ADAPTATIONS

- *A Thousand Acres* was rewritten as a screenplay by Laura Jones. It was released by Touchstone Pictures in 1997 and stars Michelle Pfeiffer, Jessica Lange, and Jason Robards. Lange was nominated for a Golden Globe Award for Best Actress in a Motion Picture-Drama.

- *A Thousand Acres* was recorded as an unabridged audiobook and released in 1996 by Recorded Books.

- A performance of *King Lear* (on which *A Thousand Acres* is loosely based) starring Ian McKellen as Lear was filmed at Pinewood Studios in Iver Heath, England, and released in March 2009 on Public Broadcasting System.

behavior of others. Rose chose a husband, Pete, who has physically abused her in the past. She is a fighter, a woman who will not just go along with things to keep from stirring up trouble. If her choices and actions cause problems and heartache for others, Rose does not care.

Nineteen-year-old Caroline grew up the object of her father's affections. Ginny basically raised her and made sure she had everything she wanted, even if it meant sacrifice on Ginny's behalf. Caroline has been accustomed to getting what she wanted but does not always recognize that the things she got came at a price to others.

### Book 2, Chapters 8–17

Jess and Ginny grow closer. With Ty working during the day, Jess visits Ginny often, and the two find that they can open up to one another with an ease they do not feel with others.

Jess explains to Ginny that he had been living in Canada and had a fiancée who committed suicide. He had gone there to avoid serving in the Vietnam War, but his leaving cost him his relationship with both parents. Harold felt he was a coward, and Verna did not want to anger her husband, so she did not answer Jess's letters or ever try to find out where he was living. Verna died of breast cancer while Jess was away.

While Ginny and Jess are forging a relationship, Larry is acting more strange with each passing day. He gets the idea that his farmhouse needs remodeling. One spring day, a delivery truck arrives at Larry's and leaves him with thousands of dollars of solid oak cabinetry. Larry has already paid for the cabinets but has no idea where he wants to install them, so he leaves them sitting in the driveway, vulnerable to the rain and sun. When Ty and Ginny suggest he get them moved inside, Larry accuses them of trying to control him.

Caroline and Ginny get into an argument over the transfer of the farm. Because she does not live near the rest of the family, Caroline had been unaware of Larry's recent odd behavior until he paid her a surprise visit in Des Moines, Iowa. He had been drinking, and the reason for his visit was never made clear. She accuses Ginny, Ty, Rose, and Pete of mishandling the farm since taking it over. When Ginny reminds her that she suggested to Caroline to just go along with his plan, Caroline is quick to anger. "All I know is, Daddy's lost everything, he's acting crazy, and you all don't care enough to do anything about it!"

Jess and Ginny go for a walk one June day. Jess informs Ginny that people in town are talking about the farm transfer and hinting that Ginny and Rose forced their father to make that decision. Everyone knows Larry and feels the idea is too far-fetched for him to have conceived of it on his own. Ginny feels defensive but knows rumors will eventually die.

Jess talks to Ginny about how happy Harold is to have him home but worries that Harold feels the only way to keep Jess there is to give him the family farm. Jess is not sure he wants to be a farmer, and he is absolutely sure he does not want to farm using the same methods his father uses. While he was away, Jess discovered organic farming. He became a vegetarian, a lifestyle no one in Zebulon County can understand. It becomes clear that Jess is in the middle of an identity crisis, unsure of who he wants to be and how to become that person.

Ginny's friendship with Jess takes a new turn when he kisses her, and the intensity of her feelings make her uncomfortable. "It scared me to death, but still I discovered how much I had

been waiting for it." It is at this point that Ginny begins to realize she is capable of being more than the meek farm wife who tries to maintain a balance within her family. She begins to open up to new possibilities in her life.

### Book 3, Chapters 18–28

Caroline and her boyfriend, Frank, marry in a civil ceremony in Des Moines without telling any family members. The sisters find out about the wedding when Rose takes Pammy and Linda into town to buy shoes. The cashier, making small talk, tells Rose she saw the wedding announcement in the newspaper. Rose shares the news with Ginny once she gets home, and both sisters are insulted. Ginny reflects on her feelings about Caroline's decision not to invite or even inform her sisters of the event. "It reminded me of how she was, a way that Rose found annoying and I usually tried to accept. It reminded me that we could have taught her better manners." In her customary way, Ginny tries to accept the bad behavior while simultaneously taking responsibility for it.

Larry gets drunk and rolls his truck, an accident that sends him to the emergency room. Ginny and Ty drive into town to pick him up, and Larry responds with his usual refusal to talk. On the trip home, Ginny reflects on her difficult relationship with her father. While Ty indicates to her that she should just take this most recent incident in stride as she had all the others, Ginny feels something inside her shift. She wonders, if she had behaved differently all along—allowed herself a life outside of taking care of others—would that have been so bad? Instead, she spent her life accommodating and fixing, being the person she believed others needed her to be. With Larry captive in the seatbelt, she takes the opportunity to sternly tell him he cannot continue behaving so recklessly. She chastises him for not helping out around the farm since signing the transfer and warns him that his wild ways might lead to losing his driver's license.

As small as that moment was in time, it was life-changing for Ginny as she said, "It was exhilarating, talking to my father as if he were my child.... It created a whole orderly future within me, a vista of manageable days clicking past, myself in the foreground, large and purposeful."

Ginny continues living with this new feeling of power, despite the fact that Ty does not approve of it. He feels Ginny and Rose have always been too hard on Larry, and now that he has had this accident, the sisters approach him with a more united front. Ginny's change of heart causes her to look at Ty in a different way. Instead of seeing him as someone who just wanted to get along with everyone, she realizes he has always been motivated by self-serving interests. If he could keep Ginny and Larry on good terms—which means keeping Ginny submissive—he would remain on good terms with Larry as well. Being on good terms with him would mean having more authority when it came to the farming operation.

Harold Clark visits Ginny to reprimand her for taking this stern approach to her father. While there, he confides in her his frustration with Loren, Jess's brother. Loren never left the farm, but chose instead to stay and help his father. Harold is bothered by nearly everything Loren does these days, and he blames it on Jess's return. Had Jess stayed away, Harold could have kept his focus on the one son he knew and been grateful for his presence.

In the meantime, Jess shares his excitement with Ginny. He tells her he has found an organic farming association in the state and plans to join. When Ginny confides in him about her many miscarriages, Jess insists the drinking water is the cause. The two become lovers, and Ginny is at once ecstatic and concerned. She knows their relationship can never revert to what it was; she is in dangerous territory.

During a tornado watch, Larry worries his entire family by disappearing in his truck. Ty goes out to search for him and comes home hours later with Larry in tow. Larry's anger takes control, and he begins screaming at Ginny. He calls her names and accuses her of trying to get rid of him. Rose tries to defend her sister, but Larry lashes out at her as well. From his perspective, both women want him to die so they will not have to take care of him, feed him, or listen to him. He threatens to take back the farm.

A few days later, Rose and Ginny talk about what happened. The discussion eventually takes them back in time, to their childhood. Rose cautiously brings up the subject of the nighttime visits Larry used to pay to both his teenage daughters. Ginny does not understand what Rose is trying to tell her. When Rose pointedly declares that their father forced his daughters to have sex with him, Ginny is astounded and, initially, disbelieving. However, the more the women talk, the clearer

Ginny's memories become, and she soon realizes Rose is telling the truth.

Five days pass without any communication from Larry. The family attends the annual church potluck dinner in July, knowing they will see Larry. Rose and Ginny soon realize their father is telling people his daughters took his farm and are planning to put him in a home. His voice is flat, and he lacks the bravado that has long dominated his personality. Ginny feels pity; Rose is enraged. She believes it is an act, that Larry is trying to garner sympathy and manipulate the townsfolk against his daughters.

Harold Clark gathers Larry's family around a table in the middle room; Ginny thinks he wants to help his friend Larry reconcile with his daughters. However, as people begin eating, Harold publicly berates Ginny and Rose as Larry sits by with a smirk on his face. Harold then turns his wrath on his son Jess and accuses him of planning to steal his farm. The room is silent except for Harold's yelling until the minister grabs Harold from behind and Jess punches him in the face.

### Book 4, Chapters 29–34

Harold has an accident in the field and is left blind, unable to farm. He got anhydrous ammonia in his eyes and was unable to flush them out because the water tank was empty. Within two minutes, his corneas were eaten away. Jess talks with Rose and Ginny because he feels he should take pity on his father and make amends, but Rose advises him to wait it out or he will never earn Harold's respect. Jess, Ginny, Rose, and Pete avoid Harold.

Larry sues Ginny, Ty, Rose, and Pete to get the farm back on the grounds they had abused and mismanaged the operation. Caroline has sided with her father and is part of the lawsuit. Ginny calls Caroline to ask why she and Larry are suing them, but Caroline refuses to talk. Ginny sees Caroline's choice as a betrayal.

### Book 5, Chapters 35–41

Pete drowns himself in a quarry. Rose confides in Ginny that she and Jess have been having an affair and that Pete knew about it a week before his suicide. Pete had confessed to Rose that it was he who emptied the water tank in Harold's field, but that it was his intention to kill Larry, not Harold. Pete had seen Larry riding the tractor in Harold's field recently and assumed he was helping Harold. Pete had wanted to kill Larry for years because he knew about the incest and blamed all his and Rose's problems on that.

Rose knew Ginny and Jess had been having an affair, and she chose to get involved with Jess anyway. Ginny cannot forgive her sister, so she cans sausage she has poisoned with water hemlock and gives the jar to Rose. Ginny knows Pammy and Linda will not eat the sausage because they don't like it. Rose accepts the home-canned meat.

The judge rules against Larry and Caroline in the lawsuit on the grounds that Larry's mental stability is questionable and there is no proof that the farm has been mismanaged. Citing frivolous use of the court for such a case, the judge orders Larry and Caroline to pay all fees and costs related to the case. This is a major turning point in the lives of all involved, and Ginny recognizes it as such. She sees it as the place where everyone is separated from each other, as well as from their old lives. Because none of them has had an experience similar to this before, there is no chance of reconciliation. They simply do not know how to act.

Ginny takes one thousand dollars and leaves behind Ty and the rest of her life.

### *Book 6, Chapters 42–Epilogue*

Ginny settles in Minnesota and takes a job as a waitress at a Perkins restaurant. Months after relocating, she writes to Rose to let her know she is safe and well. Rose writes back to inform Ginny that Larry died five days after the settlement. He dropped dead of a heart attack in the grocery store.

Rose and Ty split the farm. She and Jess plan to farm organically. It is another two months before Rose writes again, and this time she tells Ginny that Jess returned to the West Coast. She also tells her that she is renting most of her land to Ty. Ginny realizes Rose will never eat the poisoned sausages when she learns Rose has become a vegetarian.

Years pass, and one day Ty is sitting in Ginny's section of the restaurant. He announces that he is moving to Texas to work on a corporate hog operation. He and Ginny talk about all that has come to pass, and he leaves knowing he will never see her again. He has severed all ties to the family, having signed the entire farm over to Rose.

Several months later, Ginny gets a phone call from Rose, who is in the hospital. Her cancer has returned, and this time, it will kill her. The sisters have a chance to talk about what has come between them—Jess—and they work through the issue as much as they can. Rose asks Ginny to take Pammy and Linda back to Minnesota with her, and Ginny agrees to do so. Rose dies, and the farm goes to her sisters. Too many loans had been left unpaid, forcing the farm into foreclosure, and Ginny and Caroline owe the bank tens of thousands of dollars. Together, they clean out the house so that the property can be sold. Caroline continues to act like a spoiled child, insisting that she was the sister most mistreated by Larry because he cut her out of the farm transfer. Ginny considers telling Caroline about the sexual abuse, but decides against it.

She eventually finds the canned sausages. She pours them down the sink and grinds them up with the disposal. For fifteen minutes, she blasts those meats with water, thinking about all they symbolize. She feels relief: "I had a burden lift off me that I hadn't even felt the heaviness of until then, and it was the burden of having to wait and see what was going to happen."

## CHARACTERS

### *Harold Clark*

Harold Clark is the close friend of Larry Cook, who owns the farm for which the novel is titled. Their friendship is based on common experience—farming—but they also compete with each other. It is Harold's decision to buy a new tractor without consulting Larry that drives Larry to retire and divide his farm between his daughters. Larry is tormented by the idea that Harold paid for his tractor in cash because that would mean he was more prosperous than Larry. The fact is, Harold did not pay in cash, but he does not tell his friend that, nor does he lie; he simply never discusses it with him.

Harold is the father of Jess Clark, who avoided the Vietnam War by moving to Canada. In Harold's eyes, this made his son a coward, and he severed all communication with Jess. When Jess returns to the family farm after thirteen years, Harold is suspicious about his son's motives. Outwardly, he acts proud and happy to have his son back. Inside, Harold is seething over the idea that Jess has returned to steal the farm from under Harold's nose.

Harold is blinded in a farming accident and is forced into early retirement.

### Jess Clark

Jess Clark is the elder son of Harold Clark and brother to Loren Clark. Jess left Iowa to avoid being drafted into the Vietnam War, and he stayed in Canada for thirteen years. While he was gone, he got engaged to be married, but his fiancée killed herself.

Jess returns home and finds he does not fit in. From the clothes he wears—running shorts and shoes—to his attitude—organic farming is the only method to use, and eating or raising slaughter animals is unethical—Jess recognizes that he is an outsider among his own people.

Jess begins a romantic affair with Ginny Smith and soon after becomes involved with her sister, Rose Lewis. He knew both women as children, and both are attracted to him for all the ways he is not like the other men they know. Once involved with Rose, Jess no longer continues his relationship with Ginny. Although he and Rose make plans for the future, he one day packs his bags and leaves, returning to Canada.

Where Ginny sees Jess as a free spirit, Rose interprets his behavior as self-serving and manipulative. In her eyes, Jess never makes a move or decision without figuring how it will better his own situation. He never apologizes for the trail of hurt he leaves behind. Though he is a grown man, Jess Clark is still trying to figure out who he is.

### Loren Clark

Loren Clark is Harold Clark's younger son and brother of Jess Clark. Unlike Jess, Loren chooses to stay home and help Harold run the farm.

### Caroline Cook

Caroline is the youngest daughter of Harold Cook and sister to Rose and Ginny. Unlike her sisters, Caroline chooses to move to the city and have a career. She is an attorney in Des Moines, and she marries her boyfriend, Frank, without telling anyone in her family.

Caroline grew up without a mother but was raised by Ginny and Rose. Ginny, in particular, sacrificed her childhood and own desires to ensure that Caroline had as normal an upbringing as possible. Caroline is the only daughter who had not been sexually abused by their father, Larry Cook.

When Larry proposes a three-way split of the farm so that each daughter has land, Caroline expresses doubt. She does not think the idea is in her father's best interest, but he shuts her out before she can explain herself. Somewhere in the back of her mind, Caroline thinks Ginny and Rose influenced their father to make this decision. When Larry turns around to sue his daughters for mismanagement and abuse of the farm, it is Caroline who handles the lawsuit. The line between business and personal issues blurs, and Ginny is hurt by the ease with which Caroline turns on her sisters.

As Ginny and Caroline clean out the farmhouses for the sale of the property, it becomes clear that Caroline refuses to believe her father was capable of the nasty behavior that Ginny and Rose tell her about. "You never have any evidence! The evidence just isn't there! You have a thing against Daddy. It's just greed or something. . . . I realize that some people are just evil." Ginny understands at that moment that Caroline is talking about Ginny, not Larry, and she realizes Caroline willfully chooses not to believe that her father ever abused his girls. Ginny lets go of Caroline in every way; they will never again reconcile.

### Larry Cook

Larry is the patriarch of the Cook family and owner of the most prosperous farm in Zebulon County, Iowa. An alcoholic with a terrible temper, Larry emotionally and sexually abused two of his three daughters after his wife died. When he makes the spontaneous decision to retire and transfer his farm to his daughters, his youngest daughter, Caroline, objects and is cut out of the arrangement.

Larry soon begins acting erratically, and it is not long before he is at odds with Ginny and Rose and their spouses. From his perspective, he has given everything to his ungrateful daughters, and they now want to get rid of him. He eventually sues them to regain possession of the farm, but the judge rules against him.

Larry does not understand that the way he has treated and continues to treat his daughters is wrong. He has provided them with a roof over their heads, food, clothing, and eventually work for their husbands. Given that, he believes they should unquestioningly submit to his every want and need. He is to be obeyed.

### Ken LaSalle

Ken LaSalle is the Cook family's lawyer. He advises Larry Cook against making the farm transfer. When Ginny asks him to represent her, Ty, Rose, and Pete in the lawsuit, he refuses, telling her he does not think that she and Rose have treated their father well.

### Linda Lewis

Linda is the daughter of Rose and Pete Lewis and sister to Pammy. She spends most of her time at boarding school because her mother is afraid Larry Cook may abuse her daughters as he did his own.

### Pammy Lewis

Pammy Lewis is the daughter of Rose and Pete Lewis and sister of Linda. Like her sister, she is sent to live at a boarding school to prevent her spending much time with her grandfather.

### Pete Lewis

Pete Lewis is married to Rose Cook Lewis. Theirs is a rocky relationship, and there is a history of domestic violence. Pete hates Larry Cook and blames him for damaging Rose, thereby making a normal, healthy marriage with her impossible.

Pete is responsible for the accident that leaves Harold Clark blind; his intended victim is Larry Cook. Faced with this guilt, as well as the fact that his wife is romantically involved with Jess Clark and plans to leave her marriage, Pete kills himself by driving his truck into the quarry.

### Rose Cook Lewis

Rose Cook Lewis is the middle daughter of Larry Cook. The most outspoken one, Rose lives her life in sharp contrast to her older sister, Ginny. The abuse suffered at the hands of her father left Rose with an intense anger and an insatiable desire to get what she wants at all costs. Conversely, Ginny's primary focus is on keeping the peace, and she will sacrifice her own wants and needs to that end.

Rose is unhappily married to Pete, and their union has produced two daughters, Pammy and Linda. Although Pete has never liked Rose's father, Larry, Rose's own anger is more toxic and her quest for revenge more intense. After she is diagnosed with breast cancer, Rose sends her daughters away to boarding school to ensure that they will not be molested as she was.

With a self-awareness that she is, as her mother told her, "grabby," Rose wants Jess Clark and has him, despite the fact that she is married. Jess is not her first affair, but he is the one she uses to hurt Pete. She tells Pete she is leaving him for Jess, and eventually the two do set up a home together. Jess leaves Rose without warning, however, and she is left angrier than ever.

Even as she is dying, Rose sees her purpose in life as refusing to forgive. She seems to draw power from that thought, and it drives her. After Rose dies, her daughters move to Minnesota to live with their Aunt Ginny.

### Ginny Cook Smith

Thirty-six-year-old Ginny Cook Smith is the narrator of the story and wife of Ty Smith. As eldest daughter of Larry Cook, Ginny is arguably the one who has been most intensely affected by his alcoholism, temper, and sexual abuse. Having lost her mother to cancer at the age of fourteen, Ginny grew up being the surrogate mother to Rose and Caroline. In that role, she did her best to appease her father and protect her sisters. In doing so, she learned to put her own needs aside so that those she loved could have as normal a life as possible. It was a habit that molded her into a submissive woman.

Ginny went from her father's house directly into marriage with Ty at the age of nineteen. Their marriage is steady, but not necessarily fulfilling for Ginny. Ty is a good man, a quiet man. He is the opposite of Larry and offers Ginny the possibility of stability, something she has never known. Their marriage is stressed when it becomes clear Ginny cannot have children. She has had five miscarriages, but Ty is aware of only three of them for most of their marriage. His trust in her is strained when he accidentally learns of the other two.

At the beginning of *A Thousand Acres*, Ginny is the stereotypical farm wife. Her days are filled with physical chores, and she sees herself primarily as a support for her husband, her father, and even her sisters. She would say she is content but not happy. True happiness has never been part of Ginny's life, but she does not realize that until Jess Clark comes back to town. Ginny and Jess develop a friendship that eventually turns romantic, and Ginny begins to see the faint glimmer of genuine fulfillment.

Although being a victim of incest has greatly influenced Ginny's psychological development, she has repressed those memories until Rose forces her to confront them. At first reluctant to believe in the truth, Ginny eventually acknowledges it; however, the moment of recognition is painful, "So I screamed. I screamed in a way that I had never screamed before, full out, throat-wrenching, unafraid-of-making-a-fuss-and-drawing-attention-to-myself sorts of screams that I made myself concentrate on, becoming all mouth, all tongue, all vibration." Through confronting that suffering, Ginny finds liberation and the power to move past those invisible ties that held her down for thirty-six years.

As the Cook family falls apart, Ginny is able to see all of them as they really are. It is a blessing and a curse. "The strongest feeling was that now I knew them all. . . . I saw each of them from all sides at once."

As Ginny's awareness grows, so does her restlessness and feeling of confinement. Her marriage crumbles, her relationship with Jess ends, and her ability to keep up with the day-to-day pretense that everything can be fixed becomes too much. Ginny packs her bags and leaves Iowa for St. Paul, Minnesota. There she builds a new life for herself, one in which she continues to learn more about herself with each passing day. She finds a job as a waitress and makes new friends.

Many things in Ginny's new life remind her of her old life and the pain and emptiness that accompanied it. She realizes she has not forgiven her father—perhaps cannot forgive him—but by allowing herself to remember what she could never imagine was her life, she takes away the power he held over her. Ginny triumphs, even if the victory cost her the illusion of what it meant to be a family.

### Ty Smith

Ty Smith is Ginny's husband. He is a quiet man who does not expect much from the world. Ginny once thought he tried to keep the peace because he wanted harmony and wanted everyone to get along. As her eyes are opened, she realizes Ty's peacekeeping efforts are nothing more than camouflage, a way to get what he wanted. All along, Ty had a goal: to run a prosperous, large corporate farm. He sees in Larry Cook an opportunity to have that operation,

and he progresses slowly and steadily, trying hard not to be a noticeable presence in the family but a reliable, constant one.

Even as he watches the family fall apart and with it, his opportunity, Ty keeps sight of his goal. He signs his part of the farm over to Rose and leaves Iowa for Texas, where he intends to find employment with one of the corporate hog operations there. Ty has a dream, and the people and events he involves himself with along the way seem incidental.

## THEMES

### *Appearance versus Reality*

The contrast between appearance and reality is possibly the most important theme of *A Thousand Acres*. Appearances are important in rural communities where the population is small and most people know one another. Because of this familiarity, it is of major importance that families and individuals give the appearance that all is well, even when it is not.

Ginny, the narrator of the story, is particularly aware of this unspoken rule. She says, "Most issues on a farm return to the issue of keeping up appearances. . . . It was imperative that the growing discord in our family be made to appear minor. "

Smiley sees America's heartland as a region that judges its neighbors on the appearance of their farms as well. Because the farm appears neat and prosperous, anyone would assume the water used to nourish and grow crops and livestock is plentiful and safe. Smiley uses the water throughout the book as a symbol to develop the theme of appearance versus reality. When Jess learns of Ginny's numerous miscarriages, he suggests that her problem is caused by nitrates in the water. Harold is blinded in an accident because water was not available when he most needed it. Pete drowns in a rock quarry. Finally, when Caroline is heatedly discussing her childhood with Ginny in the kitchen of the farmhouse, she turns on the faucet to get a drink only to find there is no running water.

The theme applies to people as well as events and physical places. When Jess explains to Ginny that folks in town are getting suspicious about the role she and Rose played in getting Larry to transfer the farm to them, he tells her

# TOPICS FOR FURTHER STUDY

- Watch the movie adaptation of *A Thousand Acres*. Choose one of the main characters and write a paper comparing and contrasting how he or she differs from the character Jane Smiley created for the novel.

- The Cook family is seriously dysfunctional. Read Leslie Connor's young-adult novel *Waiting for Normal* and compare the two families. Make a poster illustrating the similarities and differences.

- What character in *A Thousand Acres* do you most closely identify with? Why? Write a short essay explaining your answer.

- In small groups, go through the book and identify some of the important scenes that reveal something major about a character or that propel the plot forward. Create a soundtrack for those scenes. Put on a presentation to the class in which you play a recording of the songs in the background as you read the scenes aloud. Explain to your classmates the process used for choosing the song selection.

- Research the history of farming in the United States. Find statistics about the percentage of the population that has engaged in farming at different points over the past two hundred years. Find out reasons that the farm population has decreased. If you can, interview a farmer about the difficulties of farming today. Create an oral presentation with your information.

- Pretend you are Larry Cook. Write one paragraph for each daughter and describe her to someone who knows nothing about her.

- Consider the novel without Jess. How might the story change? Write a paper explaining your conclusion. Include at least three ways in which the novel's plot would change.

- Read William Shakespeare's *King Lear*. Choose one daughter and compare her portrayal in Shakespeare's work to that in Smiley's. Use direct passages or quotes from each work to illustrate those comparisons.

- Create a book review of *A Thousand Acres*. Develop a PowerPoint presentation of your review to share with the class. Be sure to use quotes and passages from the novel to provide supporting evidence for your claims and opinions.

- Design and illustrate a book jacket for the novel. Write the inside jacket copy, including a summary or "teaser" about the plot and a short statement about the author.

---

that people know the idea was "very out of character for your dad, which is why people don't believe what appears on the surface."

On the surface, Harold Clark encourages Ginny and Rose to make up with Larry, to stop antagonizing him. However, while he is giving the appearance of wanting to bring the family to reconciliation, he is scheming to publicly reprimand and insult Ginny and Rose at the church potluck. Likewise, he throws a homecoming party for his son Jess and outwardly acts thrilled to have him home. At that potluck dinner, though, he publicly humiliates Jess and accuses him of wanting to steal his farm.

Just who is Jess? Ginny believes he is all goodness, and she believes she has fallen in love with him. Rose sees him as an opportunist who takes advantage of others to get what he wants. In the end, Jess sneaks off again, leaving everything in his wake turned upside down. He gives the appearance of being one sort of man but is in reality quite different.

Ginny believes she and Rose are united; their bond is strong and they watch out for each other. However, Ginny discovers that Rose is having an affair with Jess, even though she knows he was also involved with Ginny. This feels to Ginny like the ultimate betrayal; Rose had given the appearance of being united with Ginny, when in reality, she was the sort of person who took what she wanted at any cost.

The friendship between Larry and Harold is another example of appearance versus reality. On the surface, the two men appear to be best friends, but there is a strong underlying competition between the two, and each man knows he has a degree of power over the other.

The entire Cook family gives the appearance that they are tightly knit, a community unto themselves that takes care of its own. That appearance cracks, however, as soon as members stop considering themselves as a unit and instead act as individuals. The reality of the Cook family shatters its appearance to both members and outsiders.

### Patriarchy

Smiley's novel is a vivid criticism of the patriarchal system in which males dominate females. For the three main female characters, life has always been lived under the shadow of their father. The only one to break away from that burden is Caroline, the youngest. She is the only one to verbally doubt Larry's plan to transfer the farm, and when she does, he cuts her out of the agreement. When time passes with no word from Caroline after the falling out between her and Larry, Ginny remarks to Rose that Caroline should be more careful, meaning more aware of her father's wrath. Rose replies, "She doesn't have to be careful. She's got an income." This income provides Caroline with independence; she does not rely on her father for anything, and so his behavior and dismissive attitude do not affect her to the extent they do her sisters.

Caroline is also the sister who was not a victim of their father's incest. This abuse is another example of the expectation that a man can do whatever he wants to a woman without consideration of her as a human being. When Ginny responds to their father's descent into mental instability, Rose demands she see him for who he really is: "You've got to remind yourself what he is, what he does, what he did. Daddy thinks history starts fresh every day, every minute, that time itself begins with the feelings he's having right now."

All the men in *A Thousand Acres* operate from the patriarchal perspective. Pete Lewis, Rose's husband, physically beat her. Ty Smith, Ginny's husband, has no problems with her until she began to speak up and stand up to Larry. So intense is his sense of domination—though it is much quieter than that of Pete and Larry—that his wife had stopped telling him when she had a miscarriage. She did not want to upset him. The last time Ty sees Ginny, in the restaurant in Minnesota, he tells her life was good and right for so many years, before she and Rose messed things up. Ginny responds, "You see this grand history, but I see blows. I see taking what you want because you want it, then making something up that justifies what you did." Even Jess Clark, the one male character who shows the potential to break out of the patriarchal mold, turns out to be self-serving.

Ginny is the last person any of the men in the novel would have suspected of pushing the boundaries of the life she knew. Ginny has always been the accepting one, the one who keeps her mouth shut and does what is expected of her. The dysfunction of the Cook family hinges on Ginny, and when she refuses to play her role any longer, the family falls apart. The patriarchy topples.

### Memory

The power of memory is illustrated throughout this novel. Larry Cook has little memory, or if he has it, he chooses not to employ it. As Rose points out to Ginny, history begins fresh every day for their father, and it is that ability that allows him to sexually abuse his daughters and not feel remorse.

Rose wears her memories like a cloak and finds that they propel her forward. Despite the fact that she is dying of cancer, Rose refuses to forgive her father for victimizing her. She actually sees this refusal to forgive as her life's mission.

For Ginny, the only way to keep up with the façade of normality is to repress her memory. It is Ginny for whom the memory is most powerful. Once she acknowledges the reality of her past, she can move forward into a more fulfilling life of her own making. She has to embrace those memories before she can let them go.

### Justice

The most unlikable characters in *A Thousand Acres* are met with justice by the end of the

*Michelle Pfeiffer as Rose and Jessica Lange as Ginny in the 1997 film version of the novel* (© *Photos 12 / Alamy*)

book. Larry Cook spends his last years in torment and then dies. Pete, a wife beater who causes Harold's accident, dies. Harold is blinded and must give up farming. Rose, who lives her life in vengeance and selfishness, dies.

The death in Smiley's retelling is both literal and figurative. Although Ginny survives, death has not passed her by. She suffered the death of her marriage, her love affair, and a life that was, if not genuine, at least familiar. Every relationship she has ever forged is destroyed, and the reader is left to decide whether the cost of truth is worth it. Smiley challenges the reader to ask whether justice is ever truly served when others suffer as well.

## STYLE

### First-Person Narrative

Ginny is the narrator of *A Thousand Acres*. The narrative is a first-person (told from the viewpoint of the main character using "I") reflection of her life that ends in the place where she now lives. By telling the story in the first person, Smiley makes it more personal for the reader and creates a sense that the reader is participating and not just reading. Ginny speaks directly to the reader, allowing the reader to partially own the tale.

### Setting

Most of the novel and its events are set in the fictitious Zebulon County of Iowa in 1979. It ends several years later in St. Paul, Minnesota. Smiley could have chosen many settings for this novel, but Iowa is considered the heartland of the Midwest, so it is a fitting choice for this particular story. In contrast, St. Paul is a very large city; this is where Ginny lives once she has left behind her old life and shed that skin for a new, more independent lifestyle.

### Tragedy

Smiley's novel is a modern retelling of William Shakespeare's tragedy *King Lear*. A tragedy is a drama in which a hero brings ruin upon himself or herself because of some major character flaw. The aging King Lear decides to retire his throne and divide his kingdom among his three daughters. He tests them first by asking each to tell him how much she loves him. Goneril and Regan flatter their father with false professions of love. Cordelia, the youngest and favorite, says she has no words to describe her love for the king. Lear is angered and disowns her. Cordelia leaves home without her father's approval. Lear realizes he has made a big mistake as Goneril and Regan undermine his authority. Their betrayal causes him to go insane, and by the tale's end, Lear and all three daughters are dead.

Smiley wrote her novel so that nearly every character represents one of Shakespeare's characters: Larry Cook is King Lear, Ginny is Goneril, Rose is Regan, Caroline is Cordelia, Harold Clark is the Earl of Gloucester, Jess is Edmund, Loren is Edgar, Pete is the Duke of Cornwall, and Ty is the Duke of Albany. However, Smiley gave the plot a twist when she decided to make the patriarch (Larry) an evil man who abused his daughters. In his critical essay, "Contemporary Retellings: *A Thousand Acres* as the Latest *Lear*," James A. Schiff explains, "Smiley's central objective then in rewriting Lear is to provide a motivation for and an understanding of the two older daughters; in so doing, she is creating a feminist version of Lear."

Although *King Lear* is a more "pure" tragedy because of the characters (such as the noble but arrogant king) and the poetic language used by Shakespeare, Smiley's novel is also a tragedy. Her heroine, Ginny, is definitely flawed, but her heart is good and her intentions are noble. Her major flaw is denial, yet it is that very flaw that allows her to live daily among her oppressors without going insane. When she is forced to confront the truth, she finds she can no longer live a lie, and her entire world crumbles.

### Flashback

Ginny recalls her story in a linear style, beginning at the start and following through in order as events happen. Smiley uses flashbacks to present the reader with events and situations that happen before and influence the main story Ginny is telling. For example, when Ginny recalls a beating by her father for misplacing a shoe as a young girl, the author is using a flashback.

Flashback is a useful technique when a writer wants to provide detail or background but does not want to work it directly into the action of the story. The use of flashback in this novel serves to underscore the theme of the power of memory.

## HISTORICAL CONTEXT

### Feminism

*A Thousand Acres* is set in an era generally considered to be the end of the "second wave" of the feminist movement. Early (first-wave) feminists focused on voting rights. Those in the second wave were more concerned with issues such as workplace equality, reproductive rights, and family. Anyone who read newspapers and magazines or watched television in the 1970s knew it was a time of change for women. Attitudes they held about themselves and their potential were in flux; women were encouraged to think more as individuals and less as support characters for family and men.

Women living in America's heartland—which includes Iowa—may have been more isolated from the feminist events and attitudes of the time, but they could not remain untouched. Smiley's novel is a strong criticism of the traditional patriarchal system in which men dominate women simply because they can. Every male character dominates, and every female character struggles against those limits and expectations imposed upon them. In the end, the men in the novel are defeated. Rose is dead, and Caroline experiences a sort of self-imposed exile. However, Ginny triumphs, moves on, and begins life anew.

### Environmentalism

The environmental movement had gained momentum by the 1970s. The first Earth Day was celebrated in 1970, and the energy crisis of that decade brought environmental issues to the forefront. The U.S. government passed a series of environmental laws, and the nation was awakening to the concerns of conservation of energy resources.

Smiley uses Jess Clark to address those environmental issues pertinent to the late 1970s and early 1980s. Jess breaks away from tradition in many ways, most noticeably in his attitude toward the environment. While away, he made

# COMPARE
# &
# CONTRAST

- **1970s:** This is an era of advancement in agriculture and farming. Diseases that were once common among farm animals are being eradicated, and the average American farmer produces enough food to feed forty-eight people. Farmers are encouraged by government agencies to take out loans to subsidize the cost of buying more land and equipment. Organic farming methods are just being introduced and considered.

  **1990s:** Too many farmers had taken on debt in the 1980s in an effort to expand upon their export production. An economic crisis ensued, and laws were passed regulating farmers and their methods. Many farms went into foreclosure. By the 1990s, farm management has become key. In order to stay competitive, farmers need to understand management strategies and familiarize themselves with computers. It is a time of great change and challenge.

  **Today:** Family farms have slowly given way to corporate farms. Agricultural scientists work closely with these large farming operations to help them stay abreast of current technology and methods. Obesity and food safety are emerging as major consumer concerns.

- **1970s:** This is the most politically active decade for the second wave of the feminist movement. Women begin to organize in their push for equality in the workplace and society in general. It is a time of great social and cultural upheaval as many women seek to break out of the confines set for them by men and traditional institutions and values.

  **1990s:** Having made great strides in their efforts for equal rights, women more commonly hold jobs outside the home. By 1990, nearly 50 percent of America's workers are women. More than 39 percent of all management, executive, and administrative jobs are held by women. Despite the progress toward equality, it is a confusing time, as changing roles and expectations cause some women anxiety and stress. Those who seek jobs outside the home are accused of not putting their families first, but those who stay home are criticized for not having greater ambition.

  **Today:** Women of the twenty-first century continue to work to abolish the laws that discriminate and distinguish between the sexes. Women continue to be paid less for doing the same jobs as men, earning seventy-eight cents for every dollar earned by men. According to the Joint Economic Committee, female-headed households saw their median income drop by 5.4 percent between 2000 and 2007.

- **1970s:** Parent-child incest is a form of child abuse that has rarely been talked about until this decade. Although it happened, victims had been shamed into keep it a secret. As women strive to overcome the patriarchal bonds that had limited their freedom and health, they begin to share their stories and pasts. As more women reveal their abuse, families are unsure as to how to respond. Counseling is not common at this time, so many choose to consider it as just an unfortunate part of a child's past.

  **1990s:** Although still a taboo subject, incest is more openly discussed as therapy and mental health counseling becomes more acceptable in mainstream society.

  **Today:** Child abuse continues to be an issue that America struggles with. According to the Wisconsin Coalition Against Sexual Assault, incest is the most common form of child abuse.

a living working at a food co-op. Although co-ops are common in the twenty-first century, they were part of the counterculture in the 1970s. He returns to farm country an ethical vegetarian: His attitude toward food animals has changed, and he can no longer eat them in good conscience. He flirts with the idea of farming, but he wants to go organic so as to grow the healthiest crops possible with the least impact on the land. Jess is looked upon with suspicion by his hometown and even by his father, who is insulted that his son has turned his back on the traditional way of life.

Smiley incorporates concern for water pollution into the story by suggesting that Ginny's inability to carry a baby to full term—and perhaps even Rose's breast cancer—is the result of toxins in the drinking water. Water is a traditional symbol of health and vitality. In *A Thousand Acres*, it is suggested to be the cause of disease and death. In addition, Harold Clark is blinded in the field because there is no water nearby with which to flush his eyes.

### A Combination

The second wave of the feminist movement and the evolution of the environmental movement are seen by many as inextricably linked. At the root of each movement is the belief that the subject (women and land, respectively) has inherent value, that is, value simply because it exists and not because it is useful to men or to humans in general.

In an interview with Martha Duffy of *Time* magazine, Smiley explains how she saw the relationship between nature and women at the time she wrote the novel: "Women, just like nature or the land, have been seen as something to be used." She crafted her story by mingling the two themes. Larry, the patriarch of the family, sees his daughters and sons-in-law in terms of what they can do for him, and he considers the land his to do with as he pleases. Generations earlier, this land had been under two feet of water; it was never meant to be farmed. However, men did farm it, using methods that eventually poisoned the water and possibly led to the deaths of Harold's wife, Larry's wife, and Rose. Smiley is juxtaposing (placing side by side) the exploitation of the land and the exploitation of women in a patriarchal society. The late 1970s and early 1980s was an effective setting for this idea because America as a nation was just beginning to awaken to the realization that the exploitation of women and the environment was going to have lasting negative effects.

## CRITICAL OVERVIEW

*A Thousand Acres* is generally considered to be Jane Smiley's breakthrough novel. It won the 1992 Pulitzer Prize for Fiction and the National Book Critics Circle Award.

Because the book is an unabashed retelling of Shakespeare's *King Lear*, most critics judge it on the basis of how it compares to the original. Some take issue with the idea of Ginny as narrator. Others do not appreciate that Smiley's version of Lear has him as the abuser rather than the abused. Overall, however, the novel was well received and highly praised.

In her critical essay for the journal *Midamerica*, Jane S. Bakerman hails the novel as a success and likens its design to a quilt pattern. "She combines individual pieces—observations, incidents, memories, realizations—into blocks which steadily reveal more and more about the families she depicts."

Many critics consider the novel a feminist revision of the original tragedy because Smiley appeals to readers to sympathize with the two elder daughters instead of the father. In Shakespeare's version, the roles are reversed, and Lear is a sympathetic protagonist from whose point of view readers see the wrongdoings of the daughters. This major revision was deliberate; Smiley could never understand the behavior of the daughters. She wanted their voices to be heard.

Smiley changed her opinion of the character King Lear after attending a symposium in Los Angeles, California. During a discussion of her novel, a panelist informed her that during the writing of *King Lear*, Shakespeare's own father was suffering from dementia. Whereas she once felt Shakespeare identified with Lear in that they were both men who wanted and expected the unquestioning loyalty of women, this news changed her outlook. She explains the shift in an interview with journalist Ron Fletcher posted on the Random House Web site, "I now think that the idea of Shakespeare identifying with his daughters is more psychologically true than that of his identifying with Lear."

# CRITICISM

## *Rebecca Valentine*

*Valentine is a freelance writer and editor who holds a bachelor's degree in English with an emphasis on literary analysis. In this essay, she considers* A Thousand Acres *from a feminist perspective, focusing on character development of the three sisters.*

Jane Smiley had doubts about the authenticity of the voices of the daughters in Shakespeare's *King Lear*, and those doubts were the catalyst for writing *A Thousand Acres*. The text can be analyzed using feminist theory in many ways: structure, metaphor, and language. It is clear that the novel is a feminist revision of a centuries-old text. Smiley made such revisionism convenient by basing her story on characters forced to live in a dysfunctional patriarchal system lorded over by an abusive, volatile father figure. Ginny, Rose, and Caroline each represent a different stage of awareness of feminist thought, and when deconstructed, their characters reveal the idea that awareness does not necessarily equal progress.

Caroline, the youngest sister, is the least developed character of the three. Judging by all outward appearances, however, she is the embodiment of feminism. The idea of androgyny (neither male nor female) is represented in this character. At the age of five, Caroline announced "When I grow up, I'm not going to be a farmwife." When her mother asked her what she would like to be, Caroline answered, "A farmer." She is the only daughter to have attended college. In traditional Western thought, education is a male pursuit. She chooses a career as an attorney, a role traditionally filled by men.

This attitude that she can be whatever she wants to be because she is equal in every way to any man is a basic tenet of feminism. Caroline never seems to doubt herself. She is full of confidence and certainty. Smiley sees this trait as one commonly belonging to the younger sister in a family. She explains her opinion to journalist Suzanne Berne in an interview for the journal *Belles Lettres*: "In my experience of pairs of daughters the older one is often more anxious and tends to wring her hands. The younger one is often more certain of everything." Despite this assessment, Smiley poses the possibility that Caroline is more certain of the world and her place in it because she has been sheltered from

> GINNY, ROSE, AND CAROLINE EACH REPRESENT A DIFFERENT STAGE OF AWARENESS OF FEMINIST THOUGHT, AND WHEN DECONSTRUCTED, THEIR CHARACTERS REVEAL THE IDEA THAT AWARENESS DOES NOT NECESSARILY EQUAL PROGRESS."

the harshness of it—and their father—by Ginny and Rose.

Caroline is the one sister capable of playing within the patriarchal system without losing her identity. When presented with her father's plan to divide the farm, Caroline says only, "I don't know." However, Ginny knows exactly what her sister means without having to hear the words. Ginny believes that "Caroline would have said, if she'd dared, that she didn't want to live on the farm"; she has prepared for a life as an attorney instead. Ginny likens their father's plan to a trapdoor that would lead right back to the farm.

Perhaps Caroline knows how her father would react if she had explained herself more fully. Maybe she knows that if she does not say the words out loud, he will eventually come to terms with her doubt, which he does. However, even if he had never turned to her for help after cutting off all communication with Ginny and Rose, Caroline would have been able to walk away without remorse. She had willingly left that life behind and will not be forced into returning to it. She can exist within patriarchal confines without losing sight of who she is.

Smiley provides readers with virtually no physical description of Caroline. The first description refers to Caroline's attitude rather than her appearance: "Caroline shook hands with Jess in her brisk, lawyer's way that Rose always called her 'take-me-seriously-or-I'll-sue-you' demeanor." She is consistently described throughout the book in terms of her actions, and the reader is never given a solid image of what she looks like. This is in keeping with the feminist tenet that physical appearances should not define a person's value or existence.

# WHAT DO I READ NEXT?

- Amy Tan's *The Joy Luck Club* (1989) is the story of four Chinese women who fled their country in the 1940s and found refuge in America. They form the Joy Luck Club and meet regularly to keep alive their stories and culture. When one of the women dies, her daughter takes her place. Through the relationships she forms with the other women, she gains a greater understanding of who her mother was, as well as insight into who she is.

- *Barn Blind* was Jane Smiley's first novel, published in 1980. Like many of her novels, this one is set in the rural Midwest. The protagonist is Kate Karlson, a rancher's wife. The story focuses on her troubled relationships with her four teenage children.

- Cris Burks's 2006 young-adult book *Neecey's Lullaby: A Novel* takes the reader inside the poverty-stricken life of African American Neecey. The story follows her from her Chicago childhood in the 1950s to her early twenties. Burks presents a story of hope and forgiveness, in the form of family and loving relationships, as Neecey dedicates herself to overcoming the scars of abuse and poverty.

- *The Worst Hard Time* (2006) is the true story of the American Midwest region known as the Dust Bowl. Author Timothy Egan interviewed survivors of the great "black blizzards" that took hold of the Dust Bowl in the 1930s, the decade of the Great Depression. From their stories he weaves a tale that includes parents feeding tumbleweeds to their children, babies who die of dust pneumonia, and years of endless drought.

- Prolific novelist Jodi Picoult published *My Sister's Keeper* in 2004. Parents Brian and Sara are desperate to find a donor to save their two-year-old daughter Kate, who is dying from a rare form of leukemia. Their daughter Anna is born for the sole purpose of being a donor match for her sister. As Kate's disease progresses, the surgeries become more invasive for both girls. Anna sues her parents for the right to take control of her own body.

- Mary E. Pearson's 2008 young-adult novel *The Adoration of Jenna Fox* is the story of teenage Jenna Fox, whose father breaks the law by using the latest medical technology to save her after a car crash. Only 10 percent of her brain can be saved, but Dad uploads the high school curriculum to her computer brain. She may live for a year or for hundreds of years. The story investigates the ideas of right and wrong when it comes to family relationships.

- *The Secret Life of Bees* (2008) is the story of motherless fourteen-year-old Lily Owen, who runs away from her peach farm and neglectful father. She finds a home with three African American adult sisters who run a bee farm. Author Sue Monk Kidd sets the story in the 1960s and explores themes of family love, memory, and racism in the American South.

---

Despite the fact that Caroline is the most evolved of the three women in terms of feminism, she is the least capable of handling conflict. In the scene toward the end of the book in which Caroline and Ginny are cleaning out the house before the sale of the farm, Caroline does not want to discuss feelings or memories with her sister. She wants to divide up the items and leave. Ginny tests her, asking her who people are in family photographs. Caroline is unable to identify anyone except her father. She tells Ginny he looks "as familiar as a father should look; no more, no less." Ginny realizes at this point, without doubt, that Caroline never suffered the abuse she and Rose did; she is completely unaware of it.

After fighting with Ginny, Caroline storms out of the house and slams the door. That is the last the reader hears of her. She deals with this final blow as she does all others—by walking away. Turning one's back is not a sign of strength but of denial. Readers are given no indication that Caroline has experienced any personal growth by the end of the book. She remains stagnant, unable to feel much of anything.

Rose, the middle sister, is also in the middle on the continuum of feminist ideology. A survivor of both incest and breast cancer at the beginning of the novel, she has designed for herself a fierce existence. She has chosen to remain a part of the patriarchal system, but instead of carving out a fulfilling life within it, she lives a life motivated by revenge and seething anger. Unlike Caroline, who removes herself from the confines of patriarchy, or Ginny, who initially quietly accepts her submissive role, Rose sees reality for what it is, does nothing to permanently improve it, and grows angrier at having to deal with it each passing day.

That anger, like the incest and the breast cancer, is a poison. It prevents Rose from moving past the wrongs imposed upon her, and so they hold a crippling power over her. Throughout the novel, Rose reveals her hatred for her father. She reviles him, wants to see him pay for the pain and suffering he has inflicted upon his daughters. In her critical essay "'The Gleaming Obsidian Shard': Jane Smiley's *A Thousand Acres*," Jane S. Bakerman points out that, more than any other daughter, Rose resembles her father. Calling her a "predator who goes after what she wants," Bakerman points to Rose's affair with Jess as an example of her callousness and selfishness. "Having attempted to submerge her father's abuse in a series of affairs, Rose . . . turns to Jess, knowing full well that he is Ginny's lover. Worse, perhaps, she regards this behavior as her right."

When Ginny is deeply hurt by this betrayal, she remarks that Rose always wants everything for herself. Rose replies, "Yeah, I always have. It's my besetting sin. I'm grabby and jealous and selfish and Mommy said it would drive people away, so I've been good at hiding it." Ironically, Rose does not recognize that it is the same flaw that allows her father to do as he pleases without remorse.

Although Rose is a strong woman who recognizes her own value as a person independent of any other entity, her strength is drawn from a well of anger, and her choices and behavior have painful consequences for those who love her. She knows this and takes no issue with the fact.

Ginny, narrator of *A Thousand Acres*, is not a woman one could describe as a feminist. By telling the story from Ginny's perspective, Smiley has given the reader a work of domestic realism, where feminist values have no place. In her critical essay, "The Daughter's Subversion in Jane Smiley's *A Thousand Acres*," Susan Stealer explains domestic realism novels. "In those novels, women's roles within the home are the ostensible focus, but they recognize that such roles are defined outside the home by large social and cultural views of women's place and value."

From the beginning of the novel, readers are given to understand that Ginny sees her job as one of peacemaker. After Caroline insults their father by doubting his plans for the farm, it is Ginny who encourages her to "make allowances" for his behavior. When she and Rose are talking about Caroline's treatment of their father, Ginny says, "I didn't argue. I never have with Rose." Throughout most of the novel, Ginny never stands up to Caroline, never corrects her, and never finds the courage to question her out loud.

The same is true of Ginny's attitude toward her father. She has repressed all memories of the years of incest and abuse. Although she took over every wifely duty at age fourteen because her mother died and has continued taking care of her father for decades, he treats her as a slave. In Larry's eyes, Ginny exists solely for his benefit; Ginny has allowed this attitude of his to be perpetuated and does not criticize it.

It is not until Jess Clark returns that Ginny begins to see life from a different perspective. Jess is at once familiar and new, comforting and thrilling. As she realizes the feelings Jess evokes, Ginny must acknowledge her dissatisfaction with her own marriage. She enters into adultery with Jess, something she never would have done before he arrived.

After Larry sues Ginny and Rose with the help of Caroline, Rose decides it is time Ginny faced the reality of her past. She forces Ginny to remember the nights her father visited her in bed, and as those memories slowly unravel in her mind, Ginny must acknowledge the power that experience has had over her for all her life.

The event that ultimately pushes Ginny out of her comfort zone is Rose's romantic involvement with Jess. With a grief that transcends even the loss of five babies, Ginny says, "My deepest-held habit was assuming that differences between Rose and me were just on the surface...that somehow we were each other's real selves, together forever on this thousand acres."

Ginny's grief turns to anger, and for the first time in her life, Ginny schemes. Although her plan to poison Rose fails, it is the last event in what will become Ginny's old life. Without so much as a word of goodbye, Ginny turns her back on the painful, restrictive life she allowed others to build for her and sets out on her own. She chooses the city over the country and strangers over family.

During their last conversation, Ty tries to unravel how everything went wrong. "For years, it was right, and we prospered and we got along and we did the way we knew we should be doing, and sure there were little crosses to bear, but it was right." When Ginny counters his argument with her newfound perception of her father, Ty longs for the "old" Ginny:

> I didn't remember you like this.
>
> I wasn't like this. I was a ninny.
>
> You were pretty and funny, and you looked at the good side of things.

It is clear by the end of the novel that Ginny has broken free of the ties that have bound her, gagged her, and suffocated her. Stealer points out in her essay that the last paragraph of the epilogue reveals that Ginny has become a woman who took that which was used as a weapon against her and turned it into a gift, a gift of understanding. Although she does not forgive her father, she can understand how he came to be who he was.

Ginny recognizes that this knowledge is the one gift she can take away from a lifetime of forgetting and protecting. However, this gift will continue to enrich her life, and it allows her to pull away from the patriarchal system that so thoroughly damaged her younger self and prevented her from seeing her life and even her loved ones as they really were.

Thus, the most oppressed sister becomes the most dedicated feminist by turning the key to that oppression into her salvation.

**Source:** Rebecca Valentine, Critical Essay on *A Thousand Acres*, in *Novels for Students*, Gale, Cengage Learning, 2010.

## *Tyler Kessel*

*In the following essay, Kessel recounts the plot of* A Thousand Acres *and finds the author's voice effective.*

Domination by an oppressor is maintained by keeping the center of power invisible to the oppressed, thereby leaving nothing for the oppressed to target. When the center becomes visible, however, the oppressed are presented with the condition for the possibility of examining the source of pain, raising the potential for combating and destroying it. In her article, "The Body as a Site of Colonization: Alice Walker's Possessing the Secret of Joy," Alyson Buckman explains this possibility:

> If the colonized refuse to forget the past, then they also refuse to be complicit in their oppression, as it will not be forgotten. [sic] While history may be painful, the Other can, in remembering, deconstruct the history of the colonizer and its falsifying representation of the colonized. Memory can then act as a catalyst against oppression. (93)

Larry Cook, the principal antagonist of Jane Smiley's *A Thousand Acres*, remained invisible to his daughter Ginny because she had blocked out the memory of Larry's rape and beating for many years. Unable to identify him as the source of her misery. Ginny could not resist her father. Ultimately, however, Ginny is able to resist her father and carve out a livable existence because she comes to see Larry as the center of the power exerted over her.

Ginny's repression of these painful memories destroys her identity. Because Larry creates the occasion for a memory so horrible that it must not be allowed into consciousness, Larry is the root of Ginny's "feathery non-existence." Ginny, as Other, is not allowed to exist as her true self or as she might want to be but must conform to Larry's idea of who she should be. In other words, she sees herself only in terms of her father: "The biggest farm farmed by the biggest farmer. That fit, or maybe formed, my [Ginny's] own sense of the right order of things." Ginny's charge that Larry never sees things from her point of view provides evidence of this situation. In fact, her father does not even consider her point of view: "When he talked, he had this effect on me. Of course it was silly to talk about 'my point of view.' When my father asserted his point of view, mine vanished. Not even I could remember it." The erasure of Ginny's point of view is explained by the fact that in Larry's world, which is imposed on Ginny, her point of view is nonexistent; it therefore does not exist.

The domination does not stop, however, with the sexual and physical abuse of Ginny's younger life; it continues into her adult life in the form of silencing, misrepresentation, and expectations. Ginny's fear of her father confines her to the role of daughter only: "On the other hand, perhaps she hadn't mistaken anything at all, and had simply spoken as a woman rather than as a daughter. That was something, I realized in a flash, that Rose and I were pretty careful never to do." Ginny can hardly speak at all. This fear has its roots in early childhood: "My earliest memories of him are of being afraid to look him in the eye, to look at him at all. He was too big and his voice was too deep. If I had to speak to him, I addressed his overalls, his shirt, his boots. If he lifted me near his face, I shrank away from him." Ginny is deathly afraid to speak to her father because she cannot use her own voice. When she does speak to him it is in the accommodated, neutralized voice of his language. Ginny erases herself—her subjectivity is destroyed and kept silent by herself, her father, and her husband, Tyler. Her thoughts illustrate her inability to recognize her father as the evil source of her condition: "How many thousands of times has this sight aroused in me a distant, amused affection for my father, a feeling of forgiveness when I hadn't consciously been harboring any annoyance." If she were to free herself, she would have to "see" him for what he was.

After Rose reveals or retrieves the secret for Ginny, Ginny is able to "deconstruct" her father, to begin to see him for what he is—a cruel imperialist. Her first memory of her father creeping into her room at night to have sex with her is one of silencing. Her father says, "Quiet, now, girl." She is not allowed to resist, and she does not. Not until she begins the reconstruction of her identity through memory retrieval does Ginny find the self that should never have been concealed. In her father's house—the place where she was beaten and raped—after everyone has either left or died, Ginny is able to speak in her own unmasked, un-neutralized, and loud voice: "I screamed in a way that I had never screamed

before, full out, throat-wrenching, unafraid-of-making-a-fuss-and-drawing-attention-to-myself sorts of screams that I made myself concentrate on, becoming all mouth, all tongue, all vibration." Had the secret been "withheld" from Ginny, or not retrieved for Ginny, she would have gone on living in her oppressed and ignorant world. Thus, Ginny's not knowing, not remembering, is at once her injury and her protection. The price of gaining her voice is devastatingly high—the total annihilation of her past life—her relationships, homes, and community. Ginny regains her subjectivity through this rebirth: "Rather than feeling 'not myself,' I felt intensely, newly, more myself than ever before."

Does Ginny's relocation and employment at Perkins Restaurant represent a total escape from the imperial structure of the farm and her father? Yes, but, importantly, without forgetting them. Her move to St. Paul marks the beginning of a new life of independence and self-control, with "children" and hope. She ultimately learns "how to refuse the gifts [she] was to be given," which is evidenced by her self-removal from Iowa, but she fortunately does not forget the legacy of her father. Ginny runs away from the farm, but she cannot deny the years of abuse and memories of her past life. On the contrary, she uses these memories constructively. With respect to the worst of these, she says, "My body reminds me of Daddy, too, of what it feels like to resist without seeming to resist, to absent yourself while seeming respectful and attentive." Even though she cannot become fully uncolonized, Ginny is, at the end, fully present, fully resistant. The ultimate proof of her victory is the retelling of her story through her eyes, in her voice. She has become, to use one of Heidegger's concepts, at-home in the not-at-home—in other words, comfortable in a completely different, new life.

**Source:** Tyler Kessel, "Smiley's *A Thousand Acres*," in *Explicator*, Vol. 62, No. 4, Summer 2004, pp. 242–45.

### Lewis Burke Frumkes

*In the following interview with Frumkes, Smiley talks about her writing methods and the possibility of writing screenplays.*

*Lewis Burke Frumkes: My guest is novelist Jane Smiley, who won the Pulitzer Prize for* A Thousand Acres. *Following that was* Moo, *a spoof of academic life, and her most recent novel,* The All-True Travels and Adventures of Lidie

> BUT NO, WHAT I SET OUT TO DO WHEN I
> WAS WRITING MY NOVELS—*THE GREENLANDERS, A
> THOUSAND ACRES, MOO,* AND *LIDIE*—WAS TO WRITE
> A NOVEL IN EACH OF THE FOUR BIG GENRES: EPIC,
> TRAGEDY, COMEDY, AND ROMANCE."

Newton, *published by Knopf. Rather than spoil it with my own description, I'll let Jane introduce it and tell you what it's about.*

*Jane Smiley:* Lidie Newton takes place in the mid-1850s, mostly in Kansas and Missouri. It's about a tall, plain woman without any prospects, and a man, associated with an abolitionist group from New England, who passes through Lidie's town in Illinois. She falls for him and he for her. She goes with him to Kansas, which she thinks is going to be a pleasant, lovely, already settled place. Instead she discovers primitive conditions and a great deal of ideological strife about slavery, and free labor. She also experiences the worst winter in a hundred years. Things are very difficult for her in Kansas. I once read that every 19th-century American novel was actually a romance, so I wanted to write a romance, a story in which the protagonist sets out on a journey and sees many amazing things.

*LBF: She marries Thomas Newton, and they set out and lead a difficult life and have a lot of adventures. It's been said that you were very upset with Mark Twain's* Huckleberry Finn, *that you felt, in fact, that it had moral problems, and you would rather have seen another book become the Great American Novel. You set out to do something equivalent, maybe. How did this influence your writing of* Lidie Newton?

*JS:* The other novel of the period is *Uncle Tom's Cabin,* which is one of my favorite novels. I like to see Huck as the dad and Harriet Beecher Stowe as the mom of my novel. Their DNA is both in here. Lidie sets out on a journey, as Huck does, but she's a woman, she's married, and she's interested in issues that Huck is not interested in. She does engage morally and intellectually with the slavery issue as the characters in *Uncle Tom's Cabin* do. So both novels are very influential on

my novel, and I don't like to kick dad or mom out of the house. I like to feel that had I not read either one, my novel would be a lesser novel. I'll always put in a plug for *Uncle Tom's Cabin.* I think it has been overlooked in the 20th century by a certain type of critic. I'm not going to say that one is better or greater than the other, but I will say that both novels stand on their own, and both are worth reading. Earlier this year I was on a radio show in which we talked about *Uncle Tom's Cabin.* Every person that called in adored it, and reading it myself changed my way of looking at many things. I like to think that Huck is in my book. There's a character in here named Frank who's a 12- or 13-year-old boy; he's clearly a Huck character. He smokes a cigar, he's all of those Huckish things.

*LBF: How much of Jane Smiley is in* Lidie Newton?

*JS:* I expected Liddie to have a soberer voice than she ended up having. One of the things readers have noticed about the novel is that a lot of it is sort of funny, even though a lot of terrible things are happening. And I think that what's in Lidie of me is a kind of ironic view of things, and a tendency to make remarks that are a little unconventional. I love horses, she loves horses; she's not very domestic, and I am. I can sew and cook. I can do those things that she can't do, but I never had to set my autonomy up against a whole culture of domesticity as she does.

*LBF: As a young girl, did you fantasize about living in other eras, when you were reading history?*

*JS:* Yes, I did. Now that you mention it. I can remember that I always wished I had been born in 1790 and died in 1859, because I thought that was a really peaceful era in which to have bred—after the Revolution and before the Civil War and the atomic bombs. And now that I've read about that period, I think it would have been.

*LBF: You won the Pulitzer Prize for* A Thousand Acres, *which was really a tour de force and has been described many times as a modern version of the King Lear story. And now* Lidie Newton *has been compared to* Huck Finn. *Is [this] a device that you like to use? You try to do a modern version of powerful books you've read? Would* Uncle Tom's Cabin *be something you might one day redo in some other way?*

*JS:* The only screenplay I think I'd ever write would be the screenplay of *Uncle Tom's Cabin.* I would love to see that book made into an epic movie with great pre-Civil War slave music. But no, what I set out to do when I was writing my novels—*The Greenlanders, A Thousand Acres, Moo,* and *Lidie*—was to write a novel in each of the four big genres: epic, tragedy, comedy, and romance. I'm sure that comes from the fact that I did graduate work in English, and I did use models. *The Greenlanders* took the Icelandic saga, which is an epic tradition. *A Thousand Acres* took as its model a tragic play. *Moo* didn't have a specific model. *Lidie Newton* took as its model the 19th century novel. I very much wanted to try out each of those genres. I saved the romance for last because I didn't feel I had a particular affinity for the romance, but this turns out to be a kind of anti-romance if you think of a romance as something that leads to transcending of real life. Lidie is destroyed by her journey. Her personality and her sense of herself—she's strengthened by the losses of her journey, her circumstances are much reduced by the time she gets home. That was my original thought. I wrote *The Greenlanders* in the early 80s, so I've been working on this project for 18 years.

*LBF: What contemporary, authors do you read for pleasure?*

*JS:* I guess my dirty little secret is that I'm a slow reader. When I'm working on a book, I can't afford to read anything other than what I'm researching. Of my fellow novelists, I love Russell Banks, Jamaica Kincaid and Alice Munro. I like Garrison Keillor a lot. I love any funny writers. I like Francine Prose. My real loves are probably big 19th century novelists like Dickens, George Eliot, the incredibly great English novelists.

*LBF: Did you ever think of yourself as a long shot when you were writing, before* A Thousand Acres?

*JS:* Not before that, but when I was in graduate school I always thought of myself as a long shot. Well. I always thought of myself as kind of out-to-lunch. That sense of being in a daze or being kind of clueless lasted well into my twenties. I also had a view of what it was to be an author, a great author—you'd be a Jane Austen. You'd sit in your room, you'd write great books, die young, and then your books would be famous long after you were dead. I had no idea I would write books and that anyone would be interested in me while I was alive. So I suppose that kind of model is the dream of a person who sees herself as a long shot.

*LBF: How do you work? How do you get your ideas? Tell us a little about your writing habits.*

*JS:* I do all my research in the bathtub. I get a stack of books, and every morning, after I get the kids off to school, I get in the bathtub and read for a couple of hours. I don't like to read except in the bathtub. Then, when I'm about halfway done with the research, I think it's time to start writing. For my new horse racing novel I'd just pushed down the toast in the toaster, and it came to me that it was time to start writing, so I ran into my office without even waiting for the toast to come up. I sat down and started writing the horse racing book.

*LBF: Long shot?*

*JS:* No. I'm using a different title. My writing habits vary. I write two, three, four pages a day. It kind of depends on the novel.

*LBF: On a word processor?*

*JS:* Yes. I write on a laptop. It's on one of those slanty desks, and I have a reclining chair that I lean back in. I'm so tall that if I lean over the computer I get back pains, so I write semi-reclining I write about two hours, and then I go do something else.

*LBF: Where did you go to college, Jane?*

*JS:* I went to Vassar and The University of Iowa. I did the Writer's Workshop at the University of Iowa and studied medieval literature, specializing in Olde Norse and Olde English.

*LBF: What advice would you give to young writers starting out?*

*JS:* My advice is to focus on your work rather than your career. I taught writing for a long time, and I used a lot of techniques and a lot of revision to break down the students' resistance to revising their own work, and to get them really fascinated with their own stories. You can be a writer for your whole life and be happy if your own work is fascinating to you but if you're always thinking, "What's happening to my career," then your writing life, your relationship to your work, has a lot of ups and downs. But if you can write your own work and love it, and love to do it, and be fascinated by it, then, in my experience, your career will take care of itself.

*LBF: Of all your books, did one give you more satisfaction in any way than another?*

*JS:* Absolutely. *The Greenlanders. The Greenlanders* has a very small but loyal group of [friends]. Most of their names end in "son" or "sen," and I am one of them. That book felt as if it was channeled from "the other side." At the end of writing that book I was writing 20 pages a day, and most of that book is rough draft.

*LBF: This is some time ago.*

*JS:* Ten years ago.

*LBF: And you're still pleased with it.*

*JS:* It's a book I entered into, rather than produced.

*LBF: It's still in print?*

*JS:* Yes. Certainly, *A Thousand Acres,* my vision of *King Lear,* owes a great deal to my writing *The Greenlanders.* But in some sense, everything I know about writing comes from my writing *The Greenlanders.*

*LBF: Were you pleased with the film version of* A Thousand Acres?

*JS:* I can't answer that question. What I saw on the screen was the process. I didn't see the product. I don't think it's possible for me to see the product. But by what I saw on the screen, I could see clearly how they managed to persuade people to make the movie. I don't feel I can have an objective opinion. I felt all the actors, the directors, the producer, everyone involved in the movie; for all of them, it was a project based on enthusiasm, love and integrity.

**Source:** Lewis Burke Frumkes, "A Conversation with ... Jane Smiley," in *Writer,* Vol. 112, No. 5, May 1999, p. 20.

### Catherine Cowen Olson

*In the following essay, Olson divides the characters and classes by the types of foods they prepare and eat.*

"I'm the angriest person in the restaurant; I'm the only angry person in the restaurant." So laments Jane Smiley in her 1993 article, "Reflections on a Lettuce Wedge." In this self-described "diatribe" against the dullness of midwestern cooking, Smiley complains that she is fed up with eating at restaurants where "the salad" is a wedge of . . . iceberg lettuce floating in bright orange 'French' dressing," where patrons gladly pay top dollar for "instant mashed potatoes" and "machine-formed turkey breast." "Why do midwesterners hold their taste buds in lower esteem than everyone else in the whole world, even the notorious British?" she demands to know.

OVER AND OVER, MEALTIME SCENES LIKE THIS SUGGEST THE COOK FAMILY'S LIFELONG HABIT OF RESTRAINING PASSIONS."

Anyone who reads *A Thousand Acres* cannot help asking this same question about the eating habits of the farmers who inhabit this midwestern novel. Smiley's aptly named Cook family is always cooking or eating, and much of the food sounds heavy and unappetizing. Most of us cringe to think of Midwest-Mex garbanzo bean enchiladas or pork liver sausages canned with sauerkraut (to say nothing of tuna noodle casserole), yet these are foods that her characters prepare and expect their family and friends to eat—never mind enjoy. What does Smiley mean by constantly placing her characters in front of a plate—especially when that plate is so often filled with bland, stick-to-the-ribs food? "Reflections on a Lettuce Wedge" gives us lots of hints. Here, she argues that mid-westerners don't demand better food because they have "internalized" an "'Anything is good enough for me' attitude." Quoting one of Garrison Keillor's radio monologues, she says that midwesterners learn "early" the "'Who do you think you are?' lesson—as in, 'Who do you think you are to aspire to something more beautiful, more exotic, or more unusual than what is put before you?'"

Every one of her characters in *A Thousand Acres* is well-versed in this midwestern asceticism. In fact, we can draw a direct connection between the blandness of the food the Cook family eats and the self-denying, pinched lives they live. This novel deals largely with the complications that lie beneath the calm, healthy appearances of midwestern farm life. And what could seem more harmless than bland food? The spiceless meat-and-potatoes dishes that the characters choke down are all so undisguised that we are tempted to assume that nothing could be simpler. However, as Smiley says, these meals where "ingredients" are "juxtaposed but not allowed to mingle" represent "despair incarnate" ("Reflections"). The lack of flavor suggests zestless living—a hunger for something more satisfying. Furthermore, even the raw ingredients that make up the Cook family meals are more insidious than they seem. Supposedly pure well water turns out to be laced with poisons that furtively kill off the women and cause their miscarriages; vegetables are chock full of insecticides, and meats are tainted with drugs. Also, cooking itself appears deceptively unimportant but proves to be a source of both power and oppression. Initially, the oldest daughter, Ginny, dutifully plays the role of family hash-slinger and views herself as a minor player next to the men who tend the profit-making cornfields and pigs. But as she awakens to her own self-worth—and to the realization that her father has slept with his own daughters, that her sister Rose has slept with her lover, and that the men in her family have sacrificed their integrity, their wives, and their children for their land—cooking food and serving it becomes her means of asserting power and gaining freedom. From the opening scene at Harold Clark's pig roast, to the last page of this novel, where Ginny reflects on the connection between her sin of poisoning Rose's sausages and her father's incest, food and the way it is served mirror her submission to and final rebellion against the Cook family patriarchy.

In an interview with the journal *Belles Lettres,* Jane Smiley says that in writing *A Thousand Acres* she wanted to use the plot of *King Lear* to make an argument against our culture's habit of treating "nature and women...as exploitable objects"—as "owned things." "Feminists," she argues in another article in *Time,* "insist that women have intrinsic value, just as environmentalists believe that nature has its own worth, independent of its use to man" (Duffy, 92). Clearly, Larry Cook does not view his daughters as having "intrinsic worth"—nor did his father or grandfather. To Larry, his daughters are possessions. "We were just his, to do with as he pleased," Rose tells Ginny at one point, "like the pond or the houses, or the hogs or the crops." So as his possessions, their time is his, and they spend their lives in a flurry of chores that he directs.

One thing that takes up much of their time is preparing their father's food. Fearing his disapproval, Ginny and Rose cook exactly what he wants and serve his meals with military punctuality at six, twelve, and five on their appointed days of each week. As the novel opens, we learn that, because of Rose's mastectomy, Ginny has spent her spring "cooking for three households,"

hers, her father's, and Rose's. She cooks breakfast in each separate kitchen every morning, in a three and a half hour schedule that "start[s] before five and [does]n't end until eight-thirty," Ginny's father refuses to have his breakfast anywhere except in his own kitchen, even though Rose lives only a few feet away across the road. Furthermore, he never goes to restaurants, except "the cafe in town"—and even then, never after his noon meal. So his daughters have to cook for him, and always he demands a strictly followed menu. At breakfast, he always wants eggs. On Tuesday evenings, when it is Ginny's turn to have him over, he has the same thing every week—"pork chops baked with tomatoes, ... fried potatoes, a salad, and two or three different kinds of pickles." On Fridays, when Rose cooks for him, she has to make the same thing every week too. If Larry's supper is not ready exactly at five, when he expects it, he is surly and impatient. "He resisted efforts to change his habits," Ginny says of their culinary treadmill, "chicken on Tuesdays, or a slice of cake instead of pie, or an absence of pickles meant dissatisfaction, and even resentment."

In short, Larry Cook is accustomed to getting his own way and ordering his daughters about as he pleases. They do not dare question him openly but just act at his prompting. It is fitting then, that we first see him wield his psychological power at a crass pig roast. Here, he cedes control of his land—but not without vindictively cutting his daughter Caroline out of his will when she expresses even a hint of doubt. The morning after this pig roast, we get another, more disturbing glimpse of how much he throws his weight around. That morning, as Ginny goes back to her usual routine of cooking breakfast for her father, we see for the first time that every time he has her cook for him, he asserts his power to crush her self-esteem. Marv Carson, Larry's banker, joins them for breakfast on this day. Annoyed with Ginny for standing by as he and Marv eat the huge breakfast of "sausage, fried eggs, hash brown potatoes, cornflakes, English muffins,...toast, coffee and orange juice" that she has laid out for them, Larry barks, "You had anything to eat? What are you looking at?" When she replies that she has already eaten "with Ty," her husband, he roars, "Well, then, sit down or go out." He is greedily unappreciative of her efforts. At this same breakfast, Mary Carson tells Ginny about his peculiar regimen of forcing his body "to shed" its "toxins." "I can spot someone in the toxic overload stage from a mile away," he tells her portentously. Next, when he asks for "hot sauce," preferably "Tabasco," to help him "sweat," her only reply is, "We don't eat much spicy food." Spiceless is exactly what her life has been for so many years, and toxins are what she will soon shed as she and her sister begin to slough off their father's control and confront his incest.

Over and over, mealtime scenes like this suggest the Cook family's lifelong habit of restraining passions. Larry has such a hold on Rose and Ginny that they practice self-denial even in his absence. Even when they dream of escaping, they cannot fathom anything beyond waitressing in restaurants. And when they want to celebrate with a meal, they cannot imagine where to go. For example, not long after this breakfast with Marv, Ginny and Rose drive to Mason City for Rose's three month check-up after her mastectomy. If the news is good, their plan is to go out for lunch afterwards at the Brown Bottle, a moderately priced restaurant. When Rose's doctor tells her she is cancer-free, she is ecstatic, and declares, "Hey! Let's eat meat!" "I want to drink it all in, all the stuff I was going to miss." Then she tells Ginny she wants to go somewhere more daring and "expensive." However, her extravagant plans quickly dwindle from the "Starlight Supper Club" (a pricey eatery with "three kinds of herring on the salad bar"), to the "Golden Corral" (a low-budget steakhouse where they can spy on the prostitutes at the brothel next door), to Rose's finally surrendering with, "I think I'd rather go home. There's food there."

Rose begins by saying she wants to do "something that would scandalize Daddy," so why does she end up with such a practical response? Is it guilt, entrenched asceticism, associations between these prostitutes, her mutilated body, and her own adolescent self having sex with her father? Any way we examine this scene, food, sex, and self-denial get intimately connected with Larry Cook. This is why Jess Clark is such an important character in this novel. He is sexy and rebellious. He traipses around without a shirt in skimpy running shorts—and he never hides what he thinks. In fact, he makes fun of the midwestern tendency to avoid delicate subjects: "The wisdom of the plains. Pretend nothing happened," he says jokingly to Ginny at his father's pig roast. Furthermore, he stirs up Ginny's sexual longings and takes away the shame and dread she has always associated with sex. Jess is also a vegetarian who wants to nurture the land through organic farming. He is the exact opposite of Ginny's wasteful father who gobbles down meat, overuses insecticides, and drains wetlands.

Moreover, Jess brings a leisure to their evening meals that contrasts sharply with her father's eat-and-run supper routine. When Jess comes over for supper just before Father's Day, Ginny notes that in her father's absence, "[they] ate with appetite and joked over [their] food in a way that was new for [them]." With Jess there, they all laugh and tell old stories over their meal. But in a scene described on the next page of the novel—at Larry's house on Father's Day, the following Sunday—everyone is visibly tense. Ginny remembers that "the contrast" between the two meals "was clear." Here, Larry Cook sits before a huge "crown pork roast," snarling, "don't tell me what to do," when Rose offers to help him carve it. "It was exhausting just to hold ourselves at the table," says Ginny. "You felt a palpable sense of relief when you gave up and let yourself fall away...and wound up in the kitchen getting something, or in the bathroom running the water and splashing it on your face."

As the novel's plot thickens, every meal with her father becomes more and more of a power struggle. In another poignant breakfast scene, after Ginny learns of Larry's reckless trip to Des Moines, his mysterious phone calls to Caroline, his new couch, and his kitchen cabinets that are rotting in the driveway outside his house, Ginny makes a "plan to let him have it." She intentionally shows up after six a.m. and ignores his "accusing" glare as she walks into his yard. However, when she reaches the kitchen, she realizes that she has forgotten to bring him eggs (since apparently she does his shopping too). Faced with what she calls a "test"—either "to keep him waiting or...fail to give him his eggs"—she is reduced to groveling. She recalls, "My choice would show him something about me, either that I was selfish and inconsiderate (no eggs) or that I was incompetent (a flurry of activity where there should be orderly procedure)." With such options, either way she fails. She ends up running back to her house to get the eggs—all the time imagining her father seeing her "naked," with her "chest heaving, breast, thighs, and buttocks jiggling" clumsily down the road. Afterwards, she is angry with herself for being manipulated and not having the nerve to confront him. "I couldn't find a voice to speak in," she recalls.

Later, though, Ginny does "find a voice," first in the car on the way home from the hospital, and again the next day at the Pike cafe. The night of her father's accident, she scolds him, saying, "Rose or I will give you your breakfast at the regular time from now on, and you can just go out and work afterwards. We aren't going to let you sit around." The next morning, she conspicuously leaves eggs off of his breakfast menu—something she knows he has always demanded—and tersely sends him out to work. Later that week, at lunch, Ginny and her father have the mealtime face-off that marks a turning point in the novel and ends all discussion between them. Ginny plans to keep him busy for a day by taking him "to the chiropractor," "so he [can] be aligned after the shock of his accident," and then out for lunch and shopping. At lunch she is fuming over his having forced her to wait in the hot car during his appointment. He had refused to walk the "block and a half" from the chiropractor's to the cafe, telling her, "You can window-shop some other time. . . . You wait. I want to ride." Fearing the neighbor's gossip, she had backed down—but not without feeling bitter and stifled. "I hated the note of pleading that crept into my voice," she confesses. "Where was the power I had felt only a few days before, the power of telling rather than being told?" When they get to the cafe, even the food they order suggests her oppression. Ginny orders a "grilled cheese" sandwich, "chips," a "pickle, and a Coke," while her father has "roast beef with gravy and mashed potatoes," a utilitarian serving of "canned string beans, ice cream, [and] three cups of coffee." His meal is hoggish, hers serf-denying. He is ravenous; she has no appetite and eats only half of her sandwich.

Ginny uses the food at this meal as an excuse for "putting him in his place." "You really shouldn't be eating all that. That's too much," she scolds initially. Then the two of them begin a volley of accusations in which he insists the "girls" are "lazy," power-hungry, and disrespectful now that they have control of the "farm," and she calls him disrespectful too and argues, "I don't think you ever think about anything from our point of view." By the time they leave the restaurant, he "begin[s] to huff and puff" so much that she backs down, promising to "try harder" after he urges, "You girls should listen to me." He wins this argument—as he always does—but mixed with remorse over her "ungrateful thoughts" is a memory of the "deliciousness [she] had felt in putting him in his place." She has spoken truth and will not turn back. That night—before he steals Pete's truck, and they all have their melee in the storm—she breaks his long-held routine and barbecues their Tuesday night pork chops, rather than baking them with tomatoes. He never shows up for this meal, though, and from this point forward, Ginny and Rose are no longer his obedient daughters.

When she sees her father five days later at the church potluck, he appears senile, almost unaware of who she is. His meal does not overpower hers anymore—in fact, their plates are matched rib for rib in their heaviness. Furthermore, he can no longer argue in his own behalf, and now Harold Clark speaks for him. This is one of the uglier, more violent scenes in the novel, where Harold tries to reclaim Larry's power by shaming his daughters at the supper table. Here, Harold strategically seats Larry's family at a table in the middle of the church hall, and then publicly proclaims Ginny and Rose "bitches" who have thrown their father "off his own farm."

After this potluck supper, Ginny continues to cook and perform her farm wife's duties, but not without being aware of acting out a role for appearance's sake. Finally recalling the long-suppressed memory of her father's incest, and realizing that her husband Ty sides with the farm and not her, she questions all of the duties she has spent her life performing. Her lawyer's advice and sheer habit allow her to maintain a facade until the trial, but the day they win their suit, she cooks Ty one last supper of chops, potatoes, and brussels sprouts, and heads out the door for St. Paul—with his food still simmering on the stove. When she sees him again nearly three years later, her reaction is to "reduce [her] links to the old life even more by investing in a microwave oven." In leaving him, she exchanges her wife's apron for that of a waitress at a Perkins's restaurant—only now, her servitude gives her independence and self-esteem. She earns her own money, has her own apartment, and ironically discovers she is a superior waitress, good at empty small talk with customers, and better at her job than her co-workers. She even begins taking night classes in psychology at the University of Minnesota.

Ginny's solidarity with Rose as an incest victim is another thing that enables her to play-act through most of the months leading up to the trial. However, once Ginny discovers Rose's affair with Jess, she turns against Rose too and plots to kill her with water hemlock-laced pork liver sausages. And what do we make of these pickled sausages anyway? Their obvious phallic associations make them laughable, despite their dark purpose. But they also have deep symbolic echoes that suggest Jane Smiley gave considerable thought to the water hemlock, pork, and liver that go into them. Let us examine these sausages more closely.

To begin, Ginny's choice of water hemlock suggests her feminine power and instinctive ties with the earth. Her poison is not manmade like the insecticides her father and husband have always used but grows wild in her part of Iowa. As she makes these sausages, she appears to be casting a spell, relishing how "Rose's own appetite [will] select her death." "It was not unlike the feeling you get when you are baking a birthday cake for someone," she recalls. "That person inhabits your mind. So I thought continuously of Rose."

Furthermore, on the most obvious level, pigs connote filth, which in this case translates into the shame and dirtiness Ginny feels after discovering her father's incest. On a more subtle level, as food historian Magelonne Toussaint-Samat tells us, the pig has traditional associations with "lust" and "egotism" (*Food,* 423)—and what could be more lustful or egotistical than Rose's knowingly committing adultery with her sister's paramour? Liver also carries interesting connotations of bile and gall. In fact, "[T]he Roman poet Horace" considered the "liver" to be "the seat of the passions, particularly sensual love and anger" (*Food,* 434). Then there is the practical function that the liver serves in the body—as a filter for toxins—only in this case Ginny's sausages represent family poisons like incest, greed, jealousy, and emotional manipulation, "toxins" that Marv Carson had innocently alluded to earlier in the novel.

If, as the sausages portend, an apocalypse is coming to this farming dynasty, so is a rebirth. In her interview with *Belle Lettres,* Smiley says she

wants the Cook family women "to not be destroyed by what [their] father has done to [them]"—but "to go into the future making lives for themselves" (37). Rose's switch to vegetarianism saves Ginny from becoming a murderer, and this is one ironic sign of hope. Also, looking more closely at the symbolism of the pig, we find that it actually suggests rebirth, in addition to filth, greed, and lust.

According to James Frazer, the pig has long been linked to regeneration myths that invoke the power of women. For example, the Egyptians linked the pig with Isis and Osiris. In one version of this myth, Osiris (a fertility god) was "slain or mangled by [his brother] Typhon [who disguised himself] in the form of a boar" (Frazer, 550). When Ginny grinds up her pork sausages in her garbage disposal at the end of the novel, her actions echo Isis's resurrecting Osiris (her husband/brother) by throwing his remains into the Nile. In Ginny's case, though, she resurrects not her father, but her own identity and self-esteem.

Furthermore, as Frazer tells us, the Greeks connected the pig with the myth of Demeter and Persephone. They saw "the pig [as] an embodiment of the corn goddess . . . , either Demeter or her daughter . . . Persephone." He writes that the Greeks annually sacrificed the pig at "an autumn festival" called the "Attic Thesmophoria." "Celebrated by women alone in October," this festival simultaneously mourned Persephone's rape and unwilling "descent . . . into the lower world" as Hades's bride, and regaled "her return" in spring when she ushered in the sprouting crops. As part of this ceremony, the women would "throw pigs" into "sacred caverns or vaults," which they called "the chasms of Demeter and Persephone." Then at "the next annual festival," they would fetch the "decayed remains of the pigs" and offer them at the "altar." "Whoever got a piece of the decayed flesh . . . and sowed it with the seed-corn in his field," says Frazer, "was believed to be sure of a good crop" (543–44).

Ginny leaves her husband and her sausages in October—the time of the Attic Thesmophoria—and does not return again until October three years later. Then, after Rose's death, she goes back to the farm in winter and retrieves her sausages from Rose's cellar—another underground cavern. Her life at the end of the novel is a tragic compromise similar to Demeter's arrangement to have Persephone return to earth for only part of each year. By this time, the Cook family has been transformed into a landless matriarchy with Ginny as hesitant guardian of Pare and Linda, the family's two remaining heirs. Ginny comes home reluctantly, initially feeling "galled" and "defeat[ed]" when she finds herself cooking fried chicken and mashed potatoes with gravy for her two nieces in her father's old "kitchen." However, her resentment is short-lived, because suddenly it dawns on her that she makes the decisions now—not Rose, her father, or her husband. Cooking for the girls then becomes a nurturing act that will "bear fruit if" she is "patient."

This novel closes with the sense that, however diminished Ginny's life may be, she can reclaim some remnants of love from her past and make a future for herself and her nieces. When she returns to the farm to divide "personal possessions" with her sister Caroline, she curiously leaves with nothing but her canned pickled sausages. That night, she dumps them down her garbage disposal, and with them go the "toxins" that weighed her down for so many years, "toxins" of repression, incest, jealousy, and greed, of unborn children, sisters, and mothers murdered by poisoned water and herbicides. In the aftermath, she may not be the ruler of a farming dynasty, as her forefathers were, but she has power over her own life and enough empathy for her father to recognize that her own dark "urge" to poison those sausages was the same "goad" that prompted him to steal his own daughters' virginity.

"Eating is our oftenest repeated connection to our agricultural roots," Smiley argues in "Reflections on a Lettuce Wedge." Ironically, in Ginny's case, it is breaking her connection with her farm and her family—her agricultural roots—that makes her wake up to the environmental and familial abuses tied to the food that she and the other Cook family women have eaten and cooked all of their lives. By the end of this novel, Ginny remains a waitress who serves mostly men. Still, she and her nieces are shifting the balance of power in their relationship with food and its preparation. Ginny's psychology classes may lead to a degree that will end her life in food service, and most importantly, Pam and Linda already have more choices than Ginny and Rose did at their age. Pam has received a degree in music education, and most

suggestively, Linda (the pre-business major) aspires not to cook food for her own family but to control its production from the corporate end at "General Foods." As this novel closes, we sense that Ginny may not be able to protect her nieces from the greed and environmental destruction that they have inherited with their world, but she and they have both taken on a new "caution" and skepticism that will enable them to avoid repeating both the abuses of their forefathers and the helplessness of their mothers.

**Source:** Catherine Cowen Olson, "You Are What You Eat: Food and Power in Jane Smiley's *A Thousand Acres*," in *Midwest Quarterly*, Vol. 40, No. 1, Autumn 1998, p. 21.

## SOURCES

"Agriculture in the Classroom," in *Growing a Nation: The Story of American Agriculture*, LetterPress Software, 2006, pp. 45–48.

Bakerman, Jane S., "'The Gleaming Obsidian Shard': Jane Smiley's *A Thousand Acres*," in *Midamerica*, Vol. 19, 1992, pp. 127–37.

Berne, Suzanne, "In an Interview," in *Belles Lettres: A Review of Books by Women*, Vol. 7, No. 4, Summer 1992, pp. 36–38.

Duffy, Martha, "The Case for Goneril and Regan," in *Time*, Monday, November 11, 1991, p. 92, http://www.time.com/time/magazine/article/0,9171,974259,00.html (accessed June 1, 2009).

Fletcher, Ron, "A Conversation with Jane Smiley," in *Random House*, http://www.randomhouse.com/catalog/display.pperl?isbn = 9780449907481&view = auqa (accessed June 1, 2009).

Hill, Roger B., "History of Work Ethic: 12. Other Changes in the Workplace," in *University of Georgia College of Education*, http://www.coe.uga.edu/work ethic/hoc.html (accessed July 18, 2009).

"Incest," in *Wisconsin Coalition against Sexual Assault*, 2004, http://www.wcasa.org/docs/incest%2004.pdf (accessed July 18, 2009).

Schiff, James A., "Contemporary Retellings: *A Thousand Acres* as the latest *Lear*," in *Critique: Studies in Contemporary Fiction*, Vol. 39, No. 4, Summer 1998, pp. 367–81.

Smiley, Jane, *A Thousand Acres*, Alfred A. Knopf, 1991.

Stealer, Susan, "The Daughter's Subversion in Jane Smiley's *A Thousand Acres*," in *Critique: Studies in Contemporary Fiction*, Spring 2000, p. 2111.

"Women and Their Families Are Being Squeezed," in *U.S. Congress Joint Economic Committee*, September

16, 2008, http://jec.senate.gov/index.cfm?FuseAction=
Reports.Reports&ContentRecord_id=7e95c6c6-0a9
9-a901-e342-3edfab861701&Region_id=&Issue_id=
(accessed August 20, 2009).

## FURTHER READING

Ackerman, Robert J., *Perfect Daughters: Adult Daughters of Alcoholics*, rev. ed., Health Communications, 2002.

> This is a revised edition of a text originally published in 1989. Dr. Ackerman identifies behavior patterns common to daughters of alcoholic parents and shares the stories of more than twelve hundred such women. The book also offers positive coping strategies and includes a reference section containing helpful resources.

Aubrey, Sarah B., *Starting & Running Your Own Small Farm Business*, Storey Publishing, 2008.

> Aubrey, a small-farm owner, shares her experience to explain how to start up and operate a successful small-farm. She helps readers learn how to secure financing, draw up paperwork, and even develop Web sites and marketing skills.

Nakadate, Neil, *Understanding Jane Smiley*, University of South Carolina Press, 1999.

> This book provides an analysis of the connections between Smiley's personal experiences and her work. Nakadate traces the themes prevalent in Smiley's fiction.

Shakespeare, William, *King Lear*, edited by Grace Loppolo, W. W. Norton, 2007.

> This edition is based on the 1623 text of Shakespeare's famous drama. It includes primary sources used by the author, as well as thirteen critical interpretations.

# *To Kill a Mockingbird*

**1962**

*To Kill a Mockingbird* is a film released in 1962, based on the novel of the same title by Harper Lee, which was published in 1960. The novel is about life in a small town in Alabama during the Great Depression, as seen through the eyes of a young girl. It won a Pulitzer Prize in 1961 and immediately became a classic of American literature. The film, directed by Robert Mulligan and produced by Alan J. Pakula, was equally successful and won three Oscars in 1963. Gregory Peck, who played Atticus Finch, the small-town lawyer who stands up against racial prejudice, won Best Actor in a Leading Role; Horton Foote received the award for Best Writing for a Screenplay Based on Material from Another Medium; and Alexander Golitzen, Henry Bumstead, and Oliver Emert won Best Art Direction-Set Decoration, Black-and-White. The film was nominated for five more awards, including a nomination for Mary Badham, who played Finch's young daughter Scout, as Best Actress in a Supporting Role. *To Kill a Mockingbird* is considered one of the best American films ever made. Viewers should be aware, however, that the offensive word "nigger" is used several times, as it is in the novel. This reflects the fact that this word was often used in the South during this period. When the young girl Scout uses it, not knowing its negative connotations, her father tells her not to use it again.

*Universal Studios / Hulton Archive / Getty Images*

## PLOT SUMMARY

After the opening credits of *To Kill a Mocking-bird* show a young girl opening a cigar box that is full of trinkets of various kinds, the story begins with a voice-over narration by the adult Jean Louise Finch, known as Scout. She looks back on Maycomb, Alabama, where she grew up in the 1930s during the Great Depression. As she speaks, the camera pans across the street that made up Scout's world in those long-gone days when she was six years old.

Walter Cunningham, a farmer from the country who has been hit hard by the Depression, drives up in a horse and cart and delivers a sack of hickory nuts to the Finch residence. He is paying a debt for legal services to Atticus Finch, Scout's defense lawyer father, in the only way he can, but he is embarrassed about it. Finch explains to Scout how poor Cunningham is.

Scout's ten-year-old brother, Jem, is up in a tree house, refusing to come down until his father agrees to play football for the Methodists. Atticus says he is too old to play. When Jem complains to Miss Maudie Atkinson, a neighbor across the

street, that his father is too old to do anything, she defends him.

Jem then sees a young boy sitting in Miss Stephanie Crawford's collard patch. This turns out to be Charles Baker "Dill" Harris, who is visiting his aunt for two weeks from Meridian, Mississippi. Dill is nearly seven, and seems a confident if unusual boy, boasting that he can read and telling tall tales about his life.

### The Mysterious Boo

Jem sees Mr. Radley, one of their neighbors, pass by. He is a mean old man, and Jem explains to Dill that he has a scary, mentally deranged son called Boo who only ever leaves the house at night. The children have never actually seen Boo, but they imagine what he is like. The three children run and gaze at the Radley house. Boo eats raw squirrels and cats, says Jem. When Miss Stephanie arrives, she says that Boo once attacked his father with a pair of scissors, stabbing him in the leg.

When the clock chimes five, they run to meet Atticus, but Jem warns them about Mrs. Dubose, a bad-tempered elderly woman who is sitting on her porch in a wheelchair. Jem says they must not answer her back or she may shoot them with the pistol she keeps on her lap. As they pass her, they ignore her while she shouts angrily at them. When they return with Atticus, Atticus is very polite to her, praising her flowers.

That night, after Scout practices reading aloud to her father, she asks Atticus about Boo, and he tells her to leave the Radleys alone. Later, in bed, Scout asks Jem whether he remembers their mother. Jem says she died when he was six and he still remembers her.

Judge Taylor stops by and asks Atticus if he will defend a black man, Tom Robinson, who is to be charged by a grand jury with an as yet unspecified crime. Although he is busy, Atticus agrees out of a sense of duty.

The children's adventures continue. On the street, Scout folds herself inside a rubber tire and Jem rolls her away. By chance, she ends up in the Radley yard, and Jem has to pull his stunned and frightened sister to safety. Jem runs up to the Radleys' front door and bangs on it. Then the children run as fast as they can to escape the perceived danger.

Dill then suggests they go downtown to the courthouse to see the room where Boo was once locked up. At the courthouse, they go to the

# FILM TECHNIQUE

- By the early 1960s, color had become the norm for Hollywood films, but until 1966 there were still Oscars given for art direction in black-and-white films. Therefore, the fact that this film was shot in black and white was not unusual for 1962, although the director and producer have since gone on record saying that they cannot imagine it being made in anything else. (Mulligan and Pakula make this comment in the documentary film that accompanies the collector's edition of the DVD.)

- One reason black-and-white cinematography succeeds in this film is because it creates a period atmosphere. The story is set in the 1930s, and in those days all movies were in black and white, so this format in *To Kill a Mockingbird* authentically evokes a movie from that period. It looks more realistic. Newsreels and still photography from that period were also in black and white. That is how people who first watched this film in the early 1960s would have remembered seeing pictures of the Depression era, so the monochrome further adds to the realistic effect of the film. Black and white also makes the film look more austere, in keeping with the setting in the Depression-era South. Color creates a more opulent, rich look, which might have been out of keeping with the time and place.

- The balance of light and shade in the frame is frequently used to enhance the mood and the atmosphere of the film. In the scene that begins with Jem and Scout on the porch at night, for example (chapter 10 in the DVD)

the artful use of light and shadow is particularly effective in creating an atmosphere. The children's faces are at least half in shadow; the wall of the house reflects moonlight or streetlight, creating shadows of the porch column, the rocking chair, and the trees in the yard. There is also light coming from a window. The effect is of a very dark night lit up unevenly by pools of light. As the children run from the porch and sneak up on to the back porch of the Radley house, which both fascinates and frightens them, the subtle patterning of light and shadow creates a Gothic atmosphere. The Radley abode is a kind of ghost house, rearing up in the dark, leading the children into the fearful unknown. Again, each child's face, seen in successive medium-distance shots (so as not to lose the sense of their environment) is half in the dark and half in the light. This shows visually that they are half in the safe world of their neighborhood and half out of it, challenging their own boundaries, entering an unknown realm that they have built up to terrifying proportions in their imaginations. As they enter this world, the tension builds. When combined with other film elements, such as the sounds of the creaking gate and porch step, these patterns of light and shadow help to create an ominous atmosphere, perfectly preparing the viewer to see the huge and terrifying shadow of Boo. This spooky night world does indeed hold terrors, for both the children and the viewer.

---

second floor, and Scout and Jem hoist Dill up so he can see in the window. The grand jury is in session in the case of Tom Robinson, and Dill reports what he sees. When Atticus emerges from the courtroom, he is shocked to see the children and orders them go to home.

After they leave Atticus is confronted by Bob Ewell, the man who has accused Robinson of

raping his daughter. Ewell berates Atticus for taking the case. Atticus replies firmly that he intends to do the job he has taken on.

In the dark of the evening, the children decide to creep up on the Radley house. They scoot under a wire fence and reach the back porch. Jem peers in one of the windows to try to see Boo. A large shadow of a man appears, approaching Jem from across the porch. A shadowy hand reaches out. The children are terrified, but the shadow retreats. The children run away, but as they go under the fence Jem get his pants caught in the wire. In order to get free, he leaves his pants behind and runs home in his underwear. When they get home, Jem decides to return for his pants to avoid being punished by his father. As Scout counts slowly, waiting anxiously for his return, a shotgun blast is heard. Jem returns safely, and Atticus tells an alarmed Miss Stephanie that Mr. Radley shot at a prowler in his collard patch.

Summer ends. Dill returns home, and Scout must attend school for the first time. A tomboy, she is embarrassed at having to wear a dress (an incident that does not occur in the novel). At school, the impulsive Scout gets into a fight with Walter Cunningham's son (also called Walter), but Jem breaks it up and invites Walter home for dinner. During the meal, Scout protests when Walter pours too much syrup over his food. She is summoned to the kitchen, where the black housekeeper Calpurnia rebukes her for bad manners. Later, Atticus talks to Scout on the porch. Scout does not want to return to school, but her father gently advises her about how to get along with others.

One day, a rabid dog appears in the street. Sheriff Heck Tate arrives with Atticus, and the sheriff hands his rifle to Atticus. Atticus takes his glasses off and drops them on the street. He takes aim and shoots the dog dead. The watching children are astonished because they thought Atticus could not do useful things like that. The sheriff tells Jem that Atticus is the best shot in the county.

That evening, Atticus takes the children with him as he visits the Robinson family to talk to Tom's wife. While he is inside, the drunken Ewell appears. He lurches toward the car and stares at the children inside. When Atticus comes out of the house, Ewell insults him. As they drive off, Jem is shaken by the encounter, but Atticus tells him not to be afraid because Ewell is harmless, despite his aggression.

Later that evening, Jem is left alone while Atticus takes Calpurnia home. He is frightened by the noises of the night, but as he wanders around he discovers an old medal that has been placed in a knot-hole in a tree on the edge of the Radley yard.

Scout gets in another fight at school, and she explains to her father that the boy she fought had

said Atticus "defends niggers." Atticus tells her not to use that word, and he explains it is his duty to defend the man. He forbids Scout to fight, no matter what the provocation.

The children find more items in the tree: two figures carved from soap, a boy and a girl. They realize that the figures resemble themselves. Mr. Radley emerges and fills the hole with cement as the children watch.

In the evening, Jem shows Scout all the items he has found in the tree. They include a crayon, marbles, a whistle, a spelling medal (which used to be given to children at school), a watch, and a pocketknife. Jem also tells her about a mystery: the other night, when he went back to collect his pants, they were folded over the fence, as if ready for him to collect.

Summer returns, as does Dill. Tom Robinson's trial is to take place the next day, and Atticus decides to spend the night sitting outside the town jail so he can make sure Robinson is not harmed by a group of men from the town of Old Sarum who are out to cause trouble. During the evening, the children run to town and see their father sitting and reading outside the front door of the jail. They are about to go home when four cars arrive noisily. As the children watch from the bushes, the armed men get out of their cars and confront Atticus. They intend to lynch Robinson; Atticus tells them to go home. The children run over to see what is going on, and Atticus, fearing for their safety, orders Jem to go home and take Scout and Dill with him. Jem refuses to leave. Then Scout sees Walter Cunningham in the crowd of men, and talks to him in a friendly, conversational way, since she knows him. Embarrassed by the candor and innocence of the child, Cunningham and the other men lose their purpose and decide to go home.

### The Trial

The trial begins the next day. The courtroom is packed. The children have been told to stay at home, but they do not want to miss the excitement. The black minister, Reverend Sykes, allows them to join the black people, who all have to sit in the balcony that surrounds three sides of the courtroom.

Sheriff Tate testifies to solicitor Mr. Gilmer that Ewell had reported that his daughter Mayella had been raped. When Tate got to the house he found that the woman had also been beaten, and Ewell told him Robinson was the culprit. In cross-examination by Atticus, the sheriff admits that no doctor was called. Atticus also establishes that the woman's right eye had been blacked, and that she had finger marks all around her neck.

Then Ewell takes the stand. He testifies that when he came home he heard Mayella screaming, found Robinson attacking her, and chased him off. He is cross-examined by Atticus, who gets him to write his name on a piece of paper, establishing that he is left-handed.

Next, Mayella gives her testimony. She says she asked Robinson into her yard to break up a chifforobe (a dresser), saying she would give him a nickel. She went toward the house, but when she turned around, Robinson attacked her. Under cross-examination, she says her father is easy to get along with, but Atticus adds, "except when he's drinking." Mayella denies, though, that her father has ever beaten her. She is uncertain about whether she had ever asked Robinson into her yard before, and at first says she cannot remember whether he hit her in the face, but then she says that he did. She identifies Tom as her assailant. Atticus asks Tom to stand, and Atticus tosses a glass at him, which he catches with his right hand. Atticus then asks him to do the same with his left, but Tom replies that his left arm is useless; it was caught in a cotton gin when he was twelve. (The film departs from the novel at this point; in the novel, Tom's left arm is visibly useless and much shorter than the other. The tossing and catching of the glass does not occur in the novel.)

Confident he has made his point, Atticus asks Mayella if she is ready to say what really happened, but she just shouts out her accusations again. Then she runs from the witness stand.

Tom then takes the stand. He says that Mayella often asked him inside the fence to do chores. On the day in question, she invited him into the house to fix a door, but he saw nothing wrong with it. He was about to leave when she asked him to get on a chair and get a box down from on top of a chifforobe. When he was on the chair she grabbed him around the legs. He got down and she hugged and kissed him and asked him to kiss her back. He tried to run away and heard Ewell at the window say he was going to kill her. Then he ran away.

Under cross-examination by Gilmer, Tom admits he is strong enough to have caused Mayella's injuries but denies having done so. He says he

did chores for her because he felt sorry for her, a statement that does not go down well with Gilmer or the white spectators.

Later, Atticus sums up his case for the jury. He says there is no evidence that a crime took place and that the case should not have been brought to trial. He points out that because Tom's left hand is useless he could not have caused Mayella's injuries, which must have been caused by a left-handed person. Atticus argues that she lied about what happened because she knew she had broken a rigid code of their society that prohibits a white woman from making sexual advances to a black man. She now feels guilty, says Atticus, and must try to get rid of the evidence, the evidence being Tom Robinson. Atticus claims that both Ewells thought they could get away with their lies; they assumed the jury would not question the ingrained belief that whites tell the truth but Negroes lie and are immoral, not to be trusted around white women. Atticus concludes by saying his client is not guilty and the jury must acquit him.

Two hours later, the jury returns and gives a verdict of guilty. Atticus tells Tom he will appeal the verdict. As Atticus walks toward the exit, the black people in the balcony stand to honor him.

Later that evening, Atticus is informed by the sheriff that Tom Robinson is dead. Atticus explains to Miss Maudie Atkinson that Tom was being taken to Abbotsville so that he would be safe, but he got away and ran. A deputy ordered him to stop but he kept running. The deputy shot him, aiming only to wound, but he was off target and Tom was killed. (In the novel, Tom is shot seventeen times by a prison guard as he climbs a fence at the prison. Some time elapses between the verdict and the killing.)

Atticus goes to the Robinson family home to convey the bad news. Tom's wife Helen collapses. As Atticus leaves, he is confronted by Ewell, who spits in his face. Atticus takes one step toward Ewell, wipes his face with a handkerchief and walks past Ewell to his car. (In the novel, the spitting incident happens earlier and is not seen, only reported by Scout, who was told by Miss Stephanie it had happened on the street.)

### The Children Are Attacked

In a voice-over, the adult voice of Scout says that by the fall, life in the town had settled back to normal. She was looking forward to the Halloween pageant that October night and was going dressed as a ham.

Jem escorts Scout to the pageant, and when they return, Scout is still in her giant ham costume, having lost her dress. She and Jem pass through the woods on their walk home. The atmosphere is spooky, and Jem thinks he hears footsteps behind them. Then Jem is attacked by a shadowy figure who throws him to the ground. The figure then attacks Scout, but she is protected by her costume. Jem calls to her to run, but then he is knocked unconscious. The assailant turns his attention again to Scout, but a mysterious man, whose arms alone are shown, intervenes. There is a struggle, which Scout watches in horror. After that struggle ends, Scout watches as the second man carries the unconscious Jem home.

At the Finch house, after ascertaining that Scout is uninjured, Atticus summons the doctor and the sheriff. The doctor reports that Jem has a broken arm. When the sheriff arrives, he informs Atticus that Ewell has been found stabbed to death in the woods.

As Scout explains what happened, she says that the man who intervened to help her is standing behind the bedroom door. The sheriff moves the door to reveal a white-faced man with a scared but gentle expression on his face. The close-up is of Boo Radley. Scout smiles at him. After the men have left, Scout leads Boo to Jem's bed to say good night. Jem is still unconscious, but Boo, encouraged by Scout, touches Jem's head gently.

On the porch, Atticus says that Jem must have killed Ewell, but the sheriff tells him that was not so. They both look at Boo, who is sitting on the swing. The sheriff decides Boo is too delicate to survive the publicity that would surround him if a trial were to he held. He thinks that justice has already been done, since the innocent Tom is dead, and now Bob Ewell, who was responsible for the false accusation, is dead also. Therefore, the sheriff makes up a story that Ewell fell on his own knife. He explains his reasons to Atticus, who ponders the matter. Then Scout tells Atticus that she agrees with what the sheriff said, and Atticus silently agrees to go along with the deception. Atticus shakes Boo's hand.

In the closing scene, Scout walks Boo back to his house, holding his hand. He goes into his house, and Scout slowly returns home. Then the adult voice of Scout is heard again, in voice-over, recalling how she then understood Boo. She recalls more memories of her childhood, and the film ends with a long shot of the Finch house as Scout recalls how Atticus sat with Jem all night until he awoke in the morning.

Because the film runs only for a little over two hours, some major incidents in the novel are omitted. These include the snowstorm and the burning down of Miss Maudie's house, the damage Jem does to Mrs. Dubose's garden and his punishment of reading to her, and her death. Also omitted are the visit the children take with Calpurnia to the black church; the school pageant that Scout attends; and the visit of Aunt Alexandra, Uncle Jimmy, and Francis (Scout and Jem's cousin) to the Finch home. Some of the order of the incidents has been altered: in the novel the children discover the knot-hole in the tree much earlier, for example. Also, in the compression demanded by the film, some important details are omitted. The film does not mention that Ewell has a grudge against everybody he thinks was against him in the trial, including Judge Taylor, whose house he tries to burgle; Helen, whom he stalks and harasses; and Atticus, whom he directly threatens. It is, therefore, less a surprise in the novel when Ewell attacks the children than it is in the film. Other small details that give richness to the novel are omitted in the film. These include how the black people deluge the Finch family with food to show their gratitude after his defense of Tom Robinson, and that one juror, a member of the Cunningham family, initially voted in the jury room to acquit Tom Robinson.

## CHARACTERS

### Miss Maudie Atkinson

Miss Maudie Atkinson (Rosemary Murphy) is one of the Finches' neighbors. Maudie is a widow of about forty. In the novel, Scout spends a lot of time with her, sitting on her front porch. Maudie is friendly to all the children, allowing them to run in her yard. When her house is burned down one winter, she does not mind and looks forward to building a smaller house. Like Atticus, she has an interest in social justice. In the film, she has a fairly small role; she is a friend of the family and admires Atticus. She tries to comfort Jem after the trial verdict.

## Calpurnia

Calpurnia (Estelle Evans) is the black cook at the Finch household. In the film she is a young, attractive woman. She is trusted by Atticus, who regards her as a member of the family. To Scout, however, she is a resented authority figure. This is seen when Calpurnia rebukes Scout for her bad manners when young Walter Cunningham comes to dinner. Calpurnia sends her back into the living room with a slap on her rear. In the novel, Calpurnia is nearsighted and squints; she has been with the Finches since Jem was born, and has many battles with Scout, all of which she wins because Atticus always takes her side.

## Aunt Stephanie Crawford

In the film, Aunt Stephanie Crawford (Alice Ghostley) is Dill's aunt, but in the novel she is simply one of the neighbors who knows all the local gossip.

## Walter Cunningham, Jr.

Walter Cunningham, Jr. (Steve Condit) is Walter Cunningham's young son. In the novel, he has hookworms and goes around barefoot because the family is too poor to buy him shoes; he is nearly as old as Jem but has not yet finished first grade because every spring his father pulls him out of school to help with chores. He goes to school but has no lunch to bring with him. Scout picks a fight with Walter and rubs his nose in the dirt, but Jem invites him home for dinner, and he eats with relish.

## Walter Cunningham, Sr.

Walter Cunningham, Sr. (Crahan Denton) is a poor farmer who pays his legal debts to Atticus Finch in loads of wood, nuts, turnip greens, or whatever else he has. He is also one of the leaders of the group of men from Old Sarum who go to the county jail intending to lynch Tom Robinson.

## Mrs. Henry Lafayette Dubose

Mrs. Dubose (Ruth White) is a crotchety old lady who lives two doors down from the Finches. She sits on her porch in a wheelchair, attended by her black maid Jessie. Jem and Scout hate her because she always interrogates them and says they will make nothing of their lives. It is rumored that she keeps a pistol on her lap under her shawl. Mrs. Dubose appears in only one scene in the film, when she shouts at the children as they pass and is then soothed by Atticus's kind words. She plays a larger role in the novel. After Jem cuts the tops off all the camellia bushes in her yard, Mrs. Dubose orders him to read aloud to her six days a week. She hardly seems to listen to the reading. After she dies, however, Atticus explains to Jem that she was addicted to morphine as a painkiller but had decided to assert her will and come off the drug before she died. Atticus calls her courageous for doing so.

## Robert E. Lee "Bob" Ewell

Bob Ewell (James Anderson) is the head of one of the most wretched families in Maycomb. He lives on welfare but spends most of his money on whiskey while his many children go hungry. In the novel, Atticus tells Scout that for three generations, none of the Ewells has done an honest day's work, and the authorities no longer compel the children to go to school, since none of the Ewells wants an education. In novel and film, Ewell shows himself to be a liar, a perjurer, and a racist who beats his own daughter. He also insults Atticus, who makes the mistake of thinking that Ewell will do no real harm. But Ewell harbors grudges. In spite of the guilty verdict in the trial, he was shown to be a liar in court. His evil intent shows when he attacks and tries to kill Jem and Scout. In the film, Anderson does a fine job bringing out the malice and hatred that motivates the character.

## Mayella Violet Ewell

Mayella Violet Ewell (Collin Wilcox Paxton) is Bob Ewell's nineteen-year-old daughter. She is an angry, uneducated young woman who has a sad, lonely life without friends. She accuses Tom Robinson of rape because she is ashamed of having herself made sexual overtures to him. Her injuries were in fact inflicted by her father, but she has either blotted that out of her mind or is deliberately lying about it. On the witness stand she is defensive and brittle but also aggressive and defiant, refusing to acknowledge that she is not telling the truth.

## Atticus Finch

Atticus Finch is a defense lawyer in Maycomb; he is the father of Jem and Scout. In the film, he is played by Gregory Peck, a performance that won Peck an Oscar for Best Actor in a Leading Role.

Atticus is a widower; his wife died when Scout was two years old. In both novel and film, Atticus is often presented from the children's point of view. Although the children love their father, they think he cannot do much. All he does is work in an office in town, and he does not hunt or fish or do anything that the other men in Maycomb do. He says he is too old to play football. The children are therefore astonished and impressed when their father is able to shoot the rabid dog dead with one shot. However, it is not Atticus's way to boast of this kind of achievement.

Atticus is unfailingly polite and courteous to everyone, even Mrs. Dubose and Bob Ewell. This is part of his natural decency. He also tends to speak quietly, with a natural authority and wisdom in his words. In the movie, however, he does reveal some fire in his concluding address to the jury. He does not exactly raise his voice, but there is a controlled passion there as he says, "In the name of God, do your duty." His core beliefs in justice and righteousness are clearly audible and visible in this scene.

Atticus has high ethical standards, and he is always fair-minded and in control of himself. This is suggested visually in the film by the fact that he is usually seen in a three-piece suit, the vest carefully buttoned. This shows his dignity. His self-control is also shown in the film when Ewell spits in his face. Atticus maintains his composure in spite of his disgust; he chooses not to descend to Ewell's level and simply walks past him to his car.

Although he is willing to impose his authority on the children when necessary, Atticus prefers to teach them simply by advising them about how to behave in a way that takes into account the needs and feelings of others.

Atticus is a static character, a character who does not develop or change during the course of book or film. He is the same at the end as he was at the beginning. The ones who develop, the dynamic characters, are his children.

### Jean Louise Finch
*See* Scout Finch

### Jeremy Finch
*See* Jem Finch

### Jem Finch
Jem Finch (Philip Alford) is the son of Atticus Finch. He is nearly ten years old when the story begins. He is a voracious reader and a football fanatic. At the beginning of the film, Jem is just a kid who gets into mischief trying to get a sighting of Boo Radley. When Walter Cunningham, Jr., comes to dinner, Jem is jealous because Walter owns a gun but Jem's father will not let him have

one yet. (This occurs only in the film. In the novel, Atticus permits Jem and Scout to own air-rifles, but he refuses to teach them how to shoot.) As the film progresses, Jem starts to lose his innocence regarding the world around him. At first, he tries to show his courage by pretending not to be afraid of Boo Radley—an imaginary threat—but later, he discovers real menace when the drunken Ewell glares at him through the car window. Jem also takes a keen interest in the trial of Tom Robinson. He is naïve and thinks that because Tom is obviously innocent, he will be acquitted. He does not see how any jury could convict him. As a result of the verdict and the death of Tom, he learns about the existence of evil and prejudice in the world.

### Scout Finch
Scout Finch (Mary Badham) is the narrator of the novel, looking back on events that took place in the 1930s, beginning when she was nearly six years old. Mary Badham was ten years old when she played the role in the film, and she was nominated for an Oscar for Best Actress in a Supporting Role. In the film, the voice-over of the adult Scout looking back is performed by Kim Stanley.

Scout is a precocious girl, already able to read. She is also high-spirited and resents Calpurnia's authority over her. She thinks that the best way to settle an argument at school is to fight. During the course of the film and novel Scout learns a great deal about life, much of it in the form of moral education initiated by her father, but also directly from her own experience. She emerges from the childish world of imagination, in which her unseen neighbor Boo is a spooky presence, to the realities of a more complicated real world. In particular, she learns to have understanding and compassion for Boo. When she finally meets him in person, she befriends him. The film shows her taking his arm and helping him home, and it is clear that she has taken a big step in growing up.

### Mr. Gilmer
Mr. Gilmer (William Windom) is the prosecutor at the trial. In his cross-examination of Tom Robinson, he is sarcastic and insulting, repeatedly calling Tom "boy" and sneering at him.

### Charles Baker Harris
*See* Dill Harris

### Dill Harris
Charles Baker "Dill" Harris (John Magna) is nearly seven years old and small for his age when

he comes to Maycomb to stay with his aunt, Stephanie Crawford, for the summer months. (In the novel, his aunt is Rachel Haverford.) His family lives in Meridian, Mississippi. He tells Scout that he does not have a father, although later he says his father is president of a railroad company. Dill is a lively, intelligent boy with a good imagination. He says he has been up in a mail plane seventeen times and that he has seen an elephant, but Scout does not believe most of his stories. Dill gets along well with Jem and Scout, and they spend the summers playing together. In the novel, Dill even proposes marriage to Scout. Over the course of two years, Dill matures and, according to Scout's Aunt Alexandra, becomes a little cynical about life; he says he would like to become a clown and laugh at everyone, because that is the only sensible attitude to take to life.

### Arthur Radley

*See* Boo Radley

### Boo Radley

Arthur "Boo" Radley is the son (in the film) of Mr. Nathan Radley. He is played by Robert Duvall in his first film role. The novel explains Boo's background. He had a difficult upbringing by parents who kept to themselves and did not socialize with their neighbors. When he was a teenager, Boo got in with the wrong crowd; after some high-spirited pranks, many of the boys were sent to a state industrial school, but Mr. Radley refused to allow his son to go there. Instead, he confined Boo to the home, and Boo has not been seen for fifteen years. There are many rumors about Boo—that he is crazy and dangerous— and the children are scared of him and believe all kinds of wild stories about him. However, Boo turns out to be a kind and also courageous man. He leaves gifts for the children in the knot-hole of the tree, and he later saves their lives by rescuing them from Bob Ewell when Ewell attacks them. In one of the most memorable images of the film, Boo is finally seen in the bedroom of the Finch house after he has carried the injured Jem home. He has a pale appearance, like someone who never sees sunlight, and there is both fear and tenderness in his expression.

### Mr. Nathan Radley

Mr. Nathan Radley (Richard Hale) is the father of Boo Radley. Jem calls him a mean old man. He is seen in close-up covering over the knot-hole in the tree, and he glares fiercely at the children as they

watch. In the novel, there are two Mr. Radleys. After the older Mr. Radley, Boo's father, dies, his son Nathan, Boo's older brother, comes to live at the house. But this distinction is not preserved in the film, since it would have introduced a needless complication.

### Doctor Reynolds

Doctor Reynolds (Hugh Sanders) takes care of Jem when he is injured.

### Helen Robinson

Helen Robinson (Kim Hamilton) is Tom Robinson's wife. She collapses when she hears the news of Tom's death.

### Tom Robinson

Tom Robinson (Brock Peters) is a black man who is accused of raping a white woman, Mayella Ewell. He is innocent of the charge. Tom is a church-going married man who lives in what is considered the Negro portion of town, beyond the town dump. When giving evidence, he speaks respectfully and with humility. He is obviously a decent, honest man, and Atticus describes him as "a quiet, respectable, humble Negro." In the film, Brock Peters plays the character with a simple and moving dignity.

### Reverend Sykes

Reverend Sykes is the minister of the First Purchase A.M.E. (African Methodist Episcopal) Church. He takes the children to the balcony of the courthouse to watch the trial. In the novel, when Calpurnia takes Scout and Jem to church one Sunday, Reverend Sykes is determined to collect enough money from the congregation to help Helen, Tom Robinson's wife, make ends meet.

### Sheriff Heck Tate

Sheriff Heck Tate (Frank Overton) is the sheriff of Maycomb County. In the novel, he is a tall man who wears a belt studded with bullets, and his appearance terrifies Scout until she sees him in an ordinary business suit on the witness stand. In both novel and film, Tate is a decent, if not particularly outstanding, man who does his best to uphold the law. He is also strong-minded and is determined not to prosecute Boo Radley for killing Bob Ewell because he thinks that justice has already been done.

## Judge Taylor

Judge Taylor (Paul Fix) presides over the trial of Tom Robinson. He plays a small role in the film but the novel gives a richer portrait of him. An amiable white-haired man, he runs the court in an informal way and sometimes appears to be asleep, but he is more alert than people give him credit for. He runs the trial fairly, and Reverend Sykes tells Jem that his charge to the jury was fair-minded, perhaps even favorable to the defense.

## Other Characters

There are a number of characters in the novel who do not appear in the film. These include the first-grade schoolteacher Miss Caroline Fisher; the third-grade teacher Miss Gates, who hates Hitler's persecution of the Jews but speaks disparagingly of black people; Tom Robinson's employer Link Deas, a white man who speaks out in the courtroom in defense of Tom's character; Mr. Underwood, the owner, editor, and printer of the *Maycomb Tribune*, who writes an editorial bemoaning the senseless killing of Tom; Dolphus Raymond, a white man who lives with a black woman and has mixed-race children, and who drinks too much. In addition, there are other members of the Finch family who either visit or host the Finches for varying periods of time: Uncle Jack (Atticus's younger brother); and Aunt Alexandra (Atticus's sister), Uncle Jimmy, and their grandson, Francis. The wider cast of characters in the novel helps to create an in-depth portrait of the range of social and cultural attitudes in this small town.

## THEMES

### Childish Imagination and Adult Reality

The film begins with the children's world. Gradually, the specter of the adult world at its worst—the upcoming trial of Tom Robinson—is introduced. These two strands of the film alternate at first, as if they are parallel realities. They gradually begin to intersect, and the children learn of some of the evils in society.

Initially, Jem, Scout, and Dill spend their time playing in the long days of summer that appear to have no end. There is an early scene in which Scout is shown in bed, contentedly about to go to sleep, with her stuffed animal at her side, after an intimate talk with her father. This is the innocent, trusting world of childhood.

The only dark elements that enter this innocent world are the rumors the children hear about the dreaded Boo. Jem's imagination works overtime creating Boo as a scary, threatening figure. He says that Boo lives chained to a bed, he comes out only at night, his face is scarred, he eats cats, and he drools most of the time. Boo is like an ugly character in a fairy tale. Early in the film, Jem's way of showing his courage is to go up to the Radley porch and bang on the front door. This is his childish way of standing up to evil, but all the dangers in their childhood world are imaginary.

The children's first exposure to the turbulence of the adult world around them comes when they go to the courthouse to see the room in which Boo was once locked up. Instead, they find the courtroom in session as the grand jury hears the Robinson case. The big closed door dramatically shows the barrier between the children's innocence and the adult world and its business. Scout and Jem hoist Dill up to see into the room. Dill then describes what he sees in a childish way; he has no way of understanding the interactions of the adults he silently observes through the glass. For the first time the child's world and the adult world of the court case have intersected, but without the children's understanding.

For a while the two worlds, child and adult, continue on parallel paths, not meeting. They intersect again when Jem and Scout go with Atticus to Tom Robinson's home. This is where Jem, waiting in the car, encounters the menacing figure of Bob Ewell and hears the insult "nigger lover" spoken by Ewell to Atticus. This scene follows closely after the scene in which Jem was frightened by the huge shadow of Boo on the porch. However, Boo means Jem no harm; in contrast, Jem is now frightened by real evil in the form of Ewell, who does mean him harm. An imaginary evil has been replaced by a real evil. By being exposed to it, Jem has taken a step from childhood to maturity.

In the next scene, Jem is scared as he sits alone at night on the porch while Atticus takes Calpurnia home, but this is still the child's fear of the dark; what he will soon learn to fear, or at least to acknowledge and understand, is the darkness in people's hearts.

Scout's introduction to the Robinson case comes when a boy at her school says that Atticus "defends niggers," and she fights him.

The two worlds of adult and child now begin to intersect at more frequent intervals. The next

# READ.
# WATCH.
# WRITE.

- Watch and listen carefully to the trial scene, in particular Atticus's summing up to the jury. Then read Atticus's summing up in the novel. What changes have been made in the film version? Were these changes made simply to make the speech shorter, while keeping the content the same, or has the meaning of Atticus's speech been altered? Give an oral presentation in which you explain your findings, using PowerPoint to list your main points.

- Write an essay in which you discuss how the African American characters are portrayed in the film. Consider the portrayals of Tom Robinson, Reverend Sykes, Calpurnia, Robinson's family, and the black spectators in the gallery during the courtroom scene. How are these portrayals typical for the time in which the film was made? Why do you think that some African Americans, in spite of the fact that book and film are clearly opposed to racial prejudice, are critical of the way the black characters are portrayed?

- Working with another student, listen carefully to the music in the film. How does the music contribute to the overall effect? For example, watch the scene in which the children creep up on the Radley house. How does the music help to create a mood, and what mood is that? How does the music reinforce the children's view of the Radley house? How is this music different from that in the opening sequence? Give a class presentation in which you contrast the music in the opening sequence with that in the Radley house scene.

- Watch the last part of the film, in which Boo Radley appears, and then read the same section in the novel. Is the film faithful to the novel in terms of how Boo is presented? Robert Duvall's performance as Boo received high praise. How does he create the character and make him convincing, given that it is a nonspeaking role? Write a short essay in which you discuss these points.

example is when the children witness the ugly crowd that congregates outside the jailhouse, ready to lynch Tom. It is Scout's childish innocence that defuses the situation. She is too young to understand what is going on. Jem, who is older, has more grasp of it, and this shows in the trial scene. This is where the world of the child and that of the adult finally come together, as the children observe the trial from the gallery. The emphasis here is on Jem. There are at least six close-ups of Jem in the gallery, taking the entire spectacle in. He is devastated by the verdict, as the close-up reaction shot of him shows—he drops his head onto his arm. In another reaction shot a few minutes later, he is shown shaking his head. He is learning that injustice exists in the world, and it is a painful lesson. Another sequence shows Maudie Atkinson trying to comfort Jem on the porch of his home, but he is inconsolable. In the novel, Jem says to Atticus, "How could they do it, how

could they?" and he and his father later have a long conversation about the criminal justice system. All this is omitted from the film, which conveys Jem's distressed emotions in just a few wordless reaction shots. His body language says it all.

Scout also learns about justice and the delicate decisions that must sometimes be made about it. At the end of the film, she hears Sheriff Tate telling Atticus that he will not bring charges against Boo, instead settling on the convenient untruth that Ewell fell on his knife. After the sheriff leaves, Atticus stands for a moment, seemingly unsure of what to do. He has neither agreed nor disagreed with the sheriff. Scout comes across the porch and says to him, "Mr. Tate was right." Atticus then holds her, as if she has helped him to make up his mind. There is a subtle difference here from the novel, where Atticus tells Scout that Ewell fell on his knife and asks her if she

© *Pictorial Press Ltd. | Alamy*

can understand what he and Tate have decided. Scout says she does understand, and she thinks Mr. Tate was right. The film version makes Scout partly responsible for the decision her father makes, but either way, Scout shows a leap in maturity and understanding.

### Racial Bigotry, Class Divisions, and Injustice

There is a rigid separation in Maycomb between the races. This is shown visually in the trial scene, when the black people all have to sit in the gallery while the whites congregate below them.

There are also divisions between the whites in this rather rigidly stratified small southern town. Atticus Finch is a member of the professional class. Along with his neighbor, Maudie Atkinson, he has enlightened opinions about justice and society. Below the Finches on the social scale are people like the farmer Walter Cunningham, who is so poor he has to pay his debts in goods rather than money. There are many people like him in

Maycomb County, a rural area where the farmers have been hard hit by the Great Depression.

Cunningham and his ilk are poorly educated and have racially prejudiced views. They do not think for themselves about such questions; they act as a group, as they do when they converge on the courthouse prepared to lynch Tom Robinson. Although in the first scene in the movie, in which Walter appears, he is polite and respectful to Atticus and Scout, when the town's men get together in a group, they are capable of ugly deeds. It is from these poor country folk that the twelve anonymous men who serve on the jury are drawn. They cannot see beyond their own prejudice, ingrained in them all their lives. It is notable that in the film the jurors are never distinguished individually. They are never presented in close-up shots or in the center of the frame.

Below both the small professional class and the working poor in Maycomb are the Ewells, who are the lowest on the social scale. They are ignorant, uneducated people—at the trial Atticus pointedly asks Ewell whether he can write—and they are racial bigots. It seems they have to have someone to whom they can feel superior. Distressingly, the twelve local men on the jury still take the word of the disreputable Ewells against that of a black man. Bob Ewell may be despised, but racial solidarity still rules the day. Atticus is the shining example of a man who can hold up a mirror to the bigoted citizens of Maycomb and give them the opportunity to look at themselves and reflect. Unfortunately, the guilty verdict they hand down shows they are not capable of such rational thinking.

## STYLE

### *Symbolic Title Sequence*

The title sequence (also called the opening credits) acts as a kind of overture to the rest of the film, encapsulating its main themes from the child's point of view. The camera looks down from overhead as a young girl, who is singing and humming, opens an old cigar box. The camera moves closer, to reveal that the box contains a number of different items, including crayons, two figurines carved out of soap (one male and one female), a pocket watch, a pocket knife, a medal, marbles, a penny, a key, a pencil, and other items. These are the items the children have collected from the knot-hole in the tree; they are gifts from Boo, although, of course, the viewer does not yet know this. The camera tracks from left to right, showing some of the items in magnified close-up, this time including a black-and-white marble that rolls and collides with a black marble. The child is shown drawing with a crayon on paper. She draws what is intended to be a mockingbird, and then tears the paper in half, right through the figure of the bird. This foreshadows what will happen in the film. The mockingbird is a symbol of innocence. In the novel, Maudie Atkinson explains to Scout what Atticus meant when he told her it was a sin to kill a mockingbird: "Mockingbirds don't do one thing but make music for us to enjoy. They don't eat up people's gardens, don't nest in corncribs, they don't do one thing but sing their hearts out for us." In the film, these words are spoken by Atticus. There are two mockingbirds in the novel and film: Tom Robinson, an innocent man accused of a heinous crime, and Boo Radley, a shy, troubled man who means no one any harm.

Reinforcing the child's perspective in this opening sequence is the music. The very first thing the viewer hears, coming even before any of the images, is a simple tune on a piano, a series of notes played one at a time, exactly as a child would try to pick out notes on a piano and play a tune. This melody, later reinforced by a flute and other instruments such as bells and harps, recurs at key moments in the film to suggest the child's world.

### *Point of View*

The novel is narrated from the point of view of Scout, and the film frequently presents the story from her point of view. A shot taken from a child's point of view means that the camera shows what the child is seeing. Often such a shot will be immediately followed by a reaction shot of the child that shows the viewer how the child is experiencing that particular moment. The effect of this point of view is that the viewer can experience the child's way of seeing the world.

The child's point of view can be seen in the low-angle shots of Atticus, for example. In a low-angle shot, the camera is tilted up, so Atticus is seen as the child would see him. (This also has the effect of reinforcing the considerable authority that Atticus carries, in his roles as both parent and defense lawyer.)

The shots of the Radley house are all seen from the children's point of view and capture the spookiness of the house as it appears to them. Particularly notable is the empty swing that sways back and forth in the wind; it suggests to them the ghostly presence of Boo. When the children approach the house from the rear and see Boo's terrifying shadow, the entire sequence is from their point of view. It is especially notable in the three successive reaction shots, one of each child, as they see the shadow.

Other notable point of view shots include the children's climb up the courthouse steps and their sight of the big closed doors of the courtroom, and Jem's view of the drunken figure of Ewell getting smaller and smaller as Jem watches from the back seat of the car as Atticus drives away. The scene with the lynch mob at the courthouse also contains many shots from a child's point of view.

The child's point of view helps viewers recapture that imaginative way of seeing and understanding that characterizes a child's world. It also reminds viewers that the events portrayed, especially the trial, are important not only in themselves but for the effect they have on the children's growing awareness.

# CULTURAL CONTEXT

## The Great Depression

The novel and film are set in the South during the Great Depression, which began in October 1929 when the stock market crashed and lasted throughout the 1930s. The voice-over comment in the film that Maycomb County "had recently been told that it had nothing to fear but fear itself" is a reference to the famous words of President Franklin Delano Roosevelt, spoken during his first inaugural address on March 4, 1933.

In the Great Depression, rural areas that depended on farming were especially hard hit. Bartering systems sprang up, as shown in the film when Walter Cunningham pays his debts with goods. A doctor or lawyer might trade services for a chicken, or a grocer might trade food for clothing. In Alabama, where the novel and film are set, the Great Depression caused enormous hardship. In Birmingham, employment declined from 100,000 to 15,000. Relief agencies were overwhelmed.

Alabama voted overwhelmingly for Roosevelt in 1932 and again in 1936 and 1940. The New Deal programs Roosevelt created helped to revive the state's fortunes. These programs, including the Civil Works Administration and the Civilian Conservation Corps, provided employment.

## Jim Crow Laws

The racial segregation that is so important in the film was the result of what were known as Jim Crow laws. These were laws first enacted in the post-Civil War South that required legal segregation through separate facilities for black and white people. This included separate drinking fountains and rest rooms and separate sections within theaters, restaurants, and public transportation. The laws are named after a nineteenth-century minstrel character called Jim Crow, the last name being a reference to a black bird. Thus, a law having to do with blacks was known as a Jim Crow law. Jim Crow laws were gradually repealed in the decades following World War II, culminating in the Civil Rights Act of 1964, but they were very much a part of life in Maycomb County, Alabama, in the 1930s.

## The Scottsboro Boys

There was a real-life case in Scottsboro, Alabama, in the 1930s that resembles the situation in the film. In 1931, nine young black men, ages twelve to nineteen, were accused of raping two white women on a freight train the boys were riding illegally. Eight of the boys were quickly convicted by an all-white jury in a series of rushed and unfair trials. As in *To Kill a Mockingbird*, it was never established that the rapes did, in fact, occur. The convicted boys were sentenced to death, but their sentences were commuted by the Supreme Court. Instead, they served long prison sentences, ranging from six to nineteen years.

## Emmett Till

The case of Emmett Till took place in 1955, long after the time period in the film but still a timely exemplar of the situation in the South at the time of the film. Till was a fourteen-year-old African American boy from Chicago who was visiting his relatives in the South. He allegedly tried to flirt with a white woman in a grocery store. Days later, Till was kidnapped and killed by two white men, one of whom was the woman's brother. The two men were tried and acquitted by an all-white jury. Later, unrepentant and knowing they could not be charged again for the same crime, the men admitted their guilt. The case became nationally known and gave an impetus to the growing civil rights movement in the South. Although in the Till trial, white men are acquitted and in the fictional Tom Robinson trial, a black man is convicted, there are similarities between the two. As R. Barton Palmer notes in *Harper Lee's "To Kill a Mockingbird": The Relationship between Text and Film*, in both trials, "the law fails for precisely the same reason: the conflict between its abstract principles and prevailing community standards and beliefs." Palmer adds that the juries resolve their dilemma "by acting in ways that would ensure their continued good standing within their respective communities."

## Civil Rights Movement

*To Kill a Mockingbird* was published in 1960, when the civil rights movement was continuing to gain momentum. The movement had begun in 1955 in Montgomery, Alabama, when a black woman, Rosa Parks, refused to give up her seat on the bus for a white person. The success of the resulting Montgomery bus boycott led to a gradual desegregation of public facilities in the

*Hulton Archive | Getty Images*

South. In 1957, for example, President Dwight Eisenhower ordered the National Guard to Little Rock, Arkansas, to enforce a court order integrating Central High School. The novel and film were thus contributions to the growing national awareness of racial injustice in the South. Both works appealed to the national conscience, calling for a more enlightened social attitude on matters of race. In the film, however, the issues of justice and racial prejudice are more prominent than they are in the novel. As Palmer notes, the trial takes up 30 percent of the running time of the film but only 15 percent of the novel. In spite of this, the film softens the indictment of the justice systems at the state and local level that is noticeable in Lee's novel. For example, in the novel, the guards at the prison deliberately shoot to kill Tom Robinson, and they shoot him seventeen times, which strongly suggests excessive, racially motivated violence. In the film, the killing is an accident. The deputy shoots to wound, not to kill.

## CRITICAL OVERVIEW

*To Kill a Mockingbird* generally received high praise from movie reviewers. In the *Hollywood Reporter*, James Garner (quoted in Palmer's *Harper Lee's "To Kill a Mockingbird": The Relationship between Text and Film*) writes, "One of the finest pictures of this or any other year . . . a genuine experience, so penetrating and pervasive it lingers long after the last image has faded." In the *New York Times*, Bosley Crowther describes it as "a rewarding film," particularly the early

sequences showing Jem and Scout's adventures. Crowther comments, "The director, Robert Mulligan, achieves a bewitching indication of the excitement and thrill of being a child." However, when the issue of the trial emerges, involving the adult world, Crowther feels that the children are relegated to mere observers. He comments that it is "on the level of adult awareness of right and wrong . . . that most of the action . . . occurs. And this detracts from the camera's observation of the point of view of the child." In Crowther's view, this leaves the viewer in the dark regarding how the children feel about the events they witnessed.

Over the years, *To Kill a Mockingbird* has established itself as a classic. The American Film Institute ranked it twenty-fifth in a list of the greatest American films. In a recent review on the Web site *ReelViews*, film critic James Berardinelli showed that the film has lost none of its power to enthrall modern viewers. Calling the film "an astonishing motion picture by any standards," Berardinelli particularly admires Mulligan's direction, which "avoids grandstanding and allows the emotional power of the story to work without overt manipulation."

## CRITICISM

### Bryan Aubrey

*Aubrey holds a Ph.D. in English. In this essay on* To Kill a Mockingbird, *he discusses the differences between the novel and the film, and the character of Atticus as presented in the film.*

Novelists sometimes express dissatisfaction when their works are translated into the very different realm of film. Whereas a novel relies on the written word, a film is a predominantly visual experience. In an adaptation of a novel to the screen, carefully constructed literary themes and symbolism may get altered or obscured, characters may be misrepresented (at least in the eyes of the complaining author), long stretches of dialogue may be cut to a few pithy exchanges, and plots may get simplified and subplots eliminated so the film can fit into the running times of the average Hollywood movie. The extent to which a movie successfully represents the book on which it is based is often the subject of heated discussion by moviegoers as they leave the theater. Some people judge films by how closely they stick to their source, although it might also be argued that

# WHAT DO I SEE NEXT?

- *Twelve Angry Men* is a classic courtroom drama, based on a play by American playwright Richard Rose. The original film was made in 1957 and stars Henry Fonda. There was also a 1997 remake, starring Jack Lemmon. In the film, a young Hispanic man is charged with capital murder. The jury is made up of twelve white men. Eleven jurors believe the defendant is guilty, while one juror, defying group opinion, tries to persuade the others of the possibility of the man's innocence.

- *Intruder in the Dust* is based on a 1948 novel by William Faulkner, in which a black farmer (played by Juano Hernandez) in a small southern town is accused of murdering a white man. A lynching seems possible, but the man is eventually exonerated. The black-and-white film, directed by Clarence Brown, was made in 1949 and was nominated for two Golden Globe Awards in 1950.

- *Guess Who's Coming to Dinner* (1967) treats the topic of interracial marriage. This was a controversial subject when the film was made, since in seventeen U.S. states, interracial marriage was still illegal. It was legalized in the year of the film's release, by the Supreme Court ruling in the *Loving v. Virginia* case. In the film, a young white woman gets engaged to a black man she met on a vacation, and she brings him home to meet her parents. The film stars Spencer Tracy, Sidney Poitier, and Katharine Hepburn, and was directed by Stanley Kramer.

- *A Lesson before Dying* (1999), starring Don Cheadle, Cicely Tyson, and Mekhi Phifer, is a made-for-television adaptation of a 1993 novel by Ernest J. Gaines. It was released on DVD in 2000. Set in Louisiana in the late 1940s, the film features a black man who is falsely convicted of the murder of a white shopkeeper and has been sentenced to death. A black schoolteacher is persuaded to befriend him.

- *Inherit the Wind* (1960), starring Spencer Tracy and Fredric March and directed by Stanley Kramer, is a courtroom drama based on the famous Scopes Monkey Trial in Tennessee in 1925. John Scopes, a teacher, is prosecuted for teaching the theory of evolution in a public school. This film is another fine example of the cultural biases of the South in the early 1900s, as well as a classic courtroom drama. Based on a 1955 play by Jerome Lawrence and Robert Edwin Lee, the film received four Academy Award nominations.

- *The Learning Tree* (1969) is an adaptation of an autobiographical novel by Gordon Parks. Parks wrote the screenplay and also composed the music for the film. Set in small-town Kansas in the 1920s, the film is the coming-of-age story of an African American teenager as he learns to cope with a series of traumatic events.

---

the only valid question, bearing in mind the difference between the two media, is whether the film succeeds as a work of art in its own right, regardless of its fidelity to its source.

Harper Lee, the author of *To Kill a Mockingbird*, did not join the ranks of novelists dissatisfied with what the movie studios had done to their work. After she watched the film, she declared herself very pleased with it, grateful that her

story had been recreated as "a beautiful and moving motion picture" (quoted in R. Barton Palmer's *Harper Lee's "To Kill a Mockingbird": The Relationship between Text and Film*). She also commented that the film faithfully represented the novel.

In many respects, Lee was correct. The film preserves a great deal of the novel, including the main characters and their relationships, especially

> IN HIS MOST NOBLE ASPECT, ATTICUS STANDS FOR ENLIGHTENMENT, THE LIGHT OF REASON AND TRUTH. THIS IS BROUGHT OUT MOST VIVIDLY IN THE SCENE IN THE FILM WHEN THE MOB DESCENDS ON THE JAIL, READY TO LYNCH TOM ROBINSON."

Atticus and the children, and two major strands of the plot: the children's imaginative world as it relates to Boo Radley, and the trial of Tom Robinson in which Atticus Finch plays such as large role. No major details are altered, although the cast of characters is much reduced. There is no room in the film for the episode in which Jem damages Mrs. Dubose's flowers and is required to read to her as a punishment, nor does the film show the burning down of Maudie Atkinson's house or the visit of Aunt Alexandra, Atticus's sister. All these incidents are important for the novelist's re-creation of the life of a small town in the South during the 1930s, with its social rituals and seasonal events. However, the filmmakers needed to hold the viewers' attention with a building narrative rather than a series of self-contained episodes. With this in mind, they compressed the action, as Palmer points out, so that it takes place over a period of only one year, in contrast to three years in the novel. The filmmakers also reduced the number of incidents involving the children and increased the importance of the trial. In the novel, the first mention of the Robinson case does not come until chapter 9, and it does not assume much importance until chapter 15, just over halfway through the novel, when the lynch mob descends on the jail. In contrast, the film introduces the trial much earlier, after only about sixteen minutes, when Judge Taylor asks Atticus if he will take the case on (although he explains none of the details, as Atticus already knows about the case). A few minutes later comes the scene, written just for the film since it does not occur in the novel, when the children rush down to the courthouse and Dill reports on what he sees of the grand jury session. Immediately after this, Bob Ewell confronts Atticus, another incident that does not occur (at this time and place) in the novel. Overall, in the novel, the trial itself occupies about fifty

pages of a three-hundred-page book, but in the film it occupies proportionately about twice as much time. The effect is to give the viewer the impression that the main message of *To Kill a Mockingbird* is the call to overcome racial prejudice, while the children's adventures and their gradual maturation is presented as a secondary theme. The filmmakers' strategy correspondingly increases the importance of Atticus. This can be seen from the fact, as Palmer points out, that they introduce him in an important scene right at the beginning, with Walter Cunningham and Scout, in an incident that is much expanded from its occurrence in chapter 3 of the novel.

In terms of the dialogue in the film, in many scenes screenwriter Horton Foote was very faithful to the novel. He chopped and rearranged the dialogue where necessary for greater economy, and he showed a lot of ingenuity in doing so, but many of the most memorable lines in the film are exactly as Lee wrote them. Who can forget, for example, the dignity and determination of Sheriff Heck Tate—up to this point not a very forceful or decisive character—near the end of the film, when he says, referring to his decision not to drag Boo into the limelight for killing Ewell in self-defense, "I may not be much, Mr. Finch, but I'm still sheriff of Maycomb County and Bob Ewell fell on his knife." The force of the line is all in the acting. Frank Overton neither understates it nor charges it with too much emotion, but there is no mistaking the quick straightening of the coat that suggests a man rising to fulfill his obligations as he sees them and being absolutely certain he is doing the right thing.

Most of Tate's speech leading up to that point is taken almost verbatim from the novel, but there is one small but significant difference. In the novel Tate says, "There's a black boy dead for no reason, and the man responsible for it's dead." Tom Robinson of course is a man, not a boy. In the novel he is twenty-five years old, married with three children. "Boy" was the term often used by whites to refer to blacks of any age (as Bob Ewell does in the movie), reinforcing their perceived inferior status. The film softens this edge, not wanting to identify the well-meaning sheriff with this demeaning language. So in the film, Tate's line begins "There's a black man dead for no reason."

Even Atticus, in the novel, refers once to Tom as a "boy," but he does not do so in the film. To have allowed that would have been unthinkable; it would have been seen as a blemish on his immaculate fairness and sense of human dignity. In the film, Atticus is presented as an almost perfect character. Palmer points out that after Gregory Peck, who was very eager to accept the role, saw a rough cut of the film, he pressured the director and producer for a number of changes that would bring Atticus more to the fore, and the final result was, as Palmer notes, "essentially a hagiography [the story of a saint] of Atticus Finch, most of whose more obvious imperfections and limitations were . . . carefully and thoroughly eliminated."

This is not to say that Atticus is not an admirable and virtuous character in the novel. He is portrayed with great affection by Scout as she looks back at her childhood. It is Atticus who carries one of the themes of the novel, which is education. He is, as Scout says, able to explain everything and everyone. Atticus is, in short, an educator, even though his profession is that of a lawyer. He provides a moral education for his children. He teaches Scout the meaning of compromise and that a person should try to walk in other people's shoes in order to understand them and not judge them harshly. He explains that a man must honor his individual conscience. Atticus also serves as moral exemplar for the town in his courageous defense of Tom Robinson, although the townspeople offer him scant regard for so doing.

In his most noble aspect, Atticus stands for enlightenment, the light of reason and truth. This is brought out most vividly in the scene in the film when the mob descends on the jail, ready to lynch Tom Robinson. Atticus knows this may happen, and he deliberately puts himself in a vulnerable position. He has brought his own floor lamp with him, and a book. Not surprisingly, Atticus loves to read. He fully intends to spend the entire night sitting outside the jail to protect his client. It is an act of great courage.

In this scene, Atticus is first seen twice in long shot at the center of the frame, from the children's point of view. He is sitting reading under the light of the lamp. Just before the mob arrives he is shown, still in long shot, but not quite so far away, looking up from his book at the sound of the approaching cars. A medium shot then shows him steeling himself for the confrontation, the lamp at the top right of the frame symbolizing the light of reason and truth about to come face to face with the spirit of lawlessness and violence.

Another dramatic long shot from the perspective of the children who are watching at a distance shows Atticus and the lamp, small but still at the center of the frame, as the armed men get out of their cars and approach him. The entire frame is very dark except for the lamp and the light it sheds on the immediate surroundings. Atticus stands his ground. Fortunately, Scout's innocent intervention saves the day, but this does not take anything away from Atticus who, unarmed himself (in the novel he says that carrying a gun merely encourages others to shoot you), is prepared to face down a lawless mob. The scene is a wonderful evocation of how the light of truth, of reason, of justice, embodied in just one man of steadiness and clear purpose, can be stronger than a gang of violent individuals.

This scene is certainly Atticus's finest hour, and the final shot is memorable. After the mob and the children leave, Atticus, still immaculate in his three-piece suit, returns to his solitary vigil. He knows he has won, and he reassures Tom Robinson that the mob will not bother him again. The camera then reverts to the same long shot of Atticus with which the scene began, with the lamp illuminating just a small area in the surrounding darkness. Then there is a fade-out, which gives the impression, since the outer parts of the frame are already dark, of fading out from the outer to the inner. Since Atticus is in the center of the frame, he and the light shed by the lamp are the last to fade. All is black except that lone figure and the light. The light is still visible even after Atticus himself has been faded out. That sliver of light in a vast dark is the light that stands against the darkness of intolerance, prejudice, and violence. Although it may not be enough to save Tom Robinson from an unjust fate, it serves as a telling visual symbol of the message of the film. As long as there are people like Atticus to embody it, the light of truth will not be vanquished.

**Source:** Bryan Aubrey, Critical Essay on *To Kill a Mockingbird*, in *Novels for Students*, Gale, Cengage Learning, 2010.

### Richard Armstrong

*In the following review, Armstrong clearly lays out some of the main issues surrounding the film and novel: gender, class, and civil rights.*

When Harper Lee first submitted her manuscript of *To Kill a Mockingbird* to the publisher, she was told that it seemed more like a series of

> **IT IS SIGNIFICANT THAT TRADITIONAL GENDER CHARACTERISTICS ARE DEEPLY INVOLVED WITH ONE ANOTHER IN SCOUT, SINCE THE FILM IS MOST POIGNANTLY ABOUT DEFINING MASCULINITY."**

short stories than a novel. Echoing Lee's Alabama girlhood, Robert Mulligan's 1962 film often feels like a series of moments and parts, incidents in search of a film. Only after watching it several times do the parts merge. Like the cigar box in the opening credits, it is a treasury of scenes, each evoking the specific atmospheres of childhood.

Notice how we see the objects in the box in close up: pocket watch, safety pin, marble, pennies, crayons, a mirror, a whistle, wooden dolls. Indeed, the credits sequence recalls the trick photographs of familiar objects shot from unfamiliar angles that once appeared in children's comics and annuals. Seeing these objects in this way, we focus on their status as singular, rather unusual, things divorced from their purposes in the wider world. There is something obsessive about this sequence, as if we are examining clues in an investigation of events past but still somehow alive. As we shall see, this pregnant quality is significant to the moment the film appeared.

The de-familiarization of everyday objects is consonant with the film's overall perspective. We see Scout's experience through her six-year-old eyes so things, events and people do not come with the easy context and definition that they do for adults. Part of the film's achievement is to make us look at the world again and to see it in a fresh light. It is an achievement that has concrete and far-reaching consequences for the characters and for us.

### THE DIRECTOR

*To Kill a Mockingbird* was directed by Robert Mulligan. One of postwar America's most underrated directors, Mulligan made his name with his first film, the TV drama *Fear Strikes Out* (1957), an intimate and disturbing account of a baseball player's experience of mental illness.

Collaborating with producer Allan J. Pakula in the 1960s, Mulligan made a series of features for theatrical release. *Love with the Proper Stranger* (1963), *Baby the Rain Must Fall* (1965), and *Inside Daisy Clover* (1966) combined sensitive performances, a feeling for environment, and an exploration of character psychology that has come to seem increasingly seductive. *To Kill a Mockingbird* was the first of the Pakula-Mulligan collaborations. If critics have called these films ambiguous and fey, they remain the happy outcomes of unpretentious television camera work and editing combined with the enhanced production values available to feature filmmakers. It is worth comparing Mulligan's approach to performance and *mise-en-scène* in *To Kill a Mockingbird* with that of a Hollywood Tennessee Williams adaptation of the 1950s, such as *A Streetcar Named Desire* (1951) or *Suddenly Last Summer* (1959). Russell Harlan's unfussy cinematography and lighting bring a matter-of-fact quality to Mulligan's film that seems thoroughly naturalistic. Another characteristic of the Pakula-Mulligan films is their feeling for music. *Love with the Proper Stranger* is set in the world of New York jazz clubs. *Inside Daisy Clover* explores the life of a musical starlet during the 1930s. Notice how in the credits sequence in *To Kill a Mockingbird*, a child's singing seems to invoke Elmer Bernstein's memorable score, with its sure sense of American folk idiom.

### THE ACTOR

Scout's father is the lawyer Atticus Finch, played by Gregory Peck. Peck made his name playing a series of decent men standing up for just causes, becoming an icon of integrity and high-mindedness for American audiences in the middle decades of the twentieth century. With his dark looks and authoritative voice, in *Days of Glory* (1944) Peck was the Russian partisan fighting the Nazi invaders; in *Gentleman's Agreement* (1947), he was the undercover journalist rooting out anti-semitism. For David Thomson, Peck was a figurehead for a mass audience; 'a protagonist for middle American aspiration, pathfinder of the straight and narrow ... He is Kennedy-like, preferring to act in crisis, and always cosmetically vindicated.'

To defend the rights of Tom Robinson, the African-American accused of raping a white woman, whose trial forms the high point of the film, Atticus must stand up to the whole town. Peck's contemplative *mien* and measured tones entirely suit the role. Hollywood films like to show a thoughtful intelligent man become a man of action. He may admonish Scout for fighting at school, and merely sets his jaw when the father of the raped woman spits in his face, but Atticus is prepared to pick up a rifle to shoot a rabid dog straying into the town. Clumsily placing his reading glasses down in the dust, he briefly becomes an expert marksman. It is a scene that would have reminded some in the audience of Peck's backwoods hunter in *The Yearling* (1946).

Whilst the ornery Bob Ewell seems inarticulate, Atticus is articulate, coherent and assertive. During his cross-examination of Ewell's daughter Mayella, she hysterically accuses Atticus of fancy speechifying and high falutin' attitudes, railing as much against what Atticus represents as what he actually says. James Anderson and Collin Wilcox Paxton's performances depend on their ability to recall the backwoods temper of what Americans denigrate as 'white trash.' In his summing up, Atticus speaks of the 'cruel poverty and ignorance' which Mayella has had to endure all her life. The film is as much about class as it is about racial prejudice, a preoccupation resonating as much with the moment of its release as with the novel's Depression setting.

The climactic courtroom scene is organized so that Scout and Jem see their father from the gallery where the black spectators sit. There they can look down on the proceedings as if they took place on a stage. It is difficult to resist the impression that the characters are avidly enjoying a movie at the local cinema, agog at the hero's performance. If you think about it, a good many Hollywood films act as metaphors for the dynamics that are played out by the actors themselves. For example, in *Cape Fear* (1961), Gregory Peck played a lawyer in a small southern town whose family is threatened by a dangerous ex-convict whom he once defended. The 1991 remake cleverly subverted movie history by casting Peck as the ex-con's shady lawyer! Elaborating star trajectories is not the most interesting thing Hollywood movies do. But the use of space in the courtroom in *To Kill a Mockingbird* does tend to underline this movie's appeal as what critics and industry insiders call a star vehicle. As if this were not enough, Atticus' neighbour Maudie Atkinson (Rosemary Murphy) could be talking about Peck himself when she tells Jem: 'Some men in this world are born to do an unpleasant job for us. Your father's one of them.'

## THE CIVIL RIGHTS STRUGGLE

In his summing up, Atticus re-affirms that in the United States a man, no matter what his race, creed or status, is entitled to equal protection under the law. But *To Kill a Mockingbird* appeared at a particularly crucial moment in American history. In 1962 America was in the throes of the struggle for African-American civil rights.

Although slavery was declared unconstitutional after the American Civil War of 1861-1865, it would take another century before African-Americans could assume the rights that white Americans take for granted. The civil rights movement grew in strength and impetus throughout the 1950s and 1960s. Whilst lunch counters, restrooms (toilets) and other public facilities across the southern states were still segregated, in 1964 the Civil Rights Act declared discrimination based on race to be unconstitutional. In 1965 the Voting Rights Act gave African-Americans full suffrage. *To Kill a Mockingbird* appeared the same year as the Supreme Court ruled that segregation was unconstitutional in all transportation facilities. Also in 1962, President Kennedy sent federal troops to the University of Mississippi to quell riots attendant upon its first black student registration. (Remember: education is a key issue in *To Kill a Mockingbird*.)

Harper Lee's novel was published in 1960 and won the Pulitzer Prize in 1961. Although based upon the infamous Scottsboro trial, in which nine African-American men were tried and convicted for raping a white woman in 1931, the book chimed with more recent events. With the newspapers full of the civil rights struggle and the television news pumping pictures into living rooms across America, it is easy to imagine what an impact the film would have had on the mass audience for which it was intended. With hindsight, it seems the ideal Oscar candidate. *To Kill a Mockingbird* was a high profile release based on a best-selling book dealing with controversial subject matter. It starred Hollywood's paean of civic virtue. It was nominated for Best Actor, Best Director, Best Picture, Best Adapted Screenplay, Best Supporting Actress, and Best Art Direction. Peck received Best Actor, screenwriter Horton Foote received the Best Adapted Screenplay statuette, and Alexander Golitzen, Henry Bumstead and Oliver Emert received the statuette for Best Art Direction.

## JEAN LOUISE 'SCOUT' FINCH

*To Kill a Mockingbird* owes its moral centre to Scout and to Mary Badham who played her. Badham was nine when she was nominated for an Oscar. Pulling off the complex assignment of playing a little girl with all the spirit and energy of a tomboy yet all the imagination and sensitivity of the woman Scout will become, Badham brings a favourite Hollywood screenwriter's model to life. Her performance is natural, assured and never cloying.

Sweet and caring, Scout is also crafty and rambunctious! At the heart of many scenes is her refusal to act like little girls are supposed to. Many roles for mature Hollywood actresses depend upon this apparent contradiction. Think of Holly Hunter in *Broadcast News* (1987) or *Copycat* (1995), or Geena Davis in *Thelma and Louise* (1991) or *The Long Kiss Goodnight* (1996). Uncomfortable in the dress the Finches' maid Calpurnia makes Scout wear for her first day at school, Badham/Scout slouches and whines through the scene until deserting her breakfast and racing through the fly-screen door. Count up how many times you see Scout dashing along the streets of the town whilst adult extras sedately go about their business. At one point, she climbs inside an old truck tyre and Jem pushes it along the road, Scout rotating inside it. (The children constantly interact with their environment. How often do you see them swinging on gates or straddling railings? Do you remember taking your environment for granted as a child?)

When the lynch mob mass on the jail steps and threaten Atticus as he guards Tom before the trial, Scout races to be with him. As she charges through the mob we see the massed legs of the men as the camera barrels among them. As much of the film follows the children's adventures, we often see things at waist height. Their opinions and prejudices unavailable to the children, the men of the town seem mysterious and dangerous. Until the courtroom scene, Tom Robinson's story unfolds in scenes between adults, only becoming central to the film as she and Jem become curious about what's going on at the courthouse and Scout feels the prejudice of other children. We see Mr Cunningham (Crahan Denton) through her eyes as she speaks to him on the steps of the jail. It is a powerful scene, like others in the film that are dependent upon alignment of the audience's perspective with that of a child. Through a child's eyes, adults often seem inscrutable. Whilst Badham/Scout addresses Mr Cunningham straight to camera, Denton/Cunningham looks away, his hat obscuring his face. The tension in the scene arises from our being unsure what he is thinking or what he will do next. At last he looks straight at Scout and responds to her concern for him and his family: 'Thank-you, young lady.' By addressing Scout as 'young lady', he acknowledges both her true gender and her more genteel social status. Mr Cunningham's words reinforce distinctions that the film is anxious to uphold.

## GENDER AND CLASS

As the mature Jean Louise remembers her father saying: 'You never really knew a man until you stood in his shoes and walked around in them.' When we first meet Mr Cunningham, Scout learns that the Cunninghams are poor and poverty makes a proud man ashamed. When we next see Cunningham, he heads a lynch mob of farmers who, like him, were hit hardest by the Depression. Harper Lee's book was set during a period in American history when millions of men were out of work. Notice how in scenes with Cunningham, Atticus stands on steps, raising him slightly above the other man. The actor placement suggests a difference in social standing between characters. Notice that the Finches always have plenty to eat. At one point, Scout brings Cunningham's son back for dinner. Look how much of everything there is, as cinematographer Russell Harlan dwells on Atticus ladling sweet potato and spinach, the children tuck into plates of meat, and Cunningham Jr. drowns his meat in gravy!

Social standing is central to the problems the film works through. It is significant that traditional gender characteristics are deeply involved with one another in Scout, since the film is most poignantly about defining masculinity. *To Kill a Mockingbird* appeared at a time when millions of Americans were experiencing the most affluent and comfortable lives that any Americans had ever experienced. The economy was booming and unemployment was low. There was a young, dynamic and charismatic President Kennedy in the White House and much talk in academic circles of the 'Affluent Society'. America had come a long way in thirty years. For millions of Americans in the rich white suburbs of the 1960s this was how things should be and their values were the right values. The 1960s had seen the emergence of a college-educated white-collar class of lawyers, teachers and corporation executives whose trim grey suits and Kennedy crew cuts earned them the epithet 'Corporation Man'. Atticus does not belong to this generation, so does not conform to this image. But the film shows him as an educated man who can also act tough when necessary, answering whatever misgivings around the virility of the Corporation Man may have persisted in this traditionally masculine society.

Enjoying the highest standard of education provision in its history, in America in the 1960s, language and literature were prized among the dominant middle class which comprised most of this film's audience. *To Kill a Mockingbird* compares Scout's environment, full of books and knowledge, with that of the Ewells and the Cunninghams, in which more pressing needs have taken precedence. According to Jem, Scout had been reading 'since she was born'. Whilst the film illustrates Atticus and Scout's relatively affluent family life, we must infer from the court proceedings that Ewell sexually abuses Mayella and beats her when he is drunk. If Mayella is a gibbering idiot, Scout is a well-adjusted little girl, vindicating the liberal democratic ideal of a sensible diet, lots of affection, and a rounded education. One suspects that nobody ever called Mayella 'young lady'.

Most of *To Kill a Mockingbird* is shot in brightly-lit stable compositions that suggest an objective 'normal' environment. But in certain scenes, the film mobilizes conventions that suggest more menacing characteristics. When Jem makes his way onto the porch of the old Radley place, an apparently dilapidated shack often accompanied by 'spooky' music, Boo's shadow passes over him in spine-chilling fashion. When Bob Ewell appears out of the gloom at the Robinsons, demented and clawing at the car window, lighting and performance generate a Gothic atmosphere. When the children are attacked in the woods by a groaning figure, his spindly hand appears like a claw before Scout's petrified stare. (Indeed, this scene recalls the opening scene of Charles Dickens' *Great Expectations*). The style and execution of these scenes evokes horror movies such as *Frankenstein* (1931). In that film, a little girl is frightened by Frankenstein's Monster near a lake. What horror movies seek to do is to explore issues that are too controversial to be discussed in more mainstream genres such as melodrama, crime or soap operas. Horror movies use ghastly or monstrous images or effects as metaphors for real but 'difficult' problems such

as rape, incest or homosexuality. In *To Kill a Mockingbird* Ewell's excessive behaviour with his daughter is channelled into his Gothic representation. To the film's middle-class family audience, Ewell becomes a monster.

Because horrible gossip has surrounded the figure of Boo Radley, this gentle backward man has also become demonized. Boo's 'awful' reputation is carefully built up until the climactic moment when we actually see this quiet figure in Jem's room. The townsfolk don't understand so they have deployed metaphors that the film echoes with horror movie conventions. Like Cunningham, Bob Ewell is poor and feels less of a man for it. In an era when the Kennedy administration committed itself to conquering all social ills, Cunningham, Ewell and Boo Radley are seen as the victims of 'cruel poverty and ignorance.'

### TO KILL A MYTH...

Big mainstream releases like *To Kill a Mockingbird* tend to embody easily understood and assimilated attitudes. After all, expensive to produce, they must appeal to a wide range of people if they are to turn a profit. Seeing the film from an early twenty-first century perspective, what do you think of a white lawyer defending an African-American victim of racial hatred whilst keeping an African-American maid? How would an audience in America in 1962 have read this? How do you think contemporary African-Americans would have responded to that scene in which black people in the gallery rise in tribute to Gregory Peck's white lawyer defending their rights? How should we deal with the prospect of a little girl befriending a grown man with learning difficulties? Such questions invite us to ask why the film was made as it was and whether we have changed. Finally, how would you reconcile Atticus' philosophy with what you would see as you stepped out of an afternoon showing of *To Kill a Mockingbird* in a Mississippi picture theatre in 1962?

**Source:** Richard Armstrong, "The World in a Fresh Light: *To Kill A Mockingbird*," in *Australian Screen Education*, No. 35, Winter 2004, pp. 84–87.

### Dean Shackelford

*In the following review, Shackelford focuses on the loss of the female narrative voice in the film* To Kill a Mockingbird, *as well as a shift in focus from Scout to Atticus Finch.*

> AND IT IS PERHAPS THIS ELEMENT OF THE FEMALE VOICE IN HARPER LEE'S *TO KILL A MOCKINGBIRD* WHICH MOST MAKES HORTON FOOTE'S SCREEN ADAPTATION LARGELY A COMPROMISE OF THE NOVEL'S FULL POWER."

Aunt Alexandra was fanatical on the subject of my attire. I could not possibly hope to be a lady if I wore breeches; when I said I could do nothing in a dress, she said I wasn't supposed to be doing anything that required pants. Aunt Alexandra's vision of my deportment involved playing with small stoves, tea sets, and wearing the Add-A-Pearl necklace she gave me when I was born; furthermore, I should be a ray of sunshine in my father's lonely life. I suggested that one could be a ray of sunshine in pants just as well, but Aunty said that one had to behave like a sunbeam, that I was born good but had grown progressively worse every year. She hurt my feelings and set my teeth permanently on edge, but when I asked Atticus about it, he said there were already enough sunbeams in the family and to go about my business, he didn't mind me much the way I was.

This passage reveals the importance of female voice and gender in Harper Lee's popular Pulitzer Prize-winning novel, *To Kill a Mockingbird*, first published in 1960. The novel portrays a young girl's love for her father and brother and the experience of childhood during the Great Depression in a racist, segregated society which uses superficial and materialistic values to judge outsiders, including the powerful character Boo Radley.

In 1962, a successful screen version of the novel (starring Gregory Peck) appeared. However, the screenplay, written by Horton Foote, an accomplished Southern writer, abandons, for the most part, the novel's first-person narration by Scout (in the motion picture, a first-person angle of vision functions primarily to provide transitions and shifts in time and place). As a result, the film is centered more on the children's father, Atticus Finch, and the adult world in which Scout and Jem feel alien. As several commentators have noted, the film seems centered on the racial issue much more than on other, equally successful dimensions of the novel. Clearly, part of the novel's success has to do with the adult-as-child perspective. Lee, recalling her own childhood, projects the image of an adult reflecting on her past and attempting to recreate the experience through a female child's point of view.

That the film shifts perspectives from the book's primary concern with the female protagonist and her perceptions to the male father figure and the adult male world is noteworthy. While trying to remain faithful to the importance of childhood and children in the novel, Foote's objective narration is interrupted only occasionally with the first-person narration of a woman, who is presumably the older, now adult Scout. However, the novel is very much about the experience of growing up as a female in a South with very narrow definitions of gender roles and acceptable behavior. Because this dimension of the novel is largely missing from the film's narrative, the film version of *To Kill a Mockingbird* may be seen as a betrayal of the novel's full feminist implications—a compromise of the novel's full power.

Granted, when a film adaptation is made, the screenwriter need not be faithful to the original text. As Robert Giddings, Keith Selby, and Chris Wensley note in their important book *Screening the Novel,* a filmmaker's approaches to adapting a literary work may range from one of almost complete faithfulness to the story to one which uses the original as an outline for a totally different work on film. Foote's adaptation seems to fall somewhere in between these extremes, with the film decidedly faithful to certain aspects of the novel. His story clearly conveys the novel's general mood; it is obvious he wishes to remain close to the general subject matter of life in the South during the Great Depression and its atmosphere of racial prejudice and Jim Crow. Reflecting on the film, Harper Lee herself states, "For me, Maycomb is there, its people are there: in two short hours one lives a childhood and lives it with Atticus Finch, whose view of life was the heart of the novel."

Though admittedly Atticus Finch is at the heart of the film and novel, there are some clear and notable discrepancies between the two versions that alter the unique perspective of the novel considerably—despite what Lee herself has commented. Only about 15% of the novel is devoted to Tom Robinson's rape trial, whereas in the film, the running time is more than 30% of a two-hour film. Unlike the book, the film is primarily centered on the rape trial and the racism of May-comb which has made it possible—not surprising considering it was made during what was to become the turbulent period of the 1960s when racial issues were of interest to Hollywood and the country as a whole. Significant, though, are the reviewers and critics who believe this issue, rather than the female child's perspectives on an adult male world, is the novel's main concern and as a result admire the film for its faithfulness to the original.

Many teachers of the novel and film also emphasize this issue to the neglect of other equally important issues. In 1963 and again in the year of the film's twenty-fifth anniversary, the Education Department of Warner Books issued Joseph Mersand's study guide on the novel, one section of which is an essay subtitled "A Sociological Study in Black and White." Turning the novel into sociology, many readers miss other aspects of Lee's vision. In an early critical article, Edgar Schuster notes that the racial dimensions of the novel have been over-emphasized, especially by high school students who read it, and he offers possible strategies for teaching students the novel's other central issues, which he lists as "Jem's physiological and psycho-logical growth" (mentioning Scout's growth in this regard only briefly as if it is a side issue), the caste system of Maycomb, the title motif, educa-tion, and superstition. What is so striking about Schuster's interpretation is his failure to acknowl-edge that the issue of Scout's gender is crucial to an understanding not only of the novel but also of Scout's identification with her father. As femi-nists often note, male readers sometimes take female perspectives and turn them into commen-taries from a male point of view. Because the novel and film center so much on Atticus, he, rather than Scout, becomes the focus.

With regard to the film, I do not mean to suggest that Foote has not attempted to make some references to Scout's problems with gender identity. When he does, however, the audience is very likely unable to make the connections as adequately as careful readers of the novel might. Of particular interest are two scenes from the film which also appear in the novel. During one of their summers with Dill, Jem insults Scout as the three of them approach the Radley home and Scout whines, fearful of what may happen. As in the novel, he tells her she is getting to be more like a girl every day, the implication being that boys

are courageous and non-fearful and girls are weak and afraid (a point which is refuted when Jem's fears of Boo Radley and the dark are demon-strated). Nevertheless, what is most important in the scene is Scout's reaction. Knowing that being called a girl is an insult and that being female is valued less than being male in her small Southern town, she suddenly becomes brave in order to remain acceptable to her brother.

In another scene, as Scout passes by Mrs. Dubose's house and says "hey," she is repri-manded for poor manners unbecoming of a Southern lady. This scene occurs in both film and novel. However, in the novel Lee clarifies that the presumed insult to Mrs. Dubose origi-nates with Mrs. Dubose's assumptions as a South-ern lady, a role which Scout, in the novel especially, is reluctant to assume. The film's lack of a consistent female voice makes this scene as well as others seem unnecessary and extraneous. This is only one example of the way in which the superior narrative strategy of the novel points out the weakness of the objective, male-centered nar-ration of the film.

One scene from the film concerning girlhood does not appear in the novel. Careful not to sug-gest that the Finches are churchgoers (for what reason?), as they are in the novel, Foote creates a scene which attempts to demonstrate Scout's ambivalence about being female. As Scout becomes old enough to enter school, she despises the thought of wearing a dress. When she appears from her room to eat breakfast before attending school for the first time, Jem ridicules her while Atticus, Miss Maudie, and Calpurnia admire her. Scout comments: "I still don't see why I have to wear a darn old dress." A weakness of the film in this regard is that until this scene, there has been little indication that Scout strongly dislikes wear-ing dresses, let alone has fears of growing up as a female. The novel makes it clear that Scout pre-fers her overalls to wearing dresses, which is per-haps why Foote found it necessary to create this particular scene. However, the previous two cru-cial scenes, while faithful to the novel's general concerns with gender, create loose ends in the film which do not contribute to the success of the narration and which compromise the novel's feminist center.

The intermittent efforts to focus on the female narrator's perspective prove unsuccessful in revealing the work's feminist dimensions. As the film opens, the audience sees the hands of a small girl, presumably Scout, coloring. After the credits, a woman's voice, described by Amy Lawrence as a "disembodied voice exiled from the image," is heard reflecting on her perceptions of Maycomb. By introducing the audience to the social and spatial context, this first-person narrator provides a frame for the whole. The audience at this point, without having read the novel first, may not, however, recognize who the speaker is. As Scout appears playing in the yard, the viewer is left to assume that the voice-over opening the film is the female character speaking as a grown woman. The camera zooms down to reveal Scout and soon thereafter shifts to the standard objective narration of most films.

When the disembodied narrator is heard again, she reflects on Scout's views of Atticus after he insists she will have to return to school; yet, despite what her teacher says, father and daughter will continue reading each night the way they always have. Here the voice-over is designed to emphasize the heroic stature of Atticus and perhaps even to suggest that one reason for Scout's identification with him is his freedom of thought and action: "There just didn't seem to be anyone or thing Atticus couldn't explain. Though it wasn't a talent that would arouse the admiration of any of our friends. Jem and I had to admit he was very good at that but that was all he was good at, we thought" (Foote, p. 35). This intrusion becomes little more than a transition into the next scene, in which Atticus shoots the mad dog.

In the next intrusion the female voice interrupts the objective narration when, at school, Scout fights Cecil Jacobs for calling Atticus a "nigger lover." She states: "Atticus had promised me he would wear me out if he ever heard of me fightin' any more. I was far too old and too big for such childish things, and the sooner I learned to hold in, the better off everybody would be. I soon forgot. . . Cecil Jacobs made me forget" (Foote, p. 42). Here again, the first-person narration provides coherence, allowing the scene of Scout's fight with Cecil Jacobs to be shortened and placing emphasis on the relationship between Atticus and Scout. The subtext of their conversation could perhaps be viewed as a reflection of traditional views that women should not be too aggressive or physical, but this scene, coupled with earlier scenes reflecting social values, is not couched in terms of Scout's transgressive behavior as a woman-to-be. The female voice in the film is not used to demonstrate the book's concern

with female identity; rather, it reinforces the male-centered society which Atticus represents and which the film is gradually moving toward in focusing on the trial of Tom Robinson.

Another instance during which the female narrator intrudes on the objective, male-centered gaze of the camera occurs when Jem and Scout discuss the presents Boo Radley leaves for them in the knot-hole. At this point in the film, the attempt to convey the book's female narrative center falls completely apart. Not until after the very long trial scene does the camera emphasize the children's perceptions or the female narrator's angle of vision again. Instead, the audience is in the adult male world of the courtroom, with mature male authority as the center of attention. Immediately after the trial, the film seems most concerned with Jem's reactions to the trial, Jem's recognition of the injustice of the verdict in the Tom Robinson case, and Jem's desire to accompany his father when he tells Helen Robinson that Tom has been killed. Scout is unable to observe directly the last event, and, as a result, the narration is inconsistent—by and large from the rape trial to the end of the film.

The film does, however make use of voice-over narration twice more. In the first instance, the female narrator again provides the transition in time and place to move from the previous scene, the revelation of Tom Robinson's death to his wife, into the confrontation between Atticus and Bob Ewell. As the camera focuses on an autumn scene with Scout dressed in a white dress, Jean Louise prepares the audience for the climax, which soon follows: "By October things had settled down again. I still looked for Boo every time I went by the Radley place. This night my mind was filled with Halloween. There was to be a pageant representing our county's agricultural products. I was to be a ham. Jem said he would escort me to the school auditorium. Thus began our longest journey together" (Foote, p. 72). Following this passage is the climactic scene, when Bob Ewell attacks Scout and Jem and Boo Radley successfully rescues them.

Shortly thereafter, the camera focuses on Scout's recognition of Boo as the protector and savior of Jem and her, and for the remainder of the film, the narration, arguably for the first time, is centered entirely on Scout's perception of the adult male world. She hears Heck Tate and Atticus debate over what to do about exposing the truth that Boo has killed Ewell while defending the children. The movement of the camera and her facial expression clearly indicate that Scout sees the meaning behind the adult's desires to protect Boo from the provincial Maycomb community which has marginalized him—and this scene signifies Scout's initiation into the world of adulthood.

As the film draws to a close, Scout, still in her overalls which will not be tolerated much longer in this society, walks Boo home. For the last time the audience hears the female voice:

> Neighbors bring food with death, and flowers with sickness, and little things in between. Boo was our neighbor. He gave us two soap dolls, a broken watch, and chain a knife, and our lives. One time Atticus said you never really knew a man until you stood in his shoes and walked around in them. Just standin' on the Radley porch was enough...The summer that had begun so long ago ended, another summer had taken its place, and a fall, and Boo Radley had come out... I was to think of these days many times;—of Jem, and Dill and Boo Radley, and Tom Robinson...and Atticus. He would be in Jem's room all night. And he would be there when, Jem waked up in the morning. (Foote, pp. 79–80)

The film ends, when, through a window, Scout is seen climbing into Atticus's lap while he sits near Jem. The camera gradually moves leftward away from the two characters in the window to a long shot of the house. By the end, then, the film has shifted perspective back to the female voice, fully identified the narrator as the older Scout (Jean Louise), and focused on the center of Scout's existence, her father (a patriarchal focus). The inconsistent emphasis on Scout and her perceptions makes the film seem disjointed.

Noting the patriarchal center of the film, Amy Lawrence suggests the possibility for a feminist reading. She argues that the disembodied narrator—as well as the author, Harper Lee, and the characters of Scout and Mayella Ewell—provides a "disjointed subjectivity" on film which is characteristic of "the experience of women in patriarchy" (p.184). Such "disjointed subjectivity" is, however, missing from the novel, which centers on Scout's perceptions of being female in a male-dominated South. The novel's female-centered narration provides an opportunity for Lee to comment on her own childlike perceptions as well as her recognition of the problems of growing up female in the South. The feminine voice, while present in the film, receives far too little emphasis.

In the novel the narrative voice allows readers to comprehend what the film does not explain. Though some critics have attacked Lee's narration as weak and suggested that the use of first person creates problems with perspective because the major participant, first-person narrator must appear almost in all scenes, the novel's consistent use of first person makes it much clearer than the film that the reader is seeing all the events through a female child's eyes. Once the children enter the courtroom in the film, the center of attention is the adult world of Atticus Finch and the rape trial—not, as the book is able to suggest, the children's perceptions of the events which unravel before them.

Although it is clear in the film that Scout is a tomboy and that she will probably grow out of this stage in her life (witness the very feminine and Southern drawl of the female narrator, who, though not seen, conveys the image of a conventional Southern lady), the film, which does not openly challenge the perspective of white heterosexuals (male or female) nearly to the degree the novel does, does not make Scout's ambivalence about being a female in an adult male world clear enough. Because the novel's narrative vision is consistently first person throughout and as a result focused on the older Scout's perceptions of her growing-up years, the female voice is unquestionably heard and the narration is focused on the world of Maycomb which she must inevitably enter as she matures.

Furthermore, a number of significant questions about gender are raised in the novel: Is Scout (and, by implication, all females) an outsider looking on an adult male world which she knows she will be unable to enter as she grows into womanhood? Is her identification with Atticus due not only to her love and devotion for a father but also to his maleness, a power and freedom she suspects she will not be allowed to possess within the confines of provincial Southern society? Or is her identification with Atticus due to his androgynous nature (playing the role of mother and father to her and demonstrating stereotypically feminine traits: being conciliatory, passive, tolerant, and partially rejecting the traditional masculine admiration for violence, guns, and honor)? All three of these questions may lead to possible, even complementary readings which would explain Scout's extreme identification with her father.

As in the passage quoted at the beginning of this essay, the novel focuses on Scout's tomboyishness as it relates to her developing sense of a female self. Also evident throughout the novel is Scout's devotion to her father's opinions. Atticus seems content with her the way she is; only when others force him to do so does he concern himself with traditional stereotypes of the Southern female. Especially significant with regard to Scout's growing sense of womanhood is the novel's very important character, Aunt Alexandra, Atticus's sister, who is left out of the film entirely. Early in the novel, readers are made aware of Scout's antipathy for her aunt, who wishes to mold her into a Southern lady. Other female authority figures with whom Scout has difficulty agreeing are her first-grade teacher, Miss Fisher, and Calpurnia, the family cook, babysitter, and surrogate mother figure. When the females in authority interfere with Scout's perceptions concerning her father and their relationship, she immediately rebels, a rebellion which Atticus does not usually discourage—signifying her strong identification with male authority and her recognition that the female authority figures threaten the unique relationship which she has with her father and which empowers her as an individual.

Exactly why Scout identifies with Atticus so much may have as much to do with his own individuality and inner strength as the fact that he is a single parent and father. Since the mother of Scout and Jem is dead, Atticus has assumed the full responsibility of playing mother and father whenever possible—though admittedly he employs Calpurnia and allows Alexandra to move in with them to give the children, particularly Scout, a female role model. However, Atticus is far from a stereotypical Southern male. Despite his position as a respected male authority figure in Maycomb, he seems oblivious to traditional expectations concerning masculinity (for himself) and femininity (for Scout). The children in fact see him as rather unmanly: "When Jem and I asked him why he was so old, he said he got started late, which we felt reflected on his abilities and his masculinity." Jem is also upset because Atticus will not play tackle football. Mrs. Dubose criticizes Atticus for not remarrying, which is very possibly a subtle comment on his lack of virility. Later the children learn of his abilities at marksmanship, at bravery in watching the lynch mob ready to attack Tom Robinson, and at the defense of the same man.

Perhaps this is Lee's way of suggesting that individuals must be allowed to develop their own sense of self without regard to rigid definitions of gender and social roles.

Scout's identification with Atticus may also be rooted in her recognition of the superficiality and limitations of being a Southern female. Mrs. Dubose once tells her: "'You should be in a dress and camisole, young lady! You'll grow up waiting on tables if somebody doesn't change your ways . . .'." This is one of many instances in the novel through which the first-person narrator reveals Lee's criticism of Southern women and their narrowmindedness concerning gender roles. Even Atticus ridicules the women's attitudes. In one instance he informs Alexandra that he favors "'Southern womanhood as much as anybody, but not for preserving polite fiction at the expense of human life'." When Scout is "indignant" that women cannot serve on juries, Atticus jokingly says, "I guess it's to protect our frail ladies from sordid cases like Tom's. Besides . . . I doubt if we'd ever get a complete case tried—the ladies'd be interrupting to ask questions'." This seemingly sexist passage may in fact be the opposite; having established clearly that Atticus does not take many Southern codes seriously, Lee recognizes the irony in Atticus's statement that women, including his own independent-minded daughter, are "frail."

Admittedly, few women characters in the novel are very pleasant, with the exceptions of Miss Maudie Atkinson, the Finches' neighbor, and Calpurnia. Through the first-person female voice, Southern women are ridiculed as gossips, provincials, weaklings, extremists, even racists—calling to mind the criticism of Southern manners in the fiction of Flannery O'Connor. Of Scout's superficial Aunt Alexandra, Lee writes: ". . . Aunt Alexandra was one of the last of her kind: she has river-boat, boarding-school manners; let any moral come along and she would uphold it; she was born in the objective case; she was an incurable gossip." Scout's feelings for Alexandra, who is concerned with family heritage, position, and conformity to traditional gender roles, do alter somewhat as she begins to see Alexandra as a woman who means well and loves her and her father, and as she begins to accept certain aspects of being a Southern female. As Jem and Dill exclude her from their games, Scout gradually learns more about the alien world of being a female through sitting on the porch with Miss Maudie and observing Calpurnia work in the kitchen, which makes her begin "to think there was more skill involved in being a girl" than she has previously thought. Nevertheless, the book makes it clear that the adult Scout, who narrates the novel and who has presumably now assumed the feminine name Jean Louise for good, is still ambivalent at best concerning the traditional Southern lady.

Of special importance with regard to Scout's growing perceptions of herself as a female is the meeting of the missionary society women, a scene which, like Aunt Alexandra's character, is completely omitted from the film. Alexandra sees herself as a grand host. Through observing the missionary women, Scout, in Austenian fashion, is able to satirize the superficialities and prejudices of Southern women with whom she is unwilling to identify in order to become that alien being called woman. Dressed in "my pink Sunday dress, shoes, and a petticoat," Scout attends a meeting shortly after Tom Robinson's death, knowing that her aunt makes her participate as "part of . . . her campaign to teach me to be a lady." Commenting on the women, Scout says, "Rather nervous, I took a seat beside Miss Maudie and wondered why ladies put on their hats to go across the street. Ladies in bunches always filled me with vague apprehension and a firm desire to be elsewhere . . ."

As the meeting begins, the ladies ridicule Scout for frequently wearing pants and inform her that she cannot become a member of the elite, genteel group of Southern ladyhood unless she mends her ways. Miss Stephanie Crawford, the town gossip, mocks Scout by asking her if she wants to grow up to be a lawyer, a comment to which Scout, coached by Aunt Alexandra, says, "Nome, just a lady"—with the obvious social satire evident. Scout clearly does not want to become a lady. Suspicious, Miss Stephanie replies, "'Well, you won't get very far until you start wearing dresses more often'." Immediately thereafter, Lee exposes even further the provincialism and superficiality of the group's appearance of gentility, piety, and morality. Mrs. Grace Meriwether's comments on "'those poor Mruna'" who live "'in that jungle'" and need Christian salvation reflect a smug, colonialist attitude toward other races. When the women begin conversing about blacks in America, their bigotry—and Scout's disgust with it—becomes obvious.

Rather than the community of gentility and racism represented in the women of Maycomb, Scout clearly prefers the world of her father, as this passage reveals: ". . . I wondered at the world of women . . . There was no doubt about it, I must soon enter this world, where on its surface fragrant ladies rocked slowly, fanned gently, and drank cool water." The female role is far too frivolous and unimportant for Scout to identify with. Furthermore, she says, "But I was more at home in my father's world. People like Mr. Heck Tate did not trap you with innocent questions to make fun of you . . . Ladies seemed to live in faint horror of men, seemed unwilling to approve wholeheartedly of them. But I liked them . . . [N]o matter how undelectable they were, . . . they weren't 'hypocrites'." This obviously idealized and childlike portrayal of men nevertheless gets at the core of Scout's conflict. In a world in which men seem to have the advantages and seem to be more fair-minded and less intolerant than women with their petty concerns and superficial dress codes, why should she conform to the notion of Southern ladyhood? Ironically, Scout, unlike the reader, is unable to recognize the effects of female powerlessness which may be largely responsible for the attitudes of Southern ladies. If they cannot control the everyday business and legal affairs of their society, they can at least impose their code of manners and morality.

To Scout, Atticus and his world represent freedom and power. Atticus is the key representative of the male power which Scout wishes to obtain even though she is growing up as a Southern female. More important, Lee demonstrates that Scout is gradually becoming a feminist in the South, for, with the use of first-person narration, she indicates that Scout/Jean Louise still maintains the ambivalence about being a Southern lady she possessed as a child. She seeks to become empowered with the freedoms the men in her society seem to possess without question and without resorting to trivial and superficial concerns such as wearing a dress and appearing genteel.

Harper Lee's fundamental criticism of gender roles for women (and to a lesser extent for men) may be evident especially in her novel's identification with outsider figures such as Tom Robinson, Mayella Ewell, and Boo Radley. Curiously enough, the outsider figures with whom the novelist identifies most are also males. Tom Robinson, the male African American who has been disempowered and annihilated by a fundamentally racist, white male society, and Boo Radley, the reclusive and eccentric neighbor about whom legends of his danger to the fragile Southern society circulate regularly, are the two "mockingbirds" of the title. Ironically, they are unable to mock society's roles for them and as a result take the consequences of living on the margins—Tom, through his death; Boo, through his return to the protection of a desolate isolated existence.

Throughout the novel, however, the female voice has emphasized Scout's growing distance from her provincial Southern society and her identification with her father, a symbol of the empowered. Like her father, Atticus, Scout, too, is unable to be a "mockingbird" of society and as a result, in coming to know Boo Radley as a real human being at novel's end, she recognizes the empowerment of being the other as she consents to remain an outsider unable to accept society's unwillingness to seek and know before it judges. And it is perhaps this element of the female voice in Harper Lee's *To Kill a Mockingbird* which most makes Horton Foote's screen adaptation largely a compromise of the novel's full power.

**Source:** Dean Shackelford, "The Female Voice in *To Kill a Mockingbird*: Narrative Strategies in Film and Novel," in *Mississippi Quarterly*, Vol. 50, No. 1, Winter 1996, pp. 101–14.

# SOURCES

Berardinelli, James, Review of *To Kill a Mockingbird*, in *ReelViews*, http://www.reelviews.net/php_review_template.php?identifier = 864 (accessed May 27, 2009).

Corrigan, Timothy, *A Short Guide to Writing about Film*, 7th ed., Longman, 2009.

Crowther, Bosley, "'To Kill a Mockingbird': One Adult Omission in a Fine Film, Two Superb Discoveries Add to Delight," in *New York Times*, February 15, 1963.

"The Great Depression, the New Deal, and Alabama's Political Leadership," Alabama Department of Archives and History, in *Alabama Moments in American History*, http://www.alabamamoments.state.al.us/sec48det.html (accessed May 29, 2009).

Lee, Harper, *To Kill a Mockingbird*, J.B. Lippincott, 1960.

Mulligan, Robert, *To Kill a Mockingbird*, DVD, Collector's Edition, Universal Studios, 1998.

Nelmes, Jill, *An Introduction to Film Studies*, Routledge, 1999.

Palmer, R. Barton, *Harper Lee's "To Kill a Mockingbird": The Relationship between Text and Film*, Methuen, 2008, pp. 96, 134, 222, 243–44.

Pramaggiore, Maria T., *Film: A Critical Introduction*, 2nd ed., Allyn & Bacon, 2007.

Till-Mobley, Mamie, and Christopher Benson, *Death of Innocence; The Story of the Hate Crime That Changed America*, One World/Ballantine, 2004.

# *Typee*

## HERMAN MELVILLE
## 1846

*Typee*, by American novelist and poet Herman Melville, was the first of several adventure tales the author wrote based on his experiences at sea. As such, *Typee* is part novel, part travelogue, and part autobiography. Throughout the late 1840s and the 1850s the reading public was enthusiastic about these early sea adventures, which included not only *Typee* (1846), whose subtitle is *A Peep at Polynesian Life*, but also *Omoo: A Narrative of Adventures in the South Seas* (loosely a sequel to *Typee* and published in 1847), *Redburn, His First Voyage: Being the Sailor-Boy Confessions and Reminiscences of the Son-of-a-Gentleman, in the Merchant Service* (1849), *Mardi and a Voyage Thither* (1849), and *White-Jacket; or, The World in a Man-of-War* (1850). *White-Jacket* is often credited with helping put an end to the practice of flogging sailors on U.S. naval vessels. With the exception of *Mardi*, these early novels were critically acclaimed, but Melville's later, more thematically rich novels such as *Moby Dick* (1851), *Pierre; or, The Ambiguities* (1852), the short story "Benito Cereno" (1855) as part of the collection *The Piazza Tales*, and the posthumously published short novel *Billy Budd* (1924) are generally regarded as representing the fullest development of the author's art.

*Herman Melville* (*The Library of Congress*)

## AUTHOR BIOGRAPHY

Herman Melville was born on August 1, 1819, in New York City, although his family later moved to Albany, New York. After his father died in debt in 1832, Melville embarked on a series of occupations, including that of bank clerk, farmer, bookkeeper, and schoolteacher. His career as a seaman began in 1839 when he was a crew member on a ship that sailed to England and back. He then took a job on a whaling ship that sailed to the South Seas. There he deserted the ship with another sailor and made land in the Marquesas Islands, part of French Polynesia in the South Pacific. This incident, which took place in 1842, provided the germ of *Typee*. The trip was the start of an adventurous career at sea, which included time spent in Tahiti and the Hawaiian Islands, as well as a stint in the U.S. Navy.

Melville returned to the United States in 1844 and the following year began writing a novel based on his adventures. He actually found two publishers for the novel. The British publisher titled the book *Narrative of a Four Months' Residence among the Natives of a Valley of the Marquesas Islands*. The American publisher called the

book *Typee*. The novel was well received by the public, although some readers objected to its frank discussion of sexuality among the islanders. A "revised American edition" cut most of the offending passages, but these passages are likely to be restored in modern editions of the novel.

With *Typee*, Melville began a period of intense literary activity that culminated in the publication of his masterpiece, the allegorical whaling novel *Moby Dick*, and *Pierre*, a dark tale about an impoverished writer and his illegitimate half-sister. He followed these with *The Confidence Man: His Masquerade* (1857), a pessimistic tale about greed and charlatanism on a Mississippi riverboat. It was the last of his novels published during his lifetime. He also wrote short stories (the most famous of which is "Bartleby the Scrivener"), sketches, and poems, including a series of Civil War poems. Melville never earned a great deal of money from his writing—a total of just over $10,000 from all his books—so he supported himself in other ways, such as public speaking and working as a customs inspector. Meanwhile, he had recurrent bouts of depression, and his wife's family, concerned about Melville's financial instability and mood swings, regarded him as insane.

In the final years of Melville's life, *Typee* was still in print and available to book buyers. Ironically, what would be his most famous book, *Moby Dick*, was out of print. In the final months of his life he wrote the short novel *Billy Budd*, a morality tale about a simple sailor who is provoked by a false charge, lashes out at a ship's officer, killing him, and is hanged. The novel remained unpublished when Melville died on September 28, 1891, but it was finally published in 1924. Melville's death was hardly noticed in the newspapers, and for some twenty years he was a forgotten literary figure.

## PLOT SUMMARY

### Chapters 1–4

The novel opens as the narrator is aboard a whaling ship, the *Dolly*. The ship has not seen land for six months, little remains in the way of fresh food, and the ship's captain, Vangs, treats the crew with cruelty by overworking them, withholding food, and punishing them when they complain about conditions. The captain decides to sail to the Marquesas Islands to get

# MEDIA ADAPTATIONS

- A free audiobook version of *Typee* is available from LibriVox. The reading, by Michael Sherer, runs eleven hours and forty-three minutes.
- In 1958, a very loose adaptation of *Typee*, titled *Enchanted Island*, was released by RKO Radio Pictures. The movie stars Dana Andrews and Jane Powell and was directed by Allan Dwan. It is available in VHS format from VCI Home Video. Running time is ninety-three minutes.

provisions. The crew, including the narrator, look forward to making land, though they are apprehensive because of the islands' reputation as being inhabited by cannibals. After about a week, the ship arrives at the largest of the islands, Nukuheva, where the men discover a small fleet of French ships docked in the bay. The French have claimed the islands for France.

The narrator reflects on the influence of Europeans and Americans on South Sea islanders. He is troubled by a scene of debauchery that takes place involving the members of his crew and island maidens. He is also troubled by the islanders' treatment at the hands of the French, who appoint a puppet chief, Mowanna, and brutalize the islanders under a veneer of civilization. The narrator believes that the islanders would be better off, and more civilized, if they were left to themselves. He digresses into a discussion of the presumed "savagery" of the islanders, regarding this presumption as false.

Weary of life aboard ship, the narrator resolves to remain on the island until he can board another ship that will take him home. He decides to flee to a mountaintop that separates the bay from two valleys where the islanders live. One is home to the Happar tribe, which is reputed to be peaceful. The other is home to the Typee tribe. He resolves to keep clear of the Typee because of their reputation for ferociousness and cannibalism.

## Chapters 5–8

The narrator fears that the captain would prevent his escape if he knew about it. Thus, he keeps silent about his intentions until, one evening on deck, he encounters Toby, a quiet and capable sailor, and shares his plan, thinking it would be to his benefit to have a companion. Toby agrees to flee the ship with him the next day. The following morning, Captain Vangs gives the crew permission to spend the day on land. The narrator takes with him a few provisions and joins the crew onshore. A drenching rain falls, and the crew takes shelter under a bamboo structure. When sleep overtakes the rest of the crew, the narrator and Toby make their escape. The narrator details the rigors of climbing the mountain. The two men arrive at the top of the mountain ridge and look back at the ships in the bay. The narrator is thrilled to have made his escape.

The escape, though, is not without its difficulties. The narrator's bread has dissolved, and some biscuits Toby brought have turned into a gummy mass because of the rain. The two men are cold, wet, and hungry, and the narrator's leg is injured, possibly, he thinks, because a snake bit him. The men expected to see valleys on the other side of the mountain ridge, but instead they see only high ground. They wander about, then improvise a shelter, which fails to keep out the rain. Finally, they spot a valley, but they are uncertain about whether Happars or the Typee live in the valley, so they continue to explore their surroundings. The next morning they conclude that they need food and shelter, so they resolve to descend into the valley, regardless of the danger.

## Chapters 9–11

Toby and the narrator begin their descent into the valley. At one point they have to descend a deep ravine with a waterfall by lowering themselves down on tree roots. The descent does not get any easier when they have to get down from a rock wall by jumping into a tree, allowing the branches to break their fall. Now in the valley, the men come across a fruit tree and eat from it. Then they see a breadfruit that appears to have been put there, and as they approach, they spot a boy and a girl. The two islanders are apprehensive, but Toby and the narrator, using their limited knowledge of Polynesian as well as pantomime, indicate that they are hungry. They inquire whether they are among the Happars or the Typee, but they are uncertain about the response they get.

The two men follow the boy and girl to their village. The people in the village are curious about them and ask them questions. The village chief arrives and introduces himself as Mehevi. The narrator reveals his name as Tom, but the islanders cannot quite pronounce the name, so they call him Tommo. The chief asks Tommo a question that seems to be a demand that he choose between the Happars and the Typee. Tommo is uncertain how to respond, but the Typee are supposedly ferocious and he does not want to risk offending them, so he says "Typee . . . good." When the villagers laugh and become animated, Tommo and Toby conclude they are among the Typee, not the Happars. The villagers bring him a breadfruit dish called poee-poee and other food. The next morning, Mehevi appears and engages the men in conversation about the French. He calls a healer in to tend to Tommo's injured leg. He appoints a young man, Kory-Kory, to be the Americans' servant. Tommo and Toby meet Kory-Kory's father, Marheyo, and his mother, Tinor, along with several others at Kory-Kory's home. Tommo is immediately heart-struck by one of them, the beautiful Fayaway.

### Chapters 12–15

In the days that follow, the villagers treat Tommo and Toby with every kindness. Kory-Kory feeds Tommo regularly, even placing the food in Tommo's mouth, and bathes him in the stream each day. Mehevi takes the men to the "taboo groves," the tribe's sacred grounds. There they find a structure called a Ti and the area where religious observances, called the Hoolah Hoolah, are held. Roast meat is brought to the men. Toby refuses to eat it, believing it is human flesh, but Tommo concludes that the meat is pork.

Tommo's leg continues to be painful. Toby volunteers to go to Nukuheva to get medicine from the French. Marheyo leads Toby as far as the boundary between the Typee and the Happars. Some hours later, Toby is carried back, bloodied and beaten. After he regains consciousness, he explains that Happars attacked him but that fortunately a group of Typee found him. The men's assumption about the two tribes is overturned; the Happars appear to be the fierce tribe.

Commotion erupts at the news that French ships have arrived in the Typee bay. The villagers gather food and other items to take to the

French. Toby volunteers to accompany the villagers in another effort to procure medicine for Tommo. The party leaves and at sunset begin returning in small groups. Toby is not with them. Tommo finds Fayaway, who explains that Toby boarded one of the French vessels but that he plans to return in three days. Tommo is disheartened, but Fayaway and Kory-Kory continue to treat him attentively. Marheyo prepares a seaweed dish for Tommo, which Tommo does not like but eats out of politeness. Tommo describes at length how poee-poee is made.

### Chapters 16–18

This group of chapters details Tommo's life on the island in the absence of Toby. The islanders continue to treat him with kindness, but more and more Tommo feels that he is a captive. He explores the valley, but he is never allowed to go anywhere alone. Always with him is Kory-Kory and usually Fayaway; although riding in canoes by women is taboo, Tommo secures an exception that allows Fayaway to take a canoe ride with him. One day at the Ti, Tommo hears a rumor that ships have arrived. His hopes rise that Toby has returned, but Mehevi orders Tommo to remain in the Ti. Tommo later puts aside his clothing and begins to wear Typee clothing. The islanders are amused by his use of a needle to tighten the clothing. They are also intrigued by his razor, which he uses to shave an islander named Narmonee.

As the condition of Tommo's leg improves, he wanders around the valley more. He reflects on the life of the islanders and concludes that island life is superior to life in supposedly civilized countries. The islanders have all that they need, and they lead a peaceful life. Tommo never witnesses quarreling, and the people act with honesty and compassion. He even offers a defense of cannibalism, concluding that it is no worse than some of the brutal legal punishments used in European countries. Nevertheless, relations between the Typee and the Happars are strained, as evidenced by a skirmish that erupts between the two tribes.

An islander named Marnoo arrives, causing excitement in the village. Tommo is surprised to discover that Marnoo speaks English; he served on a ship that traveled to Australia, where he learned English. Marnoo is "taboo," meaning that he can travel about the islands and no one will bother him. Tommo questions Marnoo about Toby, but Mehevi puts an end to the discussion because it relates to Tommo's possible escape. Tommo is disappointed that Marnoo leaves.

### Chapters 19–23
This cluster of chapters details life on the island. At first, Tommo is disturbed because Mehevi and others—even Kory-Kory—appear to be annoyed with him, presumably because he was exploring avenues of escape with Marnoo. But this passes, and Tommo takes part in island life. He spends time at the Ti with the other men—women are not allowed in the Ti—where he enjoys conversation and the best food. His leg has largely healed, so he is able to move about freely. Tommo makes blowguns out of bamboo, to the delight not only of the children but also of the adults. Mehevi is intrigued by Tommo's shoes, so Tommo gives them to the chief, who wears them as a necklace. Tommo details a typical day, which consists of breakfast, pipe smoking, tending to chores, hut repair, checking food provisions, bathing, and the like. The islanders nap in the afternoon, and after a dinner of poee-poee, girls often dance before their huts. Tommo describes the process of making cloth, called tappa, out of the fibers of boiled tree branches. He also describes a medicinal spring and a series of ancient stone terraces.

One day at the Ti, Tommo learns that a festival is planned for the next day. He does not know its purpose, but he calls it the Festival of the Calabashes, since roast pig, poee-poee, bananas, and other foods are served in calabashes, or gourdlike bowls. Everyone dresses in their finest clothing for the three-day festival, which includes smoking, drinking the local liquor, and religious observances at the Hoolah Hoolah. Women whose husbands have been killed in battle mourn their loss.

### Chapters 24–26
In this sequence of chapters, Tommo turns into a bit of an anthropologist by describing, first, the religious practices of the Typee. He reflects on the belief among European missionaries that the islanders are savages, and he disputes this belief. With Kory-Kory, he inspects religious statues, including one of an ancient warrior chief. He learns that the Typee's chief god is called Moa Artua and that the island's chief priest, Kolory, performs a religious ritual that enables him to talk to Moa Artua.

Tommo then comments on the appearance of the islanders. He notes that all are fit, healthy, and attractive. Everyone in the tribe appears to be equal to everyone else, with the exception of the chiefs. While the chiefs' commands are carried out, they are not as imperious and formal as European kings, or even other South Sea kings. Tommo then describes the relationships between men and women. He notes that there are more women than men on the island and that typically each woman has two lovers. Sometimes the second lover actually moves in with the woman and her first husband. None of the men seem disturbed by this arrangement. Tommo contrasts these practices with those of other tribes, such as the Tahitians, where women have relationships with numerous men.

### Chapters 27–30
Tommo continues in the role of anthropologist. He notes (again) that he never witnesses any kind of quarreling, nor is there any evidence of crime. The islanders all get along and are generally unanimous in their opinions about matters. There does not appear to be much in the way of personal property other than such items as calabashes. Food, such as fish, is held in common and distributed to everyone in amounts based on family size. One night, a fishing party returns with fish and Marheyo goes to the Ti to get his portion. Tommo notes that the people eat fish raw and in their entirety. Tommo makes observations about the island's creatures. He learns that it is taboo to kill one of the island's dogs. He discovers a domestic cat and wonders how it got there. He takes note of the island's golden lizards and beautiful tame birds and the absence of mosquitoes and snakes. The island's weather is ideal, although there are frequent rains.

Tommo is walking with Kory-Kory. The two arrive at the hut of a tattoo artist named Karky. Karky wants to tattoo Tommo, but Tommo resists. Karky and Kory-Kory try to force him, but he pushes them away and flees. Later, Mehevi joins the effort to get Tommo's face tattooed, but Tommo is repulsed by the notion and manages to escape tattooing.

### Chapters 31–33
Tommo has been on the island for three months. After he describes the islanders' nighttime chanting, their musical ability with a flutelike instrument, and the process of making coconut oil used in the hair, events begin to come to a

climax. He returns to his hut to discover Marheyo and a group of men examining a package that contains three shrunken heads, including one of a European. He wonders whether the head is that of Toby. A week later, conflict breaks out between the Typee and the Happars. After a battle, the bodies of slain Happars are carried back to the village and taken to the Ti. Tommo is never allowed to witness what takes place at the Ti, but he strongly suspects that the village chiefs are engaging in cannibalism. His suspicion is confirmed the next day when he is allowed to visit the Ti. There he discovers a vessel that contains the half-eaten body of a Happar warrior. This incident, combined with the shrunken heads, renews Tommo's fears that the Typee might kill him and eat him.

Tommo is determined to escape. He believes that his best chance lies with Marnoo, who has returned to the village. He shares with Marnoo his desire to escape. Marnoo tells him to sneak away at night, then follow a certain path that will lead him to Marnoo's home; from there, Marnoo will take him to Nukuheva. Tommo keeps trying to sneak away, but the door to the hut makes noise that awakens the others when it is opened. When he tries to leave the door open, someone closes it. Tommo is increasingly frustrated.

### Chapters 34–Appendix–The Sequel

In the final chapter of the novel proper, Tommo makes his escape, despite the return of pain in his leg. He is told that Toby is at the Nukuheva Bay, and he begs Mehevi for permission to join him there. Mehevi finally consents, but as Tommo, Kory-Kory, and a party of islanders approach the bay, they learn that Toby is in fact not there. Tommo is detained in a hut by one of the chiefs, Mow-Mow. Tommo persuades Mow-Mow to release him, but a dispute erupts about whether Tommo should be allowed to go. When Tommo and others, including Fayaway, reach the water, they encounter a man named Karakoee, who is trying to buy Tommo's freedom. Arguing continues, and after Tommo embraces Fayaway, he leaps into the water. He and Karakoee are pulled into a boat, and with Typee warriors, including Mow-Mow, in pursuit, the boat is rowed away. Tommo is taken on board an Australian ship, where he discovers that Marnoo had informed Karakoee that he, Tommo, was being held captive. The Australian ship's captain came to rescue Tommo, who entertains the ship's crew with tales of his adventures on the island.

The novel contains an appendix that has nothing to do with the story. It concerns a dispute that arose about the behavior of Lord George Paulet in the Hawaiian Islands, then called the Sandwich Islands. Melville's purpose is to defend Paulet's behavior.

The novel concludes with a sequel titled "The Story of Toby." The story is written in Toby's voice. Toby assumed that his friend was dead, but with the publication of *Typee*, he learned that was not the case. He feels obliged to account for what happened to him. The reader learns that on the day he disappeared, he and the Typee accompanying him encountered a European named Jimmy, who agrees to help Toby escape and says that someone will return to release Tommo. Toby learns, though, that Jimmy is treacherous and has in effect sold him to the captain of a whaling ship. Toby feels forced to go, even though no one intends to rescue Tommo.

## CHARACTERS

### Fayaway

Fayaway provides a love interest for Tommo. Tommo frequently dwells on her physical beauty, including her blue eyes, long black tresses, and olive skin. He sees her as a kind of "Eve" to his "Adam," referring to the biblical story of the first humans in the Garden of Eden. She appears to be a kindly character, but she remains two-dimensional, for the reader never learns of her thoughts and motivations, and she rarely speaks. The reader does not know whether she returns Tommo's affections.

### Jimmy

Jimmy is a treacherous European who appears to be saving Toby but who is in effect selling Toby as a crew member on a ship and has no intention of seeing to it that Tommo is rescued. Like Marnoo, he holds the status of "taboo" and thus can move about the island freely.

### Karakoee

Karakoee is an islander who appears to live around the Nukuheva Bay and who plays a role in Tommo's escape from the island.

### Karky

Karky is a tattoo artist who expresses great enthusiasm about the possibility of practicing his art on Tommo.

### Kolory

Kolory is the chief priest of the Typee. He frequently conducts religious rituals and is believed to be able to communicate with the islanders' chief god, Moa Artua.

### Kory-Kory

Kory-Kory is a young man who is appointed to be Tommo's servant. He is depicted as kind, attentive, and industrious. He is a bit of a comic character, for he often has to engage in pantomime to communicate with Tommo, and his appearance, with two tufts of hair protruding from an otherwise shaven head, is comic as well.

### Marheyo

Marheyo is Kory-Kory's father and the husband of Tinor. He is depicted as kind and sympathetic to Tommo's plight. At the novel's conclusion, he supports Tommo's desire to leave the island and return to his home and his mother.

### Marnoo

Marnoo, like Mehevi, is depicted as noble and dignified, and Tommo and the islanders find him attractive. He is "taboo," so he is able to move about freely on the island in safety. He shows his kindness by helping Tommo escape.

### Mehevi

Mehevi is a chief of the Typee; although there are several chiefs, Mehevi appears to fulfill the role of king. He is striking in appearance, and Tommo stresses his nobility, dignity, and kindness. Mehevi is symbolic of the "noble savage" celebrated by the eighteenth-century French writer Jean-Jacques Rousseau, who believed that people were better when they lived in a state of nature, before the advent of civilization. Tommo frequently contrasts Mehevi with European monarchs, who rule with cruelty and scorn their subjects.

### Mow-Mow

Mow-Mow is a fierce, one-eyed Typee warrior who tries to prevent Tommo's escape in the boat that is rowed out to sea in the novel's climactic scene.

### Narmonee

Narmonee is a Typee warrior. Tommo uses his razor to shave Narmonee's head.

### Tinor

Tinor is Marheyo's wife and Kory-Kory's mother. She is industrious and a good cook, but beyond that her character remains undeveloped.

### Toby

Toby is Tommo's companion, and the two escape from their ship into the island's interior. Toby is described as quiet and a capable seaman. Like Fayaway, though, he remains two-dimensional, for he rarely speaks, and the reader learns little of his thoughts and motivations. He serves as a foil—that is, a contrast—to Tommo, for while Tommo is open-minded and willing to learn about Typee culture, Toby seems more skeptical, suspicious, and close-minded.

### Tommo

Tommo is the narrator of the novel, so everything the reader learns is from his perspective. During the early chapters of the novel, the narrator is unnamed. The islanders call him Tommo because they have difficulty saying just "Tom." Tommo is a young man looking for adventure and freedom. He proves to be open-minded about the Typee and their customs. He frequently reflects on the contrasts between the Typee culture and that of European Americans. He is a character caught between two worlds. On the one hand, he frequently argues that Typee culture is superior to that of civilization, and he tries to take part in Typee customs. On the other hand, he wants to escape from the island, even though he is treated with kindness. His refusal to be tattooed is symbolic of his unwillingness to fully immerse himself in the island's culture. Despite his admiration for the Typee and his strong attraction to Fayaway, he still feels the pull of his American roots and wishes to escape.

### Captain Vangs

Vangs, with a name that sounds like "fangs," is the cruel and despotic captain of the ship that carries Tommo and Toby to the Marquesas Islands. He stands in implicit contrast to a ruler such as Mehevi.

## THEMES

### *Colonization*

During the nineteenth century, the European powers, including France, Germany, Belgium, and Britain, established empires around the world. These countries maintained control over large swaths of Africa, the Middle East, Asia, and the Pacific. The chief motives behind this empire building were two. One was economic. The colonies provided a market for European-made goods, but more importantly they provided a source of raw materials, including wood, precious metals, jewels, foodstuffs, fabrics, minerals, and other items. In many instances, colonizers simply plundered these nations, but in at least some cases, colonizers believed that they could bring the benefits of civilization to nations that did not enjoy such benefits. The second motive was religious. In the eyes of many Europeans and Americans, the inhabitants of these lands were backward savages. Accordingly, they needed to be converted to Christianity. Although such a view is less widely held today, at the time many missionaries were sincere in their belief that traveling to these countries to convert the "natives" was their duty as Christians. Unfortunately, colonization usually meant exploitation. More importantly, it usually meant that indigenous cultures were disrupted and in many cases nearly destroyed by the influence of the colonizers.

The theme of colonization is implicit throughout *Typee*. When Tommo and his ship arrive at the Marquesas Islands, they discover that a fleet of French ships has already arrived and laid claim to the islands for France. Characters such as Jimmy have decided to stay on the island where *Typee* is set and in the process have become corrupted. Throughout the novel, Tommo reflects on the matter of colonization. A representative passage occurs in Chapter 4:

> The enormities perpetrated in the South Seas upon some of the inoffensive islanders well-nigh pass belief. These things are seldom proclaimed at home; they happen at the very ends of the earth; they are done in a corner.... But there is, nevertheless, many a petty trader that has navigated the Pacific whose course from island to island might be traced by a series of cold-blooded robberies, kidnappings, and murders.

In this respect, *Typee* was an early entry in a long list of anticolonial novels written during the nineteenth and early twentieth centuries,

perhaps the most famous of which is Joseph Conrad's *Heart of Darkness* (1902). These novels stressed the brutality of colonialism.

### *Return to Eden*

A common theme that runs through much early American literature is that the Americas represented a return to Eden, the biblical paradise that was home to Adam and Eve before they fell from God's favor and were driven out. In the consciousness of many early Americans, Europe represented decay, corruption, monarchy, and social structures that denied people their freedom. The Americas, with their vast resources and verdant lands, represented a kind of new Eden, a place where people could find redemption as part of a natural order of things. This search for an Edenic experience continued in the United States as the frontier was pushed ever farther west, but among eastern seaboard intellectuals such as Melville, American civilization was becoming as life-spoiling as old Europe. The search for Eden, then, often took the form of high-seas adventure. In places like the Marquesas Islands, Tahiti, the Hawaiian Islands, and others, Americans could find an idyllic world where people lived simple lives, uncorrupted by civilization, money, competition, industrialization, political structures, and the like.

Tommo stresses the Edenic nature of life on the island at virtually every turn. He regards himself as a kind of Adam, while Fayaway is an uncorrupted Eve before the fall and the expulsion from paradise. On the island, the people live in harmony with nature, which provides them with all their needs. The people are not driven by ideology, so there are few disputes, and they all live in harmony with one another as equals. The people are generally described as beautiful, healthy, and strong. They do not conform to the rigid morality of civilized societies, as evidenced by their sexual practices, marriage arrangements, and lack of shame about their bodies. In Chapter 17, Tommo reflects on the Edenic nature of the islanders' life:

> In a primitive state of society, the enjoyments of life, though few and simple, are spread over a great extent, and are unalloyed; but Civilization, for every advantage she imparts, holds a hundred evils in reserve;—the heart burnings, the jealousies, the social rivalries, the family dissensions, and the thousand self-inflicted discomforts of refined life.

The treatment of sexuality also illustrates the theme. When the ship arrives at the islands, the men (but not Tommo) take part in a scene of

# TOPICS FOR FURTHER STUDY

- Conduct an Internet study of the whaling industry in the nineteenth century. Try to answer such questions as: Why did Americans and the people of other nations hunt whales? How did they hunt whales? What would a typical whaling ship have looked like? Under what kinds of conditions did the crew of a whaling ship live? Present your findings in a PowerPoint presentation.

- At the time of the action of *Typee*, the South Sea islands were far away indeed, although European exploration of these islands began in the eighteenth century. Research the history of exploration of the South Seas. Who were some of the most well-known explorers? What did they find when they arrived at the various islands? How were they received by the inhabitants? Why did they tend to regard the inhabitants as "savages"? Create a map to orient your findings and trace the routes of explorers.

- During the same time period that *Typee* was written, the African continent was being colonized by Europeans. The nations of Europe turned large regions of Africa into parts of their empires. Prepare a timeline that compares the history of Asian and African colonization by European nations.

- Conduct research into the religious practices of indigenous cultures in Oceania, including but not limited to the Hawaiian Islands, Tahiti, the Marshall Islands, and others. Are there any commonalities in these cultures' religious beliefs and practices? How do they differ? In what ways have indigenous religions merged with Western religions, or with Islam? What role does the breadfruit that appears regularly in *Typee* play in religious traditions? Prepare a comparative report, perhaps using columns to trace similarities and differences.

- Watch the film version of the musical *South Pacific*, which is set on a South Sea island during World War II. The play and the film feature a wealthy French planter and a love story between a U.S. sailor and an island girl. Now imagine that you are Herman Melville. Write a review of the movie, recording the response you imagine Melville would have, based on his views in *Typee*.

- Read *The Greenlander* by Mark Adlard. It is a coming-of-age novel set during the height of whaling days. It focuses on a young sailor looking for excitement and adventure. Write an essay comparing Adlard's character Arthur with Tommo and Toby from *Typee*.

---

debauchery with island maidens. On board ship sexuality is seen as something depraved. On the island, though, sexual relations are seen as much more natural. They are not driven by lust or the desire to dominate but by genuine affection.

### Life at Sea

A relatively minor theme in *Typee* has to do with conditions of life at sea. While this theme is not stressed, it was important in all of Melville's sea tales, including not only his early novels but also his later masterpieces such as *Moby Dick* and *Billy Budd*. Conditions aboard whaling ships, naval vessels, and trading ships were harsh. The captain was often a despot—though he often had to be because the crew was made up of rough sailors who responded only to the lash. Floggings as a form of discipline were commonplace. That aside, ships often spent weeks if not months at sea, so food and fresh water were frequently in short supply. Men fell victim to disease because of poor nutrition and unsanitary conditions. The threat of shipwreck from storms was ever present.

Melville raises this theme early in *Typee*. The captain of the *Dolly*, Vangs, is given a

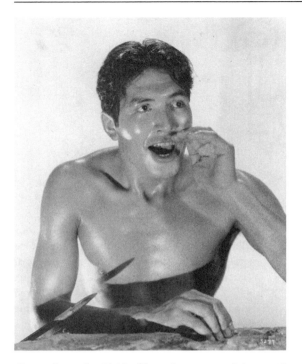

*Scene from the 1940s film adaptation of the novel*
*(Hulton Archive / Getty Images)*

name that sounds harsh and suggests his cruelty, as though he has "fangs." Tommo yearns to escape from the ship, which he and Toby do, trading shipboard life for the Eden of the island. In this respect, the ship becomes symbolic of the basic tension of the novel. The ship represents all that is wrong with civilization: its rigid social structure (captains, mates, crew), its disease, its crowded conditions, its dependence on technology, its dangers, and its essential cruelty. The ship becomes a microcosm of civilization, which Tommo wants to escape in his efforts to find himself. Having done so, he is able to make his escape from the island and find refuge on a ship where he and the men are treated well.

## STYLE

### First-Person Narrator

*Typee* is narrated in the first person by Tommo, and the events of the novel are filtered through his point of view. The novel does not explore the point of view of other characters, some of whom, like Kory-Kory and Fayaway, rarely speak.

Although a first-person narrator should generally not be confused with the author, in Melville's case, there are strong affinities between the author and his fictional narrator. The novel is in part autobiographical, based on Melville's own escape from a whaling ship. Further, many of the views that Tommo expresses are close to the views that Melville held. Some readers might find *Typee* rather unsophisticated as a work of fiction. The novel bears many characteristics of a travelogue or an anthropological treatise, with Tommo explaining at great length the things that he sees and experiences. Thus the reader is given explanations of how coconut oil and fabrics are made. The narrator expounds at great length on the religious and social practices of the islanders. This information does not arise organically from the novel's incidents but rather is presented in a form that seems almost nonfictional. *Typee*, though, was Melville's first attempt at fiction. He continued to serve his apprenticeship as a fiction writer in the novels that immediately followed it. In *Moby Dick* he returned to first-person narration much more effectively.

### Symbolism

In a larger sense, *Typee* as a whole could be considered symbolic. Tommo is representative of civilization. The island is representative of a kind of Garden of Eden. The novel then symbolizes the interaction of two widely different cultures, looked at from the perspective of an open-minded person eager to learn about the Typee.

Symbolism, though, is used in a more particular way. Many of the characters serve symbolic functions in the novel. Fayaway, with her beauty and simplicity, is symbolic of primitive innocence. Mehevi becomes symbolic of the idealized "noble savage." Jimmy, in contrast, becomes symbolic of corruption and greed.

More specific symbols include tattooing. Tommo is willing to enter into the life of the islanders. For example, he casts off his clothing and dresses like the Typee, and he is curious about all aspects of the Typee's life and culture. But he resists tattooing because he does not want to be marked with the symbols of primitivism and savagery. Another symbol is the ravine into which Tommo and Toby have to descend to reach the valley of the Typee. As they descend, they leave behind the more civilized, settled life of Nukuheva and enter into the more idyllic valley, with its lush greenery and great natural

# COMPARE
# &
# CONTRAST

- **1840s:** The practice of whaling is commonplace among American sailors, as well as sailors from other parts of the world.

  **Today:** Whaling is the subject of great controversy, as many people oppose the practice and are concerned about the survival of the species. Where it is practiced, whaling is subject to international treaties and government oversight.

- **1840s:** The search for lucrative colonies is widespread. European nations use their might to claim ownership of colonies in the South Pacific, Asia, Africa, the Middle East, and South America, a process that gains momentum throughout the century and into the 1900s.

  **Today:** Beginning after World War II, the European nations relinquish their colonies,

  and their former colonies become independent nations. Those that are still colonies are largely self-governing.

- **1840s:** Missionary activity is commonplace in colonies, with Catholics and Protestants establishing missions with a view to converting the people to Christianity.

  **Today:** While missionary activity continues, much of it has a more charitable purpose, with efforts made to alleviate poverty, provide medical care, educational opportunities, and the like. Indigenous religious beliefs are accorded more respect, and many Westerners who are born nominally Christian are adopting non-Christian belief systems.

---

beauty. The arduous experience is symbolically a reverse birth experience. The ravine can be regarded as a kind of birth canal through which the characters have to pass in order to arrive at a new kind of life. As a physical birth is a passage from the "innocence" of the womb into a world of harsh experience, the passage into and beyond the ravine is a passage from harsh experience to a world of innocence.

## HISTORICAL CONTEXT

During the mid-nineteenth century, Americans debated the issue of colonization. Although slavery continued to exist in the United States, the slave *trade* had been ended decades before by legislation. Slavery and colonization, though, were intertwined, for both had to do with European Americans imposing a way of life on supposedly primitive peoples and exploiting those peoples for their own economic gain. The Marquesas Islands were prominent in

that debate. Many Americans opposed colonization, just as they opposed slavery, but many Americans, too, supported the view that colonization was a way to bring civilization and Christianity to places like the Marquesas. The islands had been claimed by the British when they were discovered by the explorer Captain James Cook in 1774. In 1791 they were annexed by the French in the wake of the French Revolution and in the context of ongoing war between France and England. Then in the War of 1812, the islands became the first colony of the United States when they were claimed by Captain David Porter in 1813. Disputes over the islands among the United States, France, and Britain continued until just before Melville's arrival there in 1842. At that time, they were again under the control of the French. The effects of colonization on the islands were devastating; the historian Thomas Walter Herbert, in *Marquesan Encounters*, estimates that during the century, the islands' population declined from about 100,000 to under 5,000.

*Four young women in the Typee Valley* (*Eliot Elsofon* / *Time & Life Picture* / *Getty Images*)

## CRITICAL OVERVIEW

*Typee* was well received on both sides of the Atlantic. Most reviewers were taken with the adventure side of the novel. A reviewer in the London *Spectator* finds the novel "very interesting," though the reviewer faults it for its "tendency to make too much of things by writing about them." A reviewer in the London *Critic* finds the novel "a most entertaining and refreshing book," though the writer objects to the "obtrusive earnestness with which its author supports a favourite notion that savage is preferable to civilised life." A review in the London *John Bull* finds the novel "bewitching" and compares it favorably with Daniel Defoe's *Robinson Crusoe*. These reviews are primarily concerned with the book as a feat of storytelling.

A number of British reviewers take up the question of the authenticity of the novel. The book was written by a common seaman, a fact that some British readers, steeped in a caste system of educated officers and illiterate seamen, find hard to accept. A number of reviewers concede that they have no reason to doubt the novel's authenticity, but some do just that. An reviewer for the London *Times* writes that the novel "is introduced to the English public as authentic, which we by no means think it to be." The reviewer goes on to say, "We have called Mr. Melville a

common sailor; but he is a very uncommon common sailor, even for America, whose mariners are better educated than our own.... [H]is style throughout is rather that of an educated literary man than of a poor outcast working seaman on board of a South Sea whaler."

In the United States, a review in the New Bedford, Massachusetts, *Daily Mercury* calls *Typee* "a singularly attractive and delightful work," while Nathaniel Hawthorne, writing in the Salem, Massachusetts, *Advertiser*, concludes that "the narrative is skillfully managed, and in a literary point of view, the execution of the work is worthy of the novelty and interest of its subject." Similarly, Margaret Fuller, writing in the New York *Tribune*, asserts that the book is "a very entertaining and pleasing narrative." Fuller also praises Melville's ability to create "pretty and spirited pictures." Many American reviewers, including Fuller, commented favorably on the book because they wanted a wider audience exposed to the social issues the book raises.

Modern scholarship places less emphasis on overall evaluation of the work and more on the novel's grounding in historical fact. It also attempts to resolve some of the problems inherent in the type of novel Melville wrote; *Typee* poses difficulties for readers because it is part fiction, part travelogue, and part autobiography, difficulties that some of the early British reviewers alluded to. In an essay titled "The Early Novels," for example, Newton Arvin refers to the "real and equivocal quality of narrative that is constantly vibrating between the poles of 'truthfulness' and fantasy." Arvin concludes that "Melville is far too much the born artist not to keep bathing the plain truth in a medium of imaginative intensity." In *White Lies: Melville's Narratives of Facts*, John Samson tries to resolve the difficulty of balancing truth and fiction by arguing that "the history of the white culture's exploration, grounded in the dubious concepts of progress and primitivism, is itself fiction, every bit as much a romantic tale as Tommo's *Typee*. Melville's *Typee*, however, ... is an account of the collective fiction that is the white culture's history."

Milton R. Stern, in *Critical Essays on Herman Melville's "Typee,"* summarizes the directions that criticism of the novel has taken: "*Typee* criticism ... lends itself rather clearly to two summary conclusions. First, the early evaluations addressed four simple and defined issues (missionaries, primitivism, verity-and-verisimilitude, and storytelling)....

Second, evaluations since the 1940s have addressed one complex and amorphous issue (symbolic structures, subsuming myth, psychology, politics, and linguistics.... [T]he sophisticated examinations of *Typee* in the twentieth century are ... developments of the issues raised in the nineteenth."

# CRITICISM

## Michael J. O'Neal

*O'Neal holds a Ph.D. in English literature. In this essay on* Typee, *he explores the issue of point of view in Melville's first-person narration.*

Identifying the point of view in a novel such as *Typee* at first blush seems easy. From the first page it is apparent that the novel is narrated in the first person, by an "I" narrator who records events and shares perceptions and through whose consciousness the work is filtered. In general, the first-person narrator of a work of fiction is the central character. It is that character whose emotional and physical space the reader inhabits and who grows and changes as the novel proceeds. This is not always the case; some novels are told in the first person by a minor character who functions primarily as an observer and record keeper, but this type of novel is the exception rather than the rule. Clearly, in *Typee* the focus is on Tommo, the work's narrator and central character. The fiction the novel maintains is that this character has taken a trip to the South Seas, has lived for a period of time among the Typee, and has returned home to record his adventures for the benefit of anyone who might be interested.

The problem that *Typee* presents, though, is that Herman Melville really did take a trip to the South Seas, live for a period of time among the Typee, and return home to record his adventures for the benefit of anyone who might be interested. In this respect, the novel differs from a novel such as Mark Twain's *The Adventures of Huckleberry Finn*, also a first-person narration. While Twain based his novel to some extent on personal experience, the reader does not confuse Twain with Huckleberry Finn. Finn is entirely a fictional creation who might at various times express points of view that resemble the author's. But no reader thinks that *Huckleberry Finn* is an autobiographical novel. In contrast, *Typee* is very much an autobiographical novel,

and early readers and reviewers were intrigued with the question of how true, how factual, the novel really was.

From a literary standpoint, the narrative problem that Melville faced, and indeed that any writer of a first-person narrative faces, is that the narrator "knows" the work in advance. Sitting at his fictional desk, the fictional narrator has a bird's-eye view of his creation. He knows the outcome from the very first page. This problem is most difficult in any work of fiction that depends on mystery and suspense. Perhaps a classic example is Agatha Christie's *The Murder of Roger Ackroyd*, a classic murder mystery that keeps the reader in suspense as to the perpetrator of the murder until it is revealed that the narrator is the murderer. The narrator, though, "knows" that he is the culprit, so the narration has to carefully conceal that fact for the mystery to remain intact until the novel's climax.

Melville's novel does not create this kind of mystery. The only real suspense of the novel is the question of whether and how Tommo will make his escape, but the very fact that Tommo is "writing" the novel makes it clear that he has in fact escaped. Accordingly, the novel has to rely on other methods to sustain the fiction and to enter into the world that Tommo/Melville creates. In this sense, then, the point of view of the novel is not simply a matter of the mechanics of narration, of who is going to tell the story. Rather, narrative point of view becomes something closer to the everyday meaning of "point of view," that is, an attitude, a perspective on events and characters. Yet here, too, *Typee* raises questions, for it presents a picture of a man who arrives at the island bearing preconceptions about what he will experience. He enters into those experiences, but then he returns to his former way of life. So the fundamental question for the reader is this: Has Tommo changed as a result of his sojourn among the Typee?

Here is Tommo's reaction when he first learns that the *Dolly* is putting in at the Marquesas Islands:

> The Marquesas! What strange visions of outlandish things does the very name spirit up! Naked houris—cannibal banquets—groves of cocoa-nut—coral reefs—tattooed chiefs ... savage woodlands guarded by horrible idols—*heathenish rites and human sacrifices.*

Thus far, Tommo responds with the same prejudices as earlier European Americans. He

# WHAT DO I READ NEXT?

- *The Beach of Falesá* is an 1892 novella, or short novel, by Robert Louis Stevenson. The novella is a critique of imperialism and colonization and marks a departure from Stevenson's earlier romantic tales, such as *Treasure Island*, in favor of a grimmer, more realistic approach.

- Spanish-speaking readers can find Robert Louis Stevenson's *South Sea Tales* (1999), a collection of short stories, under the title *Cuentos de los Mares del Sur*.

- Robert Barclay's young-adult novel *Melal: A Novel of the Pacific* (2002) explores relationships between Americans and the indigenous inhabitants of a small island in the Marshall Islands in the South Pacific from a contemporary perspective.

- Melville's 1851 masterpiece, *Moby Dick*, is the definitive novel about whaling, but it is also a darkly allegorical tale about the ship's captain Ahab and his quest to hunt down and destroy the white whale that had taken off his leg.

- Joseph Conrad's 1902 brooding short novel *Heart of Darkness* is set in Africa, yet it takes up the theme of colonialism and what happens when the institutions of civilization intrude on indigenous cultures.

- Charles Nordhoff and James Norman Hall wrote a trilogy of novels, *Mutiny on the Bounty*, *Men against the Sea* (1933), and *Pitcairn's Island* (1934) that are fictionalized accounts of the famous mutiny that took place aboard *The Bounty* in 1789. The novels, and the film adaptations they led to, present a romanticized account of the mutineers' life on the South Sea island of Tahiti.

- K. R. Howe's *Nature, Culture, and History: The "Knowing" of Oceania* (2000) is a brief nonfiction examination of how Pacific islanders have been seen and represented by Westerners over the past two centuries.

- *First Contact* (1987), by Bob Connolly and Robin Anderson, is a work of popular anthropology set in New Guinea during the 1930s. It explores some of the themes in *Typee*, including the impact of Christian missionaries and colonial officers who impose their own versions of justice.

---

sees not only the exoticism of the islands but the dangers they pose from the heathen savagery of their inhabitants. Little time passes, though, before the narrator has concluded that the islanders are not in fact savages but that the Typee culture is superior to that of civilization. He states: "I must confess that I experienced something like a sense of regret at having my hideous anticipations thus disappointed."

In spite of the idyllic quality of life among the Typee, Tommo is eager to escape. He continues to have suspicions that the Typee plan to kill him and eat him; whenever his anxieties grow, his injured leg begins to throb. He remains a man caught between two cultures. He dresses as the Typee do, but he refuses to be tattooed. He enjoys the camaraderie of the men at the Ti, yet he discovers that the Ti is the site of cannibalistic rituals. He argues that the Typee are a peaceful race, yet they are in a state of constant tension, with outbursts of combat with the neighboring Happar tribe—in much the same way that Europeans live in fear and distrust of their own neighbors. He is enamored of Fayaway, yet he never seems interested in attempting to consummate the relationship.

In the novel's climactic scene, as Tommo and Karakoee make their escape from the pursuing Typee, here is the last image the reader is left with:

> By the time we had reached the headland, the savages were spread right across our course.... After a few breathless moments I discerned

Mow-Mow. The athletic islander, with his tomahawk between his teeth, was dashing the water before him till it foamed again. . . . [N]ever shall I forget the ferocious expression of his countenance. Only one other of the savages reached the boat.

The reader, then, is left with a fundamental question: Have Tommo's perceptions of the Typee truly changed? The Typee were "savages" at the beginning of the novel, and in our last glimpse of them, they are still savages, seemingly bent on killing Tommo simply because he wants to leave the island. These incongruities have several possible explanations. One is that Tommo is simply homesick, as anyone in his situation might be. A deeper explanation might be that individuals are a product of their culture; Tommo can no more "become" a Typee than he could become a member of another species. Perhaps, too, Melville is suggesting that Eden can also be a prison. Western thought has often posited the concept of the "fortunate fall," the idea that the fall of humankind and the expulsion of Adam and Eve from paradise was fortunate, for it gave humans the opportunity to redeem themselves and exercise their free will. Perhaps the incongruities are an expression of Melville's pessimistic view that widely differing cultures will always be at odds with one another. More optimistically, perhaps Tommo had to escape from paradise to make his case to a reading public who largely shared his preconceptions. In this sense, it is Tommo who is the Christian redeemer.

**Source:** Michael O'Neal, Critical Essay on *Typee* in *Novels for Students*, Gale, Cengage Learning, 2010.

### Owen Elmore

*In the following essay, Elmore links Melville's writing of* Typee *and* Moby Dick*, finding similar symbols and archetypal truths.*

As a young man, Herman Melville abandoned a whaling voyage to take up temporary residence among a tribe of Marquesan Islanders in the South Seas. The result of this experience is reflected in Melville's popular record of his stay in the Islands, *Typee.* This book employs a far different ethnographic method than that used in the majority of records of missionary and scientific exploration of cultural difference. *Typee* is filled with debasive-regenerate content, all of which appears designed to force Western readers to doubt their glorified self-opinions regarding civilized and/or virtuous behavior and to re-

> MELVILLE'S PERCEPTIONS HAD EXPANDED AS HE EXPLORED THESE MATTERS; THE HERMAN WHO WROTE THE *TYPEE* IS NOT THE SAME HERMAN WHO WROTE THE *MOBY-DICK* AND THE LATTER HERMAN WANTS TO MAKE AMENDS FOR THE FORMER."

examine religious, scientific, and other colonial procedures and goals in the South Seas. Melville's direct experience in the South Seas caused his doubt; by pulling readers vicariously through the beachcomber experience, he manages to make them doubters, too. For the author, the experience of the islands changed the world; the signified concept "human" could, and would, never again be encompassed by the limiting signifier "civilized Western man." That signifier had broken down for Melville, and the break down expanded from there; in *Typee,* you can feel his disillusionment unfolding in the writer's words as he, writing after the fact, ponders his discomfort over his ambivalence toward the Marquesans and the still unanswered questions about his experiences with them. As the inexorable expansion continues in Melville's mind, other signifiers begin falling for him, until, like a chain of dominos, signifiers topple into signifieds everywhere, and vice versa, on all intellectual levels; the young Melville, of course—as anyone would do to save his diffusing socialized self—quickly supplied new distinctions, but even as he did, as in Claude Levi-Strauss's admission of the limitations of structural linguistics, dimensions were reduced on one plane only to be increased on another. And once the contradictions start, they just kept coming. *Moby-Dick* is the result of the contradictions generated by Melville's experience in *Typee.*

In *Moby-Dick,* Ishmael's relationship with Queequeg is a direct outgrowth from, and a representation of, Melville's integration with the society at *Typee.* The deepest significance of this relationship can be shown through a closer examination of *Moby-Dick*'s unified central theme—a complex theme, much more difficult to generalize about than *Typee*'s. It seems very clear, however, that the experiences described in the *Typee* greatly influenced the complexity of the *Moby-Dick*. *Moby-Dick* is organically indiscrete; each part, no matter how small, connects both outwardly and inwardly to Melville's central theme of a mysterious, yet complexly unified universe; from animal to action, the ambiguous and ambivalent nature of Nature is always pervasive, making it possible to view even small pieces of the book to get to its stereoptic whole. Take, for instance, this passage from chapter 110:

> With a wild whimsiness, [Queequeg] now used his coffin for a seachest; and emptying into it his canvas bag of clothes, set them in order there. Many spare hours he spent, in carving the lid with all manner of grotesque figures and drawings; and it seemed that hereby he was striving, in his rude way, to copy parts of the twisted tattooing on his body, and this tattooing, had been the work of a departed prophet and seer of his island, who, by those hieroglyphic marks, had written out on his body a complete theory of the heavens and the earth, and a mystical treatise on the art of attaining truth; so that Queequeg in his own proper person was a riddle to unfold; a wondrous book in one volume; but whose mysteries not even himself could read, though his own live heart beat against them; and these mysteries were therefore destined in the end to moulder away with the living parchment whereupon they were inscribed, and so be unsolved to the last. And this thought it must have been which suggested to Ahab that wild exclamation of his, when one morning turning away from surveying poor Queequeg—"Oh, devilish tantalization of the gods!" (524)

The first short sentence connects the passage's ensuing parts with the book's larger motifs. The alliterative phrase "wild whimsiness" signals more of the unpredictability of action readers have, by chapter 110, grown accustomed to; that Queequeg's coffin, which had been living trees, is now a sea chest raises no suspicion when even the bones of whales have become human legs. In the box, where Queequeg had before set his body in order, he now orders his clothes. The interchange of form and usage and indeterminance of meaning of organic materials is so often a favorite thematic device of Melville's that we are prepared for, and satisfied by, the sea chest's eventual transformation into a lifebuoy. Next, a figure is drawn between the coffin/sea chest and Queequeg himself; just as the man's skin (which holds safe and ordered his internal organs) is inscribed, so Queequeg now inscribes his man-made, taxonomizing box. Besides this microconnection, there is also a macroconnection with the White Whale's

wrinkled, lined, inscrutable skin; hence, connections occur not just in singular space across time (diachronically), as in the transformations of the tree-coffin/chest/buoy, but in singular time across space (synchronically); the organic interweavings are complete and total. Something platonic, as well, is going on here, for if the marks on Moby-Dick's skin can be read as an original, heavenly form, then Queequeg, the tattooed human, is the whale's physical, earthly duplication, while Queequeg's self-duplicating inscriptions on his coffin/seachest/lifebuoy are humanity's artistic attempt at copying the copy of the original: it is Plato's "Third Bed" all over again—making Melville making his book, then, a fourth-generation attempt. The archetypal truths hammered out into the very human flesh of Queequeg are being transferred to the box—the box that will save Ishmael, who, significantly, will later tattoo himself in an effort to understand the whale, making his skin both light and dark, like Queequeg's; Ishmael makes himself over in Queequeg's image.

The symbols on Queequeg, though in his own language, carry a meaning that has been lost to all, making them as indecipherable as Ishmael's tattooings of whale measurements. Nevertheless, the indecipherable mystery holds power (indeed, the mysterious is powerful because it remains indecipherable: Moby-Dick is never caught and dissected, just as the tattoos remain unreadable), for this is the power Ishmael embraces both literally and figuratively when Queequeg's rendered coffin pops up from below as lifebuoy. Perhaps Queequeg's "living parchment" sank to the bottom to "moulder away," but that "wondrous book in one volume" survived on the coffin, survived with Ishmael, survives in Ishmael's book: *Moby-Dick*, the copy of a copy of a copy of . . . what? If there are any platonic "original forms," then they cannot be known, and to say you know them does not make them known or knowable. The impulse to know is a forgivable human weakness, but it was his mistake to think that he ever could know. There are no universal meanings—so far as they would be any good to us. Ahab makes this same mistake, thinking he can define the universal. What Queequeg's skin represents literally is Ahab's problem in the third and final sentence of the passage, akin to his unkillable whale problem, and Ahab's problem is the central conflict in the book. Although readers are spiritually with Ishmael as he is learning to accept life's ambiguities, we are also struggling—again, with Ishmael—with our ambivalent emotions regarding the Pequod's mad captain, Ahab. Why can we never decipher those marks, the ones on the savage as well as the ones on the White Whale? Ahab is our best hope; he is the mercenary for humankind, the "hired gun" strong enough, smart enough, or clever enough to track down the answers to the universe and make them serve rather than baffle and destroy. Here at the end of the passage, Melville is connecting the stuff of the book's center with the whole, and propelling the plot forward as he does. The symbols on Queequeg are a code just beyond cracking, and it is the very nearness of this cracked code that so tantalizes Ahab.

But the taxonomic box is a mere limiting concept, definitive of nothing really, despite the Western empirical scientific method of dissection and classification thinking itself the singular and valid way of knowing reality. The world, however, continues to develop according to its lights; Ahab's empiricism cannot check it. And we keep up only as long as Ishmael, the sole survivor of the Pequod, continues to catch on to Queequeg's transmogrifying box—Ishmael, the artist, the Westerner willing and capable of opening himself up to the ambiguities of otherness.

Here, very clearly, is the winding stream Melville's mind followed from *Typee* to *Moby-Dick*—a gradual process, accounting for why his questions and frustrations in the former book (which are the beachcomber-bricoleur's hesitantly shifting signifiers) are so much more agonistic and less subversive than Ishmael's artistic acceptance of ambiguity in all its forms. Melville's perceptions had expanded as he explored these matters; the Herman who wrote the *Typee* is not the same Herman who wrote the *Moby-Dick* and the latter Herman wants to make amends for the former. This is what we are seeing early in the book when Ishmael bonds with Queequeg: Herman getting another chance to embrace his "family" at Typee.

**Source:** Owen Elmore, "Melville's *Typee* and *Moby Dick*," in *Explicator*, Vol. 65, No. 2, Winter 2007, pp. 85–89.

### Rita K. Gollin

*In the following essay, Gollin finds Tommo's struggles to reach the ultimate paradise an allegory of the Garden of Eden.*

> IMPLICITLY CONFLATING THE IMAGE OF THE FORBIDDEN TREE WITH THE APPLES OF SODOM, MELVILLE SUGGESTS THAT APPETITES AND EXPECTATIONS ARE NEVER WHOLLY GRATIFIED IN THIS FALLEN WORLD."

Melville's readers from the nineteenth century to the present have interpreted Tommo's interlude among the cannibals in *Typee* as fulfillment of his quest for a primitive paradise. But the quest and its consummation are more complex. From the start, Tommo not only wants sensual pleasures; he perversely desires to encounter horrors. He finds both—on the island, among the Typees, and within himself.

During Tommo's struggles near the beginning of *Typee* to reach the idyllic paradise he and Toby hope to find on Nukuheva, Melville uses the Garden of Eden as an analogue both for anticipated delights and ensuing disappointments. When Tommo first sees the beautiful Typee valley from on high, much as Satan first viewed Eden in *Paradise Lost,* an analogue, conditional in structure, expresses his admiration: "Had a glimpse of the gardens of Paradise been revealed to me I could scarcely have been more ravished with the sight." But the paradise proves hard to reach: the young men climb a hazardous course up and down intervening ridges; and by the time they reach a tempting stream, Tommo is feverishly thirsty.

Again he anticipates physical delight, this time of a more immediate kind: "What a delicious sensation was I now to experience! I paused for a second to concentrate all my capabilities of enjoyment, and then immerged my lips in the clear element before me." The result is an unpleasant shock. Once again Tommo uses a conditional analogue, this time of a lost Paradise instead of an imminent one: "Had the apples of Sodom turned to ashes in my mouth, I could not have felt a more startling revulsion. A single drop of the cold fluid seemed to freeze every drop of blood in my body.... I fairly loathed the water." The water does not provide refreshment but "death-like chills."

Melville's allusion to the apples of Sodom derives from God's punishment of the fallen angels in *Paradise Lost*. They are turned into serpents and, like Tommo, feel "parch't with scalding thirst." God then creates a fruit grove "to aggravate / Thir penanace," and "greedily they pluck'd / The fruitage fair to sight, like that which grew / Near that bituminous Lake where *Sodom* flam'd." But the serpents "instead of Fruit / Chew'd bitter Ashes, which th'offended taste / With spattering noise rejected" (*PL* X, 547–567). Like Tommo, the serpents suffer frustration of appetite in a world after the fall.

The scene of the serpents plucking fruit apparently remained in Melville's mind as he described the first fruits Tommo and Toby pick in the Typee valley. After completing their dangerous descent, the hungry young men see fruit trees, and greedily race toward them. Toby picks some of the fruit; but "to our chagrin they proved to be much decayed; the rinds partly opened by the birds, and their hearts half devoured." Once again, hope of simple physical gratification is thwarted; but the fruit is not as repellent as the freezing water. In fact, despite the decay, the fruit is delicious. It thus offers an emblematic foretaste of life in the Typee valley.

Two earlier passages also associate Tommo with serpents, both immediately preceding his Satanic glimpse of the Paradise he will soon defile. The first describes Tommo and Toby crawling to avoid detection as they approach Nukuheva's first summit, "screened from observation by the grass through which we glided, much in the fashion of a couple of serpents." In the second and more portentous passage, Tommo tries to account for the swollen leg which will plague him throughout his stay in the Typee valley. Although he knows the Marquesas are supposedly free of such snakes, he says, "I half suspected I had been bitten by some venomous reptile." From the beginning of the novel, Tommo seems at once a serpent and a serpent's victim.

All these passages, drawing more or less directly on *Paradise Lost,* are part of a larger structural pattern which unifies *Typee*—the perverse desire for what is forbidden. From the very beginning of the novel, as Tommo plans his escape from the badly managed shipboard civilization of the *Dolly,* he acknowledges the possibility of capture by the cannibal Typees as a "rather unpleasant drawback"; yet his first eager meditation about the

Marquesas suggests that this drawback is in part an incentive:

> The Marquesas! What strange visions of outlandish things does the very name spirit up! Naked houris—cannibal banquets—groves of cocoa-nut—coral reefs—tatooed chiefs—and bamboo temples; sunny valleys planted with bread-fruit trees—carved canoes dancing on the flashing blue waters—savage woodlands guarded by horrible idols—*heathenish rites and human sacrifices.*

In "Melville and the Fortunate Fall: Typee as Eden," Richard Ruland argues that Tommo found in the Typee valley the primitive paradise he was looking for; but in his argument he omits crucial phrases from the above passage: "cannibal banquets," and "savage woodland guarded by horrible idols—*heathenish rites and human sacrifices.*" Tommo anticipates primitive delights but also primitive horrors; and he is eager for both. "Such were the strangely jumbled anticipations that haunted me," he says. "I felt an irresistible curiosity to see those islands." Tommo's "jumbled anticipations" provide not only his initial motivation for jumping ship but his subsequent motivation as well. At no point does he expect or desire a simple idyllic paradise.

This hypothesis helps the reader to understand episodes puzzling to Tommo. When he first meets the natives, they ask if he thinks they are Happars or the reputedly cannibal Typees, and Tommo answers, "I know not by what impulse it was that I answered, 'Typee'." By "impulse," Tommo voices the possibility he feared but also desired. Even more explicitly, Melville dramatizes Tommo's fear and desire to see evidence of "cannibal banquets." The natives continually try to keep him from prying into the secrets of their banquets, but he persists in what they forbid him, until finally he sees human remains at the Ti, proof of corruption at the heart of Typee existence. Although he had expected to find evidence of cannibalism, and eagerly sought it, he is horrified, and is now eager to leave the valley.

But he himself has brought corruption to the valley. Although he knew that the taboo against women in canoes was part of an institution that served to maintain tribal unity, he wheedled a dispensation for Fayaway. More insidiously, although he knew the Typees like to speak the truth, he invited deception by prying into tribal secrets. Predictably, they equivocated about cannibal rituals; understandably, Kory-Kory insisted the human remains were pork. Tommo had repeatedly complained about the "contaminating contact" of European civilization on primitive cultures; yet he himself is a contaminating force.

He does not realize this until he is about to leave the valley. The Typees had charmed him by their freedom from materialism, but now he offers them his ransoming articles, and observes that they seem "vastly willing to take them." His departure has a more serious effect: it causes dissension among the Typees, who had never before quarreled among themselves. "A new contest arose between the two parties who had accompanied me to the shore; blows were struck, wounds were given, and blood flowed." Worst of all, Tommo directly becomes an agent of bloodshed himself.

As one of the warriors tries to impede the rescue boat, Tommo prepares to perform his one act of violence in the novel. "I felt horror at the act I was about to commit," he says, but "I dashed the boat-hook at him. It struck just below the throat, and forced him downwards." At this moment, he is fully aware of his own destructive role; then, like Dante about to enter the Inferno, "I fell back fainting." Tommo's perverse eagerness to encounter what horrifies and finally repels him gives shape and meaning to Melville's first published novel.

Such interest in perversity is, of course, characteristic of the entire romantic period. Poe analyzed man's irrational desire for what will harm him in "The Imp of the Perverse;" Hawthorne explored perverse desires in "The Birthmark" and "Rappacinni's Daughter." Melville pursued this interest in *Mardi, Pierre,* and *The Confidence Man* as well as in *Moby-Dick*. Ishmael's explanation of his decision to embark on a whaler is as explicit as Poe and as densely suggestive as Hawthorne; he hopes yet fears to encounter the "nameless perils of the whale:"

> I love to sail forbidden seas, and land on barbarous coasts. Not ignoring what is good, I am quick to perceive a horror, and could still be social with it—would they let me—since it is but well to be on friendly terms with all the inmates of the place one lodges in.

Tommo's yearning is much the same. Though not as self-aware as Ishmael, he is also "quick to perceive a horror" yet willing—at least at the beginning—to "be social with it." Like Ishmael, he knows that sharks and other predators swim beneath the beautiful Pacific, and that cannibals inhabit beautiful valleys; but this keeps him from neither the seas nor the valleys. "I love to sail forbidden seas," says Ishmael, and Tommo might say the same. Like the tree in the garden of Eden, what is forbidden is enticing; but pursuit of the forbidden leads to knowledge and experience at once delightful and horrible.

Tommo did taste the fruit of the valley and found it sweet despite its decay; he had longed for the world of "cannibal banquets" and he entered it for a time. Implicitly conflating the image of the forbidden tree with the apples of Sodom, Melville suggests that appetites and expectations are never wholly gratified in this fallen world. And as the double image also suggests, Tommo is from the first a snake in the grass, a Satanic tempter in the garden; he is a polluter of the flawed paradise of Typee—the only kind of paradise to survive the fall.

**Source:** Rita K. Gollin, "The Forbidden Fruit of *Typee*," in *Modern Language Studies*, Vol. 5, No. 2, Autumn 1975, pp. 31–34.

## SOURCES

Arvin, Newton, "The Early Novels: *Typee, Omoo, Redburn, White-Jacket*," in *Herman Melville: Modern Critical Views*, edited by Harold Bloom, Chelsea House, 1986, p. 39.

Fuller, Margaret, Review of *Typee* in *Melville: The Critical Heritage*, edited by Watson G. Branch, Routledge & Kegan Paul, 1974, p. 77, originally published in *New York Tribune*, April 4, 1846.

Hawthorne, Nathaniel, Review of *Typee* in *Melville: The Critical Heritage*, edited by Watson G. Branch, Routledge & Kegan Paul, 1974, p. 68, originally published in *Advertiser*, March 25, 1846.

Herbert, T. Walter, Jr., *Marquesan Encounters: Melville and the Meaning of Civilization*, Harvard University Press, 1980, p. 19.

Melville, Herman, *Typee*, Library of America, 1982, pp. 13, 37–38, 149, 153, 290–91.

Review of *Typee*, in *Melville: The Critical Heritage*, edited by Watson G. Branch, Routledge & Kegan Paul, 1974, p. 64, originally published in *John Bull*, March 7, 1846.

Review of *Typee*, in *Melville: The Critical Heritage*, edited by Watson G. Branch, Routledge & Kegan Paul, 1974, pp. 56, 57, originally published in *Critic*, March 7, 14, 28, 1846.

Review of *Typee*, in *Melville: The Critical Heritage*, edited by Watson G. Branch, Routledge & Kegan Paul, 1974, p. 66, originally published in *Daily Mercury*, March 23, 1846.

Review of *Typee*, in *Melville: The Critical Heritage*, edited by Watson G. Branch, Routledge & Kegan Paul, 1974, p. 53, originally published in *Spectator*, February 28, 1846.

Review of *Typee*, April 6, 1846, in *Melville: The Critical Heritage*, edited by Watson G. Branch, Routledge & Kegan Paul, 1974, pp. 78, 79, originally published in *Times* (London), April 6, 1846.

Samson, John, *White Lies: Melville's Narratives of Facts*, Cornell University Press, 1989, p. 56.

Stern, Milton R., Introduction to *Critical Essays on Herman Melville's "Typee,"* G. K. Hall, 1982, p. 1.

## FURTHER READING

Gidmark, Jill B., ed., *Encyclopedia of American Literature of the Sea and Great Lakes*, Greenwood Press, 2000.
This edited volume contains entries on authors and literary works, important characters, vessels and places, and the themes and ideas that informed American writing about the sea.

Meltzer, Milton, *Herman Melville*, Twenty-first Century, 2004.
Meltzer's volume is an introductory biography of the author written principally for young adults.

Parker, Hershel, *Herman Melville: A Biography*, Johns Hopkins University Press, 2005.
Parker's book is widely regarded as the definitive biography of Herman Melville.

Robertson-Lorant, Laurie, *Melville: A Biography*, University of Massachusetts Press, 1998.
This biography of Melville draws on a large number of recently discovered letters to develop a psychological portrait of the author, focusing on his depression, his alcohol use, and his tortured relationships with family members.

# The Wings of the Dove

**HENRY JAMES**

**1902**

*The Wings of the Dove* by Henry James is a classic story, a simple one, really, in which lovers are victims of the sorrows and inequities of life and are at the same time perpetrators of harm to each other. One of James's later novels, published in 1902, this morality tale is widely acclaimed as his most brilliant work. It is tied to two of his other novels written in the same time period, *The Golden Bowl* (1904) and *The Ambassadors* (1903), which also deal with the psychology of the cruelty of humanity and the struggle to find one's conscience.

This is the love story of Kate Croy and Merton Densher. They are beautiful but poor, although Kate has access to London high society through her Aunt Maud. Into the lives of these characters enters Milly Theale, a young American heiress who is gravely ill. Her naive and innocent presence brings with it the opportunity for charity or for treachery from the worldly and clever Kate and Densher.

The character Milly is based on Minny Temple, James's young cousin to whom he felt an immense attachment. Her death at the young age of twenty-four affected him deeply, and he reveals in his autobiography that the image of her death remained with him for a long time. Her influence on his life and works is seen especially in James's later works; but she appears as early as 1881 as Isabel Archer in *The Portrait of a Lady*.

*Henry James* *(The Library of Congress)*

The language and construction of *The Wings of the Dove* can be difficult to maneuver and some determination and desire is required to understand James's long passages, the ambiguity of his descriptions, and the importance of the silences of his characters in order to know them. The experience of mastering the elusive and rich text is satisfying beyond expectation.

## AUTHOR BIOGRAPHY

Henry James was born on April 15, 1843, on Washington Place in New York City to Mary Robertson Walsh James and Henry James, Sr. His father was from a wealthy family and was a noted intellectual and theologian who was well known among the most influential writers and philosophers of the time. The Jameses had five children whom they tutored in several languages and in literature.

After attending Harvard Law School for a short time when he was nineteen, the young Henry realized that he was better suited for writing than for studying law. He published his first short story, "A Tragedy of Error," in 1864 and also became a writer for the literary magazine the *Atlantic Monthly*. His first novel, *Watch and Ward*, was published as a serial in the magazine in 1871 and in book form in 1878.

James moved to Europe in 1875, and his book *Roderick Hudson* was published the next year in 1876. It is the story of a struggling American sculptor living in Rome. *Transatlantic Sketches*, a rendering of the tales of his travels, was published in 1875. *The American*, completed in 1877 while James was living in Paris, deals with the struggles of an American millionaire who is navigating relations with an arrogant, aristocratic French family in Paris. These books constitute the early phase of his career.

Feeling himself ever an outsider, James decided he would never be anything but a foreigner in France and moved back to London in 1878. There he wrote *Daisy Miller* (1879) and *The Europeans* (1878), continuing his theme of contrasting the American spirit with rigid European society. *The Portrait of a Lady* and *Washington Square* were both published in 1881.

James continued to write prolifically during the middle portion of his career. He received great acclaim for *The Portrait of a Lady* at the age of thirty-eight, but critics felt his next offerings, *The Princess Casamassima* and *The Bostonians*, both published in 1886, did not meet their expectations. When *The Tragic Muse* met with little acclaim in 1889, James was bereft of both muse and money. He persevered, and with *What Maisie Knew* in 1897, the short story "The Turn of the Screw" in 1898, and *The Awkward Age* in 1899, he began to reposition himself in the marketplace.

The later years of James's life are his most important in literary terms. These produced his three greatest novels: *The Wings of the Dove* in 1902, *The Ambassadors* in 1903, and *The Golden Bowl* in 1904. He paid a visit to the United States after completing his last novel but found his native country greatly changed. In 1907 he published *The American Scene* that spoke of the troublesome images he had seen in America. Industrialism had taken over, and his despair at America's pollution, ruination, and greed echoed in these essays.

James became a British subject in 1915, but he is regarded as one of the most prolific and influential American writers. He died in London in 1916.

## PLOT SUMMARY

### Book One: Chapters 1–2

In *The Wings of the Dove*, two young London lovers, Kate Croy and Merton Densher, are engaged to be married. Beautiful and resilient, Kate faces poor prospects. Her father has squandered the family money allotted to her mother, who is now dead. Densher is also poor, handsome, and intelligent. Unfortunately, being poor is the greatest thing a man must overcome in England's Victorian age. Densher makes a modest sum of money as a journalist, and Kate lives as the ward of her mother's sister, Maud Lowder. She insists that Kate must marry well, both socially and materially, not making the same mistake as her poor dead mother. Kate is obliged to do what her aunt prescribes, as it is the wish of her father. He is a miserable, conniving man who will no longer have Kate live with him and sees her opportunity with her aunt as one that must surely benefit him. He implores Kate to slyly persuade Aunt Maud to accept her because the conditions under which she will help her ward are stringent: she must renounce her father in all ways possible.

### Book Two: Chapters 1–2

Aunt Maud remains insistent that Densher is not good enough for Kate, but she turns a blind eye to their encounters around London and on her magnificent estate called Lancaster Gate. She finds Densher quite attractive and seems to enjoy having him about, and she has no objection to the young couple's trysts, although she has forbidden them to marry. She does not object to his person, only to his inferiority as a suitor for Kate.

### Book Three: Chapters 1–2

The story quickly moves its focus to Milly Theale, a young American heiress from New York, who has come to Europe to experience its culture. Her friend Mrs. Susan Stringham, a writer for American society magazines, has decided to join her as an escort, and she arranges for them to visit her old friend Aunt Maud Lowder in London. The truth is that Milly Theale is dying, and although she is determined to keep it a secret, Mrs. Stringham, her traveling companion, quickly reveals it to her friend. It then becomes Aunt Maud's compassionate duty to introduce the ailing American "princess" to the best of London society. She almost immediately becomes the toast of the town, and many parties are arranged to stage her introduction into London society. At this

## MEDIA ADAPTATIONS

- *The Wings of the Dove* was adapted as an American/British film by Hossein Amini, and was directed by Iian Softley. It starred Helena Bonham Carter as Kate Croy, Alison Elliot as Milly Theale, Linus Roache as Densher, Charlotte Rampling as Aunt Maud, and Elizabeth McGovern as Mrs. Stringham. It was released by Miramax Films (1997) in the United Kingdom and in 1998 in the United States. The movie is opulent to watch as it clings faithfully to James's descriptions with lavish silk costumes, magnificent hats, rich furniture all buttoned and tasseled, and ornate jewelry. The film is available in DVD and VHS formats.

- *The Wings of the Dove* is available as an abridged audiobook from Naxos Audio Books and is read by William Hope, who has been the captivating voice on dozens of classic audiobooks. The three-CD set was released in 2006.

- *A Walk to Remember* by Nicholas Sparks was adapted into a screenplay by Karen Janszen and released by DiNovi pictures in 2002. It has a PG rating and is appropriate for teens. There are many correlations between this work and *The Wings of the Dove*, including themes of romance, deception, and death.

time, Milly becomes acquainted with Lord Mark, who makes frequent appearances at Lancaster Gate. Although he is now without a fortune, his position in society has made him a proper guest at Lancaster Gate. Aunt Maud thinks he would be a perfect husband for Kate.

### Book Four: Chapters 1–3

Mrs. Stringham learns from Aunt Maud that a previous attachment had been formed between Kate and Densher. Milly has become Kate's new confidante, and Aunt Maud wishes to know if she has learned from Kate whether or not the couple are still involved. Mrs. Stringham and

Milly delight in their new roles as detectives and decide to visit Kate's sister, Marian, to find out whether or not there is still an attachment between the two. They are dismayed by the mean conditions in which the widowed Marian lives with her children. After talking with her, they are quite confident that nothing remains of the relationship between Kate and Densher, as Marian has not mentioned it at all.

### Book Five: Chapters 1–7

Kate, Aunt Maud, Mrs. Stringham, Milly, and Lord Mark go to a party at Matcham, the grand home of Lord and Lady Aldershaw. Lord Mark is quite attentive to Milly, showing her an Agnolo Bronzino portrait of a beautiful woman who bears a strong resemblance to her. He means it as a great compliment, but she turns her head away in tears because it is a painting of a woman who is dead, the way she views herself. When the Aldershaws join them, Lady Aldershaw immediately concurs with Lord Mark about the resemblance. Aunt Maud invites Mrs. Stringham and Milly to stay on with her at Lancaster Gate.

While in London Milly visits a physician, Sir Luke Strett, who is very vague about her actual condition and encourages her to spend what time she has left living life to its fullest. Milly fears the worst now, but Kate, who has accompanied her, does not yet sense the foreboding of her friend.

Aunt Maud asks Milly to find out from Kate if she knows whether Densher has returned from his business trip to America. Milly is curious about Densher's inquiries as he talks with her about what her plans are. She finds out that Densher was in love with Kate, and she wants to know whether the two still have feelings for each other. Aunt Maud says that Densher is not good enough for Kate and intends for her to marry Lord Mark. Milly confides to Aunt Maud that Kate never speaks of Densher. She and Kate have a lively conversation about it that evening, and she learns that Kate does not have a favorable opinion of Lord Mark. Kate mentions nothing about Densher, and Milly thinks that Kate probably does not know when he will return. Kate calls Milly a "dove," a metaphor (a comparison between two seemingly unlike things that does not use like or as) that will have great significance as the story unfolds.

### Book Six: Chapters 1–5

Just as Milly is assured that there is no relationship between Kate and Densher, she meets them unexpectedly at the National Gallery. They keep their composure and act as if they have just met by chance. Milly is appeased and invites them to have lunch with her. A dinner is arranged at Lancaster Gate in order for Densher to get to know Milly better. Milly is unable to attend the dinner, but Densher is introduced to Lord Mark for the first time. Aunt Maud has made it clear to Mrs. Stringham that Kate no longer cares for Densher and says that Densher should make his own advances to Milly.

Kate has concocted a plan that will eventually allow her to marry Densher. Knowing that Milly is very ill, and very rich, she wants him to make advances to Milly in order that they fall in love. When Milly dies she must therefore leave her fortune to Densher which in turn will allow him to marry Kate. She does not reveal her entire plan to Densher yet, only telling him that she has one and he must trust her and follow her instructions.

Sir Luke visits Mrs. Stringham and tells her that Milly is indeed very ill. Milly, who has already been told by physicians in America that she has a serious ailment, says that she will seek diversions in Tyrol within two weeks. Kate has lied and convinced Milly that she does not care for Densher, and Milly admits to herself her own romantic feelings for him.

### Book Seven: Chapters 1–5

Sir Luke has charged Mrs. Stringham with the care of Milly and has said it is imperative that she remain happy and be loved in order to hold on as long as she can. Mrs. Stringham talks with her friend Aunt Maud and is encouraged to hear that Milly might have a chance with Densher. Aunt Maud reluctantly tells the truth that Kate does indeed have feelings for him, but that it will remain a secret between them.

The planned trip to Italy is the next diversion for Milly, and she invites Aunt Maud, Kate, and Densher to join her and her companion. Milly had met Densher in America and has already formed an acquaintance with him. Kate pushes Densher toward Milly while keeping their engagement a secret from everyone. Her plan for Densher to make advances to Milly is revealed to him. Densher is not easily persuaded, but Kate is insistent and promises to "come" to him and prove her love if he will follow her bidding.

Milly arrives in Venice at the lavish Palazzo Leporelli, which has high arched ceilings, beautiful wall hangings, and precious relics. Eugenio is there as her hired servant to make all things go smoothly for her in the palace. He intercedes when an unexpected visit from Lord Mark interrupts Milly almost immediately upon her arrival. He is told to wait in the salon, and she merely happens upon him as she is inspecting the rooms. After visiting with him, she admits to him that she is seriously ill. He uses the opportunity to facetiously tell her that he wants to take care of her and love her, but she dismisses his poor attempt at a proposal. She tells him that he has been chosen by Aunt Maud to marry Kate. A note from Eugenio that Densher is waiting to see her causes Milly to end the audience with Lord Mark abruptly.

### Book Eight: Chapters 1–3

The other members of the party are still reveling in the splendid dinners at the grand palace and enjoying the sights of Venice when Milly's health deteriorates so that she has to stay in her rooms. Aunt Maud decides that it is best that she and Kate return home. Densher promises Kate he will stay and continue to woo Milly. In return, he asks her to come to his hotel again, but she declines.

### Book Nine: Chapters 1–4

Densher devotes himself to Milly, and she quickly falls in love with him. They spend their time gaily in the lavish Venetian palace she has rented for their vacation. Densher, tormented by the deception that he and Kate have plotted, develops true feelings of admiration for Milly. She is delighted with his attentions and asks him why he has stayed behind. He first says it is to write a book, but then confesses it is in order to be with her. Milly has had another visit from Lord Mark, this time to lay before her the deception of Kate and Densher. He tells Milly that Densher is in love with Kate and that they are engaged. He also unveils their plot to inherit her money when she is dead. Densher calls on her but she refuses to see him, and Eugenio turns him away.

After three days, Mrs. Stringham visits Densher. She tells him that Milly has taken to her bed and "turned her face to the wall." She pleads with him to come and reassure her that the accusations made by Lord Mark are untrue. The doctor, Sir Luke Strett, comes to see Densher and tells him that Milly is a bit better and that she would like to see him now.

### Book Ten: Chapters 1–6

Back in London, Densher reveals to Kate that his visit with Milly has been short and heartrending. She has only wanted to see him one last time before her death, and he has revealed nothing of his and Kate's deceptions towards her. Imminently, they learn of her death. "Our dear dove, as Kate had called her, has folded her wings." Aunt Maud laments. Kate can sense Densher's torment and is sure now that he loved Milly. A letter arrives revealing that Milly has left everything to Densher. He is full of remorse and refuses to accept the money. He promises to marry Kate, but it must be without the acceptance of the money. She says she will marry him if he promises that he can love only her and not the memory of Milly. Then things can be as they were before. But he cannot promise that, and she is left to mourn the fact that "We shall never be again as we were!"

## CHARACTERS

### Lord and Lady Aldersham

Lord and Lady Aldersham own the grand house that is the site of a garden party held to introduce Milly to London society. Milly sees them as very elegant, but to her they speak meaningless words and act very superficially. In the house hangs the portrait by the Italian Renaissance painter Agnolo Bronzino that Lord Mark says resembles Milly.

### Marian Condrip

Marian is Kate's widowed sister who has three small children. Her poor husband has left a very small inheritance and she lives in poverty. She is pictured as vulgar, red, and fat, and her children survive on mere crumbs. Densher describes her house in Chelsea as "ugly almost to the point of the sinister." Her house is cluttered and dirty, and Marian is awash in self-pity. She looks to Kate to "work" Aunt Maud for more financial support, of which she expects to be the recipient. She is content to sit around with her stepsisters and moan about her condition and wait to hear what Kate has done to improve her dire situation.

### Kate Croy

James goes to great lengths to describe Kate's beauty. She has lustrous, thick black hair that falls down beside a clear, fair oval face. Outdoors, in the light, her eyes appear blue, but indoors, in the mirror, they are almost black. She is beautiful, not with the aid of adornments, but completely within the presentation of herself and her gracefulness. She is slender and cleverly underdressed to emphasize that great beauty needs no distractions.

Her father's debaucheries have caused the loss of a great inheritance that belonged to her dead mother. Kate is not undone by her circumstances, and unlike her sister, she rises to the challenge of deciding what she should do about them. She visits her father, and without anger, agrees to take care of him. This seemingly unselfish gesture provides an initial view of her as good-natured and high-minded. It conflicts with the apparently malicious actions she takes against Densher and Milly as the novel progresses. James clearly wants the reader to like Kate in spite of her later transgressions, and she simply does what is necessary for the most positive outcome of things. She is generous, also to her sister Marian, and gives a big portion of her small monthly allotment of money to her.

Kate's sense of duty extends to Densher, whom she truly loves. She tells him eagerly in Book Two, "I engage myself to you forever." When her Aunt Maud forbids them to marry, she takes the matter into her own hands and fashions a plan for Kate to marry Lord Mark. If she must be deceptive, so be it. For this reason, she must take skillful care to disguise her motives when necessary. Milly senses a friendship building between herself and Kate.

Her insincerities become more pronounced as the plot unfolds, and they begin with her half-truth compliments toward Milly: "We all adore you." Milly tells her in strict confidence about her illness and Kate promises not to reveal it to anyone. But it becomes the catalyst for her deception, the main ingredient for her plot. She uses her natural charm and grace to cover her duplicity and her exuberant spontaneity to refashion herself to work her plan into any situation that arises. She slips easily out of the potential danger of being discovered alone with Densher at the National Gallery by "making up" to Milly, giving her new friend her complete attention and basically ignoring Densher. Kate takes control of a situation, moves the circumstances around to her advantage, and skillfully rises above suspicion. She is pragmatic, mercenary, independent, and strong-willed.

She is also quite adept at manipulating others to join in her plot. Initially, she tells Densher that

he must simply trust her cleverness and that she will take care of everything. When she puts her plan in motion, she gives Densher only a piece of the puzzle. It is evident to her that Milly loves him, and Kate tells him he should begin to show Milly his favor as well. When he is reluctant, she tells him to trust her; there is more, but she will tell him that later. When she does tell all and he is repulsed, she tells him she will hate him if he "spoils" this for her. Finally, she agrees to go to him in his quarters if he will follow her plan. By pressing her will this far, James sets her up as the ultimate victim. She begins to become less exalted in Densher's eyes, he begins to lose respect for her, and at the end, feeling revulsion for what he has done, he despises her.

### Lionel Croy

Mr. Croy is Kate and Marian's father. He lives his life in gross poverty and wretchedness. Kate describes his condition as "the failure of fortune and of honour." In a letter to Kate, he lies, telling her that he is sick; when she comes and offers to live with him and care for him, he makes it clear he has no use for her other than his interest in what money she can get for him from her Aunt Maud. He is handsome and genteel in appearance. He must resort to haggling a living from her, and he, like Marian, will wait to see what the result is.

### Merton Densher

Densher appears at the beginning of Book Two as a tall, handsome young Englishman; considered a gentleman only in the sense that he is educated, not wealthy. James likes to write about him in the same manner as he does Milly; in indistinct, ambiguous terms James would rather reveal instead what Densher is not suited to achieve. He is too young for politics, too educated for the army, too skeptical for the church, and too sensible for poetry or art. He is vague without appearing weak; idle without looking empty. Because he is a refined young man who writes for the newspaper, it is acceptable for him to amble about the city on his long legs and gaze up with his head held back in his hands in communion with the sky.

He is convinced that he would be a fool to marry any woman who was not clever and independent. When he meets Kate at a party at a gallery, he immediately sees that she is the kind of woman he wants. Unfortunately, their felicity is short lived, and the naive Densher chooses to bow to the manipulations pressed hard on him by Kate and their economic dilemma. As he follows her scheme to his own "damnation," he is tormented, disgusted, and wracked with guilt. He feels trapped in a "circle of petticoats" as he bows to Kate's wishes: make love to Milly, inherit her money upon her death, and then marry Kate, which will be acceptable to Aunt Maud. His job is to be the savior to Milly and give her happiness and a reason to live. Ironically, she saves him, and he feels redeemed by her purity and brilliance. Exonerated by the refusal of her fortune, he gains the fortitude to propose again to Kate, this time under his own terms.

### Eugenio

Eugenio is the well-traveled and highly recommended servant hired by Milly Theale to help with accommodations for her travels abroad. He pays great attention to detail in the arrangements he makes for her comfort. He is very dedicated to her, and she feels he is "very dear and very deep—as probably but a swindler finished to the finger-tips," because he has one hand on his heart and the other in her pocketbook. He proves himself constant and cares for her until the end. Eugenio also plays the role of an accuser to Densher. He recognizes that Densher is only interested in Milly's money and makes the decision to show him he knows it with a look that one con man might give another.

### Aunt Maud Lowder

A wealthy London socialite, Aunt Maud Lowder is Kate's aunt and guardian. Kate submits herself as a ward to her benefactor only as a last resort and feels that her estate at Lancaster Gate is like a cage. It is quite a gilded cage and James fixes on Aunt Maud the embodiment of the decay of English society. The description of the house is the description of Aunt Maud: tall, rich, and heavy. It abounds in "rare material—precious woods, metals, stuffs, stones." Densher says he has never dreamed of anything "so fringed and scalloped, so buttoned and corded, . . . so much gilt and glass, so much satin and plush, so much rosewood and marble and malachite." Kate calls her the "Britannia of the Market Place—Britannia unmistakable." She also describes her as a wonderful lioness in the cage, a great spectacle for show, "majestic, magnificent, high-coloured, all brilliant gloss, perpetual satin." But the whip will remain always in the hand of the lioness, and she does not hesitate to wield it, as she will against Kate and Densher. The lioness uses her cunning persuasiveness when it comes to having her will accomplished by Mrs. Stringham, Milly, and Lord Mark. To Densher, though she is a formidable foe.

She is London in all its devices. She is resolved that a woman of society has but to be beautiful and marry well. How the money or the suitor is gotten is of little consequence; however, the "working" of persons is her central motivating effort. Kate is chosen for her beauty, and therefore, most of Aunt Maud's work is done. She settles upon Lord Mark as the suitor, and although he does not have much money, he does have his title, which is equally valuable.

### Lord Mark

Lord Mark is a member of the nobility, which makes him worthy and estimable in London society in spite of the fact that he is no longer wealthy. His nobility entitles him more respect than impoverished people of a lower class. He does not work in any business; like Aunt Maud, he is about the business of "working" people.

His age is unknown—he was either "a young man who looked old or an old man who looked young." He is bald, and as Milly sees him, "slightly stale." He is very prim in appearance with his pince-nez. He has an air of aristocratic indifference, and Milly's impression is that he is one of those Englishmen who conceal their thoughts as much as they show them.

Lord Mark has the appearance of cleverness, but Kate and Densher refer to him as "humbugging." Kate says that his grandeur is simply a result of the fact that he has a duke in his family. He is able to make himself respected without any effort simply by virtue of his aristocratic birth.

He uncovers his treacherous insincerity when he asks Milly to marry him under the guise that he will take care of her when he actually wishes merely to take care of her money. After she refuses him, he takes his revenge and reveals Densher and Kate's plan to her. He obviously has no desire or feelings for her, since this revelation ultimately leads to her broken heart and hastened death. Mrs. Stringham and Densher call him "an idiot of idiots."

### Sir Luke Strett

Sir Luke Strett is the physician Milly visits in London to find out more about her illness. She likes him immediately, although on her first visit he is only able to see her for ten minutes. He is so attentive in his manner that she has the impression that she will make a new friend, "wonderfully, the most appointed, the most thoroughly adjusted of the whole collection." He lives up to this impression on her second visit when he realizes that she has what must be a deadly condition (James does not reveal what it is) and goes further to find out details of her family and asks who will take care of her. A look passes between them, and then he smiles to let her know that she can count on him as a doctor, friend, and confidant. He tells her she can depend on him "for unlimited interest," and he remains true to this statement, even following the group to Venice to watch over her. He befriends Densher and goes with him to the galleries and churches there. For Densher, who says that Sir Luke's interest in Milly is "supremely beneficent," he provides relief from the "circle of petticoats." The physician and Milly are in a category of character far above the others, who are consumed with selfish pursuits and imagined injuries. Mrs. Stringham calls him an "angel," which completes Milly's first impression, that he may be a friend from "quite another world." He attends her to the end, through the nights, and then brings her body back to London.

### Mrs. Susan Stringham

Mrs. Stringham acts as the "fairy godmother" to Milly, the American heiress. She takes on that role when they leave New York to go abroad. She will help Milly forget her troubles and her illness and will be her guide, helping her to live her life to its fullest. She feels that she is capable of knowing Milly better than Milly knows herself, and she will extend to her what she has observed is lacking in the girl: culture. Mrs. Stringham believes she excels at recognizing culture.

She grasps at the opportunity to assist Milly in helping her escape her circumstances. The romance of the notion appeals to her great but so far stifled imagination. The strangeness of Milly's circumstances—rich, but not beautiful, and lacking culture—impel Mrs. Stringham to devote herself to the young girl. As a Boston writer for gossip magazines, she can present opportunities for romance and adventure. Her view of Milly's tragic situation is "to have... thousands and thousands a year, to have youth and intelligence," but "not have the opportunity to make the most of her liberty (from poverty),

and to live life to its fullest, rather in its present circumstances of confinement in New York."

Mrs. Stringham traveled widely in Europe as a child and she feels herself a woman of the world. As she leads Milly to Europe, she is delighted with the grand accommodations Milly's fortune can afford, but at the same time, she detests the grossness of those who have designs on Milly's wealth. Her motives remain unclear and we do not know whether she is genuinely Milly's champion and protector or just another one of the exploiters among the characters.

### Milly Theale

Milly is a young American heiress who has recently lost all of her family in New York. She is also stricken with an illness, the nature of which is never revealed, that is certain to kill her. James describes her in ambiguous terms, sometimes beautiful, sometimes "pale" and "haggard"; she is always portrayed through the musings, thoughts, and conversations of the society about her. She becomes an object in the plot rather than taking on a persona, and she is exploited by everyone. James sets her up as a clear symbol of goodness, generosity, compassion, and humble sacrifice. Hers are the wings of the dove, which in the end, "cover them all."

Many beneficent words can describe Milly: she is wonderful, "magnificent," beautiful, brilliant, "heroic," mysterious, "without sin," kind, graceful, adorable, and a "dove." She is James's tragic heroine who wants desperately to live and love, but as tragedy demands, she must be sacrificed.

## THEMES

### Victorian Values

The most important comment James wants to make in *The Wings of the Dove* is that Victorian mores (social customs) cause moral failure. This is a theme seen throughout many of his novels as he purports to make the superficiality of Europe's Victorian Age apparent through its materialism, arrogance, and superciliousness. The American is depicted as naive and inexperienced and is usually the object of a parallel theme: the slaughter of the innocent. In this case, it is Milly who is the tragic victim; she is young, frail, doomed, and impressionable.

# TOPICS FOR FURTHER STUDY

- Watch the film *A Walk to Remember*. Write an essay comparing the modern-day romance/tragedy with that of *The Wings of the Dove*. Include your opinions on the similarities of the situations of the main characters. How does Jamie resemble Milly Theale? What deceptions come into play in the relationship between Jamie and Landon, and how does that correspond to *The Wings of the Dove*? What are the similar themes addressed by both works? Who is the counterpart to Kate in the movie? How do the obstacles Jamie has to overcome with her father resemble Kate's struggles with Aunt Maud? Does money or social position have an impact on the characters? How are the stories different?

- Read *In the Garden* by Elsie V. Aidinoff, an Amelia Bloomberg Award selection. In this young-adult novel, the story of the Garden of Eden is told from Eve's point of view. Write an essay based on the ideas from the book that argues whether it is the serpent or Eve who is responsible for the "Original Sin." Include in your argument references to deception, serpent-dove imagery, manipulation, biblical allusions, free will, and determination.

- Write and perform a play with an alternate ending to *The Wings of the Dove*. You may start with the scene in Venice in which Lord Mark tells Milly of Kate and Densher's deception. You may end it however you like. The only requirement is that Densher and Kate act with greater compassion and responsibility toward members of society.

- Make a portfolio of sketches you have drawn of Victorian society: costumes, furniture, architecture, examples of advances in industry, medicine, technology, transportation, food, crafts, labor, cities, etc. Include at least ten pieces of artwork. As an alternative, collect images from the Internet and create a PowerPoint presentation.

- Make a short video concerning the theme of death and the fragility of life. It may be a documentary about someone you know or have read about, or it may be simply your philosophy about death. Please do not make the video humorous or macabre (gruesome).

- Using a shared blog, communicate with students from different countries concerning the differences and similarities in your cultures. Try to limit the subjects discussed to how they affect you directly, such as school, clothing, goals, money, entertainment, and the freedoms and restrictions you have. Remember to use proper Internet etiquette. Collect twenty to thirty entries and respond to each comment.

## Religion

Religious themes are prevalent in *The Wings of the Dove*. Like the spiritual dove that she represents, Milly has all the attributes of the biblical fruit of the spirit: love, joy, peace, patience, goodness, and gentleness, faith, humility, and self-control (Galatians 5:22–23). Hell and damnation plague Densher, Sir Luke acts as the "good physician," and Lord Mark has all the shrewdness and sinister qualities of deviltry. Kate, also culpable, is in some ways absolved because she too is a victim of British decadence, simply following what she has been taught by her father and by Aunt Maud. Densher is plagued by guilt and remorse, and in the end, redemption is available to him. He attains it by refusing Milly's money and risking the loss of Kate's love.

## Revenge

A theme of revenge reveals itself in the character of Lord Mark, when he attempts to destroy Densher and Kate's plan by telling Milly of it.

*Helena Bonham Carter as Kate in the 1997 film version of the novel* (*Mark Tilliee-Mirimax Films | AFP | Getty Images*)

Greed and insincerity abound among those in the London society depicted in the novel; almost everyone is interested in Milly in some way or another only for her money, and they see her as a commodity to be exploited. Aunt Maud is worthy in society and supreme only because she is wealthy. Mrs. Stringham enjoys the felicities of travel at the expense of Milly's fortune. Kate's plot to have Milly's fortune is simply mercenary. Money earned in "trade" as opposed to being the beneficiary of an inherited fortune is also a topic of note; in terms of one's place in Victorian society, the two were not equal. Lord Mark is worthy in the eyes of society because he has a title, regardless of the fact that he has no money. Densher is not good enough for Kate because he is simply employed as a newspaper writer and has had nothing handed down to him. This puts him on a lower social standing, and Aunt Maud only accepts him because he is handsome.

### Death

Death is a theme that appears repeatedly in James's novels, and in *The Wings of the Dove*, it is present as a force to reckon with almost from the beginning, with the appearance of Milly. It is talked about, not talked about, whispered about, guessed at, and speculated on throughout the entire novel. When Milly finally dies, death is pictured as a release from the vulgarity of this world, and remarkably, as Aunt Maud puts it, "Our dear dove then, as Kate calls her, has folded her wonderful wings.... Unless ... she has spread them the wider ... for a flight, I trust, to some happiness greater."

### Feminism

Feminism is a theme widely touched upon in James's novels. In *The Wings of the Dove*, the advancement of anyone in Victorian society is dependent upon money or title. In this regard, we sympathize with Kate's predicament. Her father has squandered away the inheritance she would have had. As a woman, she has no prospect of being able to earn a living. She is the victim of the devices and designs of her rich Aunt Maud. She must have a husband she did not choose, or she must choose poverty and lose her dignity by marrying the man she does love. There is not any opportunity for her to make her own way in life, to support herself, or to make her own choices.

# STYLE

## Omniscient Narrative

James uses the voice of a third-person omniscient narrator (mysterious and god-like, commenting in and out of the character's thoughts) in *The Wings of the Dove*. This narrator must be listened to very attentively if one wants to understand his meaning. The text is filled with long intricate sentences, rambling circumlocutions, and ideas quizzically tossed about in and out of his character's consciousness. The reader gets lost many times, in understanding who is talking about whom, because of an overuse of ambiguous pronouns in preference to naming the character who is being discussed. In spending so much time in the minds of his characters rather than in their conversations, James is a forerunner of the American stream-of-consciousness writers, who provide a window into the morals, hopes, motives, and feelings of a character without the use of action or dialogue. The technique, a rebellion against the formal prose of the Victorian period, had not been used before the late 1800s, and it was not well received at the time of the novel's publication. Many renowned authors were to follow this style and insight well into the twentieth century.

David Minter, in *A Cultural History of the American Novel: From Henry James to William Faulkner*, comments on the different styles of the American writer:

> We see them in the oblique confessions of Willa Cather's Jim Burden and F. Scott Fitzgerald's Nick Carraway; in the self-conscious fluidity of Gertrude Stein's prose and the self-conscious restraint of Ernest Hemingway's; and in the audacity of William Faulkner's, where concealment matches disclosure, mystification matches expression, and evasion matches revelation.

## Characters and Settings

*The Wings of the Dove* is presently considered one of James's greatest works of fiction. If the absent narrator and the deep delving into characters' consciousnesses confuse the reader, James provides us with familiar things: heroes, heroines, tragedy, love, and redemption. Privy to the rich descriptions played in the minds of the characters, we experience London in the gilded Victorian era. Densher's vision of Aunt Maud's estate is a delightful view of its materialistic decadence.

## Symbols, Metaphors, and Imagery

James's use of symbols and imagery is prolific, and the reader need simply choose one page of the extensive text to experience it. The dove (Milly) is the symbol of peace and redemption. Aunt Maud is the symbol of British materialism and greed. Lord Mark is a symbol of the decay of British high society. Metaphors abound as well: Aunt Maud is a lioness, Sir Luke is an angel, Lionel Croy is a sponge, and Marian Condrip is a relic. The images of Milly as a "priestess" in her black clothing, as a Christ figure (Luke 4:5) when she stands on the hill surveying the "kingdoms of the earth," Densher as "damned" and then "saved" provide conclusive use of religious imagery, though some critics have refused to recognize it.

# HISTORICAL CONTEXT

## Advancements in Science, Industry, Culture, and Thought in the Victorian Era

*The Wings of the Dove*, *The Portrait of a Lady*, and *The Golden Bowl* are regarded as James's three best novels; they were written in his later years, right at the beginning of the twentieth century. He was an American who had been living in Europe for over forty years. This was the later years of the Victorian era, and coincided with the gilded age in America, because it was a time of great wealth and expansion, and the opulence was apparent in the adornment of everything, from vast mansions and estates to the tassels on a shoe in both countries.

The gilded age was also a time of immense expansion in the areas of culture, science, industry, and philosophy. Hazel Hutchison, in *Seeing and Believing: Henry James and the Spiritual World*, says, "The relationship between environment and consciousness was hotly debated at the beginning of the twentieth century, in the work of psychologist Sigmund Freud." She notes that James "turned sixteen in 1859, the year that Darwin published *The Origin of Species*."

Darwin's theory of evolution, published in 1909, and Freud's books on psychoanalysis, published in 1900 and 1902, contributed to this time of new ideas. Socioeconomic ideas had been challenged as early as 1848 when Karl Marx published *The Communist Manifesto*. Feminist ideas came forth from the pages of Jane Austen to Virginia Woolf. The rights of women gained

# COMPARE & CONTRAST

- **1902:** Young women in Victorian England usually have arranged marriages. Suitable matches are men who have the same social standing and equal or greater amounts of wealth. Men may choose their own wives but are expected to marry within their own social circles.

  **Today:** An English woman may marry whomever she wishes, but it is still frowned upon if a person of nobility marries a commoner.

- **1902:** English Victorian women are unable to vote.

  **Today:** Women are able to vote and play a vital part in British politics, following in the footsteps of Margaret Thatcher, who was England's first female prime minister from 1979 to 1990.

- **1902:** Marriage is the only career for women. They must be attentive to their husbands and never create a scandal. They are unable to obtain profitable or prestigious jobs.

  **Today:** Women can aspire to the highest positions in England in business, in government, and in academia. There is a consensus, even among English businessmen, that there are not enough women in the boardroom.

- **1902:** The very poor are simply ignored by English society. The belief is that people deserve their poverty because they have made bad choices.

  **Today:** Views about poverty have changed dramatically, and a more compassionate effort is practiced in helping the poor in England. The overtures of Princess Diana towards the poor worldwide is remembered as heroic, and one of the best examples of charity work in recent times.

- **1902:** People of the English middle class with a respectable profession can mingle with those of the upper class if the proper introduction is arranged. The only difference between the middle class and upper class is the amount of wealth that has been gained.

  **Today:** Strict class distinctions in England are no longer in place, except for the nobility. Money, however, is still the great equalizer.

---

immense attention, and it appeared that English women would soon gain the right to vote. The Great Exhibition in London in 1851 had proved England the leader of the world in technology, industry, medical, and scientific advances. American industrialization followed the Civil War. In both countries social classes were changing and there was a tearing down of the old hierarchal society and the rise of a middle class.

### Money and Greed in the Victorian Era

*The Rule of Money: Gender, Class, and Exchange Economics*, by Peggy McCormack, shows the importance of money as status in the Victorian Era as depicted in James's works. "Both *The Ambassadors* and *The Wings of the Dove* are pivotal in terms of the protagonist's discovery and efforts to rework the economic exchange systems into which they enter." His characters, with the best intentions, then, are usually innocent, naive Americans. This is exactly the case with Milly Theale, who is the heroine, the sinless dove. But she must go abroad, as directed by Mrs. Stringham, to obtain what she lacks: culture. She must go to Europe to experience life and cultured civilization. If James sets up England as the ideal culture, he also portrays it as the experienced, shrewd, and knowledgeable society. This creates an immediate conflict between the naive and the experienced, which is used keenly in *The Wings of the Dove*. It depends primarily on what James saw among many in

*Milly travels to Venice after fearing she is seriously ill* (Image copyright Rostislav Glinsky, 2009. Used under license from Shutterstock.com)

British society: civilization as the art of acquiring all, especially money. To him, deception and corruption must follow. Milly falls victim to this deception and it becomes her demise. Because of Aunt Maud's wealth and social standing, she is free to arrange the lives of others who are less fortunate. Lord Mark represents the decaying of the British social hierarchy. He no longer has money, but his title still affords him a high place in society although it becomes a more pitiable one. With a distinct middle class arising in the Victorian period, a person in his situation historically must lose some regard. Kate also falls victim to the system; as a Victorian woman, she has no way to make her own money.

## CRITICAL OVERVIEW

At the time he wrote *The Wings of the Dove*, James had received great acclaim for only two of his novels, *Daisy Miller* and *The Portrait of a Lady*. After a lifetime of producing novels, short stories, plays, and literary criticism, James began to feel distanced from his readers as his novels took on a more difficult style. Critics complained that he walked around and about his characters,

never getting to the point, rambling in cumbersome prose, and unintelligible what-ifs.

Judith Woolf, in *Henry James: The Major Novels*, reveals that "the initial stumbling block with Henry James, for many of his readers, is not so much the fact that his novels are complex and oblique and idiosyncratic as a suspicious feeling that such complexity is willful and unnecessary." He began to feel the disconnection, and instead of trying to correct it, as an appeasement, he almost reveled in what he felt was a new freedom. In *The Rule of Money: Gender, Class, and Exchange Economics in the Fiction of Henry James*, Peggy McCormack explains that James spent five years in relative seclusion, out of the public view, to produce his most critically acclaimed novels. From 1899 to 1904, the happy consequence of his therapeutic withdrawal to Lamb House manifested itself in the phenomenal publications of this major phase: *The Sacred Fount*, *The Wings of the Dove*, *The Ambassadors*, *The Golden Bowl*, and *The American Scene*.

In her book *The Critical Reception of Henry James: Creating a Master*, Linda Simon, discussing an essay by H. G. Dwight that appeared in *Putnam's Review* in 1907, writes:

> James was ahead of his time, and Dwight looked forward to a later generation more

familiar with fiction that attended to the inner life of characters, more willing to validate a novelist whose interest was not plot but 'in relating the scene of every day to the background of mystery against which it moves.'

Simon goes on to quote Dwight, saying,

> If there is anything at all in what we vaguely called the *Zeitgeist* [the spirit of the times] . . . it would seem that as consciousness increases, as we become more trained to the consequence of much that we have regarded as inconsequent, books like *What Maisie Knew* and *The Sacred Fount* and *The Golden Bowl* will take on for us a new significance.

This proved to be the case as James's works began to regain popularity in the 1940s, and his influence became evident in the writings of James Joyce and Virginia Woolf, and ultimately he became the forerunner of artists of the stream-of-consciousness style, such as D. H. Lawrence, William Faulkner, and Ernest Hemingway.

## CRITICISM

### Cynthia Gower

*Gower is a freelance writer, novelist, and playwright. In this essay, she examines the inherent spirituality and transcendent qualities of Milly Theale and the tragedy of her lost innocence in* The Wings of the Dove *.*

In *The Wings of the Dove*, the tragedy of innocence lost, the robbing of life and worth, and the death of the pure are woven intricately in this story of Milly Theale, the young American woman who seeks to find life and love in Europe. This idea of the undoing of the frail, naïve, and virtuous by those who manipulate them is one that is repeated in several of James's late works. Although this concept is one of many that can be gleaned and examined in the sumptuous layers of the story, it is important for the student and first-time reader to recognize it. Milly is the tragic heroine, doomed to be torn apart by the wolves who circle around her, yet she is a spirit embodied in a dove, destined to soar above them and cover them with her wings.

What the reader knows about Milly is mainly discovered through the thoughts and conversations her companions have about her. There is never an absolute description of her, the descriptions are intentionally contradicting, but rather she takes on an ethereal quality; intangible and

# WHAT DO I READ NEXT?

- *November Blues*, published in 2007, is a Coretta Scott King Award Honor book by Sharon M. Draper, who also wrote the 2007 Coretta Scott King Literature Award winner *Copper Sun*. It is written for young-adult readers but deals with many of the same issues James did concerning deception, guilt, and death.

- *The Portrait of a Lady*, Henry James's 1909 novel, has a heroine who is a wealthy American, much like Milly Theale. Isabel Archer is also enticed to marry the friend of her companion, Merle, who is having an affair with the man. This novel ends differently, though, as Isabel actually marries Merle's lover, Gilbert. Even after she discovers their amour, she remains faithful to her husband.

- *Sister of my Heart* (2000), by Chitra Banerjee Divakaruni, is the story of a young girl from Calcutta who is unable to marry the boy she loves because he is considered unsuitable. A national best seller, it is an enchanting story of love and courage in women bound by mystical cultural beliefs.

- In Elsie V. Aidinoff's *The Garden* (2004), God introduces Eve to the Serpent and he "knows not what he does." An Amelia Bloomer Book Award winner, Aidinoff portrays the Serpent's deception, Eve's act of freeing the world, and the consequences that ensue.

- *Atonement*, by Ian McEwan, published by Doubleday in 2006, exudes the luxury and romance of James's fiction and is imbued with captivating scenes of innocence lost, deception, lies, and tragedy.

- Nicholas Sparks's *A Walk to Remember* (1999) is another tragic novel about young lovers. It includes the issues of societal barriers and the interferences of guardians, a concern throughout *The Wings of the Dove*.

> **MILLY IS THE TRAGIC HEROINE, DOOMED TO BE TORN APART BY THE WOLVES WHO CIRCLE AROUND HER, YET SHE IS A SPIRIT EMBODIED IN A DOVE, DESTINED TO SOAR ABOVE THEM AND COVER THEM WITH HER WINGS."**

complex, constantly changing and reforming. It is as though she is an object of admiration, lauded, pitied, followed, and watched. While she is being "worked" by them all, she becomes an object almost of supernatural proportions, able to become for them the magic genie who will grant them all what they wish. To Aunt Maud, she is a possible object of Densher's pursuit, leaving Kate free to marry Lord Mark, whose title makes him more suitable. For Eugenio, she is someone whose every whim is to be catered to, at great benefit to his pockets. For Mrs. Stringham, she is an escape, a project, a diversion. None of the other characters are initially aware of her as a spiritual force in their lives, although, ironically, they make it almost a prophecy by bequeathing her the title of "dove."

When Mrs. Stringham first encounters Milly, she is portrayed as an "apparition," pale and haggard, dressed in black mourning clothes, due to the recent death of her parents. Susan is inspired to help the poor creature and feels that it would be unscrupulous not to do everything in all her compassionate power to give Milly the things she lacked most: culture, romance, and knowledge of Europe. She says that the charm of Milly's situation is the greatest she has ever encountered, and she must give up everything for her "princess." Through all her musings about how enchanting, even beautiful, Milly has become to her, she deludes herself with her high intentions. James buries deep within Mrs. Stringham's encounter with the girl and the extolling of her high aspirations the simple truths about Milly that have garnered such attention: "she was alone, she was stricken, she was rich." Mrs. Stringham assures herself that she must renounce her own life; "and she honestly believed that she was thus supremely equipped for leading Milly's own." In taking on

her new identity, she becomes alarmed when danger lurks ahead, and she wonders when Milly stands upon a high peak in the Swiss Alps if she might be considering a jump. "She was looking down on the kingdoms of the earth" as in the story of Jesus in the wilderness when Satan beguiled him to jump from a mountain above the kingdoms of man (Luke 4:5). But Milly, the dove, the symbol of the Holy Spirit in Christianity, will not submit; "she knew herself unmistakably reserved for some more complicated passage."

Milly's reception in London is grand and splendid, and all those in the society of the "florid" Aunt Maud Manningham meet her with immeasurable regard. Kate "makes up to her" immensely, saying, "We all adore you." She is the first to call Milly a dove with the same condescension as before, and yet the heroine takes up the charge as if it is a "revelation," and she commits all her energies to conduct herself in all her manners and actions like a graceful, delicate winged creature.

For Kate, the dove has spread her wings across the Atlantic and flown to her and Densher. Aunt Maud has forbidden them to marry. He has no money, and he is therefore not good enough for Kate. The salvation Milly will provide for them has, in Kate's mind, no spiritual implications because Kate is materialistic and selfish. She will deceive Milly while making her believe that she is her greatest new friend and the delight of all their London society. She means simply for Densher to make Milly fall in love with him, so that when she dies of the much talked about but very elusive illness, they will have her money and will be able to marry. Densher is wary and describes the plan to Kate as the "sacrificing" of the young woman. When he sees Milly in her traveling clothes, he thinks her black attire "kept in place by heavy rows of pearls, hung down to her feet like the stole of a priestess." It is fortunate for Kate that Milly has already fallen in love with Densher following a chance meeting in New York. She has come out of desperation, aware that time for her is short, fervently seeking love. She hopes to arrive in London before his return, and somehow, in her most animated attempt, to win his love. But her naïveté will be her undoing and ultimately she is destined for a far greater love. She begins to love them all as Kate says "without sin." As they plot to devour her, each one for their own benefit, the dove spreads her wings of absolution over them all. Milly's descent of the stairs in a "wonderful white dress" on the evening of the ball at her palace in Venice, has been described as a sort of baptismal scene in which the dove is released above their heads (John baptizes Jesus in Luke 3:22, and the Holy Spirit descends in "bodily form" like a dove). Milly is portrayed as "different, younger, fairer," with a pervasive presence. Densher feels a keen aversion to profiting "by so high a tide; he felt himself too much 'in' it." He describes again the image of the wings when he says "her confessed consciousness brushed by him" after she joins her guest.

Densher says Milly has "saved" him. His guilt and remorse after complying with Kate's plan and ultimately causing Milly to "turn her face to the wall" prevents the plot from succeeding. Lord Mark has made Milly aware of the plan in an attempt at revenge after Milly refused his own proposal to her. The sins of Densher and Kate are too much for her to bear, and she no longer has the will to live. The Christian symbolism here is readily apparent in the weight of sin killing the people of Noah's generation, and he releases the dove from the ark to find life in the flooded world (Genesis 8:8). The figure of Christ and the dove that remains above his head after his baptism (Luke 3:21–22) provides new life, forgiveness, peace, and redemption. The dove forgives Densher, and leaves her fortune to him after her death so that he can marry Kate. However, the purity of the act prevents him from fulfilling the plan, and his conscience will not allow him to keep the money. His anguish over his deeds makes him wish not to be "unconscious of her—what he wished to ignore was her own consciousness, tortured, for all he knew, crucified by its pain." When questioned by Aunt Maud concerning Milly's fate, Densher gives her the message of her death. She replies, "Our dear dove, then, as Kate calls her, has folded her wonderful wings." Then she adds, "Unless it's more true . . . that she has spread them the wider." Densher agrees that she has, although the two differ in their meanings of "the wider." Aunt Maud hopes "for a flight, I trust, to some happiness greater." Densher interrupts to say, "Exactly, greater," but with trepidation as he speaks it. He fears the wings of the dove have spread a wide trap over him.

In "Ethereal Milly Theale in the *Wings of the Dove*: The Transparent Heart of James's Opaque Style" Kristin King says, "Milly is done to death in a social world whose fine manners cannot hide an irredeemable mercenary core." She also divines that "Milly suggests the Holy Spirit settling on Christ's shoulder when he is baptized in the Jordan River."

Densher tells Kate that he will marry her if they remain as they "were": poor. He cannot keep the money. It is evident to her that Densher's feelings have changed, and she fears she has lost his love forever. She has dimmed in his favor, "wanting in lustre" as Milly had become brilliant in his mind. Kate says that she will marry him if he can give his word of honor that he is not in love with the memory of Milly. She has realized the full force of her actions when she says, "I used to call her, in my stupidity . . . a dove. Well she stretched out her wings, and it was to that they reached. . . . They cover us." She understands finally the infinite divining power and strength of the wings, the quality that none of them had recognized in the dove.

**Source:** Cynthia Gower, Critical Essay on *The Wings of the Dove*, in *Novels for Students*, Gale, Cengage Learning, 2010.

## *Mark A. Eaton*

*In the following review, Eaton discusses the marketing campaigns for the Henry James's novels' adaptations to film.*

In his 1899 essay "The Future of the Novel," Henry James worried about the apparent demise of good taste, or rather the lack of *any* taste, which he thought necessary to appreciate aesthetically demanding fiction like his own:

> The sort of taste that used to be called "good" has nothing to do with the matter: we are so demonstrably in the presence of millions for whom taste is but an obscure, confused, immediate instinct. In the flare of railway bookstalls, in the shop-fronts of most booksellers, especially the provincial, in the advertisements of the weekly newspapers, and in fifty places besides, this testimony to the general preference triumphs. (101)

This triumph of the "general preference" was disturbing for James because he believed that it cheapened the value of serious literary fiction and even threatened the obsolescence of his work. The issue was not that people had stopped reading books—on the contrary, they were reading more than ever—but rather that readers were deluged with the wrong kinds of books: "The flood at present swells and swells,

NONETHELESS, THE JAMES FILMS ARE
DOOMED TO COMPETE FOR AUDIENCE SHARE
AMONG VIEWERS WHO ARE MUCH MORE
FAMILIAR WITH HIGH CONCEPT THAN WITH
HIGH CULTURE."

threatening the whole field of letters, as would often seem, with submersion. [. . .] There is an immense public, if public be the name, inarticulate, but abysmally absorbent, for which, at its hours of ease, the printed volume has no other association [than with fiction]. This public [. . .] grows and grows each year" (100). Drowning in books and lacking taste, this fast-growing mass public failed to discriminate between good books and bad ones.

James's novels have always been credited with representing highly refined mental states, "centers of consciousness" that prefigure the stream of consciousness techniques of later high modernists. Yet James's novels, according to Mark McGurl in a recent study, are at the same time complex delineations of social distinction. For the refined consciousness and exquisite taste of James's protagonists are usually set against the average intelligence of social inferiors, or even against the general stupidity of the masses: "Thus the novels of James must be understood not, or not merely, as representations of thinking, or of consciousness, but as a means of distinguishing the smart from the stupid" (McGurl 129). The celebrated inward turn of James's late phase, in this view, was an attempt "to atomize the class differences [which] had become confused by the proximity, intimacy, and capacity for imitative theatricality of different persons circulating in the same dimension of spaces" (McGurl 76). Class differences had also become confused, as the passage I started with suggests, by the emergence of what was later called the culture industry.

If James's novels have accrued the kind of cultural capital that serves to distinguish the smart from the stupid, how exactly do we account for the appeal of the recent film adaptations?

"Describing James's interest in the cultural values of art does not," as Susan M. Griffin insists, "explain the cultural capital that his own work has accrued in modern cinema. Why has James's writing proved so popular as the material for film?" (2). It seems clear that the very notion of "cultural capital" may have different valences, different consequences even, depending on the context in which it is used, and that certain high culture icons—Shakespeare or Jane Austen, say—may well have markedly different uses when translated into a cultural medium like film. In literary studies, cultural capital has been quite productively viewed as a "symbolic value," as Dale M. Bauer explains, "that registers social class distinctions; it is 'knowledge-capital' that operates as a 'mechanism of social exclusion'" (240; Guillory viii–ix). But in this sense, at least, cultural capital would seem to guarantee a limited rather than a mass audience. Indeed, Pierre Bourdieu points out that cultural capital often accrues to cultural products in inverse proportion to economic capital. The literary field operates according to a kind of anti-economy in which the "loser wins"; economic failure is strangely seen "as a sign of election," whereas success is seen as "a sign of compromise" (*Field* 38–40). Which is precisely what makes cultural capital such a problematic form of currency in the film industry, where the enormous production costs must be offset by maximizing box office grosses. Although classic art cinema certainly did acquire cultural capital once movies were legitimized as art, the demise of art cinema in the last several decades raises the question of whether knowledge of movies—that is, certain kinds of movies—gives anyone the symbolic value (and hence class status) designated by the term cultural capital.

Given Henry James's own anxiety about mass publics, it is interesting to consider how the author would have responded to the current cinematic revival of his novels. The hypothetical scenario of Henry James sitting in a theater watching a movie while munching popcorn has proved irresistible to critics assessing the latest spate of adaptations (as in the title and cover art of a recent essay collection, *Henry James at the Movies*). As early as the 1950s, movie critics used Henry James as a benchmark of high culture that cinema would have to be measured against if it were to gain artistic legitimacy in its own right. Thus in the preface to *The Immediate Experience: Movies, Comics, Theater and Other Aspects of Popular Culture*, Robert Warshow declared himself to be "sharply aware that the impulse which leads me to a Humphrey Bogart movie has little in common with the impulse which leads me to the novels of Henry James. [. . .] I have not brought Henry James to the movies or the movies to Henry James, but I hope I have shown that the man who goes to the movies is the same man who reads James. In the long run, I hope that my work may even make some contribution to the 'legitimatization' of the movies" (xli–xliii). Warshow expresses here an anxiety about appreciating popular culture at the expense of high culture that James obviously shared but which has long since diminished, thanks in part to the subsequent elevation of art cinema. Today's critics are less fastidious about bringing Henry James to the movies, or the movies to Henry James. Cynthia Ozick, for instance, cannot think of anyone who "distinguished more stringently between High and Low than this illustrious literary master," yet still believes James would have "welcomed" film adaptations of his works (H1). Daphne Merkin goes further: "[James] would have *loved* the vicarious embrace of the movies" (122; my emphasis). I'm not so sure myself. What *is* clear, though, is that the demarcations between high and low culture have profoundly shifted since James's time, first with the emergence of "middlebrow culture" in the mid-1920s, and then with the leveling of cultural hierarchies generally in postmodernism. "For more than a century," John Seabrook argues in *Nobrow: The Culture of Marketing, the Marketing of Culture:*

> [. . .] the elite in the United States had distinguished themselves from consumers of commercial culture, or mass culture. Highbrow/lowbrow was the language by which culture was translated into status—the pivot on which distinctions of taste became distinctions of caste. [. . .] In the United States, making hierarchical distinctions about culture was the only acceptable way to talk about class. (26)

However, in the last half of the twentieth century, Seabrook continues:

> [. . .] the town house of culture collapsed. [. . .] The old distinction between the elite culture of the aristocrats and the commercial culture of the masses was torn down, and in its place was erected a hierarchy of hotness. Nobrow is not culture without hierarchy, of course, but in Nobrow commercial culture is a potential source of status, rather than the thing the elite define themselves against. (69, 28)

Similarly, recent popular appropriations of high cultural texts by Jane Austen, James, and Shakespeare speak to a subtle shift in the dynamics of middlebrow culture starting in the 1990s. To begin with, the very concept of the "middlebrow," which has proved useful in assessing the pedagogical function of early twentieth-century institutions such as the Book-of-the-Month Club (Radway), seems less and less applicable to the current film industry. "I believe it is a serious mistake," writes Jim Collins, "to conceive of the current popularization of elite cultural pleasures as simply the most recent incarnation of middlebrow aesthetics" (7). The inadequacy of the middlebrow as a model for these adaptations prompts Collins to suggest a new cultural category he terms "high-pop," which depends "on the appropriation of elite cultural pleasure without quotation marks, an appropriation not just of specific icons or canonical texts but entire protocols for demonstrating taste and social distinction" (6). I suggest that we begin to describe the placement of cultural forms less around the well-worn coordinates of a spatial model of high, low, middlebrow than in terms of the different use-values taken on by various cultural forms. As Marc Bousquet suggests, the question is "not primarily one of degree on a spectrum with largely intellectual valence (i.e., highbrow, middlebrow, mass), but really one of many other specificities—so that when we say something is 'popularized,' we should also feel compelled to ask: popularized for whom, exactly?" (234). In other words, we still need to develop a fuller understanding of the interplay or overlapping of cultural forms, as well as the variety of uses to which they are put. What you read may determine who you are, as the saying goes, but what movies you see does not have quite the same identifying function in the current culture industry.

The recent Henry James films were marketed to well-educated urban professionals who can generally be relied on to seek out more intelligent fare than the latest James Bond thriller or mindless Farrelly Brothers comedies like *Dumb and Dumber* (1994) and *Shallow Hal* (2001). Paradoxically, though, this audience seems increasingly disinclined to see only art films. As Dianne F. Sadoff points out, "the art-house filmgoer, once a member of a specialized but highly coherent audience, now has a range of options as consumer" ("Intimate" 288). This range of options comprises a highly undifferentiated field of filmic entertainment, where new releases go head to head every week, and where hit movies must appeal to more than one segment of the movie-going audience. "The anxiety about opening weekends reached its peak in the mid-nineties," J. D. Connor writes. "Between 1990 and 1996, studio [. . .] production increased by a third, costs per picture rose by half, while U.S. box office went up only one sixth. Even with healthy increases in the number of screens, the number of screens per studio picture was down by a quarter. This is the bare bones of a scenario in which there are too many movies" (56). With so much competition for screens and viewers, it is no wonder that art-house-type films fail to "open big," in Hollywood parlance, not least because they are shown on far fewer screens, but also because there is more competition for box-office dollars on any given weekend: "In this tight market no film has the luxury of a weak week in order to get 'legs'" (Connor 56). And that is why the movie industry is currently dominated by what Justin Wyatt terms the "high concept" movie, one where a straightforward, simple narrative combines with obligatory star power to create the nearly perfect marketable commodity. Needless to say, film adaptations of Henry James novels are about as far from high concept as one can get. Nonetheless, the James films are doomed to compete for audience share among viewers who are much more familiar with high concept than with high culture.

**Source:** Mark A. Eaton, "Miramax, Merchant-Ivory, and the New Nobrow Culture: Niche Marketing *The Wings of the Dove* and *The Golden Bowl*," in *Literature Film Quarterly*, Vol. 34, No. 4, 2009, pp. 257–66.

## Michael McFee

*In the following essay, McFee highlights the architectural similarities and effects of the church scenes in three of Henry James's works.*

F. O. Matthiessen once observed that Henry James makes "magnificently functional use of his architectural details." Not only his details: James also employs the general setting—whether museum, court, chamber, garden, or street—very carefully as part of what he calls "the admirable medium of the scene." One such setting—which occurs only once but at a crucial position in *The Ambassadors, The American*, and *The Wings of the Dove*—is a church, a chapel or a cathedral or an oratory entered by the male protagonists for very particular (and very different) reasons.

Almost every critic remarks on the precise symmetry and balance of *The Ambassadors*, and Strether's pilgrimage to Notre Dame exactly begins the second half of the book (bk. 7, pt. 1). His relationship with Chad and Madame de Vionnet, the great changes in himself, and the communications with America are all unsteadily balanced on the precarious fulcrum of plot at the end of book 6. It is no wonder he seeks sanctuary, "a refuge from the obsession of his problem," "a sense of safety, of simplification," in the church. There is no spiritual pretension in Strether—"the great church had no altar for his worship, no direct voice for his soul"—although he does feel some longing when he sees a lady who "had placed herself, as he never did, within the focus of the shrine, and she had lost herself, as he could easily see, as he would only have liked to do." Instead, his attitude is that of someone "under the charm of a museum," and when, "in the museum mood," he drops into a seat halfway down the nave, "head thrown back and eyes aloft," he might very well be Newman at ease on his divan in the Louvre at the opening of *The American*.

Strether's scene in church is an interlude, an idle stroll under the spell of a friendly old monument. Newman's is very different, his initial moments of aesthetic leisure have disappeared, and we are nearing the conclusion of the book (chap. 24). Madame de Cintré has entered the convent, and Newman has come to the Carmelite chapel in hopes of hearing her voice. The medium is much more concentrated and intense than the diffuse, casual atmosphere of the cathedral. The chapel is small, dim and (James twice emphasizes) quite cold, every person there is desperately involved, especially after the priest begins to say mass and the nuns start to chant. Newman is not there to escape his problem, as Strether is, but to confront it, and he reaches the emotional crisis of the book." Newman felt that he needed all his self-control. He was growing more agitated; he felt tears in his eyes. At last . . . he rose abruptly and went out." Abruptly; for, unlike Strether, he found only "a mockery of consolation" and no sanctuary.

In *The Wings of the Dove* Merton Densher likewise comes to a church at his moment of crisis, which is also near the end of the book (bk. 10, pt. 3). After an agitated Christmas Eve alone—"his intelligence and imagination, his soul and his sense, had never on the whole been so intensely engaged"—and an eventful Christmas morning, during which he learns that Millie has died and Kate has left Mrs. Lowder, Densher finally realizes that his affairs with Kate must not "escape an hour longer taking their proper place in his life." That he should actually resolve all his complications at Brompton Oratory, however, is almost accidental. The idea of attending church has only just been suggested ("And now—I dare say—you'll go to church?") and assented to ("Why yes—I think I will"), and it is only because he finds himself on Brompton Road en route to Kate that he thinks of the nearby Oratory and decides to honor his word to Mrs Lowder. But once he reaches the door of the church, he feels that his previously vague "idea," so demanded by Kate at the end of part 2, has been "really consecrated," and he knows that "The Oratory, in short, to make him right, would do." James, true to his method of indirection and omission in the book and to the established pattern of passivity and indecision in Densher, ends part 3 at this point without detailing the effect of the service on his protagonist.

Besides the very different medium and effect of the three church scenes, there are several particular similarities. One is the way the men observe their fellow visitants. Just as Strether meditates upon the back of the supremely still lady, so for Newman "the praying women kept still, with their backs turned." And though Densher enters a crowded church on a holy day, he is similarly situated, looking over the backs of worshippers, behind and not among the congregation "he was, pushing in, on the edge of a splendid service—the flocking crowd told of it." This characteristic position of Densher—always "on the edge," "never one to flock"—emphasizes both his isolation and his longing for a consummation intense as the mass "which glittered and resounded, from distant depths, in the blaze of altar lights and the swell of organ and choir."

In the less festive atmosphere of *The Ambassadors* and *The Americans,* the hidden faces of "women, deeply absorbed in their devotion," naturally make the protagonists feel the inadequacy of the tourist or visitor, but they also suggest a deeper estrangement from a source of spiritual comfort for their problems, as Newman says, "they were better off than he, for they at least shared the faith to which the others had sacrificed themselves." Moreover, these women also reinforce the peculiarly female medium of these books, for whether in

church, or in interviews following these scenes, or in the whole progress of plot in the novels, the men are always at the mercy of women, not of God. *The Wings of the Dove* is perhaps the extreme case, with Densher hemmed in, as he repeatedly says, by "a circle of petticoats" and trying to be elastic enough to satisfy four demanding women at once—Kate, Mrs. Lowder, Mrs. Stringham, and Milly. This influence is pervasive: "the dove" is not the traditional Christian symbol, from Noah's hardy bird to spiritus sanctus, but a frail American heiress. And after all, Strether strolls not to Sainte-Chappelle but to Notre Dame, yet another functional, if unintentional, choice of architectural detail.

**Source:** Michael McFee, "The Church Scenes in *The Ambassadors, The Americans,* and *The Wings of the Dove*," in *Papers on Language & Literature*, Vol. 16, No. 3, Summer 1980, pp. 325–28.

## Miriam Allott

*In the following essay, Allott argues that the identification of the Bronzino portrait helps document the mind and imagination of Henry James.*

The identification of the Bronzino portrait in *The Wings of the Dove* (1902)—a portrait resembling the heroine Milly Theale and supplying the occasion for a scene which is one of the psychological climaxes of the novel—helps to enrich appreciation of this book and to fill in some of the gaps left by the *Notebooks* as a document revealing the working of James's mind and imagination.

Milly is introduced into English society by Mrs. Lowder and Lord Mark and is a success in the country-house gathering at Matcham. In one of the galleries hangs a portrait by Bronzino of a remarkable young woman whom Milly closely resembles. Everyone comments on the likeness and Lord Mark urges her to inspect it for herself. Standing before the painting she suddenly experiences a moment of significant emotion:

> . . . she found herself, for the first moment, looking at the mysterious portrait through tears. Perhaps it was her tears that made it just then so strange and fair . . . the face of a young woman, all magnificently drawn down to the hands, and magnificently dressed; a face almost livid in hue, yet handsome in sadness and crowned with a mass of hair rolled back and high, that must, before fading with time, have had a family resemblance to her own. The

lady in question at all events, with her slightly Michaelangelesque squareness, her eyes of other days, her full lips, her long neck, her recorded jewels, her brocaded and wasted reds, was a very great personage—only unaccompanied by a joy. And she was dead, dead, dead. Milly recognised her exactly in words that had nothing to do with her. 'I shall never be better than this.'

From the details supplied by James in this description it is possible to assert that here he is not inventing an imaginary Bronzino but recalling an actual portrait seen by him in the Uffizi at Florence. The portrait of Lucrezia Panciatichi, painted between 1532 and 1540, is reproduced—unsatisfactorily—in the *Enciclopedia Italiana* (VII, facing p. 928, 1930), but is also available as a Medici Society print. The pale face of the sitter stares out of the now dark setting—once probably deep green—and confronts the world with the characteristic aloofness of Bronzino's aristocratic subjects. The pallor of the face combined with the red hair 'rolled back and high,' 'the long neck,' 'the Michaelangelesque squareness,' the 'brocaded and wasted reds' and 'the recorded jewels' makes the identification irresistible. The expressive stillness of the pose suggests self-control allied to a capacity for intense feeling.

It is unnecessary to document Henry James's many visits to Florence, but it may be noted that his first visit was in 1869, the year before the death of his cousin Minnie Temple. At what point he decided to introduce the portrait of Lucrezia Panciatichi into *The Wings of the Dove* would be as difficult to determine as the point at which he became quite conscious that his figure of 'La Mourante' was to be in effect a memorial to his cousin. But that the Bronzino portrait came to carry poignant associations for him, that it was the 'right thing' for his purpose in *The Wings of the Dove,* is abundantly clear from the quality of the emotional response it arouses in Milly Theale, the novel's central character. It is clear, too, that James must have looked hard and long at the portrait in the Uffizi. The phrase 'her recorded jewels' reveals this. Carved into the longer green 'beads' of the second and larger necklace worn by Bronzino's Lucrezia is the legend 'Amour dure sans fin' [Love lasts forever]. No phrase could be more exact for the love of a Milly, the dove whose wings even from the grave 'cover us,' as Merton Densher tells Kate Croy when everything else is at an end.

**Source:** Miriam Allott, "The Bronzino Portrait in Henry James's *The Wings of the Dove*," in *Modern Language Notes*, Vol. 68, No. 1, January 1953, pp. 23–25.

## SOURCES

Berland, Alwyn, "The Related Ideas," in *Culture and Conduct in the Novels of Henry James*, Cambridge University Press, 1981, pp. 39–40.

Hutchison, Hazel, "The Vain Appearance: Vision and *The Ambassadors*," in *Seeing and Believing: Henry James and the Spiritual World*, Palgrave MacMillan, 2006, p. 81.

———, "The Sacred Hush: Death, Elegy, and *The Wings of the Dove*," in *Seeing and Believing: Henry James and the Spiritual World*, Palgrave MacMillan, 2006, pp. 107–12.

James, Henry, *The Wings of the Dove*, edited by Peter Brooks, Oxford University Press, 1984.

King, Kristin, "Ethereal Milly Theale in *The Wings of the Dove*: The Transparent Heart of James's Opaque Style," in *Henry James Review*, Vol. 21, No. 1, Winter 2000, pp. 1–13.

*Life Application Study Bible: The New Living Translation*, 2nd ed., Tyndale House Publishers, 2004.

McCormack, Peggy, "Exchange Economics after the Major Phase," in *The Rule of Money: Gender, Class, and Exchange Economics in the Fiction of Henry James*, UMI Research Press, 1990, pp. 95, 100.

Minter, David L., "A Dream City, Lyric Years, A Great War," in *A Cultural History of the American Novel: Henry James to William Faulkner*, Cambridge University Press, 1994, pp. 10–11.

Simon, Linda, "A Mirror for Americans: Contemporary Criticism, 1866–1916," in *The Critical Reception of Henry James: Creating a Master*, Camden House, 2007, p. 24.

Woolf, Judith, Introduction to *Henry James: The Major Novels*, Cambridge University Press, 1991, p 1.

## FURTHER READING

Faulkner, William, *The Sound and the Fury: the Corrected Text*, Vintage International, 1991.
   The fiction of William Faulkner, a mid-twentieth-century writer, is lauded as being among the greatest in American literature. Henry James was a nineteenth-century forerunner of Faulkner's stream of consciousness.

Novick, Sheldon, *Henry James: The Mature Master*, Random House, 2007.
   This biography of Henry James is dedicated to the latter part of his life from 1881 to the end of his life in 1916. This is the period during which he

wrote *The Wings of the Dove* and is considered to be the time of his greatest artistic achievement.

Rosenbloom, Robert, and H. W. Janson, *19th Century Art*, Pearson Prentice Hall, 2005.

This survey of art and sculpture in the nineteenth century is an enormous picture book of over 540 illustrations, 370 of which are in color. It not only gives insight into the culture of James's era, but also deals with how art was influenced by literature, politics, technology, and music.

Shandley, Mary Lyndon, *Feminism, Marriage, and the Law in Victorian England, 1850–1895*, Princeton University Press, 1993.

This study provides insight into the lives of the Victorian woman and those who sought to change the inequalities of the society. In particular, it discusses the laws concerning marriage, divorce, and married women's property, which at the time gave much greater consideration to men.

# A Wrinkle in Time

## MADELEINE L'ENGLE

## 1962

The novel *A Wrinkle in Time*, by American author Madeleine L'Engle, contains elements of both fantasy and science fiction. It was originally conceived and written as a young-adult novel, but many readers comment that the novel readily sustains the interest of adult readers and even question whether the book is truly a "young-adult" novel. The novel is the first in a series called the Time Quartet; the other novels in the series are *A Wind in the Door*, *A Swiftly Tilting Planet*, and *Many Waters*. A fifth novel, *An Acceptable Time*, turned the quartet into a quintet, yet it is still referred to as the Time Quartet.

In discussing L'Engle's work, critics also talk about the "frameworks" that organize the novels. One of these is called the "chronos" framework; the novels in this framework are written in a more or less realistic style and are all structured around a family called the Austins. In her autobiographical book *A Circle of Quiet*, L'Engle explains that chronos is everyday clock time. In contrast is the "kairos" framework. These novels sometimes have realistic settings, but they more often have elements of science fiction, fantasy, and even magic. This vision of time is God's time, where past and present are meaningless, the novels are structured around the Murry and O'Keefe families. In both frameworks, the tales deal with subsequent generations; thus, for example, Meg Murry and Calvin O'Keefe in *A Wrinkle in Time* become the parents of Polly O'Keefe, who appears as the protagonist in later books. Also,

*Madeleine L'Engle* (*AP Images*)

characters from both the chronos and kairos frameworks cross over into each other, creating an interlocking world where time and historical events are shared.

*A Wrinkle in Time* is one of L'Engle's earliest books, and it was rejected by more than two dozen publishers before John Farrar of the publishing firm Farrar, Straus & Giroux, agreed to read it. He published it not because he believed it would sell but simply because he liked it. *A Wrinkle in Time* went on to win the prestigious Newbery Medal in 1963 and has been in hard-cover print ever since it was published in 1962.

## AUTHOR BIOGRAPHY

Madeleine L'Engle Camp was born on November 29, 1918, in New York City. Her father, Charles Wadsworth Camp, was a writer and critic; her mother, also named Madeleine, was an accomplished pianist. L'Engle was a shy, awkward child, and her teachers believed she was of limited ability, so she retreated into a world of books and writing, including a journal she began keeping at the age of eight. She had a series of governesses and attended boarding schools, including one in

Switzerland and one in Charleston, South Carolina, after her family returned to the United States to settle in Florida. After graduating with honors from Smith College in 1941, she moved to New York City. There she met Hugh Franklin, an actor, when she appeared in a play with him, and the two were married in 1946. Meanwhile, in 1945, she published her first novel, *A Small Rain*. In the late 1940s, after the birth of the couple's first child, the family moved to rural Connecticut, where they lived in a two-centuries-old farmhouse called Crosswicks. But in 1959 they returned to New York City so that Hugh could resurrect his acting career. Just prior to the move, though, the family took a ten-week camping trip across the United States. L'Engle later said that it was during this trip that she conceived *A Wrinkle in Time*, which she completed in 1960.

What followed was an enormously busy time in the author's life. In addition to raising her two biological children and a third adopted child, L'Engle taught from 1960 to 1966 at St. Hilda's and St. Hugh's School in New York City. She also wrote and published numerous novels (for both adults and young adults), as well as a collection of poetry, autobiographies (in a series of four books called *The Crosswicks Journals*), and books on art and religion—a total of three dozen books in all. Additionally, she was in demand as a speaker, seminar leader, and writer-in-residence. She served a term as president of the Authors Guild, was named an Associate Dame of Justice of the Venerable Order of Saint John, directed her church choirs, and received honorary degrees from a dozen colleges and universities. She also served as the librarian and writer-in-residence at the Episcopal Cathedral of St. John the Divine in New York City for a lengthy period. Her writing has won numerous awards, including the ALAN Award and the Kerlan Award.

L'Engle was seriously injured in a car accident in 1991. In her final years, her travel schedule was limited because of osteoporosis, and she suffered a stroke in 2002. She died in a nursing home in Litchfield, Connecticut, on September 6, 2007, at the age of eighty-eight.

## PLOT SUMMARY

### Chapter 1: Mrs. Whatsit
On a wet, stormy night, fourteen-year-old Meg Murry lies awake in bed in her attic room,

# MEDIA ADAPTATIONS

- A film version of *A Wrinkle in Time* was released by Walt Disney Home Entertainment on DVD and VHS in 2004. It stars Katie Stuart and David Dorfman and was directed by John Kent Harrison. Running time is two hours and eight minutes.

- An audiobook version, read by the author, was released in 1994 by Recorded Books. Running time is approximately five and a half hours.

- An operatic version of *A Wrinkle in Time* premiered in 1991. The composer is Libby Larsen, and the librettist is Walter Green.

troubled by thoughts that she does not fit in with the other students at her high school and that her teachers are threatening to give her low grades because her classroom performance is poor. Worse, though, is the fact that her father, Dr. Alexander Murry (whose first name is revealed only in a later novel in the Time Quartet series), has been missing for over a year. When the family dog, Fortinbras, begins barking, she worries that a neighborhood tramp, who stole bed sheets from the constable's wife, Mrs. Buncombe, is hanging about. Meg goes down to the kitchen, where her brother, five-year-old Charles Wallace, appears to be waiting for her. Mrs. Murry (Katherine, or Kate) enters and tells Meg that she spoke with Mrs. Henderson, whose son Meg had beaten up at school that day. Meg laments that she is an oddball and wishes she were more normal, like her twin siblings, ten-year-old Sandy (Alexander) and Dennys. Charles Wallace says that he has discussed Meg's problems with Mrs. Whatsit, though he refuses to provide any information about the woman's identity.

The dog begins barking again, so Mrs. Murry goes outside to investigate. She returns with Mrs. Whatsit, an eccentric vagrant who is bundled in wet clothing. Mrs. Whatsit explains that while she enjoys stormy weather, the storm

has blown her off course. She also confirms that it was she who stole the bed sheets from Mrs. Buncombe. After drying her feet, she announces that there is such a thing as a tesseract. She then dashes off, leaving the family stunned by her odd statement. In particular, Mrs. Murry, who like her husband is a scientist, is mystified that Mrs. Whatsit knows about the tesseract.

## Chapter 2: Mrs. Who

The following day is a difficult one for Meg. She is puzzled by the events of the previous evening, but her mother tells her "you don't have to understand things for them to *be*." At school, a teacher sends her to the office of the principal, Mr. Jenkins, for being rude. She bristles when the principal asks her about her home life and suggests that the family needs to accept the fact that Meg's father is gone for good. After school, Meg, Charles Wallace, and Fortinbras go to a local haunted house to visit Mrs. Whatsit. Along the way they encounter Calvin O'Keefe, a popular athlete at Meg's school who admits that he is strangely fascinated by the haunted house. The three enter the house and find Mrs. Who, a plump woman wearing large glasses and sewing with Mrs. Buncombe's sheets while a black pot boils on the hearth. Mrs. Who cryptically refers to Calvin as a "good choice." She also tells them that the time is drawing near and that the three should get food and rest. Meanwhile, Charles Wallace has invited Calvin for dinner, and the three depart for the Murry home.

## Chapter 3: Mrs. Which

Chapter 3 is set in the Murry home before and after dinner. Before dinner, Meg shows Calvin a picture of her father, who used to work at Cape Canaveral but has been missing for over a year. She also helps Calvin with his math and physics, even though she is in a lower grade. Her ability in science and math was fostered by her father, who used to play number games with her. Calvin, meanwhile, enjoys the Murry family's warmth and closeness; as the third of eleven children, he feels that his parents pay little attention to him. After dinner, as Calvin reads to Charles Wallace, Meg and her mother discuss Mr. Murry's disappearance. Mrs. Murry accepts that there are some things that have no explanation, but Meg is unwilling to agree with this notion.

Meg and Calvin take a walk in the yard, where Meg tells Calvin that her father was an astrophysicist who worked first in New Mexico, then at Cape Canaveral. Calvin mentions the rumors that he has heard about Mr. Murry's disappearance, such as the one spread by the postmistress that he has run off with another woman, but Calvin reassures Meg that he does not believe the rumors. Calvin and Meg hold hands, and Meg blushes when Calvin tells her that she has beautiful eyes. Suddenly Charles Wallace appears and tells them that it is time for them to go in search of Mr. Murry. Mrs. Who appears in the moonlight, and Mrs. Whatsit, wearing Mrs. Buncombe's sheets, climbs over a fence into the yard. Then Mrs. Which announces her presence in a gust of wind but says that for her to fully materialize would be too tiring. The three are collectively referred to as the Mrs. Ws.

### Chapter 4: The Black Thing

Chapter 4 takes place on the planet Uriel. Meg feels herself cast into a silent darkness until Calvin and Charles Wallace appear, along with Mrs. Whatsit, Mrs. Who, and Mrs. Which, who tell the children where they are. Calvin asks how they arrived on Uriel, and Mrs. Whatsit explains that they are able to "tesser," or "wrinkle," through space. She also tells the children that they are searching for Mr. Murry, who is facing a threat. Mrs. Whatsit then transforms herself into a beautiful creature with the body of a horse but the torso of a human. She rebukes Calvin for falling to his knees, as though he is worshipping her. The children climb onto her back and she flies over the planet, showing them green fields, a rocky plateau, and visions of beautiful creatures doing a dance in a garden to music set to words from the biblical book of Isaiah, including the famous verse "Sing a new song unto the Lord." She gives each of the children a bouquet of flowers and tells them to breathe through it if the air becomes too thin. Their travels continue, allowing them to see one of Uriel's moons. Most importantly, they see a blackness above the clouds. Meg feels the blackness, the Black Thing, as an embodiment of evil and asks Mrs. Which if this evil is what her father is fighting.

### Chapter 5: The Tesseract

While Chapter 4 is dominated by images of religion, Chapter 5 is dominated by a discussion of science. Mrs. Whatsit tells Meg that her father is trapped behind the Dark Thing and that they are traveling to meet him by tessering, a mode of travel that takes shortcuts through space and time. Charles Wallace, who is a precocious boy,

explains that tessering involves a fifth dimension; if the first dimension is a line, the second is a square, the third is a cube, the fourth is time, and the fifth is a tesseract, which enables them to travel through "a wrinkle in time" and space. Suddenly, the children feel themselves tessering, but Meg feels that her body is flattened and that she cannot breathe. Mrs. Which apologizes, telling the children that they are on a two-dimensional planet and that she momentarily forgot that humans cannot live in two dimensions.

The group arrives at a foggy planet in the constellation Orion. They enter a cave, where they meet the Happy Medium, a jolly woman with a crystal ball. She shows the children a vision of Earth, which is being surrounded by the Dark Thing. Mrs. Which explains that they are the latest in a long line of those who have fought the Dark Thing, including Jesus, Shakespeare, Leonardo da Vinci, Johann Sebastian Bach, Albert Einstein, and Mahatma Gandhi. Mrs. Which tells Meg that her father is a captive on a planet that has surrendered to the Dark Thing.

### Chapter 6: The Happy Medium

Using her crystal ball, the Happy Medium shows the children a battle between the Dark Thing and the stars, explaining that one of the stars has just sacrificed itself in battling the Dark Thing. Charles Wallace guesses that Mrs. Whatsit was once a star who made a similar sacrifice. The Happy Medium gives the children a vision of their mothers: Mrs. O'Keefe is paddling one of her children, but Mrs. Murry is writing her daily letter to her husband.

The group then tessers to the planet of Camazotz, where Mr. Murry is being held. On a hill overlooking a town, the Mrs. Ws tell the children that they can accompany them no farther. Each gives the children a gift to help them. Mrs. Whatsit's gift is to strengthen each child's natural characteristics; she helps Meg overcome her faults, enhances Calvin's ability to bond with all sorts of people, and reinforces Charles Wallace's childhood resilience. Mrs. Who gives Meg her spectacles, Calvin a quotation from Shakespeare's play *The Tempest*, and Charles Wallace a quotation from the German poet Johann Wolfgang von Goethe. Mrs. Which's gift is to enjoin the children to remain strong together. The children descend the hill into the town, where all the houses are uniform and the children all seem to play in a synchronized rhythm, a pulsing that Charles Wallace senses as he tries to divine the thoughts of the people. One mother is horrified at the "aberration" of her child dropping a ball. A paper delivery boy informs them that the town is ruled by IT in the CENTRAL Central Intelligence building. The children are resolved to confront the danger they know they will face in the CENTRAL Central Intelligence building.

### Chapter 7: The Man with Red Eyes

At the CENTRAL Central Intelligence building, a door opens and the children see a dull entryway and anonymous-looking men in business suits. They ask one of the men how things in the building work, but in response they get meaningless references to a spelling machine, the S papers, the B slot, and the like. The man fears that if he does not report them, he will be "reprocessed." He tells them to "just relax and don't fight it and it will all be much easier for you." A wall before them dissolves, revealing a room with machines, robotic attendants, and a man with red eyes on a platform. The children sense that he is a manifestation of the Dark Thing. He communicates with the children telepathically, without moving his lips. He tries to hypnotize them by having them recite multiplication tables, but Calvin resists by reciting the Gettysburg Address, as does Charles Wallace by reciting nursery rhymes. The man is unable to understand why they want to see Mr. Murry. He says that of the three children, Charles is the only one complex enough to understand him. He offers the children a turkey dinner, but the food is synthetic and tastes like sand. He asks Charles to accompany him so that the boy can learn about IT, and Charles agrees over Meg's protests. The Man with Red Eyes stares into Charles's eyes, and Charles becomes a different person. He appears to have been absorbed by IT. He chastises his sister for being belligerent and now claims that the food is delicious.

### Chapter 8: The Transparent Column

Charles has gone over to the IT. He tells Meg and Calvin that the Man with the Red Eyes is their friend and that the Mrs. Ws are enemies. The Man with the Red Eyes identifies himself as the Prime Coordinator. He tells Meg and Calvin that Charles will lead them to Mr. Murry. As the boy leads them down a long white hallway, Meg urges Calvin to use his ability to communicate with people to talk to Charles in an effort to reclaim him. Charles, though, continues to speak in the

voice of IT, telling his companions that the Man with the Red Eyes is the Boss and that because of the conformity on Camazotz, there are no wars and no unhappiness. Charles waves his hand and a wall dissolves. Inside a room they see the boy who earlier had dropped the ball; as his punishment, he is bouncing the ball in a rhythmic fashion, but every time it hits the floor, he feels pain. In another small room, Charles shows them a transparent cylinder. Mr. Murry is trapped inside.

### Chapter 9: IT

Meg tries to reach her father, but she cannot penetrate the cylinder. She attacks Charles, but her brother punches her. Calvin nearly gets Charles back from IT's clutches by quoting the lines from *The Tempest*, but Charles remains under the control of IT. Meg remembers the glasses from Mrs. Who. She puts them on and is able to penetrate the cylinder. Her overjoyed father can now see her if he puts the glasses on. By holding Meg, he is able to escape the cylinder. Charles behaves rudely to his father, but Meg assures Mr. Murry that Charles is not really himself. Charles tells the others that he has to lead them to IT. He takes them to another building, which is filled with nothing but a pulsing violet glow and a large living brain on a dais. Mr. Murry shouts to the children that they have to resist succumbing to the control of the pulsations. Meg tries by reciting the Declaration of Independence, the periodic table of the elements, and irrational square roots, but she feels herself slipping away. Calvin, sensing that Meg is being lost to IT control, orders everyone to tesser. Mr. Murry holds Meg's hand, and she feels herself caught in a swirl of tessering.

### Chapter 10: Absolute Zero

Having tessered through the absolute zero cold of the Black Thing, Meg experiences a drop in body temperature and loses the ability to move or speak, but she can hear her father discussing his disappearance with Calvin. He was part of a team that wanted to tesser to Mars but somehow he wound up on Camazotz. He was in a state of despair and was in danger of giving in to IT when the children rescued him. Meg begins to regain the ability to move and speak and unfairly demands to know why her father did not save Charles. Mr. Murry responds by saying that "all things work together for good to them that love God." As he massages her fingers, Meg feels pain, which her father tells her is good, for she is regaining the ability to feel. Three creatures approach them, each with four arms and tentacles for hair. Meg is frightened, but when one of the creatures touches her, she feels warmth spread through her.

### Chapter 11: Aunt Beast

Calvin tries to explain to the creatures that he is from a planet that is striving to fight off the Dark Thing. Meg is still very weak, so the creatures take her into their care. She nestles against the furry chest of one and feels well-being. The creature rubs something over her, clothes her, and gives her delicious food. The creature asks Meg to give it a name; Meg settles on Aunt Beast. She tries to explain the concept of vision to Aunt Beast, but to no avail, for the creatures have no eyes. After a profound sleep, Meg awakens feeling refreshed. Aunt Beast explains to Meg that she and the other two creatures are from the planet Ixchel and that her planet, too, is fighting off the Dark Thing. After Aunt Beast sings her a beautiful song, Meg feels peaceful. The creatures return Meg to Calvin and her father. Meg asks whether the creatures can summon the Mrs. Ws. She tries to describe them, but again the effort is fruitless because the creatures have no eyes. To summon them herself, Meg tries to concentrate on their essence. Suddenly, in a booming voice, Mrs. Which announces the three women's arrival.

### Chapter 12: The Foolish and the Weak

The Mrs. Ws join the group on Ixchel. They say that they can do nothing to retrieve Charles from Camazotz. Mr. Murry, then Calvin, offer to go, but the Mrs. Ws oppose them. Meg realizes that only she would have any chance of success in breaking through to Charles, for she was the one closest to her brother. She is terrified about having to return to Camazotz, but she is determined to try. Mrs. Which offers to tesser through the Dark Thing with Meg. Each of the Mrs. Ws gives Meg a gift: Mrs. Whatsit strengthens Meg's power of love, and Mrs. Who gives her a passage from St. Paul's Epistle to the Corinthians that empowers "the foolish and the weak," who can succeed in spite of their inadequacies. Mrs. Which's gift is to strengthen in Meg the thing that IT lacks, but Meg will have to learn what that is on her own.

Meg and Mrs. Which tesser safely to Camazotz, and Meg goes to the IT building that houses the brain, where she discovers Charles. She tries to determine the nature of Mrs. Which's gift, but Charles insists that IT has everything Meg has.

When Charles tells Meg that Mrs. Whatsit hates her, the nature of the gift dawns on her: She has the power to love. She concentrates all of her love on Charles, which breaks the spell of IT. Charles runs to Meg's embrace, and the two tesser through the darkness to Calvin and Mr. Murry, who are in the garden at the Murry home on Earth. During a merry family reunion, the Mrs. Ws appear to apologize for not saying good-bye. Mrs. Whatsit starts to explain that the three have a new mission, but before she can finish, a gust of wind rises and the three women disappear.

## CHARACTERS

### Aunt Beast

Aunt Beast, the name given to her by Meg, is one of three creatures on the planet Ixchel who approach the travelers after their escape from Camazotz. Like her companions, she has tentacles for hair, fur, and four arms, and she has no eyes, so she is unable to understand the concepts of vision and light. She is depicted as warm and caring; she nurses Meg after she is caught in the whirlwind of tessering through the Dark Thing.

### Mrs. Buncombe

Mrs. Buncombe is the wife of the town constable. Twelve of her bed sheets are stolen by Mrs. Whatsit.

### Happy Medium

The Happy Medium is a jolly clairvoyant dressed in satin and wearing a silk turban. She has a crystal ball that she uses to give Meg, Charles, and Calvin visions of Earth and of the Dark Thing.

### Mr. Jenkins

Mr. Jenkins is the principal of Meg's high school. He is depicted as cold and unfeeling, and he annoys Meg by suggesting that Meg's family has to accept that Mr. Murry is gone for good.

### Man with the Red Eyes

The man is under the control of IT on the planet Camazotz. He tries to absorb Meg, Charles Wallace, and Calvin by hypnotizing them with his eyes. He tells the group that he is the Prime Coordinator on the planet.

### Alexander Murry

Mr. Murry (whose first name is provided in a later book) is an astrophysicist who, with a team of scientists, was experimenting with the tesseract, a mode of time and space travel. He and his team intended to "tesser" to Mars, but Mr. Murry wound up on the plant Camazotz, which had succumbed to the Dark Thing. Mr. Murry remains a captive on the planet until Meg and Charles Wallace, accompanied by Calvin O'Keefe, arrive to rescue him. At the start of the novel, no one on Earth has heard from him for over a year.

### Charles Wallace Murry

Charles Wallace is just five years old, yet he is quite precocious and capable of understanding scientific concepts. He also seems to have the ability to read people's minds and know what they are thinking. Perhaps because of his raw intelligence, IT is able to capture him on the planet Camazotz, though he is later saved by his sister, Meg.

### Katherine Murry

Katherine, or Kate, is the mother of four children, including Meg and Charles Wallace. She is also a biologist who works out of a lab in her home; she even cooks meals for her children using a Bunsen burner. She is also described as beautiful. Meg is almost jealous of her mother, for her mother's beauty and accomplishments seem to stand in contrast to Meg's awkwardness and homeliness.

### Meg Murry

Meg is the protagonist in *A Wrinkle in Time*. She is fourteen years old and a high school student. At the start of the novel, she is awkward, shy, impatient, and sometimes belligerent. She feels that she does not fit in with the other students at school, and her academic performance is shaky, although she is very intelligent. She wishes that she could be more normal, like her siblings, the twins Sandy and Dennys. She is almost completely lacking in self-confidence. Her journey through space and time, though, changes her. Despite her fears, she journeys to Camazotz to save her father, and she willingly returns to save her brother, Charles Wallace. Along the way she is accompanied by Calvin O'Keefe, a popular boy at school, and their story contains hints of a potential love relationship between the two. At the end of the novel, Meg is more confident and self-assured, and she has learned that love is a powerful weapon against evil.

### Sandy and Dennys Murry

Sandy (Alexander) and Dennys are ten-year-old twins and brothers of Meg and Charles Wallace. Unlike Meg, they are athletic and socially popular.

### Calvin O'Keefe

Calvin is an older boy at Meg's high school. Unlike Meg, he is popular, and he is a gifted athlete. He is also capable of loving, affectionate relationships. Just as Meg feels that she does not belong, Calvin feels like a bit of an outcast in his large family, where he is the third of eleven children. When he visits the Murry home for dinner, he is impressed by the close, loving relationship Mrs. Murry has with her children, in contrast to his own mother, who he thinks will not even notice that he's missing for dinner. It is clear that Calvin is interested in Meg romantically.

### Mrs. Whatsit

Mrs. Whatsit, along with Mrs. Who and Mrs. Which, functions as a guide, a kind of guardian angel, as Meg, her brother, and Calvin make their journey to save Mr. Murry. Mrs. Whatsit stole Mrs. Buncombe's bed sheets to sew clothing. She used to be a star, but she gave up her existence as a star to combat the Dark Thing.

### Mrs. Which

Mrs. Which is one of the three celestial figures who act as guides to Meg, her brother, and Calvin as they journey to find Meg's father. Unlike her companions, Mrs. Whatsit and Mrs. Who, Mrs. Which has difficulty becoming fully materialized, so she appears as something of a haze. She also has trouble speaking, so her words have repeated letters; for example, "Nnoww, cchilldrenn, yyouu musstt nott bee frightened att whatt iss ggoingg tto hhappenn."

### Mrs. Who

Mrs. Who, along with Mrs. Whatsit and Mrs. Which, functions as a guide and guardian angel to Meg, her brother, and Calvin as they make their journey to save Mr. Murry. She finds it difficult to speak using her own sentences, so she communicates largely through quotations from famous writers and thinkers.

# TOPICS FOR FURTHER STUDY

- The tesseract is not entirely L'Engle's fictional creation. Mathematicians describe a tesseract as a kind of four-dimensional cube, and the term was first used as far back as 1888. Investigate the mathematical concept of the tesseract. Does it bear in mathematics any relationship to the concept as it is used in *A Wrinkle in Time*? Present your findings in a report.

- Read any of the ten novels in D. J. MacHale's *Pendragon Adventure* young-adult series, published from 2002 to 2009. The series is about a boy, Bobby Pendragon, who is joined by a group of Travelers to race across space and time to confront and defeat evil in the figure of Saint Dane. Prepare a chart drawing comparisons and contrasts between the novel you selected and *A Wrinkle in Time*.

- At the time L'Engle wrote *A Wrinkle in Time*, there was tremendous interest in the United States in science and especially in space travel. Prepare a timeline of key events in the history of space travel from the late 1950s through the 1960s.

- In 1960, many observers of American culture and society were becoming concerned about conformity, rather like the conformity depicted on the plant Camazotz. A key document in this examination of conformity was Sloan Wilson's 1955 novel *The Man in the Gray Flannel Suit*, a widely read novel about conformity in American business.

Read Sloan's novel and prepare a chart that lists the similarities you see between Sloan's vision of conformity and L'Engle's in *A Wrinkle in Time*.

- One way of looking at *A Wrinkle in Time* is that it is an attempt to reconcile religion and science, two fields of thought that are often regarded as antithetical to each other. Research the relationship between science and religion. What do major religious groups, such as Christianity, Judaism, Islam, Buddhism, Hinduism, and others believe about science versus religion? Summarize your findings in an oral presentation.

- Using the Internet, conduct research about wormholes, or bridges in the space-time continuum that theoretically might allow time travel or travel that is faster than the speed of light. How have artists, mathematicians, and astrophysicists rendered the concept of the wormhole visually? How do they explain the concept of the wormhole? Present your findings in a PowerPoint presentation.

- In Chapter 9, Calvin quotes lines from Shakespeare's play *The Tempest* that were Mrs. Who's gift to him. These lines can be found in act 1, scene 2, of the play, and they are spoken by the main character, the magician Prospero, to Ariel. Read Shakespeare's play and write an essay on its relevance to *A Wrinkle in Time*. Explain why L'Engle used this particular quotation as Mrs. Who's gift.

## THEMES

### Good versus Evil

A major theme of *A Wrinkle in Time* is the ongoing battle between good and evil in the universe. Clearly, the Dark Thing represents evil, a malevolent force that surrounds planets and stars and forces them to succumb to its numbing qualities. All of the characters in the novel are clearly identified as "good" or "bad." Meg and her family, along with Calvin O'Keefe, the three Mrs. Ws, the Happy Medium, and Aunt Beast, all represent the forces of good, of resistance to the Dark Thing. In contrast, the Man with the Red Eyes is an embodiment of the evil effects of the Dark Thing and of IT.

*A Wrinkle in Time involves travel through the universe* (*Image copyright Jurgen Ziewe, 2009. Used under license from Shutterstock.com*)

## The Power of Love

A central message in *A Wrinkle in Time* is that love is a powerful force that humans use to combat evil. From the beginning, Calvin is impressed by the love that permeates the Murry household, in contrast to his own home, where he meets with indifference. Although Mr. Murry has been gone for over a year, Mrs. Murry sustains her love for her husband by writing him a daily letter. As the novel approaches its climax, Meg returns to Camazotz to rescue her brother, but not before Mrs. Which gives her a gift. That gift is to strengthen in Meg the thing that IT lacks, but Meg has to learn what that thing is on her own. When she encounters Charles Wallace, he tells her that Mrs. Whatsit hates her. It is then that Meg understands that the thing she has and that IT does not is the power of love. She is able to release Charles from the clutches of IT by concentrating her power of love on him.

## Self-Knowledge and Growth

Meg is an imperfect heroine. Unlike the heroines of traditional romances and fairy tales, she is by no means beautiful. At the start of the novel she is depicted as shy, awkward, and homely. She is impatient and sometimes has a bad temper. She is rude to a teacher, and she gets into a fight. She feels the insecurities that are common to fourteen-year-olds. She wishes that she could be more "normal," more like the other students at her school, or more like her popular, athletic younger brothers, the twins Sandy and Dennys. She even has bad handwriting. Later, after her father is rescued, everyone tessers away from Camazotz, but Meg unfairly upbraids her father for not saving Charles from IT and the Dark Thing. By the end of the novel, though, Meg has become more self-assured. She learns from her journey that her need to conform is a flaw. She learns that her own power of loving and that the love of her family are more important than social conformity. Early in the novel she thinks, "A delinquent, that's what I am. . . . That's what they'll be saying next. Not Mother. But them. Everybody Else." The pronoun "them" foreshadows the pronoun IT of Camazotz. At the end, though, she is capable of thoughts such as this: "I love you. Charles Wallace, you are my darling and my dear and the light of my life and the treasure of my heart."

## STYLE

### *Symbolism*

*A Wrinkle in Time* is fraught with symbolism. The most prominent symbol is the use of light and dark. In particular, the Dark Thing is symbolic of evil—an evil that is not identified with any particular actions or behaviors. It is a presence, an entity, that surrounds planets and is capable of subduing them. IT is symbolized by the brain that is housed in the Central Intelligence building on Camazotz. The use of a disembodied brain to represent IT suggests that intelligence is not enough to lead a good life. Rather, love is a necessary complement to the intelligence of such characters as Mr. and Mrs. Murry, Charles Wallace, and even Meg herself.

Much of the symbolism of the novel is religious. The three Mrs. Ws have witchlike characteristics, but they suggest the concept of guardian angels who shepherd people through the difficulties of life. Eyes are also used symbolically. The emphasis on eyes is foreshadowed early in the novel when Calvin tells Meg that she has beautiful eyes. The Man with Red Eyes uses his eyes to hypnotize people; his eerie eyes bore into them and force them to submit to IT. In contrast, Aunt Beast and her fellow creatures have no eyes, but they have other characteristics that enable them to communicate with people. Meg is able to rescue her father by putting on Mrs. Who's glasses, enabling her to see her father; Mr. Murry is able to see Meg by putting on the glasses, and at the end of the novel he announces that he needs new glasses. All of these references to vision, sight, eyes, and glasses symbolize the notion of sight, the ability to truly see what is important and what is good.

### *Place Names*

Closely related to symbolism is the author's use of place names. Little emphasis is placed on the New England location where the Murrys and O'Keefes live. The suggestion is that the lessons of the novel are universal, not bounded by place or time. To rescue her father, Meg first travels to Uriel, where she has visions of both good and evil. Uriel is the name of one of the archangels of biblical tradition. She then has to travel to Camazotz. This is not a name of L'Engle's invention; Camazotz is the name of a malevolent Mexican god, an evil vampire that people worshipped. Similarly, the name of the planet Ixchel is not made up. Ixchel is the name of an ancient Mayan goddess associated with rainbows and healing. It indirectly alludes to the rainbow at the end of the biblical story of Noah and the Ark, when evil has been conquered and the earth renews itself. It is an appropriate name, for it is here that the beasts, including Aunt Beast, nurse Meg back to health and restore her for her return to Camazotz to rescue Charles.

### *Journey Motif*

Every author faces the practical problem of how to embody themes, characters, and ideas in a compelling story. If the protagonist of a story is going to grow and change, that character has to be made to confront experiences that promote growth. A common method authors use is structuring the character's growth around a journey. One of the appeals of science fiction and fantasy is that the author encounters essentially no limits in creating the journey. Boundaries of time and place can easily be transcended, and the characters can encounter magical worlds and otherworldly characters that define the experience. While an author such as Mark Twain placed his character Huckleberry Finn on a raft on the Mississippi River, L'Engle has her characters tesser through time and space, traveling to different planets, encountering magical characters such as the Happy Medium and Aunt Beast, and returning home as though no actual time has passed. Meg's journey, then, is clearly not a literal journey, like Huck's. It is a psychological and emotional journey that changes her.

## HISTORICAL CONTEXT

Some readers and critics have contended that *A Wrinkle in Time* is an oblique commentary on the specter of Communism in the 1950s and 1960s. At the time L'Engle wrote the novel, the cold war between the West and the Soviet Union and its satellite countries was at its height. After World War II, the Soviet Union expanded its Communist empire into Eastern Europe. In the late 1940s and early 1950s, there was widespread fear that Communists had infiltrated American

# COMPARE & CONTRAST

- **1960s:** Space travel is entirely new; the first human, the Russian cosmonaut Yuri Gagarin, is launched into space in 1961, followed less than a month later by the first American, Alan Shepard.

  **Today:** In spite of catastrophes such as the space shuttle *Challenger* explosion in 1986 and the *Columbia* explosion in 2003, travel in earth orbit is almost routine, astronauts live on the international space station for months at a time, and communications satellites are launched with regularity.

- **1960s:** The European Organization for Nuclear Research, known widely by the acronym of its French acronym, CERN, is formed in 1954 and begins undertaking research in high-energy physics at its massive facility near Geneva, Switzerland.

  **Today:** CERN continues to operate, and in 1990 a project called ENQUIRE became the prototype for the World Wide Web.

- **1960s:** The civil rights movement in America is gaining momentum under the leadership of such figures as Martin Luther King, Jr.

  **Today:** Despite some continuing prejudice and discrimination, African Americans and other minorities have seen significant gains in such areas as housing, access to professional careers, and education.

- **1960s:** Christian religions, including Catholicism, emphasize traditional beliefs and forms of worship, though movement toward more openness and a more ecumenical spirit is taking hold, especially with the convening of the Catholic Church's Second Vatican Council.

  **Today:** Conflict over religion continues to exist, although earlier conflict between Christian denominations (or between Catholicism and Protestantism) has in large part been replaced by religious intolerance between Christianity, Judaism, and Islam.

---

education, government, and media. In 1949, Communists assumed power in China after a long civil war, and many political observers believed that China wished to export its form of government to other Asian nations, including Korea and Vietnam. By 1960, the United States sent its first troops to Vietnam, beginning America's involvement in a long war whose goal was to stop the spread of Communism. In 1957, the Soviet Union forged a lead in the space race with the launch of the world's first satellite, and many observers were panicked that the Soviets now had the ability to deliver nuclear weapons using missiles. In 1959, the famous "Kitchen Debate" between U.S. Vice President Richard Nixon and Soviet Premier Nikita Khrushchev about the merits of Communism and capitalism took place. That same year, Fidel Castro seized power in Cuba, transforming the island into a Communist nation. Tensions increased in 1960 when the Soviets downed an American U-2 spy plane over the Soviet Union and captured the pilot, Gary Powers. Khrushchev scored propaganda points in Paris that year at a failed summit conference, pointing to the spy plane incident as evidence of American aggression.

All of these incidents combined to create a fear that Communism was spreading, much like the Dark Thing in *A Wrinkle in Time*. It was believed that Communism was atheistic and that it promoted a drab conformity—that it was an evil regime that had to be fought, for it drained individuality and genuine love out of people in the furtherance of its economic, political, and imperialistic goals. At the same time, it is difficult not to think of the American Central Intelligence Agency (CIA) in passages about Camazotz's CENTRAL Central Intelligence.

*A centaur appears near the end of the novel* (Image copyright Christos Georghiou, 2009. Used under license from Shutterstock.com)

The CIA's involvement in espionage and the overthrowing of governments that were not friendly to the West in itself suggests a kind of conformity being imposed by a secretive, authoritarian government.

Conformity was an issue that was entering the public discourse in the late 1950s and early 1960s. During these years, the civil rights movement was gathering steam. Martin Luther King, Jr., was becoming a well-known civil rights leader, and on February 1, 1960, four African American university students broke the color barrier by "sitting in" at a segregated lunch counter in Greensboro, North Carolina. This event, along with numerous others that took place in the late 1950s, began a revolution against conformist, traditional ways of thinking that accelerated during the 1960s. Further, many social observers were concerned about the homogenization of American culture and society. For example, in the wake of World War II, many housing developments sprang up in the suburbs of American cities. One of the most famous was Levittown, on Long Island, New York, though similar developments could be found in and around most major cities. The purpose of these developments was to provide affordable housing. They accomplished that goal, but often the houses and streets were bland and uniform, much like the town the travelers first encounter on Camazotz. It was believed that these suburbs created a high degree of social conformity, with people leading similar lives, watching the same television shows, wearing the same clothes, buying the same furniture, cars, and charcoal grills, and adopting the same social attitudes—that is, living lives according the pulse that drives the lives of those under the control of IT on Camazotz.

## CRITICAL OVERVIEW

*A Wrinkle in Time* won the Newbery Medal in 1963, as well as the Sequoyah Award in 1965 and the Lewis Carroll Shelf Award the same year. It was also a runner-up for the Hans Christian Andersen Award in 1964. It was ironic that the novel was so well received, for L'Engle had great difficulty finding a publisher for it. She submitted the book to publisher after publisher and received in response one rejection slip after another. The chief objection to the book was that publishers were unclear what the market for it would be, whether it was a children's book or whether it was written for adults. Quoting Jean Feiwel, Jennifer Mattson notes in *Booklist*, "Wrinkle wasn't a book for children, and it wasn't a book for adults, and it was kind of unreal, and it just didn't fall into any existing category. So she who couldn't be classified became a class by herself."

*A Wrinkle in Time* was controversial, and in fact continues to be so. Many readers object to the book— and to many of L'Engle's books— because in their view the books are too religious. Ironically, though, many Christian bookstores have refused to stock the book, or any of L'Engle's books, because they object to the version of Christianity that pervades her writing. For example, they argue that L'Engle believes in universal salvation, that is, that God would never condemn anyone to hell for eternity. She also expressed doubts about her religious beliefs, and these doubts found their way into her novels. She was an avid reader of Einstein and other theoretical physicists, and she tried in her novels to reconcile science and religion, thus rejecting a literal interpretation of the Bible. Donald R. Hettinga, quoting *Dare to Be Creative*, notes in *Presenting Madeleine L'Engle* that "Mrs. What [sic], Mrs. Who, and Mrs. Which were witches practicing black magic." In *Sojourners Magazine*

Suzanne St. Yves notes, "*A Wrinkle in Time* is vastly misunderstood by some fundamentalists. A well-researched book (ask any physicist)... ended up being labeled as 'dangerous.' Angels were thought to be witches; the Naked Brain, Satan." Accordingly, *A Wrinkle in Time* has been a frequently "challenged" book, meaning that parents and citizens raise formal objections to its inclusion in school curricula or in public libraries. According to the American Library Association, the novel has consistently been on frequently challenged and banned books lists, appearing as recently as 2005.

From the start, though, *A Wrinkle in Time* was well received. The *Saturday Review* wrote: "It has the general appearance of being science fiction but it is not.... There is mystery, mysticism, a feeling of indefinable brooding horror... original, different, exciting" (quoted by Zarin, "The Storyteller"). The reception of *A Wrinkle in Time* gathered momentum over the years, and many critics look back on the impact the book had on them, on other writers, and on readers. Jennifer Mattson, writing in *Booklist*, refers to the novel's "groundbreaking qualities" and "resilience" and concludes that "it's no surprise that the book had an impact on many contemporary writers of sf/fantasy." Writing in the *New Yorker*, Cynthia Zarin says, "*A Wrinkle in Time*, and a number of L'Engle's other books, became inextricably part of who I was. They influenced how I thought about religion and politics, about physics and mystery, and how I imagined what family life could be." She goes on to note that a college friend said, "There are really two kinds of girls. Those who read Madeleine L'Engle when they were small, and those who didn't."

## CRITICISM

### Michael J. O'Neal

*O'Neal holds a Ph.D. in English literature. In this essay on* A Wrinkle in Time*, he discusses the author's use of parallelism and contrast as a structuring principle in the novel.*

That the major structuring device of *A Wrinkle in Time* is the journey motif is readily apparent to even the most casual reader. What is slightly less obvious is L'Engle's reliance on parallelism and contrast as a further structuring principle. This device enables the author to achieve unity in the book; rather than presenting

> LIFE HAS A 'FORM,' PERHAPS ONE DICTATED BY GOD, YET WITHIN THE BOUNDARIES OF THAT FORM, EACH PERSON HAS TO WRITE THE SONNET OF HIS OR HER OWN LIFE."

the reader with a series of events strung out like beads on a string, parallelism and contrast link the several parts of the novel into a single, organic whole.

Examples of parallelism and contrast abound. Perhaps the most significant one is the implied comparison between the world of Camazotz and the world that Meg inhabits in her daily life. The chief characteristic of Camazotz is that nobody there seems to really care. The people live their lives in conformity with the pulse that locks their lives into a predictable pattern. When Meg and her companions enter the Central Intelligence building, they encounter a man who cares little for who they are or why they are there; his only concern is with making the machines work and dealing correctly with forms. The mother of the child who mishandled the ball punishes the child by calling his fault an "aberration" and locking him in a room where he experiences pain every time his ball hits the floor.

Put simply, Camazotz is a world where there is no love. In many respects, this world parallels the world that Meg inhabits daily. The boy whose mishandling of the ball is an "aberration" contrasts with the athletic prowess of Calvin and of Meg's twin siblings, Sandy and Dennys. Meg gets into a fight at school because other children make fun of her brother. She has conflicts with her teachers and the school principal, whose attitudes parallel those of the man in the Central Intelligence building. Residents of her community spread malicious gossip about Mr. Murry's disappearance. Calvin O'Keefe comes from a family that pays little attention to him; after Charles invites him to the Murry home for dinner, he muses that his mother will likely not notice that he is not at home. When the Happy Medium shows Calvin a vision of home, all he sees is his mother punishing one of his siblings. Most importantly, Meg longs to be an accepted

# WHAT DO I READ NEXT?

- The other novels in L'Engle's Time Quartet series are *A Wind in the Door* (1973), *A Swiftly Tilting Planet* (1978), and *Many Waters* (1986). *An Acceptable Time* (1989) completes the story of the Murry and O'Keefe families.

- *The Chronicles of Narnia* (1950–1956), a series of seven fantasy novels by C. S. Lewis, have become staples in both the fantasy genre and classical literature. Like L'Engle's works, they contain religious elements.

- Philip Pullman's trilogy of fantasy novels, *His Dark Materials* (1995–2000), is a young-adult series that has been described as rejecting the Christian themes of C. S. Lewis's *The Chronicles of Narnia* and by implication those of other fantasy novels with Christian themes.

- *Dark Matter: A Century of Speculative Fiction from the African Diaspora*, edited by Sheree R. Thomas and published in 2001, is a collection of fantasy and science fiction stories by such prominent African American writers as Amiri Baraka, Derrick Bell, Walter Mosley, and Ishmael Reed. It also contains several essays by black writers on black science fiction and fantasy.

- *The Girl from Playa Blanca* (1995) by Ofelia Dumas Lachtman tells the story of Elena and her younger brother Carlos who set out on a journey from their Mexican village to Los Angeles to find their missing father.

- *The Dark Is Rising* is the title of a five-book series of young-adult novels by Susan Cooper that uses elements of Celtic and Norse legends and the tales of King Arthur. It is also the title of the second book in the series. Published in the 1960s and 1970s, the fantasy series depicts the struggle between the forces of good, called The Light, and those of evil, called The Dark.

- Orson Scott Card's *Homecoming* series of five young-adult novels published in the early to mid-1990s tells the tale of a super-computer that controls the world and communicates telepathically with humans. It features a fourteen-year-old girl who knows that the computer is breaking down. The novels contain strong religious themes.

- Margaret Mahy's *The Changeover: A Supernatural Romance* (1994) is slightly eerier than *A Wrinkle in Time*. It features a fourteen-year-old girl who, with the help of an older boy, rescues her younger brother from a spirit that is taking over his life-essence. The novel contains a hint of romance between the girl and her sidekick.

- Christina Askounis's *The Dream of the Stone* (2007) is a young-adult fantasy/science fiction novel about a girl who receives cryptic advice from a mysterious old woman; the girl's brother has disappeared from the science institute where he works, and she travels to another world to confront the forces of evil.

---

part of her conformist world at school, to be more "normal" and not be such an "oddball." The reader is told that conformity on Camazotz eliminates wars and conflict, the kind of conflict that Meg takes part in when she beats up a boy at school for picking on Charles. Yet conformity exacts its own price. Meg's sense of alienation at the start of the novel parallels and contrasts with the utter lack of alienation on Camazotz. In effect, Camazotz is a parody of what Meg longs for in her daily life.

By creating parallel worlds such as this, L'Engle drives home her message in the novel. While the reader regards Meg's physical journey as "real," the more underlying reality is that the journey is psychological. When she returns home, it is apparent that no real clock or calendar time has passed. Meg is left in the same place and at the same time as when she left. But she has returned with a new outlook, a new perspective on good and evil, on her own faults, and on her place in the world. Thus, even though a kind of evil surrounds her, just as it did on Camazotz, she can triumph over that evil through the force of her own will, persistence, and love.

This kind of parallelism plays out in many of the details of the novel. For example, the novel's first words are "It was a dark and stormy night." This expression, which has become a cliché, is the opening line of British author Edward Bulwer-Lytton's 1830 novel, *Paul Clifford*. The passage in L'Engle's novel goes on to describe the "frenzied lashing of the wind." Clouds "scudded frantically across the sky," and the moon "ripped through them." The imagery captures the turmoil of Meg's thoughts; the term "pathetic fallacy" is often used to refer to this kind of imagery, in which the author uses nature to reflect the inner workings of a character's mind. The imagery in the novel's opening lines prepares the reader for similar disruptions in the natural environment that pervade the novel. The Dark Thing is like a massive storm cloud. The act of tessering is described in terms that suggest a storm, a whirlwind, a dizzying experience that leaves Meg exhausted and weak. Images of clouds, wind, and cold dominate Meg's travels through her psychological landscape. But after passing through the trials that steel her, Meg arrives back on Earth: "A whirl of darkness. An icy cold blast. An angry, resentful howl that seemed to tear through her. Darkness again.... And then the feel of earth beneath her, of something in her arms, and she was rolling over on the sweet smelling autumnal earth." The images of tearing, slashing, and piercing are replaced by more pastoral images, even to the point where Charles announces that they have landed "in the twins' vegetable garden! "And we landed in the broccoli!" The gray world of Camazotz has been replaced by the golden, autumnal world of Meg's home. Autumn, the season of fulfillment, of harvest, of maturation, has arrived, reflecting the maturation of Meg as a result of her journey.

Yet other details provide linkages of parallelism and contrast. Early in the novel, Charles Wallace invites Calvin O'Keefe to the Murry home for dinner. While he is there, Meg tries to explain scientific concepts to him, even though she is in a lower grade at school. Calvin asks her what a megaparsec is, and Meg explains that it is a nickname her father had given her, but that it is also equal to 3.26 million light years. Calvin then asks about the famous Einstein equation $E = mc^2$. Meg patiently explains what the terms of the equation mean. But then Calvin asks her what countries share boundaries with Peru, and Meg is not even entirely sure that Peru is a country in South America. Calvin continues to quiz her about other subjects until she finally confesses that she is not very good at English.

This theme is picked up near the end of the novel when Mrs. Whatsit quizzes Calvin about the sonnet, a type of poem with fourteen lines and a strict rhyme scheme. Mrs. Whatsit, though, goes on to note that the sonnet form embodies a valuable life lesson: "But within this strict form the poet has complete freedom to say whatever he wants, doesn't he?" Calvin responds, "You mean you're comparing our lives to a sonnet? A strict form, but freedom within it?" Mrs. Whatsit replies, "You're given the form, but you have to write the sonnet yourself. What you say is completely up to you."

Taken together, the two parallel scenes form a reconciliation. The earlier scene presents scientific knowledge—pure information—that is devoid of meaning. Meg's ignorance about other matters suggests that science cannot provide all the answers to the questions that Meg has about her life and her place within it. She knows the science by rote, but it has no application in her life. The later scene, to which Meg is a witness, begins with dry knowledge: A sonnet is a particular type of poem with a particular form—the type of information that any diligent student can commit to memory. More importantly, though, the sonnet is a metaphor for life: Life has a "form," perhaps one dictated by God, yet within the boundaries of that form, each person has to write the sonnet of his or her own life. Life is not predetermined by fate. Rather, each individual has free will within the confines of God's creation. This is the wisdom that is lacking on Camazotz, which is dominated by the disembodied Brain, and it is the wisdom that Meg and her companions win through their trials. Science and knowledge—the Brain—provide answers, but they do not always ask the right questions.

**Source:** Michael J. O'Neal, Critical Essay on *A Wrinkle in Time* in *Novels for Students*, Gale, Cengage Learning, 2010.

### Sally Thomas

*In the following essay, Thomas offers a personal reflection on the literature of Madeleine L'Engle.*

The winter I was ten, my teacher read *A Wrinkle in Time* aloud to our class, a chapter a day. It was, in my view, the sole reason for getting up and going to school. I loved the novel's Meg Murry, a girl neither beautiful nor graceful nor socially gifted—yet entrusted with a dangerous and salvific mission. She was an icon of unlikely heroic potential for bespectacled girls everywhere, and I was no exception. I can remember almost panting with impatience for the teacher to take the book out of her desk drawer. I can remember feeling, as she shut the book at the end of another chapter, as if I'd been pushed suddenly and rudely back through a curtain from Meg's world into my own—which looked rather like Meg's, minus the interplanetary travel and the extraterrestrials stealing sheets off the clothesline.

The novels of Madeleine L'Engle that I read in those awkward transitional years of late elementary school and junior high—chiefly *A Wrinkle in Time,* over and over, and its first sequel, *A Wind in the Door*—answered some deep longing in me for there to be more to the universe than meets the eye. The idea of cherubim and other supernatural "Servants," the idea that there might really be angels and that they wouldn't be fat babies with wings, but something as unimaginable and terrifying as they were good, was compelling and new to me. I devoured those novels even as I devoured the *Chronicles of Narnia* and *The Lord of the Rings,* not because they satisfied my inchoate yearning for something beyond the world I knew, but because they stoked it.

Much has already been written on the death of Madeleine L'Engle on September 6 at age eighty-eight, all of it celebrating her contributions to children's literature. In fact, L'Engle bridled at being labeled a "children's author" and insisted that she would not "write down" to her audience. It's true that her fiction was largely marketed for children, whatever her intent, and she was often awarded honors such as the Newbery Medal for children's books. But she was willing, as most children's authors are not, to engage ideas both challenging and strange in the world of children's books.

The tesseract, for instance—the conceit around which *A Wrinkle in Time* revolves— derives from geometry and describes a four-dimensional construction consisting of three conjoined cubes. Other novels deal with *kything,* a form of intuitive and extra-verbal communication that can transport the practitioner, in his mind, into other times, places, and bodies. L'Engle's characters include centaurs, snakes, disembodied brains, and cherubim, as well as relatively ordinary human children and adults whose workaday misadventures, in the hands of another writer, might have been the sum of the story. It's perhaps not surprising that a daydreamy child would be irresistibly drawn, through a story, to a potent imaginative crossroads.

Not insignificantly, L'Engle also bridled at being labeled a Christian writer, preferring instead to be known as "a writer who is struggling to be a Christian." Any artist's resistance to religious pigeonholing is understandable, especially when the pigeonhole is already full of substandard efforts raised to a dubious level of art by virtue of being "religious." We have all encountered novels, poems, paintings, and music of sincere and unimpeachable sentiment that were nevertheless so bad they made our teeth hurt. What L'Engle intuited about art was a principle that Flannery O'Connor named: "The sorry religious novel comes about when the writer supposes that, because of his belief, he is somehow dispensed from the obligation to penetrate concrete reality. . . . But the real novelist, the one with an instinct for what he is about, knows that he cannot approach the infinite directly, that he must penetrate the natural human world as it is."

The world of L'Engle's *Time* trilogy resembles the fictional worlds of C.S. Lewis, one of her acknowledged heroes. Like Lewis, L'Engle posits the presence of other worlds whose fates hinge on the actions and decisions of human children. To penetrate the natural human world, to strip characters down to both their essential flaws— pride, shortsightedness, fear, lack of faith—and their innate but unexplored potential for heroism and sacrifice, L'Engle's impulse, like Lewis', is to remove them from their own world for a time and then to return them from their adventures safe and outwardly unchanged but with new understanding.

Their stories are conversion stories. L'Engle's protagonists are called from their nets to follow; they do so with fear and grumbling and little vision in the beginning for what is at stake or the grace they will need in the end. In *A Wrinkle in Time,* the clumsy, myopic, awkward Meg, confronted at every turn with her own incompetence, ultimately saves both her imprisoned father and her beloved little brother Charles Wallace—an awkward and inadvertently unlikable character in himself—by discovering that the one thing she can do, and the one thing that the disembodied totalitarian brain *IT* cannot do, is love the people she loves.

In *A Wind in the Door,* Meg is called one step further, to move beyond the easy emotion with which she loves her family and her friend Calvin, to love her human nemesis, the school principal Mr. Jenkins. Likewise, Mr. Jenkins, a pallid, timorous, incompetent sort himself, discovers his own capacity for courage as he is drawn with Meg and Calvin, in company with an alarming "cherubim" named Proginoskes and other supernatural personages, into a battle between good and evil that takes place, simultaneously, everywhere in the universe. In *A Swiftly Tilting Planet,* the now teenage genius Charles Wallace must lay aside his reliance on his own intellect to enter into the minds and lives of other characters in other times to avert a course of events leading to disaster in the present, while Calvin's angry, inscrutable mother, now Meg's mother-in-law, reveals herself in her final hours to be a character of depth and dignity on whom, unexpectedly enough, the fate of the known world turns.

Clearly what's at stake in L'Engle's fantasy is no mere matter of pushing the witch into the oven; on the other hand, that's precisely what does happen in these heady fairy tales, with the crucial difference that the witch keeps coming back, in wildly different guises: an alien brain, a troupe of shape-shifting annihilators called Echthroi, and finally a human madman, his finger poised over a fatal button. Each novel in L'Engle's time trilogy leaves the door ajar.

All is well—for the moment—but there can always be a sequel. Evil is never a single entity on whom the forces of good can concentrate their strength; it is an ever-fluid force like running bamboo, which, after you've eradicated it in the back fence corner, sprouts up anew under the swing set. Perhaps this is why thoughtful children who have read the entire Harry Potter series without flinching report feeling "really creeped out" by something in L'Engle's books that they are unable to put their fingers on.

Though I adored these books as a child, and still find much to admire in them, I think it's quite possible to find aspects of them creepy, or at least irritating. The happy, loving family at the heart of the *Time* trilogy, for example, happens to be a family of geniuses: The "ordinary" twins in the middle only go to boring old medical school in the end, instead of reading minds.

A vein of aestheticism, in fact, runs through all of L'Engle's fiction: Her central characters are almost always artists of one kind or another, or scientists who listen to Bach. Even the lovably awkward Meg does higher math for fun. Meanwhile, workaday nonintellectuals often appear (as in the case of Calvin's large family and other inhabitants of the Murrys' New England village) as crude, inarticulate caricatures, seemingly incapable of any real human feeling.

Some readers of L'Engle's fantasy perceive a more general foundational disorder at work. In *A Landscape With Dragons,* a discussion of the merits and dangers of contemporary children's literature, Michael O'Brien categorizes L'Engle's work as "good on the surface, but fundamentally disordered," operating from a theological base that is gnostic and neopagan instead of Christian. L'Engle, a lifelong communicant in the Episcopal Church, often made declarations of belief that tend toward a theological fuzziness: "We've built up an image of . . . a comfortable God. It must be shattered," and that sort of thing, of a piece with the arguments with which people justify, for example, the official blessing of nonmarital cohabitation.

But we are talking about children's literature. And despite her protestations to the contrary, L'Engle will be remembered chiefly as the author of challenging books that—whatever the writer's intent—are read by children. The question remains, I suppose, of whether the deeper theological problems that are arguably in L'Engle's work render it dangerous to the spiritual formation of children.

My intuitive answer is no, though I base that intuition on the simple, anecdotal, and utterly unreliable basis of my own reading of them. As a child, raised on a relatively secular diet of mainstream Protestantism and utterly unaware of the existence of any theological problem beyond being mean to somebody on the playground, I was captivated by the notion that there *was* such a thing as evil and, conversely, that there was such a thing as *good.* The idea, further, that even the weak and the flawed were called to the battle—that there even *was* a battle—roused something in my imagination that years of Sunday School had somehow failed to touch.

What these novels provided me with was something I cannot remember having possessed before I encountered them: a religious imagination. Perhaps I should have been reading them through the lens of the Bible; instead, as a teenager, I turned anew to the Bible with these stories alive in my mind.

The novels themselves were not the gospel, and I don't think I ever mistook them as such. But they awakened my mind to the idea of a universe in which, even in distant galaxies, God is praised in the familiar words of the Psalms, as the creatures on Uriel sing: *Sing unto the Lord a new song, and his praise from the end of the earth, ye that go down to the sea, and all that is therein.... Let the inhabitants of the rock sing, let them shout from the top of the mountains. Let them give glory unto the Lord.*

**Source:** Sally Thomas, "Fantasy and Faith," in *First Things: A Monthly Journal of Religion and Public Life*, Vol. 177, November 2007, pp. 15–16.

## Jennifer Mattson

*In the following review, Mattson reflects on the impact of* A Wrinkle in Time *on science fantasy.*

One need only look at lists of Newbery Medal winners in the decades prior to Madeleine L'Engle's *A Wrinkle in Time* to recognize the novelty of the 1963 committee's choice. Even today, the relative scarcity of youth science fiction is reflected in more recent crops of medalists; how much more surprising, then, that the historical and realistic stories dominating the pre-1963 Newbery Medalists came to be joined by a book involving tesseracts, theoretical physics, and, perhaps most startling of all, a heroine at a time when male characters like Tom Swift were most strongly associated with children's sf.

Certainly, the success of *A Wrinkle in Time* must have been a shock to the more than 20 publishers who initially rejected the tale of an awkward adolescent, Meg Murry, who must rescue her scientist father from a disembodied brain called IT. Charlotte Jones Voiklis, L'Engle's granddaughter, recently offered insights about the book's long journey to print on behalf of her grandmother, who is approaching her ninetieth birthday.

> ITS RESISTANCE TO CONCLUSIONS THAT POP FULLY FORMED FROM THE MUFFIN TIN MAY BE ONE OF THE SECRETS TO *A WRINKLE IN TIME*'S RESILIENCE— THAT, ALONG WITH ITS PERENNIALLY REASSURING MESSAGE ABOUT THE ABILITY OF FRAIL HUMANS TO AVERT DOOMSDAY."

After many rounds of rejection, said Voiklis, L'Engle decided to give up on her manuscript, originally titled *Mrs. Whatsit, Mrs. Who, and Mrs. Which*, after Meg's three mystical chaperones. What came next is the sort of break most aspiring novelists only dream of: "[L'Engle's] mother went to the same church as John Farrar [of Farrar, Straus & Giroux], and talked with him about the book at a dinner party. Although *Wrinkle* had already been rejected by FSG, Farrar had read [L'Engle's] first novel, *The Small Rain* (1945), and admired it, and so agreed to read it himself. They published it not because they expected it to be successful, but because they liked it."

In hindsight, it's not so difficult to imagine why the time was ripe for *A Wrinkle in Time*; having been released the same year as the Cuban missile crisis, and in the thick of the race to land a man on the moon, a novel that projected youngsters into space to fight a looming "Dark Thing" must have plugged directly into children's most immediate interests and concerns. (In a fan letter from 1963, one fifth-grader even noted that IT reminded her of Khrushchev.)

But many novels that precisely fit their moment eventually age into quaint set pieces, while *Wrinkle* has endured through 69 hardcover printings (and numerous paperback, audio, and audiovisual formats) to enjoy its forty-fifth anniversary this year. The occasion is being marked in style by Square Fish books, Holtzbrinck Publishing's debut reprint line, which will be releasing paperback editions of *Wrinkle* and its sequels in two formats, with two sets of new covers, and marketing bells and whistles such as a Web site and teacher's-edition giveaways. (They're also being launched, at L'Engle's request, as the

Time Quintet, as opposed to the original quartet; the series now concludes with *An Acceptable Time*, 1989).

Jean Feiwel, senior vice president and publisher of Square Fish, says that she sees the relaunch of *Wrinkle* as an opportunity to bring the limelight back to an author who may have been overshadowed by the Harry Potter–fueled "onslaught of fantasy," citing the book's mix of genres—the very thing that gave its earliest readers pause—as one of its major strengths. As Feiwel puts it, "*Wrinkle* wasn't a book for children, and it wasn't a book for adults, and it was kind of unreal, and it just didn't fall into any existing category. So she who couldn't be classified became a class by herself."

Susan Chang, senior editor of the children's and young adult division at Tom Doherty Associates (a leading publisher of fantasy and sf), agrees, explaining that the term *science fantasy*, rather than *science fiction* per se, best suits L'Engle's creative approach. "She was doing something so unusual that it didn't spawn many imitators; it remains as original today as when it was published in 1962. The only person I can think of who would be comparable is William Sleator [*Interstellar Pig,* 1984, and others], in that L'Engle took real scientific concepts—like the tesseract, or mitochondria in *A Wind in the Door* [1973]—and wove them into amazing stories."

Given *A Wrinkle in Time*'s groundbreaking qualities, it's no surprise that the book had an impact on many contemporary writers of sf/fantasy.

Diane Duane, author of numerous sf novels for adults as well as her Young Wizards series for children, said that she would have been one of L'Engle's first-generation readers: "My preferences were gradually being skewed toward a more scientifically oriented side of fantasy by books like Eleanor Campbell's Mushroom Planet series," she recalls. "I was (unknowingly) hunting for . . . the shadow of something larger, deeper, and more important leaning over the mere circumstance of story: a sense of imminence. When I picked up *A Wrinkle in Time,* I knew I was really onto something, on both counts."

Scott Westerfeld, whose Uglies trilogy imagines a world of enforced conformity that wouldn't have seemed out of place on Planet Camazotz, likewise encountered *Wrinkle* as a child. "It won the Newbery the same year I was born. I read it a decade later, and three decades further on still shiver as Meg puts on those glasses and sees the awful truth of her world. I try to give all of my protagonists some version of that moment," he said.

For his part, William Sleator admits to reservations about some aspects of *A Wrinkle in Time.* "I believe that in reality you can say 'I love you' a million times and it will not kill the evil brain controlling that other planet," he said, referring to the climactic showdown between Meg and IT. What he admires, though, is L'Engle's portrayal of Meg's scientific family. "I seem to remember that [Meg's] mother made stew over a Bunsen burner in her lab, which is a great touch."

And what about children today—those who may have Duane's, Westerfeld's, Sleator's, and other, newer works of science fiction to choose from? Are they still greeting *A Wrinkle in Time* enthusiastically, despite dated elements (such as those enormous punch card computers on Camazotz)? Yes, said Andrew Medlar, Youth Materials specialist at the Chicago Public Library.

"This is one of those books where you can tell if someone has read it by how their eyes light up when you mention the title," Medlar says. "It's such a great combination of so many things, all of which appeal to different types of people and readers." His library's circulation figures back up these personal impressions: "It definitely is one of the most popular Newbery titles that we have in the collection."

Of course, the book has less enthusiastic interpreters as well; *Wrinkle* landed at number 22 on the ALA's Top 100 Most Frequently Challenged Books of 1999–2000. Fond readers may have difficulty imagining where the trouble lies—Meg and her friend Calvin share only the most chaste of romances, and the book reflects L'Engle's own strong spirituality (at one point, Mrs. Who reassures Meg with verses from I Corinthians).

"I've never understood it," said Voiklis, "but *Wrinkle*'s challengers object to the three Mrs. Ws and the Happy Medium because they think they are thought to be witches and involved in black magic." She also remembers controversy over a scene where the children are naming people who have fought the darkness, and non-Christians are named. "One foreign-language publisher wanted permission to add 'but Jesus was the best,'" said Voiklis. "That permission was not forthcoming!"

Not surprising, given the book's central message about preserving intellectual and creative freedom over "totalitarian, absolutist, and fundamentalist thinking on any level" (Voiklis' words.) Indeed, in an era of No Child Left Behind controversy, L'Engle's comments in her Newbery acceptance speech have the same timeless resonance as her fiction: "There are forces working in the world as never before in the history of mankind for standardization, for the regimentation of us all, or what I like to call making muffins of us, muffins all like every other muffin in the muffin tin."

Its resistance to conclusions that pop fully formed from the muffin tin may be one of the secrets to *A Wrinkle in Time*'s resilience—that, along with its perennially reassuring message about the ability of frail humans to avert doomsday. As Voiklis reflected, "*Wrinkle* doesn't offer answers, but I think it does offer people who are trying to understand their place in the universe a model for how to ask questions, and how to listen, and how to live joyfully in the midst of struggle."

**Source:** Jennifer Mattson, "Another Look at *A Wrinkle in Time*," in *Booklist*, Vol. 103, No. 18, May 15, 2007, pp. 58–59.

## SOURCES

Hettinga, Donald R., *Presenting Madeleine L'Engle*, Twayne Publishers, 1993, p. 16.

L'Engle, Madeleine, *A Wrinkle in Time*, Dell, 1962, pp. 11, 12, 29, 45. 92, 109, 157, 179, 188.

Mattson, Jennifer, "Another Look at *A Wrinkle in Time*," in *Booklist*, Vol. 103, No. 18, May 15, 2007, p. 58.

St. Yves, Suzanne, "Madeleine L'Engle's Search for God," in *Sojourners Magazine*, March–April, 1995.

Zarin, Cynthia, "The Storyteller," in the *New Yorker*, April 12, 2004, pp. 60 ff.

## FURTHER READING

Hettinga, Donald R., *Presenting Madeleine L'Engle*, Twayne Publishers, 1993.

This volume is a brief, basic introduction to the author and her works.

L'Engle, Madeleine, "Kerlan Award Lecture," in *Kerland Collection Newsletter*, University of Minnesota, Fall 1990, pp. 5–7.

In her lecture, the author explains her efforts to reconcile science and religion and notes the profound impact Albert Einstein had on her thinking.

Tuck, Donald H., ed., *The Encyclopedia of Science Fiction and Fantasy*, 3 Vols., Advent Publishers, 1974–1982.

These volumes form a massive reference set on science fiction and fantasy, including works, author biographies, bibliography, and information about series and interconnected works.

Westfahl, Gary, ed., *The Greenwood Encyclopedia of Science Fiction and Fantasy*, 3 Vols., Greenwood, 2005.

These volumes update Donald Tuck's *The Encyclopedia of Science Fiction and Fantasy*. Volumes 1 and 2 are organized thematically, discussing 400 science fiction and fantasy themes and putting them into historical and social contexts. The third volume contains entries on classic novels, along with films and television series.

# Glossary of Literary Terms

## A

**Abstract:** As an adjective applied to writing or literary works, abstract refers to words or phrases that name things not knowable through the five senses.

**Aestheticism:** A literary and artistic movement of the nineteenth century. Followers of the movement believed that art should not be mixed with social, political, or moral teaching. The statement "art for art's sake" is a good summary of aestheticism. The movement had its roots in France, but it gained widespread importance in England in the last half of the nineteenth century, where it helped change the Victorian practice of including moral lessons in literature.

**Allegory:** A narrative technique in which characters representing things or abstract ideas are used to convey a message or teach a lesson. Allegory is typically used to teach moral, ethical, or religious lessons but is sometimes used for satiric or political purposes.

**Allusion:** A reference to a familiar literary or historical person or event, used to make an idea more easily understood.

**Analogy:** A comparison of two things made to explain something unfamiliar through its similarities to something familiar, or to prove one point based on the acceptedness of another. Similes and metaphors are types of analogies.

**Antagonist:** The major character in a narrative or drama who works against the hero or protagonist.

**Anthropomorphism:** The presentation of animals or objects in human shape or with human characteristics. The term is derived from the Greek word for "human form."

**Anti-hero:** A central character in a work of literature who lacks traditional heroic qualities such as courage, physical prowess, and fortitude. Anti-heroes typically distrust conventional values and are unable to commit themselves to any ideals. They generally feel helpless in a world over which they have no control. Anti-heroes usually accept, and often celebrate, their positions as social outcasts.

**Apprenticeship Novel:** See *Bildungsroman*

**Archetype:** The word archetype is commonly used to describe an original pattern or model from which all other things of the same kind are made. This term was introduced to literary criticism from the psychology of Carl Jung. It expresses Jung's theory that behind every person's "unconscious," or repressed memories of the past, lies the "collective unconscious" of the human race: memories of the countless typical experiences of our ancestors. These memories are said to prompt illogical associations that trigger powerful emotions in the reader. Often, the emotional process is primitive, even primordial. Archetypes are the literary images that grow out of the "collective unconscious." They appear in literature as incidents and plots that repeat basic patterns of life. They may also appear as stereotyped characters.

**Avant-garde:** French term meaning "vanguard." It is used in literary criticism to describe new writing that rejects traditional approaches to literature in favor of innovations in style or content.

## B

**Beat Movement:** A period featuring a group of American poets and novelists of the 1950s and 1960s—including Jack Kerouac, Allen Ginsberg, Gregory Corso, William S. Burroughs, and Lawrence Ferlinghetti—who rejected established social and literary values. Using such techniques as stream of consciousness writing and jazz-influenced free verse and focusing on unusual or abnormal states of mind—generated by religious ecstasy or the use of drugs—the Beat writers aimed to create works that were unconventional in both form and subject matter.

**Bildungsroman:** A German word meaning "novel of development." The *bildungsroman* is a study of the maturation of a youthful character, typically brought about through a series of social or sexual encounters that lead to self-awareness. *Bildungsroman* is used interchangeably with *erziehungsroman*, a novel of initiation and education. When a *bildungsroman* is concerned with the development of an artist (as in James Joyce's *A Portrait of the Artist as a Young Man*), it is often termed a *kunstlerroman*.

**Black Aesthetic Movement:** A period of artistic and literary development among African Americans in the 1960s and early 1970s. This was the first major African-American artistic movement since the Harlem Renaissance and was closely paralleled by the civil rights and black power movements. The black aesthetic writers attempted to produce works of art that would be meaningful to the black masses. Key figures in black aesthetics included one of its founders, poet and playwright Amiri Baraka, formerly known as LeRoi Jones; poet

and essayist Haki R. Madhubuti, formerly Don L. Lee; poet and playwright Sonia Sanchez; and dramatist Ed Bullins.

**Black Humor:** Writing that places grotesque elements side by side with humorous ones in an attempt to shock the reader, forcing him or her to laugh at the horrifying reality of a disordered world.

**Burlesque:** Any literary work that uses exaggeration to make its subject appear ridiculous, either by treating a trivial subject with profound seriousness or by treating a dignified subject frivolously. The word "burlesque" may also be used as an adjective, as in "burlesque show," to mean "striptease act."

## C

**Character:** Broadly speaking, a person in a literary work. The actions of characters are what constitute the plot of a story, novel, or poem. There are numerous types of characters, ranging from simple, stereotypical figures to intricate, multifaceted ones. In the techniques of anthropomorphism and personification, animals—and even places or things—can assume aspects of character. "Characterization" is the process by which an author creates vivid, believable characters in a work of art. This may be done in a variety of ways, including (1) direct description of the character by the narrator; (2) the direct presentation of the speech, thoughts, or actions of the character; and (3) the responses of other characters to the character. The term "character" also refers to a form originated by the ancient Greek writer Theophrastus that later became popular in the seventeenth and eighteenth centuries. It is a short essay or sketch of a person who prominently displays a specific attribute or quality, such as miserliness or ambition.

**Climax:** The turning point in a narrative, the moment when the conflict is at its most intense. Typically, the structure of stories, novels, and plays is one of rising action, in which tension builds to the climax, followed by falling action, in which tension lessens as the story moves to its conclusion.

**Colloquialism:** A word, phrase, or form of pronunciation that is acceptable in casual conversation but not in formal, written communication. It is considered more acceptable than slang.

**Coming of Age Novel:** See *Bildungsroman*

**Concrete:** Concrete is the opposite of abstract, and refers to a thing that actually exists or a description that allows the reader to experience an object or concept with the senses.

**Connotation:** The impression that a word gives beyond its defined meaning. Connotations may be universally understood or may be significant only to a certain group.

**Convention:** Any widely accepted literary device, style, or form.

# D

**Denotation:** The definition of a word, apart from the impressions or feelings it creates (connotations) in the reader.

**Denouement:** A French word meaning "the unknotting." In literary criticism, it denotes the resolution of conflict in fiction or drama. The *denouement* follows the climax and provides an outcome to the primary plot situation as well as an explanation of secondary plot complications. The *denouement* often involves a character's recognition of his or her state of mind or moral condition.

**Description:** Descriptive writing is intended to allow a reader to picture the scene or setting in which the action of a story takes place. The form this description takes often evokes an intended emotional response—a dark, spooky graveyard will evoke fear, and a peaceful, sunny meadow will evoke calmness.

**Dialogue:** In its widest sense, dialogue is simply conversation between people in a literary work; in its most restricted sense, it refers specifically to the speech of characters in a drama. As a specific literary genre, a "dialogue" is a composition in which characters debate an issue or idea.

**Diction:** The selection and arrangement of words in a literary work. Either or both may vary depending on the desired effect. There are four general types of diction: "formal," used in scholarly or lofty writing; "informal," used in relaxed but educated conversation; "colloquial," used in everyday speech; and "slang," containing newly coined words and other terms not accepted in formal usage.

**Didactic:** A term used to describe works of literature that aim to teach some moral, religious, political, or practical lesson. Although didactic elements are often found in artistically pleasing works, the term "didactic" usually refers to literature in which the message is more important than the form. The term may also be used to criticize a work that the critic finds "overly didactic," that is, heavy-handed in its delivery of a lesson.

**Doppelganger:** A literary technique by which a character is duplicated (usually in the form of an alter ego, though sometimes as a ghostly counterpart) or divided into two distinct, usually opposite personalities. The use of this character device is widespread in nineteenth- and twentieth-century literature, and indicates a growing awareness among authors that the "self" is really a composite of many "selves."

**Double Entendre:** A corruption of a French phrase meaning "double meaning." The term is used to indicate a word or phrase that is deliberately ambiguous, especially when one of the meanings is risqué or improper.

**Dramatic Irony:** Occurs when the audience of a play or the reader of a work of literature knows something that a character in the work itself does not know. The irony is in the contrast between the intended meaning of the statements or actions of a character and the additional information understood by the audience.

**Dystopia:** An imaginary place in a work of fiction where the characters lead dehumanized, fearful lives.

# E

**Edwardian:** Describes cultural conventions identified with the period of the reign of Edward VII of England (1901-1910). Writers of the Edwardian Age typically displayed a strong reaction against the propriety and conservatism of the Victorian Age. Their work often exhibits distrust of authority in religion, politics, and art and expresses strong doubts about the soundness of conventional values.

**Empathy:** A sense of shared experience, including emotional and physical feelings, with someone or something other than oneself. Empathy is often used to describe the response of a reader to a literary character.

**Enlightenment, The:** An eighteenth-century philosophical movement. It began in France but had a wide impact throughout Europe and America. Thinkers of the Enlightenment valued reason and believed that both the individual and society could achieve a state of perfection. Corresponding to this essentially humanist vision was a resistance to religious authority.

**Epigram:** A saying that makes the speaker's point quickly and concisely. Often used to preface a novel.

**Epilogue:** A concluding statement or section of a literary work. In dramas, particularly those of the seventeenth and eighteenth centuries, the epilogue is a closing speech, often in verse, delivered by an actor at the end of a play and spoken directly to the audience.

**Epiphany:** A sudden revelation of truth inspired by a seemingly trivial incident.

**Episode:** An incident that forms part of a story and is significantly related to it. Episodes may be either self-contained narratives or events that depend on a larger context for their sense and importance.

**Epistolary Novel:** A novel in the form of letters. The form was particularly popular in the eighteenth century.

**Epithet:** A word or phrase, often disparaging or abusive, that expresses a character trait of someone or something.

**Existentialism:** A predominantly twentieth-century philosophy concerned with the nature and perception of human existence. There are two major strains of existentialist thought: atheistic and Christian. Followers of atheistic existentialism believe that the individual is alone in a godless universe and that the basic human condition is one of suffering and loneliness. Nevertheless, because there are no fixed values, individuals can create their own characters—indeed, they can shape themselves—through the exercise of free will. The atheistic strain culminates in and is popularly associated with the works of Jean-Paul Sartre. The Christian existentialists, on the other hand, believe that only in God may people find freedom from life's anguish. The two strains hold certain beliefs in common: that existence cannot be fully understood or described through empirical effort; that anguish is a universal element of life; that individuals must bear responsibility for

their actions; and that there is no common standard of behavior or perception for religious and ethical matters.

**Expatriates:** See *Expatriatism*

**Expatriatism:** The practice of leaving one's country to live for an extended period in another country.

**Exposition:** Writing intended to explain the nature of an idea, thing, or theme. Expository writing is often combined with description, narration, or argument. In dramatic writing, the exposition is the introductory material which presents the characters, setting, and tone of the play.

**Expressionism:** An indistinct literary term, originally used to describe an early twentieth-century school of German painting. The term applies to almost any mode of unconventional, highly subjective writing that distorts reality in some way.

## F

**Fable:** A prose or verse narrative intended to convey a moral. Animals or inanimate objects with human characteristics often serve as characters in fables.

**Falling Action:** See *Denouement*

**Fantasy:** A literary form related to mythology and folklore. Fantasy literature is typically set in non-existent realms and features supernatural beings.

**Farce:** A type of comedy characterized by broad humor, outlandish incidents, and often vulgar subject matter.

**Femme fatale:** A French phrase with the literal translation "fatal woman." A *femme fatale* is a sensuous, alluring woman who often leads men into danger or trouble.

**Fiction:** Any story that is the product of imagination rather than a documentation of fact. characters and events in such narratives may be based in real life but their ultimate form and configuration is a creation of the author.

**Figurative Language:** A technique in writing in which the author temporarily interrupts the order, construction, or meaning of the writing for a particular effect. This interruption takes the form of one or more figures of speech such as hyperbole, irony, or simile. Figurative language is the opposite of literal language, in which every word is truthful, accurate, and free of exaggeration or embellishment.

**Figures of Speech:** Writing that differs from customary conventions for construction, meaning, order, or significance for the purpose of a special meaning or effect. There are two major types of figures of speech: rhetorical figures, which do not make changes in the meaning of the words, and tropes, which do.

**Fin de siecle:** A French term meaning "end of the century." The term is used to denote the last decade of the nineteenth century, a transition period when writers and other artists abandoned old conventions and looked for new techniques and objectives.

**First Person:** See *Point of View*

**Flashback:** A device used in literature to present action that occurred before the beginning of the story. Flashbacks are often introduced as the dreams or recollections of one or more characters.

**Foil:** A character in a work of literature whose physical or psychological qualities contrast strongly with, and therefore highlight, the corresponding qualities of another character.

**Folklore:** Traditions and myths preserved in a culture or group of people. Typically, these are passed on by word of mouth in various forms—such as legends, songs, and proverbs—or preserved in customs and ceremonies. This term was first used by W. J. Thoms in 1846.

**Folktale:** A story originating in oral tradition. Folktales fall into a variety of categories, including legends, ghost stories, fairy tales, fables, and anecdotes based on historical figures and events.

**Foreshadowing:** A device used in literature to create expectation or to set up an explanation of later developments.

**Form:** The pattern or construction of a work which identifies its genre and distinguishes it from other genres.

# G

**Genre:** A category of literary work. In critical theory, genre may refer to both the content of a given work—tragedy, comedy, pastoral—and to its form, such as poetry, novel, or drama.

**Gilded Age:** A period in American history during the 1870s characterized by political corruption and materialism. A number of important novels of social and political criticism were written during this time.

**Gothicism:** In literary criticism, works characterized by a taste for the medieval or morbidly attractive. A gothic novel prominently features elements of horror, the supernatural, gloom, and violence: clanking chains, terror, charnel houses, ghosts, medieval castles, and mysteriously slamming doors. The term "gothic novel" is also applied to novels that lack elements of the traditional Gothic setting but that create a similar atmosphere of terror or dread.

**Grotesque:** In literary criticism, the subject matter of a work or a style of expression characterized by exaggeration, deformity, freakishness, and disorder. The grotesque often includes an element of comic absurdity.

# H

**Harlem Renaissance:** The Harlem Renaissance of the 1920s is generally considered the first significant movement of black writers and artists in the United States. During this period, new and established black writers published more fiction and poetry than ever before, the first influential black literary journals were established, and black authors and artists received their first widespread recognition and serious critical appraisal. Among the major writers associated with this period are Claude McKay, Jean Toomer, Countee Cullen, Langston Hughes, Arna Bontemps, Nella Larsen, and Zora Neale Hurston.

**Hero/Heroine:** The principal sympathetic character (male or female) in a literary work. Heroes and heroines typically exhibit admirable traits: idealism, courage, and integrity, for example.

**Holocaust Literature:** Literature influenced by or written about the Holocaust of World War II. Such literature includes true stories of survival in concentration camps, escape, and life after the war, as well as fictional works and poetry.

**Humanism:** A philosophy that places faith in the dignity of humankind and rejects the medieval perception of the individual as a weak, fallen creature. "Humanists" typically believe in the perfectibility of human nature and view reason and education as the means to that end.

**Hyperbole:** In literary criticism, deliberate exaggeration used to achieve an effect.

# I

**Idiom:** A word construction or verbal expression closely associated with a given language.

**Image:** A concrete representation of an object or sensory experience. Typically, such a representation helps evoke the feelings associated with the object or experience itself. Images are either "literal" or "figurative." Literal images are especially concrete and involve little or no extension of the obvious meaning of the words used to express them. Figurative images do not follow the literal meaning of the words exactly. Images in literature are usually visual, but the term "image" can also refer to the representation of any sensory experience.

**Imagery:** The array of images in a literary work. Also, figurative language.

**In medias res:** A Latin term meaning "in the middle of things." It refers to the technique of beginning a story at its midpoint and then using various flashback devices to reveal previous action.

**Interior Monologue:** A narrative technique in which characters' thoughts are revealed in a way that appears to be uncontrolled by the author. The interior monologue typically aims to reveal the inner self of a character. It portrays emotional experiences as they occur at both a conscious and unconscious level. images are often used to represent sensations or emotions.

**Irony:** In literary criticism, the effect of language in which the intended meaning is the opposite of what is stated.

# J

**Jargon:** Language that is used or understood only by a select group of people. Jargon may refer to terminology used in a certain profession, such as computer jargon, or it may refer to any nonsensical language that is not understood by most people.

# L

**Leitmotiv:** See *Motif*

**Literal Language:** An author uses literal language when he or she writes without exaggerating or embellishing the subject matter and without any tools of figurative language.

**Lost Generation:** A term first used by Gertrude Stein to describe the post-World War I generation of American writers: men and women haunted by a sense of betrayal and emptiness brought about by the destructiveness of the war.

# M

**Mannerism:** Exaggerated, artificial adherence to a literary manner or style. Also, a popular style of the visual arts of late sixteenth-century Europe that was marked by elongation of the human form and by intentional spatial distortion. Literary works that are self-consciously high-toned and artistic are often said to be "mannered."

**Metaphor:** A figure of speech that expresses an idea through the image of another object. Metaphors suggest the essence of the first object by identifying it with certain qualities of the second object.

**Modernism:** Modern literary practices. Also, the principles of a literary school that lasted from roughly the beginning of the twentieth century until the end of World War II. Modernism is defined by its rejection of the literary conventions of the nineteenth century and by its opposition to conventional morality, taste, traditions, and economic values.

**Mood:** The prevailing emotions of a work or of the author in his or her creation of the work. The mood of a work is not always what might be expected based on its subject matter.

**Motif:** A theme, character type, image, metaphor, or other verbal element that recurs throughout a single work of literature or occurs in a number of different works over a period of time.

**Myth:** An anonymous tale emerging from the traditional beliefs of a culture or social unit. Myths use supernatural explanations for natural phenomena. They may also explain cosmic issues like creation and death. Collections of myths, known as mythologies, are common to all cultures and nations, but the best-known myths belong to the Norse, Roman, and Greek mythologies.

# N

**Narration:** The telling of a series of events, real or invented. A narration may be either a simple narrative, in which the events are recounted chronologically, or a narrative with a plot, in which the account is given in a style reflecting the author's artistic concept of the story. Narration is sometimes used as a synonym for "storyline."

**Narrative:** A verse or prose accounting of an event or sequence of events, real or invented. The term is also used as an adjective in the sense "method of narration." For example, in literary criticism, the expression "narrative technique" usually refers to the way the author structures and presents his or her story.

**Narrator:** The teller of a story. The narrator may be the author or a character in the story through whom the author speaks.

**Naturalism:** A literary movement of the late nineteenth and early twentieth centuries. The movement's major theorist, French novelist Emile Zola, envisioned a type of fiction that would examine human life with the objectivity of scientific inquiry. The Naturalists typically viewed human beings as either the products of "biological determinism," ruled by hereditary instincts and engaged in an endless struggle for survival, or as the products of "socioeconomic determinism," ruled by social and economic forces beyond their control. In their works, the Naturalists generally ignored the highest levels of society and focused on degradation: poverty, alcoholism, prostitution, insanity, and disease.

**Noble Savage:** The idea that primitive man is noble and good but becomes evil and corrupted as he becomes civilized. The concept of the noble savage originated in the Renaissance period but is more closely identified with such later writers as Jean-Jacques Rousseau and Aphra Behn.

**Novel:** A long fictional narrative written in prose, which developed from the novella and other early forms of narrative. A novel is usually organized under a plot or theme with a focus on character development and action.

**Novel of Ideas:** A novel in which the examination of intellectual issues and concepts takes precedence over characterization or a traditional storyline.

**Novel of Manners:** A novel that examines the customs and mores of a cultural group.

**Novella:** An Italian term meaning "story." This term has been especially used to describe fourteenth-century Italian tales, but it also refers to modern short novels.

# O

**Objective Correlative:** An outward set of objects, a situation, or a chain of events corresponding to an inward experience and evoking this experience in the reader. The term frequently appears in modern criticism in discussions of authors' intended effects on the emotional responses of readers.

**Objectivity:** A quality in writing characterized by the absence of the author's opinion or feeling about the subject matter. Objectivity is an important factor in criticism.

**Oedipus Complex:** A son's amorous obsession with his mother. The phrase is derived from the story of the ancient Theban hero Oedipus, who unknowingly killed his father and married his mother.

**Omniscience:** See *Point of View*

**Onomatopoeia:** The use of words whose sounds express or suggest their meaning. In its simplest sense, onomatopoeia may be represented by words that mimic the sounds they denote such as "hiss" or "meow." At a more subtle level, the pattern and rhythm of sounds and rhymes of a line or poem may be onomatopoeic.

**Oxymoron:** A phrase combining two contradictory terms. Oxymorons may be intentional or unintentional.

# P

**Parable:** A story intended to teach a moral lesson or answer an ethical question.

**Paradox:** A statement that appears illogical or contradictory at first, but may actually point to an underlying truth.

**Parallelism:** A method of comparison of two ideas in which each is developed in the same grammatical structure.

**Parody:** In literary criticism, this term refers to an imitation of a serious literary work or the signature style of a particular author in a ridiculous manner. A typical parody adopts the style of the original and applies it to an inappropriate subject for humorous effect. Parody is a form of satire and could be considered the literary equivalent of a caricature or cartoon.

**Pastoral:** A term derived from the Latin word "pastor," meaning shepherd. A pastoral is a literary composition on a rural theme. The conventions of the pastoral were originated by the third-century Greek poet Theocritus, who wrote about the experiences, love affairs, and pastimes of Sicilian shepherds. In a pastoral, characters and language of a courtly nature are often placed in a simple setting. The term pastoral is also used to classify dramas, elegies, and lyrics that exhibit the use of country settings and shepherd characters.

**Pen Name:** See *Pseudonym*

**Persona:** A Latin term meaning "mask." *Personae* are the characters in a fictional work of literature. The *persona* generally functions as a mask through which the author tells a story in a voice other than his or her own. A *persona* is usually either a character in a story who acts as a narrator or an "implied author," a voice created by the author to act as the narrator for himself or herself.

**Personification:** A figure of speech that gives human qualities to abstract ideas, animals, and inanimate objects.

**Picaresque Novel:** Episodic fiction depicting the adventures of a roguish central character ("picaro" is Spanish for "rogue"). The picaresque hero is commonly a low-born but clever individual who wanders into and out of various affairs of love, danger, and farcical intrigue. These involvements may take place at all social levels and typically present a humorous and wide-ranging satire of a given society.

**Plagiarism:** Claiming another person's written material as one's own. Plagiarism can take the form of direct, word-for-word copying or the theft of the substance or idea of the work.

**Plot:** In literary criticism, this term refers to the pattern of events in a narrative or drama. In its simplest sense, the plot guides the author in composing the work and helps the reader follow the work. Typically, plots exhibit causality and unity and have a beginning, a middle, and an end. Sometimes, however, a plot may consist of a series of disconnected events, in which case it is known as an "episodic plot."

**Poetic Justice:** An outcome in a literary work, not necessarily a poem, in which the good are rewarded and the evil are punished, especially in ways that particularly fit their virtues or crimes.

**Poetic License:** Distortions of fact and literary convention made by a writer—not always a poet—for the sake of the effect gained. Poetic license is closely related to the concept of "artistic freedom."

**Poetics:** This term has two closely related meanings. It denotes (1) an aesthetic theory in literary criticism about the essence of poetry or (2) rules prescribing the proper methods, content, style, or diction of poetry. The term poetics may also refer to theories about literature in general, not just poetry.

**Point of View:** The narrative perspective from which a literary work is presented to the reader. There are four traditional points of view. The "third person omniscient" gives the reader a "godlike" perspective, unrestricted by time or place, from which to see actions and look into the minds of characters. This allows the author to comment openly on characters and events in the work. The "third person" point of view presents the events of the story from outside of any single character's perception, much like the omniscient point of view, but the reader must understand the action as it takes place and without any special insight into characters' minds or motivations. The "first person" or "personal" point of view relates events as they are perceived by a single character. The main character "tells" the story and may offer opinions about the action and characters which differ from those of the author. Much less common than omniscient, third person, and first person is the "second person" point of view, wherein the author tells the story as if it is happening to the reader.

**Polemic:** A work in which the author takes a stand on a controversial subject, such as abortion or religion. Such works are often extremely argumentative or provocative.

**Pornography:** Writing intended to provoke feelings of lust in the reader. Such works are often condemned by critics and teachers, but those which can be shown to have literary value are viewed less harshly.

**Post-Aesthetic Movement:** An artistic response made by African Americans to the black aesthetic movement of the 1960s and early '70s. Writers since that time have adopted a somewhat different tone in their work, with less emphasis placed on the disparity between black and white in the United States. In the words of post-aesthetic authors such as Toni Morrison, John Edgar Wideman, and Kristin Hunter, African Americans are portrayed as looking inward for answers to their own questions, rather than always looking to the outside world.

**Postmodernism:** Writing from the 1960s forward characterized by experimentation and continuing to apply some of the fundamentals of modernism, which included existentialism and alienation. Postmodernists have gone a step further in the rejection of tradition begun with the modernists by also rejecting traditional forms, preferring the anti-novel over the novel and the anti-hero over the hero.

**Primitivism:** The belief that primitive peoples were nobler and less flawed than civilized peoples because they had not been subjected to the tainting influence of society.

**Prologue:** An introductory section of a literary work. It often contains information establishing the situation of the characters or presents information about the setting, time period, or action. In drama, the prologue is spoken by a chorus or by one of the principal characters.

**Prose:** A literary medium that attempts to mirror the language of everyday speech. It is distinguished from poetry by its use of unmetered, unrhymed language consisting of logically related sentences. Prose is usually grouped into paragraphs that form a cohesive whole such as an essay or a novel.

**Prosopopoeia:** See *Personification*

**Protagonist:** The central character of a story who serves as a focus for its themes and incidents and as the principal rationale for its development. The protagonist is sometimes referred to in discussions of modern literature as the hero or anti-hero.

**Protest Fiction:** Protest fiction has as its primary purpose the protesting of some social injustice, such as racism or discrimination.

**Proverb:** A brief, sage saying that expresses a truth about life in a striking manner.

**Pseudonym:** A name assumed by a writer, most often intended to prevent his or her identification as the author of a work. Two or more authors may work together under one pseudonym, or an author may use a different name for each genre he or she publishes in. Some publishing companies maintain "house pseudonyms," under which any number of authors may write installations in a series. Some authors also choose a pseudonym over their real names the way an actor may use a stage name.

**Pun:** A play on words that have similar sounds but different meanings.

# R

**Realism:** A nineteenth-century European literary movement that sought to portray familiar characters, situations, and settings in a realistic manner. This was done primarily by using an objective narrative point of view and through the buildup of accurate detail. The standard for success of any realistic work depends on how faithfully it transfers common experience into fictional forms. The realistic method may be altered or extended, as in stream of consciousness writing, to record highly subjective experience.

**Repartee:** Conversation featuring snappy retorts and witticisms.

**Resolution:** The portion of a story following the climax, in which the conflict is resolved.

**Rhetoric:** In literary criticism, this term denotes the art of ethical persuasion. In its strictest sense, rhetoric adheres to various principles developed since classical times for arranging facts and ideas in a clear, persuasive, appealing manner. The term is also used to refer to effective prose in general and theories of or methods for composing effective prose.

**Rhetorical Question:** A question intended to provoke thought, but not an expressed answer, in the reader. It is most commonly used in oratory and other persuasive genres.

**Rising Action:** The part of a drama where the plot becomes increasingly complicated. Rising action leads up to the climax, or turning point, of a drama.

**Roman à clef:** A French phrase meaning "novel with a key." It refers to a narrative in which real persons are portrayed under fictitious names.

**Romance:** A broad term, usually denoting a narrative with exotic, exaggerated, often idealized characters, scenes, and themes.

**Romanticism:** This term has two widely accepted meanings. In historical criticism, it refers to a European intellectual and artistic movement of the late eighteenth and early nineteenth centuries that sought greater freedom of personal expression than that allowed by the strict rules of literary form and logic of the eighteenth-century neoclassicists. The Romantics preferred emotional and imaginative expression to rational analysis. They considered the individual to be at the center of all experience and so placed him or her atthe center of their art. The Romantics believed that the creative imagination reveals nobler truths—unique feelings and attitudes—than those that could be discovered by logic or by scientific examination. Both the natural world and the state of childhood were important sources for revelations of "eternal truths." "Romanticism" is also used as a general term to refer to a type of sensibility found in all periods of literary history and usually considered to be in opposition to the principles of classicism. In this sense, Romanticism signifies any work or philosophy in which the exotic or dreamlike figure strongly, or that is devoted to individualistic expression, self-analysis, or a pursuit of a higher realm of knowledge than can be discovered by human reason.

**Romantics:** See *Romanticism*

# S

**Satire:** A work that uses ridicule, humor, and wit to criticize and provoke change in human nature and institutions. There are two major types of satire: "formal" or "direct" satire speaks directly to the reader or to a character in the work; "indirect" satire relies upon the ridiculous behavior of its characters to make its point. Formal satire is further divided into two manners: the "Horatian," which ridicules gently, and the "Juvenalian," which derides its subjects harshly and bitterly.

**Science Fiction:** A type of narrative about or based upon real or imagined scientific theories and technology. Science fiction is often peopled with alien creatures and set on other planets or in different dimensions.

**Second Person:** See *Point of View*

**Setting:** The time, place, and culture in which the action of a narrative takes place. The elements of setting may include geographic location, characters' physical and mental environments, prevailing cultural attitudes, or the historical time in which the action takes place.

**Simile:** A comparison, usually using "like" or "as," of two essentially dissimilar things, as in "coffee as cold as ice" or "He sounded like a broken record."

**Slang:** A type of informal verbal communication that is generally unacceptable for formal writing. Slang words and phrases are often colorful exaggerations used to emphasize the speaker's point; they may also be shortened versions of an often-used word or phrase.

**Slave Narrative:** Autobiographical accounts of American slave life as told by escaped slaves. These works first appeared during the abolition movement of the 1830s through the 1850s.

**Socialist Realism:** The Socialist Realism school of literary theory was proposed by Maxim Gorky and established as a dogma by the first Soviet Congress of Writers. It demanded adherence to a communist worldview in works of literature. Its doctrines required an objective viewpoint comprehensible to the working classes and themes of social struggle featuring strong proletarian heroes.

**Stereotype:** A stereotype was originally the name for a duplication made during the printing process; this led to its modern definition as a person or thing that is (or is assumed to be) the same as all others of its type.

**Stream of Consciousness:** A narrative technique for rendering the inward experience of a character. This technique is designed to give the impression of an ever-changing series of thoughts, emotions, images, and memories in the spontaneous and seemingly illogical order that they occur in life.

**Structure:** The form taken by a piece of literature. The structure may be made obvious for ease of understanding, as in nonfiction works, or may obscured for artistic purposes, as in some poetry or seemingly "unstructured" prose.

**Sturm und Drang:** A German term meaning "storm and stress." It refers to a German literary movement of the 1770s and 1780s that reacted against the order and rationalism of the enlightenment, focusing instead on the intense experience of extraordinary individuals.

**Style:** A writer's distinctive manner of arranging words to suit his or her ideas and purpose in writing. The unique imprint of the author's personality upon his or her writing, style is the product of an author's way of arranging ideas and his or her use of diction, different sentence structures, rhythm, figures of speech, rhetorical principles, and other elements of composition.

**Subjectivity:** Writing that expresses the author's personal feelings about his subject, and which may or may not include factual information about the subject.

**Subplot:** A secondary story in a narrative. A subplot may serve as a motivating or complicating force for the main plot of the work, or it may provide emphasis for, or relief from, the main plot.

**Surrealism:** A term introduced to criticism by Guillaume Apollinaire and later adopted by Andre Breton. It refers to a French literary and artistic movement founded in the 1920s. The Surrealists sought to express unconscious thoughts and feelings in their works. The best-known technique used for achieving this aim was automatic writing—transcriptions of spontaneous outpourings from the unconscious. The Surrealists proposed to unify the contrary levels of conscious and unconscious, dream and reality, objectivity and subjectivity into a new level of "super-realism."

**Suspense:** A literary device in which the author maintains the audience's attention through the buildup of events, the outcome of which will soon be revealed.

**Symbol:** Something that suggests or stands for something else without losing its original identity. In literature, symbols combine their literal meaning with the suggestion of an abstract concept. Literary symbols are of two types: those that carry complex associations of meaning no matter what their contexts, and those that derive their suggestive meaning from their functions in specific literary works.

**Symbolism:** This term has two widely accepted meanings. In historical criticism, it denotes an early modernist literary movement initiated in France during the nineteenth century that reacted against the prevailing standards of realism. Writers in this movement aimed to evoke, indirectly and symbolically, an order of being beyond the material world of the five senses. Poetic expression of personal emotion figured strongly in the movement, typically by means of a private set of symbols uniquely identifiable with the individual poet. The principal aim of the Symbolists was to express in words the highly complex feelings that grew out of everyday contact with the world. In a broader sense, the term "symbolism" refers to the use of one object to represent another.

# T

**Tall Tale:** A humorous tale told in a straightforward, credible tone but relating absolutely impossible events or feats of the characters. Such tales were commonly told of frontier adventures during the settlement of the west in the United States.

**Theme:** The main point of a work of literature. The term is used interchangeably with thesis.

**Thesis:** A thesis is both an essay and the point argued in the essay. Thesis novels and thesis plays share the quality of containing a thesis which is supported through the action of the story.

**Third Person:** See *Point of View*

**Tone:** The author's attitude toward his or her audience may be deduced from the tone of the work. A formal tone may create distance or convey politeness, while an informal tone may encourage a friendly, intimate, or intrusive feeling in the reader. The author's attitude toward his or her subject matter may also be deduced from the tone of the words he or she uses in discussing it.

**Transcendentalism:** An American philosophical and religious movement, based in New England from around 1835 until the Civil War. Transcendentalism was a form of American romanticism that had its roots abroad in the works of Thomas Carlyle, Samuel Coleridge, and Johann Wolfgang von Goethe. The Transcendentalists stressed the importance of intuition and subjective experience in communication with God. They rejected religious dogma and texts in favor of mysticism and scientific naturalism. They pursued truths that lie beyond the "colorless" realms perceived by reason and the senses and were active social reformers in public education, women's rights, and the abolition of slavery.

## U

**Urban Realism:** A branch of realist writing that attempts to accurately reflect the often harsh facts of modern urban existence.

**Utopia:** A fictional perfect place, such as "paradise" or "heaven."

## V

**Verisimilitude:** Literally, the appearance of truth. In literary criticism, the term refers to aspects of a work of literature that seem true to the reader.

**Victorian:** Refers broadly to the reign of Queen Victoria of England (1837-1901) and to anything with qualities typical of that era. For example, the qualities of smug narrowmindedness, bourgeois materialism, faith in social progress, and priggish morality are often considered Victorian. This stereotype is contradicted by such dramatic intellectual developments as the theories of Charles Darwin, Karl Marx, and Sigmund Freud (which stirred strong debates in England) and the critical attitudes of serious Victorian writers like Charles Dickens and George Eliot. In literature, the Victorian Period was the great age of the English novel, and the latter part of the era saw the rise of movements such as decadence and symbolism.

## W

**Weltanschauung:** A German term referring to a person's worldview or philosophy.

**Weltschmerz:** A German term meaning "world pain." It describes a sense of anguish about the nature of existence, usually associated with a melancholy, pessimistic attitude.

## Z

**Zeitgeist:** A German term meaning "spirit of the time." It refers to the moral and intellectual trends of a given era.

# Cumulative Author/Title Index

## Numerical

*1984* (Orwell): V7

## A

*The A.B.C. Murders* (Christie): V30
Abe, Kobo
   *The Woman in the Dunes:* V22
*Absalom, Absalom!* (Faulkner): V13
*The Accidental Tourist* (Tyler): V7
Achebe, Chinua
   *Things Fall Apart:* V2
Adams, Douglas
   *The Hitchhiker's Guide to the
     Galaxy:* V7
Adams, Richard
   *Watership Down:* V11
*The Adventures of Huckleberry Finn*
   (Twain): V1
*The Adventures of Tom Sawyer*
   (Twain): V6
*The Age of Innocence* (Wharton):
   V11
Agee, James
   *A Death in the Family:* V22
*Alas, Babylon* (Frank): V29
*The Alchemist* (Coelho): V29
Alcott, Louisa May
   *Little Women:* V12
Alexie, Sherman
   *The Lone Ranger and Tonto
     Fistfight in Heaven:* V17
   *Reservation Blues:* V31
*Alias Grace* (Atwood): V19
*Alice's Adventures in Wonderland*
   (Carroll): V7

*All Quiet on the Western Front*
   (Remarque): V4
*All the King's Men* (Warren): V13
Allende, Isabel
   *Daughter of Fortune:* V18
   *Eva Luna:* V29
   *The House of the Spirits:* V6
Allison, Dorothy
   *Bastard Out of Carolina:* V11
Alvarez, Julia
   *How the García Girls Lost Their
     Accents:* V5
   *In the Time of the Butterflies:* V9
*Always Coming Home* (Le Guin): V9
*The Amazing Adventures of Kavalier &*
   *Clay* (Chabon): V25
*The Ambassadors* (James): V12
*American Pastoral* (Roth): V25
*An American Tragedy* (Dreiser): V17
Anaya, Rudolfo
   *Bless Me, Ultima:* V12
Anderson, Laurie Halse
   *Speak:* V31
Anderson, Sherwood
   *Winesburg, Ohio:* V4
Angelou, Maya
   *I Know Why the Caged Bird Sings:*
     V2
*Animal Dreams* (Kingsolver): V12
*Animal Farm* (Orwell): V3
*Anna Karenina* (Tolstoy): V28
*Annie John* (Kincaid): V3
*Anthem* (Rand): V29
*Appointment in Samarra* (O'Hara):
   V11
*Around the World in Eighty Days*
   (Verne): V30

*As I Lay Dying* (Faulkner): V8
Asimov, Isaac
   *I, Robot:* V29
*The Assistant:* V27
*Atlas Shrugged* (Rand): V10
*Atonement* (McEwan): V32
Atwood, Margaret
   *Alias Grace:* V19
   *Cat's Eye:* V14
   *The Handmaid's Tale:* V4
   *Surfacing:* V13
Auel, Jean
   *The Clan of the Cave Bear:* V11
Austen, Jane
   *Emma:* V21
   *Mansfield Park:* V29
   *Northanger Abbey:* V28
   *Persuasion:* V14
   *Pride and Prejudice:* V1
   *Sense and Sensibility:* V18
*The Autobiography of an Ex-
   Coloured Man* (Johnson): V22
*The Autobiography of Miss Jane
   Pittman* (Gaines): V5
*The Awakening* (Chopin): V3

## B

*Babbitt* (Lewis): V19
Baldwin, James
   *Go Tell It on the Mountain:* V4
Ballard, J. G.
   *Empire of the Sun:* V8
Banks, Russell
   *The Sweet Hereafter:* V13
*Bastard Out of Carolina* (Allison):
   V11

Baum, L. Frank
  *The Wonderful Wizard of Oz:* V13
*The Bean Trees* (Kingsolver): V5
*Bel Canto* (Patchett): V30
*The Bell Jar* (Plath): V1
Bellamy, Edward
  *Looking Backward: 2000–1887:*
    V15
Bellow, Saul
  *Herzog:* V14
  *Humboldt's Gift:* V26
  *Seize the Day:* V4
*Beloved* (Morrison): V6
Benitez, Sandra
  *A Place Where the Sea
    Remembers:* V32
*Betsey Brown* (Shange): V11
*The Big Sleep* (Chandler): V17
*Billy Budd, Sailor: An Inside
    Narrative* (Melville): V9
*Black Beauty* (Sewell): V22
*Black Boy* (Wright): V1
Blair, Eric Arthur
  *Animal Farm:* V3
*Bleak House* (Dickens): V30
*Bless Me, Ultima* (Anaya): V12
*Bless the Beasts and Children*
    (Swarthout): V29
*Blindness:* V27
*The Bluest Eye* (Morrison): V1
Blume, Judy
  *Forever...:* V24
*Body and Soul* (Conroy): V11
*The Bone People* (Hulme): V24
*The Bonesetter's Daughter* (Tan):
    V31
*The Book of Laughter and Forgetting*
    (Kundera): V27
Borland, Hal
  *When the Legends Die:* V18
Boulle, Pierre
  *The Bridge over the River Kwai:*
    V32
Bowen, Elizabeth Dorothea Cole
  *The Death of the Heart:* V13
Bradbury, Ray
  *Dandelion Wine:* V22
  *Fahrenheit 451:* V1
  *Something Wicked This Way
    Comes:* V29
Braithwaite, E. R.
  *To Sir, With Love:* V30
*Brave New World* (Huxley): V6
*Bread Givers* (Yezierska): V29
*Breathing Lessons* (Tyler): V10
*Briar Rose* (Yolen): V30
Bridal, Tessa
  *The Tree of Red Stars:* V17
*The Bride Price* (Emecheta): V12
*Brideshead Revisited* (Waugh): V13
*The Bridge of San Luis Rey* (Wilder):
    V24

*The Bridge over the River Kwai*
    (Boulle): V32
Brontë, Anne
  *The Tenant of Wildfell Hall:*
    V26
Brontë, Charlotte
  *Jane Eyre:* V4
Brontë, Emily
  *Wuthering Heights:* V2
Brookner, Anita
  *Hotel du Lac:* V23
Brooks, Geraldine
  *March:* V26
*The Brothers Karamazov*
    (Dostoevsky): V8
Brown, Rita Mae
  *Rubyfruit Jungle:* V9
Buck, Pearl S.
  *The Good Earth:* V25
Bulgakov, Mikhail
  *The Master and Margarita:* V8
Bunyan, John
  *The Pilgrim's Progress:* V32
Burdick, Eugene, and
    William J. Lederer
  *The Ugly American:* V23
Burgess, Anthony
  *A Clockwork Orange:* V15
Burney, Fanny
  *Evelina:* V16
Burns, Olive Ann
  *Cold Sassy Tree:* V31
Butler, Octavia
  *Kindred:* V8
  *Parable of the Sower:* V21

**C**

*The Caine Mutiny: A Novel of World
    War II* (Wouk): V7
*The Call of the Wild* (London): V8
Camus, Albert
  *The Plague:* V16
  *The Stranger:* V6
*Candide* (Voltaire): V7
*Cane* (Toomer): V11
*Cannery Row* (Steinbeck): V28
Card, Orson Scott
  *Ender's Game:* V5
Carroll, Lewis
  *Alice's Adventures in Wonderland:*
    V7
  *Through the Looking-Glass:* V27
*Catch-22* (Heller): V1
*The Catcher in the Rye* (Salinger): V1
Cather, Willa
  *Death Comes for the Archbishop:*
    V19
  *My Ántonia:* V2
*Cat's Cradle* (Vonnegut): V28
*Cat's Eye* (Atwood): V14
*Ceremony* (Silko): V4

Chabon, Michael
  *The Amazing Adventures of
    Kavalier & Clay:* V25
Chandler, Raymond
  *The Big Sleep:* V17
*Charming Billy* (McDermott): V23
*The Chocolate War* (Cormier): V2
Choi, Sook Nyul
  *Year of Impossible Goodbyes:* V29
Chopin, Kate
  *The Awakening:* V3
*The Chosen* (Potok): V4
Christie, Agatha
  *The A.B.C. Murders:* V30
  *Ten Little Indians:* V8
*A Christmas Carol* (Dickens): V10
*Chronicle of a Death Foretold*
    (García Márquez): V10
Cisneros, Sandra
  *The House on Mango Street:* V2
*The Clan of the Cave Bear* (Auel):
    V11
Clavell, James du Maresq
  *Shogun: A Novel of Japan:* V10
Cleage, Pearl
  *What Looks Like Crazy on an
    Ordinary Day:* V17
Clemens, Samuel Langhorne
  *The Adventures of Huckleberry
    Finn:* V1
  *The Adventures of Tom Sawyer:* V6
*A Clockwork Orange* (Burgess): V15
Coelho, Paulo
  *The Alchemist:* V29
Coetzee, J. M.
  *Dusklands:* V21
*Cold Mountain* (Frazier): V25
*Cold Sassy Tree* (Burns): V31
*The Color Purple* (Walker): V5
Conan Doyle, Arthur, Sir
  *The Hound of the Baskervilles:* V28
*A Connecticut Yankee in King
    Arthur's Court* (Twain): V20
Conrad, Joseph
  *Heart of Darkness:* V2
  *Lord Jim:* V16
Conroy, Frank
  *Body and Soul:* V11
Cooper, James Fenimore
  *The Deerslayer:* V25
  *The Last of the Mohicans:* V9
  *The Last of the Mohicans* (Motion
    picture): V32
Cormier, Robert
  *The Chocolate War:* V2
  *I Am the Cheese:* V18
*The Count of Monte Cristo* (Dumas):
    V19
*The Country of the Pointed Firs*
    (Jewett): V15
Courtenay, Bryce
  *The Power of One:* V32

Crane, Stephen
   *Maggie: A Girl of the Streets:*
     V20
   *The Red Badge of Courage:* V4
*The Crazy Horse Electric Game*
   (Crutcher): V11
*Crime and Punishment*
   (Dostoyevsky): V3
Crutcher, Chris
   *The Crazy Horse Electric Game:*
     V11
   *Staying Fat for Sarah Byrnes:*
     V32
*Cry, the Beloved Country* (Paton):
   V3
Cunningham, Michael
   *The Hours:* V23

**D**

*The Damnation of Theron Ware*
   (Frederic): V22
*Dandelion Wine* (Bradbury): V22
Dangarembga, Tsitsi
   *Nervous Conditions:* V28
Danticat, Edwidge
   *The Dew Breaker:* V28
*Darkness at Noon* (Koestler): V19
*Daughter of Fortune* (Allende): V18
*David Copperfield* (Dickens): V25
Davis, Rebecca Harding
   *Margret Howth: A Story of*
     *To-Day:* V14
*A Day No Pigs Would Die* (Peck):
   V29
*The Day of the Locust* (West): V16
de Cervantes Saavedra, Miguel
   *Don Quixote:* V8
*The Dead of the House* (Green): V10
*Death Comes for the Archbishop*
   (Cather): V19
*A Death in the Family* (Agee): V22
*Death in Venice* (Mann): V17
*The Death of the Heart* (Bowen): V13
*The Deerslayer* (Cooper): V25
Defoe, Daniel
   *A Journal of the Plague Year:* V30
   *Moll Flanders:* V13
   *Robinson Crusoe:* V9
DeLillo, Don
   *White Noise:* V28
*Deliverance* (Dickey): V9
*Demian* (Hesse): V15
*Democracy* (Didion): V3
Desai, Kiran
   *Hullabaloo in the Guava Orchard:*
     V28
*The Dew Breaker* (Danticat): V28
Dick, Philip K.
   *Do Androids Dream of Electric*
     *Sheep?:* V5
   *Martian Time-Slip:* V26

Dickens, Charles
   *Bleak House:* V30
   *A Christmas Carol:* V10
   *David Copperfield:* V25
   *Great Expectations:* V4
   *Hard Times:* V20
   *Oliver Twist:* V14
   *A Tale of Two Cities:* V5
Dickey, James
   *Deliverance:* V9
Didion, Joan
   *Democracy:* V3
Dinesen, Isak
   *Out of Africa:* V9
*Dinner at the Homesick Restaurant*
   (Tyler): V2
*Do Androids Dream of Electric*
   *Sheep?* (Dick): V5
*Doctor Zhivago* (Pasternak): V26
Doctorow, E. L.
   *Ragtime:* V6
*Don Quixote* (de Cervantes
   Saavedra): V8
Dorris, Michael
   *A Yellow Raft in Blue Water:* V3
Dos Passos, John
   *U.S.A.:* V14
Dostoyevsky, Fyodor
   *The Brothers Karamazov:* V8
   *Crime and Punishment:* V3
   *Notes from Underground:* V28
Doyle, Arthur Conan, Sir
   *The Hound of the Baskervilles:*
     V28
*Dr. Jekyll and Mr. Hyde* (Stevenson):
   V11
*Dracula* (Stoker): V18
Dreiser, Theodore
   *An American Tragedy:* V17
   *Sister Carrie:* V8
du Maurier, Daphne
   *Rebecca:* V12
Dumas, Alexandre
   *The Count of Monte Cristo:* V19
   *The Three Musketeers:* V14
*Dune* (Herbert): V31
Duong Thu Huong
   *Paradise of the Blind:* V23
*Dusklands* (Coetzee): V21

**E**

*East of Eden* (Steinbeck): V19
Eco, Umberto
   *The Name of the Rose:* V22
*The Edible Woman* (Atwood): V12
*Einstein's Dreams* (Lightman): V29
Eliot, George
   *Middlemarch:* V23
   *The Mill on the Floss:* V17
   *Silas Marner:* V20
*Ellen Foster* (Gibbons): V3

Ellis, Bret Easton
   *Less Than Zero:* V11
Ellison, Ralph
   *Invisible Man:* V2
   *Juneteenth:* V21
*Elmer Gantry* (Lewis): V22
Emecheta, Buchi
   *The Bride Price:* V12
   *The Wrestling Match:* V14
*Emma* (Austen): V21
*Empire Falls* (Russo): V25
*Empire of the Sun* (Ballard): V8
*The End of the Affair* (Greene): V16
*Ender's Game* (Card): V5
*The English Patient* (Ondaatje): V23
Erdrich, Louise
   *Love Medicine:* V5
Esquivel, Laura
   *Like Water for Chocolate:* V5
*Ethan Frome* (Wharton): V5
Eugenides, Jeffrey
   *Middlesex:* V24
*Eva Luna* (Allende): V29
*Evelina* (Burney): V16

**F**

*Fahrenheit 451* (Bradbury): V1
*Fallen Angels* (Myers): V30
*Far from the Madding Crowd*
   (Hardy): V19
*Farewell My Concubine* (Lee): V19
*A Farewell to Arms* (Hemingway):
   V1
*Fathers and Sons* (Turgenev): V16
Faulkner, William
   *Absalom, Absalom!:* V13
   *As I Lay Dying:* V8
   *Light in August:* V24
   *The Sound and the Fury:* V4
Fielding, Henry
   *Joseph Andrews:* V32
   *Tom Jones:* V18
Fitzgerald, F. Scott
   *The Great Gatsby:* V2
   *This Side of Paradise:* V20
   *Tender Is the Night:* V19
*The Fixer* (Malamud): V9
Flagg, Fannie
   *Fried Green Tomatoes at the*
     *Whistle Stop Café:* V7
Flaubert, Gustave
   *Madame Bovary:* V14
*Flowers for Algernon* (Keyes): V2
Foden, Giles
   *The Last King of Scotland:* V15
*For Whom the Bell Tolls*
   (Hemingway): V14
Ford, Ford Madox
   *The Good Soldier:* V28
Ford, Richard
   *Independence Day:* V25

*Foreign Affairs* (Lurie): V24
*Forever...* (Blume): V24
Forster, E. M.
   *Howards End:* V10
   *A Passage to India:* V3
   *A Room with a View:* V11
*The Fountainhead* (Rand): V16
Fowles, John
   *The French Lieutenant's Woman:*
     V21
Fox, Paula
   *The Slave Dancer:* V12
Frank, Pat
   *Alas, Babylon:* V29
*Frankenstein* (Shelley): V1
*Franny and Zooey* (Salinger): V30
Frazier, Charles
   *Cold Mountain:* V25
Frederic, Harold
   *The Damnation of Theron Ware:*
     V22
*The French Lieutenant's Woman*
   (Fowles): V21
*Fried Green Tomatoes at the Whistle*
   *Stop Café* (Flagg): V7
Fuentes, Carlos
   *The Old Gringo:* V8

# G

Gaines, Ernest J.
   *The Autobiography of Miss Jane*
     *Pittman:* V5
   *A Gathering of Old Men:* V16
   *A Lesson Before Dying:* V7
García Márquez, Gabriel
   *Chronicle of a Death Foretold:* V10
   *Love in the Time of Cholera:* V1
   *One Hundred Years of Solitude:*
     V5
Gardner, John
   *Grendel:* V3
*A Gathering of Old Men* (Gaines):
   V16
*Giants in the Earth* (Rölvaag): V5
Gibbons, Kaye
   *Ellen Foster:* V3
Gide, André
   *The Immoralist:* V21
*Gilead* (Robinson): V24
*The Giver* (Lowry): V3
*Go Tell It on the Mountain* (Baldwin):
   V4
*The God of Small Things* (Roy): V22
*The Godfather* (Puzo): V16
Golden, Arthur
   *Memoirs of a Geisha:* V19
*The Golden Notebook* (Lessing): V27
Golding, William
   *Lord of the Flies:* V2
Goldman, William
   *The Princess Bride:* V31

*Gone with the Wind* (Mitchell): V9
*The Good Earth* (Buck): V25
*The Good Soldier* (Ford): V28
Gordimer, Nadine
   *July's People:* V4
Grahame, Kenneth
   *The Wind in the Willows:* V20
*The Grapes of Wrath* (Steinbeck): V7
*The Grass Dancer* (Power): V11
Graves, Robert
   *I, Claudius:* V21
*Gravity's Rainbow* (Pynchon): V23
*Great Expectations* (Dickens): V4
*The Great Gatsby* (Fitzgerald): V2
Green, Hannah
   *The Dead of the House:* V10
Greenberg, Joanne
   *I Never Promised You a Rose*
     *Garden:* V23
Greene, Bette
   *Summer of My German Soldier:* V10
Greene, Graham
   *The End of the Affair:* V16
   *The Power and the Glory:* V31
*Grendel* (Gardner): V3
Guest, Judith
   *Ordinary People:* V1
*Gulliver's Travels* (Swift): V6
Guterson, David
   *Snow Falling on Cedars:* V13

# H

Haley, Alex
   *Roots: The Story of an American*
     *Family:* V9
Hammett, Dashiell
   *The Maltese Falcon:* V21
*The Handmaid's Tale* (Atwood): V4
*Hard Times* (Dickens): V20
Hardy, Thomas
   *Far from the Madding Crowd:* V19
   *Jude the Obscure:* V30
   *The Mayor of Casterbridge:* V15
   *The Return of the Native:* V11
   *Tess of the d'Urbervilles:* V3
Harris, Marilyn
   *Hatter Fox:* V14
*Hatter Fox* (Harris): V14
Hawthorne, Nathaniel
   *The House of the Seven Gables:*
     V20
   *The Scarlet Letter:* V1
Head, Bessie
   *When Rain Clouds Gather:* V31
*The Heart Is a Lonely Hunter*
   (McCullers): V6
*Heart of Darkness* (Conrad): V2
Hegi, Ursula
   *Stones from the River:* V25
Heller, Joseph
   *Catch-22:* V1

Hemingway, Ernest
   *A Farewell to Arms:* V1
   *For Whom the Bell Tolls:* V14
   *The Old Man and the Sea:* V6
   *The Sun Also Rises:*V5
Herbert, Frank
   *Dune:* V31
   *Soul Catcher:* V17
*Herzog* (Bellow): V14
Hesse, Hermann
   *Demian:* V15
   *Siddhartha:* V6
   *Steppenwolf:* V24
Highsmith, Patricia
   *The Talented Mr. Ripley:* V27
Hijuelos, Oscar
   *The Mambo Kings Play Songs*
     *of Love:* V17
Hinton, S. E.
   *The Outsiders:* V5
   *Rumble Fish:* V15
   *Tex:* V9
   *That Was Then, This Is Now:*
     V16
*The Hitchhiker's Guide to the Galaxy*
   (Adams): V7
*The Hobbit* (Tolkien): V8
Høeg, Peter
   *Smilla's Sense of Snow:* V17
*Hotel du Lac* (Brookner): V23
*The Hound of the Baskervilles*
   (Conan Doyle): V28
*The Hours* (Cunningham): V23
*House Made of Dawn* (Momaday):
   V10
*The House of Mirth* (Wharton): V15
*The House of the Seven Gables*
   (Hawthorne): V20
*The House of the Spirits* (Allende):
   V6
*The House on Mango Street*
   (Cisneros): V2
*How Green Was My Valley*
   (Llewellyn): V30
*How the García Girls Lost Their*
   *Accents* (Alvarez): V5
*Howards End* (Forster): V10
Hudson, Jan
   *Sweetgrass:* V28
Hughes, Langston
   *Tambourines to Glory:* V21
Hugo, Victor
   *The Hunchback of Notre Dame:*
     V20
   *Les Misérables:* V5
*Hullabaloo in the Guava Orchard*
   (Desai): V28
Hulme, Keri
   *The Bone People:* V24
*Humboldt's Gift* (Bellow): V26
*The Hunchback of Notre Dame*
   (Hugo): V20

Hurston, Zora Neale
  *Their Eyes Were Watching God:* V3
Huxley, Aldous
  *Brave New World:* V6

## I

*I Am the Cheese* (Cormier): V18
*I, Claudius* (Graves): V21
*I Know Why the Caged Bird Sings* (Angelou): V2
*I Never Promised You a Rose Garden* (Greenberg): V23
*Ida* (Stein): V27
*The Immoralist* (Gide): V21
*In Babylon* (Möring): V25
*In Country* (Mason): V4
*In the Castle of My Skin* (Lamming): V15
*In the Time of the Butterflies* (Alvarez): V9
*Independence Day* (Ford): V25
*Invisible Man* (Ellison): V2
*I, Robot* (Asimov): V29
Irving, John
  *A Prayer for Owen Meany:* V14
  *The World According to Garp:* V12
Ishiguro, Kazuo
  *The Remains of the Day:* V13
*Ivanhoe* (Scott): V31

## J

James, Henry
  *The Ambassadors:* V12
  *The Portrait of a Lady:* V19
  *The Turn of the Screw:* V16
  *The Wings of the Dove:* V32
*Jane Eyre* (Brontë): V4
Japrisot, Sébastien
  *A Very Long Engagement:* V18
Jen, Gish
  *Typical American:* V30
Jewett, Sarah Orne
  *The Country of the Pointed Firs:* V15
Jin, Ha
  *Waiting:* V25
Johnson, James Weldon
  *The Autobiography of an Ex-Coloured Man:* V22
Jones, Edward P.
  *The Known World:* V26
*Joseph Andrews* (Fielding): V32
*A Journal of the Plague Year* (Defoe): V30
*The Joy Luck Club* (Tan): V1
Joyce, James
  *A Portrait of the Artist as a Young Man:* V7
  *Ulysses:* V26
*Jude the Obscure* (Hardy): V30
*July's People* (Gordimer): V4

*Juneteenth* (Ellison): V21
*The Jungle* (Sinclair): V6

## K

*Kaddish for a Child Not Born* (Kertész): V23
Kafka, Franz
  *The Trial:* V7
Keneally, Thomas
  *Schindler's List:* V17
Kerouac, Jack
  *On the Road:* V8
Kertész, Imre
  *Kaddish for a Child Not Born:* V23
Kesey, Ken
  *One Flew Over the Cuckoo's Nest:* V2
Keyes, Daniel
  *Flowers for Algernon:* V2
Kidd, Sue Monk
  *The Secret Life of Bees:* V27
*The Killer Angels* (Shaara): V26
*Kim* (Kipling): V21
Kincaid, Jamaica
  *Annie John:* V3
*Kindred* (Butler): V8
Kingsolver, Barbara
  *Animal Dreams:* V12
  *The Bean Trees:* V5
  *Pigs in Heaven:* V10
  *Poisonwood Bible:* V24
Kingston, Maxine Hong
  *The Woman Warrior:* V6
Kinsella, W. P.
  *Shoeless Joe:* V15
Kipling, Rudyard
  *Kim:* V21
*Kitchen* (Yoshimoto): V7
*The Kitchen God's Wife* (Tan): V13
Knowles, John
  *A Separate Peace:* V2
*The Known World* (Jones): V26
Koestler, Arthur
  *Darkness at Noon:* V19
Kogawa, Joy
  *Obasan:* V3
Kosinski, Jerzy
  *The Painted Bird:* V12
Kundera, Milan
  *The Book of Laughter and Forgetting:* V27
  *The Unbearable Lightness of Being:* V18

## L

Lahiri, Jhumpa
  *The Namesake:* V31
Lamming, George
  *In the Castle of My Skin:* V15
*The Last King of Scotland* (Foden): V15

*The Last of the Mohicans* (Cooper): V9
*The Last of the Mohicans* (Motion picture): V32
Laurence, Margaret
  *The Stone Angel:* V11
Lawrence, D. H.
  *The Rainbow:* V26
  *Sons and Lovers:* V18
Le Guin, Ursula K.
  *Always Coming Home:* V9
  *The Left Hand of Darkness:* V6
*The Learning Tree* (Parks): V32
Lederer, William J., and Eugene Burdick
  *The Ugly American:* V23
Lee, Harper
  *To Kill a Mockingbird:* V2
  *To Kill a Mockingbird* (Motion picture): V32
Lee, Lilian
  *Farewell My Concubine:* V19
*The Left Hand of Darkness* (Le Guin): V6
L'Engle, Madeleine
  *A Wrinkle in Time:* V32
Leroux, Gaston
  *The Phantom of the Opera:* V20
*Les Misérables* (Hugo): V5
*Less Than Zero* (Ellis): V11
Lessing, Doris
  *The Golden Notebook:* V27
*A Lesson Before Dying* (Gaines): V7
Lewis, C. S.
  *The Lion, the Witch and the Wardrobe:* V24
Lewis, Sinclair
  *Babbitt:* V19
  *Elmer Gantry:* V22
  *Main Street:* V15
*Life of Pi* (Martel): V27
*Light in August* (Faulkner): V24
Lightman, Alan
  *Einstein's Dreams:* V29
*Like Water for Chocolate* (Esquivel): V5
*The Lion, the Witch and the Wardrobe* (Lewis): V24
*The Little Prince* (de Saint-Exupéry): V30
*Little Women* (Alcott): V12
*Lives of Girls and Women* (Munro): V27
Llewellyn, Richard
  *How Green Was My Valley:* V30
*Lolita* (Nabokov): V9
London, Jack
  *The Call of the Wild:* V8
  *White Fang:* V19
*The Lone Ranger and Tonto Fistfight in Heaven* (Alexie): V17
*A Long and Happy Life* (Price): V18

*Look Homeward, Angel* (Wolfe): V18
*Looking Backward: 2000–1887*
    (Bellamy): V15
*Lord Jim* (Conrad): V16
*Lord of the Flies* (Golding): V2
*The Lord of the Rings* (Tolkien):
    V26
*Losing Battles* (Welty): V15
*Love in the Time of Cholera*
    (García Márquez): V1
*Love Medicine* (Erdrich): V5
Lowry, Lois
    *The Giver:* V3
Lurie, Alison
    *Foreign Affairs:* V24

**M**

Machiavelli, Niccolo
    *The Prince:* V9
*Madame Bovary* (Flaubert): V14
*Maggie: A Girl of the Streets*
    (Crane): V20
*The Magic Mountain* (Mann): V29
Mailer, Norman
    *The Naked and the Dead:* V10
*Main Street* (Lewis): V15
Malamud, Bernard
    *The Assistant:* V27
    *The Fixer:* V9
    *The Natural:* V4
*The Maltese Falcon* (Hammett):
    V21
*Mama Day* (Naylor): V7
*The Mambo Kings Play Songs of
    Love* (Hijuelos): V17
*The Man Who Loved Children*
    (Stead): V27
Mann, Thomas
    *Death in Venice:* V17
    *The Magic Mountain:* V29
*Mansfield Park* (Austen): V29
*March* (Brooks): V26
*Margret Howth: A Story of To-Day*
    (Davis): V14
Markandaya, Kamala
    *Nectar in a Sieve:* V13
Martel, Yann
    *Life of Pi:* V27
*Martian Time-Slip* (Dick): V26
Mason, Bobbie Ann
    *In Country:* V4
*The Master and Margarita*
    (Bulgakov): V8
Maugham, W. Somerset
    *The Razor's Edge:* V23
*The Mayor of Casterbridge* (Hardy):
    V15
McCullers, Carson
    *The Heart Is a Lonely Hunter:*
        V6
    *The Member of the Wedding:* V13

McDermott, Alice
    *Charming Billy:* V23
McEwan, Ian
    *Atonement:* V32
Melville, Herman
    *Billy Budd, Sailor: An Inside
        Narrative:* V9
    *Moby-Dick:* V7
    *Typee:* V32
*The Member of the Wedding*
    (McCullers): V13
*Memoirs of a Geisha* (Golden): V19
Méndez, Miguel
    *Pilgrims in Aztlán:* V12
*Middlemarch* (Eliot): V23
*Middlesex* (Eugenides): V24
*Midnight's Children* (Rushdie): V23
*The Mill on the Floss* (Eliot): V17
Mitchell, Margaret
    *Gone with the Wind:* V9
*Moby-Dick* (Melville): V7
*Moll Flanders* (Defoe): V13
Momaday, N. Scott
    *House Made of Dawn:* V10
More, Thomas
    *Utopia:* V29
Mori, Kyoko
    *Shizuko's Daughter:* V15
Möring, Marcel
    *In Babylon:* V25
Morrison, Toni
    *Beloved:* V6
    *The Bluest Eye:* V1
    *Sula:* V14
    *Song of Solomon:* V8
*Mrs. Dalloway* (Woolf): V12
Munro, Alice
    *Lives of Girls and Women:* V27
Murdoch, Iris
    *Under the Net:* V18
*My Ántonia* (Cather): V2
Myers, Walter Dean
    *Fallen Angels:* V30
*My Name is Red* (Pamuk): V27

**N**

Nabokov, Vladimir
    *Lolita:* V9
*The Naked and the Dead* (Mailer):
    V10
*The Name of the Rose* (Eco): V22
*The Namesake* (Lahiri): V31
*Native Son* (Wright): V7
*The Natural* (Malamud): V4
*Nausea* (Sartre): V21
Naylor, Gloria
    *Mama Day:* V7
    *The Women of Brewster Place:* V4
*Nectar in a Sieve* (Markandaya): V13
*Nervous Conditions* (Dangarembga):
    V28

*Night* (Wiesel): V4
*No-No Boy* (Okada): V25
Norris, Frank
    *The Octopus:* V12
*Northanger Abbey* (Austen): V28
*Notes from Underground*
    (Dostoyevsky): V28

**O**

Oates, Joyce Carol
    *them:* V8
    *We Were the Mulvaneys:* V24
*Obasan* (Kogawa): V3
O'Connor, Flannery
    *The Violent Bear It Away:* V21
    *Wise Blood:* V3
*The Octopus* (Norris): V12
*Of Mice and Men* (Steinbeck): V1
O'Hara, John
    *Appointment in Samarra:* V11
Okada, John
    *No-No Boy:* V25
*The Old Gringo* (Fuentes): V8
*The Old Man and the Sea*
    (Hemingway): V6
*Oliver Twist* (Dickens): V14
*On the Beach* (Shute): V9
*On the Road* (Kerouac): V8
*The Once and Future King* (White):
    V30
Ondaatje, Michael
    *The English Patient:* V23
*One Day in the Life of Ivan
    Denisovich* (Solzhenitsyn): V6
*One Flew Over the Cuckoo's Nest*
    (Kesey): V2
*One Hundred Years of Solitude*
    (García Márquez): V5
*The Optimist's Daughter* (Welty): V13
Orczy, Emmuska
    *The Scarlet Pimpernel:* V31
*Ordinary People* (Guest): V1
Orwell, George
    *Animal Farm:* V3
    *1984:* V7
*Out of Africa* (Dinesen): V9
*The Outsiders* (Hinton): V5

**P**

*The Painted Bird* (Kosinski): V12
Pamuk, Orhan
    *My Name is Red:* V27
*Parable of the Sower* (Butler): V21
*Paradise of the Blind* (Duong): V23
Parks, Gordon
    *The Learning Tree:* V32
*A Passage to India* (Forster): V3
Pasternak, Boris
    *Doctor Zhivago:* V26
Patchett, Ann
    *Bel Canto:* V30

Paton, Alan
   *Cry, the Beloved Country:* V3
   *Too Late the Phalarope:* V12
*The Pearl* (Steinbeck): V5
Peck, Robert Newton
   *A Day No Pigs Would Die:* V29
*Persuasion* (Austen): V14
*The Phantom of the Opera* (Leroux):
   V20
*Picture Bride* (Uchida): V26
*The Picture of Dorian Gray* (Wilde):
   V20
*The Pigman* (Zindel): V14
*Pigs in Heaven* (Kingsolver): V10
*Pilgrims in Aztlán* (Méndez): V12
*The Pilgrim's Progress* (Bunyan): V32
Pirsig, Robert
   *Zen and the Art of Motorcycle
     Maintenance:* V31
*A Place Where the Sea Remembers*
   (Benitez): V32
*The Plague* (Camus): V16
Plath, Sylvia
   *The Bell Jar:* V1
*Poisonwood Bible* (Kingsolver): V24
Porter, Katherine Anne
   *Ship of Fools:* V14
*The Portrait of a Lady* (James): V19
*A Portrait of the Artist as a Young
   Man* (Joyce): V7
Potok, Chaim
   *The Chosen:* V4
Power, Susan
   *The Grass Dancer:* V11
*The Power and the Glory* (Greene):
   V31
*The Power of One* (Courtenay): V32
*A Prayer for Owen Meany* (Irving):
   V14
Price, Reynolds
   *A Long and Happy Life:* V18
*Pride and Prejudice* (Austen): V1
*The Prime of Miss Jean Brodie*
   (Spark): V22
*The Prince* (Machiavelli): V9
*The Prince and the Pauper* (Twain):
   V31
*The Princess Bride* (Goldman): V31
Puzo, Mario
   *The Godfather:* V16
Pynchon, Thomas
   *Gravity's Rainbow:* V23

### R

*Rabbit, Run* (Updike): V12
*Ragtime* (Doctorow): V6
*The Rainbow* (Lawrence): V26
Rand, Ayn
   *Anthem:* V29
   *Atlas Shrugged:* V10
   *The Fountainhead:* V16

*The Razor's Edge* (Maugham): V23
*Rebecca* (du Maurier): V12
*The Red Badge of Courage* (Crane):
   V4
*The Red Pony* (Steinbeck): V17
*The Remains of the Day* (Ishiguro):
   V13
Remarque, Erich Maria
   *All Quiet on the Western Front:*
     V4
*Reservation Blues* (Alexie): V31
*The Return of the Native* (Hardy):
   V11
Rhys, Jean
   *Wide Sargasso Sea:* V19
*Robinson Crusoe* (Defoe): V9
Robinson, Marilynne
   *Gilead:* V24
Rölvaag, O. E.
   *Giants in the Earth:* V5
*A Room with a View* (Forster): V11
*Roots: The Story of an American
   Family* (Haley): V9
Roth, Philip
   *American Pastoral:* V25
Roy, Arundhati
   *The God of Small Things:* V22
*Rubyfruit Jungle* (Brown): V9
*Rumble Fish* (Hinton): V15
Rushdie, Salman
   *Midnight's Children:* V23
   *The Satanic Verses:* V22
Russo, Richard
   *Empire Falls:* V25

### S

Saint-Exupéry, Antoine de
   *The Little Prince:* V30
Salinger, J. D.
   *The Catcher in the Rye:* V1
   *Franny and Zooey:* V30
Saramago, José
   *Blindness:* V27
Sartre, Jean-Paul
   *Nausea:* V21
*The Satanic Verses* (Rushdie): V22
*The Scarlet Letter* (Hawthorne): V1
*The Scarlet Pimpernel* (Orczy): V31
*Schindler's List* (Keneally): V17
*Scoop* (Waugh): V17
Scott, Walter
   *Ivanhoe:* V31
*The Secret Life of Bees* (Kidd):
   V27
*Seize the Day* (Bellow): V4
*Sense and Sensibility* (Austen): V18
*A Separate Peace* (Knowles): V2
Sewell, Anna
   *Black Beauty:* V22
Shaara, Michael
   *The Killer Angels:* V26

Shange, Ntozake
   *Betsey Brown:* V11
Shelley, Mary
   *Frankenstein:* V1
Shields, Carol
   *The Stone Diaries:* V23
*Ship of Fools* (Porter): V14
*Shizuko's Daughter* (Mori): V15
*Shoeless Joe* (Kinsella): V15
*Shogun: A Novel of Japan* (Clavell):
   V10
Shute, Nevil
   *On the Beach:* V9
*Siddhartha* (Hesse): V6
*Silas Marner* (Eliot): V20
Silko, Leslie Marmon
   *Ceremony:* V4
Sinclair, Upton
   *The Jungle:* V6
*Sister Carrie* (Dreiser): V8
*Slaughterhouse-Five* (Vonnegut):
   V3
*The Slave Dancer* (Fox): V12
Smiley, Jane
   *A Thousand Acres:* V32
*Smilla's Sense of Snow* (Høeg): V17
Smith, Betty
   *A Tree Grows in Brooklyn:* V31
*Snow Falling on Cedars* (Guterson):
   V13
*So Far from the Bamboo Grove*
   (Watkins): V28
Solzhenitsyn, Aleksandr
   *One Day in the Life of Ivan
     Denisovich:* V6
*Something Wicked This Way Comes*
   (Bradbury): V29
*Song of Solomon* (Morrison): V8
*Sons and Lovers* (Lawrence): V18
*Sophie's Choice* (Styron): V22
*Soul Catcher* (Herbert): V17
*The Sound and the Fury* (Faulkner):
   V4
Spark, Muriel
   *The Prime of Miss Jean Brodie:*
     V22
*Speak* (Anderson): V31
*Staying Fat for Sarah Byrnes*
   (Crutcher): V32
Stead, Christina
   *The Man Who Loved Children:*
     V27
Stein, Gertrude
   *Ida:* V27
Steinbeck, John
   *Cannery Row:* V28
   *East of Eden:* V19
   *The Grapes of Wrath:* V7
   *Of Mice and Men:* V1
   *The Pearl:* V5
   *The Red Pony:* V17
*Steppenwolf* (Hesse): V24

Stevenson, Robert Louis
    *Dr. Jekyll and Mr. Hyde:* V11
    *Treasure Island:* V20
Stoker, Bram
    *Dracula:* V18
*The Stone Angel* (Laurence): V11
*The Stone Diaries* (Shields): V23
*Stones from the River* (Hegi): V25
Stowe, Harriet Beecher
    *Uncle Tom's Cabin:* V6
*The Strange Case of Dr. Jekyll and*
    *Mr. Hyde* (Stevenson): see
    *Dr. Jekyll and Mr. Hyde*
*The Stranger* (Camus): V6
Styron, William
    *Sophie's Choice:* V22
*Sula* (Morrison): V14
*Summer* (Wharton): V20
*Summer of My German Soldier*
    (Greene): V10
*The Sun Also Rises* (Hemingway): V5
*Surfacing* (Atwood): V13
Swarthout, Glendon
    *Bless the Beasts and Children:* V29
*The Sweet Hereafter* (Banks): V13
*Sweetgrass* (Hudson): V28
Swift, Graham
    *Waterland:* V18
Swift, Jonathan
    *Gulliver's Travels:* V6

## T

*A Tale of Two Cities* (Dickens): V5
*The Talented Mr. Ripley*
    (Highsmith): V27
*Tambourines to Glory* (Hughes): V21
Tan, Amy
    *The Bonesetter's Daughter:* V31
    *The Joy Luck Club:* V1
    *The Kitchen God's Wife:* V13
*Ten Little Indians* (Christie): V8
*The Tenant of Wildfell Hall* (Brontë):
    V26
*Tender Is the Night* (Fitzgerald): V19
*Tess of the d'Urbervilles* (Hardy): V3
*Tex* (Hinton): V9
Thackeray, William Makepeace
    *Vanity Fair:* V13
*That Was Then, This Is Now*
    (Hinton): V16
*Their Eyes Were Watching God*
    (Hurston): V3
*them* (Oates): V8
*Things Fall Apart* (Achebe): V2
*This Side of Paradise* (Fitzgerald):
    V20
*A Thousand Acres* (Smiley): V32
*The Three Musketeers* (Dumas):
    V14
*Through the Looking-Glass:* V27
*The Time Machine* (Wells): V17

*To Kill a Mockingbird* (Lee): V2
*To Kill a Mockingbird*
    (Motion picture): V32
*To the Lighthouse* (Woolf): V8
Tolkien, J. R. R.
    *The Hobbit:* V8
    *The Lord of the Rings:* V26
Tolstoy, Leo
    *Anna Karenina:* V28
    *War and Peace:* V10
*Tom Jones* (Fielding): V18
*Too Late the Phalarope* (Paton): V12
Toomer, Jean
    *Cane:* V11
*To Sir, With Love* (Braithwaite): V30
*Toward the End of Time* (Updike):
    V24
*Treasure Island* (Stevenson): V20
*A Tree Grows in Brooklyn* (Smith):
    V31
*The Tree of Red Stars* (Bridal): V17
*The Trial* (Kafka): V7
Turgenev, Ivan
    *Fathers and Sons:* V16
*The Turn of the Screw* (James): V16
Twain, Mark
    *The Adventures of Huckleberry*
        *Finn:* V1
    *The Adventures of Tom Sawyer:* V6
    *A Connecticut Yankee in King*
        *Arthur's Court:* V20
    *The Prince and the Pauper:* V31
Tyler, Anne
    *The Accidental Tourist:* V7
    *Breathing Lessons:* V10
    *Dinner at the Homesick*
        *Restaurant:* V2
*Typee* (Melville): V32
*Typical American* (Jen): V30

## U

*U.S.A.* (Dos Passos): V14
Uchida, Yoshiko
    *Picture Bride:* V26
*The Ugly American* (Burdick and
    Lederer): V23
*Ulysses* (Joyce): V26
*The Unbearable Lightness of Being*
    (Kundera): V18
*Uncle Tom's Cabin* (Stowe): V6
*Under the Net* (Murdoch): V18
Updike, John
    *Rabbit, Run:* V12
    *Toward the End of Time:* V24
*Utopia* (More): V29

## V

*Vanity Fair* (Thackeray): V13
Verne, Jules
    *Around the World in Eighty Days:*
    V30

*A Very Long Engagement* (Japrisot):
    V18
*The Violent Bear It Away*
    (O'Connor): V21
Voltaire
    *Candide:* V7
Vonnegut, Kurt, Jr.
    *Cat's Cradle:* V28
    *Slaughterhouse-Five:* V3

## W

*Waiting* (Jin): V25
Walker, Alice
    *The Color Purple:* V5
*War and Peace* (Tolstoy): V10
*The War of the Worlds* (Wells):
    V20
Warren, Robert Penn
    *All the King's Men:* V13
*Waterland* (Swift): V18
*Watership Down* (Adams): V11
Watkins, Yoko Kawashima
    *So Far from the Bamboo Grove:*
    V28
Waugh, Evelyn Arthur St. John
    *Brideshead Revisited:* V13
    *Scoop:* V17
*The Waves* (Woolf): V28
*We Were the Mulvaneys* (Oates): V24
Welch, James
    *Winter in the Blood:* V23
Wells, H. G.
    *The Time Machine:* V17
    *The War of the Worlds:* V20
Welty, Eudora
    *Losing Battles:* V15
    *The Optimist's Daughter:* V13
West, Nathanael
    *The Day of the Locust:* V16
Wharton, Edith
    *The Age of Innocence:* V11
    *Ethan Frome:* V5
    *The House of Mirth:* V15
    *Summer:* V20
*What Looks Like Crazy on an*
    *Ordinary Day* (Cleage): V17
*When Rain Clouds Gather* (Head):
    V31
*When the Legends Die* (Borland):
    V18
*White Fang* (London): V19
*White Noise* (DeLillo): V28
White, T. H.
    *The Once and Future King:* V30
*Wide Sargasso Sea* (Rhys): V19
Wiesel, Eliezer
    *Night:* V4
Wilde, Oscar
    *The Picture of Dorian Gray:* V20
Wilder, Thornton
    *The Bridge of San Luis Rey:* V24

*The Wind in the Willows* (Grahame): V20

*Winesburg, Ohio* (Anderson): V4

*The Wings of the Dove* (James): V32

*Winter in the Blood* (Welch): V23

*Wise Blood* (O'Connor): V3

Wolfe, Thomas
*Look Homeward, Angel:* V18

*The Woman in the Dunes* (Abe): V22

*The Woman Warrior* (Kingston): V6

*The Women of Brewster Place* (Naylor): V4

*The Wonderful Wizard of Oz* (Baum): V13

Woolf, Virginia
*Mrs. Dalloway:* V12
*To the Lighthouse:* V8
*The Waves:* V28

*The World According to Garp* (Irving): V12

Wouk, Herman
*The Caine Mutiny: A Novel of World War II:* V7

*The Wrestling Match* (Emecheta): V14

Wright, Richard
*Black Boy:* V1
*Native Son:* V7

*A Wrinkle in Time* (L'Engle): V32

*Wuthering Heights* (Brontë): V2

## Y

*Year of Impossible Goodbyes* (Choi): V29

*A Yellow Raft in Blue Water* (Dorris): V3

Yezierska, Anzia
*Bread Givers:* V29

Yolen, Jane
*Briar Rose:* V30

Yoshimoto, Banana
*Kitchen:* V7

## Z

*Zen and the Art of Motorcycle Maintenance* (Pirsig): V31

Zindel, Paul
*The Pigman:* V14

# Cumulative
# Nationality/Ethnicity Index

## African American

Angelou, Maya
  *I Know Why the Caged Bird Sings:*
    V2
Baldwin, James
  *Go Tell It on the Mountain:* V4
Butler, Octavia
  *Kindred:* V8
  *Parable of the Sower:* V21
Cleage, Pearl
  *What Looks Like Crazy on an*
    *Ordinary Day:* V17
Danticat, Edwidge
  *The Dew Breaker:* V28
Ellison, Ralph
  *Invisible Man:* V2
  *Juneteenth:* V21
Gaines, Ernest J.
  *The Autobiography of Miss Jane*
    *Pittman:* V5
  *A Gathering of Old Men:* V16
  *A Lesson before Dying:* V7
Haley, Alex
  *Roots: The Story of an American*
    *Family:* V9
Hughes, Langston
  *Tambourines to Glory:* V21
Hurston, Zora Neale
  *Their Eyes Were Watching God:* V3
Johnson, James Weldon
  *The Autobiography of an*
    *Ex-Coloured Man:* V22
Kincaid, Jamaica
  *Annie John:* V3
Morrison, Toni
  *Beloved:* V6

  *The Bluest Eye:* V1
  *Song of Solomom:* V8
  *Sula:* V14
Myers, Walter Dean
  *Fallen Angels:* V30
Naylor, Gloria
  *Mama Day:* V7
  *The Women of Brewster Place:*
    V4
Parks, Gordon
  *The Learning Tree:* V32
Shange, Ntozake
  *Betsey Brown:* V11
Toomer, Jean
  *Cane:* V11
Walker, Alice
  *The Color Purple:* V5
Wright, Richard
  *Black Boy:* V1

## Algerian

Camus, Albert
  *The Plague:* V16
  *The Stranger:* V6

## American

Agee, James
  *A Death in the Family:* V22
Alcott, Louisa May
  *Little Women:* V12
Alexie, Sherman
  *The Lone Ranger and Tonto*
    *Fistfight in Heaven:* V17
  *Reservation Blues:* V31
Allende, Isabel
  *Daughter of Fortune:* V18

  *Eva Luna:* V29
  *The House of the Spirits:* V6
Allison, Dorothy
  *Bastard Out of Carolina:* V11
Alvarez, Julia
  *How the García Girls Lost Their*
    *Accents:* V5
Anaya, Rudolfo
  *Bless Me, Ultima:* V12
Anderson, Laurie Halse
  *Speak:* V31
Anderson, Sherwood
  *Winesburg, Ohio:* V4
Angelou, Maya
  *I Know Why the Caged Bird Sings:*
    V2
Asimov, Isaac
  *I, Robot:* V29
Auel, Jean
  *The Clan of the Cave Bear:* V11
Banks, Russell
  *The Sweet Hereafter:* V13
Baum, L. Frank
  *The Wonderful Wizard of Oz:* V13
Bellamy, Edward
  *Looking Backward: 2000–1887:* V15
Bellow, Saul
  *Herzog:* V14
  *Humboldt's Gift:* V26
  *Seize the Day:* V4
Benitez, Sandra
  *A Place Where the Sea*
    *Remembers:* V32
Blume, Judy
  *Forever...:* V24
Borland, Hal
  *When the Legends Die:* V18

Bradbury, Ray
   *Dandelion Wine:* V22
   *Fahrenheit 451:* V1
   *Something Wicked This Way*
     *Comes:* V29
Bridal, Tessa
   *The Tree of Red Stars:* V17
Brown, Rita Mae
   *Rubyfruit Jungle:* V9
Buck, Pearl S.
   *The Good Earth:* V25
Burdick, Eugene J.
   *The Ugly American:* V23
Burns, Olive Ann
   *Cold Sassy Tree:* V31
Butler, Octavia
   *Kindred:* V8
   *Parable of the Sower:* V21
Card, Orson Scott
   *Ender's Game:* V5
Cather, Willa
   *Death Comes for the Archbishop:*
     V19
   *My Ántonia:* V2
Chabon, Michael
   *The Amazing Adventures of*
     *Kavalier & Clay:* V25
Chandler, Raymond
   *The Big Sleep:* V17
Choi, Sook Nyul
   *Year of Impossible Goodbyes:* V29
Chopin, Kate
   *The Awakening:* V3
Cisneros, Sandra
   *The House on Mango Street:* V2
Clavell, James du Maresq
   *Shogun: A Novel of Japan:* V10
Cleage, Pearl
   *What Looks Like Crazy on an*
     *Ordinary Day:* V17
Clemens, Samuel Langhorne
   *The Adventures of Huckleberry*
     *Finn:* V1
   *The Adventures of Tom Sawyer:*
     V6
   *A Connecticut Yankee in King*
     *Arthur's Court:* V20
   *The Prince and the Pauper:* V31
Conroy, Frank
   *Body and Soul:* V11
Cooper, James Fenimore
   *The Deerslayer:* V25
   *The Last of the Mohicans:* V9
   *The Last of the Mohicans*
     (Motion picture): V32
Cormier, Robert
   *The Chocolate War:* V2
   *I Am the Cheese:* V18
Crane, Stephen
   *The Red Badge of Courage:* V4
   *Maggie: A Girl of the Streets:*
     V20

Crutcher, Chris
   *The Crazy Horse Electric Game:*
     V11
   *Staying Fat for Sarah Byrnes:* V32
Cunningham, Michael
   *The Hours:* V23
Danticat, Edwidge
   *The Dew Breaker:* V28
Davis, Rebecca Harding
   *Margret Howth: A Story of*
     *To-Day:* V14
DeLillo, Don
   *White Noise:* V28
Desai, Kiran
   *Hullabaloo in the Guava Orchard:*
     V28
Dick, Philip K.
   *Do Androids Dream of Electric*
     *Sheep?:* V5
   *Martian Time-Slip:* V26
Dickey, James
   *Deliverance:* V9
Didion, Joan
   *Democracy:* V3
Doctorow, E. L.
   *Ragtime:* V6
Dorris, Michael
   *A Yellow Raft in Blue Water:* V3
Dos Passos, John
   *U.S.A.:* V14
Dreiser, Theodore
   *An American Tragedy:* V17
   *Sister Carrie:* V8
Ellis, Bret Easton
   *Less Than Zero:* V11
Ellison, Ralph
   *Invisible Man:* V2
   *Juneteenth:* V21
Emecheta, Buchi
   *The Bride Price:* V12
Erdrich, Louise
   *Love Medicine:* V5
Eugenides, Jeffrey
   *Middlesex:* V24
Faulkner, William
   *Absalom, Absalom!:* V13
   *As I Lay Dying:* V8
   *Light in August:* V24
   *The Sound and the Fury:* V4
Fitzgerald, F. Scott
   *The Great Gatsby:* V2
   *Tender Is the Night:* V19
   *This Side of Paradise:* V20
Flagg, Fannie
   *Fried Green Tomatoes at the*
     *Whistle Stop Café:* V7
Ford, Richard
   *Independence Day:* V25
Fox, Paula
   *The Slave Dancer:* V12
Frank, Pat
   *Alas, Babylon:* V29

Frazier, Charles
   *Cold Mountain:* V25
Frederic, Harold
   *The Damnation of Theron Ware:*
     V22
Gaines, Ernest J.
   *The Autobiography of Miss Jane*
     *Pittman:* V5
   *A Gathering of Old Men:* V16
   *A Lesson Before Dying:* V7
Gardner, John
   *Grendel:* V3
Gibbons, Kaye
   *Ellen Foster:* V3
Golden, Arthur
   *Memoirs of a Geisha:* V19
Goldman, William
   *The Princess Bride:* V31
Green, Hannah
   *The Dead of the House:* V10
Greenberg, Joanne
   *I Never Promised You a Rose*
     *Garden:* V23
Greene, Bette
   *Summer of My German Soldier:* V10
Guest, Judith
   *Ordinary People:* V1
Guterson, David
   *Snow Falling on Cedars:* V13
Hammett, Dashiell
   *The Maltese Falcon:* V21
Harris, Marilyn
   *Hatter Fox:* V14
Hawthorne, Nathaniel
   *The House of the Seven Gables:*
     V20
   *The Scarlet Letter:* V1
Heller, Joseph
   *Catch-22:* V1
Hemingway, Ernest
   *A Farewell to Arms:* V1
   *For Whom the Bell Tolls:* V14
   *The Old Man and the Sea:* V6
   *The Sun Also Rises:* V5
Herbert, Frank
   *Dune:* V31
   *Soul Catcher:* V17
Highsmith, Patricia
   *The Talented Mr. Ripley:* V27
Hijuelos, Oscar
   *The Mambo Kings Play Songs of*
     *Love:* V17
Hinton, S. E.
   *The Outsiders:* V5
   *Rumble Fish:* V15
   *Tex:* V9
   *That Was Then, This Is Now:* V16
Hughes, Langston
   *Tambourines to Glory:* V21
Hurston, Zora Neale
   *Their Eyes Were Watching God:*
     V3

Irving, John
   *A Prayer for Owen Meany:* V14
   *The World According to Garp:* V12
James, Henry
   *The Ambassadors:* V12
   *The Portrait of a Lady:* V19
   *The Turn of the Screw:* V16
   *The Wings of the Dove:* V32
Jen, Gish
   *Typical American:* V30
Jewett, Sarah Orne
   *The Country of the Pointed Firs:*
     V15
Johnson, James Weldon
   *The Autobiography of an
     Ex-Coloured Man:* V22
Jones, Edward P.
   *The Known World:* V26
Kerouac, Jack
   *On the Road:* V8
Kesey, Ken
   *One Flew Over the Cuckoo's Nest:*
     V2
Keyes, Daniel
   *Flowers for Algernon:* V2
Kidd, Sue Monk
   *The Secret Life of Bees:* V27
Kincaid, Jamaica
   *Annie John:* V3
Kingsolver, Barbara
   *Animal Dreams:* V12
   *The Bean Trees:* V5
   *Pigs in Heaven:* V10
   *Poisonwood Bible:* V24
Kingston, Maxine Hong
   *The Woman Warrior:* V6
Knowles, John
   *A Separate Peace:* V2
Lahiri, Jhumpa
   *The Namesake:* V31
Le Guin, Ursula K.
   *Always Coming Home:* V9
   *The Left Hand of Darkness:* V6
Lederer, William J.
   *The Ugly American:* V23
Lee, Harper
   *To Kill a Mockingbird:* V2
   *To Kill a Mockingbird*
     (Motion picture): V32
L'Engle, Madeleine
   *A Wrinkle in Time:* V32
Lewis, Harry Sinclair
   *Babbitt:* V19
   *Elmer Gantry:* V22
   *Main Street:* V15
Lightman, Alan
   *Einstein's Dreams:* V29
London, Jack
   *The Call of the Wild:* V8
   *White Fang:* V19
Lowry, Lois
   *The Giver:* V3

Lurie, Alison
   *Foreign Affairs:* V24
Mailer, Norman
   *The Naked and the Dead:* V10
Malamud, Bernard
   *The Assistant:* V27
   *The Fixer:* V9
   *The Natural:* V4
Mason, Bobbie Ann
   *In Country:* V4
McCullers, Carson
   *The Heart Is a Lonely Hunter:*
     V6
   *The Member of the Wedding:* V13
McDermott, Alice
   *Charming Billy:* V23
Melville, Herman
   *Billy Budd:* V9
   *Moby-Dick:* V7
   *Typee:* V32
Méndez, Miguel
   *Pilgrims in Aztlán:* V12
Mitchell, Margaret
   *Gone with the Wind:* V9
Momaday, N. Scott
   *House Made of Dawn:* V10
Mori, Kyoko
   *Shizuko's Daughter:* V15
Morrison, Toni
   *Beloved:* V6
   *The Bluest Eye:* V1
   *Song of Solomon:* V8
   *Sula:* V14
Myers, Walter Dean
   *Fallen Angels:* V30
Norris, Frank
   *The Octopus:* V12
Oates, Joyce Carol
   *them:* V8
   *We Were the Mulvaneys:* V24
O'Connor, Flannery
   *The Violent Bear It Away:* V21
   *Wise Blood:* V3
O'Hara, John
   *Appointment in Samarra:* V11
Okada, John
   *No-No Boy:* V25
Parks, Gordon
   *The Learning Tree:* V32
Patchett, Ann
   *Bel Canto:* V30
Peck, Robert Newton
   *A Day No Pigs Would Die:* V29
Pirsig, Robert
   *Zen and the Art of Motorcycle
     Maintenance:* V31
Plath, Sylvia
   *The Bell Jar:* V1
Porter, Katherine Anne
   *Ship of Fools:* V14
Potok, Chaim
   *The Chosen:* V4

Power, Susan
   *The Grass Dancer:* V11
Price, Reynolds
   *A Long and Happy Life:* V18
Puzo, Mario
   *The Godfather:* V16
Pynchon, Thomas
   *Gravity's Rainbow:* V23
Rand, Ayn
   *Anthem:* V29
   *Atlas Shrugged:* V10
   *The Fountainhead:* V16
Robinson, Marilynne
   *Gilead:* V24
Rölvaag, O. E.
   *Giants in the Earth:* V5
Roth, Philip
   *American Pastoral:* V25
Russo, Richard
   *Empire Falls:* V25
Salinger, J. D.
   *The Catcher in the Rye:* V1
   *Franny and Zooey:* V30
Shaara, Michael
   *The Killer Angels:* V26
Shange, Ntozake
   *Betsey Brown:* V11
Silko, Leslie Marmon
   *Ceremony:* V4
Sinclair, Upton
   *The Jungle:* V6
Smiley, Jane
   *A Thousand Acres:* V32
Smith, Betty
   *A Tree Grows in Brooklyn:* V31
Stein, Gertrude
   *Ida:* V27
Steinbeck, John
   *Cannery Row:* V28
   *East of Eden:* V19
   *The Grapes of Wrath:* V7
   *Of Mice and Men:* V1
   *The Pearl:* V5
   *The Red Pony:* V17
Stowe, Harriet Beecher
   *Uncle Tom's Cabin:* V6
Styron, William
   *Sophie's Choice:* V22
Swarthout, Glendon
   *Bless the Beasts and Children:*
     V29
Tan, Amy
   *The Bonesetter's Daughter:* V31
   *Joy Luck Club:* V1
   *The Kitchen God's Wife:* V13
Toomer, Jean
   *Cane:* V11
Twain, Mark
   *The Adventures of Huckleberry
     Finn:* V1
   *The Adventures of Tom Sawyer:*
     V6

*Cumulative Nationality/Ethnicity Index*

*A Connecticut Yankee in King*
 *Arthur's Court:* V20
*The Prince and the Pauper:* V31
Tyler, Anne
 *The Accidental Tourist:* V7
 *Breathing Lessons:* V10
 *Dinner at the Homesick*
  *Restaurant:* V2
Uchida, Yoshiko
 *Picture Bride:* V26
Updike, John
 *Rabbit, Run:* V12
 *Toward the End of Time:* V24
Vonnegut, Kurt, Jr.
 *Cat's Cradle:* V28
 *Slaughterhouse-Five:* V3
Walker, Alice
 *The Color Purple:* V5
Warren, Robert Penn
 *All the King's Men:* V13
Watkins, Yoko Kawashima
 *So Far from the Bamboo Grove:* V28
Welch, James
 *Winter in the Blood:* V23
Welty, Eudora
 *Losing Battles:* V15
 *The Optimist's Daughter:* V13
West, Nathanael
 *The Day of the Locust:* V16
Wharton, Edith
 *The Age of Innocence:* V11
 *Ethan Frome:* V5
 *House of Mirth:* V15
 *Summer:* V20
Wilder, Thornton
 *The Bridge of San Luis Rey:* V24
Wolfe, Thomas
 *Look Homeward, Angel:* V18
Wouk, Herman
 *The Caine Mutiny:* V7
Wright, Richard
 *Black Boy:* V1
 *Native Son:* V7
Yezierska, Anzia
 *Bread Givers:* V29
Yolen, Jane
 *Briar Rose:* V30
Zindel, Paul
 *The Pigman:* V14

### Asian American

Jen, Gish
 *Typical American:* V30
Kingston, Maxine Hong
 *The Woman Warrior:* V6
Lahiri, Jhumpa
 *The Namesake:* V31
Okada, John
 *No-No Boy:* V25
Tan, Amy
 *The Bonesetter's Daughter:* V31

*The Joy Luck Club:* V1
*The Kitchen God's Wife:* V13
Uchida, Yoshiko
 *Picture Bride:* V26
Watkins, Yoko Kawashima
 *So Far from the Bamboo Grove:*
  V28

### Asian Canadian

Kogawa, Joy
 *Obasan:* V3

### Australian

Brooks, Geraldine
 *March:* V26
Clavell, James du Maresq
 *Shogun: A Novel of Japan:* V10
Keneally, Thomas
 *Schindler's List:* V17
Stead, Christina
 *The Man Who Loved Children:*
  V27

### Barbadian

Lamming, George
 *In the Castle of My Skin:* V15

### Brazilian

Coelho, Paulo
 *The Alchemist:* V29

### Canadian

Atwood, Margaret
 *Alias Grace:* V19
 *Cat's Eye:* V14
 *The Edible Woman:* V12
 *The Handmaid's Tale:* V4
 *Surfacing:* V13
Bellow, Saul
 *Herzog:* V14
 *Humboldt's Gift:* V26
 *Seize the Day:* V4
Hudson, Jan
 *Sweetgrass:* V28
Kinsella, W. P.
 *Shoeless Joe:* V15
Kogawa, Joy
 *Obasan:* V3
Laurence, Margaret
 *The Stone Angel:* V11
Martel, Yann
 *Life of Pi:* V27
Munro, Alice
 *Lives of Girls and Women:* V27
Ondaatje, Michael
 *The English Patient:* V23
Shields, Carol
 *The Stone Diaries:* V23
Waugh, Evelyn Arthur St. John
 *Brideshead Revisited:* V13

### Chilean

Allende, Isabel
 *Daughter of Fortune:* V18
 *Eva Luna:* V29
 *The House of the Spirits:* V6

### Chinese

Jin, Ha
 *Waiting:* V25
Lee, Lilian
 *Farewell My Concubine:* V19

### Colombian

García Márquez, Gabriel
 *Chronicle of a Death Foretold:*
  V10
 *Love in the Time of Cholera:* V1
 *One Hundred Years of Solitude:*
  V5

### Czechoslovakian

Kundera, Milan
 *The Book of Laughter and*
  *Forgetting:* V27
 *The Unbearable Lightness of*
  *Being:* V18

### Danish

Dinesen, Isak
 *Out of Africa:* V9
Høeg, Peter
 *Smilla's Sense of Snow:* V17

### Dominican

Alvarez, Julia
 *How the Garcia Girls Lost*
  *Their Accents:* V5
 *In the Time of Butterflies:* V9
Rhys, Jean
 *Wide Sargasso Sea:* V19

### Dutch

Möring, Marcel
 *In Babylon:* V25

### English

Adams, Douglas
 *The Hitchhiker's Guide to the*
  *Galaxy:* V7
Adams, Richard
 *Watership Down:* V11
Austen, Jane
 *Emma:* V21
 *Mansfield Park:* V29
 *Northanger Abbey:* V28
 *Persuasion:* V14
 *Pride and Prejudice:* V1
 *Sense and Sensibility:* V18

Ballard, J. G.
   *Empire of the Sun:* V8
Blair, Eric Arthur
   *Animal Farm:* V3
Bowen, Elizabeth Dorothea Cole
   *The Death of the Heart:* V13
Braithwaite, E. R.
   *To Sir, With Love:* V30
Brontë, Anne
   *The Tenant of Wildfell Hall:* V26
Brontë, Charlotte
   *Jane Eyre:* V4
Brontë, Emily
   *Wuthering Heights:* V2
Brookner, Anita
   *Hotel du Lac:* V23
Bunyan, John
   *The Pilgrim's Progress:* V32
Burgess, Anthony
   *A Clockwork Orange:* V15
Burney, Fanny
   *Evelina:* V16
Carroll, Lewis
   *Alice's Adventurers in
      Wonderland:* V7
   *Through the Looking-Glass:* V27
Christie, Agatha
   *The A.B.C. Murders:* V30
   *Ten Little Indians:* V8
Conan Doyle, Arthur, Sir
   *The Hound of the Baskervilles:*
      V28
Conrad, Joseph
   *Heart of Darkness:* V2
   *Lord Jim:* V16
Defoe, Daniel
   *A Journal of the Plague Year:*
      V30
   *Moll Flanders:* V13
   *Robinson Crusoe:* V9
Dickens, Charles
   *Bleak House:* V30
   *A Christmas Carol:* V10
   *David Copperfield:* V25
   *Great Expectations:* V4
   *Hard Times:* V20
   *Oliver Twist:* V14
   *A Tale of Two Cities:* V5
Doyle, Arthur Conan, Sir
   *The Hound of the Baskervilles:*
      V28
du Maurier, Daphne
   *Rebecca:* V12
Eliot, George
   *Middlemarch:* V23
   *The Mill on the Floss:* V17
   *Silas Marner:* V20
Fielding, Henry
   *Joseph Andrews:* V32
   *Tom Jones:* V18
Foden, Giles
   *The Last King of Scotland:* V15

Ford, Ford Madox
   *The Good Soldier:* V28
Forster, E. M.
   *A Passage to India:* V3
   *Howards End:* V10
   *A Room with a View:* V11
Fowles, John
   *The French Lieutenant's Woman:*
      V21
Golding, William
   *Lord of the Flies:* V2
Graves, Robert
   *I, Claudius:* V21
Greene, Graham
   *The End of the Affair:* V16
   *The Power and the Glory:* V31
Hardy, Thomas
   *Far from the Madding Crowd:*
      V19
   *Jude the Obscure:* V30
   *The Mayor of Casterbridge:* V15
   *The Return of the Native:* V11
   *Tess of the d'Urbervilles:* V3
Huxley, Aldous
   *Brave New World:* V6
Ishiguro, Kazuo
   *The Remains of the Day:* V13
James, Henry
   *The Ambassadors:* V12
   *The Portrait of a Lady:* V19
   *The Turn of the Screw:* V16
Kipling, Rudyard
   *Kim:* V21
Koestler, Arthur
   *Darkness at Noon:* V19
Lawrence, D. H.
   *The Rainbow:* V26
   *Sons and Lovers:* V18
Lessing, Doris
   *The Golden Notebook:* V27
Lewis, C. S.
   *The Lion, the Witch and the
      Wardrobe:* V24
Llewellyn, Richard
   *How Green Was My Valley:* V30
Maugham, W. Somerset
   *The Razor's Edge:* V23
McEwan, Ian
   *Atonement:* V32
More, Thomas
   *Utopia:* V29
Orwell, George
   *Animal Farm:* V3
   *1984:* V7
Rhys, Jean
   *Wide Sargasso Sea:* V19
Rushdie, Salman
   *The Satanic Verses:* V22
Sewell, Anna
   *Black Beauty:* V22
Shelley, Mary
   *Frankenstein:* V1

Shute, Nevil
   *On the Beach:* V9
Spark, Muriel
   *The Prime of Miss Jean Brodie:*
      V22
Stevenson, Robert Louis
   *Dr. Jekyll and Mr. Hyde:* V11
Swift, Graham
   *Waterland:* V18
Swift, Jonathan
   *Gulliver's Travels:* V6
Thackeray, William Makepeace
   *Vanity Fair:* V13
Tolkien, J. R. R.
   *The Hobbit:* V8
   *The Lord of the Rings:* V26
Waugh, Evelyn
   *Brideshead Revisited:* V13
   *Scoop:* V17
Wells, H. G.
   *The Time Machine:* V17
   *The War of the Worlds:* V20
White, T. H.
   *The Once and Future King:*
      V30
Woolf, Virginia
   *Mrs. Dalloway:* V12
   *To the Lighthouse:* V8
   *The Waves:* V28

## European American
Hemingway, Ernest
   *The Old Man and the Sea:* V6
Stowe, Harriet Beecher
   *Uncle Tom's Cabin:* V6

## French
Boulle, Pierre
   *The Bridge over the River Kwai:*
      V32
Camus, Albert
   *The Plague:* V16
   *The Stranger:* V6
Dumas, Alexandre
   *The Count of Monte Cristo:*
      V19
   *The Three Musketeers:* V14
Flaubert, Gustave
   *Madame Bovary:* V14
Gide, André
   *The Immoralist:* V21
Hugo, Victor
   *The Hunchback of Notre Dame:*
      V20
   *Les Misérables:* V5
Japrisot, Sébastien
   *A Very Long Engagement:* V18
Leroux, Gaston
   *The Phantom of the Opera:* V20
Saint-Exupéry, Antoine de
   *The Little Prince:* V30

*Cumulative Nationality/Ethnicity Index*

Sartre, Jean-Paul
  *Nausea:* V21
Verne, Jules
  *Around the World in Eighty Days:*
    V30
Voltaire
  *Candide:* V7

## German
Hegi, Ursula
  *Stones from the River:* V25
Hesse, Hermann
  *Demian:* V15
  *Siddhartha:* V6
  *Steppenwolf:* V24
Mann, Thomas
  *Death in Venice:* V17
  *The Magic Mountain:* V29
Remarque, Erich Maria
  *All Quiet on the Western Front:*
    V4

## Guyanese
Braithwaite, E. R.
  *To Sir, With Love:* V30

## Haitian
Danticat, Edwidge
  *The Dew Breaker:* V28

## Hispanic American
Allende, Isabel
  *Daughter of Fortune:* V18
  *Eva Luna:* V29
  *The House of the Spirits:* V6
Benitez, Sandra
  *A Place Where the Sea*
    *Remembers:* V32
Cisneros, Sandra
  *The House on Mango Street:* V2
Hijuelos, Oscar
  *The Mambo Kings Play Songs of*
    *Love:* V17

## Hungarian
Koestler, Arthur
  *Darkness at Noon:* V19
Orczy, Emmuska
  *The Scarlet Pimpernel:* V31

## Indian
Desai, Kiran
  *Hullabaloo in the Guava Orchard:*
    V28
Markandaya, Kamala
  *Nectar in a Sieve:* V13
Roy, Arundhati
  *The God of Small Things:* V22

Rushdie, Salman
  *Midnight's Children:* V23
  *The Satanic Verses:* V22

## Irish
Bowen, Elizabeth Dorothea Cole
  *The Death of the Heart:* V13
Joyce, James
  *A Portrait of the Artist as a Young*
    *Man:* V7
  *Ulysses:* V26
Murdoch, Iris
  *Under the Net:* V18
Stoker, Bram
  *Dracula:* V18
Wilde, Oscar
  *The Picture of Dorian Gray:* V20

## Italian
Eco, Umberto
  *The Name of the Rose:* V22
Machiavelli, Niccolo
  *The Prince:* V9

## Japanese
Abe, Kobo
  *The Woman in the Dunes:* V22
Ishiguro, Kazuo
  *The Remains of the Day:* V13
Mori, Kyoko
  *Shizuko's Daughter:* V15
Watkins, Yoko Kawashima
  *So Far from the Bamboo Grove:*
    V28
Yoshimoto, Banana
  *Kitchen:* V7

## Jewish
Asimov, Isaac
  *I, Robot:* V29
Bellow, Saul
  *Herzog:* V14
  *Humboldt's Gift:* V26
  *Seize the Day:* V4
Kafka, Franz
  *The Trial:* V7
Kertész, Imre
  *Kaddish for a Child Not Born:*
    V23
Malamud, Bernard
  *The Assistant:* V27
  *The Fixer:* V9
  *The Natural:* V4
Roth, Philip
  *American Pastoral:* V25
Salinger, J. D.
  *The Catcher in the Rye:* V1
  *Franny and Zooey:* V30
West, Nathanael
  *The Day of the Locust:* V16

Wiesel, Eliezer
  *Night:* V4
Yezierska, Anzia
  *Bread Givers:* V29
Yolen, Jane
  *Briar Rose:* V30

## Korean
Choi, Sook Nyul
  *Year of Impossible Goodbyes:*
    V29

## Mexican
Esquivel, Laura
  *Like Water for Chocolate:* V5
Fuentes, Carlos
  *The Old Gringo:* V8

## Native American
Alexie, Sherman
  *The Lone Ranger and Tonto*
    *Fistfight in Heaven:* V17
  *Reservation Blues:* V31
Dorris, Michael
  *A Yellow Raft in Blue Water:*
    V3
Erdrich, Louise
  *Love Medicine:* V5
Momaday, N. Scott
  *House Made of Dawn:* V10
Silko, Leslie Marmon
  *Ceremony:* V4
Welch, James
  *Winter in the Blood:* V23

## New Zealander
Hulme, Keri
  *The Bone People:* V24

## Nigerian
Achebe, Chinua
  *Things Fall Apart:* V3
Emecheta, Buchi
  *The Bride Price:* V12
  *The Wrestling Match:* V14

## Norwegian
Rölvaag, O. E.
  *Giants in the Earth:* V5

## Polish
Conrad, Joseph
  *Heart of Darkness:* V2
  *Lord Jim:* V16
Kosinski, Jerzy
  *The Painted Bird:* V12

## Portuguese

Saramago, José
*Blindness:* V27

## Romanian

Wiesel, Eliezer
*Night:* V4

## Russian

Asimov, Isaac
*I, Robot:* V29
Bulgakov, Mikhail
*The Master and Margarita:* V8
Dostoyevsky, Fyodor
*The Brothers Karamazov:* V8
*Crime and Punishment:* V3
*Notes from Underground:* V28
Nabokov, Vladimir
*Lolita:* V9
Pasternak, Boris
*Doctor Zhivago:* V26
Rand, Ayn
*Anthem:* V29
*Atlas Shrugged:* V10
*The Fountainhead:* V16
Solzhenitsyn, Aleksandr
*One Day in the Life of Ivan
Denisovich:* V6
Tolstoy, Leo
*Anna Karenina:* V28
*War and Peace:* V10

Turgenev, Ivan
*Fathers and Sons:* V16
Yezierska, Anzia
*Bread Givers:* V29

## Scottish

Grahame, Kenneth
*The Wind in the Willows:* V20
Scott, Walter
*Ivanhoe:* V31
Spark, Muriel
*The Prime of Miss Jean Brodie:*
V22
Stevenson, Robert Louis
*Treasure Island:* V20

## South African

Coetzee, J. M.
*Dusklands:* V21
Courtenay, Bryce
*The Power of One:* V32
Gordimer, Nadine
*July's People:* V4
Head, Bessie
*When Rain Clouds Gather:* V31
Paton, Alan
*Cry, the Beloved Country:* V3
*Too Late the Phalarope:* V12

## Spanish

de Cervantes Saavedra, Miguel
*Don Quixote:* V8

## Sri Lankan

Ondaatje, Michael
*The English Patient:* V23

## Swiss

Hesse, Hermann
*Demian:* V15
*Siddhartha:* V6
*Steppenwolf:* V24

## Turkish

Pamuk, Orhan
*My Name is Red:* V27

## Uruguayan

Bridal, Tessa
*The Tree of Red Stars:* V17

## Vietnamese

Duong Thu Huong
*Paradise of the Blind:* V23

## West Indian

Kincaid, Jamaica
*Annie John:* V3

## Zimbabwean

Dangarembga, Tsitsi
*Nervous Conditions:* V28

# Subject/Theme Index

## Numerical

1950s (Decade)
  *To Kill a Mockingbird:* 237–238

## A

Abandonment
  *Atonement:* 10
  *A Place Where the Sea
    Remembers:* 136
  *Staying Fat for Sarah Byrnes:* 175,
    177
Abortion
  *A Place Where the Sea
    Remembers:* 137
  *Staying Fat for Sarah Byrnes:* 173,
    175, 176, 181, 187, 188, 193
Absolutism
  *Staying Fat for Sarah Byrnes:* 178,
    181, 187
  *A Wrinkle in Time:* 314
Absurdity
  *The Bridge over the River Kwai:* 48
Adultery
  *Joseph Andrews:* 58
  *A Thousand Acres:* 200, 205, 213,
    221
Adventure fiction
  *The Bridge over the River Kwai:* 36
  *The Last of the Mohicans:* 81, 90
  *Typee:* 253, 263
Aesthetics
  *A Wrinkle in Time:* 311
African American history
  *To Kill a Mockingbird:* 243
  *The Learning Tree:* 103–105
African Americans
  *The Learning Tree:* 93, 96–97, 102
African history
  *The Power of One:* 160, 162

Agriculture
  *A Thousand Acres:* 222
Alcoholism
  *The Learning Tree:* 99
Alienation
  *A Wrinkle in Time:* 301, 308
  *See also* Outsiders
Allegories
  *The Bridge over the River Kwai:* 28
  *The Pilgrim's Progress:* 114–115,
    120, 125
  *Typee:* 269–271
Allusions
  *Atonement:* 17–22, 24
Ambiguity
  *Atonement:* 13, 25
  *Typee:* 268, 269
Ambition
  *The Bridge over the River Kwai:* 49
American culture
  *The Last of the Mohicans:* 78–79,
    81–82, 92
  *A Wrinkle in Time:* 306
American Revolution, 1775-1783
  *The Last of the Mohicans:* 82
Androgyny
  *To Kill a Mockingbird:* 249
Anger
  *A Thousand Acres:* 212, 213
Anthropology
  *Typee:* 257
Apartheid
  *The Power of One:* 160, 162
Apocalypse
  *A Thousand Acres:* 221
Appearance *vs.* reality
  *Joseph Andrews:* 58–59
  *Staying Fat for Sarah Byrnes:*
    180–181, 187
  *A Thousand Acres:* 203–205

Archetypes
  *Typee:* 268
Aristocracy
  *The Wings of the Dove:* 279
Arrogance
  *The Bridge over the River Kwai:* 32
  *The Wings of the Dove:* 280
Art
  *The Wings of the Dove:* 292–293
Asceticism
  *A Thousand Acres:* 217–219
Atonement
  *Atonement:* 1
Atrocities. *See* Brutality
Authenticity
  *Typee:* 264
Authority
  *To Kill a Mockingbird:* 230, 231,
    236, 250
  *Staying Fat for Sarah Byrnes:* 179
Autobiographical fiction
  *The Learning Tree:* 93, 103
  *The Power of One:* 159
  *Typee:* 253, 265

## B

Beauty
  *The Pilgrim's Progress:* 120
  *Typee:* 258, 262
  *The Wings of the Dove:* 277–278,
    279
  *A Wrinkle in Time:* 301
Betrayal
  *Atonement:* 16
  *A Thousand Acres:* 204–205
Bildungsroman
  *The Power of One:* 159
  *See also* Coming of Age
Bravery. *See* Courage
Brutality

*The Bridge over the River Kwai:*
33–35, 41
*The Learning Tree:* 99
*The Power of One:* 147–148, 149,
150, 153, 155, 157, 158–159,
163, 166, 168
Bureaucracy
*The Bridge over the River Kwai:*
32

## C

Captive-captor relationship
*The Bridge over the River Kwai:*
29–32, 33–35, 39
*The Last of the Mohicans:* 90
Censorship
*Staying Fat for Sarah Byrnes:*
184–185
*A Wrinkle in Time:* 307
Change (Philosophy)
*Staying Fat for Sarah Byrnes:*
185
Characterization
*Atonement:* 24–25
*The Bridge over the River Kwai:*
46–49
*Joseph Andrews:* 63–64, 65
*To Kill a Mockingbird:* 240–241
*The Last of the Mohicans:* 88–89,
91
*Staying Fat for Sarah Byrnes:* 185,
193
*The Wings of the Dove:* 283
Charity
*Joseph Andrews:* 58
Child abuse
*Staying Fat for Sarah Byrnes:* 172,
175, 178, 179, 180, 183–185,
186, 188, 191–192
*A Thousand Acres:* 195, 201,
211–213, 213–214, 222
Childhood
*Atonement:* 22
*To Kill a Mockingbird:* 233–235,
236, 244, 246
Christianity
*The Last of the Mohicans:* 92
*The Pilgrim's Progress:* 116, 119,
124–125
*Staying Fat for Sarah Byrnes:* 178,
179, 181, 187
*The Wings of the Dove:* 287, 288,
291–292
*A Wrinkle in Time:* 306, 310
Cold War
*A Wrinkle in Time:* 304–306
Colonial Africa, 1870-1960
*The Power of One:* 159, 160, 162
Colonial America
*The Last of the Mohicans:* 71–72,
76, 79–80, 89–90

Colonialism
*The Bridge over the River Kwai:* 44
*Typee:* 255, 260, 263
Comedy
*Joseph Andrews:* 56, 57
Coming of age
*To Kill a Mockingbird:* 232, 233
*The Learning Tree:* 101
*The Power of One:* 163
*Staying Fat for Sarah Byrnes:* 182
*See also* Bildungsroman
Communications
*Atonement:* 9–10
Communism
*A Wrinkle in Time:* 304–306
Community
*The Pilgrim's Progress:* 123–124
Compassion
*To Kill a Mockingbird:* 231
*The Learning Tree:* 93, 111
*Staying Fat for Sarah Byrnes:* 178
*The Wings of the Dove:* 280
Confidence
*A Thousand Acres:* 210
Confinement
*A Thousand Acres:* 203
Conflict
*To Kill a Mockingbird:* 251
*A Thousand Acres:* 211
Conformity
*To Kill a Mockingbird:* 250
*A Wrinkle in Time:* 303, 306,
307–308, 314
Confusion
*Atonement:* 9, 10, 11
Contradiction
*The Bridge over the River Kwai:* 42
*Typee:* 267
Contrast. *See* Opposites
Control (Psychology)
*A Thousand Acres:* 219
Corruption
*Joseph Andrews:* 57, 58, 59, 60, 63
*The Pilgrim's Progress:* 122
*Typee:* 262
Courage
*To Kill a Mockingbird:* 230, 232,
241
*The Pilgrim's Progress:* 116
*The Power of One:* 158
*Staying Fat for Sarah Byrnes:* 193
Cruelty
*The Bridge over the River Kwai:*
33–34
*The Learning Tree:* 93
*The Power of One:* 167
*Staying Fat for Sarah Byrnes:* 178
*Typee:* 259
Cultural conflict
*The Bridge over the River Kwai:*
29, 32–33, 36
*Typee:* 259, 266, 267

Cultural identity
*The Bridge over the River Kwai:* 35
Culture
*The Wings of the Dove:* 283–284,
284–285, 289–291
Cynicism
*To Kill a Mockingbird:* 232

## D

Death
*Atonement:* 22
*The Learning Tree:* 93, 95, 98,
101–102, 106–108
*The Pilgrim's Progress:* 118
*A Place Where the Sea
Remembers:* 136, 137, 138
*The Power of One:* 150
*A Thousand Acres:* 206
*The Wings of the Dove:* 277, 282,
286
Deception
*Atonement:* 19
*To Kill a Mockingbird:* 229
*The Wings of the Dove:* 287
*See also* Insincerity
Dedication. *See* Devotion; Loyalty
Deformity
*Staying Fat for Sarah Byrnes:* 172,
173, 177, 178
Denial
*A Thousand Acres:* 207, 212
Desolation
*The Last of the Mohicans:* 91
Despair
*The Pilgrim's Progress:* 117
Determination
*The Bridge over the River Kwai:* 49
*The Power of One:* 157
Devil
*The Wings of the Dove:* 281
Devotion
*The Power of One:* 157
*See also* Loyalty
Dignity
*To Kill a Mockingbird:* 231, 232,
241
Disfigurement. *See* Deformity
Disillusionment
*Typee:* 267
Distance
*The Power of One:* 156
Doubt
*Atonement:* 13
Dreams
*The Pilgrim's Progress:* 118
Duty
*The Bridge over the River Kwai:*
32, 41
*To Kill a Mockingbird:* 225
*The Wings of the Dove:* 278

# E

Education
   *To Kill a Mockingbird:* 241, 245
   *The Learning Tree:* 101, 109–110
   *The Power of One:* 147–148, 152, 153, 154, 158
Emotions
   *Atonement:* 22
   *The Bridge over the River Kwai:* 49
Empathy
   *To Kill a Mockingbird:* 241
   *A Thousand Acres:* 222
English history
   *Atonement:* 11–12
   *Joseph Andrews:* 61–63
   *The Pilgrim's Progress:* 125–126
   *The Wings of the Dove:* 283–285
Environmentalism
   *A Thousand Acres:* 207, 209, 222
Equality
   *The Last of the Mohicans:* 92
Escape
   *The Last of the Mohicans:* 74
   *The Pilgrim's Progress:* 117
   *Typee:* 255, 258, 259, 266–267
Ethics
   *Joseph Andrews:* 66
   *To Kill a Mockingbird:* 231
Evil
   *Atonement:* 22
   *To Kill a Mockingbird:* 231, 233
   *The Wings of the Dove:* 281
   *A Wrinkle in Time:* 299, 301, 311
Exoticism
   *Typee:* 266

# F

Failure (Psychology)
   *The Pilgrim's Progress:* 119
   *A Thousand Acres:* 219
Fairness
   *To Kill a Mockingbird:* 231, 233, 241
   *Staying Fat for Sarah Byrnes:* 174
Faith
   *The Pilgrim's Progress:* 116, 125
   *The Wings of the Dove:* 281
Family relationships
   *Atonement:* 1, 4–5, 9–10
   *To Kill a Mockingbird:* 246
   *The Last of the Mohicans:* 84–85
   *A Thousand Acres:* 195, 197–200, 204–205, 217–222
Fantasy fiction
   *A Wrinkle in Time:* 295, 311, 312–314
Father-child relationships
   *To Kill a Mockingbird:* 249–250
   *The Last of the Mohicans:* 84–85
   *The Learning Tree:* 100

*A Place Where the Sea Remembers:* 134–135, 138–139, 144
*A Thousand Acres:* 195, 200–201, 201–202, 207, 209
Fear
   *The Bridge over the River Kwai:* 33
   *To Kill a Mockingbird:* 227, 232, 233, 245
   *The Learning Tree:* 93
   *The Pilgrim's Progress:* 116, 117, 119
   *Staying Fat for Sarah Byrnes:* 180
   *A Thousand Acres:* 214
Fear of death
   *The Learning Tree:* 98, 101, 102, 106–108
Female-male relations
   *The Pilgrim's Progress:* 128–130
Femininity
   *To Kill a Mockingbird:* 250
   *The Pilgrim's Progress:* 128
Feminism
   *To Kill a Mockingbird:* 247–252
   *A Thousand Acres:* 207, 209, 210–213
   *The Wings of the Dove:* 282, 283–284
Feudalism
   *The Pilgrim's Progress:* 120
Flashbacks
   *Staying Fat for Sarah Byrnes:* 183
   *A Thousand Acres:* 207
Foreshadowing
   *To Kill a Mockingbird:* 236
Forgiveness
   *Atonement:* 8, 13
   *The Last of the Mohicans:* 92
   *A Place Where the Sea Remembers:* 143–145, 145
Freedom
   *To Kill a Mockingbird:* 251
   *A Thousand Acres:* 203, 218
   *A Wrinkle in Time:* 309, 314
French history
   *The Bridge over the River Kwai:* 39–43, 42–44
Friendship
   *The Learning Tree:* 99
   *The Power of One:* 155, 156, 167, 168
   *Staying Fat for Sarah Byrnes:* 172, 175, 179, 180, 181, 188
   *A Thousand Acres:* 202, 205
Frontier life
   *The Last of the Mohicans:* 71–72, 77, 79–80, 85

# G

Garden of Eden. *See* Paradise
Gender roles. *See* Sex roles

Generosity
   *The Wings of the Dove:* 278, 280
God
   *A Wrinkle in Time:* 312
Good and evil
   *Atonement* 23
   *The Bridge over the River Kwai:* 46
   *The Last of the Mohicans:* 91
   *The Power of One:* 159–160
   *A Wrinkle in Time:* 302, 309, 311
Good life
   *The Pilgrim's Progress:* 117
   *A Wrinkle in Time:* 304
Goodness
   *Joseph Andrews:* 63–64, 66
   *The Wings of the Dove:* 278, 280, 281
   *A Wrinkle in Time:* 304
Great Depression
   *To Kill a Mockingbird:* 224, 225, 237, 243, 244, 246
Greed
   *Joseph Andrews:* 58
   *The Pilgrim's Progress:* 122
   *Typee:* 262
   *The Wings of the Dove:* 282, 283, 284–285, 287, 288
Grief
   *A Place Where the Sea Remembers:* 143
   *A Thousand Acres:* 213
Guilt (Psychology)
   *Atonement:* 1, 5, 7, 8, 13
   *A Place Where the Sea Remembers:* 143, 145
   *Staying Fat for Sarah Byrnes:* 176, 188
   *A Thousand Acres:* 202
   *The Wings of the Dove:* 279, 281, 288

# H

Happiness
   *Joseph Andrews:* 60
   *A Place Where the Sea Remembers:* 136, 144
   *Staying Fat for Sarah Byrnes:* 181
Hatred
   *The Bridge over the River Kwai:* 33
   *To Kill a Mockingbird:* 230
Heritage
   *To Kill a Mockingbird:* 250
Heroes
   *The Last of the Mohicans:* 89
Heroines
   *The Wings of the Dove:* 280
Heroism
   *The Bridge over the River Kwai:* 42, 47

*Subject / Theme Index*

*Staying Fat for Sarah Byrnes:*
182–183, 186
*A Wrinkle in Time:* 310
Historical fiction
*The Last of the Mohicans:* 81–82
Honesty
*To Kill a Mockingbird:* 232
Honor
*The Last of the Mohicans:* 76, 91
Hope
*Staying Fat for Sarah Byrnes:* 177,
179
*A Thousand Acres:* 221
Human condition
*The Bridge over the River Kwai:* 28
*The Pilgrim's Progress:* 120
Human nature
*The Last of the Mohicans:* 90
Human potential
*A Wrinkle in Time:* 314
Humanity
*Joseph Andrews:* 63–64
Humiliation
*The Bridge over the River Kwai:*
33, 41
Humility
*To Kill a Mockingbird:* 232
*The Wings of the Dove:* 281
Hypocrisy
*Joseph Andrews:* 56, 58, 64
*Staying Fat for Sarah Byrnes:* 178,
180, 187

**I**

Identity
*The Power of One:* 157–158
Ignorance (Theory of knowledge)
*To Kill a Mockingbird:* 243, 245
Imagery (Literature)
*The Wings of the Dove:* 283
*A Wrinkle in Time:* 309
Imagination
*Atonement:* 1, 7, 25, 26
*To Kill a Mockingbird:* 232,
233–235, 244
*A Wrinkle in Time:* 312
Imprisonment
*The Last of the Mohicans:* 75
*The Power of One:* 151
*Typee:* 267
Incest
*To Kill a Mockingbird:* 245
*A Thousand Acres:* 195, 199–200,
201, 202, 203, 205, 212,
213–214, 218, 219, 221
Independence
*The Last of the Mohicans:* 80, 92
*A Thousand Acres:* 220
*The Wings of the Dove:* 278
Individualism
*The Last of the Mohicans:* 88

*The Pilgrim's Progress:* 124
*The Power of One:* 163
Inequality
*The Learning Tree:* 102
Inheritance
*The Last of the Mohicans:* 85
*A Thousand Acres:* 197
Injustice
*To Kill a Mockingbird:* 234,
235–236
*The Last of the Mohicans:* 92
*The Wings of the Dove:* 273
Innocence
*Atonement:* 1, 5
*To Kill a Mockingbird:* 231, 234,
236, 241
*The Last of the Mohicans:* 77
*Typee:* 262
*The Wings of the Dove:* 273, 280, 286
Insincerity
*The Wings of the Dove:* 278, 279,
282
*See also* Deception
Integrity
*To Kill a Mockingbird:* 241, 242
Intellectualism
*A Wrinkle in Time:* 314
Intelligence
*To Kill a Mockingbird:* 232, 243
*The Power of One:* 167
*Staying Fat for Sarah Byrnes:* 193
*A Wrinkle in Time:* 304
Irony
*Atonement:* 11, 18, 19, 22, 26
*The Bridge over the River Kwai:*
35–36, 40, 42
*Joseph Andrews:* 60–61
*To Kill a Mockingbird:* 250, 251
*The Last of the Mohicans:* 91
*Staying Fat for Sarah Byrnes:* 174
*A Thousand Acres:* 220, 222
*The Wings of the Dove:* 287
Irresponsibility
*The Learning Tree:* 98
Isolation
*To Kill a Mockingbird:* 252

**J**

Jealousy
*Joseph Andrews:* 58
*The Power of One:* 156
*A Thousand Acres:* 221
*A Wrinkle in Time:* 301
Joy
*A Place Where the Sea
Remembers:* 131
*The Wings of the Dove:* 281
Justice
*To Kill a Mockingbird:* 229, 231,
232, 234, 241, 242
*A Thousand Acres:* 205–206

**K**

Kindness
*Joseph Andrews:* 60
*To Kill a Mockingbird:* 232
*The Power of One:* 154, 155, 166
*Typee:* 259
Knowledge
*The Pilgrim's Progress:* 122–123
*Staying Fat for Sarah Byrnes:*
185–188
*A Thousand Acres:* 213
*A Wrinkle in Time:* 309

**L**

Language and languages
*A Place Where the Sea
Remembers:* 142
*The Power of One:* 163, 165
Leadership
*The Learning Tree:* 98
Life (Philosophy)
*A Wrinkle in Time:* 309
Light and darkness
*A Wrinkle in Time:* 304, 309
Loneliness
*To Kill a Mockingbird:* 230
*Staying Fat for Sarah Byrnes:* 178,
180, 184–185
Love
*Atonement:* 3, 4, 5, 8, 14, 22
*Joseph Andrews:* 53
*The Last of the Mohicans:* 73, 74,
83, 91
*The Learning Tree:* 93, 100
*A Place Where the Sea
Remembers:* 144, 145
*The Power of One:* 156
*Staying Fat for Sarah Byrnes:*
180
*A Thousand Acres:* 222
*Typee:* 258
*The Wings of the Dove:* 273, 276,
277, 281
*A Wrinkle in Time:* 300, 301, 303,
304, 309, 311
Loyalty
*Joseph Andrews:* 57
*The Wings of the Dove:* 279
*See also* Devotion

**M**

Magic
*A Place Where the Sea
Remembers:* 136
Manipulation
*Staying Fat for Sarah Byrnes:*
179
*A Thousand Acres:* 219–220, 221
*The Wings of the Dove:* 278, 279,
286

Marginalization
*Staying Fat for Sarah Byrnes:* 178, 184–185
Marriage
*Atonement:* 9
*Joseph Andrews:* 56, 66
Masculinity
*To Kill a Mockingbird:* 244, 245, 249, 250
Materialism
*Joseph Andrews:* 65
*To Kill a Mockingbird:* 246
*The Pilgrim's Progress:* 120
*The Wings of the Dove:* 280, 282, 283, 287
Memory
*A Place Where the Sea Remembers:* 134–135
*A Thousand Acres:* 203, 205, 212–213, 213–214
Metamorphosis (Literature)
*The Last of the Mohicans:* 89
Metaphors
*The Wings of the Dove:* 276, 283
*A Wrinkle in Time:* 309
Mexican culture
*A Place Where the Sea Remembers:* 140–142, 145
Mexican history
*A Place Where the Sea Remembers:* 140–142
Middle class
*The Wings of the Dove:* 284
Midwestern United States
*A Thousand Acres:* 206, 217–219
Mistakes
*Atonement:* 10
*A Place Where the Sea Remembers:* 134
Misunderstanding
*A Place Where the Sea Remembers:* 133
Modern life
*Joseph Andrews:* 60
Morality
*The Bridge over the River Kwai:* 46
*Joseph Andrews:* 56, 58, 61, 63–64, 66
*To Kill a Mockingbird:* 231, 241, 244, 251
*The Last of the Mohicans:* 76
*The Learning Tree:* 100, 101
*Staying Fat for Sarah Byrnes:* 178, 179, 181, 187
*The Wings of the Dove:* 273
Mortality
*The Learning Tree:* 106–108
Mother-child relationships
*The Learning Tree:* 101
*A Place Where the Sea Remembers:* 134, 135–136, 143–144
*The Power of One:* 156
*Staying Fat for Sarah Byrnes:* 177, 179–180
Motherhood
*A Place Where the Sea Remembers:* 145
Motivation
*The Pilgrim's Progress:* 116
*The Power of One:* 167
*Staying Fat for Sarah Byrnes:* 176
*The Wings of the Dove:* 278
Murder
*The Learning Tree:* 103
Mystery
*Typee:* 268
*A Wrinkle in Time:* 307
Mysticism
*A Place Where the Sea Remembers:* 145
*A Wrinkle in Time:* 307
Mythology
*The Last of the Mohicans:* 81–82

## N

Narrators
*Atonement:* 11, 14, 18–19
*Joseph Andrews:* 60
*To Kill a Mockingbird:* 247–248
*Typee:* 262, 265–267
*The Wings of the Dove:* 283
Nationalism
*The Power of One:* 165, 183
Native American culture
*The Last of the Mohicans:* 78, 83–85
Native American history
*The Last of the Mohicans:* 70–71, 81–82, 83–85
Native Americans
*The Last of the Mohicans:* 72–75, 75–79, 83–85, 87–88, 89–90
Nature
*The Power of One:* 159
*Typee:* 262–263, 268
*A Wrinkle in Time:* 309
Noble savage
*Typee:* 259, 262

## O

Opposites
*A Wrinkle in Time:* 307–309
Oppression (Politics)
*A Thousand Acres:* 213–214, 218, 220
Optimism
*Atonement:* 21
Outsiders
*To Kill a Mockingbird:* 246, 251–252
*Staying Fat for Sarah Byrnes:* 172, 173, 178, 181, 184–185
*See also* Alienation

## P

Pain
*Staying Fat for Sarah Byrnes:* 178, 188
*A Thousand Acres:* 203
Paradise
*The Pilgrim's Progress:* 119, 128
*Typee:* 256, 258, 260–261, 266, 267, 269–271
Parallelism
*A Wrinkle in Time:* 307–309
Passion
*Atonement:* 4
*Joseph Andrews:* 57
Patience
*The Wings of the Dove:* 281
Patriarchy
*To Kill a Mockingbird:* 249
*A Thousand Acres:* 195, 205, 207, 209, 210–213, 218
Peace
*The Wings of the Dove:* 281, 283
Perception (Psychology)
*Atonement:* 19
Persecution
*The Pilgrim's Progress:* 115
Point of view (Literature)
*Atonement:* 13, 19
*To Kill a Mockingbird:* 236–237, 242, 244, 246–252
*Typee:* 265–267
Politics
*Joseph Andrews:* 62–63
*The Power of One:* 163–166
*A Wrinkle in Time:* 307
Poverty
*To Kill a Mockingbird:* 230, 235–236, 244, 245
*The Wings of the Dove:* 275, 277, 278
Power (Philosophy)
*To Kill a Mockingbird:* 251, 252
*The Power of One:* 166
*Staying Fat for Sarah Byrnes:* 179
*A Thousand Acres:* 205, 213–214, 218, 219, 220, 222
*Typee:* 268
Prejudice
*The Bridge over the River Kwai:* 32, 36
*To Kill a Mockingbird:* 231, 235–236, 243, 244
*The Learning Tree:* 100, 101, 102
*A Place Where the Sea Remembers:* 137
*The Power of One:* 158, 167
*Typee:* 265
Pretension
*Joseph Andrews:* 64, 67–69
Pride
*The Bridge over the River Kwai:* 33

*Joseph Andrews:* 67
*To Kill a Mockingbird:* 244
Primitivism
*Typee:* 264
Progress
*Typee:* 264
Protestantism
*Joseph Andrews:* 61–62

# Q

Questing
*The Pilgrim's Progress:* 116–120,
122, 123–124

# R

Race relations
*The Bridge over the River Kwai:*
32–33, 41
*To Kill a Mockingbird:* 246
*The Last of the Mohicans:* 76, 77,
83–85, 87–88, 90, 91, 92
*The Learning Tree:* 96–97, 102,
103–105, 111–112
*The Power of One:* 156
Racism
*The Bridge over the River Kwai:*
35, 36, 41, 49
*To Kill a Mockingbird:* 230,
237–238, 246–247, 251
*The Learning Tree:* 93, 96–97, 100,
102, 103–105, 111–112
*The Power of One:* 147, 158, 167,
168, 169
Rape
*Atonement:* 4, 7, 14
*A Place Where the Sea
Remembers:* 145
Rationality
*The Last of the Mohicans:* 76
*See also* Reason
Reality
*Atonement:* 10–11, 22, 23–24, 26
*To Kill a Mockingbird:* 233–235
*A Place Where the Sea
Remembers:* 145
*Staying Fat for Sarah Byrnes:* 182,
183–184
*See also* Appearance *vs.* reality
Reason
*To Kill a Mockingbird:* 241
*Staying Fat for Sarah Byrnes:*
179
*See also* Rationality
Rebellion
*To Kill a Mockingbird:* 250
*The Power of One:* 163, 166
*A Thousand Acres:* 214, 218, 219
Rebirth
*A Thousand Acres:* 221
Reconciliation
*The Last of the Mohicans:* 92

Redemption
*The Wings of the Dove:* 281, 283
Reflection
*Atonement:* 13
Regimentation. *See* Rigidity
(Psychology)
Relativism
*Staying Fat for Sarah Byrnes:*
181
Reliability (Trustworthiness)
*Atonement:* 14
Religion
*Joseph Andrews:* 61–62
*The Pilgrim's Progress:* 122
*Staying Fat for Sarah Byrnes:*
188
*Typee:* 257, 259
*The Wings of the Dove:* 281, 283,
291–292
*A Wrinkle in Time:* 298, 304, 307,
310–312
Religious beliefs
*The Pilgrim's Progress:* 115–116,
119
*Staying Fat for Sarah Byrnes:* 176,
178, 181, 187, 193
*A Wrinkle in Time:* 306
Religious conflict
*Joseph Andrews:* 61–62
*The Pilgrim's Progress:* 114,
125–126
Religious tolerance
*The Pilgrim's Progress:* 115
*Staying Fat for Sarah Byrnes:*
172–173, 179
Remorse
*A Place Where the Sea
Remembers:* 145
*A Thousand Acres:* 220
*The Wings of the Dove:* 277, 279,
281, 288
Rescue
*Joseph Andrews:* 54, 57
*To Kill a Mockingbird:* 232
*The Last of the Mohicans:* 89
*Typee:* 258
Resentment
*The Learning Tree:* 99
*A Thousand Acres:* 222
Respect
*To Kill a Mockingbird:* 232, 235
*Staying Fat for Sarah Byrnes:* 179,
180
Responsibility
*A Place Where the Sea
Remembers:* 143, 145
*Staying Fat for Sarah Byrnes:*
185–188
Restlessness
*A Thousand Acres:* 203
Revelation
*The Pilgrim's Progress:* 118

Revenge
*The Last of the Mohicans:* 73, 76,
77
*The Power of One:* 157, 166
*Staying Fat for Sarah Byrnes:* 176
*A Thousand Acres:* 212
*The Wings of the Dove:* 279,
281–282
Righteousness
*To Kill a Mockingbird:* 231
Rigidity (Psychology)
*Staying Fat for Sarah Byrnes:*
187
*A Wrinkle in Time:* 314
Rituals
*To Kill a Mockingbird:* 240
Romantic love
*The Last of the Mohicans:* 72, 76,
84, 87–88
Romanticism
*The Last of the Mohicans:* 80–81
*Typee:* 271
Rural life
*Joseph Andrews:* 59–60
*To Kill a Mockingbird:* 224
*The Learning Tree:* 93, 94, 102,
108
*A Place Where the Sea
Remembers:* 131
*A Thousand Acres:* 206

# S

Sacrifice
*The Wings of the Dove:* 280
Salvation
*The Pilgrim's Progress:* 118, 119,
120, 122
*A Thousand Acres:* 213
*A Wrinkle in Time:* 306
Satire
*Joseph Andrews:* 51–52, 60, 61, 63,
65
*The Last of the Mohicans:* 90
Science
*The Learning Tree:* 98
*Typee:* 269
*The Wings of the Dove:* 283–284
*A Wrinkle in Time:* 298, 309
Science fiction
*A Wrinkle in Time:* 295, 307,
312–314
Seafaring
*Typee:* 253, 254–255, 261–262
Seduction
*Joseph Andrews:* 53
Self confidence
*The Learning Tree:* 101
Self control
*To Kill a Mockingbird:* 231
*The Wings of the Dove:* 281
Self esteem. *See* Self worth

Self identity
    *The Power of One:* 163–164, 165
    *A Thousand Acres:* 213–214
Self image
    *Staying Fat for Sarah Byrnes:* 173,
        188
Self knowledge
    *A Thousand Acres:* 203
    *A Wrinkle in Time:* 303–304
Self reliance
    *Atonement:* 3
Self worth
    *A Thousand Acres:* 218, 220
Selfishness
    *Joseph Andrews:* 57, 65
    *A Place Where the Sea
        Remembers:* 144
    *The Wings of the Dove:* 280, 287
Setting (Literature)
    *A Thousand Acres:* 206
    *The Wings of the Dove:* 283, 291
Sex roles
    *To Kill a Mockingbird:* 246–252
    *The Pilgrim's Progress:* 128–130
    *A Thousand Acres:* 195, 205, 212
Sexism
    *The Pilgrim's Progress:* 128–130
    *A Thousand Acres:* 205, 207, 209,
        210–213
Sexual behavior
    *The Learning Tree:* 95, 100, 101
Sexuality
    *A Thousand Acres:* 219
    *Typee:* 260–261
Shame
    *Atonement:* 13
    *To Kill a Mockingbird:* 230, 244
    *Staying Fat for Sarah Byrnes:* 186
Sibling relations
    *A Place Where the Sea
        Remembers:* 137, 139, 144–145
    *A Thousand Acres:* 195, 200, 201
Silence
    *A Thousand Acres:* '214
Simplicity
    *Typee:* 262
Sin
    *The Pilgrim's Progress:* 118
    *The Wings of the Dove:* 288
Social change
    *The Learning Tree:* 103–105
Social class
    *Joseph Andrews:* 58, 61, 65
    *To Kill a Mockingbird:* 235–236,
        243, 244
    *The Power of One:* 165
    *The Wings of the Dove:* 275, 282,
        284–285
Social commentary
    *The Learning Tree:* 108
Social satire
    *Joseph Andrews:* 65–66

Sociology
    *To Kill a Mockingbird:* 247
Sorrow
    *A Place Where the Sea
        Remembers:* 131, 136, 143
    *The Wings of the Dove:* 273
Southern gothic
    *To Kill a Mockingbird:* 245
Southern United States
    *To Kill a Mockingbird:* 224, 237,
        240, 246, 249, 250, 251
Spirituality
    *The Last of the Mohicans:* 78
    *The Pilgrim's Progress:* 122,
        123–124
    *A Place Where the Sea
        Remembers:* 137
    *The Wings of the Dove:* 286–288
    *A Wrinkle in Time:* 311, 313
Stereotypes (Psychology)
    *The Last of the Mohicans:* 77, 78
    *The Power of One:* 160
Stoicism
    *The Last of the Mohicans:* 76
Storytelling
    *Atonement:* 23–24
    *Typee:* 264
Submission
    *A Thousand Acres:* 202
Success
    *The Learning Tree:* 110–111
    *The Power of One:* 158, 166, 168,
        169
Suffering
    *The Last of the Mohicans:* 92
    *A Thousand Acres:* 203, 206
Suicide
    *The Learning Tree:* 97, 100
    *Staying Fat for Sarah Byrnes:* 176,
        180, 181, 187, 188
Superiority
    *The Bridge over the River Kwai:*
        32, 36, 41, 49
    *To Kill a Mockingbird:* 236
    *The Power of One:* 147, 158
    *Typee:* 266
Survival
    *The Last of the Mohicans:* 77
    *The Power of One:* 159, 166, 168,
        170
Suspense
    *The Bridge over the River Kwai:*
        45, 49
Symbolism
    *The Bridge over the River Kwai:*
        49
    *To Kill a Mockingbird:* 236, 241,
        252
    *The Last of the Mohicans:* 82, 92
    *The Pilgrim's Progress:* 125
    *A Thousand Acres:* 221
    *Typee:* 262–263, 268

*The Wings of the Dove:* 283, 287,
        288, 292
    *A Wrinkle in Time:* 304

**T**

Temptation
    *The Pilgrim's Progress:* 120, 122
    *Typee:* 271
Tension
    *The Last of the Mohicans:* 72
Time
    *A Wrinkle in Time:* 295
Totalitarianism
    *A Wrinkle in Time:* 314
Tradition
    *To Kill a Mockingbird:* 250, 251
Tragedies (Drama)
    *A Thousand Acres:* 206–207
    *The Wings of the Dove:* 280,
        286–288
Tragedy (Calamities)
    *A Place Where the Sea
        Remembers:* 138–139, 145
Transcendence
    *The Wings of the Dove:* 286–288
Transformation
    *The Last of the Mohicans:* 91
Travel
    *Typee:* 253
    *A Wrinkle in Time:* 304, 308, 309
Treason
    *The Bridge over the River Kwai:*
        41, 43
Triumph
    *The Power of One:* 167, 169
    *A Thousand Acres:* 203, 207, 213,
        214
    *A Wrinkle in Time:* 309
Trust (Psychology)
    *A Place Where the Sea
        Remembers:* 134, 139–140
Truth
    *Atonement:* 1, 6, 8–9
    *To Kill a Mockingbird:* 241
    *Staying Fat for Sarah Byrnes:* 175,
        187
    *A Thousand Acres:* 207, 220
    *Typee:* 264
    *A Wrinkle in Time:* 304

**U**

Understanding
    *To Kill a Mockingbird:* 231, 233,
        235, 236
Unity
    *Typee:* 268
Urban life
    *Joseph Andrews:* 59–60
    *The Pilgrim's Progress:* 122

## V

Values (Philosophy)
  *Joseph Andrews:* 65
  *To Kill a Mockingbird:* 244
  *The Last of the Mohicans:* 77
Vanity
  *Joseph Andrews:* 57, 65, 67–69
  *The Pilgrim's Progress:* 128
Vengeance. *See* Revenge
Victimization
  *The Power of One:* 165, 167
  *Staying Fat for Sarah Byrnes:* 181,
    183–184, 191–192
  *A Thousand Acres:* 202, 203,
    211–213, 213–214
Victorian values
  *The Wings of the Dove:* 280
Viewpoint. *See* Point of view
    (Literature)
Violence
  *To Kill a Mockingbird:* 241
  *The Last of the Mohicans:* 92

*The Learning Tree:* 93, 96, 97, 100,
    112
*The Power of One:* 149, 150,
    153, 155, 157, 158–159, 163,
    165, 166
*Typee:* 271
Virtue
  *Joseph Andrews:* 64, 66
  *To Kill a Mockingbird:* 243
  *The Last of the Mohicans:* 90
  *The Wings of the Dove:* 286

## W

Wars
  *Atonement:* 20–21, 25
  *The Bridge over the River Kwai:*
    28, 29–32
  *The Last of the Mohicans:* 72–73,
    74, 77, 90
Weakness
  *The Power of One:* 158

Wealth
  *Joseph Andrews:* 60, 65
  *The Pilgrim's Progress:* 120
  *The Wings of the Dove:* 279,
    284–285
Western culture
  *The Bridge over the River Kwai:*
    29, 49
  *Typee:* 267
Wilderness
  *The Last of the Mohicans:* 77
  *The Pilgrim's Progress:* 122
Wisdom
  *To Kill a Mockingbird:* 231
  *A Wrinkle in Time:* 309
Women's rights
  *The Wings of the Dove:* 283–284
Work
  *The Power of One:* 168
World War II, 1939-1945
  *Atonement:* 4–5, 11–12
  *The Bridge over the River Kwai:*
    29–32, 33–35, 36–39, 39–43